Library of
Davidson College

Reprints of Economic Classics

THE BRITISH EMPIRE IN AMERICA

Volume II

[JOHN OLDMIXON]

THE BRITISH EMPIRE

IN

AMERICA

CONTAINING

The HISTORY of the DISCOVERY,

SETTLEMENT, PROGRESS and STATE

OF THE

BRITISH COLONIES

ON THE

CONTINENT AND ISLANDS of AMERICA

TWO VOLUMES
VOLUME II

[1741]

REPRINTS OF ECONOMIC CLASSICS

AUGUSTUS M. KELLEY · PUBLISHERS
NEW YORK 1969

First Edition 1708

Second Edition, Corrected and Amended 1741

(London: *Printed for* J. Brotherton,
J. Clarke *in Duck-Lane,* A. Ward, J. Clarke
at the Royal-Exchange, C. Hitch, J. Osbourn,
E. Wicksteed, C. Bathurst, Timothy Saunders
and T. Harris, 1741)

Reprinted 1969 by
Augustus M. Kelley • Publishers
New York New York 10010

973.2
O446
v.2

SBN 678 00524 9

Library of Congress Catalogue Card Number
68-56558

84-9605

PRINTED IN THE UNITED STATES OF AMERICA
by SENTRY PRESS, NEW YORK, N.Y. 10019

The British Empire
IN
AMERICA,
CONTAINING
The HISTORY of the Discovery, Settlement, Progress and State of the

BRITISH COLONIES
ON THE
Continent and Islands of AMERICA.

VOL. II.

Being an ACCOUNT of the Country, Soil, Climate, Product and Trade of

BARBADOS,	MONTSERRAT,	ANGUILIA,
ST. LUCIA,	NEVIS,	JAMAICA,
ST. VINCENTS,	ST. CHRISTOPHERS,	BAHAMA, and
DOMINICO,	BARBUDA,	BERMUDAS.
ANTEGO,		

SECOND EDITION, Corrected and Amended.

With the Continuation of the HISTORY, and the Variation in the State and Trade of those COLONIES, from the Year 1710 to the present Time. Including OCCASIONAL REMARKS, and the most feasible and useful Methods for their Improvement and Security.

LONDON:

Printed for J. BROTHERTON, J. CLARKE in *Duck-Lane*, A. WARD, J. CLARKE at the *Royal-Exchange*, C. HITCH, J. OSBOURN, E. WICKSTEED, C. BATHURST, TIMOTHY SAUNDERS, and T. HARRIS. MDCCXLI.

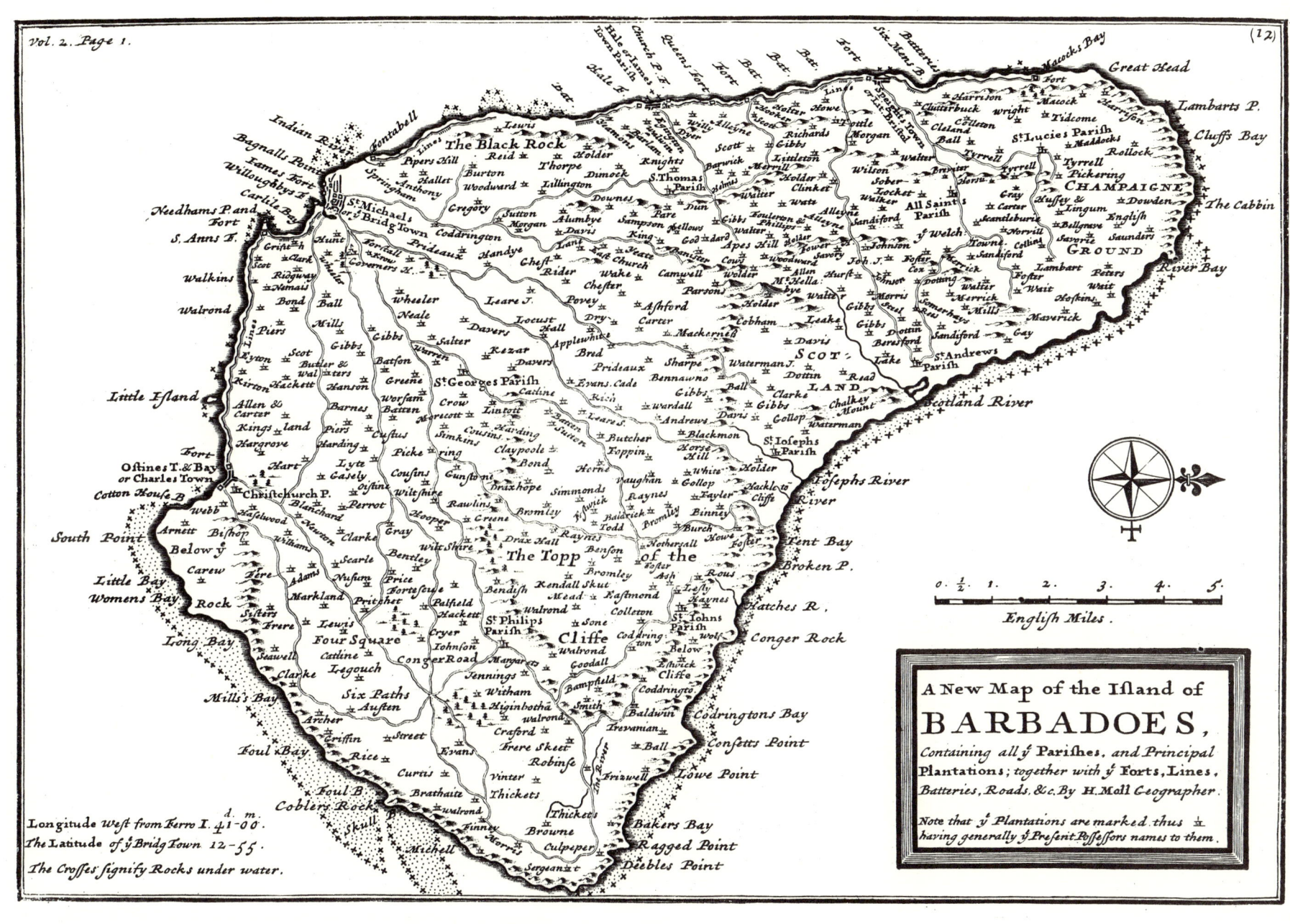

THE HISTORY OF BARBADOS.

CHAP. I.

Containing an Account of its Discovery, Settlement, the Progress of it, the Perfection, the Decrease and Present State.

'TIS agreed by all Historians, that have made mention of this Island, as 'twas first settled by the *English*, that the *Portuguese* were the first who discovered it; and it lying convenient for their stopping in their Voyages to and from the *Brasils*, they left some Hogs here, which multiplied, according to the general Report of Writers, so prodigiously, that when the *English* came hither, they found the Isle over-run with them. But this, in all Probability, is a Fiction; for the Island was entirely covered with Woods, and those Woods affording only a few Berries, for the Nourishment of these Animals, 'tis not likely there should be such Abundance of them.

About the Year 1696, there was a Person living, who came to *Barbados* with the first *Englishmen* that settled there; and he assured a very worthy Gentleman, from whom the Writer of this History had this Information, that when they had lived there some Time on Salt Provisions, he long'd so much to taste some fresh, that he would have sold himself for a Slave to any *Englishman*, who would then have supplied him

with

with a Meal of fresh Meat. Now if there were such Plenty of Hogs, and the Flesh of them so delicious, as will be mentioned hereafter, we cannot imagine he could be in such great Want of fresh as well as salt Provisions.

The same Man confirmed the Account we have given of the Thickness of the Woods; and from thence argued, as we do, that 'twas impossible for the pretended infinite Numbers of Hogs to subsist.

We cannot ascertain at what Time the *Portuguese* discover'd it, nor when the *English* first found it out after them. We suppose the Former might have been there 100 Years before the *English* discovered it: For *Alvarez Cabral* landed in *Brasil, A. D.* 1501, and 'tis not probable his Countrymen, the *Portuguese*, should sail by *Barbados* 20 Year, and not find it out; the Coast of *Brasil* being not far from the *Charibbee* Islands, of which *Barbados* is the chief.

As to the Time when the *English* first came hither, tho' we cannot fix the Year, we are sure it must be in the Reign of King *James* I. For it appears by an Act of Assembly in *Barbados*, that 'twas settled in his Time. This Act is entitled, *An Act for the better ascertaining the Laws of this Island*; and passed, *A. D.* 1666. In which 'tis said, That all Acts *confirmed by any Governor and Counsellor, President and Council, by Virtue of any Commission from King* James *or* Charles *the* Ist, &c. Which is a plain Proof, that 'twas discovered by the *English* before the Year 1625.

What we know of the Matter, is, about the Year 1624. a Ship of Sir *William Curteen*'s returning from *Fernambock*, in *Brasil*, was driven by Stress of Weather on this Coast; as the *Portuguese* had been before, it being not, as *Ligon* says, *far out of the Way*; *for 'tis the most windwardly Island of the* Charibbees, Tobago *only excepted.* As indeed it is, *Tobago* lying in 11 Degrees, 16 Minutes North Latitude, above a Degree nearer the Line than *Barbados*.

That this Ship touched here about the Year 1624, we may conclude, for these Reasons: 'Tis plain there was no sailing to *Brasil* for any *Englishman*, but under the Protection of the *Dutch West-India* Company; the *Spaniards* and *Portuguese* making it Death for any Stranger to come among them on this Part of the Continent.

Now tho' the *Dutch West-India* Company, after the Expiration of the Truce with *Philip* III. King of *Spain* and *Portugal*, began, by Permission of the *States General*, to trade thither; yet they never sent any Fleet, till the Beginning of the Year 1624. before which Time we cannot imagine the *English* would venture to *Brasil*, the *Dutch* having
not

not made any Settlement, and King *James* dying, *Anno* 1625. We think 'tis proved plain enough, that Sir *William Curteen*'s Ship came to *Barbados, Anno* 1624.

Sir *William* was one of the greatest Merchants of that Time in *London,* and is often mentioned by Writers, on Account of a very rich Sugar Ship of his taken by the *Dutch,* for which Satisfaction was required and obtained in subsequent Treaties. *Ligon* tells us only, *a Ship of Sir* William Curteen's was driven upon this Coast, and anchored before it. The Men aboard it landed, and stayed some Time, to inform themselves of the Nature of the Place; which, as before hinted, they found to be so over-grown with Woods, that there was no Champion Ground, no *Savana's,* for Men to dwell in; nor were there any Beasts, but the above-mention'd Hogs; and those, says Mr. *Ligon, in Abundance*; *the* Portuguese *having long before put some ashore, for Breed, in Case they should at any Time be driven by foul Weather upon the Island, that they might there find fresh Meat, to serve them upon such an Extremity.* He adds, *The Fruits and Roots that grew there, afforded them so great Plenty of Food, as they multiplied abundantly.*

Wherein he is not only contradicted by the old Man we have spoken of in the foregoing Pages, but by all the later Accounts written of *Barbados:* For they all agree, that there was no Plant, Root, or Herb found here, except *Purcelain;* and indeed he confesses as much himself: *I know no Herb, naturally growing in the Island, that has not been brought thither from other Parts, but* Purcelain, &c. P. 97.

'Tis very certain, that the *Charibbeans* never inhabited this Island, for there were no Remains nor Signs of any of their Villages or Dwellings; and they had not been so long possessed of the Islands, to which they give Name, as that one can suppose they might have dwelt there many Ages before.

This, 'tis probable, was one of the Islands they used to visit for Pleasure, of which we shall say more in the History of St. *Christophers,* where we shall speak of the *Charibbeans,* and return now to our present Subject.

Before we continue the History of *Barbados,* 'twill not be improper to observe, that this Name was given it by the *Portuguese*; and no doubt relates to the Barbarity of the Country, which they found wild to the last Degree, and consequently believed it to be inhabited by Barbarians. There are some weak People in this Island, who think the Word is formed from the *Beards* of the Fig-Trees, and that it should be called *Beardbados.* But this Etymology is equally groundless and ridiculous. The *Portuguese* name it *Los Barbados*;

from

The History of Barbados.

from whence 'twas a long Time called, *The Barbados*; tho' we do not see what Occasion there is for the *The* in our Language. The *French* at first gave it the Name of *Barboude*. They now call it, *La Barbade*; and the *English*, all at least who have any Acquaintance with the Place or People, *Barbados*.

How it came to be inhabited by our Countrymen, is our next Business to relate. The *English*, who landed there out of Sir *William Curteen*'s Ship, when they returned to *England*, gave Advice to their Friends of the Discovery they had made; and several Persons, Noblemen, and others, undertook to settle a Colony here. Ships were sent, with Men, Provisions, and working Tools, to cut down the Woods, and clear the Ground, to plant Provisions for their Subsistence: which till then they found but straggling among the Woods.

Ligon, p. 24.
Thus says the Writer of the Book, which he calls, the *Barbados History*. If by Provisions, he means Corn, 'twas impossible they should find that there which never was sown. If he means the Hogs, we have often mentioned, how comes it they found them *stragglingly?* This confirms what the old Man said of their Want of fresh Meat.

Having cleared some Part of the Ground, the *English* planted Potatoes, Plantanes, and *Indian* Corn, with some other Fruits; *Which*, says the same Author again, *with the Hogs Flesh they found, served only to keep Life and Soul together*. And the Supplies from *England* came so slow, and so uncertainly, that they were often driven to great Extremities.

Pag. 23.
William Earl of *Pembroke* was a great Adventurer in the first settling of this Island, of which he possessed himself of a good Part; but we do not find he had any Grant from the King, for the whole Island was given away afterwards.

Capt. Cannon Governor.
This Lord sent over Capt. *Cannon*, to manage his Affairs there, and we may look upon *Cannon* as the first Governor, the rest of the Colony being under his Direction. These new Comers found here certain Pots, or Pans of several Sizes, made of Clay, so finely tempered, and turned with such Art, that they could hardly think them to be the Workmanship of Barbarians or Savages. Yet 'twas thought they were brought thither by the *Charibbeans*, who coming thither in their Canoos and Periaguas, hunted the Hogs, killed them, and boiled their Meat in them. Which Conjecture will seem very probable, to any one that reads what is said of the *Charibbeans*, their little Voyages, and their neat Pots, in the History of *St. Christophers*.

Capt.

The History of Barbados.

Capt. *Cannon* told Mr. *Ligon*, that this was a gross Mistake in the Planters, and that no *Indians* ever came there; but those Pots were brought by the Negroes that were fetched from *Angola*, and some other Parts of *Africa*; and that he had seen them make of them at *Angola*, with the greatest Art that may be.

What this Author writes in Answer to *Cannon*, is not the least curious Part of his Book: *Tho' I am willing to believe this Captain, who delivered upon his Knowledge, that the Negroes brought some Pots thither, and very finely and artificially made; yet it does not hinder any Man from believing, that the* Indians *brought some too: And who knows which were the most exactly made; for 'tis certain, in some Parts of the Island, you may see, in a clear Day, St.* Vincents *perfectly. And if we can see them, why may they not see us? And they will certainly venture to any Place they see, so far as they know they can reach before Night, setting out very early in the Morning.*

This Account of the *Charibbeans* Voyages agrees with the *French* Authors, translated by Mr. *Davies* of *Kidwelly*, and made Use of by him in the Article of St. *Christophers*.

'Twas not long before all the first Adventurers were either forced to abandon their Settlements, or hold them of the Earl of *Carlisle*, of the Family of *Hay*; who was a great Favourite in the Reign of King *James* I. This Lord begged the Propriety of the Island of King *James* I. and obtained a Grant of it; but not of King *James*, for it seems he did not live long enough; King *Charles* I. granting it to *James* Earl of *Carlisle*, in the first Year of his Reign. Upon which all that transported themselves thither to settle, were obliged to purchase their Lands of him; and the Rates being easy, and the Country pleasant, the Colony soon began to grow populous, no other Settlement thriving so fast.

The first Comers made Choice of the Bottom of the Bay, where the Bridge-Town now stands, to inhabit; and there-abouts, and all along the *Leeward* Shore, were the first Settlements. Then the *South-Eastern* Coast was planted, and afterwards the Windward, and *North-Western*.

'Tis a very great Misfortune to us, that about the Year 1666. the Bridge-Town was burnt, and all the chief Records lost, insomuch that if we are out in our Chronology before that Time, we must be excused; for this Government having been 30 Years a Proprietary's, no publick Records were kept of it in *England*; and tho' we believe we are right, yet taking our Account from Tradition, and from several Passages in History, 'tis not unlikely we may err in our Chronology.

The History of Barbados.

The Inhabitants of *Barbados* at their first coming fell to planting Tobacco; which, whatever is said of the *Barbados* Tobacco now, proved so earthy and worthless, that it yielded little or nothing in *England*, or elsewhere; so that for a while they lost their Labour, and their Industry did not turn to Account.

The Woods were so thick, and most of the Trees so large and massy, that 'twas not a few Hands could fell them; which was another Discouragement to them. When the Trees were down, their Branches were so thick and unmanageable, as required more Help than could be procured, to lop and remove them off the Ground.

By this Means, twenty Years afterwards, Mr. *Ligon* writes; he found both Potatoes, Maize, and Bonavists, planted between the Boughs; the Trees lying along upon the Ground; so far short was it then of being cleared.

Sir Henry Hunks Governor. The first Governor that I can learn was sent thither with a regular Commission, was Sir *Henry Hunks*; but I cannot ascertain what Year he went. Notwithstanding all the Discouragements the new Colony lay under, it still thrived; for Indigo and Cotton-Wool coming up plentifully, great Quantities of those Commodities, as also of Fustick, were ship'd off for *London*; and meeting with a good Market, other Ships were sent to *Barbados*, loaden with such Goods as were wanted there; Working Tools, Iron, Steel, Clothes, Shirts and Drawers, Stockings, Shoes and Hats.

More People also came over; their Trade encreased with their Company; and about the Year 1646. 'twas looked upon to be a flourishing Colony. Capt. *Swan*, who was then Surveyor of the Island, drew a Draught of it, and gave it to the Governor; which he carried with him to *England*, and so 'twas lost; but he gave Mr. *Ligon* a Copy of it from his Memory, and loose Papers, which was engraved, and is the same that he put before his History.

The most considerable of the first Planters were Mr. *Hilliard*, Mr. *Holduppe*, Mr. *Silvester*, Mr. *Walrond*, Mr. *Raines*, Mr. *Kendall*, Mr. *Middleton*, Mr. *Standfast*, and Mr. *Drax*; for Mr. *Modiford* did not come over till about the Year 1647. The Planters were so neglected by the Proprietor, that they refused to honour him with the Name; and his Governor taking no Care to have their Grievances redressed, nor due Provision made for the Defence of the Island, 'twas a great Baulk to these first Adventurers; who were most of them Men of moderate Fortunes, that had brought Stocks thither to be improved, and were uneasy, to find no Care was taken to defend what they had already got, and what they might acquire. The

The History of Barbados.

The Earl of *Carlisle* granted 10000 Acres of Land, in that Part of the Island, which now makes the Parish of St. *George*'s, to *Marmaduke Rawden*, Esq; Mr. *William Perkins*, Mr. *Alexander Banister*, Mr. *Edmund Foster*, Capt. *Wheatly*, and others, on certain Covenants and Conditions, which 'tis to be supposed were not complied with: For those Lands, a few Years afterwards, returned to the Proprietor; who, upon Sir *Henry Hunks*'s Return to *England*, appointed Capt. *Philip Bell*, who, says *Ligon*, had been Governor of the Isle of *Providence*, to have the same Character in *Barbados*; where there was now a Council, an Assembly, and several Laws were made; and among others, one to raise 40 Pound of Cotton a-Head, on all the Inhabitants, for the Proprietary; but this Tax, and other Duties and Rents, were abolished, in the Government of *Francis* Lord *Willoughby*. *Capt Philip Bell Governor.*

Sugar was not as yet planted, and probably was not so soon as Sir *Dalby Thomas* makes it, in a Pamphlet he published *Anno* 1690. *About* 50 *Years ago,* says he, *during the War between the* Hollanders *and* Portuguese *in* Brasil, *a* Hollander *happened to arrive from thence upon our Island of* Barbados, *where, tho' there were good Sugar-Canes, the* English *knew no other Use of them, than to make refreshing Drinks for that hot Climate, intending by planting Tobacco there to have equalled those of the* Verinas; *on which, on Ginger, Cotton, and Indigo, they meant to rely.* *Hist. Account of the Rise and Growth of the West-India Colonies, &c.*

Ligon seems to hint, that the Planters made Experiments of Sugar, before they were taught by the *Dutch*. His Words are these: ' At the Time we landed on this Island, which
' was in the Beginning of *September* 1647. we were inform'd
' partly by those Planters we found there, and partly by our
' own Observations, that the great Work of Sugar-making
' was but newly practised by the Inhabitants, some of the
' most industrious Planters having gotten Plants from *Fer-*
' *nambock*, in *Brasil*, and made Trial of them at *Barbados*;
' and finding them to grow, they planted more and more as
' they grew and multiplied on the Place, till they had such a
' considerable Number, as they were worth the while to
' set up a very small *Ingenio*, and so try what Sugar could be
' made upon that Soil: But the Secrets of the Work being
' not well understood, the Sugars they made were very in-
' considerable, and little worth for two or three Years, till
' at last finding their Errors by their daily Practice, they be-
' gan a little to mend; and by new Directions from *Brasil*,
' sometimes by Strangers, and now and then by their own Peo-
' ple, who (being covetous of the Knowledge of a Thing
' which so much concerned them in their Particulars, and
' for *Pag. 83. A Cattle-Mill.*

'for the general Good of the whole Island) were content
'sometimes to make a Voyage thither, to improve their
'Knowledge in a Thing they so much desired; being now
'made abler to make their Queries of the Secrets of that
'Mystery, by how much their often Failings had put them
'to often Stops and Nonplusses in their Work; and so re-
'turning with more Plants, and better Knowledge, they
'went on upon fresh Hopes, but still short of what they
'should be more skilful in: For at our Arrival there, we
'found them ignorant of three main Points, that much con-
'duced to the Work, the Manner of Planting, the Time
'of Gathering, and the right placing of their Coppers in
'their Furnaces; as also, of the true Way of covering their
'Rollers with Plates, or Bars of Iron. We found many
'Sugar-Works set up, and at work, but yet the Sugars they
'made were but bare Muscovado's, and few of them mer-
'chantable Commodities, so moist, and full of Molosses,
'and so ill cured, they were hardly worth the bringing
'Home for *England*.' Let us compare this with what Sir
Dalby Thomas said above, and what he farther says on the
same Subject, which he places about the Year 1640, seven
Years before Mr. *Ligon* arrived in *Barbados*, *This* Hollander
understanding Sugar, was, by one Mr. Drax, *and some other
Inhabitants there, drawn in to make a Discovery of the Art he
had to make it.* If so, how comes it they were such Novices
7 or 8 Years afterwards?

Ligon's Account of it seems to be most natural, and therefore we shall continue it, being one of the most considerable Parts of the *Barbados* History, to know when the
Cane was first planted. He goes on, ' About the Time I
' left the Island, which was in 1650. the Planters were much
' bettered, for then they had the Skill to know when the
' Canes were ripe, which was not till they were 15 Months
' old, and before they gathered them at 12; which was a
' main Disadvantage to their making good Sugar. Besides,
' they were grown Proficients, both in boiling and curing
' them, and had learnt the Knowledge of making them
' White, such as you call Lump-Sugars here in *England*.'

One may see what an Improvement the Canes made of
the Lands, by what the same Author says of Major *Hilliard*'s
Plantation, which, before the working of Sugar began,
might have been purchased for 400 *l*. tho' it was 500 Acres;
and when he came over, about which Time also came Col.
Thomas Modiford, the latter gave 7000 *l*. for the half of it;
and he adds, *'Tis evident all the Land there, which has been
employed to that Work, has found the like Improvement.*

'Tis

The History of Barbados.

'Tis not to be doubted, but that the Hopes of making Sugar tempted over those Gentlemen in the Civil War, whose Fortunes had been almost ruined by it at Home: The Chief of these were Col. *Humphry Walrond*, Mr. *Thomas Kendall*, and others, whose Names and Families are very well known in *Devonshire* and *Cornwall*.

By the Addition of these Refugees, and other Adventurers, the Island, especially the Leeward Part of it, was very well settled in Mr. *Bell's* Government; and 'twill not be improper to take Notice what Settlements there were in his Time. The most Eastern was one *Oystine's*, who was a mad Spark, and made himself talked of for his Extravagance and Debauchery; insomuch, that 'twas for his Infamy, and not for his Honour, the Bay was so called, and the Town afterwards. Next to *Oystine's* was *Webb's*, then *Place's*, then *Isham's*, then *Trott's*, then *Knott's*, then *Battyn's*, then *Thompson's*, then *Bar's*, then *Webb's*, then *Wetherfoll's*, then *Scriven's*, then *Ross's*, then *Hotherfoll's*, whose Posterity enjoy it at this Day: Then *Glegitt's*, then *Birch's*, then *Baldwin's*, then *Rouse*, then *Freer*, whose Plantation is now in the Possession of his Descendant Col. *Freer*. Then *Allen's*: This Gentleman was originally of *Kent*, and of a good Family. His Son, Lieutenant General *Abel Allen*, held this, and several other Estates to his Death; and they are now enjoy'd by his Sons, the eldest of which is Col. *Thomas Allen*. More within Land was Major *Hilliard's*, where Col. *Thomas*, afterwards Sir *Thomas Modiford*, first settled; and then *Allen* again; and then Col. *James*, afterwards Sir *James Drax*: The latter from 300 *l.* acquired an Estate of 8 or 9000 *l.* a Year, and married the Earl of *Carlisle's* Daughter. There's no Male-Issue of this Family left, and the Estate is in several Hands. Near *Drax* was *Brome's* Plantation, then *Stringer's*, of whose Posterity some still remain in this Island. Then *Mallin's*, then *Redwood*, then *Knot* again, then *Lacy*, then *Sam's*, then *May*, then *Hayes*, then *Trott*. Next to *Allen*, near the Coast, was *Boben*, then *Fawcet*, then *Warmell*, then *Kitteridge*, then *Hamond*, then *Wafer*, then *Butler*, then *Jones*, then *Birch*, then *Webb* again; and then *Needham*, who gave Name to the Point, on which the Fort was afterwards built, from thence called *Needham's* Fort. Next to him was *Cieves*, then *Wood*, then *Sanders*, then *Moss*, and then Mr. *Bell* the Governor's, near *Indian* River, so the Stream that ran into *Carlisle* Bay was called; and the Town, consisting of about 100 Houses, was built on the South Side of it. 'Twas in *Ligon's* Time as big as *Hounslow*. More up in the Country was *Minor's*, *Marshal's*, *Coverly*, and *Lee's* Plantation; and above the Governor's nor's was *Marten, Dorels, Howard, Digby, Green,* and *Buckley*'s Plantations. On the Coast, beyond the Bridge, was *Curtis*'s. Higher up *Hill*'s, then *Holdip*'s, then *Perk*'s, then *Bix*'s, then *Bower*'s, then *Fortescue*; of which Family there are some still remaining in the Island. Then *Chambers*, then *Rich*, whose Son, *Robert Rich*, Esq; was a Counsellor in King *William*'s Reign. Then *Haw*, and then *Peter*. Nearer the Coasts was *Davies, Edward*'s, *Belman*'s, *Yrish, Reid*'s, whose Descendant was the late *John Reid*, Esq; a Member of the Council; and then *Mills*; of which Name there was lately several in *Barbados*, and Col. *John Mills* is at this present Time a Member of the Council, and Chief Baron of the Exchequer; next to *Curtis*'s was *Reid*'s again, near the Shore; then *Ashton*'s, then *Lambert*'s, then *Cox*'s, *Wincott*'s, *Ball*'s, *Martyn, Swinow, Howard, Eastwick, Stone, Morgan, Stallinidge, Fydes, Andrews, Whitaker, Weeks, Thompson, Hutton, Brown,* and then the *Hole* Town; beyond which was *Ball*'s, *Legouch, Woodhouse*.

Higher up, were *Alven*'s, *Watt*'s, and *Ball*'s Plantations. The Governor had also a Plantation between the *Hole* and *Speight*'s. Next to which was *Futter*'s, then *Holland*'s, then *Smith*'s, then *Pearce*'s, then *Marshall*'s, then *Terrell*'s, whose Grandson, *Michael Terrel*, Esq; was a Member of the Council. About *Speight*'s were *Day*'s, *Powel*'s, *Russel*'s, *Flech*'s, *Treacle*'s Settlements. More within Land beyond *Speight*'s, were *Saltonstal, Walker, Senex, Buck*'s, *Well*'s, *Hale*'s, *Sympson*'s, *Smith*'s, *Tring*'s, *Wascot*'s, *Rowland, Wright, Nelson, Ware, Humphrey*'s, *Sandford, Hemingsworth,* and *Hauley*'s Plantation. The latter was one of the Governors of the Island, as will be shewn hereafter. Then *Guy*'s, a very considerable Name in *Barbados*; then *Parish*; and within Land, *Yate*'s, *Duke*'s, *Bushell*'s, and *Biron*'s. Next to *Parish*'s was *Dotten*'s, whose Descendant, *William Dotten*, Esq; was lately a Representative in the Assembly for the Parish of St. *Andrews*. Then *Brown*'s, *Stretton*'s, *Parvi*'s, *Cook*'s, *Hargrave*'s, *Week*'s, *Conyer*'s, *Ogles*, *Stevens*, and *Macock*, whose Posterity enjoy his Estate to this Day. Then *Patrick, Cater, Lawrence,* and *Downman*'s Plantations, where now is *Lambert*'s *Point*.

There were no Plantations on the Windward Shore, till you come to *Chalky* Mount, and not above 10 or 12 along that Coast; yet the Island was so populous, that there were mustered 10000 good Foot, and 1000 Horse; and the Number of Souls, of the Whites only, were computed to be 50000, when there were not ¼ Part as many Plantations as there are now.

For

The History of Barbados.

For the Defence of the Country, a few flight Works were raifed on the Coafts, where it was not naturally fortified. And one Capt. *Burroughs*, who pretended to be a Soldier and an Engineer, undertook to make the Fortifications, and furnifh them with fuch a Store of Artillery as fhould be fufficient to maintain them, provided he might have the Excife paid to him, for 7 Years; which was promifed by the Governor and Affembly. Upon which he went to Work, and made fuch a Fort, as when abler Engineers came upon the Ifland, they found to be moft pernicious for commanding all the Harbour, and not being ftrong enough to defend it felf; if it had been taken by an Enemy, it would have done much Harm to the Landward. For which Reafon, in a very little Time, it was pulled down, and in its ftead, Trenches, Rampiers, Pallifadoes, Horn-works, Curtains, and Counterfcarps, were made. Three Forts were alfo built, one for a Magazine to lay their Ammunition and Powder in, the other two to make a Retreat to upon all Occafions.

And now a Form of Government was fettled by a Governor and ten Counfellors. The Ifland was alfo divided into 4 Circuits, for the Adminiftration of Juftice; and into 11 Parifhes, which were to fend two Reprefentatives to the Affembly. Minifters were alfo fettled, and Churches built, but very indifferent ones.

The Inhabitants driving a confiderable Trade with all Parts of the World, grew rich; and Col. *Drax* already began to boaft, he would not think of Home, meaning *England*, till he was worth 10000 *l.* a Year, which he acquired, or at leaft very near it.

Their Hands confifted in white Servants, Negroes, and a few *Charibbeans*. The firft they had from *England*, the fecond from *Africa*, and the laft from the Continent, or the neighbouring Iflands, by Stealth or Violence, and always with Difhonour: For the *Charibbeans* hating Slavery as much as any Nation in *America*, abhorred the *Englifh* for impofing their Yoke upon them; and 'twas very few they could get into their Power by their Pyracies and Invafions. They had not fuch great Numbers of Slaves, Blacks and *Indians*, as they have now; fewer Hands were required to cultivate the Ground, and 100 Negroes would manage the greateft Plantation in the Ifland, with the white Servants upon it.

However, the Negroes were more numerous than the *Europeans*, and began early to enter into Confpiracies againft their Mafters. The firft I meet with in my Memoirs of this kind, was about 1649, when they were fo exafperated by their ill Ufage, that Hopes of Revenge and Liberty put thofe
Thoughts

Thoughts into their Heads, which one would have thought they had not Senfe enough to be Mafters of. We muft confefs, the Planters had not yet learnt to govern their Slaves by any other Ways than Severity. Befides, they were all Foreigners, and confequently had not the leaft Affection for the Country, or their Mafters; whereas now of 60 or 70000 Negroes, which are fuppofed to be in *Barbadoes*, 40000 of them are Natives of the Ifland, as much *Barbadians* as the Defcendants of the firft Planters, and do not need fuch a ftrict Hand to be held over them as their Anceftors did, tho' their Numbers and their Condition make them ftill dangerous.

The Confpirators in Governor *Bell*'s Time, complaining to one another of the intolerable Burdens they laboured under, the Murmur grew general, and the Defire of Revenge univerfal. At laft, fome among them whofe Spirits were not able to endure fuch Slavery, refolved to break their Chains, or perifh in the Attempt. They communicated their Refolution to their Fellow-Sufferers, who were all ready to join in the Enterprize, and a great Number of thefe Malecontents were drawn into the Confpiracy, infomuch that they were the Majority. A Day was appointed to fall upon their Mafters, cut all their Throats, and by that Means not only get Poffeffion of their Liberty, but alfo of the Ifland. This Plot was carried on fo clofely, that no Difcovery was made till the Day before they were to put it in Execution; and then one of them, either by the Failing of his Courage, or fome new Obligations from the Love of his Mafter, revealed this Confpiracy, which had been carrying on a long while. The Negro belonged to Judge *Hotherfall*, and to him the Difcovery was made; who by fending Letters to all his Friends, and they to theirs, gave all the Planters fuch timely Notice of the Confpiracy, that the Confpirators were all fecured, and the chief Contrivers of the Plot made Examples.

There were many of this Kind, and none of them were faved; for they were fo far from repenting of the Treafon, that the Planters were afraid, if they had been fuffered to live, they would have entered into a fecond Plot.

As to the *Indians*, there were not fuch Numbers of them as to be dangerous; yet many there were, and fome Plantations had a Houfe on Purpofe for them, called the *Indian Houfe*.

'Tis too true, the *Englifh* made ufe of indirect Practices to get them; but there was one young Fellow fo very cruel and ungrateful towards a young *Indian* Woman, that 'tis a Story not eafily to be parallel'd. We find it in *Ligon*. This
Indian

The History of Barbados.

Indian dwelt on the Continent near the Shore, where an *English* Ship happening to put into a Bay, some of the Crew landed, to try what Provisions or Water they could find, for they were in Distress: But the *Indians* perceiving them go up so far into the Country, as they were sure they could not make a safe Retreat, intercepted them in their Return, fell upon them, chasing them into a Wood; and being dispersed there, some were taken, and some killed; but a young Man amongst them straggling from the rest, was met by this *Indian* Maid, who, upon the first Sight, fell in Love with him, and hid him close from her Countrymen in a Cave, where she kept him, and fed him, till they could safely go down to the Shore, the Ship lying still in the Bay, expecting the Return of their Friends. When they came there, the *English* aboard the Ship, spying him and his beautiful Savage, for she was very handsom, sent the Long-Boat for them, took them aboard, and brought them away: But the Youth, when he came to *Barbados*, forgot the Kindness of the *Indian* Maid, who had ventured her Life to save his, and sold her for a Slave. Thus the unfortunate *Yarico*, for that was her Name, lost her Liberty for her Love. An Instance of Ingratitude hardly credible in an *Englishman*. What could a *Spaniard*, or a *Frenchman*, Nations that have distinguished themselves for their Cruelty and Treachery, have done more? Would not one have thought, this base young Man had been born in the Land where the Inquisition and the Galleys are the Punishments of light Offences, and sometimes the Reward of Virtue and Merit.

This *Yarico* was so true a Savage, that after she had been some time in *Barbados*, she refused to wear Clothes, but went still naked. Mr. *Ligon* commends her Shape and Complexion, and her Beauty was not without Admirers, for we find she was so kind to a white Servant belonging to her Master, that she had a Child by him; and my Author tells it with this Circumstance, that when she found her Hour was come, she left the Company she was in, went to a Wood, was absent about three Hours, and *then returned Home with her Child in her Arms, a lusty Boy, frolick and lively.* P. 54, 55.

We have before observed, that there were 50000 Inhabitants, Men, Women, and Children, besides Negroes and *Indians*, in *Barbadoes*, in the Year 1650. Thus *Ligon* tells us; but the *French* Author of *the History of the Charibbee-Islands*, done into *English* by Mr. *Davies*, writes, that *about the Year* 1646, *there were accounted in it about* 29000 *Inhabitants, not comprehending in that Number the Negro Slaves, who were thought to amount to a far greater.*

There's

There's such a vast Difference between those two Authors, that there's no pretending to reconcile them; and 'tis most likely, that Mr. *Ligon*, who was on the Spot, should know better than a Foreigner, whose other Part of the Account of *Barbados* shews it was very populous.

' There are many Places, says he, in this Island, 'which
' may justly be called Towns, as containing many fair, long,
' and spacious Streets, furnished with a great Number of
' noble Structures, built by the principal Officers and Inha-
' bitants of this noble Colony. Nay indeed, taking a full
' Prospect of the whole Island, a Man might take it for one
' great City, inasmuch as the Houses are at no great Dis-
' tance one from another; that many of those are very well
' built, according to the Manner of Building in *England*;
' that the Shops and Store houses are well furnished with all
' Sorts of Commodities: That there are many Fairs and
' Markets. And lastly, that the whole Island, as great Cities
' are, is divided into several Parishes. The most considerable
' Inhabitants think themselves so well settled, that 'tis seldom
' seen they ever remove thence.'

Such was the State of *Barbados* about the Year 1650; and 'tis Matter of Astonishment to think what Progress this Colony had made in 20 Years Time. The People that went thither from *England*, could not be so mean as those that transported themselves to other Parts of *America*, because to raise a Plantation required a Stock of some Thousands of Pounds, which were not so common then, as they are now, tho' we do not live in the most abounding Times.

As Persons went hither chiefly to raise their Fortunes, and not to enjoy the Liberty of their Consciences; so this Island was not settled by *Puritans*, as *New-England*, and some other Colonies are. The Inhabitants were for the most Part Church of *England* Men, and Royalists; yet some there were who were of the Party called *Round-Heads*, or Parliamentarians. However both Sides, for many Years, lived peaceably and amicably; and by an Agreement made among themselves, every Man who called another Cavalier, or Round-Head, was to forfeit a small Sum to the Person offended.

This good Correspondence did not last long after the King's Death; for the Royalists, who were the most powerful Party, resolved not to own the usurped Authority of the Rump; and the Parliamentarians were of another Opinion. After the King's Friends were entirely suppressed in *England*, 'twas not likely the *Barbadians* could stand out against the new Republick. However Col. *Modiford*, Col. *Walrond*,

and

The History of Barbados.

and others, were very high, and the major Part of the Island, was for proclaiming King *Charles* II. Yet in the Acts paſt by the Aſſembly, which ſat in the Year 1648, we do not find that there was any Thing done, that might give Offence to the Government in *England*, which was then in the Hands of the Parliament.

Mr. *Bell* ſtill continued Governor, and having the Lord Proprietor's Commiſſion, wanted no new one from the Rump; againſt whom moſt of the Iſlands in the *Britiſh Weſt-Indies* declared, particularly *Barbados*, as has been hinted.

King *Charles* I. being beheaded by his unnatural Subjects; as ſoon as News came of it to this Iſle, the People proclaimed his Son, *Charles* II. who having received Advice, that not only this Iſland, but others, and *Virginia* alſo, remained in their Obedience, his Miniſters conceived vain Hopes, that Men might be raiſed even in *America*, to help him againſt the Rebels in *England*; whereas our Colonies were all then in their Infancy, and Men could ill be ſpared from their Labour, to defend their Works againſt an Enemy.

However, the Lord *Willoughby* of *Parham* was declared Governor of *Barbados*, by the King in *Holland*; and accordingly he went thither. But the Planters who were in the Intereſt of the Parliament, as Col. *Allen*, and others, removed to *England*, being apprehenſive of the Reſentment of their Enemies.

Becauſe the Government of this Iſle was above 20 Years in this Lord and his Brother's Poſſeſſion, it will not be amiſs to ſay ſomething of him; he was one of the firſt who raiſed Forces againſt King *Charles* I. notwithſtanding his Majeſty ſent him poſitive Orders to the contrary, and generally acted in the *Eaſtern* aſſociated Counties, in Conjunction with the Earl of *Mancheſter* and *Oliver Cromwell*: But when the latter, by his Courage and Intrigues, had got the ſtart of both of them, and the Sectarian Faction began to prevail in Parliament, the Lord *Willoughby*, who was a Presbyterian, ſided with thoſe of his own Profeſſion, that were Malecontents, oppoſed the Army, and being one of thoſe Peers who was accuſed of Treaſon by them, he fled to *Holland*, where he embraced the King's Intereſt.

The Earl of *Carliſle* had alſo granted a Commiſſion to this Lord to be Governor of *Barbados*. And upon his Arrival, Mr. *Bell*'s was ſuperſeded. While he was here he undertook an Expedition againſt the King's Enemies in the *Leeward* Iſlands; which being all reduced, the King appointed Major General *Pointz*, another Presbyterian Deſerter, to be Governor of them. *Francis Lord Willoughby Governor.*

He

He summoned an Assembly, and they past an Act, entitled, *An Acknowledgment and Declaration of the Inhabitants of the Island of* Barbados, *of his Majesty's Right to the Dominion of this Island; and the Right of the Right Honourable the Earl of* Carlisle, *derived from his said Majesty; and by the Earl of* Carlisle, *to the Right Honourable the Lord* Willoughby *of* Parham; *and also for the unanimous Profession of the true Religion in this Island, and imposing condign Punishment upon the Opposers thereof.*

Some place the passing this Act upon his being made a second Time Governor of *Barbados*; 'twas not to be expected, that this Government would be of any long Duration; for after that in *England* had triumphed over all its Enemies in *Europe*, there was no Reason to hope they would leave those in *America* in Possession of any Power.

Col. *Allen*, and the other Gentlemen who came from *Barbados*, had no Need to sollicite Succours; the Powers then uppermost, were too jealous of their Honour, to admit of any one's disputing their Authority; especially, when they understood, that Prince *Rupert* was designed for the *West-Indies*, to confirm the Inhabitants of the Island and the Continent in their Loyalty.

They were also provoked against the *Barbadians* for trading wholly with the *Dutch*, with whom they were about to make War; wherefore they resolved to send a stout Squadron of Men of War, and a good Body of Land-Forces aboard, to reduce not only *Barbados*, and the *Leeward* Islands, but all the *English* Colonies in *America*.

The Command of this Squadron was given to Sir *George Ayscue*, and also of the Land Troops; and with them returned Col. *Allen*, and those other *Barbadians*, who would not submit to the Lord *Willoughby*.

Sir *George* was ordered to cruize a little off *Spain* and *Portugal*, to endeavour to intercept Prince *Rupert*; which not being able to do, he set sail for *Barbados*; and arrived in *Carlisle* Bay, the 16th of *October*, 1651. He found 14 Sail of *Hollanders* in the Road; and, to prevent their running ashore, sent in the *Amity Frigat*, Capt. *Peck* Commander, with three other Men of War, to seize them.

The Captain immediately ordered the Masters of those Ships aboard; which Orders they obeyed, finding all Resistance would be in vain. Thus he took all those Vessels, and made them Prize, for trading with the Enemies of the Commonwealth in that Island. Sir *George* also took three other *Hollanders*, as they were sailing to the other Islands.

The History of Barbados.

The Governor made as if he would defend the Island to the last Extremity; the Alarm was given, and 400 Horse and Foot appeared in Arms, to dispute the Parliamentarians landing.

The Forts in *Carlisle-Bay* defended that Harbour; so Sir *George* plied up and down the Island, seeking for a Landing-place. The Inhabitants saw him, and the Sight of such a Fleet, coming in a hostile Manner, was far from being pleasant.

The Loss of the Ships in the Harbour, the Impossibility of their being relieved, and their certain Expectations of Want, staggered the Resolutions of the most Brave. However their Loyalty remained firm for some Time, especially among the meaner Sort, who had little to lose: For the Men of Substance considered, that they were about a very rash Business, and that they endangered their Persons and Estates, without hoping to be serviceable to the King: For 'twas now very easy for the Enemy to starve them, if they did not attempt to land.

Sir *George* at last anchor'd in *Speight*'s Bay, and stayed there till *December*; when the *Virginia* Merchant Fleet arriving, he resolved to take that Opportunity, to land with the greater Advantage; for he made as if 'twas a Reinforcement that had been sent him, and he had only waited for them till then. Whereas the Truth was, he had not above 2000 Men; and the Sight of the little Army on Shore made him cautious of venturing his Men, till he thought the Inhabitants had conceived a greater Idea of his Strength than they had done before.

The *Virginia* Ships were welcomed as a Supply of Men of War; and he presently ordered his Men to go ashore; 150 *Scots* Servants, aboard that Fleet, were added to a Regiment of 700 Men, and some Seamen to them, to make the Number look the more formidable.

The Command of them was given to the before-mention'd Col. *Allen*, who having a considerable *Interest* in the Island, 'twas supposed he would be the fittest Man to lead the Soldiers to gain it. The *Barbadians* were posted on the Shore very regularly, yet on the 17th of *December* the *English* landed, and beat them up to their Fort; which was on a sudden deserted by them, after the Loss of 60 Men on both Sides. On Sir *George*'s, was that brave *Barbadian*, the before-mentioned Col. *Allen*, who was killed with a Musket-Shot, as he attempted to land; and was very much lamented, being a Man of Worth and Honour; the Soldiers and

Seamen

Seamen who followed him gained the Fort, and 4 Pieces of Cannon in it.

The Sailors returned to their Ships, which cruized up and down, to prevent any Succours coming to the Iſlanders, or any Merchants trading with them. The Soldiers poſted themſelves in the Fort, and from thence made Incurſions into the Country; upon which the chief of the Inhabitants grew weary of the War; which Sir *George* underſtanding by the Correſpondence he had in the Iſland, he, by the ſame Means, procured Col. *Modiford*, who was the moſt leading Man on the Place, to enter into a Treaty with him; and this Negotiation ſucceeded ſo well, that *Modiford* declared publickly for a Peace, and joined with Sir *George*, to bring the Lord *Willoughby*, the Governor, to *Reaſon*, as they phraſed it.

Sir *George*'s Men were now all aſhore, and made up a Body of 2000 Foot, and 100 Horſe, for many Deſerters had come over to him. If Col. *Modiford* had joined him with his Party, there was no Hope of the Governor's eſcaping, who having before deſerted the Parliament, could expect no Mercy from them, if he was taken without a Treaty. This he knew the beſt of any Man, and accordingly conſented to treat; tho' to ſpeak more properly, we ſhould ſay, Sir *George Ayſcue* conſented to the Treaty; for being the ſtronger, he might, if he had pleaſed, have ſpoken *En Maitre*.

But to avoid the Effuſion of Chriſtian and of *Engliſh* Blood, both Parties appointed Commiſſioners to treat: Sir *George* named Capt. *Peck*, Mr. *Searl*, Col. *Thomas Modiford*, and *James Colliton*, Eſq; The Lord *Willoughby*, Sir *Richard Peers*, *Charles Pym*, Eſq; Col. *Ellice*, and Major *Byham*; who on the 17th of *January* agreed on Articles of Rendition, which were alike comprehenſive and honourable. The Lord *Willoughby* had what he moſt deſired, Indemnity, and Freedom of Eſtate and Perſon. Upon which, ſome Time after, he returned to *England*; and we hear no more of him till the Reſtoration.

―― Searl, Eſq; Governor.

The Rump having thus reduced this Iſland, without conſulting the Earl of *Carliſle* on the Matter, made ―― *Searl*, Eſq; Governor of it; who called an Aſſembly, which paſt ſeveral good Acts; as, *An Act for Weights, Numbers, and Meaſures*, according to the *Weights, Numbers, and Meaſures uſed in the Commonwealth of England*. An Act *to prevent frequenting of Taverns and Ale-houſes by Seamen*. An Act *for the keeping clear the Wharfs, or Landing-Places, at the* Indian *Bridge, and on* Speight's *Bay, alias* Little-Briſtol. An Act, *That the bringing Writs of Errors, and other equitable Matters, before the Governor and Council, to be by them determined,*

determined, be, and *do* continue in Force, *according to the ancient Customs of this Island.* An Act *for prohibiting all Persons to encroach upon their Neighbours Line.* An Act *for the certain and constant Appointment of all Officers Fees within this Island.*

And here we cannot but observe a great Oversight in Mr. *Rawlins*'s late Collection of the Body of the Laws of *Barbados,* in not taking Care to tell us, in what Year, and what Governor's Time, such Laws past, which would have been a great Help to the Chronology of this Island; whereas few of his Statutes are dated, and the Governor's Name seldom mentioned, till about Sir *Jonathan Atkins*'s Time.

We know certainly what Governors succeeded Mr. *Searl*; but the before-mentioned Accident may perhaps occasion some Error in the Succession, tho' we think we are in the right, and that his immediate Successor was Col. *Thomas Modiford*; who had been very instrumental in bringing this Island into the Power of the Parliament. And 'twas after this Reduction of the Island of *Barbados*, that *England* began to taste some of the Sweets of the Trade thither: For the Inhabitants before traded chiefly with the *Dutch*, and other Nations, insomuch that if we might believe *Ligon*, they had Beef from *Russia*; but herein he is to be suspected, and that Part of his Book, as well as others, notwithstanding the Bishop of *Salisbury*'s Epistolary Preface, favours of Romance. That they traded with the *Hollanders* mostly is not to be doubted. Sir *Dalby Thomas* tells us, in the Treatise we have already spoken of; ' That as it was the Happiness of
' this Island, to learn the Art of making Sugar from a *Dutch-*
' *man*; so the first and main Support of them in their Pro-
' gress, to that Perfection they are arrived to, exceeding all
' the Nations in the World, is principally owing to that Na-
' tion; who being eternal Searchers for moderate Gains by
' Trade, did give Credit to these Islanders, as well as they did
' to the *Portuguese* in *Brasil*, for black Slaves, and all other
' Necessaries for Planting, taking, as their Crops throve, the
' Sugars they made.'

The *Dutch* War happening soon after Sir *George Ayscue*'s Expedition, hindered their trading with that Nation; and their future Traffick returned to its proper Center, *which was dealing with their native Country.* 'Tis very true, for our Advantage the proper Center of the *Barbados* Trade is *England*.

But let us do the Colony and our selves Justice, to confess, we consulted our own Interest more than theirs, when we tied them to one Market, and obliged them to send all their

margin: Col. Tho. Modiford, Governor.
Pag. 37.
Pag. 36.

Com-

Commodities to us. Choice of Markets is the greatest Advantage of any Trade: And when about the Time of Col. *Modiford*'s Government, the Parliament in *England* past the Act of Navigation, requiring, among other Things, that the Product of all the Colonies should be shipped for *England*, a Stop was put to the flourishing State of this Island; and if it continued as it was, without decaying much, the Duties afterwards laid upon it, has so reduced it, that well might Mr. *William Rawlins* say of it, in the Epistle Dedicatory before his Collection of the Laws, *This once flourishing (but alas! now withering) Isle.*

Col. Tufton *Governor.*
As soon as *Jamaica* was conquered, Col. *Modiford* resolved to remove thither, and Col. *Tufton* was appointed Governor in his Stead, we suppose by the Rump, or *Oliver*; for we are now in the Dark as to Years, and the Order of Succession; but such as has been the Information, we have received from the best Tradition.

Henry Hawley, *Esq; Governor.*
'Twas in this Gentleman's Time that the Revolutions in *England* came about quick, and none of the Governors abroad were sure who were their Masters. In this Uncertainty, *Henry Hawley*, Esq; procured a Commission from the Earl of *Carlisle*, the Lord Proprietary, possessed himself of the Government; and Col. *Tufton* making some Opposition, was taken Prisoner, tried for High Treason, and condemned to be shot to Death; which Sentence was put in Execution off the Bay.

Thus *Hawley* became Governor of this Island, and solemnized his Inauguration with the Blood of a worthy Gentleman, of a very good Family, being a Relation of the Earl of *Thanet*. Yet we do not find, that after the Restoration he was called to an Account, for such vigorous Measures were then thought necessary, to strike an Awe into the People, and peaceable Justice was to effect that which Arms could not do before.

In his Time an Assembly was holden, who passed an Act, *for limiting the Assembly's Continuance*; confining their Session to one Year; the former Assembly having sat several Years, and the Islanders not approving of their Conduct.

Francis, Lord Willoughby *Governor.*
King *Charles* II. to reward the good Services of *Francis*, Lord *Willoughby* of *Parham*, restored him to the Government of *Barbados*, with the Title of, *Captain General and Governor in chief of the Island of* Barbados, *and all other the* Charibbee *Islands.* But my Lord did not think fit to remove thither then; neither did he name a Deputy-Governor, but contenting himself with the Profits arising by his Government, stayed in *England*, leaving the Administration in

Barbados

The History of Barbados.

Barbados to the Council, and they, of Course, devolved the executive Power on their President; which has been ever since observed, in the Absence of the Governor and Deputy-Governor.

'Twas in the Year 1661 that King *Charles* purchased the Propriety of this Island of the Lord *Kinowl*, Heir to the Earl of *Carlisle*, who was to have 1000 *l.* a Year for it (and now it being a Royal Propriety, there was no Occasion for any Commission from any one but the King himself.) But the Purchase was with the *Barbadians* Money, out of the $4\frac{1}{2}$ per *Cent.* about that Time granted to the King for ever by the Assembly; the History of which the Lord *Clarendon* thus relates in his *Vindication.*

The Earl of *Clarendon* says it was granted by King *Charles* I. to the Earl of *Carlisle*, and his Heirs for ever, *on a Supposition that it had been first discovered, possessed, and planted, at the Charge of the said Earl.* If these Allegations are not true in Fact, for which we refer to the History, that *Supposition* is without Ground, and consequently the Fabrick built upon it had no solid Foundation. However, the Earl of *Carlisle*'s Son, after the Earl's Trustees had *totally neglected* it, as the Lord *Clarendon* says, assigned to the Lord *Willoughby* of *Parham*, in the Year 1647, half of the Profits made of this Plantation by a Lease of 21 Years. Thus these noble Lords were buying and selling the Soil of a Country, that one of them had perhaps scarce heard of before, and the other took up the Right to, after it had been abandoned by his Representatives. But the Truth is, these noble Lords were so far from having any real Property in the Island at this Time, that the Earl of *Clarendon* writes, *Citizens, Merchants, Gentlemen and others transported themselves thither, without asking any Body Leave, or without being opposed or contradicted by any Body*; but the Lease to the Lord *Willoughby* from the Earl of *Carlisle* was corroborated by a Commission to the said Lord *Willoughby* from the Prince of *Wales*, to be Governor of *Barbados*, and all the *Charibbee* Islands, all which, St. *Christophers, Antego, Montserat, Nevis,* and others, were included in the Earl of *Carlisle*'s Grant, and consequently under the same Supposition of his having discovered, possessed and planted them all. Many of the like valuable Considerations of these *Plantation* Grants, would have the like merry Aspect, if they were viewed in their true and natural Light. As the People who went to and settled at *Barbados*, did not regard this Grant enough, or enquire whether there was such a Thing in being or not, so it is to be observed, that the Lease and Commission to the Lord *Willoughby*,

loughby, was at a Time when his Lordship, who had all along been serving in the Parliament Armies against the King, was fallen under the Parliament's Displeasure, and no more employed by them; when the Prince of *Wales* was in very great Straits in *Holland*, and his Father King *Charles* I. in the Hands of the Parliament Army; which render all these Regulations about the Island of *Barbados*, rather whimsical than important, that Island being possessed and planted, as the Lord *Clarendon* tells us, by Persons who only had a just Title to it by the Charge they were at in acquiring such Possessions. The Earl of *Clarendon* acknowledging, that the Planters insisted that *They alone had been at the Charge of settling the Plantation, when the Lord* Carlisle *had not been at the least Expence thereupon.* And this is so apparent, that the Earl of *Clarendon* himself owns, The Earl of *Marlborough* had a Grant of the Island of *Barbados*, long before the Earl of *Carlisle* had any Pretence thereunto by his *Grant* from the same King, on a Supposition that it was discovered, possessed, and planted at his Charge. This very valuable Consideration will doubtless excite the Curiosity of some Persons to enquire how much that *Supposition* has cost the Island of *Barbados*, before and since it was declared void by King *Charles* II's Council at Law, not for the Interest of the Planters, the only true and well grounded Interest in this Island, or any other *English* Colony, but to put the Property of it so much into the King's Hands, that he might make a Bargain for it with the present Possessors. Several Planters came Home to sollicit the voiding of the *Carlisle* Patent, which they were so intent upon, that Mr. *Kendal*, one of them, fell in with a Proposition of a Duty upon Sugar, now the 4 *per Cent.* at least the Origin of it, in Lieu of the Demands upon the Grant. After what has been said, what needed my Lord *Clarendon* have enlarged so much upon the Earl of *Carlisle*'s Assignment of it by *Will*, for the Payment of 50000 *l* Debts, which the Planters of *Barbados* were no more obliged to concern themselves in the Payment of, than his Lordship or his Trustees were obliged to concern themselves in the Payment of theirs. The other Agent in *England* for the Planters, upon this Occasion dropt Mr. *Kendal* in his frank Acquiescence with the Duty to be laid on Sugar, alledging the Island could not bear such a Burthen as 10000 *l.* a Year, which it was computed it would amount to, and the Produce has very well answered the Computation. Besides they added, nothing could be done without the Assembly's Consent, to procure which the Lord *Willoughby* was ordered to call one as soon as he arrived at *Barbados*, the Government of which
was

The History of Barbados.

was continued to him, and how well he deserved it, by his Regard to the only true Interest of the Island, appears by his bargaining with the Earl of *Carlisle* for half of the Profits arising from the *Supposition* Grant, and after he came thither a second Time to procure the 10000 *l.* a Year for his Master's Use, by his throwing Col. *Farmer* into Jail, for his zealous Defence of the Country against the oppressive Impositions the Governor would have imposed on them, if the Assembly would have consented. This Col. *Farmer* did his utmost to prevent, which so provoked his Wrath, that he gave Orders for arresting him, and for his being sent Prisoner to *England*. When Col. *Farmer* appeared before the King and Council at *Oxford*, in 1665. the Lord *Clarendon* promoted the imprisoning him, for which with other Things he was 21 Years after impeached. But let the Reader take the Account of it in his own Words, it being the indispensable Duty of an Historian to let the Lights he gives have all the Views they will bear. The Lord *Willoughby* sent a full Charge of Mutiny, Sedition and Treason against him, and by his Letter ' informed the Secretary of State, of all the ' Behaviour and Carriage of the said *Farmer*, with all the ' Circumstances thereof; and that he had by his seditious ' Practices prevailed so far upon a *disaffected Party* in that ' Island.'——One cannot avoid observing here, that by *disaffected Party* is meant no more nor less, than every honest reasonable Man in the Place; and by *seditious* Practices, his zealous Endeavours to obstruct any unreasonable Impositions, of no manner of Use towards the Advantage and Security of the Colony. Again, ' That the Lord *Willoughby* was obliged ' in the Instant to send him aboard the Ship, without which he ' did apprehend a *general Revolt* ;' the major Part, and indeed the wealthier, soberer, as well as greater Part, being intirely in the same Way of thinking with Col. *Farmer*. Again, ' The Lord *Willoughby* likewise desired, that *Farmer* might ' not be suffered to return, before the Island was reduced to ' a better Temper.' That is to say, that Col. *Farmer* should be kept in Jail or Banishment from his Estate and Family, till this Governor had carried his Point against the *Country Interest*, and removed whatever Letts might stand in his Way, to punish Col. *Farmer* as a Traytor. The Charge against him was Sedition and *Treason*. His only Crime was *Opposition*, but that Opposition was in a legal Way, his Interest or Influence in the *Assembly*. The Earl of *Clarendon* confesses, he was for sending him back to be tried and punished for Treason and Sedition, because, says his Lordship, *The Governor could not preserve his Majesty's Right*, if he were
discharged

Pag. 32.

discharged according as *Magna Charta* directed. I have read many Letters from this Col. *Farmer* to his Correspondent in *London*, Sir *John Bawdon*, and never met with any from our *American* Colonies, among many Thousands I have read, writ with so much good Sense, Politeness and Knowledge of Men and Things. His Prudence, his Knowledge, his Fortune, was as directly contrary to the Lord *Willoughby*'s Letter, as Truth is to Falshood. His Character is so well known in this Island, that I am certain I shall not meet with *Opposition* in asserting he was a wise Man and a good Patriot, and when called to it, a good Governor.

How the long *Parliament* in King *Charles* II. Reign resented this Behaviour of the Earl of *Clarendon* towards Col. *Farmer*, late President of *Barbados*, is seen in the IXth Article of the Impeachment against him, *That he intruded an arbitrary Government in his Majesty's foreign Dominions, and has caused such as complained thereof before his Majesty and Council, to be long imprisoned for so doing.* What the Earl in his *Vindication* says, shews that he was principally concerned in that long Imprisonment. His Lordship's Words are in his Discourse before the King and Council, he behaved himself peremptorily and insolently. This needs no Explanation, every Body knowing that in the *Cant* of Lawyers and Officers, whatever is said for the Liberty of the Subject, for Property, or Privilege, to such as have offended by asserting them, is insolent and peremptory. The Truth is, Col. *Farmer* was a Man of Spirit as well as Sense, he had a great Property to protect, and almost the whole Country on his Side, and it was impossible for him not to be bold and firm under the like Oppression. But to return to our History; The next President of the Council was *Humphry Walrond*, Esq; a Gentleman who had suffered for his Loyalty in *England*; and his Sufferings obliged him to leave that Kingdom, and settle in *Barbados*. And when he entered on the Administration, an Assembly was called, which past several notable Laws. As an Act, entitled,

Humphry Walrond, Esq; President.

An Act for the Encouragement of such as shall plant or raise Provisions to sell.

An Act for the better amending, repairing, and keeping clean the common Highways, and known Broad-Paths within this Island, leading to Church and Markets ; and for laying out new Ways, where it shall be needful.

An Act concerning the Conveyance of Estates.

An Act for the good governing of Servants, and ordering the Rights between Masters and Servants.

An

The History of Barbados.

An Act for the Encouragement of all faithful Ministers in the Pastoral Charge within this Island; as also for appointing and regulating of a convenient Maintenance for them for the future.

An Act concerning written Depositions, produced in Courts, and appointing how the Evidence of sick and lame Persons, and of Persons intended off this Island, shall be valid and good.

An Act establishing the Courts of Common Pleas In this Island; declaring also a Method and Manner of Proceedings, both to Judgment and Execution; which are to be observed in the said Courts.

An Act appointing a special Court, for the speedy deciding Controversies between Merchant and Merchant, or Mariner and Mariner, or Merchant and Mariners, about Freight, Damage, or other maritime Causes.

They also confirmed the Act about Officers Fees, past in Governor *Searl*'s Time; as the King and Parliament did the *Act of Navigation* in *England*, to the great Disgust of the Colonies.

During Mr. *Walrond*'s Administration, the Militia were often regulated by the Assembly; and a Regiment of Horse was settled. Care was also taken to repair and maintain the Breast-Works and Fortifications: And this Gentleman gave general Satisfaction in the Discharge of his Post. Indeed 'tis most natural to suppose, that a Person who has himself an Interest in a Country, should be more concerned for the good Government of it, than one who looks upon it as a temporary Dwelling, whither he has procured himself to be sent, to raise a Fortune, or patch up one going to Decay.

Mr. *Walrond* signed these Acts after the Arrival of the Lord *Willoughby*, which was about *August*, 1663. For the Act above-mentioned, *concerning written Depositions*, &c. is said to be *by the Governor, Council, and Assembly*; yet his Name is to it: Whereas in the other Acts signed by him, 'tis only said, by the *President, Council, and Assembly*.

It appears by the Act, which settles that fatal Duty of the $4\frac{1}{2}$ *per Cent.* that the Lord *Willoughby* took out a new Commission for Governor, when he embarked for the *West-Indies*; which Commission was dated the 12th of *June*, 1663, and that Act passed the 12th of *December*.

Since in the following Chapters we shall have frequent Occasion to make Mention of it, 'twill not be improper to recite the Causes which moved the Assembly to settle that Impost for ever on the Crown. *As nothing conduceth more to the Peace and Prosperity of any Place, and the Protection of every*

single

single Person therein, than that the publick Revenue thereof may be in some Measure proportioned to the publick Charges and Expences; and also well weighing the great Charges that there must be of Necessity, in the maintaining the Honour and Dignity of his Majesty's Authority here, the publick Meeting of the Sessions, the often Attendance of the Council, the Reparation of the Forts, the building a Session's House, and a Prison, and all other publick Charges incumbent on the Government: We do in Consideration thereof give and grant unto his Majesty, his Heirs and Successors for ever, &c. That is to say, upon all dead Commodities, of the Growth or Produce of this Island, that shall be shipped off the same, four and a half in Specie for every five Score.*

Now if the publick Charges and Expences have been defrayed out of this Duty, if the Honour and Dignity of the Sovereign' Authority there have been maintained, if the Charges of the meeting of the Sessions, and the often Attendance of the Council, have been paid out of it; if the Forts have been repaired, a Session's House and a Prison been built, and all other publick Expences, incumbent on the Government, answered by this Impost, what Reason have the *Barbadians* to complain? But if on the contrary, not one of those Articles were in the least complied with in all King *Charles* and King *James*'s Reign; if the Inhabitants have themselves, by other Taxes, been obliged to defray all the Charges of the Government in this Island, have they not Reason to wish the Name of *Willoughby* had never been heard of there?

He shewed he deserved the Post the King had given him, when for his 1200 *l.* a Year Salary, he got the Settlement of 10000 *l.* a Year on the Crown. That King took Care it should be laid out to the Service of his Privy-Purse, by assigning Pensions out of it to his Favourites, and others.

Thus was all the 4$\frac{1}{2}$ per Cent. Money lost to the *Barbadians*, and the Lord *Kinowl* was the only Person, who had any Interest in the Island, that got any Benefit by it; for his 1000 *l.* a Year was settled to be paid out of the Monies arising by this Duty.

The Lord *Willoughby*'s Family coming over with him, *Henry Willoughby*, Esq; who was his Son, Brother, or Nephew, settled on the Island; and his Plantation to this Day goes by the Name of *Willoughby*'s Plantation.

My Lord *Willoughby* undertook an Expedition against the *Spanish West-Indies*, as some report; but there being then no Wars between the *English* and *Spaniards*, we rather suppose it might be against the *Dutch* Plantations, King *Charles*

having

having declared War with the States. Be it either on a private or publick Account, he sailed towards the Continent, and appointed *Henry Willoughby*, Esq; *Henry Hawley*, Esq; and *Samuel Berwick*, Esq; to be Governors in his Absence.

That they were Joint-Governors, appears by an Act, *For the better ascertaining the Laws of this Island*, passed by them; *The present Governors subscribing their Names to this Act, shall be deemed*, &c.

<small>Henry Willoughby, Esq; Henry Hawley, Esq; and Samuel Berwick, Esq; Governors.</small>

By Virtue of this Act, *Philip Bell*, Esq; *Constant Silvester*, Esq; *Robert Hooper*, Esq; *Simon Lambert* and *Richard Evans*, Esqrs; and Mr. *Edward Bowden*, Secretary of the Island, were appointed Commissioners to collect what Laws should be in Force there; and in Pursuance of their Commission, they collected the following Acts from the Books of the Office, and other such Books, the Original Rolls being lost in the Hurricane or Fire; *An Act for Officers putting in Security*; *An Act appointing Security to be given by the Clerks,* &c. *of the several Courts within this Island*; *An Act giving Power to Church-Wardens to make Sale of Lands,* &c. *and concerning Surplus of Land within old Bounds,* &c. *An Act for the Transcription and safe keeping of Records*; *An Act concerning Trespass done by Hogs*; *An Act declaring what Proofs to Bonds, Bills, Procurations, Letters of Attorney, or other Writings shall be sufficient in Law*; *An Act concerning Vestries*; *An Act to order the Publication and Execution of the Acts concerning the Uniformity of Common Prayer*; *An Act concerning Morning and Evening Prayer in Families*. They confirmed the Acts in Mr. *Searl*'s and Mr. *Walrond*'s Time, at least all that we have mentioned to be passed then; as also, *An Act to prevent the Prejudice that may happen to this Island, by loose and vagrant Persons, in and about the same*; *An Act for the disposing of several Fines, that are imposed upon several Persons for several Misdemeanors done within this Island*; *An Act for regulating and appointing the Fees of the several Officers and Courts of this Island*; *An Act for the Relief of such Persons as lie in Prison, and others, who have not wherewith to pay their Creditors*: An Addition to an Act, entitled, *An Act for settling the Estates and Titles of the Inhabitants of this Island to their Possessions in their several Plantations within the same*; *An Act concerning the Sale of Lands by Attorneys, Executors and Administrators*; *An Act for the Prevention of Firing of Sugar Canes*.

These Laws are very well abridged in the Collection of the Plantation Laws, to which we often have referred the Reader, and may be seen at large in Mr. *Rawlins*'s Collection.

The Commissioners above-named made the following Return to their Commission.

'We, the Committee appointed for the compiling of the Laws, having caused them to be collected and transcribed, as appears by a Writing under our Hands, expressed in the Page, the first Line entered in this Book, and are therein expressed, and be comprehended in one hundred fifty three Sheets of Paper; which being now fairly engrossed in this Book, do appear to be fifty eight Laws, and are comprehended in fifty eight next preceding Pages. And to the End that our first Declaration may be rightly understood, in regard that relateth to the one hundred fifty three Sheets of Paper, wherein the Laws were first digested, we have thought good here to insert this present Explanation. Given under our Hands the 14th of *Nov.* 1667.

'*Philip Bell.*
'*Constant Silvester.*'

'Tis well for the Inhabitants of *Barbados*, that those Laws are more intelligible than this Return; for we fear the Reader will find it somewhat obscure as well as the Historian.

This Collection of Laws was by an Act of Assembly ordained and established to be in full and absolute Force and Virtue, and were duly published in all the Parishes of the Island, and returned to the Clerk of the Assembly. They were also sent to *England* for his Majesty's Approbation, and were fully approved and confirmed by the King to be of full Force and Authority, as the *Standing Laws of* Barbados, none of which have been since repealed. We speak of those whose Titles are inserted in this History.

Francis Lord *Willoughby* was cast away, and perished in the Expedition we have mentioned in the foregoing Pages. Upon which King *Charles* the IId. gave his Commission of Captain General and Governor in chief of the Island of *Barbados*, to his Brother *William* Lord *Willoughby*, who arrived in that Island, *A. D.* 1667, and 'twas by the Assembly summoned on his Arrival, that the Laws the Commissioners collected were confirmed.

[margin: William Lord Willoughby Governor.]

There's one Thing very remarkable in their Address to the Governor, Council, and Assembly, dated the 18th of *July,* 1667, wherein, after they have declared that their Laws are the only Laws and Statutes which they found either originally made and enacted, or revived, collected, amended, and confirmed, *&c.* they say, There are two Acts only excepted, wherein they could not determine, which of them was valid, they both importing Customs on

all

all the Commodities of this Island, hence exported, but only one of them could be in Force. The first of which Acts, say they, is entitled, *An Act importing the Customs*, &c. dated the 17th Day of *January*, 1650, which was made and enacted by Governor, Council, and the Representatives of this Island, lawfully impowered by Commission from the Earl of *Carlisle*, thereto impowered by Letters Patent from the King; and that Act we cannot say is repealed, by Reason that the other Act, dated the 12th of *September*, in the Year 1663, importing *the Custom of* 4½ *per Cent. and intended to repeal the former Act, is not free from Objections and Exceptions of several Persons, who conceive the Assembly, which consented to the said last Act, was an Assembly not legally continued* at the Time of the making the said Act.

This Address or Declaration was signed by all the seven Commissioners before-mentioned, who were the most considerable Gentlemen of the Island, for Wisdom and Wealth. Men, whom their Country had such an Opinion of, that they thought fit to entrust them with their Laws; and we see they declared the 4½ *per Cent.* Act was not *free from Objections and Exceptions*, &c. If so, the Gentlemen of *Barbados* have paid 300,000 *l*. out of Complacency; for those Objections and Exceptions have not been made Use of to excuse them of this Duty.

The Hurricane mentioned to have been the Occasion of the Loss of some publick Rolls, happened the same Year that the Bridge Town was burnt, and that Fire deprived us of several Records, which would have been useful to us in settling the Chronology of this Island.

We shall hereafter be more certain. The Hurricane was far from being so terrible as to deserve such publick Notice; and if it destroyed the Rolls, it must be more through the Fear or Negligence of the Keeper, than through the Fury of the Storm.

About the Time of *William* Lord *Willoughby*'s coming to *Barbados*, Sir *Tobias Bridge* arrived there with a Regiment of Soldiers, for an Addition of Strength to the Island. The Assembly provided Accommodations for both Officers and Soldiers, as appears by several Acts now expired; and we make Mention of none but such as are now in Force. The Assembly also impowered the Governor of the Island, for the Time being, to appoint a Provost Marshal there, and passed an Act, directing how the Clerks and Marshals for the several Courts of Common-Pleas, within this Island, shall be appointed, and what they shall receive; as also, *An Act concerning the Commission of the Judges and their Assistants*.

We

We are now at a Loss how to reconcile the Stile of the Acts of this Assembly with the History; for in all of them before the 10th of *March*, 1667, 'tis expressed, *Be it ordained and enacted, by his Excellency* William *Lord* Willoughby *of* Parham, *&c.* and such Acts are signed *William Willoughby:* Whereas from the 10th of *March* aforesaid, to the *November* following, 'tis only said in the Acts that passed, *Be it enacted and ordained by the Deputy Governor, Council and Assembly*; yet those Acts are signed *William Willoughby.* By which it appears there then was a Deputy-Governor of the same Name with my Lord; for no Governor could sign the Act, when his Deputy's Name was in the Stile of it.

William Willoughby, Esq; Deputy Governor.

We take this *William Willoughby* to be some Relation of my Lord's, whom he left Deputy Governor in his Absence, which was probably in a Voyage to the *Charibbee* Islands, of which he was also Governor.

The several Acts signed by the Deputy-Governor *Willoughby*, are as follow: *An Act to prevent forcible and clandestine Entries into any Lands or Tenements within this Island; An Act for reducing the Interest to ten Pounds for one hundred in a Year. An Act for preventing the selling of Brandy and Rum in tippling Houses, near the Broad Paths and Highways, within this Island; An Act declaring the Negro Slaves of this Island to be real Estate; An Act for repealing a former Act, establishing Market-Days.* The next Act that passed, was by his Excellency, *William* Lord *Willoughby* of *Parham, &c.* entitled, *An Act for regulating and appointing the Fees of the several Officers in this Island, and other publick Ministers;* which is signed by my Lord: And I must either be right in my Conjecture, that there was a Deputy-Governor named *William Willoughby* also, or my Lord confirmed the Acts which his Deputy-Governor passed in his Absence, without being named, and without signing them; which is very unreasonable to believe; for till they were signed, they were not Laws.

William, Lord Willoughby, Governor.

My Lord reassuming the Government after 8 Months Absence, passed another Act *for advancing and raising the Value of Pieces of Eight,* and soon after that removed to *England,* as we imagine by his long Stay, for he was absent 4 Years; or to the *Charibbee* Islands, to settle *Antego*; which, as we are informed, was his Propriety.

In the mean Time, the Damage done by the late Fire at the Bridge was more than repaired, for the Town was rebuilt and enlarged; the Buildings being of Stone, more beautiful, and not so much exposed to a second Conflagration, as the former Houses.

The History of Barbados.

The Assembly, by a particular Act, appointed what Materials the Town should be built of; for the Inhabitants having begun to run up slight Houses of Timber again, a Stop was put to further Building by a former Act of Assembly, till they had taken that Matter into further Consideration.

The Lord *Willoughby* left Col. *Christopher Codrington*, his Deputy; who in *Feb.* 1668, passed an Act, *prohibiting wandering Persons from carrying Goods and Wares, in Packs or otherwise, from House to House, in this Island*; and an Act *for repealing a Clause in an Act, entitled,* An Act *reducing Interest to ten Pounds of Sugar for one hundred Pounds of Sugar for one Year.* In *May,* 1669, he signed an Act, called, *An additional Act concerning the Conveyance of Estates.* On the 22d of *December*, he passed two other Bills; the one, entitled, *An Act appointing Bench Actions, and the Manner of proceeding therein*; the other, An Act *concerning* Spanish *Money.* The next Day he signed another Bill, called, *An Act appointing Overseers of Plantations to officiate and act as Surveyors of the High-ways, and Constables.* The 11th of *August,* 1670, he passed two other Acts; one entitled, *An additional Act to the Act concerning the Conveyance of Estates*; the other, *An Act to prevent spiriting People off this Island.* In *October* he signed four other Bills: *An additional Act to the Act for establishing the Courts of Common-Pleas within this Island; An Act to prevent Abuse of Lawyers, and Multiplicity of Law-Suits; An Act for the trying of all petty Larcenies at the several Quarter-Sessions within this Island; An Act for regulating and appointing the Fees of the Secretary of this Island.*

About the same Time, *James Beek*, Esq; procured an Act of Assembly, impowering him to build a publick Wharf in the Town of St. *Michael's*; and Mr. *Richard Rumney*, Receiver General of the Island, having embezzled the publick Money, a Bill passed to recover the publick Debt from his Estate.

In *July*, 1671, the Deputy Governor signed the Bill *for Prevention of firing Sugar Canes*; and Mr. *William Withington* having disbursed Money relating to the publick Affairs, the Committee of the publick Accounts were appointed to repay him as much as the Country had benefited by his Disbursements.

In *February*, An Act passed *to prohibit the transporting of uncured Ginger of this Island*; and two other Acts on the 5th of *May,* 1672, viz. *An Act for the annual rating of Liquors*; and *An Act concerning Forestallers and Ingrossers of Provisions*: The last Act passed by the Deputy-Governor, was signed the 9th of this Month, and was a very useful one, as has been found

Christopher Codrington, Esq; Deputy-Governor.

found since by Experience; 'twas called, *An Act concerning Persons intended to depart this Island, and the setting up their Names in the Secretary's Office, and Warrants of Arrest.*

<small>William Lord Willoughby, Governor.</small>
Not long after this, the Lord *Willoughby* returned to *Barbados* from *England* or the *Charibbee* Islands, and stayed here till about the Time that there was a new Governor named in *England*, which was in 1674.

We have not learned whom this Lord appointed to be his Deputy-Governor, or who was President of the Council, when he left the Island; or whether he stayed after Sir *Jonathan Atkins*, the new Governor's Arrival, which was towards the latter End of the Year 1674. But sure we are, the Lord *Willoughby* signed a Bill the 29th of *January*, 1672, entitled, *A declarative Act upon the Act making Negroes real Estate*; and that we hear no more of him in this Island, where the *Willoughby*'s had been long Masters.

<small>Sir Jonathan Atkins Governor.</small>
Upon Sir *Jonathan Atkins*'s Arrival at the Assembly, he took up his Residence at *Fontabell*, about a Mile and an half from the Bridge, a Plantation lately belonging to Mr. *Springham*, which was rented for him at 500 *l.* a Year, and the Assembly confirmed the Lease of it to him, enacting, that the Rent should be defrayed at the publick Charge.

The first Act passed by Sir *Jonathan*, was called *An Act for taking off the* 80 *Days, after Execution for future Contracts.* At this Time, Mr. *Edwyn Stede*, was Deputy Secretary, and Mr. *John Higginbotham*, Clerk of the Assembly. This Bill was signed the 25th of *March*, 1675. By which we may see the Governor came hither in the Year before. In *April*, he passed an Act *for regulating the Gage of Sugar.*

'Twas in this Governor's Time, that the Merchants of *London* and at *Barbados* were severely and unjustly dealt with by a Society of Men, calling themselves the *Royal* African *Company of* England; who under the Protection of the Duke of *York*, did as many arbitrary Things as Men could do, who were not Sovereigns as well as Tyrants. We shall speak of them more largely elsewhere.

Sir *Jonathan Atkins* had Orders to seize all Interlopers; so those fair Merchants were called, who, at the greatest Hazard, endeavoured to supply the Plantations with Negroes, which none were to import, but such as had subscribed to the Monopoly.

We shall not pretend to give an Account of all the Ships taken by the Men of War, Governor, and Agents, to feed the Rapine of this Company, nor how many Families were ruined by them, who afterwards were ruined themselves, and became the most contemptible Society of Merchants

The History of Barbados.

in *Europe*, with the most pompous Name: We are now come to speak of one of the most dreadful Events that ever happened to *Barbados*, which Island had lately escaped the Terrors of the War; for *de Ruyter* with a Fleet of *Dutch* Men of War came to attack it, but found the Inhabitants so well prepared for their Defence, that after having made a Bravo of a few Shot against the Forts at the Bridge, he drew off. 'Tis true, he had no Number of Land Forces aboard, and *Barbados* was never more populous than at this Time, for the Island could spare 10000 Men able to bear Arms, and have as many more to follow the Business of the Field, besides *Blacks*. The Government ordered a good Body of Troops to the Coasts, and they appeared in such Crouds on the Shore, that the *Dutch* Admiral contented himself with throwing away some Powder and Ball to no Purpose, and sailed away.

The Hurricane that happened the 31st of *August*, 1675, was the worst Enemy this Island ever knew, except it were the *Projectors*, and Contrivers of *Taxes* in *England*.

The Leeward Part of the Country suffered most; for the Sugar-Works, and Dwelling-Houses were all thrown down; very few Wind-mills, except Stone-mills, stood out the Storm. The Houses and Sugar-Works to the Windward were very much shattered; the Canes were blown down flat, and some up by the Roots. All the Ships in the Road were brought ashore; the Pots in the Curing-Houses were all broken. Windward the Storm was not so violent. From thence Leeward, and all over *Scotland*, there was neither Dwelling-house, Out-work, or Wind-mill standing, except a few Stone-mills. All the Houses in the Bay were blown down, as were most of the Churches; and almost all the Corn in the Country was destroy'd.

One may guess at the Loss, when at two Plantations, belonging to Mr. *John Bowden*, and Mr. *John Spark*, the Damage came to no less than 6000 *l*. Others, who could not so well bear the Loss, were totally ruined.

There had been a Hurricane the Year before, when the Damage done was not inconsiderable, but none of the Houses fell; and Mr. *Spark* before-mentioned, writing to his Partner Mr. *Bowden*, then living in *London*, has this Expression in his Letter; ' I have been in two Hurricanes since my ' last coming hither, which were nothing comparable, and ' but Flea-bitings to this.'

'Tis somewhat out of the Way indeed, to compare a *Hurricane* to a *Flea-biting*; but considering this Man's Business was not *Metaphor* and *Simile*, one may conceive an Idea of the Terribleness of the last Tempest by the Comparison.

Sir *Jonathan Atkins* immediately summoned the Assembly together; and when they met, they took under Consideration, how to prevent Creditors being too hasty on their Debtors after this Calamity. For the latter would have been forced to desert the Island, had those they owed Money to come upon them at that Time. Had they gone, those who remained would have been in great Danger of their Negroes whom the Inhabitants were at that Time very much afraid of.

The Assembly agreed to send Home a Petition to the King, to take off the 4½ *per Cent.* Duty, as the only Means to save the Colony from Destruction : For besides that their Canes in the Ground were all ruined, the Planters were forced to take off so many of their Hands, to employ them about re-building their Houses, that there was no Likelihood of their having a Crop the next Year. At the same Time they suffered also by Want; for the Supplies of Provisions that used to be sent from *New-England*, were in a great Measure stop'd, that Colony labouring under two severe Judgments, Pestilence and War; insomuch 'twas feared the *Indians* would overrun them, which however did not come to pass, as we have shewn elsewhere.

The Leeward People made very little Sugars for two Years; and the Distresses of the Planters were such, that 'twas thought, if ever the 4½ *per Cent.* would be taken off, 'twould be then. But there was no such good News for the *Barbadians*. King *Charles* had his Necessities for Money, as well as his Subjects, tho' perhaps not for as justifiable Occasions. The 4½ *per Cent.* was a good Fund for 100,000 *l.* And who could expect such a Gift, at a Time when even the Exchequer was under the Scandal of Bankrupts?

We do not find the Assembly passed any Act to relieve the Sufferers in the late Hurricane, nor any Thing tending thereto, unless it was, *An Act for Allowance of a second free Entry for the dead Production of this Island, lost or taken, relating to the* 4½ per Cent. For the Commissioners of the Customhouse would not allow the Planter, if he had paid the Duty of 10000 Pound Weight of Sugar, and 'twas lost in the Harbour, to ship off a like Quantity, by Virtue of the first Entry, as now he was allowed to do by this Act.

The Houses being levelled with the Ground by the Hurricane, the best Planters in the Island lived in Hutts; and when they built again, were afraid to run up their Houses to any Height for a long Time. The Terror of this Tempest stuck so upon the Inhabitants, that few People cared to meddle with Estates, tho' they had Money to buy them, seeing to what Accidents they were exposed.

The History of Barbados.

In *April*, 1676, we see by the Statutes of *Barbados*, that the Quakers were very industrious, in their Endeavours to convert the Negroes. Upon which Occasion an Act past to prevent it, with a whimsical Preamble; *Whereas of late many Negroes have been suffered to remain at the Meeting of Quakers, as Hearers of their Doctrine, and taught in their Principles,* whereby the Safety *of this Island may be much hazarded,* &c.

In this Act Care was taken to bring in a Clause against any Dissenters keeping Schools: For, according to the Humour in *England,* the Governors of this Colony, as well as others, have been always careful to act.

At this Time there was a wicked Practice in the *West-Indies,* of which the *English* are accused; and that was their stealing and enslaving *Indians,* which they took on the *Continent,* or the Islands. And one Col. *Warner* being charged with this unlawful Traffick, if it deserves that Name, was made a Prisoner in *England,* and sent aboard the *Phoenix* Frigat to *Barbados,* to take his Trial there; but he found so many Friends, that he came off.

There was another unfair Way of dealing in this Island, much complained of: Some Merchants knowing the Necessity of the Inhabitants, used, by Forgery, and other Deceits, to engross Beef, Pork, Fish, and Salt, into their Possessions; and the Planters not being able to live without Provisions, were forced to buy them of them at their own exorbitant Prices.

This Grievance became so great at last, that the Governor, Council, and Assembly, past an Act to redress it, and *prevent the Inconveniences upon the Inhabitants of this Island, by Forestallers, Ingrossers, and Regrators.*

On the same Day, the 29th of *November,* 1676, an Act past, to explain a Clause in the Act for establishing the Courts of Common Pleas in this Island. On the 15th of *March,* Sir *Jonathan Atkins* signed another Act, *appointing the Sale, in open Market, of Effects attached for the Excise, the Parish Dues, and Servants Wages.*

The Governor and Assembly raised Money to repair and finish the Fortifications and Breast-Works, and build new ones, where Occasion required. In the Year the Popish Plot broke out in *England,* we find the Government of *Barbados* providing against the Papists, by an Act, entitled, *An Act for the more effectual putting in Execution a Statute of* England, entitled, *An Act for preventing Dangers which may happen from Popish Recusants:* Which was signed the 19th of *February,* 1678.

The History of Barbados.

The same Year Capt. *Delaval*, in the *Constant Warwick Man of War*, convoyed the Fleet of Merchant Ships from *Barbados* as far as in 20 Degrees of Latitude, the Inhabitants being apprehensive of a War with *France*, and that the Enemy might intercept them; but King *Charles* and *Lewis* XIV. understood one another too well.

The *Constant Warwick* returning to *Barbados*, as she came near the Island, took an Interloper, commanded by one Capt. *Golding*, and bound to this Island with Negroes. The Ship belonged to Mr. *Richard Walter*, a Merchant there, and Mr. *John Bowden*, a Merchant in *London*.

Sir *Jonathan Atkins*, according to his Instructions, presently condemned the Ship and Cargo, because the Master had not the Royal *African* Company's Licence to trade; and Mr. *Walter* was forced to pay 1400 *l*. to get Capt. *Golding* his Ship and Cargo discharged.

We might have remembered several such Captures, but they are Events too *mercantile* to be inserted among such as are purely historical; of which Kind are only those that relate to the Publick, as indeed this Oppression did; which *Edward Littleton*, Esq; Judge of *Speight*'s or St. *Peter*'s Precinct, has set forth, in a Pamphlet called *The Groans of the Plantations*, with equal Force and Reason.

' It cannot be imagined how the Company and their A-
' gents lord it over us, having us in their Power; and if any
' offer at the Trade besides themselves, they make such Ex-
' amples of them, that few dare follow them. If they catch
' us at *Guinea*, they use us as downright Enemies; and at
' Home, we are dragged into the Admiralty-Courts, and
' condemned in a trice; there is not such speedy Justice in
' the World. The Word is, that we are found Prize, or
' condemned as Prize, as if we were Foreigners, taken in
' open War. They have got a Trick of State, to bring In-
' terlopers within the Acts of Navigation or Trade; which
' are the severe Acts about Plantations. But even in this
' Case we are brought into the Admiralty, whatever the
' Law says to the contrary: Nor doth it avail us to plead,
' that all Offences against Statutes must be tried by Jury.
' The Forfeitures of the Acts before-named (which are ne-
' ver less than Ship and Goods) are given to the King, the
' Governor, and the Informer. The Governor in these
' Matters sits Chief Judge of the Court, &c.

Such was the Tyranny of this *African* Monopoly; and Sir *Jonathan Atkins* not pleasing the Company, in his Proceedings against *Interlopers*, a frightful Name given fair and honest Dealers, he was recalled, tho' he had done enough to deserve

The History of Barbados.

deserve the Favour of the Society: But they wanted a Man of more Severity, and less Honour, and procured one in his Successor, Sir *Richard Dutton*; a Man of such Principles, that in any other Reign he would not have been trusted with the Government of *Providence*. He was a compleat Tool of the Court, had been the Duke of *York*'s Creature, and was like to do any Thing he should be commanded. *Sir Richard Dutton, Governor.*

Sir *Richard* set sail for *Barbados* in *February*, 1680, touched at the *Maderas*, and arrived at *Barbados* in *April*, where he was received with great Kindness and Respect, and found the Island in a very flourishing Condition.

The Assembly confirmed the Lease of *Fontabell* to him, and having past an Act, for settling the Militia, the Governor would have it inserted, that all the Soldiers should appear in Red Coats; which put the Inhabitants to an extraordinary Charge; and, says Judge *Littleton* above-mentioned, *has driven many a poor House-keeper from off the Island*. The same Assembly past an Act, *to revive and continue an Act*, entitled, An Act *for taking off the* 80 *Days after Execution, for future Contracts*.

Sir *Richard*, to shew his Loyalty, got the Grand Jury, at the General Sessions of the Peace, holden for the Island of *Barbados*, on *Tuesday*, the 16th Day of *August*, 1681, to draw up an Address to the King; which the Governor sent to *England*, and his Majesty graciously accepted of it, and was pleased to declare the great Satisfaction he had, in this Testimony of the Duty and Affection of those his Subjects, to his Person and Government. And this Address was one of the earliest of all those Addresses of Abhorrences, &c. which all good Men have since so much abhorred.

In *July*, 1682, the Governor signed two Bills, which the Assembly had past. One *for the better regulating the Manner of giving Tickets out of the Secretary's Office*. The Preamble of this Act tells us on what Occasion it past: ' Whereas sundry ' Persons have of late departed this Island, to *Jamaica*, the ' *Leeward-Islands*, and other new Settlements, and left be-' hind them their Wives and Children, many of which are, ' and others may become burdensom to the Parishes they ' are left in; To prevent, &c.'

'Tis said the severe Proceedings of this Governor drove several off the Island, and made such an Act necessary. The other Bill he then signed, was an Act *appointing the Sale in open Markets of Effects attached for Arrears*.

In *March* following he signed another Bill, *for the ascertaining the Bounds of the several Parishes, and enclosing the Church-Yards within this Island*. And soon after he returned

Henry Walrond, Esq; Lieut. Governor of Barbados.

turned to *England*: For in *April*, 1683, we find *Henry Walrond*, Esq; Lieutenant General of the Island of *Barbados*; and a Session of the Peace, of *Oyer* and *Terminer*, was holden before him the 2d of that Month.

The Grand Jury drew up an Address, of the same Stamp with the former; which, to use their own Words, was presented *by their noble and high deserving Governor.*

In it the Gentlemen were pleased to rejoice in King *Charles* the Second's known Piety, and in the Loyalty and Prudence of their *Religious Governor*; who had *stifled and discountenanced Faction and Fanaticism in the very Embrio.* They tell the King, ' Their Mind had been infinitely ruffled and ' disturbed, at the Notices they had of the many Attempts ' and Offers that had been lately made in their native Country ' of *England*, and by the rebellious Heat of some Spirits, ' hatched in Hell, to shake his Majesty's Royal Throne, &c.' They declared, ' their Detestation of that cursed Paper, ' the *Association*; and that they were hearty *Lovers* and *Admirers* of his *dearest* Brother.'

Indeed there's something so very extraordinary in the Truth, Eloquence, Grammar, and Moderation of this excellent Address, that we are sorry we have not Room for the Entertainment of the Reader, to shew him what a noble Address Sir *Richard* gave himself the Trouble to carry three thousand Miles, and present as a grateful Offering to his Master, who, 'tis said, was pleased to receive it very graciously.

But little did these worthy Gentlemen of the Grand Jury think how soon they would have Reason to turn their Addresses to Remonstrances, as will be related in its proper Place.

Sir Richard Dutton Governor.

Sir *Richard Dutton* returned to *Barbados* in the following Year, held an Assembly, and past an Act, *for more speedy Remedy in Distresses taken Damage fesant, and Trespasses done by Horses, Cattle, and other living Chattels.* As also another, *to impower Attornies to confess Judgment upon particular Warrants.* And another, *declaring how Piracies and Felonies done upon the Sea, shall be tried and punished.*

At this Time a Law was made, for appointing a Treasurer for the Island, who was Col. *Rich. Salter:* And the Rebellion in the *West* happening in the next Year, the Government of *Barbados* passed a severe Act against those Rebels that were sent thither; whereby their Condition was rendered almost as bad as the Negroes. But 'twas then the Mode in *England*, to make all Merit center in an implicit Loyalty; and why should not the *Barbadians* be as mad as others? The Bill was called, An Act *for the governing and retaining within*

The History of Barbados.

within this Ifland, all such Rebels convict, as by his Majesty's most sacred Order, or Permit, have been, or shall be transported from his European *Dominions to this Place.*

Lieutenant General *Walrond*, notwithstanding his loyal Address, and the Post Sir *Richard Dutton* left him, fell under his Displeasure; for what, my Author does not inform us; but how severely and unjustly he was prosecuted, will appear by his Representation of the Matter.

'Another remarkable Example of the Inconveniences they *Sir Dalby* 'have been, and are liable to, is that of the before-men- *Thomas,* 'tioned Col. *Walrond*; who upon a bare Suggestion against *Hist. Ac.* &c.
'him, made by a Man fairly tried before a Court of *Oyer* 'and *Terminer*; wherein he was but one, tho' the first in 'Commission, that was commanded from *Barbados* hither '(to *England*) where he has been detained above three Years.
'And at last upon a full Trial at an Assizes in the Country, 'where his Adversary was powerful, and himself utterly a 'Stranger, there was given against him but 30 *l.* Damage; 'and that for no other Reason, but that the Court-Judge 'was pleased to over-rule this Plea: Whereby such a Disor- 'der, Ruin, and Distraction of his Wife, Children, Fami- 'ly, Plantation and Estate, has happened to him, that as 'the Calamity is not to be expressed, and for some Respects 'is not fit to be related; so it could never have been sup- 'ported by any Man, but one of an extraordinary Fortitude 'and Understanding; which he has demonstrated, by his 'constant Endeavours under his unjust Oppressions, to serve 'the publick Interest of those Colonies, and rightly to repre- 'sent their sad Condition at Court; especially that of *Barba-* '*dos*, who was so kind and just to him at his coming thence, 'as by the Representative Body of that Ifland, together with 'his Majesty's Governor and Counil, to make a Present to 'him of five Hundred Pounds Sterling, in Acknowledgment 'of his good Service he had done that Country, together 'with a publick Declaration of his just Proceedings in that 'Court of *Oyer* and *Terminer*, and especially in this Case he 'was brought over upon.'

And this I must farther observe to the Reader; 'That it 'was not the least Crime of State was so much as alledged 'against him, for banishing him from *Barbados* into *England*; 'but merely private Malice, supported by the partial Tyran- 'ny of some great Men, occasioned all his Sufferings.'

This Gentleman was the Son of Col. *Humphry Walrond*, once Governor of the Ifland; a Gentleman whose Loyalty had banished him his native Country.

'Twas

'Twas in this Year 1685, that the new Duty was laid upon Sugar, which has almoſt ruined this Colony: But it being in King *James*'s Reign, 'tis neceſſary we ſhould take Notice of the Death of King *Charles*, and his Brother's Succeſſion.

When Sir *Richard Dutton* received Advice from the Privy Council in *England* of King *Charles*'s Death, he immediately ſummoned the Members of the Council to meet the Day following; and upon the 23d, which was St. *George*'s Day, King *James* was proclaimed with great Solemnity and Order, in the Manner following: Firſt the Officers of two Regiments of Foot, marching from *Fontabell* to the Town of St. *Michael*, or the *Bridge*. Next the Officers of two Regiments of Horſe; next the Juſtices of the Peace; the Reverend the Clergy; the Lawyers in their Gowns; the Maſters and Regiſters of *Chancery* in their Gowns; the King's Council at Law in their Gowns; the Judges in their Gowns: Next the Honourable the Council of *Barbados*. After which marched ſeveral Trumpets ſounding; the Marſhals of the ſeveral Courts, and their Deputies, and the Provoſt Marſhal General with his Men; next the Governor, attended by the King's Life Guard of Horſe. His Majeſty's Regiment Royal of Foot Guards was drawn up in St. *Michael*'s Town, to receive the Governor, and perform their Duty in the more ſolemn proclaiming his Majeſty; which being done in the Place called *Cheapſide*, the Governor march'd from thence to *James Fort*, where the Guns in that Fort, and at the ſame Time thoſe in all other Forts, Platforms, Lines and Batteries, were fired three Times, with great Shouts; the like being done by the *Diamond* Man of War, and all the Merchant Ships in the Bay.

But this Pomp and Parade was of no Service to the Iſlanders, in obtaining Relief in the heavy Duties now laid upon them; for the Duke of *Monmouth* landing, raiſed a War that was thought more dangerous than it proved to be. The Court laid hold of that Opportunity to get vaſt Sums of Money granted to the Crown; and among other Taxes they got the additional Duties on Tobacco and Sugar. The Caſe of the Planters, as ſtated by Judge *Littleton*, with Reference to the Taxes on Sugar, was this;

Groans of the Plantations.
' Upon the coming of King *James* to the Crown, the
' Parliament being called, they were preparing a Complaint
' againſt the Commiſſioners of the Cuſtoms, who had taken
' a Liberty of late, to their grievous Prejudice, to call that
' *white* Sugar, which had never been accounted ſuch before;
' and whatever they pleaſed to call *Whites*, muſt pay the Duty
' of 5 s. the Hundred. But they were ſoon obliged to lay
' aſide

'aside these Thoughts, to provide against a new Storm that
' threatned: For they were told, to their great Astonishment,
' that a Project was set on Foot, to lay more Load upon us;
' no less than 2 s. and 4 d. a Hundred more upon Musco-
' vado Sugar; and 7 s. upon Sugars fit for Use; for that
' was now the Word. They saw this tended plainly to their
' Destruction; but the Thing was driven on furiously by
' some *Empsons* and *Dudleys* about the late King, who did
' not care how many People they destroyed, so they might
' get Favour and Preferment themselves. Since they were
' put into the Herd of Foreigners, and paid Duties with
' them, they hoped they should fare no worse than other
' Foreigners did. But that the Plantations should be singled
' out as the hunted Deer, and the Burden upon their Com-
' modities should be doubled, and almost trebled, when all
' others was untouched, was Matter of Amazement and
' Consternation. They humbly moved, that if the whole
' Tax must be laid upon Trade, it might be laid upon all
' Commodities alike; They said, that a small Advance upon
' all the Customs might serve every Purpose, as well as a
' great one upon some; and that this might be born with
' some Ease, there being so many Shoulders to bear it.
' But they would hearken to nothing of that Kind, being re-
' solved and fixed to lay the whole Burden upon the Planta-
' tions. The Projectors stood stoutly to it in the Parliament
' House, that the new Tax upon Sugars would not burden
' them; but this was esteemed such barbarous Nonsense,
' that there was little Fear of their prevailing, had not King
' *James* been so strangely earnest for this Tax, which yet
' that Parliament, who then denied him nothing, had never
' granted, but that some Privy-Counsellors assured them in
' the King's Name, and by his Order, that if the Duty
' proved grievous to the Plantations, it should be taken off.
' So the Act passed, and the Plantations were ruined. The
' Planters made their humble Application several Times to
' the late King, and laid their Distresses before him, but he
' was not pleased to take off their Burthens, or any Part of
' them, nor to give them the least Ease or Mitigation. One
' Time they were referred to the Commissioners of the Cus-
' tom; among whom, to their Comfort, they found their
' Friends the Projectors. Another Time they were told by
' a great Minister of State (who was a principal Projector
' also, and who was to give them their Answer) *That it was
' very indecent, not to say undutiful, to tax the King with his
' Promise*; when as they had only said in their submissive
' Petition, *That they had been encouraged to address to his
' Majesty*

'Majesty by the gracious Expressions he had been pleased to use in Parliament concerning his Plantations.'

This Tax lasted many Years, and the Wars coming on, when the State had Occasion for all the Money that could be raised, the Planters could not hope to be relieved; for tho' the Duty is not now the same, 'tis as high, and they are very ill able to pay it.

Governor *Dutton*, who was a zealous Friend to the *African* Company, used always to sit in Court to judge of the Forfeitures; the Company's Agents were the Informers, and as soon as Sentence was given, they divided the Spoil.

Edwyn Stede, Esq; Lieutenant Governor.

Mr. *Edwyn Stede*, who was but Deputy Secretary, because he was one of the Royal Company's Agents, was left Deputy Governor by him; and the same *Stede* had afterwards a Commission to be Lieutenant Governor from *England*. The Assembly presented him with 1000 *l*. and confirmed the Lease of *Fontabell* to him.

It now became a Custom for the Country to make the Governor Presents; which, with their Salary from the Crown, Perquisites, Fees, and Administrations, made the Place worth 4 or 5000 *l*. a Year.

In the Year 1687, the Duke of *Albermarle* put into *Barbados*, as he was going to *Jamaica*; the Lieutenant Governor received him with great Honours, the Life-Guard of Horse waiting upon him at his Landing, and conducting him to *Fontabell*: They also did Duty during his Stay there, which was three Weeks or a Month.

About the same Time, there was a Conspiracy of the Negroes to rise against their Masters, and possess themselves of the Island; all the Planters were to be killed, their Wives to be kept for the chief of the Conspirators, their Children, and white Servants to be their Slaves.

The Time for putting this damnable Plot in Execution, was near come; and some of the Negroes had provided Arms, which they hid, to make Use of on this Occasion; but being discovered in Time, Notice was given the Government, the Inhabitants were all armed, the chief Conspirators seized, put to the Torture, and executed: And many of them being the best Slaves, the Losses their Masters had, were not inconsiderable. About twenty of them were put to Death.

In the same Year, Mr. *Dalby Thomas*, since Knighted, Col. *Walrond*, and some others, procured a Sort of Monopoly for the *Facture* of all Goods from the *West-Indies*; which, if it had passed, no Man who was not of their Company was to be allowed to sell any Sugars or other Commodities from the Plantations. This

The History of Barbados.

This was oppofed with good Reafon by Sir *John Bowden*, and Mr. *John Gardner*, who had then the largeft Commiffions from *Barbados* of any Merchants in *England*, and perhaps the largeft that ever were lodged in one Houfe in the *Weft-India* Trade. Thefe Gentlemen, one would think, did this for their own Intereft only; but the Author fpeaks of his own Knowledge, they were applauded for it by the Gentlemen who had the beft Intereft in *Barbados*: For no Planter of any Note was willing to be obliged to fend his Goods to Perfons he did not know; nor were others willing to expofe their Wants to a Society, which a private Merchant might affift them in, with lefs Notice. And indeed this Monopoly was fo unjuft and chimerical, that even the Lord Chancellor *Jefferies* would not hear of it. 'Tis true, King *James* was not much againft it; but that unhappy Prince might perhaps like it merely becaufe 'twas irregular, becaufe it put a Conftraint on the Subject, and was againft Law.

But becaufe Sir *Dalby Thomas*, in the before-mentioned Tract, values himfelf mightily upon this Defign of his, let us fee what an eminent Planter, *John Rede*, Efq; lately a Member of the Council of *Barbados*, wrote to the Merchants above-named, with whom he correfponded: ' I thank ' you kindly for fending me the new Project. We look upon ' it as a moft ridiculous prepofterous Thing; and that if it ' take Effect (as God forbid) will certainly be our Ruin. ' If the chief Projector *Walrond* did but know, how his ' Plantation here is torn to Pieces, his Negroes and Cattle ' brought to Market, and fold at Outcry, it would probably ' haften him to *Barbados* (where I am fure he will not be ' welcome to many) and make him ufe his Endeavours to ' keep together what he left. Something might be faid to ' every Particular, but it would be too tedious, and the ' Subject is hardly worth writing upon.' The fame Judgment did Mr. *Richard Walter*, and the moft confiderable Planters in *Barbados*, make of it.

The firft Act now in Force, which we find paffed in Mr. *Stede*'s Time, was, *An additional and explanatory Act to an Act entitled, An Act for the governing of Servants, and ordaining Rights between Mafters and Servants*, which he figned the 15th of *May*, 1688.

The Inhabitants were fo alarm'd by the late Plot of the Blacks, that the Affembly pafs'd a very long Act, entitled, *An Act for the governing of Negroes*, which the Lieutenat-Governor fign'd the 10th of *July*, 1688. and the 2d of *October*, he pafs'd another, call'd, *An Act for binding out and ordering poor Apprentices*.

The

The History of Barbados.

The Assembly presented him with 1000 *l.* Sterling, and pass'd a Bill *for the better regulating of Outcries in open Market*; another *for the securing the Possession of Negroes and Slaves*; and another, *to repeal an Act, entitled, An Act to prevent Depopulation*; which Mr. *Stede* sign'd the 19th of *December*; and is the last Act he pass'd, that is not obsolete or expir'd.

Upon the Revolution in *England*, his late Majesty King *William* the IIId. of glorious Memory, continu'd this Commission to the Lieutenant Governor, till he appointed *James Kendall*, Esq; to be Captain General, and Chief Governor of *Barbados*, and other the *Charibbee*-Islands. This Gentleman had an Interest upon the Place, to use the *Barbados* Phrase, (for the Islanders always call an Estate an Interest) and was the more welcome to the Inhabitants.

We find the Assembly pass'd a Bill, *for the further Accommodation of his Excellency in his intended Voyage*; which being done before his Arrival, we cannot well comprehend what they meant by it. It could not relate to Mr. *Stede*, for they never gave him the Title of Excellency, he being only Lieutenant Governor.

Before he left *Barbados*, or Col. *Kendal* arriv'd there, the People of St. *Christophers*, and the other Leeward Islands, being distress'd by the *French*, apply'd themselves to the Government of *Barbados* for Assistance. Mr. *Stede* referr'd the Matter to the Assembly; who, upon Sir *Timothy Thornhill*'s offering to go himself at the Head of a Regiment, to their Relief, assented to it, as did also the Governor and Council.

While the Administration was in Mr. *Stede*'s Hands, a Difference happen'd between the Lieutenant Governor and Sir *Timothy Thornhill:* The former prosecuted him at Law, and Sir *Timothy* appeal'd to the King and Council; who were so far from giving him Relief, that he was condemn'd to pay 500 *l.* to the King, and 1500 *l.* to the Lieutenant Governor. The Matter, which, as I am inform'd, were Words spoken, had some small Relation to both Governments, but nothing that was worth taking Notice of.

Having this Warrant for it, Sir *Timothy* order'd the Drums to beat up for Volunteers; and in less than a Fortnight's time, he rais'd a Regiment of 700 able Men, who were all of them (the Commission Officers excepted) furnish'd with Arms, &c. for this Expedition, at the Charge of the Island of *Barbados*. Transport Ships were also provided to carry them to St. *Christophers*. The Soldiers embark'd the

1st

The History of Barbados.

1st of *August*, 1689. and fail'd the same Day. What Sir *Timothy* did in this Enterprize, will be spoken of in the History of these Places, where the Actions pass'd.

Col. *Kendal* embark'd for his Government aboard a Squadron of Men of War, commanded by Commodore *Wright*, with whom went also the Earl of *Inchiqueen*, appointed Governor of *Jamaica*. The 3d of *May* this Fleet arrived at *Madera*, and at *Barbados* about the beginning of *June*. Aboard *Wright's* Ships was the Duke of *Bolton's* Regiment, which was for the intended Expedition against the *French* in the Leeward Islands, where Sir *Timothy Thornhill*, now Major General of the Army, remain'd with his *Barbados* Regiment.

James Kendal, Esq; Governor.

In *April*, 1990. there was an Earthquake at *Barbados*, but it did no manner of hurt to Men or Cattle. Two very great Comets appear'd in those Parts of the World; and in an Hour and a Quarter's time, the Sea ebb'd and flow'd, at an unusual Degree, three times.

Mr. *Stede*, the late Lieutenant Governor, removed to *England*, and settled in *Kent*, where his Family have long had a Seat at *Stede-hill*.

Col. *Kendal*, on his Arrival at *Barbados*, contributed his utmost Endeavours towards carrying on the Leeward Expedition with great Application and Success. Several Gentlemen of *Barbados* went upon it, and in a Fortnight's time the Fleet was dispatch'd at the Bridge, and sail'd to *Nevis*, as will be mention'd elsewhere.

The new Governor having summon'd an Assembly, they pass'd an Act *to encourage Artificers and others to take Apprentices*, which he sign'd the 1st of *October*, 1690. At which time *George Paine*, Esq; was Clerk of the Assembly, and Mr. *John Whetstone*, Deputy Secretary; it being customary for those two Officers to sign all Bills in *Barbados*, as well as the Governor.

In *November*, an Act pass'd *for the better ascertaining how the Bonds forfeited for carrying Persons off this Island without a Ticket, shall be employ'd;* which the Governor sign'd the 17th of *December*; as also a Bill *to establish and ascertain the Bushel Weight, by which all sorts of Corn, Pulse, or other the Produce of this Island, shall be bought and sold*.

At this time, Freight of Sugars ran so high, and Masters of Ships were so exorbitant in their Demands, that the Government of *Barbados* was forc'd to intermeddle in the Matter, and an Act pass'd *for regulating the exorbitant Rates demanded and receiv'd by Masters of Ships and others, for Freight of Sugars*, &c. *for* Europe. By which no Commander of a Ship was to have more than 6 s. 6 d. a Hundred

Freight

Freight for Muscovado Sugar; 7 *s.* 6 *d.* for *Whites*; 5 *s.* a Hundred for scalded, 6 *s.* a Hundred for scrap'd Ginger; and 2 *d.* a Pound for Cotton; whereas the Prices were double before: But the Inhabitants found so many Inconveniencies in this Act, that the Assembly either repeal'd or suspended it. Indeed the Owners and Masters threatned they would not send Ships, nor go to *Barbados*, till Freight was left free in its Price. Sugars now sold well in *England*, and that was a great Relief to the Planters, under the Hardships of heavy Duties and high Freights.

Sir *Timothy Thornhill*, continu'd with his *Barbadians* in the Leeward Islands, and he and they signaliz'd themselves at the taking of St. *Christophers*, and in several other Enterprizes.

In *January* this Year, a Fleet of stout Ships arriv'd from *London*, and 6 of them were immediately taken up, by Order of the Governor and Council, and sent as Men of War to reinforce Rear Admiral *Wright*. These Ships were commanded by Capt. *Daniel*, Capt. *Leech*, Capt. *Champney*, Capt. *Harding*, Capt. *Man*, and Capt. *Willey*, and sail'd from *Barbados* the 11th of *February*. Captain *Carter* was ordered with a Packet for *England*, to give the Ministers an Account of the Proceedings here.

King *William* having been graciously pleased to order Col. *Kendal* to procure the Liberty of such Men as were in Servitude in *Barbados*, for their Rebellion under the Duke of *Monmouth*; the Governor got an Act passed *Nemine contradicente*, the 17th of *March*, 1690. to that Purpose, which he signed the same Day: It was entitled, *An Act to repeal an Act for the governing and retaining within this Island all such Rebels convict*, as by his Majesty's most sacred Order or Permit, have been or shall be transported from his European *Dominions to this Place*.

In *August*, 1691. the Governor passed another Act, *for prohibiting the several Clerks of the Courts of Common Pleas within this Island, to practise as Attorneys in the Courts where they are Clerks*.

The Assembly, the same Year, taking into their Consideration how necessary it was that they should have Agents at *London*, to take Care of their Affairs, and solicit for them at the Court, and elsewhere, as Occasion required; they chose *Edward Littleton*, Esq; and *William Bridges*, Esq; to be their Agents, and allowed them a Salary of 250 *l*. a Year each. That they did very prudently in this, is not to be questioned; and had they done as honourably as they did wisely, their Wisdom would probably have succeeded better.

'Tis

The History of Barbados.

'Tis no News to the Inhabitants of *Barbados*, that Mr. *John Gardener* before-mentioned, had been their constant and indefatigable Solicitor for many Years; that 'twas, in a great measure, to him they owed the Ease they found in the *African* Trade after the Revolution; he having so fully proved the Oppressions of the Royal Company at that time, in Parliament and elsewhere, that the Interlopers were no longer afraid of being seized and condemned; and the Company no more made use of that Part of their Prerogative.

This was a Piece of Service, which then they thought so considerable, that, besides the frequent Thanks that was sent him from *Barbados* by his own Correspondents, he had the same Acknowledgments paid him by such as he had no Commerce with; yet when it was put to the Vote, whether he should be one of the Agents of this Island, it was carried in the *Negative*, notwithstanding he had by his Agency done more for them, without that Title, than has been done since by those who have had it: For as the Ruin of the Monopoly Project, and the opening the *African* Trade was (let it be said by a Relation of his, without Vanity or Partiality) more owing to his Contrivance and Industry, than any other Person or Persons whatsoever; if the Island of *Barbados* has received two such Obligations from their Agents, in 17 Years, I am a Stranger to its Concerns. This is said without any other Design, but to pay Homage to Truth; and by the fair Representation I have made of all their Grievances and Pressures, the Gentlemen of *Barbados* will see, that no ill Usage has been able to provoke me to sacrifice my Sincerity to my Resentment.

'Tis below the Dignity of History to record private Matters; and this Digression is not perhaps of so private a Nature as may at first View be imagin'd.

These Agents have been continued ever since, and this Salary paid, but 'tis to be doubted, whether the 15000*l*. that has been paid them, would not have been as well laid out on the Uses the four and a half *per Cent*. was given for. No prudent Man can think, that a Gentleman, who is not bred up in the Business, and has no Interest in the Island, can be fit to make an Agent; nor even a Merchant, who has many Commissions: For there is no kind of Affairs that makes a Man so busy, and keeps him in such continual Hurries, as Factorage. 'Tis, without doubt, proper the Agent should fully understand the true Interest of *Barbados*, that he should have full Leisure to carry on his Agency, be a Man of Sense and Honour, and one that needs not make use of

a bora borrowed Pen to set forth its Grievances, and Petition for Redress.

I had put these few Reflections in the Chapter of *Trade*, but that as much as I have seemed to digress, they come in more naturally here.

The Act for establishing the first Agents was to expire in two Years; but others of the same Nature have been passed, and 'tis probable will pass, till the *Barbadians* have no Cause of Complaints, or have Friends that will make them for nothing.

The opening of the Trade to *Africa* was not soon accomplished, but at last 10 *per Cent.* was given to the *Royal Company* towards maintaining their Forts, &c. The honourable *John Farmer*, Esq; who was afterwards President, wrote thus to his Correspondent on this Head, after a sad Representation of the then State of *Barbados:* ' I hope ' yours, and other our Friends Endeavours against the ' *Royal Company*, have met with the desired Effect, which ' will be a sovereign Cordial to revive our drooping Spirits,&c.

The People of *England* had form'd great Expectations, as well as the *Barbadians*, of the Leeward Expedition; but the Gentlemen of *Barbados* soon saw those Expectations would come to nothing; for notwithstanding the Accounts of it printed in *England*, 'tis very certain they did nothing there, neither Admiral nor General, worth the Expences they put both *England* and *Barbados* to.

Col. *Farmer* was a Man of Penetration, and the Reader will not be displeased with his Account of our Affairs there, and his Reflections upon them, in a Letter dated the 3d of *April*, 1691. about 7 Weeks after the Fleet sailed from *Barbados*, with the Reinforcements mentioned before.

' Most of our Ships Men being pressed, and gone with the
' Fleet for the *Leeward* Expedition, they will not be able to
' sail for want of them, and so must stay for their Return.
' I wish I may then be able to give you such an Account of
' their Proceedings there, as may be pleasing to you; but by
' what they have hitherto done, I much doubt I shall not:
' For Capt. *Wright*, with all the King's Ships, reinforced
' with 6 of our best Merchant-Men, equal to fourth and
' fifth Rates, well manned, has been these seven Weeks
' down there; and tho' great Matters were talked of here
' before he went, as of taking and destroying all the *French*
' Islands in a short Time, yet talking is all that has hitherto
' been done, except the taking a small Fisher-boat: But the
' *French* have been more active; for while these mighty
' Things were performing by our Fleet in the Roads and
' Bays

' Bays of St. *Christophers*, *Antego*, and *Nevis*, they with
' Sloops and other small Vessels, are busied in taking (both
' Windward and Leeward of this Island) our Vessels in-
' ward and outward bound, of which we have Advice of
' 13 of all sorts already taken by them; so that in a very
' short time we shall be in a miserable Condition for want
' of Provisions.

And Mr. *Reid*, another Member of the Council, in a Letter dated the 2d of *July* following, writes:

' Our Crops this Year have been very small; in all Pro-
' bability the next will be smaller, we not having had the
' usual Seasons to plant. We have been annoyed extremely
' with a little *French* Snow, who has, notwithstanding the
' King's Fleets, taken by Report 28 or 30 of our small
' Vessels to Leeward of this Island, which has occasioned
' Provisions to be scarce and dear. Our Admiral, of whom
' we are like to be happily rid, has been slothful in their
' Majesty's Service; he and General *Codrington* deserted
' *Guardaloup* without any Reason, only their own Jealousies
' and Fears of the *French* Fleet, when we had three times
' the Number of Men that the *French* had. They left
' their Mortar Piece behind, tho' the *French* at the same
' time deserted the Island also, concluding we were going
' to attack *Martinico*. This Expedition is one of the most
' unaccountable things I ever heard of.

The little Care *Wright* took to scour those Seas of Privateers, put the Islanders to the Expence of equipping and fitting out two Ships for its Defence; which we find by the Title of an Act then passed, to *secure and reimburse the honourable Col. Richard Salter, Treasurer of this Island, all such Sums of Money, together with the Interest of the same, after the Rate of 10 per Cent. per Annum, he shall lend and accommodate towards the hiring, equipping, and fitting out two Ships, Sloops, or other Vessels of War, for the Defence of this Island.*

We perceive the Fleet and Land Forces did not secure the *Barbadians* from Fear; for another Act past *for entrenching and fortifying this Island, in such Places as his Excellency shall direct.*

This Fleet did not only do a great deal of Mischief to the *Barbadians*, by taking away their Landmen and Seamen, but the Soldiers had a pestilential Distemper among them, with which the Islanders were infected; and the Island, which before was reckoned to be the healthiest of all the Isles thereabouts, has ever since been very sickly, vast Numbers of Merchants, Captains of Ships, Planters, La-
bourers,

bourers, and Negroes have been swept away by this Disease; and 'tis to be wished, they may have such Supplies of Men sent them, as they want for their Defence.

Wright, for his Negligence and Cowardice, was sent Home a Prisoner; but the Affairs of the *French* in the *Charibbee* Islands did not receive that Turn which we threatned them with.

The *Assistance* Frigat meeting with a *French* Fly-boat of 800 Tuns, and 60 Guns, loaden with 30 Masts, and all Manner of Stores, for the Use of the *French* Men of War, took her, and brought her into *Barbados*; one of the best Things that was done by the Maritime Officers in that Expedition.

On the 16th of *January*, Capt. *Wren*, who succeeded Admiral *Wright* in the Command of the Leeward Fleet, arrived with a Fleet of Merchant Ships under his Convoy, he having 8 Men of War.

On the 24th of the same Month, Col *Kendal* having received Intimation, that 9 *French* Men of War were plying to the North-East of the Island, with the Advice of the Council, ordered 2 Merchant Men to be taken into their Majesties Service, and fitted for Men of War: Which was done accordingly; and being joined with their Majesties Ships, the *Norwich*, the *Mary*, the *Antelope*, the *Mordaunt*, and the *Diamond*, with 2 Sloops, they set sail the 30th, but having cruized several Days off the North East of this Isle, and in the Latitude of *Martinico*, without meeting with the Enemy, they returned to *Barbados* the 5th of *February*. After which it was resolved, that Capt. *Wren*, with the same Ships, should set sail to the Leeward Islands, together with the Merchant Men bound thither, and to *Jamaica*; and at his Arrival there, take into his Company the *Assistance*, the *Hampshire*, and the St. *Paul* Fireship; and then endeavour to find out the Enemy.

In order to this he set sail on the 17th of *February*, and the 21st in the Evening, being off the *Delcadas*, he saw 16 *French* Men of War, and 2 Fireships, commanded by the Count *de Blenac*, Governor of the *French* Islands. They sailed together all Night without any Action, tho' they were very near one another. About two the next Morning the *French* were on his Weather Quarter. At five he spread his Flag at the Fore-top Mast Head. At 6 the *French* Admiral made his Sign for a Council of War, and drew his Fleet into a Line of Battle. From 6 till past 7 they had little Wind, Calms, and much Rain. About 8 in the Morning the *French* having a Gale, bore down upon Capt. *Wren*. The
Mary

The History of Barbados.

Mary then bringing up the Rear, they first engaged with her, and afterwards with the rest of his Squadron; which lasted from 8 till 12 at Noon, and gave all his Merchant Men the Opportunity of getting clear. In the mean Time the Enemy had got the *Mordaunt*, commanded by Capt. *Butler*; the *Mary*, by Lieutenant *Wyat*; and the *England* Frigat, by Capt. *Stubbles*, in the midst of them; but they cleared themselves with all the Conduct and Bravery imaginable.

Capt. *Wren*'s Squadron consisted but of 7 Ships: Against which the *French* had 14, from 40 to 60 Guns, and 2 from 30 to 40 Guns, besides 2 Fire-Ships: Which is but an ill Proof of their boasted Courage and Conduct; for, notwithstanding all this Disparity, Capt. *Wren* brought all his Squadron into *Barbados* on the 25th of *February*, except the *England* Frigat, who bore away to *Jamaica*. Neither did any of the Merchants Ships fall into the Enemies Hands.

This was a very brave Action of Capt. *Wren*'s, and one of the best that has been done in the *West-Indies* in the late Wars.

The Mortality continued all this Year at *Barbados*, especially among the Sailors; insomuch that 'twas common to bury 10, 15, and 20 a Day at the *Bridge-Town*; and the Sickness abated little the next. Most of the Ships Crews, Men of War, and Merchant Men died of it: And the Inhabitants taking the Contagion, decreased daily.

The King's Ships could not go out a Cruising, for Want of Men. Capt. *Wren* was among the Number of the Dead; and the Ships were justly said to be *Graves*.

On the Revolution in *England* several Members of the Council of *Barbados* were misrepresented, as disaffected to the Government: But Col. *Kendal* having informed himself of the Injustice that had been done them, gave such a Recommendation of them at Home, that all such as desired it, were restored to their Seats at that Board.

About this Time his Majesty was pleased to appoint certain Lords and Gentlemen, of whom eight had Salaries, and the other were honorary Members, or rather Members by their Places, to be a Committee for Trade and the Plantations. This Committee are since better known by the Appellation of, *The Lords of Trade*, &c. Their Stile shews what their Business was to be; and every Thing relating to the Plantations, or Trade, is now brought before them.

The Island of *Barbados* being under their Care, and one of the most considerable Parts of it, 'twas necessary to mention

tion the establishing this Committee; of whom we may have Occasion to speak in this and other Parts of our History.

Besides the Mortality in *Barbados* in the Year 1692, there was very unseasonable Weather, and such Rains, that the Planters could not send their Sugars to the Ports. Most of the Masters of Ships who came to this Island at this Time, were buried here; and the Condition of the People was truly deplorable.

The Assembly passed an Act *concerning Trade*; which the Governor signed the 2d of *August*. And another to *raise, arm, and accouter* 1000 *Men, for an Expedition against the* French; tho' Hands were then so scarce in *Barbados*, that they could ill spare them. Another Act passed, and was signed in *October, appointing an Oath to be taken by all such, as by the Laws of this Island are, or shall be impowered to hear and determine Writs of Error, and Petitions of Grievances, and all other Matters of Equity whatsoever.* Another very necessary Act past, and was signed the same Month; entitled, *An Act for Encouragement of all Negroes and Slaves that shall discover any Conspiracy.*

The Assembly earnestly pressed the Governor, and desired their Agents in *England*, to write to, and petition the Lords of the Committee, to permit a Regiment of Soldiers, designed for the Leeward Expedition against the *French*, to remain in *Barbados* when the Expedition was over; and past an Act for free Quarter for them: But we never understood that a Regiment was granted them while this Governor staid here.

The Assembly passed an *Act, for prohibiting the selling of Rum, or any strong Liquors, to any Negro, or other Slave*; which the Governor signed: But this *Act*, like others in other Places, has been easily and often evaded.

The Governor had a Present from the Country this Session; and the Grand Jury sitting at the *Bridge* drew up a very loyal Address to their Majesties King *William* and Queen *Mary*; which was presented them by Col. *Edwyn Stede*, introduced by the Earl of *Rochester*. At which Time his Majesty conferred the Honour of Knighthood on Col. *Stede*, in Consideration of his faithful Services.

The Reader may have the Curiosity to know the Reason of their passing the Act concerning the Negroes above-mentioned. The Preamble to the Act for their discovering Conspiracies, tells us : *Whereas sundry of the Negroes and Slaves of this Island, have been long preparing, contriving, and designing a most horrid, bloody, damnable and detestable Rebellion, Massacre, Assassination, and Destruction, by them to be committed,* &c. This

The History of Barbados.

This Plot was the most general the Slaves ever hatched, and brought nearest to Execution. The Villains were so cunning, as to observe the Want of Inhabitants, occasioned by the Pestilence and War, and thought they should never have a better Opportunity to accomplish their diabolical Purposes, tho' one would think, that Wretches capable of so foolish, as well as bloody a Design, could never have much thought of the Matter: For what could they pretend to do? Could they maintain themselves there without Provisions? Would it have mended their Condition to have changed their Masters? And instead of serving Free-men, have been Slaves to Slaves, the *French*. Or did they imagine the Christians would have suffered them to set up a Negro Monarchy, or Republick, in the midst of their Governments, *English*, *Dutch*, and *French*? They would rather have leagued, than have suffered such an unnatural and dangerous Independence. Would they have returned to their original Barbarity? How could they have got to *Africa*? They would have been looked upon as common Enemies by all Nations: And if *England* had not thought fit to have chastized them, as they most certainly and severely would have done, every Christian People would have thought it fair to have attacked them, and carried them into worse Slavery, than what they basely endeavoured to free themselves from, by Treason, Murder, and hellish Ingratitude.

Before we reflect any farther upon it, the Reader will expect to know more of the Particulars, which are these.

This Design, as has been said, had been carried on a long Time; but the Conspirators met with several Disappointments about the Execution of it. The Conspiracy was to kill the Governor; and at the same Time those who were chiefly trusted in each Plantation, were to fall upon their Masters and Overseers; and afterwards to rendezvous with what Arms, Ammunition, and Horses they could seize, at the *Bridge-Town*; where they were to form themselves into several Regiments of Horse and Foot; of which they had agreed who were to be the principal Officers. They were to have been farther supplied with Arms and Ammunition out of the publick Magazine, by a Negro employed there under the Store-keeper, who was to have been murdered by his Slave. They designed also to surprize the Fort, and from thence to batter the Ships in the Harbour. But their wicked Contrivances were happily brought to Light by two of the chiefest of the Conspirators, who were over-heard as they were discoursing of it; and being immediately seized, were condemned to be hanged in Chains, till they were starved to

Death;

Death; which they endured four Days, and then finding they were not relieved by the Succour they hoped for from their Accomplices, they promised to declare the whole Design; and accordingly did it, making a full Confession, and discovering the principal Conspirators; who were secured, put to the Torture, and several of them executed.

The Laws made on this Occasion are in the Abridgment of the Laws of the Plantations, and in the Statutes at large of the Island of *Barbados*. When we consider that above half of the Blacks are *Creolians*, or Natives of the Isle, their Folly and Madness appear the more unaccountable; that they should be willing to change their natural Lords for foreign. If they imagined they could get to *Guinea*, or could maintain themselves at *Barbados*, they must be Fellows of the poorest Capacities upon Earth, and their Understanding be as vile as their Condition.

This was the greatest Danger the *Barbadians* were ever exposed to from their Slaves: And the good Laws that were made for preventing the like Conspiracies for the future, have in a great Measure answered the End.

As for the Dispute that happened in this Governor's Time, between him and Col. *Hallet*; and the Process thereupon, having no sufficient Memoirs to make a just Report of the Matter, we can only mention it, and proceed with our History.

The thousand Men, of which we have spoken, were rais'd, according to the Act of the Assembly, and formed two Regiments; one commanded by Col. *Richard Salter*; the other by Col. *John Boteler*, both Planters in this Island; and were intended to join with some Forces expected from *England*, in order to undertake an Expedition against *Martinico*. A good Squadron of Men of War were equiped in *England*, and sailed for *Barbados*, about the latter End of the Year 1692, having on Board Col. *Foulk*'s and Col. *Godwin*'s Regiments of Foot, and 200 Recruits of Col. *Lloyd*'s.

Sir *Francis Wheeler* was Commander of the Men of War; and Col. *Foulks* of the Land-Forces, who arriving at *Barbados*, was joined by Col. *Salter*, and Col. *Boteler*.

The Fleet sailed from that Island the 30th of *March*, 1693, and on the 1st of *April* arrived at *Martinico*, where they anchored in the *Cul de Sac Marine*. We must observe, that the two *Barbados* Regiments, when raised, the Gentlemen and others, Volunteers, that went from thence with them, made the whole Number of *Barbadians* 13 or 1400 Men, above half of the Land-Forces.

The

The History of Barbados.

The Place where Sir *Francis* anchored was the South-East Part of the Island, about a Mile and half from the Shore. Himself, Col. *Foulk*, and Col. *Lloyd*, went in a Sloop, to see for a convenient Place, in order to land their Men.

The *French* had several small Guards along the Shore; from one of which a Musket Shot struck Sir *Francis* under the Right Pap, and fell down at his Feet, having only made a great Contusion. Orders were given for landing of the Forces, but the Wind blowing very fresh, 'twas deferred till next Day; when, about 9 in the Morning, Col. *Foulk* landed with 1500 Men, without any Opposition. The Boats were immediately sent back, and towards Evening the rest of the Forces also landed. On the 3d of *April* they continued ashore, and destroyed all the Houses and Plantations about *Cul de Sac Marine*; most of which were good Sugar-Works; the Inhabitants and Negroes flying into the Woods.

The 4th the Forces returned on Board. The 5th Sir *Francis Wheeler* went ashore, with a Detachment of 500 Men, in the Bay towards the *Diamond*, burnt several Houses and Plantations; and at Night came on Board again. The same Day a Lieutenant of one of the *Barbados* Regiments going ashore without Orders, with 6 or 7 Soldiers, besides the Boat's Crew, fell into an Ambuscade: Two of them were killed, and the rest taken Prisoners.

The 6th Lieutenant Colonel *Lilliston* was sent ashore with a strong Party, to destroy the Country on the Side of the Bay towards the *Diamond*; and having performed the same, returned on Board with his Men towards Night.

The 9th Col. *Codrington* joined them with Col. *Lloyd's* Regiment, and the Leeward Forces. But Col. *Foulk* remained without Action till the 12th, when 'twas resolved, in a Council of War, to sail to St. *Pierre*, where the Fleet arrived the 15th, and anchored within Musket Shot of the Shore.

On the 17th the *English* landed, and their advanced Parties had some Skirmishes with the Enemy. Col. *Foulk* commanded an Eminence to be possessed, and sent out several Parties, who advancing into the Country, destroyed all before them.

On the 18th the *English* posted themselves on a Hill, within Cannon Shot of the Town of St. *Pierre*; and several Field-pieces were brought ashore; which played upon the Enemy, who lay behind their Entrenchments.

The 19th the *French* made a Sally upon *Foulk's* Out-guards, but were repulsed by Part of Col. *Foulk's* Regiment, led by Capt. *Sproston*, who pursued them to their Trenches;

where

where the Officer that commanded them was killed. Col. *Blackstone* supported Capt. *Sproston* with a Leeward Regiment; and the Enemy was so discouraged, that they ventured out of their Lines no more.

Such was the End of this *Martinico* Expedition, wherein the *Barbadians* were rather too forward, than otherwise; and had the Officers who came from *England* done their Duty, as well as these that came from *Barbados*, we might probably have given a better Account of it. For a Council of War being held, 'twas resolved that the Men and Artillery should be re-imbarked; which was done: And the only Reason I ever heard of, was, because the Fort was a regular Work; and that, 'tis to be supposed, was known before the *English* landed there. 'Tis said, the Men were sickly: If so, the keeping them aboard, and carrying them to the Leeward, was not the Way to cure them.

The Forces made all together 4 or 5000 Men, and were enough to have dispossessed the *French* of all their Sugar-Islands. Col. *Salter*, and Col. *Boteler*, returned to *Barbados*; which Island had only lost more Hands, and no Soldiers were left to supply their Places.

Col. *Foulk*, Col. *Goodwin*, Major *Abrahall*, and other Officers died a Ship-board, and met with an inglorious Death, in avoiding a glorious one. 'Tis true, the *French* at *Martinico* were enough frighten'd, and most of the richest Inhabitants ship'd themselves and their valuable Effects for *France*; some of whom were intercepted by the *English*.

Col. Francis Russel, Governor. His Majesty King *William* having recalled Col. *Kendal*, appointed Col. *Francis Russel*, Brother to the Right Honourable the Earl of *Orford*, to be Governor of *Barbados*, and gave him a Commission for a Regiment of Soldiers, which were to be transported to that Island, and there to remain. Accordingly the Assembly took Care for their Accommodation against their Arrival, which was in the Year 1694. And Col. *Kendal* being returned to *England*, his Majesty was pleased to make him one of the Lords of the Admiralty.

Tho' some Accounts brought Advice, that the Sickness in *Barbados* was abated, yet 'tis certain, that the Men, both ashore and aboard, died as fast as ever; and the two Men of War in *Carlisle-Bay*, the *Tyger* and *Mermaid*, wanted Hands so much, that the Assembly were forced to pass an Act, for speedy supplying them with Men.

With Col. *Russel* went his Lady, the Lady *North* and *Grey*, and her Daughter, Sister to the present Lord *North*, who both died there.

The first Act now in Force, which the new Governor Mr. *Ruffel* passed, was, *to prevent the breaking up or taking away of any Rocks or Stones in any Part of the Sea, or Sea-Shores before this Island*; which Act is signed by Mr. *Thomas Brewster*, who, 'tis said, acted as Deputy Secretary, by the Governor's Order; and *George Pain*, Esq; Clerk of the Assembly. The latter being some time after made Deputy Secretary, the present Sollicitor-General was chosen Clerk of the Assembly in his stead.

The Government here thought fit to set forth the *Brigantine Marygold* to go to Leeward, and fetch up the Remainder of the Men that were left there, after the *Martinico* Expedition.

The Assembly advanced 700 *l*. to victual the *Bristol* Man of War, and *Play Prize*; and added Mr. *Francis Eyles*, a worthy Merchant of *London*, to the two Agents beforementioned, ordering by an Act, that 1500 *l*. should be remitted to him for the Service of the Island. They presented the Governor with 2000 *l*. and maintained his Regiment. The Governor, Council, and Assembly, transmitted a very loyal Address of Condolance to his Majesty King *William*, on the never enough lamented Death of his Royal Consort, our Sovereign Queen *Mary*, Sister in all things to our present Gracious and Glorious Queen *Anne*; which the King was pleased to receive very graciously, and some time after knighted Col. *Willoughby Chamberlayne*, for his good and faithful Services in this Island; who being since dead, his Lady married Mr. *Mitford Crow*, a Merchant of *London*, of whom more hereafter.

The *Child's Play* Man of War convoyed a Fleet of Merchant Ships from *Barbados* to *England*; and 'tis observable, that the Islanders were in a great measure at the Expence of it: For without they had victual'd her, she could not have sailed.

Besides these Charges, the Governors began now to be a sort of Grievance, by their exacting Presents from the Country, and looking upon those Gifts to be their Right, which were only extraordinary Benevolences of the Inhabitants.

Col. *Ruffel* had 2000 *l*. more, *A. D.* 1695. tho', if Report is true, he did not deserve it; for we have been credibly informed, there were not seven Rounds of Powder in the Forts when Monsieur *Pointy* came in Sight of *Barbados*, as he was sailing to *Carthagena*; and had he known what Circumstances the *Barbadians* were in, perhaps he had ended his Expedition before he reached the Continent. There

was

was Powder enough in *Barbados* not long before; but the Pirates had their Agents in this Island as well as other Places, and some how or other Means were made use of to supply those at *Madagascar* with it. 'Tis not to be questioned, but they paid a good Price for it ; and if the Gentlemen of *Barbados* had any Jealousy of such an infamous Traffick, we wonder they did not, by their Agents in *England*, take Care to complain of it.

<small>Francis Bond, Esq; Governor.</small>

Col. *Russel* dying, just as this Matter began to make a Noise, *Francis Bond*, Esq; President of the Council, undertook the Administration, till a Governor arrived from *England*: And the President, Council, and General Assembly, having Advice of the damnable Assassination Plot, sent over a hearty and loyal Address to his Majesty, *to congratulate his Majesty's wonderful and happy Deliverance from the most barbarous and bloody Assassination lately designed against his Royal Person by execrable Villains, and Monsters of Mankind, who are the Dishonour of the present, and will be the Horror and Detestation of future Ages.*

A very loyal Address was also presented to his Majesty on the same Occasion, from the Grand-Jury of the Island of *Barbados*.

In this President's Time several good Laws were made, which remain still in Force ; and which we shall particularize in the Order of Time, as they passed. The first is an Act *declaring the Decision of all controverted Elections of Members to serve in the General Assembly, to be legally and rightfully in the Representatives of his Majesty's liege People of this Island*; which was signed the 10th of *February*, 1696. And on the 16th of the same Month, another Bill passed, being *A supplemental and explanatory Act to an Act, entitled, An Act for binding and ordering poor Apprentices*. And the 3d of *March* following, another, entitled, An Act *that the solemn Affirmation and Declaration of the People called* Quakers, *shall be accepted instead of an Oath in the usual Form.*

About this time, Vice-Admiral *Nevil* arrived at *Barbados*, with a Squadron of Men of War ; and the 28th of *April*, 1697. sailed from this Island, to look after Monsieur *Pointy*.

The Assembly still sitting, an Act passed the 18th of *May, to disable the Judges from pleading and practising in any of the Courts of this Island* ; as also, another *to repeal an Act, entitled, An Act for laying a Duty on Shipping, for the Publick Building of Peers, and clearing the Bar in* Carlisle *Road*.

Two Ships, the *Providence* and *Benjamin*, were fitted out, employed and paid by the Country, according to an

Act

Act passed for that Purpose: And in *June* 1697. a Bill was read, and passed the President and Council, *to keep inviolate and preserve the Freedom of Elections, and appointing who shall be deemed Freeholders, and be capable of electing, or being elected Representatives, Vestry Men, or to serve as Jurors to try real Actions within this Island:* A Law of very great Importance in the present Constitution of the Government of *Barbados*; as is that *for the Settlement of the* Militia *of this Island.*

The *Barbadians* had not then heard of the Conclusion of the Peace at *Reswyck,* and this Bill was enacted for their Security against Invasions. Guns were to be placed on *Lesley*'s Hill, *Ramsay*'s Hill, the Mount, *Brigg*'s Hill, and other convenient Places, for the speedy carrying on of an Alarum.

About the Beginning of *January,* the Earl of *Bellomont* arrived at *Barbados,* in the *Deptford* Man of War. He was bound for his Government of *New-England* and *New-York,* and driven hither by Stress of Weather.

News coming to this Island of the Peace, one may imagine by their Losses, that the Inhabitants, in whose Name, as well as their own, the President, Council, and Assembly, addressed King *William,* were heartily glad of the Security he had given them, by bringing *France* to Reason.

The last Act now in Force, passed in Mr. *Bond*'s Presidency, was an Act *for the better securing the Liberty of his Majesty's Subjects within this Island, and preventing long Imprisonment.*

In 1698, his Majesty was pleased to appoint the Honourable *Ralph Grey,* Esq; Brother to the Right Honourable the Earl of *Tankervill,* to be Governor of *Barbados,* and he sailed from St. *Hellens* on board the *Soldados Prize,* the 1st of *June.* He arrived at *Madera* the 24th of *June,* and having been nobly entertained by the Governor, during his Stay, sailed thence the 1st of *July,* and on the 26th arrived at *Barbados.*

The Honourable Ralph Grey, *Esq; Governor.*

The *Speedwell,* Capt. *Coulsea,* came thither in Company with the *Soldados;* aboard which Ship, in their Passage from *Madera,* a villanous Design was discovered, carried on by one *Jonathan Bear,* a Midship Man, to surprize and murder the Captain, and afterwards to run away with the Ship. Upon which *Bear,* and two other Seamen, who were chiefly concerned in the Plot, were secured; and when they came to *Barbados,* were put aboard the *Sheerness,* and sent in Chains to *England.*

The

The new Governor, Mr. *Grey*, upon his Arrival near the Shore, was faluted by the Cannon from the Caftles and Forts; and coming to an Anchor, was complimented by the Council and Affembly. The next Day he came afhore, the Men of War and the Forts firing all the while. Major *Garth*'s independent Company of Regular Soldiers, and fome Militia Horfe, were drawn up to receive him; and upon his Landing, the Council waited upon him, and conducted him to the Council-Chamber, where his Commiffion was read, and the ufual Oaths adminiftred to him, and to the Members of the Council; after which they entertained him at Dinner. In the Evening the Governor, attended by feveral of the Council, went to Mr. *Bond*'s Houfe, two Miles from the *Bridge-Town*; where he continued till Mr. *Hotherfall*'s Plantation was taken for him, and the Houfe fitted up for his Reception.

On *Tuefday* the 2d of *Auguft* the Affembly met, and attended him in the Council Chamber; and their Speaker, *Thomas Maxwell*, Efq; made a Speech, expreffing great Loyalty and Duty to his Majefty, and congratulating the Governor's fafe Arrival.

The Reader will not be difpleafed with a Lift of this Council and Affembly; by which he will have a clearer View of the Form of Government in *Barbados*, and the Governor's Stile.

The NAMES of the *Governor, Council*, and *Affembly* of *Barbados*, as they were in the Year 1698.

His Excellency *Ralph Grey*, Efq;
Captain General and Chief Governor of the Ifland of *Barbados, Sancta Lucia*, St. *Vincent's, Dominico*, and the reft of his Majefty's Iflands, Colonies, and Plantations in *America*, known by the Name of the *Charibbee*-Iflands, lying and being to Windward of *Guardaloup*.

The Honourable the Members of his Majefty's COUNCIL, at that Time.

Francis Bond, Efq; late Prefident.

John Gibbs,	*Michael Terrill,*	
John Farmer,	*David Ramfey,*	
George Lillington, Efquires.	*Richard Scot,*	Efquires.
George Andrews,	*Benjamin Cryer,*	
William Sharp,	*Richard Walter,*	
Tobias Frere,	*Thomas Merrick,*	

The Members of the then General ASSEMBLY, viz.

For the Precincts of

St. *Michael.*	George Peers, Esq;
	William Wheeler, Esq;
Chrift-Church.	Thomas Maxwell, Esq; Speaker.
	Daniel Hooper, Esq;
St. *Philips.*	William Fortefcue, Esq;
	Henry Markland, Esq;
St. *John.*	John Lefslie, Esq;
	James Colliton, Esq;
St. *George.*	Peter Flewellin, Esq;
	Miles Toppin, Esq;
St. *Jofeph.*	John Holder, Esq;
	Henry Gallop, Esq;
St. *Andrew.*	William Cleeland, Esq;
	William Doten, Esq;
St. *James.*	Abel Alleyne, Esq;
	William Holder, Esq;
St. *Thomas.*	Thomas Sadleir, Esq;
	Jonathan Downes, Esq;
St. *Peter.*	Samuel Maynard, Esq;
	Robert Harrifon, Esq;
St. *Lucyes.*	John Gibbs, Esq;
	Thomas Englifh, Esq;

Upon the Governor's Arrival, the Affembly fell prefently to Bufinefs, were unanimous and fpeedy in their Debates, and in a Week's Time had two Bills ready; as an Act *to declare and afcertain the Rights and Powers of the General Affembly of this Ifland*; and an Act *to fettle five hundred Pounds* per Annum *on his Excellency, for his Habitation.* At which time we find Mr. *William Hart* was Deputy Secretary. The Preamble to the laft Act gives us the Reafons why the Governor did not think fit to take up his Refidence at *Fontabell: Whereas it is neceffary and expedient for the Inhabitants of this Ifland to find and provide an Habitation for his Majefty's Governor of this Ifland; and by Reafon of the Decay, and want of Repairs at* Fontabell, *the late Habitation of the Governor, and the Danger he will be expofed to in Cafe of War, fo that it is no ways fit for his Excellency's Reception,* &c. But fince it had done in time of War, that Argument in time of Peace might have been left out of the Preamble.

The 500 *l.* a Year was paid for *Hotherfall*'s House and Plantation, which, 'tis probable, the Governor liked better, and thought to be a better Bargain than the other.

'Tis very certain, this Gentleman was much in the good Graces of the People of *Barbados*; never any Governor was so well beloved. He was a Man of Honour; his Soul noble as well as his Birth, and he was not capable of doing an ill thing by them for his own Interest. Such Men will soon gain the Affections of a Colony, and they will in the main find their Advantage by it too; for People give more when they see Governors are not greedy, than when they are always begging, or doing worse.

On the 7th of *September* an Act passed *for two thousand Pounds for his Excellency's Charges of his Voyage, towards the better Support for the Government*; the Title of which is not very grammatical. Mr. *George Payne* signed it, acting as Deputy Secretary *pro hac vice:* And Mr. *Rawlins*, Clerk of the Assembly, the same Day procured an Act to appoint him to collect the Body of the Laws, and *for printing the Laws of the Island of* Barbados, *contained in the ensuing Volume:* The Volume he published, from which the Writer of this History took some of his Matter, as the Titles of the *Acts*, &c. and that Collection going down no farther than the above-mentioned 7th of *September*, 1698, we have no farther Helps from him. The same Day the Governor, Council, and Assembly, passed the Act *concerning the General Sessions.*

This being a Time of Peace, few Events happened here worth recording. The Mortality continued till the Year 1698, but grew less and less from the Year 1694. In the first of Mr. *Grey's* Government it ceased, and the Island grew healthful again, but not in such a Degree as it was twenty or thirty Years before; for two Years afterwards, *A. D.* 1700, the Sickness returned: And at the same Time there was a great Scarcity of Corn and Provisions; but as the Mortality did not last long, so the Scarcity was supplied by Imports from *New-England.*

About this Time *William Welby*, Esq; was made Secretary of the Island; a very worthy Gentleman, who served the late Duke of *Devonshire*, and his Grace the present Duke, in the same Capacity. This Office was afterwards made over to *Alexander Skeyne*, Esq; the present Secretary of *Barbados.*

The same Year, 1700, Sugars were scarce and dear; and there happened also a Hurricane, which did much Damage, threw down several Warehouses, and drove two Ships and two Sloops ashore.

The History of Barbados.   63

In the following Year, 1701, the Governor being indisposed in his Health, removed to *England*, leaving the Administration in the Hands of the then President of the Council, *John Farmer*, Esq; in whose Time his Majesty King *William* dying, the Privy-Council in *England* notified her present Majesty's Accession to the Throne, to the President and Council in *Barbados*. Upon which Col. *Farmer* immediately gave Directions for proclaiming the Queen; and on the 18th of *May*, 1702, the President and Council, being accompanied by Mr. *Skeyne* the Secretary, Mr. *George Hannah* the Provost-Marshal, and other publick Officers, the Clergy, and Gentlemen of the *Bridge-Town*, and other Parts of the Island, attended by several Troops of Horse, and the Regiment of Foot Guards, went in a solemn Procession from *James* Fort to the common Parade, where the Proclamation was made. After which the Forts and Ships discharged their Guns three Times, and the People gave all publick Demonstrations of their Joy on this Occasion. The President and Council, together with the principal Officers and Inhabitants of the Island, drew up a very handsom Address of Congratulation to the Queen, and condoled heartily with her on the Death of his late Majesty: Which was presented by the Right Honourable *Ralph* Lord *Grey* of *Werk*, their late Governor; for the Earl of *Tankervill* being dead, his Brother, Mr. *Grey*, succeeded him in the Barony, but not in the Earldom.

John Farmer, Esq; Governor.

The War was no sooner proclaimed between *France* and *England*, but the Gentlemen and Merchants of *Barbados* fitted out a good Number of Privateers, to act against the *French*. Sixteen of them meeting together near *Guardaloup*, the Men landed on the Island, burnt a great Part of the West End of it, and brought off a good Number of Negroes. In the same Year an Earthquake was felt at *Barbados*, which lasted a Minute and a half, but did no considerable Damage. The Inhabitants were at this Time more healthy than they had been for several Years before.

'Tis said the Blacks then formed another Design to burn the *Bridge-Town*, and seize the Forts; but the Plot was timely discovered, and the chief Conspirators executed.

In the following Year, 1703, her Majesty was pleased to appoint Sir *Bevill Greenvill* to be Governor of *Barbados*; and it having been found burthensome to the Country to make Presents of 2000*l*. and other large Sums to the Governors, Orders were sent to put a Stop to that Custom; and as a Compensation for this, the Governor's Salary was encreased from 1200 to 2000*l*. a Year.

Sir Bevill Greenvill Governor.

This

This Government in King *William*'s Time had been promised to Mr. *Mitford Crow*, a Merchant of *London*, who had served an Apprenticeship to a *Barbados* Merchant, Mr. *Abraham Tillard*, and married the Lady *Chamberlayne* of this Island. He kissed the King's Hand for it, and prepared his Equipage; but when his Majesty was dead, Sir *Bevill Greenvill* put in for it, and obtained it.

The Assembly, to compliment the new Governor, appointed Sir *John Stanly*, Secretary to the Lord Chamberlain, and Sir *Bevill*'s Brother in Law, to be one of their Agents; in which their Conduct was courtly indeed, but not very politick; for how is it possible any Man should be able to serve the Island as an Agent ought, who is not fully apprized of her Concerns, who does not perfectly understand her true Interest, and has other Avocations of more Importance, to him at least, than his Agency?

Sir *Bevill* arriving at *Barbados*, a House was built for him and his Successors, on *Pilgrim*'s Plantation, where he resided.

There was a Novelty in the Ministry here, which was a little extraordinary; the Sex was shifted, and the fair Favourite did not lose her Time nor her Market.

On the 27th of *September*, her Majesty's Ship the *Blackwall*, Capt. *Samuel Martin* Commander, brought into *Carlisle* Bay a *French* Privateer of 12 Guns, and 120 Men, which he took in that Latitude; as also, an *Irish* Ship bound for *Barbados*, which had been taken the Day before by the same Privateer.

On the 2d of *February* her Majesty's Ship the *Dreadnought*, having on Board Col. *Seymour*, Governor of *Maryland*, arrived there; where he stayed a few Days, and then proceeded in his Voyage, having been driven thither by Stress of Weather.

The Island of *Barbados* was at this Time miserably divided into Factions; one was for the Governor, and the other against him. The latter sent Complaints to *England*, which were contradicted by those of the other Interest, tho' 'twas generally reported, that Sir *Bevill Greenvill* had done several unfair Things; the Particulars of which not being come to our Hands, they are like to be forgotten.

In his Time one *Chilton*, who made the References to *Cook*'s *Reports*, was Attorney General of *Barbados*. He had the Misfortune to kill a Man there, and being guilty of many male Practices, was suspended: When he came to *England*, he also joined with the Complainants against the Governor, and succeeded almost as well as if he had been innocent.

The History of Barbados.

The Faction in *Barbados* ran so high, that one Gentleman was accused of Designs against the Governor's Life; but tho' he was fined 2000 *l.* yet 'twas generally thought, there was more Malice than Reason in the Accusation. The Gentleman was one of the Council, and had we believed he had been guilty, we should have named him.

In the Year 1705, the Assembly taking into Consideration the great Want of Money in the Island, occasioned by the sending away all the Silver from thence, upon the Proclamation for reducing Pieces to a certain Standard in the *West-Indies*, passed an Act to allow 65000 *l.* Paper Credit, impowering the Treasurer to give out Bills for such a Sum, and lend them to the Planters, on Security of Land and Negroes. *John Holder*, Esq; Speaker of this Assembly was appointed Treasurer, and was to have 5 *per Cent.* for managing these Bills. The Money'd Men were generally against this Project; for they found their Debtors were glad of an Opportunity to pay them in Paper.

The Assembly who passed the Act being dissolved, the next that sat proceeded vigorously against those who were concerned in it, and sent an Address to *England* to complain of it.

On the 4th of *July*, 1706. the Squadron of her Majesty's Ships, under the Command of Captain *Kerr*, arrived at *Barbados*; from whence they sailed to the Leeward Islands, having on board Colonel *Park*, who was appointed Governor of those Islands.

Sir *Bevill Greenvill* being either recalled, or having obtained Leave to come for *England*, her Majesty was pleased, in Consideration of Mr. *Crow*'s eminent Services at *Barcelona*, to let him succeed Sir *Bevill* in the Government. The latter embarked on board the *Kingsale* Man of War, bound for *England*, and died in his Voyage homewards, as the late President, Colonel *Farmer*, had done some time before.

Mr. *Crow* arrived in *Barbados*, in the Year 1707. and, according to his Instructions, removed those Gentlemen that had been concerned in the Paper Credit Act from their Places at the Council Board, and from all other that were in the Governor's Power. This bred Discontents, and has occasioned more Remonstrances to be sent to *England*.

Mitford Crow, *Esq* *Governor.*

The Treasurer, Mr. *Holder*, was obliged to refund the 5 *per Cent.* he had received for managing the Paper Credit; and he appealing, the Matter depends at this time.

Some Months before Mr. *Crow*'s Arrival, a very odd Accident happened here to one Mr. *Samuel Frazon*, a Merchant, who coming from on board a Man of War, a Storm arose,

arose, and drove him in his Boat out to Sea ; so that 'twas feared he was lost. At last News came of him, that after having driven upon the Ocean six Days, without any Subsistence, not so much as Bread and Water, he fell upon St. *Vincents*; where, as soon as he had landed with his Sailors and Negro, the Indians stripped them stark naked. The two Sailors died in a little time of the Fatigue, but the Merchant and his Black survived it. Mr. *Frazon* continued in that Condition three Months; at the end of which the Indians carried him over to *Martinico*; where he paid 17 or 18 Pistoles for his Ransom, but they would not let him redeem his Negro. Form *Martinico* the *French* sent him to *Nevis*; from whence he returned to *Barbados*.

Another Boat at the same time, with two Negroes, drove off to Sea, and they landed the same Day at St. *Vincents*; where the *Charibbeans* do not always deal so civilly by the *English*, who are driven thither by Storms, as they did by Mr. *Frazon*, tho' they used him ill.

Whatever was the Issue of the Paper Credit Project, 'tis certain the Contests it raised in the Island were not over when more warm and dangerous ones arose between the Governors and the Inhabitants of the Island. Mr. *Crow*'s Successor in this Government was *Robert Lowther*, Esq; whose first Stay here was short; for I find he was recalled in 1713. whether for Irregularities in his Conduct, or for the Ill-will the Ministry in *England* bore him on Account of his being preferred to that Post by their Predecessors before the *Utrecht* Peace, I know not; but the former seems most probable; for after he was recalled, and *William Sharp*, Esq; President of the Council was ordered to take upon him the Administration, he was so loth to part with his Authority, that *Samuel Cox*, Esq; and *Timothy Salter*, Esq; Members of the Council, were obliged to remonstrate against his keeping it so strenuously, that he endeavoured to have it understood to be an Act of Rebellion, and to have them prosecuted accordingly, of which we must speak farther in the Sequel. Mr. *Sharp* behaved so well in his Station the first time he was Commander in Chief, that the Earl of *Sunderland*, then Secretary of State, approved his Conduct by Letter, and this his second Administration was as wise and as well approved. He continued as President till Mr. *Lowther* returned to *Barbados* with his former Character after his late Majesty's Accession to the Throne, and in a worse Disposition to abuse his Power there than when he formerly held it. How can a good Subject, without the deepest Regret observe, that so just, so gracious a Prince as our late Sovereign should have

Counsellors

Robert Lowther, Esq; Governor.

William Sharp, Esq; President.

The History of Barbados.

Counsellors near his Royal Person, capable of recommending one so obnoxious to his Majesty's Favour for a Post of that Trust and Honour. But this History of our *American* Colonies abounds with Instances of the like Recommendations. Mr. *Lowther* was not long in *Barbados* before he fell out with the Rev. Mr. *Gordon*, Rector of St. *Michael's-bridge*, and Commissary or Vice-bishop of the Island, and wrote against him to his Diocesan the Bishop of *London*, representing him as a Man of ill Principles and Morals. He wrote also against him to the *Barbados* Agents, and they made the Contents of his Letter the Subject of a Memorial to the Board of Trade; where Mr. *Gordon* succeeded not so well as at the Board of Regency. The Proceedings of the Agents and their Success at the Board of Trade obliged Mr. *Gordon* to quit the Island, to take proper Measures in *England* for his Defence, by an Appeal to the Lords Justices, from whom he found such Relief as the Goodness of his Cause deserved against the Oppression and Ruin that threatened him. Their Lordships Decree runs thus.

Governor Lowther's Prosecutions.

'His Majesty having been pleased by his Order in Council of the 15th of *March* 1718. to refer unto a Committee the humble Petition of *William Gordon*, Clerk, Rector of the Parish of St. *Michael*, in *Barbados*; complaining as well against a Petition of the Agents of the said Island, and a Report of the Board of Trade thereupon, as against a Letter wrote by the Governor of the said Island to the Lord Bishop of *London*, highly reflecting on the said *Gordon's* Conduct as Commissary, and on his Principles and Character, &c.' The Lords Justices ordered Depositions to be taken at *Barbados*, as well on the Part of the Governor, as of Mr. *Gordon*, who returning thither had the said Order served on the Governor, who instead of proceeding regularly thereon, caused a Copy of it to be proclaimed by beat of Drum in the *Bridge-Town*, and again published in all the Churches in the Island; and farther, Mr. *Gordon* was sent to the common Goal by Warrant under the Governor's Secretary's Hand without assigning any Cause. And the above-mentioned Depositions not being returned in the appointed Time, and nothing farther offered to make good the Allegations against Mr. *Gordon*, their Lordships reported it as their Opinion, that the Charges of the Governor and *Agents* of *Barbados* against Mr. *Gordon* are groundless, and ought to be dismissed.

Mr. *Francis Lanfa*, Merchant of *Bridge-Town*, having had a Ship unlawfully seized by Order of Governor *Lowther*, presented a Petition to the King in Council, complaining of the

the said Seizure, upon which an Order was sent to *Barbados*, directing an Enquiry into the Matter of Mr. *Lanfa*'s Complaint against the Governor, and Mr. *Henry Lafcelles*, Collector of the Customs, and Mr. *Ifaac Lenoir* the Governor's Secretary. But the Governor far from obeying the Order, treated it contemptuously, and abufed *Jonathan Blenman*, Efq; Mr. *Lanfa*'s Counfel, took from him the original Order, and refufed to redeliver it, and detained Mr. *Lanfa*'s Letter of Attorney, declaring it to be forged, and committed Mr. *Blenman* to Prifon, and caufed him to be bound over in a thoufand Pound Bail, which he forfeited on his coming to *England* to complain. But upon hearing the Caufe, the Lords Juftices ordered, that *all Proceedings on the Recognizance be vacated, and if any Levy had been made upon the Forfeiture, that the fame be forthwith returned to Mr.* Blenman *or his Agent.*

1720.

Some time before this, Sir *Charles Cox*, Member in frequent Parliaments for the Borough of *Southwark*, prefented a Petition to the King in Council, in Behalf of his Brother *Samuel Cox*, Efq; againft Governor *Lowther*, who removed Mr. *Cox* from the Council Board without any juft Caufe or Reafon, as is faid in his Petition; this Caufe being afterwards heard by the Lords Juftices, they declared that Sir *C. Cox* had made out the Allegations of his Petition, that the Governor's Reafons for the Sufpenfion of Mr. *Cox* were without the leaft Ground, and that the faid Governor had acted *arbitrarily* and *illegally*. They alfo ordered that *Samuel Cox*, Efq; be reftored to his Place and Seniority in the Council, and put into, and take upon him the Exercife of the Government of the Ifland during the Abfence of the Governor, who was recalled, and had appointed *John Frere*, Efq; his Nephew, to take his Place in the Government of the Ifland; and the Lords Juftices farther ordered the faid *John Frere*, Efq; to repair forthwith before the Council Board in *England*, to anfwer for his having acted in Contempt of his Majefty's Order, relating to the Adminiftration of the Government, fignified to him fince Governor *Lowther*'s Departure by Mr. Secretary *Craggs*.

The Lords Juftices at the fame time took into Confideration the Cafe of *Alexander Walker* and *Timothy Salter*, Efqrs; both of whom, together with Mr. *Cox*, had been turned out of the Council, at which Board Mr. *Salter* and Mr. *Cox* had been charged with Rebellion, as has been beforementioned; and at the fame Time demonftrated to the Governor the Injuftice of fuch a Charge, and diffented to the Publication of it, and the Governor repeated with

Vehemence

Vehemence that they should be punished as Rebels against him. For this Governor, as did Colonel *Park* of *Antegoa*, and as all ill Governors probably will always do, endeavoured to terrify the People they govern with branding all Offences, even personal ones, with the odious name of Rebellion against them, a Term they should never be suffered to abuse. The Charge against Mr. *Cox* and Mr. *Salter* was declared, after hearing by the Lords Justices, to be *without the least Grounds*, who ordered a Stop to be put to the Prosecution, and the two Members, Mr. *Salter* and Mr. *Walker*, to be also restored to their Seats at the Council Board. I have observed, that ill Governors do generally distinguish the most worthy Persons in their Governments to be the Objects of their Hatred and Oppression, probably because they are jealous of the good Understanding of such Men, and consequently that they will not tamely submit to their intended Tyranny.

At the same Time the Lords Justices proceeded to examine farther Complaints against Governor *Lowther*, and heard the Petition of Sir *Robert Davers*, Knight of the Shire for *Suffolk*, *John Walter*, Esq; Knight of the Shire for *Surrey*, Mr. *Alleyne* his Brother-in-law, &c. Men of great Interest in *Barbados*; and after a long hearing of the Case, the Lords Justices declared that the Petitioners had made good their Allegations, by which it appeared that the Governor had taken from the Assembly above 28,000 *l*. *Barbados* Currency, contrary to his Majesty's express Instructions; and also that he had permitted a *Spanish* Vessel to trade contrary to the Acts of Trade and Navigation, and in Breach of his Oath; all which Charges having been proved against him, he was taken into the Custody of a Messenger, and ordered to be prosecuted, of which, to my very great Regret, I can say no more. The Council for the Petitioners at the Hearing were the Sollicitor General, and Mr. *Talbot*, afterwards Lord Chancellor; and for the Governor Sir *William Thompson*, and Mr. *Bootle*. The Attorney General who had appeared for *Lowther* returned his Brief before the second Hearing, and refused to be farther concerned in his Cause, not on Account of his extorting 28,000 *l*. nor for the Breach of his Oath; not for the prosecuting the most worthy Planters in the Island on a Pretence of Rebellion, and *Jonathan Blenman*, Esq; late Attorney General of *Barbados*, and Mr. *Gordon*, Commissary or Vice-bishop of the Island, but for being uncivil to certain Missionaries, whose Characters are found delineated in the History of *Jamaica*.

By

The History of Barbados.

By the barbarous Usage of *Bernard Cook*, we shall see how well Justice was distributed in Mr. *Lowther's* Government, and what sort of Magistrates he employed in the Distribution of it. *Cook's* Case will appear in his Petition to the King, setting forth, ' That *Robert Lowther*, Esq; Go-
' vernor of *Barbados*, having conceived a Displeasure, and
' threatned him for no other Cause, as he knows of, but that
' of his discovering the said Governor's contemptuous
' Treatment of his Majesty's most gracious Letter to him,
' the said Governor, in Favour of the Petitioner, concern-
' ing his Estate in *Barbados*, which is wrongfully detained
' from him by several Persons of great Interest and Autho-
' rity there, and particularly *John Frere*, Esq; the said
' Governor's Nephew; and that the said Governor, to gratify
' such his Resentments, did, together with *Robert Warren*,
' and *Samuel Adams*, Gent. contrive to oppress and injure
' the Petitioner, under a false Pretence that the Petitioner had
' uttered some Words reflecting on the Modesty of the said
' *Warren's* Wife, and the Wife of the said *Adams*, by
' causing the Petitioner to be bound over to a *Petit*
' Sessions of the Peace, where several Justices from dif-
' ferent Precincts were sent by the said Governor and
' *Guy Ball*, Esq; presided in order to punish the Petitioner
' for the said pretended Words without any Trial. That
' the said Petitioner well knowing the Attachment of the
' said Justices to the Governor, moved to traverse the said
' Complaint to the Grand Sessions, that it might be tried by
' a Jury of twelve Men. But the said Justices absolutely
' refused to let the Petitioner traverse the same; and did,
' without any legal Trial by a Jury, condemn the Petitioner
' for the said pretended Words, to be publickly whipped, and
' he was accordingly publickly whipped by the common
' Whipper of Slaves in a barbarous manner, *&c*.' This Petition being referred to the Lords Committee of Council, they reported, ' that the Justices of the Peace proceed-
' ed against the Petitioner without any Crime alledged; for
' that scandalous Words spoken of private Persons are no
' Grounds for criminal Prosecutions; and that the said
' Justices had proceeded illegally, for that they had not
' proper Cognizance of the Matters before them, and had
' taken upon them to examine Witnesses and determine Mat-
' ters of Fact without a Jury, and have given two Sentences
' of *whipping*, which were arbitrary and illegal.' His Majesty was graciously pleased to approve of this Determination of the Lords Committees, and to order in Council *Jan.* 20. 1721. ' that *Guy Ball, Francis Bond, Thomas Maycock*,
' Junior,

The History of Barbados. 71

'Junior, *Robert Bishop, George Barry, John Fercherson, Stephen
'Thomas*, and *William Kirkham*, Esqrs; who were Justices
'present in Court at the time of the Proceedings against the
'Petitioner, be all removed from the Commission of the
'Peace.' We shall find several of these Names among the
Prosecutors of President *Cox*, and if we had found them
under a Sentence of *Lex Talionis*, we should have thought
their Punishment no more than adequate to their Crime;
for the wrongfully whipping an *English* Freeman, is capable
of no other Satisfaction.

The late Governor Mr. *Lowther*, expecting to be recalled, and knowing Mr. *Cox* as President of the Council would succeed him in the Administration, by Virtue of his Presidency, till a new Governor was appointed; he, as we have said, suspended Mr. *Cox* from the Council Board, that his own Nephew *Frere*, next in Council to the President, might, as senior Counsel, assume the Government, and by that Means the effectual Examination and Detection of Mr. *Lowther's* Misdemeanors be prevented. But the Lords Justices Order to restore Mr. *Cox* and suspend Mr. *Frere*, put the Administration in the Hands of the President, who found all Places of Trust and Profit filled with Creatures of the said *Lowther*, who to keep them in those Places, procured an Act of *Assembly* to be passed, entitled, *An Act to preserve the Peace and Tranquillity of this Island*, still known in *Barbados* by the Name of the *Tranquillity Act*, it being in Truth the very reverse of the Preamble, and instead of *Peace* and *Tranquillity*, to preserve *Division* and *Discord*; for by this Law all the Instruments of Mr. *Lowther's* tyrannical Government were kept in Power, and the President disabled to remove there, tho' the King's Commission authorised him so to do, and the Peace and Prosperity of the Island rendered it necessary. Mr. *Frere* assumed the Government upon Mr. *Lowther* his Uncle's return to *England*, notwithstanding President *Cox's* Right, nay, notwithstanding Secretary *Craggs*, by Letters dated the 25th of *March*, 1720, signified to the Council of *Barbados*, his Majesty's Pleasure, that *on no Pretence whatsoever, Mr. Cox should be excluded from the Administration*. President *Cox* asserts in his printed Case, that *Thomas Maxwell*, Esq; *Thomas Maycock*, Esq; *John Lucia Blackman*, Esq; *Guy Ball*, and *Francis Bond*, Esqrs; Members of the Council, advised *Frere* to disobey the royal Orders, and that Mr. *Maxwell* accompanied with *Gelasius Macmahon*, a Practitioner in the Law, came to the Gate of the President's House, and calling aloud for his Majesty's royal Order, said, *Rascal, Rascal*, all *Rascals*, by G—d. We have seen how

Samuel Cox, Esq; President.

the

the late Governor *Lowther* acted in that high Office: We have taken the Proofs from Records, and even have but very little better Opinion of his Creatures than of himself. However, considering the Duty of an Historian is to carry an even Hand between contending Parties, and we have not so large Memoirs for what relates to Mr. *Cox*'s Opponents, as what relates to himself, and especially considering a full Discussion of this Contention in *Barbados*, would take up as much Room as is allowed me for the Continuation of this whole History of our Colonies, I shall only give Hints of the Events, without expatiating on *Affirmatives* and *Negatives*.

The royal Order came the Beginning of *December*, 1720, and Mr. *Cox* having pursuant thereunto taken upon him the Administration, made a healing Speech to the Council; some of whom, the Members before-mentioned, insisted on the Validity of the *Tranquillity Act*, and immediately formed Cabals to obstruct the Powers vested in him, to place and displace Officers, as was most for the Interest and Security of the Island; and the refractory Counsellors insisting still on the Tranquillity Act and the President's strict Observance of it contrary to the royal Prerogative and his Commission, he was necessitated to suspend the said Counsellors, which Proceeding of his was the more justifiable by the Repeal of the said Act in *England*. This happened so soon after his entering on the Administration, that in a Fortnight's Time a Petition against the President was signed by Messrs. *Maxwell, Maycock, Ball, Blackman, Carter, Bond,* and *Colleton,* Members of the Council, and Confidents of Mr. *Lowther*. The Complaints in the Petition referring chiefly to their own displacing and others, it was answered by the President, by the Reason and Necessity of his making Use of his Commission therein, to which we must refer. Not only these Counsellors, but Mr. *Lowther*'s Assembly also then sitting, addressed against the President and the Gentlemen who had opposed the said *Lowther*'s arbitrary and illegal Proceedings, of which so much had been said and proved, that it is astonishing to find the said *Lowther*'s Administration not only justified but applauded by them in calling his Government the *greatest of Blessings*. Besides the passing the *Tranquillity Act*, so contrary to the royal Authority and the Constitution of the Island. It was these Counsellors that insisted on Mr. *Cox*'s admitting Mr. *Frere* to sit at the Council Board notwithstanding he was regularly suspended and re-called to *England* by an Order from Home. These Counsellors, *Maxwell, &c.* concurred with the late Governor in the arbitrary, illegal and oppressive Proceedings against Mr. *Gordon*, Mr. *Blenman, &c.* but my

Compass

Compass will not allow me to enter into Particulars of the Misbehaviour charged upon them by President *Cox*, in Articles he exhibited against them, to his Successor in the Government. One of these Articles is sufficient to let us into it.

ARTICLE IV. ' The said Messieurs *Maxwell*,
' *Maycock*, *Blackman*, *Ball*, *Bond*, did endeavour to per-
' plex and distress the Administration, and throw the whole
' Island into Confusion, by denying the Legality of the As-
' sembly then sitting, and refusing after they were restored
' to the Council, to join in any Act of Government, or to
' consent to any *Law*, tho' they had themselves allowed the
' Substance of it to be good, and of publick Utility; by
' which Means the *Excise Bill*, the only Fund for the Sup-
' port of the Government, was endanger'd, &c.'

The President shews how little Reason he had to expect that they would grow more cool and discreet, by his Suspension for former Miscarriage; for when by Order from Home they were restored to their Seat in Council, they exulting on that Turn in their Favour, talked as if their Commander in Chief would be thrown out of his Office, and with an Air of Insult asked at the President's House, *If he was not run away to* Martinico.

I do not wonder such Men as these were restored to Council. I have been acquainted with the Means made Use of by the Correspondents of Counsellors in *Barbados* at *London*, to procure them to be made and kept in. President *Cox* suspended or displaced the Judges who had been Abettors of Mr. *Lowther's* Misgovernment; as *Edmund Sutton*, Esq; *John Waterman*, Esq; *James Dotten*, Esq; and if his Articles against them are true, they are unworthy of the Favour they met with, in being re-instated on the Bench of Justice.

ARTICLE VI. ' *Edmund Sutton, John Waterman*,
' *James Dotten*, together with *Samuel Husbands* and *John*
' *Carter*, Esqrs; a little before the Election of the Assembly,
' were in *Sept.* 1720, entered into a Confederacy not to
' take, as Judges, the Probate of Deeds for *Freeholders*, but
' of their own Party, and did actually refuse the Probates
' of many Deeds of *Freeholds*, in order to obtrude an As-
' sembly to their own liking on the Island.'

We see by this what a Condition the People of *Barbados* were reduced to, by the Countenance given now to one, now to another Party; by alternately putting Men into and turning them out of Places, according as they made Interest at Court, and the employing of such as had been Instruments of Mr. *Lowther* in the worst of his Practices, for which he

was

was censured and confined by the Regency in *England*, could hardly avoid giving Occasion of continuing the Contention and Discord in the Government of this Island, where Mr. *Lowther*'s Confidents and Creatures found Means to disturb and perplex it.

'Tis certain Mr. *Cox* in more Cases than one, let his Resentment carry him too far against such as had offended him personally, as in the Case of Mr. *Sutton*, who was ordered to be prosecuted by himself and 5 of his Counsellors, for unmannerly Expressions in Letters; which shews us that his Counsellors, as well as Mr. *Lowther*'s, were but too ready to do what the Commander in Chief would have them. Mr. *Carter*, the Attorney General, evaded entering upon that Prosecution by the following Reasons offered to the Governor. *As to the Letters there is nothing in them which appears libellous, scandalous or defamatory, to make up the necessary Ingredients of an Indictment or Information for a Misdemeanor by Writing.*

Had the Lord *Belhaven*, to whom this Government was given in the Year 1721, arrived at *Barbados*, the People might have expected to have seen a quick End put to the Discord and Contention, this Lord being a Person of great Capacity and Honour, incapable of being influenced by his own or other Mens Interest, against Reason and Equity. 'Tis not to be doubted, but the late Governor *Lowther* supported the Party who persecuted President *Cox*, with the whole String of his Personal and Family Interest in *England*; and it was no hard Matter to procure a Reference of their Case to the Lord *Belhaven* for his Inquiry. But that Lord being shipwrecked near the *Lizard Point*, soon after his embarking for *Barbados*, that Enquiry was transferred to the next Governor, *Henry Worseley*, Esq;

Henry Worseley, Esq; Governor. 1721.

During Mr. *Cox*'s Presidency, there happened a furious Hurricane at this Island, in which several Ships and Sloops were lost, and other considerable Damage done. But this Storm had nothing to distinguish it from other Hurricanes, excepting that it did not reach the *French Islands*, as all former Hurricanes here have been wont to do.

The Duke of Portland at Barbados.

On the 28th of *November* the *Kingston* Man of War arrived at *Barbados* in her Way to *Jamaica*, having on Board their Graces the Duke and Dutchess of *Portland*, the Duke having been lately appointed Governor of that Island, Lady *Ann Bentinck* their Graces Daughter, and several Persons of Distinction of both Sexes, who came ashore with the Duke and Dutchess in Barges. They had been waited on aboard by several Members of the Council, who came to invite

vite them to land. The Guns of the Forts fir'd when they left the Ship, and at their landing, while they were received by President *Cox* and the Body of the Council, and the Dutchess, Lady *Ann*, and the rest of the Ladies being handed into Coaches, each with six Horses, the Procession began. The Duke walked on Foot on the right Hand of the President, thro' the principal Streets of *Bridge-Town*, to the President's own House, followed by the Gentlemen who came with his Grace, and all the Members of the Council and Assembly, as also by the Life Guard of Horse. The Streets were lined on each Side by several Companies of *Militia*; and the Life Guard being afterwards drawn up on the Green before the President's House, saluted his Grace in a very gallant Manner. The Balconies were all filled with People of the best Fashion, who came from all Parts of the Island to be Spectators of a Sight, like which nothing had ever been seen there since the Arrival of the Duke and Dutchess of *Albemarle*; whose Persons were far from giving the like Grace to such a Spectacle, as did those of the Duke and Dutchess of *Portland*, equally beautiful and grand. The Duke and Dutchess seemed highly pleased with the gay Appearance of so numerous a Concourse of People. At Night there was a Ball at the President's House, where the Duke and Dutchess both danced, and the Time past very pleasantly till almost Morning. The next Day being St. *Andrew's*, the *Scots* Anniversary, the Stewards of that Feast waited on the Duke, and invited him to their Entertainment. His Grace accepted of the Invitation, but before Dinner he visited *Pilgrims*, the Seat of the Governor of *Barbados*. From thence he returned to the *Bridge*, and heard a Sermon preached by the Rev. Mr. *Gordon*, in St. *Michael* his Parish Church. My Lord after Sermon went with the Stewards and other Gentlemen, to the House where the *Scots* Feast is annually kept, and was seated at the Head of the Table, President *Cox* being at his left Hand. The Feast was in every Thing manag'd with Order and Decorum, with which his Grace expressed himself equally pleased and surprized.

A Letter from *Barbados* tells us, that when the Duke and Dutchess assisted at divine Service the next Sunday in St. *Michael's*, the Appearance there was very splendid and showy, and *I question*, says the Writer, *whether any Church in England was ever filled with a Congregation more richly habited.*

Indeed, *Thomas Tryon*, a *Barbados* Trader, in a Tract of his censures this expensive Vanity of the *Barbadians*, as it makes a false Appearance, and gives Occasion to mistake their Profusion for Wealth; which has been a Hinderance to the Relief

lief they might otherwise have hoped for, in Cases of Taxes and publick Grievances. But as this was written by a Man who wrote also for a Regimen of Diet at 2 *d.* a Day, it doubtless will have very little Weight with so gay and gallant a People as the Inhabitants of this Island. The Divisions among them at this Time mingled even with their Festivals and Compliments. For the President not having invited the Members of the Council and Assembly, who had sent Complaints Home against him, to dine with him at the Time that he was to entertain the Duke at his House, tho' they had attended him thither, the Complainants resolved to have the Honour also of the Duke's Company, and a great Number of them waited on his Grace, to invite him, the Dutchess, and the Ladies and Gentlemen who came with them, to an Entertainment of their own; and one of the most forward of these Gentlemen made a Speech to his Grace, which tho' florid, is too long for this History. I shall only abridge a Paragraph of it, because it seems to intimate that the *Anti-President* Party, which in Truth was made up mostly of such as had been Confidents and Creatures of Mr. *Lowther*, had it early in their Thoughts to cajole and engage on their Side the new Governor Mr. *Worseley,* the Paragraph is this.

Parties divide in feasting the Duke.

The Advantage of your Grace's immediate Presence, is what we can hardly forbear envying our Neighbour Island, even tho' we are ourselves in Expectation of the Arrival of a Governor every Way qualified by the Character, which is arrived here before, to reconcile our fatal Differences, and make us a happy People. The Entertainment these Gentlemen gave their Graces and their noble Company, was at least as sumptuous and as elegant as that of the President, which cost 800 *l.* and was looked upon as a Charge on the Island. Mr. *Joseph French,* and Mr. *Henry Elliot,* Quakers, presented an Address to his Grace in Behalf of *Friends,* which the Duke received with his wonted Ease and Affability. On the 8th of *December* his Grace, and all who came with him, returned on Board the Man of War, being attended to the Water-side, almost in the same Manner as at their landing, and the next Day set sail for *Jamaica.*

While his Grace was at the *Bridge-Town* arrived there the *Winchelsea* Man of War, having on Board Mr. *Vring,* whom his Grace my Lord Duke of *Montagu* had appointed Governor of a Colony intended for St. *Lucia.* The People aboard that Ship and the Transports were then well and healthy, and how far the Government of *Barbados* was to be concerned in that Enterprize, appears by the following

ing Inftructions in the Governor of *Barbados*'s Commiffion.

If any of the Subjects of a foreign Prince or State have already planted themfelves upon any of the Iflands of St. Lucia, *Dominico, St. Vincent, Tobago, or fhall hereafter attempt to do the fame, you are to affert our Right to the faid Iflands, exclufive of others, and in Order to hinder the Settlement of any Colony there, you are to give Notice to fuch Foreigners that fhall pretend to make fuch Settlements, that unlefs they fhall remove within fuch Time as you in your Difcretion fhall affign, you fhall be obliged by Force to difpoffefs and fend them off the Iflands.*

<small>Governor of Barbados's Inftructions about St. Lucia.</small>

Prefident *Cox* receiving a Letter from Mr. *Vring* at St. *Lucia*, informing him that on the Colony's Arrival there, he was forbidden to proceed to a Settlement by Monf. *de Feuquieres*, Governor of *Martinico*, by Orders from *France*, as is related in an Account of Mr. *Vring*'s Proceeding in that Ifland; upon this the Prefident fent *William Boteler*, Efq; to *Martinico*, with a Letter to Monf. *de Feuquieres*, to reprefent the Injuftice of fuch Orders, and the Matter of his foregoing Inftructions, all which availed nothing, as might eafily have been, and probably was forefeen. The *French* were come to a Point to hinder any *Englifh* Settlement there by Force, and had Force fufficient to do it. The *Englifh* were fortified with a Claim and an Inftruction only, without a fufficient Force to fupport them: If they had in Earneft refolved to have poffeffed themfelves of that Ifland, they fhould have done it while we were in War with *France*; on other Accounts, when the ftrong Squadrons of *Wright* or *Wheeler* were in thofe Seas, and the *Englifh* had 5 or 6000 Men in Arms in the *Charibbee* Iflands, regular Troops and Militia; a Strength the *French* there were then in no Condition to oppofe, and St. *Lucia* might have been fo fortified during that War, that the Enemy would have found it more difficult to have reduced it, than any other of the *Charibbees*.

Prefident *Cox*, to juftify his Conduct as to the before-mentioned Inftruction, held a Council by *fpecial* Call at Mr. *Lamplee*'s Houfe in the *Bridge-Town*, where were prefent,

Samuel Cox, Efq; Prefident.
Timothy Salter, Efq;
Thomas Maxwell, Efq;
John Lucia Blackman, Efq;
Richard Lightfoot, Efq;
Henry Peers, Efq;

Who

Who resolved that Directions should be given Capt. *Charles Brown*, Commander of his Majesty's Ship *Feversham*, to assist Mr. *Vring* pursuant to his Instructions, and to certify to him, that this Island would supply him with what Forces and Ammunition he may have Occasion for; but the *French* were so quick and so powerful in their Proceeding against the *English* in St. *Lucia*, that the latter were obliged to withdraw from thence, as is particularly related in its proper Place.

Henry Worseley, Esq; Governor.

Not long after the Evacuation of St. *Lucia* by Mr. *Vring*, Mr. *Worseley* the new Governor arrived at *Barbados*; he was complimented on his Arrival by a Letter from Monf. *de Feuquieres*, in which he expressed some Resentment at Mr. *Vring*'s Terms of menacing as he phrases it. Mr. *Worseley* answered the *French* Governor's Letter the 12th of *February*, 172$\frac{2}{3}$, and in his own has this Paragraph. *Since you are pleased to communicate to me your Conduct in the Affair of St. Lucia, I must say I have a very great Esteem for every Officer that punctually obeys his Master's Orders, and had I been in my Government when this Affair happened, I should have used my utmost Endeavours to have maintained the Duke of* Montagu *in the Possession of those Islands, to which the King my Master has an incontestable Right.* But I am apt to believe those Endeavours of his would have amounted to no more than President *Cox*'s, with whose Administration he shewed himself highly dissatisfied, prepossessed by the Representations of the male-contented Counsellors, whose Representations were referred to his Inquiry and Judgment, upon the unhappy Wreck of that truly and excellent Man the Lord *Belhaven*. But before Mr. *Worseley* discovered his Bias on the other Side, he gave the President's Party Hopes of answering their Expectations, and continuing them in the Station wherein he found them, insomuch that the Assembly then sitting, settled on him 6000 *l*. a Year for the Support of his Government, by a Tax so far exceeding the Ability of the People to pay it, no less than 2 *s*. 6 *d*. a Head on Negroes, that it was equally monstrous to give or receive it. This Governor having secured this intolerable Burthen on the Island for himself, faced about to the other Side, and took the late President *Cox*'s Case in Hand.

1722.

His Proceedings against President Cox.

It boded not well for the late President, that Governor *Worseley*, instead of managing his Inquiry by acquainting himself with the Matter by impartial Informations, should erect a Sort of Tribunal for himself to sit in Judgment, and the late President taking a Seat when the Governor had seated himself, that his Excellency should more than once reprimand

mand his Predeceffor in the Government, for prefuming to make ufe of a vacant Chair in the Room. But I meet with fo much of this Kind of Arrogance in delegated Power, that it is not at all fuprizing.

It will be feen by the following Minute of Council, that feveral of the Complainants againft Mr. *Cox* were at the Board when his Caufe was in Queftion.

Pilgrims, Thurfday, 30th of *May,* 1723.

PRESENT

His Excellency Colonel *Worfeley.*

The Hon. *Samuel Cox,* Efq; *Richard Lightfoot,* Efq;
Timothy Salter, Efq; *Edmund Sutton,* Efq;
Thomas Maxwell, Efq; *James Elliot,* Efq;
John Lucia Blackman, Efq;

Mr. *Cox* prepared a general Anfwer to the Charge againft him, in which he cleared himfelf of all the Particulars therein contained, proving them to be part falfe in Fact, and part in Reprefentation, and that with fuch Circumftances, as add Malice to the other Infirmities. They charge him with ufing infolent Language in Council, when they themfelves were the Aggreffors therein. See his own Words: ' I had a Tafte of their Conduct the fecond Time I fat with them in Council after their Reftoration; feveral of them roundly charged me with having faid what I am certain never entered into my Thoughts, which occafioned my telling them, that if they could accufe me in fuch a Manner, I fhould not think it fafe to fit with them at that Board, unlefs fome impartial Perfons were prefent, who might be Witneffes of our reciprocal Behaviour. Whereupon they, or fome of them, in a very infulting Manner, afked me if I were afraid, that if I were, they would lay by their Swords; to which I replied, *It is not your Swords, but your Tongues I am afraid of.*' The complaining Counfellors accufed the Prefident of needlefs and frequent calling of Councils, when they themfelves had been the fole Occafion by their Artifices, to prevent the meeting of a Council to do Bufinefs, by each ftaying away in his Turn as they could beft frame Excufes. They charged Mr. *Cox* with injurious Treatment of Mr. *Le Noyer* Clerk of the Council, by turning him out of his Place, tho' it was done with his own Confent, and he himfelf defired that his Succeffor might be fworn into his Office. But I cannot enlarge on the Complaints and the Defence, fo fhall clofe

with

with what concerns Mr. *Mac Mahon,* a very active Man for Mr. *Lowther,* and against Mr. *Cox.* The latter words it thus: ' I am charged with having committed Gentlemen at ' the Bar for speaking for their Clients, and abusing them in ' *set Speeches.* I beg Leave to aver, that I paid as much ' Respect to the Gentlemen of that Profession, and gave them ' as much Liberty, as any one in my Station ever did. 'Tis ' true, I once committed Mr. *Mac Mahon* for his very rude ' Behaviour to me, and notorious Contempt of the Court of ' Errors, for which he was afterwards found guilty by a Jury. ' Wherefore I am not able to conceive the Reason of a ' Charge so egregiously false, unless it were with Design to ' make evil Impressions against me, as being guilty of the ' very same Crime of which Mr. *Lowther,* whom these Gen- ' tlemen seem determined never to forsake, was so plainly ' convicted, and for which he was so justly censured in the ' Case of Mr. *Blenman.*' This confirms what I had before suggested, that Mr. *Cox* was thus prosecuted at the Instigation of Mr. *Lowther's* Creatures and Confidents, and the Favour they met with in his Prosecution, and the Hardships himself laboured under, being largely set forth in his printed Case, I thereto refer. The late President exhibited Articles against *Thomas Maxwell, Thomas Maycock, John Lucia Blackman, William Carter,* Esqrs; Members of the Council; *Edmund Sutton, John Waterman,* and *James Dotten,* Esqrs; *John Le Noyer,* late Deputy Secretary, *Richard Carter,* Esq; Attorney General, *Henry Lascells,* Esq; Collector of the Customs, and *Robert Gibbs,* Water Waiter; which are full of Matter very unjustifiable and insolent towards a chief Governor, and did not want apparent Proofs, but they are of small Use to the President, whose Fate seems to have been determined by the Representations against him, not by his own Vindication and the admirable Arguments of his Council *William Walker,* Esq; *Jonathan Blenman,* Esq; *Thomas Baxter,* Esq; whose Pleadings would have distinguished their Learning and their Reasoning in *Westminster-Hall.* But they had no Effect in Mr. *Worseley's Court,* his *Hall* or Chamber, so stiled on this Occasion, and after his Excellency had heard as much on the Complainants Side, as their Council thought proper; and on the Defendant's Side as he himself thought fit, the definitive Sentence remained in his own Breast, till a Petition from Mr. *Cox* to his Excellency, drew the following Declaration of it from him by his Secretary.

His Excellency commands me to acquaint you, in Answer to your Petition, in which you have prayed a Copy of the Judgment his Excellency had given in your Affair, that upon his

hearing

The History of Barbados.

hearing the Evidences on both Sides, he did determine that you had acted corruptly, arbitrarily and illegally; and therefore he not only removed you from being of his Majesty's Council here, but also declared you uncapable of ever being one. And that 'twas his farther Opinion, you ought to be prosecuted in the Manner that the Nature of the Crimes proved against you required. I am with very great Respect, Sir,

Your most humble Servant,

Nicholas Hammond.

There is something so dry and shocking in this Answer, that 'tis far from giving one Reason to take Pleasure in the Superiority which their Commission gives Colony Governors, and Mr. *Worseley*, by this unreasonable and ungenerous Treatment of the late President, made but very ill Returns to his Party, who were most forward in settling upon him that prodigious and amazing Salary of 6000 *l.* a Year, besides customary Fees and Perquisites, the latter sufficient for his personal and houshold Expences. This Salary was so intolerable a Burthen, that the Party, who had been most bitter against the late President, refused to acquiesce in the Continuance of it; and though the Governor had Interest enough in both Parties to prevent the Repeal of the Act, yet he could not prevent the almost general Resolution of the Inhabitants not to pay the Tax any longer, which occasioned his applying at Home for Orders to put the Law in full Execution; and it must be confessed, that Governors have, in such Cases, found the several Persons concerned in the issuing of such Orders more ready to join with them than with the People, whose Money is to go for the Discharge of them.

While the Payment of these Thousands yearly to the Governor went smoothly on, that of Government here went on smoothly also, till the Pressure of that exorbitant *Negro* Tax began to squeeze out the vital Substance of the Planters, whose Eyes were burst open by it, and who could then see worse Management in this Governor, than had been complained of against President *Cox.* In the mean Time the Plantation Merchants were very much distressed in their Trade, chiefly from the Increase and Extent of the *French* and *Dutch* Sugar Plantations; which, while those of the *English* were labouring under high Imposts both in the Colonies and at Home, were visibly getting Ground upon them in *Works* and in Markets. They were enabled to encrease their Sugar

Works

Works, by the great Quantities of Provisions which they were supplied with by our Continent Colonies, for the Subsistence of their Hands employed in them, and they there found Markets for their Product and Commodities, *Sugar*, *Molasses*, and *Rum*, which they stockt our *Northern* Provinces with; and by the Increase of their Growths and Product in their Sugar Islands they supplied not only *France*, *Holland*, *Germany*, and the *Streights*, which the *English* had done 40 or 50 Years, but *Ireland* in a great Measure. This they could the better do, for that the *French* and *Dutch* Imposts on their *West-India* Commodities are light and trivial in Comparison with *English*. They paid no 4½ *per Cent.* in their Islands, and scarce 1 *per Cent.* at Home. They exported their Plantation Goods to what Part they pleased, without the chargeable and troublesom Incumbrance of first landing them in some of their own Ports, which was 15 or 20 *per Cent.* Loss to the *English*, enough to knock any Trade on the Head. Their Governors durst not extort excessive Donatives from them. Their Security was at the publick Charge, and carefully provided for, and their Mother Countries cherished them as their most dear and most useful Children. By a late Law in *England*, the Planters in our Sugar Colonies have the Benefit of foreign Markets, without the before-mentioned Incumbrances; but there are still so many Restrictions in that Law, that the Trade still remains extremely clogged, and is by no Means on so good a Footing, as is that between the *French* and *Dutch* Sugar Colonies and *Europe*.

The Trade between the *English* and *French* in *America*, licite or illicite, has been extended so far, that our Sugar Islands have dealt with the *French* Sugar Islands even for Sugar; and I have met with a Complaint against a Collector of the Customs in *Barbados*, for sending *Martinico* Sugar to *London*, in Remittances for the 4½ *per Cent.* which should have been returned in the Growth of the Country, much better than that of the *French* Islands; and there is no Doubt, but the Goodness of our Commodity, and the Advantage we have or may have of the *French* in the *Guinea* Trade, and the Trade of the *Northern* Provinces, would with like Care and Encouragement, as the *French* have in their Sugar Trade, restore our's to its former Extent and Benefit.

1727.
Tho' the People of *Barbados* bore for some Time the Negro Tax patiently, but not willingly, yet in the Year 1727, their Complaints concerning that and other Grievances, reached the Representatives. In the following Year the Assembly drew up a Petition to be presented to the King for their Relief, which was transmitted to *England*, but is said to be lost

The History of Barbados.

oft there for want of proper Agents to folicit it; a very hard Cafe, that an Ifland which paid 10,000 *l.* a Year to the un-appropriated Revenue, and 50,000 *l.* a Year in Cuftoms, fhould lofe Redrefs of their Grievances becaufe not properly folicited. This Affair came again on the *Tapis* in *Barbados* in 1730, as will appear by the following Minutes.

At a Meeting of the General Affembly, at the Houfe of *Willoug'by Duffoy*, Gent. in the Parifh of St. *Michael*, on *Monday* the 15th Day of *Feb.* 1730.   1730;

PRESENT

The Hon. *Henry Peers*, Efq; Speaker.

The Hon. *Tho. Maycock*, Efq;
John Pickering, Efq;
Gelafius Mac Mahon, Efq;
Samuel Palmer, Efq;
Othniel Haggat, Efq;
James Thorne, Efq;
John Walcott, Efq;
George Worrall, Efq;

John Braithwaite, Efq;
Hardis Jordan, Efq;
Philip Scott, Efq;
Francis Ford, Efq;
John Bignal, Efq;
John Cobham, Efq;
James Bucce, Efq;

This Affembly referred the Matter of the Petition before- *Affembly against the Negro Tax.* mentioned to a Committee, who reported the Caufe of its Mifcarriage, as we before have related it, and added thereto the Particulars of its Contents, the principal of which we muft not omit, becaufe we fhall there find the beft Reprefentation of the State of this Ifland at that Time.

Their firft Grievance is the 6000 *l.* Sterling a Year to the Governor, thus expreffed in their Petition. ' When his
' Excellency *Henry Worfeley*, Efq; took the Adminiftration
' of this Government upon him, the Gentlemen of the
' Ifland, having for many Years before been haraffed with
' Parties and Divifions, in Hopes to put an End to the fame,
' and to obtain the Redrefs of feveral Grievances, were
' wrought upon to fubmit to a Settlement of 6000 *l.* Sterling
' *per Annum* on the faid Governor during his Refidence here,
' yet notwithftanding this extravagant Settlement, the Ifland
' was fo far from reaping any Advantage from their in-
' difcreet Generofity, that on the contrary, the publick Good *Grievances complain'd of.*
' had been entirely neglected, and no Meafures taken to re-
' drefs the Grievances of the Ifland; but his Excellency and
' his Creatures had thereby been the better enabled, and
' more at Leifure to opprefs the Inhabitants; the Militia had
' been totally neglected, the Forts, Breaft-Works and Bat-
' teries were gone to Ruin, the publick Stores were imbezzled

'bezzled and wasted, and all Persons in Office under his Excellency busied in nothing but how to raise Fortunes from the Ruins of the People;' of which they give too many Instances to be here inserted; and after having enumerated many enormous Grievances they add, ' The said Grievances, and many others, tending to the impoverishing and Ruin of the Island, were still the more insupportable, from the dismal Apprehensions his Majesty's Subjects here lie under in Case of a War, the Forts and Fortifications of the island having gone to Ruin, warlike Stores of all Kinds necessary for the Defence of the Island being wholly wanted, and no Possibility of purchasing a sufficient Quantity of Powder and other Stores, and the Inhabitants not in a Condition of bearing the necessary Charges, either of buying Powder sufficient were the same to be purchased, or repairing the Forts and Fortifications, while the heavy Tax which they had for so many Years paid, chiefly for his Excellency's Use, was continued; by which Tax almost all the current Cash of this Island was annually brought together and hoarded in his Excellency's Coffers, Trade was stagnated, and the Value of the Produce of the Island was very considerably lowered, to the vast Damage of the distressed Inhabitants, who were forced to part with their Goods at any Price, to raise their Quota of a Tax not only heavy in itself, but much more so in Regard of the ill Effects it had upon Trade and the Markets in the Colony.'

'Tis here to be noted, that the Assembly's chief Inducement for granting that Tax to the Governor, was his Promise ' that he would be satisfied with that Settlement, and make no other Demand upon the Publick during his Government.' But instead thereof, he demanded and had actually paid him at once, upwards of 2000 *l.* for *supposed* Repairs of his House and Gardens, a Sum sufficient to have bought them; and several other Sums for which we must refer to the Petition.

The Report after this touches on a Petition transmitted to *England* by some particular Persons, representing their Grievances in general; which the Committee of Assembly say was opposed at the Board of Trade by the Governor's Agent. They also complain in very significant Terms of the unjustifiable Dependency of the Council on his Excellency, of their servile Compliances and partial Behaviour on all Occasions, to the Prejudice of their Liberties and Properties.

Notwithstanding their Remonstrances the Assembly had drawn up against Mr. *Worseley's* Administration, we find the Body of the People were not so unanimous in it, but that the

Grand

The History of Barbados. 85

Grand Jury of the whole Island presented an Address, wherein among other Things they say, *Tho' the most cautious and inoffensive Conduct on your Excellency's Part has not entirely freed you from some Attempts to make you uneasy, yet we have Reason to think many, who once gave too much Countenance to such Proceedings, are now convinced, that the same were impertinent and absurd,* &c. too florid and flattering for a short History. It was signed by

John Trescourt.
Christopher Lacy.
William White.
Richard Dowell.
Ambrose Whitaker.
Benjamin Philips.
Samuel Johnston.
Samuel Gittens.
John Gittens.

Samuel Clarke.
John Bullins.
Charles Burton.
William Grenidge.
Richard Alder.
Thomas Macullock.
Edward Mead.
John Kirton.

But what the Assembly of *Barbados* say of their Grand Juries at this Time shews us, that little Stress is to be laid on their Addresses. After having spoken of the Council as before-mentioned, and of new Practices to pack Assemblies, they add, ' This notorious Partiality appears not only upon Elec-
' tions of Assembly Men and Vestry Men, but also in their
' returning of Juries for the Grand Sessions, consisting of
' the meanest of the People, and out of these are pricked,
' by his Excellency's favourite Judges occasionally made for
' the Purpose, such Grand Juries as twice a Year, in their
' Panegyricks on his Excellency, rail at all those that happen
' to be of Sentiments different to theirs.' We know not what became of the Assembly's intended Petition, but we find that Governor *Worseley* removed soon after to *England*; for in the following Year 1731, *Samuel Barwick*, Esq; succeeded him as Commander in Chief in Quality of President of the Council, and so was to continue till the Arrival of the new Governor — *Chetwynd*, Esq; It would be partial and condemnable in us, if we mentioned what the Assembly said of the Council, and sunk what the Council said of the Assembly in the Council's Remarks on the Minutes of that House, touching the *Excise Bill* 1731. ' 'Tis apprehended
' that no unprejudiced Person can look back on the *Disputes*
' that have happened betwixt this Board and the General As-
' sembly for three Years past, but must easily perceive at
' least, that the Source of them has been owing more to the
' vain

1731.

vain and ambitious Views of particular Men than to any 'other Cause.'

The Difference between the Council and the Assembly, concerning the former's Amendment of the Excise Bill, contains too many Particulars to have a Place here; a Clause in that Bill in Favour of the Attorney General, being only for Services done by himself in and for the Island, was very just and reasonable, but the Clause for Services done by Lord *Micklethwaite*, &c. as Secretaries for the Island, for Services done in an Island where they never were, and never were likely to be, do not seem to stand on so good a Footing as the Attorney General's, who had frequently and personally signalized himself in its Service. *John Bignal*, Esq; Member of the Assembly excepted against this Clause in these Words, *As we have not been allowed hitherto to know the Nature and State of those Demands, we cannot in Justice to the People we represent, consent to let any of the publick Money be directed to the Payment of them.* This refers to the Council's insisting upon it, that the Assembly should pass the many Clauses in their Amendments in the lump, without inquiring into the Uses or Proportions of the several Payments. Whereas nothing is more obvious, than the Reason and Equity of the Assembly's Pretensions to know and be satisfied with the said Uses and Proportions. I here meet with no Answer to such Exceptions as these, on the Side of this or other Colony Assemblies in the like Cases, but Mandations, Letters from *England*, which leaving the Equity and Reason of the Thing still with the Representative of the People, out of whose Properties the Money demanded is to be raised, I cannot here enter any farther into a Disquisition of the Matter.

Before Mr. *Worseley* left *Barbados*, a Petition was presented him by Mr. *William Holford*, complaining of several grievous Exactions and Extortions of *Oliver Kennedy*, Esq; *Deputy Provost Marshal*. And here it is to be noted, that the most beneficial Places in the Island are patenteed to Persons living in *England*, and are rented and executed by Persons living in *Barbados*, who remit yearly many Hundreds, if not Thousands, to their Principals in *England*; where it has the Effect which Soil taken from one Ground to cultivate another always will have, the enriching the latter proportionably to the Impoverishment of the former. The Renters of the Patents being screwed up in their Rent to as high a Pitch as the several Offices will bear, make no Scruple to use their utmost Dexterity towards enlarging their Fees and Perquisites at the Expence of the aggrieved Inhabitants, whose Judge is the Governor, who holds his Commission on the same Foot, as the Aggressors hold their Patent. Mr.

The History of Barbados.

Mr. *Worseley* with great Formality referred Mr. *Holford*'s Commission to *Thomas Gallop*, Esq; Chief Baron of the Exchequer, *Othniel Haggat*, Esq; *Francis Vaughan*, Esq; *Joseph Pilgrim*, Esq; *George Foster*, Esq; *John Reeves*, Esq; Chief Judges of the Common Pleas, *Henry Dodsworth*, Esq; Judge of the Admiralty, and *Jonathan Blenman*, Attorney General; Persons well qualified to determine the Right and the Wrong, in that or any other Cause whatsoever. Accordingly they took a great deal of Pains in examining *Holford*'s Complaints, and found that he had been egregiously abused by *Kennedy*, in fraudulent and unlawful Extortion of Fees from him, and one no less than 22 *l*. of a poor Widow for laying out of a Dower, when scarce half of that Sum was his Due; but we have no Room for Particulars, and therefore shall only mention, that the Gentlemen determined in their Report, that he had enhanced the Marshal's Fees in various Articles: But I do not find that Mr. *Holford* had any pecuniary Satisfaction for the Damage he suffered by it, and am sensible of the Difficulties any particular Person in our Colonies will have to struggle with, that seeks for Redress of Patent Grievances by the Arbitrament of a Governor.

Proceedings against the Provost Marshal.

Mr. *Worseley* did not find the People of *Barbados* so ready to pay his enormous Salary of 6000 *l*. a Year, as they were to settle it upon him, and when he returned to *England*, near 20,000 *l*. of it was in Arrear. Happy it had been for the *Barbadians*, if that Arrear had been demandable by such Governors as the Duke of *Portland* or Lord *How*; but the Defaulters here were by particular Orders from Home, prosecuted in the surest Manner of Process, which falling into the Hands of a Gentleman perfectly well acquainted with the Circumstances of the Inhabitants and the Interest of the Island, he with great Capacity and Success obeyed the Orders he received, and remitted to *England* 17000 *l*. of that enormous and hated Salary, the bad Effects of which were a main Cause of the Steadiness of the *New-England* Assembly, in opposing the stated Settlement of an annual Salary on their Governor a Native, and not likely to send away the Treasures that were given him.

Mr. *Worseley* returning to *England*, the Government fell of Course to the President, *Samuel Berwick*, Esq; President of the Council, whose Name and Family had been of Distinction in this Island from its first Settlement under Governors and Assemblies. This Gentleman's prudent Management, prepared the Way for that good Agreement and Harmony, which made the Lord *Howe*'s Government so easy and happy to himself and the *Barbadians*. Now it was, that the

Samuel Barwick, Esq; President.

the famous Island Addrefs, entitled, *The humble* Petition of the Planters, Traders and other Inhabitants of your Majefty's Ifland of *Barbados*, was tranfmitted to *England*, fetting forth the Advantages of their Trade and Shipping to the Kingdom of *Great-Britain*, the Caufes of their Decay, and fome probable Means of retrieving them. The main Caufe is contained in the following Words.

That within thefe few Years, great Improvements have been made by the Dutch *and* French *in their Sugar Colonies, and great and extraordinary Encouragements have been given to them, not only from their Mother Countries, but alfo from a pernicious Trade carried on by them to and from* Ireland, *and the Northern* Britifh *Colonies; and the* French *do now from the Produce of their own Sugar Colonies, effectually fupply with Sugar not only* France *itfelf, but* Spain *alfo, and a great Part of* Ireland *and the* Britifh *Northern Colonies, and have to fpare for* Holland, Germany, Italy, *and other Parts of* Europe: *And the* French *and* Dutch *Colonies have lately fupplied the Northern* Britifh *Colonies with very large Quantities of Molaffes, for the making of Rum and other Ufes, to the vaft Prejudice of your Majefty's Sugar Colonies. As Rum is a Commodity, and which next to Sugar they moftly depend upon, and they have in Return for fuch Sugar, Rum and Molaffes, Shipping, Horfes, Boards, Staves, Hoops, Lumber, Timber for Building, Fifh, Bread, Bacon, Corn, Flower, and other Plantation Neceffaries, at eafier Rates than your Majefty's Subjects of the Sugar Colonies have. For the continual Supplies received by the* Dutch *and* French *from the* Britifh *Northern Colonies, have enabled them to put on and maintain a great Number of Slaves on their Plantations, and to enlarge their Sugar Works, and make new Settlements in new fertile Soils; and at the fame Time coft little, being now purchafed chiefly with Molaffes, which before this late Intercourfe between the foreign Colonies and the Northern* Britifh *Colonies, were flung away as of no Value.* They then reckon up the Advantages of the *French* and *Dutch* Sugar Colonies over the *Britifh,* as that they pay inconfiderable Duties, as but 1 *per Cent.* for the Sugars they carry directly to *Spain.* &c. To remedy fuch Evils, they propofe a Prohibition of *foreign Sugar, Rum, Molaffes,* &c. from being imported to *Ireland* and the *Britifh* Northern Colonies, till they have firft been imported into *Great-Britain,* or that the *Britifh* Sugar Colonies may be at leaft on the fame Footing with them. Since this Petition was confidered in *England,* fome Steps have been taken for the Relief of the Sugar Iflands. As 6 *s.* Bounty on the Re-exportation of refined Sugar. The Liberty of importing
Rum,

The History of Barbados.

Rum, &c. directly into *Ireland*. Foreign Sugar, Rum and Molasses entirely prohibited from being imported into *Ireland*, unless shipped in *Great-Britain*. A high Duty is laid on all foreign Sugar, Rum and Molasses imported into any of our Northern as well as Southern Colonies. Liberty to carry all Sugars directly from our Plantations to all the foreign Parts of *Europe* under certain Restrictions, which probably will be repealed when this Matter is reconsidered by the Legislature; as 1. *Excluding Ships built in our* American *Plantations*; an unspeakable Detriment to the Colony, and consequently to the *British* Navigation. 2. *Taking out Licences in* Great-Britain *only*; a great Incumbrance and Delay on the Sugar Trade. 3. *All Owners of Ships in this Trade to reside in* Great-Britain, *or the Sugar Islands*. 4. *All Ships bound to the Northward of* Great-Britain *to enter first there*, which besides the extraordinary Charge and Delay of Time, may very often lose a Market.

On the 11th of *April* 1733, the Lord *Howe*, whom his Majesty had appointed Governor of *Barbados*, arrived there in the *Rye* Man of War, and was received in as grand a Manner as the short Time they had to prepare could admit of; and on the 17th he met the Assembly at *Pilgrim*, and made them a very handsom Speech, the Promises of his future good Government.

1733. Lord Howe, Governor.

A short Time before his Lordship's Arrival, a News Paper was printed and published at *Bridge-Town* by *Samuel Keimer*, lately a *London* Printer. It was called the *Barbados Gazette*, and came out every *Wednesday*.

Lord *Howe's* prudent and engaging Behaviour soon reconciled all Parties in Affection and Regard for his Person and Government: The Emulation among the Inhabitants seemed to be who could give the greatest Marks of their Love and Obedience to his Person, and of Duty and Service to his Government. They looked back on the turbulent Times of former Governors, with a Pleasure which Men who have escaped Shipwreck take in surveying the Storm they were in, from the Shore. My Lord *Howe* was continually pressing the Representative to be watchful for their Safety, and zealous for the Increase of their Trade and Welfare, to which he was always ready to contribute whatever lay in him. The Assembly chearfully settled on him 4000 *l. per Annum*, which his Lordship as chearfully spent amongst them with a large Addition out of his own Revenue in *England*.

We have seen in *New York*, to what the Severities of Governors may drive them against the Press, and there was

was now an Attempt to have *Keimer* the Printer of the *Barbados Gazette* fined without any Trial by the Court of Seſſion, for ſome Offence given in that Paper to a Gentleman who had publiſhed ſeveral Mercantile and Plantation Schemes, which had produced Animadverſions upon ſome of them enough intemperate, but not Matter of Proceſs at Law; however a Preſentment was ready drawn up for the Grand Jury to ſign, under Pretence that the Paper had reflected on the Chief Juſtice, who denied he knew any Thing of it, and the Matter dropped, and it was not likely that any irregular Proceeding could paſs in ſo mild and equal a Government as my Lord *Howe's*; Of which every Heart and Tongue in *Barbados* was full, except thoſe of a Set of Men who are ſeldom eaſy themſelves, or would ſuffer any to be eaſy about them; for we ſhall ſee by the following Addreſs of the Aſſembly, that it was the Practitioners in the Law only who expreſſed any Uneaſineſs in the preſent Adminiſtration: after the greateſt Expreſſions of Thankfulneſs, Duty, Reſpect, and Affection to his Excellency, they ſay in their Addreſs, *publick Grievances, my* Lord, *let them be in what Perſons, Stations, or Profeſſions ſoever, ought to be enquired into, and proper Remedies agreeable to Juſtice be given. Your* Excellency's *Conduct manifeſtly evinces, you intended no more by the late Enquiry concerning the Lawyer's Fees,* &c. 'Twas a ſenſible Pleaſure to us, ſince we were to find ſome Oppoſition to this excellent Governor's juſt and wiſe Adminiſtration, that it ſhould come from that Quarter which has ever been moſt productive of Diſcord.

1734.

During the Government of Lord *Howe*, there happened a Quarrel at *Bridge-Town*, between Mr. *Gelaſius Mac Mahon*, and Mr. *Thomas Keiling*, in which ſeveral Perſons were engaged on both Sides, and a Scuffle enſuing, Mr. *Keiling* was unfortunately killed. Mr. *Mac Mahon* having been very active in the publick Differences for ſeveral Years paſſed, the Iſland was divided in their Judgments on this Event, and in their Hopes as to the Iſſue of it. Mr. *Mac Mahon*, Mr. *Theophilus Morris*, and *John Laurence*, quitted the Iſland on the preferring a Bill of Indictment againſt them and Mr. *William Perry*. The latter was ſeized and impriſoned, and having petitioned for a Trial, was brought to the Bar of the Grand Seſſions; but the Attorney General being ready to make it appear by Affidavits, that ſome ill Practices had been uſed in tampering with ſeveral of the King's Evidences, and that one of them was actually enticed away and carried off the Iſland, the Trial was put off by Conſent of thoſe that appeared in Behalf of the Priſoner, without reading the

Affidavits;

The History of Barbados. 91

Affidavits; whereupon the Prisoner's Council moving that he might be admitted to Bail, the Court was pleased in Regard to his ill State of Health, and the Circumstances of his Family, to admit it, and accordingly he gave four Securities in 5000 *l.* each, and himself in 10,000 *l.*

About this Time Mr. *Christopher Gillmor,* a *Romish* Priest, made a publick Recantation of the Errors of the Church of *Rome,* and embraced the Protestant Religion according to the Doctrine of the Church of *England*; declaring his Assent and Consent, &c. in due Form, in the Church of St. *Michael's* before a numerous Congregation, and a Certificate of it was signed by

A Romish Priest turns Protestant.

J. Blenman,	H O W E,
Tho. Funckes,	William Johnson, *Rector,*
Recorded in the Secretary's Office the 23d of July 1734.	Charles Game, *Church-Warden,*
	Jasper Young,
	Tho. Withers,
	Joshua Brook, *Curate,*
William Duke,	Tho. Harrison.
Dep. Secr.	

While the People of *Barbados* were flattering themselves of being many Years happy in Lord *Howe,* he was suddenly taken ill of a Fever, which held him six days; the Distemper took several different Turns, so that their Fears were mixed with Hopes, which however were of very short Duration, and *March* the 27th, 1735, he expired in the 37th Year of his Age, to the unspeakable and universal Grief of the Inhabitants of this Island, who were all thrown into outward and inward Mourning. His Lordship lived with them almost two Years, and in that short Time gained the Love of the People more than all the preceding Governors had done from its Settlement, to the present State of the Island: So much of this Subject is said in their printed Papers, of one of which above 20,000 were dispersed in the Sugar Islands, that we cannot pretend to copy it, but refer thereto, and how the Representative of the People behaved on this Occasion will be seen by the following Minutes.

Lord Howe dies.

At a Meeting of the General Assembly *Tuesday* the 22d Day of *April* 1735.

P R E S E N T.

The Honourable *Henry Peers,* Esq; Speaker.

The Hon. *John Bignall,* Esq; *Samuel Palmer,* Esq;

John

John Green,		William Jeves,	
Thomas Waterman,		Enoch Gretton,	
Edward Brace,	Esqrs;	John Lyte,	Esqrs;
John Cumberbatch,		John Cobham,	
William Gibbons,		The Hon. J. Bruce,	
J. Waterman,			

James Dottin, Esq; President.

To whom *James Dottin*, Efq; who as President of the Council, fucceeded in the Government, made a Speech, which began thus:

Gentlemen,

Little did I imagine before our Meeting, to return an Anfwer to our moft worthy Governor's Speech on the calling of that Affembly, we should be deprived of that ineftimable Life on which our Happinefs fo much depended. A Governor poffeffed of his amiable and fhining Qualities, which he exerted equally for the Honour of his Royal Mafter, and the true Intereft of this Colony; as he well deferved the Favour of his Sovereign, fo he merited every Thing from us, that we were capable of doing to him.

We were indeed fully fenfible of the Bleffing, being fatisfied that his Prefence gave Life and Vigour to all our Actions, and 'tis certain that without him, we muft have defponded under our Misfortunes; but his Chearfulnefs, and the Means he was inceffantly contriving for our Benefit, raifed our Hopes, and made us even forgetful of our own Condition, &c.

Former Governors, the longer they remained with us, ufually became the lefs refpected; but the Lord Howe daily encreafed in our Affections: But while we are regretting our Lofs, let us not forget to pay that Regard which is juftly due to his noble Family. Her Ladyfhip, whofe prudent Conduct and moft engaging Behaviour raifed the Admiration, and equally engaged the Affection of the Inhabitants, demands our more immediate Confideration, and calls for all the Affiftance in our Power to alleviate her great Affliction.

Though we made the beft and largeft Settlement on his Excellency, the Circumftances of this Ifland could afford, yet it was not fufficient to anfwer his Expences here. The Charges he was neceffarily at in coming over hither, and that which her Ladyfhip will be put to in returning will be very great, whereby inftead of receiving an Advantage by accepting of the Government, a Lofs will rather accrue to his Family, which furely the Publick ought not to fuffer. It is but too manifeft be

The History of Barbados.

lost his Life in the Service of our Country. Besides, as we were prevented (by his own express Directions) from expending a large Sum at his Funeral, our Gratitude ought to be shewn in another Way, by the Provision I would recommend to you, to make for the Payment of his Lordship's Debts here, and for the Use of her Ladyship.

Then the President laid before the House a Bill prepared for that Purpose, entitled, *An Act the better to manifest the Gratitude of the People in this Island, for the Benefits they received from the just and prudent Administration of his late Excellency*, &c. and the same was read and passed *Nemine Contradicente*.

After which the House appointed a Committee to bring in a Bill to settle the Fees of the several Officers of the Island, and ordered that the Hon. *John Bignall*, and *James Bruce*, Esqrs; *Samuel Palmer*, *John Lyte*, and *John Green*, Esqrs; do bring it in.

By this Act, 2500 *l*. was given to her Ladyship for the Uses before-mentioned. Her Ladyship soon after embarked on Board a Merchant Man with her Daughter and the Corpse of her late dear Consort, and the Captain of the Man of War, then stationed at *Barbados*, very generously offered his Service to attend her Ladyship some Days sail on her Way, and the Merchant Man in which she went arrived in *England* in 34 Days. President *Dottin* behaved to the General Satisfaction of the People of *Barbados*, and was himself very well satisfied with an Appointment of 600 *l*. a Year only granted him by the Assembly.

2500 l. given to Lady Howe.

This shews us what a vast Difference there is between the Charge that a Governor is to an Island, and that of a President. Governor *Worseley* had ten times the Salary that President *Dottin* had, and yet gave not the 10th Part of the Content which the People had in this President's Government.

Ten Weeks after Lord *Howe*'s Death, Mr. *Gelosius Mac Mahon* returned to *Barbados*, and surrendered himself to the Provost-Marshal; on the 12th of *June* 1735, he petitioned for a Trial, but the Attorney General shewed to the Court that the Petitioner, from the Circumstances of his Case, was by no Means entitled to the Benefit of the Royal Instruction in Pursuance of the *Habeas Corpus* Act, on Account of his having gone off the Island and avoided the Justice of the Court for two several grand Sessions before, and that if the Prisoner had proposed to be tried, he should have signified it sooner, and ought to have petitioned for it the first Day of Sessions. But Mr. Attorney perceiving the Court

1735.

Court generally inclined to a Trial, declared, that although he had a Right to put it off, he would notwithstanding immediately order the Witnesses to be summoned, and if possible try the Prisoner next Day. Accordingly it was expected that the Trial of Mr. *Mac Mahon* would have come on, and there was a great Concourse of People to hear it, as might well have been expected considering the Prisoner had been an Assembly Man; but in calling over the Witnesses that had been summoned, it appeared that one of them was off the Island, and two more not attending, the Trial was deferred. The Prisoner then moved that he might be bailed, which was opposed by the King's Council; but the Court were pleased, after hearing Arguments on both Sides, to admit him to Bail; and accordingly the Hon. *John Frere*, the Hon. *Thomas Applewaite*, *George Hannay*, and *Robert Warren*, Esqrs; became his Sureties in 5000 *l*. each, and himself in 10,000 *l*.

His Trial came on afterwards, and the Jury was so tender to him, that they only brought in their Verdict *Manslaughter*.

In the Beginning of the next Year President *Dottin*, summoned a new Assembly, which consisted of the following Members.

For the Parish of St. *Michael*.	The Hon. *Henry Peers*, Esq; The Hon. *John Bignal*, Esq;
Christ-Church.	*Francis Ford*, Esq; *George Hannay*, Esq;
St. *Philips*.	*Enoch Gretton*, Esq; *Ralph Weeks*, jun. Esq;
St. *John*.	*Samuel Palmer*, Esq; *Henry Leslie*, Esq;
St. *George*.	*Edward Brace*, Esq; *John Lyte*, Esq;
St. *Joseph*.	*Thomas Waterman*, Esq; *John Waterman*, Esq;
St. *Andrew*.	Hon. *James Bruce*, Esq; *William Jeeves*, Esq;
St. *Lucy*.	*Hurdis Jordan*, Esq; The Hon. *William Sandford*, Esq;
St. *Thomas*.	*John Cobham*, Esq; *Josh. Cumberbach*, Esq;
St. *James*.	*Reynold Alleyne*, Esq; *Phil. Gibbs*, Esq;
St. *Peters*.	*John Pickering*, Esq; *William Gibbons*, Esq;

The History of Barbados.

These Members made choice of *Henry Peers*, Esq; to be their Speaker, to which Station he had been annually elected ever since the Year 1727, the Duties whereof, it is universally allowed, he has discharged with the strictest Honour and greatest Abilities. A Gentleman deservedly of so great an Interest in the Island, that it would be difficult for any Member to be elected, if he should be pleased to declare he thought him unworthy of it.

In the Year 1739, President *Dottin* resigned the Administration to *Robert Byng*, Esq; who arrived here with the Character of Governor. This Gentlemen had the Misfortune to have the fine Equipage he had provided for this Voyage taken by the *Spaniards*, and the Assembly of *Barbados* very generously presented him with 2500 *l.* to make good that Loss; but being unwilling to come into such a Settlement of Salary as he insisted upon, it occasioned some Misunderstanding between him and them, which however was not of long Continuance, nor had any ill Consequences, that Matter being happily compromised; but he lived not long in his Government, being taken ill and dying about a Year after his Arrival; upon which President *Dottin* re-assumed the Government a third Time: But these Events have happened so lately, that we have little Information, and cannot enlarge farther upon them, but must not omit, that so great Care and Diligence has been used of late in repairing and improving the Fortifications that the Island is now in a good Posture of Defence.

Robert Byng, Esq; Governor. 1739.

He dies.

The following is a *List* of the Chief Officers Civil and Military now in Employment at *Barbados*.

MEMBERS of the COUNCIL.

Hon. *James Dottin*, Esq; President.
Ralph Weeks, Esq;
John Frere, Esq;
Thomas Maxwell, Esq;
Thomas Applewhaite, Esq;
Richard Salter, Esq;

John Gallop, Esq;
Charles Dunbar, Esq;
Abel Dottin, Esq;
Thomas Harrison, Esq;
John Maycock, Esq;
Reynold Hooper, Esq;

Deputy Secretary, and as such Clerk of the Council, *Samuel Husbands*, Esq;
Clerk of the Assembly, *William Duke*, Esq;

JUDGES

JUDGES.

Honourable *James Bruce*, Efq; for the *Bridge*.
Ralph Weeks, Efq; for *Oiſtin's*.
Francis Vaughan, Efq; for the *Hole*.
John Terryl, Efq; for *Speight's*.
John Bignall, Efq; for *Scotland*.

Chief Baron of the *Exchequer*, Hon. *Tho. Harriſon*, Efq;

Attorney General, *Thomas Baxter*, Efq; in the Room of *Jonathan Blenman*, Efq;

Sollicitor General, *Edmund Jenkins*, Efq;

Judge of the Admiralty, Hon. *John Fairchild*, Efq; on Mr. *Blenman's* leaving the Iſland.

Treaſurer, the Hon. *John Bignall*, Efq;

Collector of the Cuſtoms for the *Bridge*, *Edward Laſcelles* Efq; who is alſo Agent Victualler.

Surveyor General, Hon. *Charles Dunbar*, Efq;

Provoſt Marſhal, *Thomas Stevinſon*, Efq;

Agent for the Iſland in *England*, *John Sharpe*, Efq;

Commiſſary to the Biſhop of *London*, the Rev. Mr. *William Johnſon*, Rector of St. *Michael's*, who dying lately, the preſent Rector is the Rev. Mr. *Huxley*.

Lieutenant General, was *Henry Peers*, Efq; but Governor *Byng* removed him, and put *Thomas Applewhaite*, Efq; in his Room, who had been Major General.

CHAP. II.

A Geographical Deſcription of the Iſland, with its Towns, Forts, Fortifications, Ports, Harbours, Rivers, Publick and Private Buildings.

THE various Accounts that are given us of the Situation of *Barbados*, obliged us to be very exact in examining it by the lateſt Surveys that have been taken of the Iſland, and comparing them with the Informations we received from the Inhabitants of the Place.

Ligon ſays in his Hiſtory, it lies in 13 Degrees, 30 Minutes Northern Latitude; and where 'tis longeſt, is ſomewhat above 28 Miles in Length; and where 'tis broadeſt, 17 Miles in Breadth: Which Deſcription agrees exactly with the Map that was printed with this Book.

The History of Barbados.

An anonymous Author, who pretends to have been on the Spot, says, it lies in 13 Degrees, 20 Minutes, Northern Latitude, is 24 Miles long, and in some Places 15 Miles over.

Monsieur *Robbe*, the famous *French* Geographer, says, it is situated in 17 Degrees North Latitude, and is above 30 Leagues in Circumference.

The last printed Survey of this Island makes it to be situated between the 13th and 14th Degrees of North Latitude. The South Part lying in 13 Degrees, 10 Minutes; and the North Part in 13 Degrees, 27 Minutes; being in Length from the Point, below *Carew*'s Plantation in the South South-East, to the Spout below *Dowden*'s in the North North-West, 21 Miles: And from *Needham*'s Point to *Conger* Rock, 12 Miles over, and about 75 Miles in Circumference.

The Latitude is right, and so is the Breadth of the Island; but we are assured by Gentlemen who have often travelled from *Ostin*'s in the South East, to *Cluff*'s Bay in St. *Lucy*'s Parish in the North-West, that 'tis full 28 Miles long; which, reckoning the Breadth at 12, and multiplying the one by the other, makes 336 square Acres of Land; in all 215,040 Acres.

But this Calculation, however just it may be found to be according to the Rules of Arithmetick, will certainly deceive any one that shall survey it; for the Island does not contain in all above 100,000 Acres: And this vast Diminution proceeds from the Inequality of the Breadth; in the North-Western, where it is narrowest; and that in the South-Eastern Part of the Island, where it is broadest.

Barbados is the most Windwardly Island of all the *Charibbee* Islands, *Tobago* excepted, as some will have it; of an oval Form, broad towards the South End, growing narrow to the North, with a bending in on the East Side.

The nearest Islands to it are St. *Vincent* and St. *Lucia*. At St. *Vincent*'s the *English* had formerly a small Settlement. This Island may be seen from *Barbados* in a clear Day. The nearest Part of the *Continent* to it is *Surinam*, about a Day and a half's Sail off of it. The *English* were once in Possession of that Country, but the *Dutch* dispossess'd them; and the former have not thought fit to require to be restored to their Plantation.

The Country in general is gradually rising, level in some Parts, and in others, some high Hills, affording most lovely Prospects all over the Island, with a continual Verdure.

In

The History of Barbados.

In the Description of *Barbados*, we shall begin with the Capital, the *Bridge-Town*; and from thence proceed from one Parish to another, over the whole Island.

The *Bridge-Town* was at first called St. *Michael's*, from the Name of the Parish Church, which is dedicated to St. *Michael* the Arch-Angel. 'Tis situated in the Latitude of 12 Degrees, 55 Minutes, in the inmost Part of the Bay, commonly called *Carlisle* Bay; and the Choice of the Place to build this Town upon, seems to have been directed more by Convenience than Health: For the Ground thereabouts being a little lower within Land than the Sea-Banks, the Spring-Tides flow over, and make a great Part of the Flat a Bog, or Marsh: From which there used formerly to ascend noxious Vapours, that contributed very much to the Unhealthiness of the Place; but the Inhabitants have since drained the Flats, and defended it so well from the Influxes of the Sea, that they are not much troubled with those unwholesom Fumes, which before corrupted the Air, and bred Diseases.

The Bog or Morass, which is now on the East Side of the Town, is occasioned by the Freshes or Floods that sometimes overflow the whole Town; which lies at the Entrance of a Valley, that runs several Miles into the Country, and is called, the Valley of St. *George*.

There was a small River, that some Years ago fell into *Carlisle* Bay, at the *Bridge*. It was very commodious for the Planters and Merchants, being deep enough for Sloops to go up about a Mile into the Country: But now 'tis quite choked up; and without the Inhabitants be forced to get it cleared, is like to remain so; no Body thinking it their Business or Interest to set about so necessary a Work, unless the Government gave them due Encouragement.

The *Bridge-Town*, or rather City, is certainly the finest and largest in the Island. It contains 1200 Houses, built of Stone; the Windows glazed, many of them sashed; the Streets broad, the Houses high, and the Rents as dear in *Cheapside*, in the *Bridge*, as in *Cheapside* in *London*.

The Wharfs and Keys are very neat and convenient; and the Forts to the Sea so strong, that there would be no taking it by Force, if they were as well manned and furnished with Ammunition as they ought to be.

The first of these Forts Westward, is *James* Fort, near *Stewart's* Wharf. 'Tis mounted with 18 Guns. In this Fort the Lord *Grey*, when he was Governor of the Island, built a very fine Council-house. Next to this is *Willoughby's* Fort, built on a small Neck of Land, that runs out into the Sea.

'Tis

'Tis mounted with 12 Guns. The Coaſt of *Carliſle* Bay, from this Fort to *Needham's*, is fortified by three Batteries. *Needham's* Fort is mounted with 20 Guns.

Above this Fort, and more within Land, the late Governor, Sir *Bevill Granvill*, began the Royal Citadel, in Honour of our Sovereign Queen *Anne*, called St. *Anne's* Fort. This will be the ſtrongeſt in the whole Iſland, and ſtand the Country in above 30000*l*. Sterling.

The Aſſembly were frightened into ſuch a vaſt Expence, by Advice that Monſieur *Herbeville* was making vaſt Preparations at *Martinico* to attack *Barbados*, as he really intended, but durſt not venture to make any Attempt upon it: So the Storm fell on St. *Chriſtopher's* and *Nevis*; the latter of which Settlements he entirely deſtroyed, as will be related elſewhere.

There is a ſmall Fort of eight Guns to the Eaſtward of the Town; which is thus ſecured from any foreign Invaſion, or home Inſurrection; and it is this Security which makes it the richeſt Town of the *Charibbees*. The Merchants Storehouſes are here ſafe; and both thoſe, and the Tradeſmens Shops, as well furniſhed as the Shops and Ware-houſes in *London*.

The Church in the *Bridge-Town* is as large as many of our Cathedrals. There's an Organ in it as fine and as big as moſt in *England*. There belongs alſo to it a very good Ring of ſeven Bells lately put up, and a fine Clock.

Here are ſeveral large Taverns and Eating-Houſes, and a Poſt-Houſe for Receipt of Letters from all Parts. There have been, in this War, Packet-boats employed monthly by the Government, to carry Letters to and from the *Weſt-Indies*.

Carliſle Bay, at the Bottom of which the *Bridge* ſtands, is a very ſpacious one, and capable of containing 500 Sail of Ships. There was a Mole in it before the late dreadful Hurricane: It ran out from *James* Fort into the Sea; but that terrible Tempeſt entirely ruined it, in the Year 1694.

One may judge of the Populouſneſs and Strength of this Place by the Number of its Militia, which are no leſs than 1200 Men, for the Town, and St. *Michael's* Precinct: They are called the Royal Regiment, or the Regiment of Foot-Guards. Here the Governor, Council, and Aſſembly, hold their Seſſions, the Court of Chancery is kept, and all the publick Affairs of this Iſland generally tranſacted.

In ſhort, if this Town ſtood in as healthy a Place, as it does in a ſafe and advantageous one, 'twould be the beſt of

the

the Bignefs in her Majefty's Dominions, as it is the wealthieft.

On the Eaft Side of the Town is a Magazine-houfe, built of Stone, where the Stores of Powder for the whole Ifland are always kept under a good Guard. From the *Bridge*, about four Miles up in the Country, ftands the Parifh-Church of St. *George*, in a delightful Valley.

And in the Way about a Mile from the Town, the Affembly has ordered a ftately Houfe to be built for the Governor's Refidence. 'Tis called *Pilgrim's*, from the Name of the Proprietor of the Land on which it ftands. And a Mile and an half from the *Bridge*, to the Southward, is *Fontabell*, which was ufually the Seat of the Governors; the Ifland renting the Houfe for that Purpofe of the Owner Mr. *Walrond*.

From the *Bridge* to *Fontabell*, along the Shore, there's a Line fortified with a Parapet; and at *Fontabell* a Battery of 10 Guns. From *Maxwel*, near the *Chaces*, there runs along a Ridge of Hills to *Harrifon*'s, the farthermoft Weftward Plantation. The Line is continued from *Fontabell* to *Chace*'s Plantation: Under which there is a Battery of twelve Guns; and from thence, along *Mellows*'s Bay, are great Rocks and fteep Cliffs, which have naturally fortified the Ifland againft any Invader.

On *Mellows*'s Bay is a Battery of 12 Guns, and from thence Entrenchments, till you come to the *Hole-Town*, vulgarly called the *Hole*.

The *Hole* lies 8 Miles from St. *George's*, and 7 from the *Bridge*. This is a pretty Town, and confifts of a Street which comes down to the Water-fide, and thence leads up into a long one, that forms the Town. There are about 100 Houfes in it. The Road is good, and lies commodious for the Planters in St. *Thomas*'s Parifh, to fhip off their Goods. It has a regular and handfom Church, dedicated to St. *James*; from whence it is fometimes called *James-Town*. Every Month the Seffions is held there for St. *James*'s Precinct; and, for the Defence of the Port, there is a Fort, mounted with 28 Guns, and a Battery of 8 Guns at *Church-Point*, near St. *James*'s Church.

From the *Hole* to St. *Thomas*'s Parifh to the Eaft, is a Mile and an half; and from St. *Thomas*'s to *Speight*'s Town on the Coaft, about 6 Miles.

The Line is ftill continued along the Shore, from *Church-Point* to Col. *Allen*'s Plantation; under which there is a Fort of 12 Guns, that goes by the Name of *Queens Fort*. From whence the Line and Parapet are carried on to *Reid*'s Bay, where there is a Fort mounted with 14 Guns. The Entrenchment

The History of Barbados.

trenchment is thence continued to *Scot*'s Plantation; under which there is a Fort of 8 Guns. And from thence to *Baily's*; by whose Plantation there is a Battery. From *Baily's* it is carried on to *Benson's* Battery of 4 Guns. From *Benson's* it is continued to *Heathcot's* Bay: Upon which stands a Fort, mounted with 18 Guns, near *Speight's* Town; for the Security of which it was erected.

Speight's Town lies about 3 Miles and an half from the *Hole*, and was at first called *Little Bristol*. It is the most considerable Place in the Island next to the *Bridge*. It consists of one long Street, called *Jew-Street*; and three others, that lead down to the Water Side; the whole making above 300 Houses. It was much frequented by the *Bristol* Men when it was first built. The Planters in *Scotland* used to send their Goods thither, to be shipped off for *England*; which occasioned the building of Store houses, and a Concourse of People; and that in Time raised the Town to a flourishing Condition; but the *Bridge* has lately drawn most Part of the Trade thence, and the Place is falling to Decay.

There is a fair Church in it, dedicated to St. *Peter*, which gave Name to one of the 5 Precincts of the Island; and here the monthly Sessions are kept for this Division. The Town is defended by two Forts, besides that to the Southward on *Heathcot's* Bay. One of them stands in the Middle of the Town, and is mounted with 11 Guns: The other at the North End, mounted with 28 Guns.

Near this Town one Mr. *Hancock* built or gave a House for a Free-School. Whether it was endowed or not we cannot tell; but we are better informed of its present Condition, which is going to Decay, if not already a Heap of Ruins.

The Parish of St. *Peter's* is so large, that there's a Chapel of Ease built, and named *All-Saints*, two Miles and an half up in the Country, near that which was *Holloway's* Plantation. This Chapel is so large and beautiful, that it is dignified with the Name of a Church by the modern Surveyors, but it belongs to St. *Peter's* Parish; the Minister there serving both the Cures.

From *Speight's-Town* the Line and Parapet are continued to *Macock's* Bay, in Length 3 Miles and an half. There is a Fort lately built on that Bay; and from thence about 2 Miles up in the Country, is St. *Lucy's* Parish. The Church dedicated to St. *Lucy* is new built of sawed Stone, very handsom and regular.

From hence to the Northern Shore is a fine Champaign Country; and along the Coasts, from *Macock's* Bay to *Lambert's* Point, there are several little Bays, each fortified

by

by a Fort, for the Length of about 4 Miles, from *Lambert's* Point all round the Northern Shore to *Deeble's* Point.

And thence, to *Oſtin's* Town in the Eaſt, the Iſland is fortified naturally by very high Rocks and ſteep Cliffs, which make it impracticable to land there; from *Conſet* Point to *South* Point the Cliffs are very high and contiguous. The Sea alſo is ſo deep under the Shore, that there's ſcarce any Ships Cable can reach the Bottom, at leaſt ſo as to ride the Veſſel; indeed 'tis all ſo rocky that there's no approaching it.

We muſt now ſurvey the Inland Parts of the Windward Shore; where, 5 Miles from St. *Lucy's*, we find the Pariſh-Church and Precinct of St. *Andrew's*, ſituate in that Part of the Country called *Scotland*. St. *Andrew's* Church is a regular, beautiful Edifice; and the Altar-piece was painted by Monſieur *Birchet*, one of the beſt Maſters in *London*, but is not yet put up.

There's a Ridge of Hills in *Scotland*, the higheſt Part of which is called *Mount Helleby*, and is eſteemed the higheſt Ground in the Iſland. From the Top of this Place the Sea is to be ſeen all round it; and out of theſe Hills riſes the River, that is thence called *Scotland River*, which falls into the Sea near *Chaulky Mount*, forming a Sort of Lake, about a Mile from the Shore.

In this Part of the Iſland there's a running Soil, which ſometimes runs away with a Foot of the Surface of the Earth after 'tis planted, to the great Loſs of the Planter.

From St. *Andrew's* Pariſh to St. *Joſeph's*, along the ſame Shore, is about 3 Miles and a Quarter. In this Pariſh riſes *Joſeph River*, the chief in the Iſland: Its Source is in the Cliff near *Davis's* Plantation; and it falls into the Sea below *Holder's*, after it has had a Courſe of about 2 Miles from its Head. Some pretend, that both this and *Scotland River*, by the ſoaking of the ſalt Water in Spring-Tides thro' the Sand, are ſometimes a little brackiſh, which is not true. But at other Times the Floods overflow the Paſtures and Plantations about them, ſo much, that it has been very difficult for Travellers to paſs.

Beſides theſe two Rivers, there are Springs of freſh Water in almoſt every Plantation: For dig where you will, to any Depth, you are ſure to meet with a Spring; from St. *Joſeph's*, along the ſame Coaſt to St. *John's*, is about 3 Miles and a Quarter. In this Pariſh is that Part of the Iſland call'd, *The Top of the Cliff*, near which ſtands *Drax-Hall*, one of the firſt Spots of Ground that was planted: And the Owner Col. *James Drax*, from a Stock of 300 *l.* raiſed the greateſt Eſtate of any Planter of his Time, or ſince.

About

The History of Barbados.

About 3 Miles and a Quarter to the Southward of St. *John*'s, lies St. *Philip*'s and St. *Andrew*'s. A Ridge of Hills runs from *Walrond*'s to *Middleton*'s Mount; and thence to *Harding*'s in St. *George*'s. This Part of the Island was the laſt inhabited of any, except *Scotland*. For thirty Years after the *Engliſh* firſt ſettled upon it, there was no Plantation from *Codrington*'s Bay, all along the Coaſt, and ſeveral Miles up in the Country, till you come to *Cotton-houſe* Bay near *Oſtin*'s. Indeed moſt Part of the Windward Pariſhes were not then cleared of the Woods. *Scotland* was the firſt planted; and now 'tis as rare to meet a Wood from St. *Lucy*'s to St. *Oſtin*'s, except in *Scotland*, as it was then to meet with a Houſe.

From St. *Philip*'s to *Chriſt-Church* is about ſeven Miles. This Church is at *Oſtin*'s Town, which derived its Name from one *Oſtin*; whoſe Plantation was near the Shore, and being a mad extravagant Fellow, the Place became famous on his account, and ſo was called *Oſtin*'s, together with the Bay. This Town ſometimes goes by the Name of *Charles-Town*; but *Oſtin*'s is that by which 'tis beſt known.

The Town Bay is flanked by two good Forts; one towards the Sea, and the other towards the Land; a Platform being carried from the one to the other, for the Benefit of Communication. That towards the Sea is on the North-ſide of the Town; and before St. *Anne*'s Fort, or the *Royal Citadel* was built at the *Bridge*, this was the beſt in the Iſland, being mounted with above 40 Guns. The other Fort, which ſtands at the South End of the Town, is mounted with 16 or 18 Guns. Both of them are a ſure Defence to the Place, which is about the Bigneſs of the *Hole*, and is built in the ſame Form; one long Street and a Lane in the Middle. 'Tis one of the five Precincts of the Iſland, and is a Market-Town as well as the other three Towns, and has, like the reſt, a Monthly Seſſions held in it. It lies about ſix Miles from the *Bridge*, and four and an half from St. *George*'s. From the Southward Fort the Line and Parapet reach as far as the *Royal Citadel*.

Little Iſland is a Mile and an half from it, near a Quarter of a Mile from the Shore. It lies off *Allen* and *Carter*'s Plantation: And about a Mile in the Road, from *Oſtin*'s to the *Bridge*, ſtands the late Mr. *Piers*'s Seat and Plantation, famous for having the beſt Gardens in the Iſland, adorned with Variety of Orange-Walks, Citron Groves, Water-works, and all the lovely and pleaſant Fruits and Flowers of that delicious Country, as well as with the moſt curious of our own.

Thus

Thus we have gone over the whole Island, and there remains now only to mention some remarkable Places and Things, which we forbore taking Notice of in our way, because we were loth to interrupt the complete Survey we were making of the Country, as 'tis divided into Parishes.

Besides the Bays we have named, there are *River* Bay, *Tent* Bay, *Baker*'s Bay, on the Windward Coast: *Skull* Bay, *Foul* Bay, *Mill*'s Bay, *Long* Bay, and *Womens* Bay, in the East: between *Deeble*'s Point and *Ostin*'s, *Six Mens* Bay, to the South-West; and *Cliff*'s Bay the most westerly in the Island. There are many more little Bays, which either have no Name, or bear that of the Owners of the Plantations next to them.

There are also some large Brooks that are honoured with the Names of Rivers, as that at *Hockleton Cliff* in St. *Joseph*'s Parish, which runs into the Sea, about a Mile from the Mouth of *Joseph*'s River; *Hatches* River near *Haynes*'s, in St. *John*'s Parish. There's another River in the Thickets, in St. *Philip*'s Parish; but the Stream is so weak, it can't reach the Sea. There are several Pools besides, by which the Inhabitants are supplied with Water, as also by Ponds and Draw-wells. These are on the Windward or North Coast. The only Water that is allowed to usurp the Title of a River, on the Leeward, or South Coast, is the *Indian* River, between the *Bridge-Town* and *Fontabell*, and this looks much more like a Pond than a River, but in great Floods it falls into the Sea, and that is enough for it to pretend to that Honour. The Fortifications, of which we have given so particular a Description as to their Length, consist of a Line and a Parapet, which goes from Fort to Fort. The Parapet is ten Foot high, made of Sand; before it is a deep Ditch, and for the Security of it a Hedge of Thorns, of a prickly Plant, whose Prickles are very long, and if they get into the Flesh, make a very dangerous Wound.

The Strength of this Island and its Situation, being the Windwardmost Island of the *Charibbees*, give it many Advantages; by which it has, in all times of War, been the Means of preserving the rest of the *English Leeward* Settlements from the Insults of the Enemy, till the last fatal Blow given by Monsieur *Herberville*.

The Inhabitants of this Island, as they have taken a great deal of Pains to fortify it, so they had a great deal of Reason to do it; for if 'tis not the richest Spot of Ground in the World, 'tis only because the Industry of the People is not enough encouraged.

To

The History of Barbados.

To return to our Description of the Country: There are several vast Caves in it; some of them so large, as that in Col. *Allen's* Plantation, that they will hold above three hundred Men. Others are passable half a Mile or more, under the Ground; and there's one in Col. *Sharp's* Plantation, that has a Stream of Water running in it above a Quarter of a Mile from its Mouth, like that in *Okey-Hole* near *Wells* in *Somersetshire*. To these Caves the Negroes often fly from the Fury of their Masters, when they are conscious to themselves, that their Guilt deserves a severe Punishment. They hide themselves there sometimes for Weeks together, and never stir out but at Night. These Cavities are very unwholesom, because of the Damps. 'Tis thought the *Charibbeans* lived in them, when they inhabited this Island; but 'tis a Question whether any *Charibbeans* ever lived there or not.

There are few publick Buildings in *Barbados*. The Churches, Council House, and the Governor's Seat, are all that can properly be so termed. The Churches are all handsom, regular Buildings of Stone, the Pews and Pulpits are of Cedar, and all the Ornaments as decent as any where in the *British* Empire.

The private Buildings are not so stately as one would expect from the Riches of the Planters. There are many high Houses, and some low ones; for such as built immediately after the Great Storm in 1676. were so apprehensive of another, that they lowered their Buildings; but those who have built since them, not having those Apprehensions, have raised their Houses to three and four Stories high, and the Rooms are as lofty as in *England*. Hung Rooms are very scarce here; for the Walls are so damp, occasioned by the Moistness of the Air, that the Hangings would soon rot. The Planters study Convenience more than Magnificence in their Buildings, which are generally neat, and fit for the Habitations of Gentlemen: They are tiled with Pantiles; and the Out-houses and Negroes Huts are covered with Shingles.

What other things relating to it are worth Observation, will fall under other Heads; and we shall close this with the several Divisions of the Country, as it is divided into five Precincts, containing eleven Parish Churches, and one Chapel of Ease.

In the South Part of the Island,
{
In St. *Michael*'s, or *Bridge* Precinct, are,

St. *Michael*'s,
St. *George*'s, and } Parishes.
St. *John*'s,

In St. *James*'s, or the *Hole* Precinct,

St. *James*'s, and } Parishes.
St. *Thomas*'s,

In St. *Peter*'s, or *Speight*'s Precinct,

St. *Peter*'s, with
All-Saints Chapel, and } Parishes.
In the West,] St. *Lucy*'s
}

In St. *Andrew Overhil*'s, or *Scotland* Precinct,

In the North, { St. *Andrew*'s, and } Parishes.
{ St. *Joseph*'s,

In *Ostin*'s Precinct.

In the East, { *Christ-Church*, and } Parishes.
{ St. *Philip*'s,

CHAP. III.

Of the Climate, Soil, and its Productions.

HAving thus given a Geographical Account of the Island in its present State, we come now to treat of the Soil, and its Productions.

We may imagine, that this must be one of the most fruitful Soils in the World, since at the first using it with Sugar Canes, it brought forth a considerable Crop yearly, from three Years to nine, without farther planting, but only weeding, and keeping it clean. Though 'tis not now quite so fertile as before, (and how can it be expected after it has been so much worn?) 'tis yet so apt to produce, that with a little cultivating, it still brings forth a Treasure that seems scarce credible to such as are not acquainted with the Trade

of

The History of Barbados.

of the Island, every Acre, one with another, yielding 10 s. a Year Profit to the National Stock of *England*, besides what the Planter gets, and the many thousand Mouths that are maintained there and here out of it. 'Tis blessed with such a productive Faculty, that few Soils, if any, exceed it. Some Parts of it are however poorer than others; as about the *Bridge*, the Earth is sandy and light; and in *Scotland* and St. *George*'s Parish, near Mount *Helleby*, and *Middleton* Mount, the Mould is rich. In most Places 'tis a light spungy Mould, yet so fertile, that it bears Crops all the Year long. The Trees, Plants, and Fields are always green; some of its Productions always in Blossom, and Fruit on others always hanging on the Trees; there being at once to be seen in this Island the verdant Beauties of the Spring, and the mature Glories of the Summer.

The Inhabitants are always planting or sowing, but chiefly in *May* and *November*, which are the Seasons for sowing and planting Indian Corn, Potatoes, Yams, &c.

There was at first no particular Season for Sugar Canes, all were thought to be alike favourable to them; and indeed they thrived wonderfully; but since the Ground has wanted cultivating, by being so much worn for so long time, the Season for planting Sugar Canes is from *August* to the latter end of *January*, as will be shewn in another Chapter.

This Commodity is the chief of its Productions; the others are Indigo, Cotton, and Ginger. There was formerly Logwood, Fustick, *Lignum Vitæ*, and there are still Variety of Trees, Plants, Fruits, and Herbs.

Of Trees. The Physick Nut is much talked of, being, says *Ligon*, of so poisonous a Nature, that no Animal will approach it, and therefore 'tis made use of in Fences. He adds, it grows 18 Foot high; which is not true, for rarely it grows above eight or nine Foot high, and is generally reckoned a Shrub, not a Tree. There's nothing poisonous in it, but the Leaf in the Nut; which, like other Physick, if taken to Excess, might be mortal; but if used moderately, is only a gentle Purge. This Nut is often eaten, Leaf and all, and Beasts browse often near it, though not upon it.

The *Poison* Tree is as big as the *Locust*, and looks very beautiful. Its Juice, 'tis said, will strike a Man blind, if it happens to get into his Eyes: and 'tis reckoned very unhealthy to stand under its Shade; yet of this Tree the Inhabitants first used to make their Sugar Pots, afterwards of Cedar, and now of Earth.

Though the Sap of the Cassavia Tree is Poison, yet the Planters make Bread of the Root of it for their Negroes:
They

They grate it, and press the Liquor out of it as clean as possible, then bruise it, bolt it, and bake it, for the use we have before-mentioned; and this Cassavia Bread is reckoned one of the most nourishing Foods they give their Slaves.

Coloquintada bears a beautiful Fruit. The Rind smooth, of several Colours, as the green, murry, yellow, and Carnation in streaks. This is not very common now.

Cassia Fistula, a Tree of the quickest Growth of any, it having been known to rise eight Foot high in a Year's time. The Pulp of the Fruit of it is Physical, and made use of by the Apothecaries in *England* for its purgative Faculty. The Leaves in Form are like a Beach Tree.

The Tamarine Tree was first planted in *Barbados*, about threescore Years since, being then brought from the *Indies*; as was also the Palm Tree, famous for the Wine and Oil it produces.

Lowth. Abridg. Vol. III. p. 554.

Dr. *Stubs* writes, that he was credibly informed, there was a Palm Tree in this Island 300 Foot high; but I am as credibly informed there never was any such thing.

The Fig Tree bears a small Fruit, little regarded by the Inhabitants. Its Trunk is as large as an ordinary Elm. The Cherry is less; its Fruit useless and insipid. These Fig Trees shoot Beards or Fibres out of the main Trunk, which root in the Ground again; and so continuing to grow on, would make a Grove of itself, if suffered; this is what Monsieur *Legat*, in his Description of the Island of *Diego Ruys*, by Mistake calls the *Pavilion* or Tent Tree; for that Island being a Desert, it had Room there to grow to what Bigness it could. The same are to be met with in *Guinea*.

The Citron is a small Tree, but bears a large Fruit, the Weight of which often pulls it down to the Ground; the Stalk is of a darkish Colour, the Leaf like that of a Lemon, of a dark green Colour. With the Rind of this Fruit the Ladies of *Barbados* make the finest Cordial in the World; that which is imported for Sale is not so good as what they keep for their Closets; which, they taking Care to have all the Ingredients good, is infinitely above the choicest Waters at *Philips's*; and the *L'eau de Barbade*, as the nice People affect to call their Citron Water, would without doubt be esteemed more than any of his costly Cordials, did it not come from our own Plantations.

This Tree also, by the Peel of its Fruit, furnishes the Planters with another valuable Commodity, their Succats, or Sweatmeats; which are extraordinary good, and excel any the Confectioners make in *London*, when they are well prepared: Indeed, in the Art of conserving and preserving, the

The Hiſtory of Barbados.

the *Barbados* Ladies outdo the beſt in *England*; for which they have the Advantage of the fineſt Sugar, and the fineſt Fruits that Nature produces, and abundance of excellent Leaves, Roots, &c. to pickle, which are equally wholeſom and picquant.

Orange Trees thrive wonderfully in *Barbados*, and the Planters there may as eaſily have Walks of Orange, Lemon, or Citron Trees, for Avenues to their Seats, as the Country Gentlemen, in the Counties about *London*, have Rows of Lime; or of Elm Trees, at a greater Diſtance from the City. And when we conſider that theſe Trees are almoſt always either covered with Bloſſoms, or loaden with Fruit, we cannot but envy the Inhabitants the Pleaſure of theſe delightful Walks and fragrant Shades, where the Evening Breezes ſcatter a thouſand Sweets, and perfume the Groves with Variety of odorous Smells. The Deſcription of the *Elyſian* Fields, the Garden of the *Heſperides*, and all that is lovely and charming in the Fictions of the ancient Poets, are but faint Images of this real Paradiſe; and 'tis impoſſible to keep within the Bounds of the Gravity of an Hiſtorical Stile, when we treat of ſuch a tempting Solitude.

They have all ſorts of Oranges and Lemons, ſweet, ſour, and *Sevil*, in Abundance; the Fruit of which is large, and the Juice delicious; the *China* is not ſo apt to ſurfeit, as thoſe that come from *Spain*; the Fragrancy of the Lemon Juice is as remarkble, as the Beauty and Bigneſs of the Fruit.

The Lime Tree in *Barbados* is like a Holly Buſh in *England*. Fifty Years ago the Planters made Hedges of them about their Houſes; and their Prickles ſerved for a Fortification againſt the naked Negroes. It grows ſeven or eight Foot high, full of Leaves and Fruit; the former like thoſe of a Lemon Tree; and the Fruit reſembles a Lemon ſo much, that at three Yards Diſtance they can't be diſtinguiſhed one from another. The Juice of this Fruit, ſince Punch has been ſuch a faſhionable Drink in *England*, has ſold in great Quantities at good Rates, and is now a ſtaple Commodity, ſome Tuns of it having been imported at *London*, and other Ports of *England* and *Ireland*, in a Year.

The Prickled Apple bears a Fruit in Form like an Ox's Heart. Its Leaf is like that of a Walnut-tree; 'tis of a pale green Colour, and taſtes like a muſty Lemon.

The Pricked Pear is of a better Taſte and Form; it reſembles a *Greenfeild* Pear; the Rind of it, near the Stalk, is of a pale green Colour, ſtreaked with yellow; 'tis larger at the End than in the Middle; the Body of it is of a fine Red, ſtriped with prickled Spots of yellow; 'twill thrive if planted

The History of Barbados.

ed on a Wall, and the Fruit is as pleasant as a Strawberry.

The Pomegranate is a handsom Tree, the Leaves small, of a green Colour, mixt with Olive; the Fruit not so large as the *Spanish*. Here are also the Soursop, which is spoken of in *Jamaica*; the Sugar Apple, and Shaddocks, which is a sort of Orange ; the Fruit is as big as a Melon, or rather bigger. *China*, or Sweet Lemons, are frequent here, and *China* Limes ; but not of so much Use or Profit as the other.

There are several other Trees and Shrubs that bear Fruit also, of which the most valuable are the *Papa*, so soft, that when the Trunk of it is as big as a Man's Leg, it may be cut down with a Knife; the Fruit is boiled, and served instead of Turnips with salt Pork.

The *Guaver*, according to Mr. *Ligon*, resembles a Cherry-tree ; the Fruit of it is as big as a small Lemon ; the Rind as thick as a Lemon's, but soft, and of a delicate Taste. It encloses a pulpy Substance, full of small Seeds like a Fig, some white, and some of a stammel Colour within; the Fruits have different Tastes; and we are told, that if the Seeds are eaten, where-ever they are evacuated again, they grow, which in the Infancy of the Settlement did Mischief to the Plantations ; for the Cattle eating them, dropt them again every where, to the great Incumbrance of the Pasture-Ground.

This Fruit is like a Quince, and the Tree has been known to bear at half a Foot high, as well as at 18 Foot high. It makes the best Gelly and Marmalade in the World, both much beyond that of the Quince.

We must not omit the Coco-Tree, which grows 20, 30, or 40 Foot high ; the Branches shoot forth in several parts of the Trunk, with Spaces between them. It bushes pretty much at the Top, and the greatest Quantity of Boughs growing there, occasion the Coco Tree's always stooping. The Nuts grow where the lower Branches sprout out, and are of several Sizes, most of them as big as a large Foot-Ball ; the Skin of them is green without; they have a pulpy Substance between that and the Shell, which when it is dry, as like *Hemphurds*, or the Rind of the Mangrave-tree, whose Bark being well ordered makes strong Ropes ; the Shell of the Coco is near half an Inch thick; those that gather them cut a hole at the End, as big as a Crown-piece; 'tis full of a clear delicious Liquor, which has been reckoned not very wholesom, but lately 'tis found otherwise ; the Shell is lined with a Substance as thick as itself; 'tis white, and as sweet and soft as a *French* Walnut ; this Shell serves sometimes

times instead of Cups to drink out of, and in *England* are adorned for that purpose with a Rim of Silver.

The Reader must distinguish between this Tree, the Coco and the Cacao-Tree, of whose Nuts Chocolate is made; which Tree is of late cultivated very much in *Barbados*; and the best Chocolate I ever drank in my Life was made of the Nut, that grew in *Apeshill* Plantation.

The Planters of this Island finding it thrives as well there as in *Jamaica*, or *Hispaniola*, will no doubt take Pains to raise it. The Fruit being one of the most valuable Commodities that comes from *America*, we shall treat more particularly of it in the History of *Jamaica*.

The Custard Apple bears a Fruit as big as the largest Pomewater; 'tis of the Colour of a Warden: It must be kept a Day after 'tis gathered, before it should be eaten; then those who eat it, cut a Hole big enough for a Spoon to enter at the End, and the Pulp of it is so like a Custard, that thence it took its Name.

This is *Ligon*'s Description; but he is not always to be depended on: For the Colour of this Tree is a fine clear Red; and the Fruit is so ordinary, that none but the Servants and Negroes eat it.

The Macow Tree, remarkable only for its Figure, being stuck all over with Prickles: 'Tis about the Size of an ordinary Willow; neither Man nor Beast dares touch it. Here *Ligon* draws us into an Error again, for 'tis as high as a Coco Tree, some of which are about 40 Foot high.

The Mangrave Tree is a Shrub, but spreads itself to a great Width. It drops a Sort of Gum, which hangs together like Isicles, one Drop after another, till it touches the Ground, where it takes Root, and encreases the Bulk of the Tree. If all this may be reckoned to be one Tree, the Mangrave will hide a Troop of Horse; which however may be better said of the Fig-tree before-mentioned. The *Indians* make Ropes of the Bark, and Threads as fine as Flax, to weave *Hammocks*.

The Calibash Tree bears a Fruit as big as a Coco, round as a Ball, and of a fine green Colour. It grows so close to the Trunk, that till 'tis pulled or cut off, one can perceive no Stalk that it has. The Shells are employed for several Uses, according to their several Sizes; some for Dishes, some for Cups, some for Basons, and the largest for Pitchers and Pails; there being many of them that hold 2 or 3 Gallons.

There are other Trees that bear Fruit, as the Anchovie Apple, the Date Tree, the Poisonous Cane, and the Bay Tree, &c. But not designing this for a Natural History, we we shall tire the Reader no farther about the Fruit Trees and Shrubs.

Of all the Trees in the Island, the Cotton Shrub might be made to turn to most Advantage, as will be seen in the Chapter of its Trade. It grows up to the Heigth of a Peach Tree; the Bark is of a brownish Colour, the Leaves small, divided into three Parts: It bears a Flower about the Bigness of a Rose, under which there are three little Green sharp-pointed Leaves that encompass it round. This Flower consists of 5 Leaves, of a bright yellow Colour, that have several purple Streaks towards the Stem, and a yellow Button or Crown, surrounded with Fibres of the same Colour. The Flowers are succeeded by a Fruit of the same Colour, as big as a Walnut Shell; when 'tis ripe 'tis black on the Out-side. In these Pods the Cotton is contained; and as soon as they are ripe they will open of themselves, the Sun cracking them.

The Cotton Tree is of no Use; it grows vastly big, and very tall, bearing Pods 5 Inches thick, when they are ripe; and the Sun cracking them, they open, and out flies the Cotton; 'tis very fine. People wait for it, or gather it before the cracking, or 'twould be lost: 'Tis excellent for Quilting.

The Timber Trees in *Barbados* are as follows: The first and fairest of the Forest is very common there, and that is the Cedar Tree; 'tis the most useful Timber in the Island, strong, lasting, light, and proper for Building. There have been great Quantities of it sent to *England*, for Wainscoting Stair-Cases, Drawers, Chairs, and other Houshold-Furniture; but the Smell, which is so pleasing to some, being offensive to others, added to the Cost, has hindered its coming so much in Fashion, as otherwise it would.

The Leaves of this Tree are like those of an Ash; it grows sometimes to a prodigious Bigness, and the Timber has sold so well, that Col. *Alleyne* made 400 *l.* of one Tree, a Sum hardly credible to an *English* Reader; but the Truth of it is not to be questioned, the Author having received the Information from a Gentleman of Worth and Honour, and nearly related to Mr. *Alleyne*.

The Mastick Tree grows to a vast Heigth, some 60 Feet high, and in Bigness proportionable. The Timber of it is used for Wind-mill Work; as is also that of the Bulley Tree, which is something less, and bears a Fruit like Bullace in *England*, whence it takes its Name; and the Locust Tree, growing in Form like a *Tuscan* Pillar, thickening at the Foot, and lessening by Degrees to the Top of it. The Timber of it is lasting, and serves for many Uses in Building.

The History of Barbados.

There's the Bastard Locust, the Iron Wood, so called from its Weight and Hardness; it grows very tall, blossoms twice a Year, in *March* and *September*; the Wood is of a dark red Colour: The Lignum Vitæ Tree, Red Wood, Prickled Yellow Wood, and the Palmetos, the Less and the Royal Palmeto; the Less Palmeto grows about 50 Foot; the Royal Palmeto from 100 to 300, and is one of the most stately Trees in the Universe. At 12 Years Growth 'tis about 17 Foot high; at 40 Years Growth 180 Foot; and at an 100 Years Growth, when in Perfection, 300 Foot high, and but three Foot Diameter; the Bush or Head 80 Foot round; the Leaves are 18 Foot long; and yet the Roots are no bigger than Swans Quills, nor the Fruit than *French* Grapes.

The Plants that grow in *Barbados* are Ginger, whose Root shoots forth Blades, in Shape not unlike those of Wheat when 'tis ripe. The Roots are dug up and scraped by the Negroes, to clear it of the outward Skin, and kill the Spirit, otherwise 'twould be always growing. Those that have not Hands enough to scrape it, are forced to scald it; which Ginger will prove nothing near so good as the other, 'twill be as hard as Wood; whereas the scraped Ginger is white and soft: And accordingly scalded Ginger is sold 40 *per Cent.* cheaper than scraped.

Red Pepper, of which there are two Sorts; one of them so like a Child's Coral, as not to be discerned from it at two Yards Distance. The Colour of it is a Crimson and Scarlet mixed; the Fruit about two Inches long. The other, or the Bonnet-Pepper, is of the same Colour, and shines as much, but 'tis shaped like an old fashioned Cloak Button. The Quality of both the one and the other is the same, and both are so strong, that when they are broken, there comes forth such a Vapour, as will set all who are near it a Coughing, after the Pepper is removed. The *Spaniards* love it to season their Sauces, and it has such a violent Houghgoe with it, that Garlick is faint and cool to it.

There are also Cucumbers, Melons, 16 Inches long, Water Melons, like an Apple for Colour, cooling, and good for the Stone. There are Grapes, but not so good, and in such Quantities, as in the Northern Colonies.

The Plantine Tree, or Shrub, bears a Fruit, which tho' it is not very delicious, yet is of as great Use as any in the Island, being the most nourishing Food that the Negroes eat. It is of a swift Growth, and the Manner of it extraordinary; three or four Sprouts come out of one Root, and one of them getting the start of the rest, keeps its Superiority, and is always uppermost. This Sprout shoots up from the interior

terior Part of the Stem, and as it grows the Out-Leaves hang down and rot, but new ones come forth in their Places; they rise up like a Pike, as the Palmetos do; and as the Sun opens them they become Leaves.

When the Plantine Tree is 8 or 10 Foot high, it is at its full Bigness, and then the Leaves are so too; after which they shed no more. The Fruit grows much like a Long-Boat's Grapling-Iron; it is Yellow when it is ripe. The Negroes don't love it so well then, as while it is Green; they then boil it, and eat it: The *English* eat it only when it is ripe, first peeling it. It is a pleasant, wholesom, nourishing Fruit. The wild Plantine resembles the other, only it is of a Scarlet Colour, the Leaves not so broad, and the Fruit good for nothing.

The Banana is like the Plantine in the Body and Leaves, excepting that the Leaves are something less, and the Body has here and there some blackish Spots; it is of a faint Colour, with the Mixture of the Ash; the Fruit stands outright, like a Bunch of Puddings, each 4 or 5 Inches long; it is sweeter than the Plantine, eats well stewed or preserved, both in Look and Taste not unlike a Quince. The Negroes don't like it so well as the Plantine, because it is sweet, they having an Aversion to sweet Things, if my Author is not mistaken, for I am informed they are very far from hating Sugar.

In the Fruit, when it is cut, as you do the Root of Fern to find a spread Eagle, you see the lively Representation of Christ upon the Cross, the Head hanging down, the Arms extended to a full Length, with some little Elevation, and the Feet crofs one upon another.

Thus several Authors have written; but I have been told by several Gentlemen, that there is no Manner of Representation of a human Figure; it is true, there is a Sort of a Crofs, and Fancy may supply the Want of the Representation.

The last and best of all the excellent Fruits we have nam'd, is the Pine, the most beautiful and pleasant of all Nature's Productions. The Fruit is almost of the Colour of an Abricot not full ripe, it eats crisp and short as that does, is full of Pores, and those of such Forms and Colours, as render a lovely Sight to the Eye, and are tempting to the Taste. It would never endure bringing to *England*, tho' frequent Trials have been made to do it. The Smell of this Fruit is extremely fragrant; the Tree never grows to be above 4 Foot high, and the Fruit is sometimes 14 Inches long, and 6 Diameter. There are two Sorts, the King and Queen Pine, and both painted with so many different glorious

Colours,

The History of Barbados.

Colours, that it makes a moſt charming Proſpect to the Eye.

The Taſte of it is wonderfully picquant, ſharp and ſweet alternatively, and both in a very high Degree. The Pleaſure it gives is ſo delicious, and at the ſame Time ſo refreſhing, that it tranſports the Perſon who taſtes it.

There are many other Plants proper for Phyſick or Food; as Aloes, which is a beautiful Plant; the Leaves are four Inches broad, and a Quarter of an Inch thick, and a Foot and an half long, with Prickles on each Side. Out of theſe Leaves, when they are cut, the Aloes iſſue. The Trees in this Iſland continue green all the Year; and at whatever Time they are lop'd and cut, they ſprout out again.

The ſenſible Plant is common in *Barbados*, which when you touch it cloſes its Leaves, and in a little Time will open again. The Humble Plant, and the Dumb Cane are frequently met with here; alſo moſt Sorts of *Engliſh* Pot-herbs and Roots thrive. Leek-ſeed will not come up, nor Roſe-trees bear Flowers.

Mr. *Ligon* tells us this, which is however a Miſtake; for there are as good Leeks in *Barbados*, as in *England*, and fine Damask and Provins Roſes all the Year round.

Theſe Herbs were all carried thither; for when the firſt Planters landed, they found nothing of that Kind but Purcelain; with which the Place was then ſo over-run, that it was thrown away as a Weed. They have Potatoes in Abundance, and *Yams*, which is Part of their Slaves Food.

Tho' there are few Flowers in the Iſland, there are ſome very lovely ones; ſuch as the White Lily, which grows ſpontaneouſly, and is a fairer Flower than the *Engliſh*; the Red Lily is of the ſame Bigneſs, neither of them ſweet. The St. *Jago* Flower is very beautiful, but of a nauſeous Smell.

The Paſſion Flower takes its Name from the Picture of ſome of the Inſtruments of our Saviour's Paſſion there repreſented; they creep along the Ground like Ivy, if they have no Tree to grow up by. This Flower in *Barbados* is known by the Name of, the *Vinegar Pear Flower*, and is uſed to run over Arbours, as we do Honey-Suckles here; the *Water Lemon Flower* is put to the ſame Uſe. And as to other Flowers, there are few or none, the Heat of the Soil being too fierce for the cultivating Things of ſo delicate a Conſtitution.

The Four a Clock Flower, ſo named, becauſe it always opens at Sun-ſet; it is in *England* called the *Merveille de Peru*. It grows in Tufts, the Leaves in the Form of a Heart, the Point turning back; the Flower bigger than a Primrose, and of the finest purple Colour that ever Eye beheld. The Seed is Black, with an Eye of Purple, shaped like a Button, and so hard, that it might serve for the same Use.

There is a Root in the Island, the Name of which I cannot learn, but suppose it to be the *Yams*; the Seeds were brought thither by the *Negroes*, and planted there in little Hills as big as Mole-Hills. When it shoots forth its Stalks they turn down the Ground on each Side, and then there grows up a Stem, not unlike Asparagus, of a purple Colour; which being gathered, and eaten as a Sallet, with Oil, Vinegar, and Salt, is a tolerable Sauce, where no better is to be had. The Root is also good boiled with powdered Beef and Pork, eaten with Butter and Vinegar; the Cabbage which they call the *Seven Years Cabbage*, and is much sweeter than ours, when it is ripe, shoots forth many Slips, which being transplanted, produce others, that grow to be as fair, and as large, as if they rose from the Seed. But the common Cabbage is not so much minded, as otherwise it would be, on Account of the Cabbage-Tree, which grows 20 or 30 Foot high, and bears a Flower of proportionable Bigness, resembling a Cabbage in Form and Taste.

Eddoes is a Plant, the Pulp of whose Stalk they eat, as we do Artichoke Bottoms, and it is every whit as good.

We must not close this Chapter, without taking Notice of the *Withies*, which formerly crept among Bushes, and fastened on the Trees, but now are quite rooted up: They bear a beautiful and odoriferous Flower; but if they got into a Plantation, they crept about the Ground like Horse-Radish; and if not taken up, which was very difficult, ruined the Growth of the Canes.

There are all Sorts of Pulse in *Barbados*, in very great Plenty, and excellent in their Kind. Apples and Pears never thrived there, nor many of our Shrub Fruits, as Gooseberries, Currants, or Cherries.

As for Corn, the Planters never sow any *English* Wheat; and the poorer Sort of People, who spare most of their Ground for Corn, plant only *Indian* or *Guinea* Corn, which they sell to the richer, but at so great Rates, that they are forced to send to the Northern Colonies for *Indian* Corn.

That Part of the Island called the *Champaign*, and that called the *Thickets*, are entirely planted with Corn. There are many thousand Acres of Land lye waste for want of Hands to cultivate it. The *English* Corn is generally sent thither from *England* in Flower. *Indian* Corn is sometimes sold for 2 *s.* 6 *d.* and sometimes 10 *s.* a Bushel, but commonly 5 *s.* a Bushel. There

The History of Barbados.

There is no *English* Grain cultivated here; if there was, there is no doubt but all the Summer Corn would thrive; as Oats, &c. have done, when, for an Experiment, some Grains have been thrown into the Ground.

The Seasons for Planting *Indian* Corn are chiefly in *May* and *November*; but it is also planted all the Year, from *May* to *January*.

Orchards and Gardens are rare in this Island, and they are at very little Labour to cultivate any Thing besides Sugar-Canes, and the Commodities that are fit for a home Market. Nature has done, and continues to do so much for them, that they take the less Pains to do for themselves; and depending on her Bounty, and Supplies from *England*, and the Northern Colonies, they content themselves with what she produces, which is enough to satisfy the Desire of the most luxurious Taste in the World; so delicate, and so rich are the Fruits of this little, but lovely Island.

As to the Climate, one would think, by its Situation, that it is intolerably hot; and indeed for 8 Months in the Year, the Heats would be insupportable, were it not for the fresh Breezes which rise with the Sun, and blow fresher as the Sun gets higher.

The Place is sensibly cooler since it was cleared of the thick Woods, we have before spoken of. The Breezes blow from the East, with a Point or two to the North, except in the Months of *July*, *August*, *September*, and *October*; which is their Mid-summer, and then the Weather is excessively hot: But yet the Sea Breezes, the Groves and Shades, and their cool Houses, render it very tolerable; and it was reckoned the healthiest Island in *America*, till about the Year 1691, when some Forces were shipped at *Cadiz*, to go upon the Expedition against *Martinico*.

These Regiments carried with them a pestilential Fever, with which the whole Island was so infected, that in the Course of 12 or 13 Year, it carried off above a third Part of its Inhabitants, and destroyed most of the Seamen, as well in the Merchant Men, as Men of War, that came thither.

The dreadful Turnado's, or Hurricanes, that used to threaten this Island with a general Ruin, are not so frequent as formerly; and the Distemper which was called, the *Sickness*, is so much decreased, that the Island begins to recover its former Reputation for Health.

From the Situation of the Place, it follows of Consequence, that the Length of the Days must be very near equal; and the Sun rises at Six, and sets at Six, or in less than half an Hour before or after, which continues so all the Year round.

Three

Three Quarters of an Hour after Sun-set it is dark, the Twilights being no longer in these Parts.

CHAP. IV.

Of the Beasts, Birds, Fish, Insects, and other Animals in *Barbados*.

THERE were several Beasts found on the other *Charibbee* Islands, but few or none at *Barbados*; which, as has been said, was almost over-run with Hogs. Afterwards Beasts of Burthen were brought thither, and Cattle for Food.

Those that were either some Years ago, or are still to be met with there, are Camels, of which there were several imported at the first Settlement of the Island. They did not thrive, and for that Reason no more were brought over. Captain *Higginbotham* of St. *Philips* had four or five; each of them would carry 15 or 1600 Pound Weight of Sugar to the *Bridge*, and bring as good a Load to his Plantation, eight Miles from it.

Horses the Inhabitants have from *England* for their Coaches; and for their own Riding, and the Militia, from *New-England*. For Carts and common Uses, they had some from *Bonavist*, *Cape Verd Islands*, and *Curassau*.

When they first settled there, *Virginia* also used to furnish them with Horses, but now they have almost all from *Old* and *New-England*. Their own Breed are mettlesom, swift, and hardy, but small, and not very handsom.

Oxen, Bulls, and Cows, were brought from the Isle of *May* and *Bonavista*, to the first Planters. Their Posterity and Successors breed all now; for it has been found, that the black Cattle brought from foreign Parts, lick off the Pitch and Tar with their own Hair, which never passes thro' them, but occasions their Death, few of them living when they come ashore.

The *Barbados* Cattle is a midling Breed; and they seldom cut their Bulls, but yoke them, and put them to the Cart; as they do also Cows, and work them there, and in their Cattle-Mills, of which there are not many now; the meaner sort, who want Negroes, only making use of them. The Bulls are so well taught, that they will work very orderly.

Assnegoes, or Asses, are extraordinary useful, in carrying Sugar to the *Bridge*. These Beasts will run along with their Burthen, in Ways where Horses cannot pass. The former will

The History of Barbados. 119

will pick and choose their Way; and if any one of them fall, two Negroes can help him up; they will carry from one hundred and an half, to two hundred Weight. The *Assnegoes* were brought thither, as well as other Cattle.

This Island having no living Creature in it bigger than a Hog, till the *English* settled there, Hogs were in such extraordinary Plenty, that the *English* were more pestered than served by them at their first landing. It is thought they were left there by the *Portuguese*, to breed, and supply them with Provisions, in their Passage to and from the *Brasils*.

The Hogs the *Portuguese* landed there multiplied, in a few Years, so fast, that the whole Island could hardly maintain them; the *Europeans* and *Charibbeans* came from the other Islands to hunt them; and the *English* thought to have given it the Name of, *The Isle of Hogs*.

The Flesh of these Hogs, as the Inhabitants have mended the Breed, is extremely delicious, and surpasses the best Pork in *Europe*; they are some large, and some little, but all good.

Sheep don't thrive well in *Barbados*; yet there are some whose Meat is not so kindly as ours in *England*. There is greater Plenty of Goats, much of the same Nature with the *Welsh*, the Flesh tasting like that of the *Welsh* Goats. Monkeys and Racoons are there in abundance.

The Birds of this Place, says an Author who lived in the Island, are hardly worth the Pains of describing. The biggest they have there is a Buzzard, less than the *English* Grey-Buzzard, swifter of Wing, and serviceable to the Planter, by destroying the Rats, which otherwise would destroy his Canes; for there are great Numbers of them.

There's great store of the larger Turtle-Dove; a much handsomer Bird in Shape and Colour than the *English* Turtle, and much better to eat. The lesser Turtle is a finer Bird than the larger, shaped like a Partridge, her Feathers grey and red, brown under her Wings.

There's a Bird in this Island like a Thrush, which is so called; her Feathers always ruffled, and her Head hanging down, as if her Neck was broke: She has three or four Notes, loud and sweet. Another they have like a Wren, they call it the Quaking-thrush, a very merry Bird by her Motion, but she seldom or never sings; she has a long Bill. There's a Black-Bird, so called, with white Eyes; her Voice harsh like a Jay; a great Devourer of Corn and Blossoms. They fly in Flocks of many thousands; they walk, and don't hop. Another in Colour like a *Fieldfare*: It is, says *Ligon*, called a Counsellor, *because her Head seems too big for her Body*; but her true Name is a Loggerhead. She is extremely

ly wanton in her Flight, and so strange in her Note, that no Voice or Instrument can imitate it; it is a Quarter Note, which is a Discovery in Musick that no Master has yet been able to make.

There are Sparrows, Haysocks, Finches, Yellow-Hamers, Titmice, and such like Birds; for which the *English* have not thought fit to be at the trouble to invent Names, they are so little and worthless, either for Flesh, Feather, or Note.

The most famous of all the feathered Nation in *America*, is the *Colibry*, or *Humming-Bird*, which, according to an ingenious Author, is admirable for her Beauty, Shape, Smell, which is like Musk, and way of Life; it is much less than a Wren; yet though she's the least, she is the most glorious of all Birds. Some of these Birds are no bigger than the greater sort of Flies, the biggest scarce exceeding an Humble Bee in Bulk; the Colours of the Feathers of her Neck and Wings represent those of the Rain-bow: Some of them have such a bright Red under their Necks, that at a Distance one would think it were a Carbuncle; the Belly and under the Wings are of a gilt yellow, the Thighs as green as an Emerald, the Feet and Beak as black as polished Ebony, the two little Eyes shine like two Diamonds, the Head is of a Grass-green; the Plumage of the Male is finer than the Female's, and on his Head he has a Crown of Feathers, as it were to distinguish his Superiority. It is so strong in its Flight, that it makes a louder Noise, by the Agitation of its Wings, than the greatest Birds. It loves to fly near those that pass, and surprizes them like a little Whirlwind. It lives on the Dew, which it sucks with its Tongue from the Blossoms. Its Tongue is much longer than its Beak, hollow like a Reed, and about the Bigness of a small Needle. It is seldom seen on the Ground, nor standing on the Trees, but hovering in the Air, near the Tree from whence it takes its Nourishment. Humming-Birds covet the Blossoms of Cotton-Trees most, roost in that or the Orange-Tree, and are very curious in building their little Houses in the Branches. The only way of taking the *Colibry*, is by shooting it with Sand, which stuns it for the present: When you have it, you cannot keep it, for no body can furnish it with the Food it is used to feed upon.

This Description of the *Colibry* suits in most Things with the Humming-Birds of *Barbados*, which have no Smell, unless it is what is given them after they are dead; when they are perfumed, and sent for Presents to *England*. The bright Red under the Neck was never seen in *Barbados*; the Belly and under the Wings of a dark Colour; the Thighs, as well as the Feet and Beak, black: Its Neck is about the Bigness of half a Walnut Shell, split in two Parts. As

The History of Barbados.

As for Wild Fowl, the Inhabitants of *Barbados* do not often see any: They sometimes take Teal near their Ponds, and a sort of Fowl they call *Oxen and Kine*. They have a Bird which goes by the Name of the *Man of War*, because it flies out to Sea for Discoveries; and it is said, these Men of War are so much to be depended on, that whenever they return, the People cry out a *Sail*, and are never deceived in it. These Birds will meet Ships 20 Leagues from Land. Mr. *Ligon*, who gives this Account of the Wild Fowl of *Barbados*, must not here also be trusted; for when the Winds change to the South and South-West, there are great Quantities of Wild Fowl, that come in Flocks from the Continent, as Plovers, Curliews, Snipes, Wild Pigeons, a few Wild Ducks, and Teal. The Wild Pigeons are so fat, that when they are shot in the Trees, they sometimes fall down and burst; they are bigger than our Pigeons, and of a very dark Colour; some of them with a Ring of white about their Necks; 50 of these Wild Fowl have been killed at a Shot.

Their Tame Fowl is of the same Kind with ours in *England*, only the Meat of the several Sorts are better. Their Ducks, which they call *Muscovy*, are excellent Food; so are their Pigeons, Pullets, and all their Poultry.

They have some Rabbits, but no Hares, nor Venison. The Rabbits are good and scarce, so that they are generally 5 s. a Couple.

The Insects that are most frequently met with in this Island, are Snakes, some of which are a Yard long, they kill the Planters Pigeons, do the same Mischief as they do in *England*, and suck up their Milk; they will climb up a Wall, six or seven Foot high, come in at a Window, get down in the Room, where the Milk Pans are, skim them, and return back the same Way they came; they never sting any body.

The Scorpions in *Barbados* are as big as Rats; they will combat the Snakes that attack them to eat them, but they always have the worst on't; they never hurt Man or Beast. There are no Toads or Frogs. Lizards were more common in the Island than they are lately, the Cats having almost destroyed all of them; they loved to be where Men were, to gaze in their Faces, and hearken to their Discourse; they are not like those in *Europe*, their Bodies are about four Inches long, their Tails near as much, their Heads resembling a Snake's, their Backs are of a Grass-green Colour, blewish towards the Side, their Bellies yellow; they have four Legs, and are very nimble.

Musketoes

Musketoes sting and bite People in the Night, and are indeed the most troublesom Creature the *English* meet with in *America* ; they are like Gnats in *England*, and are not so frequent in *Barbados* as in the Colonies upon the Continent, where there are large Fens and low Places.

Cock-roaches are about the Bigness of a Beetle ; if they happen upon sound Sleepers, they bite till they fetch Blood; and if they awake, and hunt them, they are nimble, that 'tis not easy to catch them. The Negroes, who have thick Skins, and by Reason of their hard Labour, are not easy to be waked when they are asleep, are sometimes bitten so, that for the Breadth of both your Hands together, their Skins are razed, as if it was done with a Curry-comb. Thus it might be in Mr. *Ligon*'s Time, but now 'tis certain they are not so very mischievous : It is true, where-ever they touch, they leave a Sting; and if Children go to Bed with greazy Fingers, will nibble them unmercifully ; they are the most offensive things in *Barbados*.

Merriwings are of so small a Size, and so thin and aerial, they can hardly be discerned, but by the Noise of their Wings, which is like a small Bugle Horn, at a great Distance: Where they sting, they raise a Nob as big as a Pease, which lasts a whole Day. These Merriwings, so pompously described by Mr. *Ligon*, are nothing but what we call Gnats in *London*, and Stouts in the West-Country. All Lands that lie low will be troubled with them in Summer-time.

Caterpillars eat the Potatoes, and are eaten by Turkies. The *Chegoes* are another little mischievous kind of Insect; and there are various Sorts of smaller ones, as Ants, Pismires, &c. but none that are peculiar to the Country, and therefore not proper to be inserted in this Place, unless it be the Wood Ant and Mastick Fly ; the former of which destroys the Timber in the Houses. Upon a Deal Beam they will build a Nest as big as a Barrel; and within it is like a Honey-comb, but without any Honey ; they will eat up and destroy a Piece of *English* Oak in a very little time ; their Colour is white, and if they are squeezed, there comes out a soft Substance of the same Colour; they build upon Trees in the Woods, or in Houses.

The *Mastick Fly*, which is so called from its destroying the Mastick Trees ; the Smell of it is so fragrant, that it perfumes the Air as it flies by you. It is supposed to destroy the Tree by a Sort of a Rasp in the Bill, with which it makes thousands of Holes in the Tree, so that there will be Pecks of Dust, like Saw-dust, under it.

The History of Barbados.

The Sea of *Barbados*, if that Part of the Ocean which surrounds it, may be so called, yields almost all Sorts of Fish that are caught elsewhere; those that are rarely to be seen in other Parts of the World, are, the Parrat Fish, Snappers, and grey Cavallos, *Terbums*, Coney-fish.

The Mullets are reckoned extraordinary good of their Kind, and so are their Lobsters and Crabs.

There's a Sort of Land Crab, which lives almost always on the Shore; they hide themselves in Holes and in Houses, and sometimes in Hollow Trees: They are often met upon the Stairs, in Parlours, and Gardens, where they eat Herbs. In *March*, they all come out of their Holes, and march down to the Sea in such Multitudes, that they cover a great Part of the Ground where they go. Several Years ago the Planters used to ride over them in the Roads; they never eat them, but the Negroes love them, and frequently feast upon them.

The Parrat Fish is about 20 Pound Weight, and well tasted. It has Scales like a Carp, of a green Colour; it has no Teeth, but sharp strong Jaws, and feeds chiefly on Shell-fish.

As to the Description of the other Kinds of Fish we have mentioned above, we must be forced to leave it as we found it in general, and therefore cannot descend into Particulars: We are told they are all excellent Meat, and are often served up to the Gentlemens Tables of the Island.

As for the Tortoise, we shall speak of it more at large in the History of *Jamaica*, and shall in this Place only correct an Error of Mr. *Ligon*'s, who writes, a Tortoise has three Hearts, which Dr. *Stubs* says he found to be false; for though the Resemblance of the two Auricles be such, as also their Bodies or Flesh, as to deceive the unwary Observer, yet is there but one Heart triangular and fleshy, &c. Lowth. *Vol.* 3. *p.* 552.

In all the Rivers are Craw-fish, Maid-fish, Grigs, not *Eels*, about nine Inches long, Prawns, and several Fish that come out of the Sea, and live in the fresh Water, as Cophmirs, Snooks, Place, and some Eels.

CHAP.

CHAP. V.

Of the Inhabitants, Masters, Servants, and Negroes: Their Numbers, Strength, Manner of Living, Diet, Exercises, and Diversions.

THIS Island was the soonest peopled of all our Colonies; the Riches of the Planters produced by that of the Soil, tempted Gentlemen of good Families and moderate Estates, to transport themselves thither to improve them. And tho' it seems trivial to relate Particulars of the Honours bestowed on private Persons; yet for the Credit of *Barbados*, there have been more of that Island knighted by the Kings of *England*, than of all the rest of the *English* Plantations in *America*; for since the Settlement of the Island 13 Baronets and Knights were made, for the Incouragement of the Industry of the Inhabitants.

Created Baronets the same Day, *Feb.* 18. 1661.

Sir *John Colliton*,
Sir *James Modiford*,
Sir *James Drax*,
Sir *Robert Davers*,
Sir *Robert Hacket*,
Sir *John Yeomans*,
Sir *Timothy Thornhill*,
Sir *John Witham*,
Sir *Robert Legard*,
Sir *John Worsum*,
Sir *John Bawdon*,
Sir *Edwyn Stede*,
Sir *Willoughby Chamberlayne*,
} Baronets.

And indeed whoever will look over the Map of *Barbados* will find, the Country is not possessed by such a Set of Men as inhabit the other Plantations; the *Walronds*, the *Fortescues*, the *Collitons*, the *Thornhills*, the *Farmers*, the *Pickerings*, the *Littletons*, the *Codringtons*, the *Willoughbies*, the *Chesters*, the *Kendals*, the *Dimocks*, the *Hawleys*, the *Stedes*, the *Prideauxs*, the *Alleyns*, the *Quintines*, the *Bromley's*, and others, whose Families are of the most ancient and honourable in *England*; nor must we omit one, which is indeed a mighty Name, *Palæologus*, who had a small Plantation near the

Top

Top of the Cliff. How he came by that Imperial Name, we have not heard fairly made out; neither can we believe the Tradition of the Family, of whom one attefted to the Author, that his Anceftors were originally *Greek* Fugitives, and defcended from the Emperors of *Conftantinople* of that Name, who reigned in the *Eaft* from the driving out of the *French* by *Michael Palæologus*, in the thirteenth Century, to the Diffolution of that Empire under *Conftantine Palæologus*, in the fifteenth Century, by *Mahomet the Great*.

Enough of this Digreffion, which is only defigned to fhew, that the common Reflection made upon the Plantations, as to the Meannefs of the Planters Origins, is groundlefs as to *Barbados*, where there are as many good Families as are in any of the Counties of *England*, where Commerce and Trade flourifh. But were that Reflection true, it would be far from leffening the Reputation of the prefent Inhabitants; the vaft Eftates which many of them enjoy, as the *Draxes*, the *Guys*, the *Walters*, and the *Hallets*, are glorious Proofs of the Induftry and Wifdom of their Anceftors; and a fair Invitation for other Merchants in *England* to remove thither, and endeavour to acquire the fame Poffeffions, equal to many of our Nobility and Gentry, of the firft Rank in *England*. Indeed, the Pleafantnefs of the Country is fuch, that it might tempt over the moft profperous; and the Profit would be great enough, were it duly encouraged, to invite the moft covetous to live there. Wealth and Pleafure, which are generally Strangers, dwell there together; and an induftrious prudent Man may grow rich with as much Delight, as a Prodigal grows poor in *England*.

The Character of this Ifland was fuch, as drew over Multitudes to fee and inhabit it; infomuch that twenty Years after the firft Settlement was made there, the Militia of the Country were more in Number than that of *Virginia* is now, though the Place is not a fiftieth Part fo big. They muftered then 11000 Horfe and Foot, as good Men, and as refolute as any in the World: This Number was confiderably encreafed afterwards, and in the Year 1676, when the Ifland was in its moft flourifhing Condition, during Sir *Jonathan Atkins*'s Government, there were 20000 Men, and 50000 Souls, all *Europeans* by Birth or Defcent, and 80000 Negroes; in all above 150000 Souls; in an Ifland not much bigger than the Ifle of *Wight*.

By this we may fee how much this little Ifle had flourifhed in about 50 Years. There are few Counties in *England* that have 130000 Souls in them; and the Kingdom itfelf, taken all together, fell infinitely fhort of the Populoufnefs of *Bar-*
bados

bados at that Time; for granting there are 100000 Acres of Land in *Barbados*, and 40 Millions in *England*, as there are by the beſt Computations, as *Chamberlain*'s, *Houghton*'s, &c. *England* contains 400 Times as much Ground as that Iſland, and in Proportion, ſhould have above 50 Millions of Inhabitants, whereas it has not 8 Millions by Sir *William Petty*'s, and the largeſt Calculations.

The Number of Souls is ſince conſiderably decreaſed in *Barbados*, as well by the Removal of ſeveral of the moſt eminent Planters to *England*, where they have purchaſed Eſtates, and live in great Affluence and Splendor, as by a fatal Diſeaſe, which infected the whole Iſland. It was, as we have hinted, brought thither in the Year 1691, and ſwept away ſo many of the Inhabitants, Maſters, Servants, and Slaves, that there are not above 7000 fighting Men, and 25000 *Engliſh* Souls in the Place, nor above 60 or 70000 Negroes, Men, Women, and Children.

The Diſtemper is lately abated, and the Colony encreaſes in People daily, in which the preſent Health of the Place will, if it laſts, advance it in two or three Years to the happy State it was in formerly, if they are not too much diſcouraged from Home.

Every Freeholder, and white Servant, able to bear Arms, is liſted in the Militia of the Iſland, which conſiſts now of about 3500 Foot, and 1200 ſtout Horſe; and theſe are as good, or better, than any regular Forces; for beſides that the *Creoleans* are as brave Men as any in the World, they would certainly fight reſolutely for ſo rich and ſo pleaſant a Country.

Such Engliſhmen as are born in Barbados are ſo called.

We have ſhewn in our Geographical Account of the Iſland, how it is fortified by Nature and Art; and that the Reader might not be at a Loſs, to know how a Line of ſuch Length, above 30 Miles on the Coaſt, is manned, he muſt underſtand, that in Caſe of an Alarm, the Government can arm 10000 ſtout Negroes, dextrous at handling a Pike, who would defend thoſe Entrenchments againſt any Invader.

The Inhabitants are ranked in theſe three Orders; Maſters, who are either *Engliſh*, *Scots*, or *Iriſh*, with ſome few *Dutch*, *French*, and *Portugueſe Jews*; White Servants, and Slaves: The White Servants are either by Covenant or Purchaſe; there are two Sorts, ſuch as ſell themſelves in *England*, *Scotland*, and *Ireland*, for 4 Years, or more; and ſuch as are tranſported by the Government from thoſe three Kingdoms, for Capital Crimes.

The Gentlemen of *Barbados* ſcorned to employ any of the latter Sort, till the late Sickneſs and War had reduced them

to

The History of Barbados.   127

to great Want of Hands: And of the former, several poor Mens Children have been driven thither, by Necessity or Discontent; who behaving themselves honestly and laboriously, have raised themselves, after their Servitude was expired, to be Masters of good Plantations, and been the making of their Relations at Home.

The Masters, Merchants, and Planters, live each like little Sovereigns in their Plantations; they have their Servants of their Houshold, and those of the Field; their Tables are spread every Day with Variety of nice Dishes, and their Attendants are more numerous than many of the Nobility's in *England*; their Equipages are rich, their Liveries fine, their Coaches and Horses answerable; their Chairs, Chaises, and all the Conveniences for their travelling, magnificent.

The most wealthy of them, besides this Land-train, have their Pleasure-Boats, to make the *Tour* of the Island in, and Sloops to convey their Goods to and from the *Bridge*.

Their Dress, and that of their Ladies, is fashionable and courtly; and being generally bred at *London*, their Behaviour is genteel and polite; in which they have the Advantage of most of our Country Gentlemen, who living at great Distances from *London*, frequent the World very little; and from conversing always with their Dogs, Horses, and rude Peasants, acquire an Air suitable to their Society.

The Gentlemen of *Barbados* are civil, generous, hospitable, and very sociable. They were not, till lately, troubled with Factions and Parties; and, to prevent the growing of Divisions among them, in the Time of the Distractions in *England*, they made a Law among themselves, that whoever named the Word *Round-head*, or *Cavalier*, should give the Company, at his own House, a Pig and a Turkey; and sometimes they would make Forfeitures, on Purpose to have an Opportunity to entertain their Neighbours. But this Hospitality is now almost lost there, the Gentlemen learning in *England* to keep their good Things to themselves, and to part with them very sparingly: Yet some there are, whose Houses are still free to Strangers, and who receive all with a chearful Look, and open Heart.

Their Diet is the same with ours in *England*; they have Beef, Pork, Veal, Mutton, and Lamb, of their own breeding, or at their Markets, for 9 d. Half-penny a Pound, which is cheap there.

Their second Courses are their Poultry, as Turkeys, Geese Ducks, Fowl, Chickens, and Fish, which they have in Abundance, by the Convenience of their Situation.

All Sorts of Sauces, as Pickles, Olives, &c. they have from *England*, as alfo Tongues, Hams, Anchovies, Caveer, &c. Their Paftry and their Bread are made of *Englifh Flower*; and their Kitchin Servants are as good Cooks as any in *England*.

Their Deferts are all admirable, and the very Idea of a Table fpread with their Melons, Succats and Pines, is tranfporting.

Their Drink is chiefly *Madeira* Wine and Water: Of that Wine there are two Sorts, *Malmfey* and *Vidonia*; the former as rich, and not fo lufcious as Canary; and the latter as dry, and as vigorous as Sherry; it is Red, being coloured with *Tinto*; they alfo drink cool Tankards of Wine, excellent Lemons, fine Sugar and Spring-Water, Lemonades made of all the laft Ingredients but Wine.

The more fanguine People entertain one another with Punch, made of the beft Ingredients, Lemons, double refined Sugar, Spring-Water, and right *French* Brandy.

The good Husbands ufe their own Manufacture Rum, inftead of *French* Brandy. They have alfo all Sorts of other Wines, Malt Drinks and Cyder, from *England*. In fhort, the Inhabitants of *Barbados* live as plentifully, and fome of them as luxurioufly as any in the World. They have every Thing that is requifite for Pomp and Luxury; they are abfolute Lords of all Things, Life and Limb of their Servants excepted, within their own Territories; and fome of them have no lefs than 7 or 800 Negroes, who are themfelves, and their Pofterity, their Slaves for ever.

Every Dwelling-houfe, and other Out-houfing, looks like a handfom Town, moft being new built with Stone, and covered with Pantile or Slate, brought hither in the Ballafts of Ships, as is alfo Sea-Coal for Forges; and the Freight being by that Means made cheap, there is Plenty enough of thofe Neceffaries.

The White Servants are fold for about 20 *l.* a Piece; but if they are Mechanicks, for much more. Women, if they are handfom, 10 *l.* As foon as the Time, for which they covenanted to ferve, or at the End of which they are free by Law, is expired, they are entirely their own Mafters; and, during their Servitude, are treated more gently than the *Blacks*.

Their Clothing is made of Ozinbrig Jackets and Drawers, and fometimes of coarfe Cloth. The Male Servants have thick Drawers, Shoes, Stockings, Caps, and Canvas Waiftcoats allowed them. And the Females have Shifts, Petticoats, Waiftcoats, Shoes, and Stockings, made neat and ferviceable. We

The History of Barbados.

We must add to Mr. *Ligon's* Account, that the Servants, when they are out of their Time, have 5 *l.* for those that are *British* Servants. All others have but 40 *s.* And as for Female Servants there are now none, unless they are Natives of the Country, and hired as Servant-Maids are in *England.* 'Tis by Chance that any come from *England* to be hired, and no Women have been sold these 20 Years.

Their Labour is not very hard; much less than our Day-Labourers in *England,* and their Encouragement much more; for if they are good for any Thing when they come out of their Times, there are enough will employ them on their own Terms.

Their Diet is not so good, as those who have been used to rich Farmers Tables in *England* would desire, because they cannot be fed every Day with Beef and Mutton; however they cannot complain of any Want; and the Planters distinguish them from the Negroes, by providing them Bisket from *England.* The chief of them are supplied from their Masters Tables. The Overseers have Tables of their own in the House, when the Owner is in *England.*

The Variety of Fruits, Roots, and Herbs, that grow there, is a great Help to the Servants Diet, in furnishing them with Sauce and Change, when they are weary of the salt Beef, Pork and Fish, which is brought them from *New-England,* and other Places.

The Condition of the *Blacks* is only worse, because their Servitude is perpetual. There is as much Care taken of them, and rather more; because if a Negro dies, the Owner loses 40 or 50 *l.* whereas by the Death of a White-Man, he is at the Loss only of 2 or 3 Years Wages to another.

The *Blacks* Business lies most in the Field, unless it is those that are taken into the Boiling-House, the Curing-House, the Still-House, the Mills, the Store-House, or Dwelling-House; where the handsomest, cleanliest Maidens are bred to menial Services, and the properest, cleanest limbed Fellows, to be Coachmen, Footmen, Grooms, and Lacquies. Others often are employed in handicraft Trades, as Coopers, Joiners, Carpenters, Smiths, Masons, and the like.

A Slave that is excellent in any of these mechanick Employments, is worth 150 or 200 *l.* and I have known 400 *l.* bid for a Boiler, belonging to Sir *John Bawdon's* Plantation in *Scotland.* They are all of them worth from 40 to 50 *l.* a Head, Males; and answerable for Females at this Time, occasioned by several Accidents, which will be mentioned in our Article of Trade.

The History of Barbados.

The Slaves are purchased by Lots, out of the *Guinea* Ships. They are all viewed stark naked, and the strongest and handsomest bear the best Prices. They are allowed to have two or three Wives, that they may encrease the Planter's Stock by Multiplication: For their Posterity to all Generations are Slaves, unless their Liberties are given them: But it is questioned, whether their Polygamy does not rather hinder than promote their multiplying. The immoderate Use of such Pleasures enervates and decays Men, and no vigorous Issue can be expected from them.

If their Female Slaves were treated more gently, their Burdens and Labour lessened, the Planters would in all Probability find their Account by it, in the Increase of the Number of their Servants, if every Negro was obliged to keep to one Woman, more than now they are suffered to have two, or more.

These Women are very constant to the Man that passes for their Husband. Adultery is reckoned the most abominable of Crimes, even by those Barbarians, who are as jealous as the *Italians*.

As to the Scandal some People take at the Masters denying their Negroes the Benefit of Baptism, it is as groundless as the Notion, that their Conversion to Christianity sets them free. They and theirs are as much Slaves as before, only some more scrupulous Overseers might not be willing to handle the Cat-a-nine-tails so often against their Fellow-Christians, as they would against Infidels.

The Truth is, few of these poor Wretches shew any Disposition to hearken to the Doctrine of the Christians. They are so fond of their own Idolatry, that unless the Government of *Barbados* was impowered to set up an Inquisition, they would never be converted. But such of them as desire to receive the Sacrament of Baptism, are suffered and encouraged so far, that they are used more favourably afterwards. 'Tis true, the Planters are not over forward in promoting such Conversion; for their Slaves, in Hopes of better Usage, would all profess Christianity with their Lips, while their Hearts retained their old diabolical Idolatry: Wherefore due Care is taken to enquire into the Reality of their Conversion, before they are admitted to the Holy Sacrament of Baptism; and it would be well if the same Care was taken elsewhere, to prevent others receiving unworthily that of the Lord's Supper, which is too often prostituted to temporal Concerns.

The Negroes are generally false and treacherous. Some Instances of great Fidelity have been found among them, which

which have been related in the Historical Account of the Island; but for the most Part they are faithless, and Dissemblers. They are apt to swell with a good Opinion of themselves, on the least Occasion for it to be very stubborn, are sullen and cruel, and their Masters are almost under a fatal Necessity to treat them inhumanly, or they would be ungovernable.

Their Numbers render them very dangerous, they being three to one to the Whites; and by their frequent Attempts to get the Mastery one may see, that the Planters are forced to carry a strict Hand over them.

The Stories that are told of the Severities they suffer from the Overseers, are aggravated; and few *English* have been so barbarous, as they are all represented to be, by the Enemies of the Plantations; tho' according to the Nature or Understanding of the Masters, the Slaves are used the better or the worse. Their whipping them with Thongs, till they are all a-gore of Blood; their tying them up by their Hands or Feet, to endure such Stripes, and the pickling afterwards with Brine, are Bugbears to frighten Children with, like Tales of *Raw-head, and Bloody-bones*. And yet when we consider how lazy they are apt to be, and how careless, and that the Fortune of their Masters depends almost entirely on their Care and Labour, one can't blame the Overseers, for punishing the Idle and Remiss severely. Some of them have been so negligent, as by laying Fire too near the Canes, to set whole Lands of Canes, and Houses too, in a Flame; the knocking out a Tobacco Pipe against a dry Stump of a Tree, by others of them, has set it on Fire, and the Wind fanning it, and a Land of Canes being near it, has caught and burnt down all that were before the Wind. Mr. *James Holduppe*, and Mr. *Constantine Silvester*, several Years ago, lost 10000 *l.* by such an Accident.

Their Diet is very coarse, and yet they are very well contented, being perhaps better than any they had in their own Country. Their choicest Fare is Plantines, which they boil or roast, and then eat. They have now, twice or thrice in a Week, salt Fish, Mackarel, or salt Pork.

They have some Bread made of *Indian* Corn, of the Produce of the Country, or fetched from *Carolina*. But of this there is not too great Plenty amongst them; each Family has a Cabbin belonging to it, for the Men, his Wives, and Children. They are built with Sticks, Withs, and Plantine-Leaves, which makes every Plantation look like a little *African* City, and the Planter's House like the Sovereign's in the midst of it.

To

To each Hut there is a little Plot of Garden set out, where the Negroes plant Potatoes, Yams, Caſſavia-Roots, &c. They have alſo another Sort of Food, called *Loblolly*, made of Maize, the Ears of which they roaſt, and then eat it. The White Servants are ſometimes dieted with this Maize, which is thus dreſſed for them; it is pounded in a Mortar, and boiled in Water, to the Thickneſs of Frumenty, then meſſed out to them, with ſome Salt. This is a poor Kind of Food, and ſeldom uſed of late, unleſs in a Time of great Scarcity.

If an Ox, Bull, or Cow, or any Sort of Cattle, die accidentally, the Negroes feaſt upon it, and the White Servants have often not diſdained to come in for a Share.

All the Inhabitants of the Iſland run ſo much upon making of Sugar, that they will not ſpare Ground for Paſtures, which renders Fleſh-Meat very ſcarce, and fit only for the Maſters Table.

The White Servants and Negroes make Caſſavy and Potatoe-Bread. The latter many ordinary Planters were contented with at their firſt Settlement on the Iſland; but now Meal, Flower, and Bisket are plentier, few Maſters will deign to eat any Thing but Wheat-Bread.

The Servants and Slaves Drinks are *Mobbie*, brewed with Potatoes, Water, and Sugar; *Kowwow* of Molaſſes-Water, and Ginger; *Perino* of the Caſſavy-Root; after the old Women had chawed the Juice, they uſed to ſpit it out into the Water, where in 3 or 4 Hours it would work, and purge itſelf of the poiſonous Quality. The Root is put in with the Juice, and this Drink is the moſt like the *Engliſh* Beer of any. 'Tis a very beaſtly Preparation, and one would think by its fine Taſte that it had been ſome more delicate Drink.

Plantine Drink is made of Plantines maſhed in Water, and well boiled; ſtrained the next Day, and bottled; it will be fit to be drunk in a Week's Time, is pleaſant and ſtronger than Sack.

There is another Liquor, called *Kill-Devil*, made of the Skimmings of Sugar, it is ſtrong, but not very palatable, and ſeldom falls to the Servants Lot.

Pine Drink is made by preſſing the Fruit, and ſtraining the Liquor; it ſhould be bottled: This is one of the beſt Drinks that the Iſland affords; the Planters themſelves will often drink of this pleaſant Liquor, and when it was firſt made, it was compared to *Nectar*.

The Negroes have often large Drams of Rum given them to hearten them at their Work; and a Pipe of Tobacco

and

The History of Barbados.

and a Dram is the moſt acceptable Preſent that can be made them.

They are rung up every Morning at 6 a Clock, and at eleven are ſet to Dinner ; at one they are rung out again to the Field, and muſt work till ſix.

Their Mens Clothing is coarſe Woollen Jackets, or Ozinburg Waiſtcoats and Drawers. The Women have Petticoats and Waiſtcoats of the ſame ; the Men *Monmouth* Caps, and the Women the ſame. They had formerly alſo in ſome Plantations Rug-Gowns to wrap over them when they were hot; which Cuſtom was introduced by Col. *Walrond*, and is much better than burning out their Lungs with Rum.

Sundays are the only Days of Pleaſure to the Negroes; and the moſt induſtrious of them, inſtead of diverting themſelves, or reſting, as it was intended they ſhould, ſpend it in making Ropes of the Rind of certain Trees fit for that Uſe, which they ſell to other Servants, Whites or Blacks, for what Neceſſaries they can furniſh them with.

There is a great deal of Difference between the Negroes; thoſe that are born in *Barbados* are much more uſeful Men, than thoſe that are brought from *Guinea*. Mr. *Ligon* could not make this Obſervation, the Colony was too young; but the *Creolian* Negroes are every Way preferable to the new Comers (which they call *Salt-Water* Negroes) whom they deſpiſe, and value themſelves much on being born in *Barbados*. The Children that come over young from *Africa* are alſo better Servants, when they are grown up, than thoſe that come thence Men or Women.

As for their Living : By the Allowance of Ground, which the Maſter allows them, they have Opportunities to ſow ſeveral Roots and Plants, to breed Goats, Hogs, and Fowl, which they either ſell or eat themſelves; and ſome of them, by their Induſtry, eſpecially if they are Mechanicks, come to be worth 40 or 50 *l.* and ſometimes more, which they are cunning enough to keep from their Maſters. Such of them as can afford it, buy Clothes finer than their Maſter allows them; as the Men, white Holland Waiſtcoats, and Breeches, a Shirt, and Silver-Claſps. The Women alſo will make their rich Huſbands purchaſe them a Shift, a fine Waiſtcoat and Petticoat, and Lace for their Heads, to ſet themſelves out for a Holiday. They often buy Part of the Share of the White Mens Proviſions, who are ſuch Sots as to part with it for Money to purchaſe Rum, which is the *Kill-Devil* mentioned by *Ligon* ; and a mean Spirit, that no Planter of any Note will now deign to drink; his Cellars are better furniſhed.

If the Negroes could come at a dead Bull, Cow, or Horse, it is likely they would dispatch it; but the Planters are careful to keep them out of their Way, by burying them immediately, or otherwise disposing of them, that they may not come at them, for Fear of their eating them, and being infected by it with some contagious Distemper. Thus it is plain, no Gentleman admits of his Servants being fed with Carrion, whatever Inclination they may have to it; for it must be owned the new Comers are very greedy, for such a Repast, when they come first to *Barbados*; an Instance of which is told us in an Accident that happened to Col. *Helms*, who having some Years ago bought a Lot of Negroes, sent them to his Plantation; where it happened that a Cow had lately died by some ill Hap: He ordered it to be flung into a Well 40 Fathom deep, not thinking any of the Slaves would have ventured down after her; but the Negroes not having fathomed the Well, and thinking they might get up as easily as the Cow got down, one of them leapt first into the Well, and was followed by another, then by a third, a fourth followed him, and him the fifth, at several Times, till at last the Owner mistrusting what had happened, discovered his Misfortune in the Death of his Slaves, and prevented the sixth going after the other. The Notice *Ligon* takes of the Planters eating Potatoe Bread is so true, that several have affirmed to me they preferred it to Wheaten Bread.

As for the old Womens chawing the Cassavy Root, 'tis a Falsity, or at least has not been practised in *Barbados* in the Memory of Man, the Perino being made of the Cassavy, worked up with Sugar, after it is baked. There's now no Drink made of Plantines. Pine Drink, something of the Colour of Mead, tastes sharp like the Pine, is a cooling Drink, and too good to fall to the Servants or Slaves, who would perhaps prefer a strong Spirit to it.

As for the Rug-Gowns, mentioned by Mr. *Ligon*, they are now quite out of Use; whether the Reason of them is not as good in our Times, as in his, let the Gentlemen of *Barbados* determine.

In the Plat of Ground allowed them, besides their little Gardens to each Cottage, which is now built of Poles, and covered with Thatch, having several Partitions round about it, they set Plantine Trees, so that their Houses are not to be seen; they are not contiguous, but at a little Distance from each other, for fear of Fire.

As for their Diversions on *Sundays*, the Generality of them dance, or wrestle all Day, the Men and Women together. In Mr. *Ligon's* Time, the Men danced by themselves, and
the

The History of Barbados.

the Women by themselves, but it is not so in ours. They have two Musical Instruments, like Kettle-Drums, for each Company of Dancers, with which they make a very barbarous Melody. They have other Musical Instruments, as a *Bangil*, not much unlike our Lute in any thing, but the Musick; the *Rookaw*, which is two Sticks jagged, and a *Jinkgoving*, which is a Way of clapping their Hands on the Mouth of two Jars. These are all play'd together, and accompany'd with Voices, in a most terribly harmonious manner.

They are so far superior in Number to the Whites, that one would think it should be unsafe for the *English* to dwell among them; and yet the Danger by that Superiority is very little, especially since the Government there has taken Care to build such strong Forts as are lately built.

The Reasons of the Planters Security are these: The Slaves are brought from several Places in *Guinea*, which are different from one another in Language, and consequently they cannot converse freely in *Barbados*; or if they could, they hate one another so mortally, that some of them would rather die by the Hands of the *English*, than join with other *Africans*, in an Attempt to shake off their Yoke. None of them are allowed to touch any Arms, unless it is by their Master's Command: They are kept in such Awe, that they are afraid even to think of Liberty; and when they see the *English* muster and exercise, there can be no Terror in the World greater than what they lie under at that Time. It is true, the *Creolian* Negroes are not of this Number; they all speak *English*, and are so far from fearing a Muster, that they are very familiar with it, and can exercise very well.

The Way of the *English* Merchants trafficking for them was, till lately, by sending Ships with Beads, Pewter, Jars, Cloth, Hats, Copper Bars, Knives, and Toys, to *Africa*; but now the Trade is by Perpetuanoes, Guns, Powder, Flints, Tallow, and Spirits. They trade from *Sierra Leona* to Cape *Negro*, a vast Territory on the Coasts, near fifteen hundred Miles in Length; in which are many petty Kingdoms, where the Kings sell their Subjects and Prisoners of War; some mean Men their Servants, their Children, and sometimes their Wives. They are all Idolaters, and the Object of their abominable Worship is the Devil, if it has any Object, or have any Worship at all. The *Creolian* Negroes are far from such a Diabolical Religion; and if they have any at all, it must be the *English*, for they have no Opportunity to learn any other. The Foreign Slaves believe they return to their own Country; which Belief they brought from thence with them. Some of these Wretches are very ingenious, and others of them as stupid. Indeed such of them as are dull, are so to Brutality; and such as are ingenious are as apt to learn as any People. They make good Mechanicks when they take to it, and such are the Treasure of a Planter; for the chief Riches of the Island consists in the Slaves, of whom some have so great a Multitude, that their Stocks in that one Article would amount to above 20000 *l.* When a Mortality seizes them, the Planter is undone, unless he is a Monied Man, and can renew his Stock; which must be replenish'd every Year, or he would soon want Hands for his Work, for there must be great Numbers of them, almost half in half die in Seasoning, the Polygamy of his Negroes serving little to the Stocking his Plantation. Every *Pickaninny,* or Infant Negro, is valued at 6 *l.* at a Month old; and the Commodity in general rises or falls, like any other of the Market.

Lowth.

The Blood of the Negroes is almost as black as their Skins. Doctor *Towns* says, I have seen the Blood of at least twenty drawn forth, both Sick and in Health, and the Superficies of it is all as dark as the Bottom of any *European* Blood, after standing a while in a Dish; which is an Argument that the Blackness of Negroes is likely to be inherent in them, and not caused by the scorching of the Sun, especially seeing that other Creatures that live in the same Clime and Heat with them, have as florid Blood as those that are in *England.*

Whatever this Doctor has been pleased to communicate to the *Royal Society,* I have been informed by Gentlemen, who have seen the Blood of a thousand of them, that there is no manner of Difference between the Colour of the Blood of a Negro and that of an *European*; as an Instance of which he told me, Col. *Titcomb* had a Negro scalded with Sugar in several Parts of his Body, which left in it white Spots; and these white Spots wore into one another till the Negro was perfectly white; and his Skin grew so tender, that it blistered and freckled with the Sun, which, had his Blood been black, would never have been so. This Change of the *Æthiopian's* Skin, both in the Colour and Nature of it, obliged the Owner to clothe him as a white Servant. Besides, all the Physicians that lived on the Place, and have dissected several, assured the same Gentleman, there was no Blackness in the Blood of the Negroes, nor any other Difference between the Bodies of them and the Whites.

One may imagine, that the Charge of a Plantation, where often there are 2 or 300 Mouths to be fed, must be very great; and this is managed under the Master by a Head Overseer, at 100 or 150 *l.* a Year Salary and Maintenance, 2 or 3 Under-

The History of Barbados.

3 Under-Overseers, Accomptants, and other Officers; who have all enough to do to keep things in Order.

What has been said of *Barbados*, with Relation to Servants and Slaves, may serve for *Jamaica*, they being the Riches of that Island as well as of this, their Work and their Manner of Living the same.

Before we conclude this Chapter, we should take some Notice of the Diversion of the Whites, as well Masters as Servants, who have their times of Recreation; the Servants on Holidays and Festivals, the Masters when they please, as in other Places.

Gaming, as Cards, Dice, Tables, was much more frequent and extravagant in *Barbados* than it is now; but they are obliged to use sedentary Diversions more than active, on Account of the Disposition of the Country, which is not fit for Hunting or Hawking. Some have attempted to hunt Hogs, which have been left wild in the Woods, or Goats with Mongrels, but it may properly be called a Mungrel Sport without the Offence of a Pun.

The Turf, according to *Ligon*, will never be fine enough, nor the Ground soft enough to make a Bowling-Green in *Barbados*. But my Lord *Grey*, when he was Governor of the Island, quite ruined this Author's Reasons, for he made one at Mr. *Hotherfall*'s Plantation, which he rented; and there was another long before to the Windward, upon the Cliff.

Bares they might have, but there has as yet been no Trial made of one; wherefore the Diversion of the Gentlemen in this Island are most within Doors.

The Gallant People delight most in Balls and Consorts; the good Fellows, in Drink and good Company; and though one would imagine, that Men should be afraid to drink such a hot Wine as *Madeira*, in such a hot Country, yet it has been known that some of them have drank their five and six Bottles a Day, and held it on for several Years. Sweating is an admirable Relief to them in this Case, and has been practised by many with Success.

Madeira Wine, white and red, which is drunk here, is in Nature contrary to all other, for 'twill not endure a cool Cellar. *French* and *Rhenish* Wines neither keep in *Barbados*, nor agree well with the Stomachs of the Inhabitants, if so constantly drunk as in *England*. Few care for *Canary* Wine.

There was once a Company of Poppet Strollers in this Island; they came from *England*, and set up their Fairy Drama at the *Bridge*, where, for the Novelty of the Matter, they found a good Market: From thence they went to
the

the Leeward Iflands, and thence home. We wonder their Example has not been followed by fome of the young Fry of Poppet Players at *London*, who would do better to go over, and either play or work at *Barbados* voluntarily, than rake at home till they are fent thither by the Magiftracy againft their Wills.

The Servants in *Barbados* follow the Sports and Exercifes of the common People in *England*, as far as confifts with the Heat of the Climate ; and being all *Englifhmen* like our felves, the Reader is not to expect much Difference in their way of Living, Exercifes, or Diverfions, from our own.

CHAP. VI.

Of the Government of the Ifland, Civil and Military : Of the Laws, Courts of Judicature, Publick Offices, Revenues, and Church-Affairs.

THE Government of *Barbados* is like that of the other Colonies, by a Governor and Council, who are named by the King or Queen of *England* ; and an Affembly, chofen by the Freeholders of each Parifh, two for each.

The Governor is the King or Queen's Reprefentative in this, as in the other Plantations. He is Captain General, Admiral, and Chancellor of the Ifland, and has Power to iffue out all Sorts of Commiffions under that of a General ; to fummon and diffolve Affemblies, to make Counfellors, to pardon all Crimes, but Treafon and Murder ; and even in thofe Cafes to grant Reprieves ; to place and difplace all Officers, who are not by Patent. In a Word, to act with Sovereign Authority, taking Advice of his Council, under the King or Queen of *England*, according to the Laws of this Ifland ; and he has a Negative Voice in the paffing of all Acts of the Affembly : As he is Chancellor of *Barbados*, he is impowered to grant Adminiftrations and Executorfhips of Eftates, of Perfons dying inteftate, to whom he pleafes ; which has been a profitable Branch of the Prerogative in fome ill Governments.

The prefent Governor is *Mitford Crow*, Efq; whofe Salary is 2000 *l.* a Year. It formerly was but 1200 *l.* but then the Ifland ufed to make large Prefents to each Governour on his Arrival, and fo much every Year, to engage his Favour, which in time grew to a Sort of a Prefcription, and was expected by the Governors as their Right. Her

The History of Barbados.

Her present Majesty put an end to this Grievance, by forbidding any such Benevolences for the future; and, to make amends for it, encreased the Salary to 2000 *l.* a Year. There are however some lawful Perquisites and Advantages, which renders the Government worth near 4000 *l. per Annum*, besides the 500 *l.* a Year for the Rent of the House, which is built for his Residence, at the publick Charge, on *Pilgrim*'s Plantation; which is also for his Use.

The Council are Twelve in Number, and are generally Men of the best Estates and Quality in the Country. They are appointed by Letters of *Mandamus* from the King or Queen: And on the Death or Dismission of any of the Members, the Governor has Power to fill up their vacant Places with others.

Their Business is to advise and assist the Governor in all Matters relating to the Government; and to be a Check upon him if he exceeds the Bounds of his Commission. In the Assembly they make the Upper-House, and claim an intire Negative Voice, as the House of Lords in *England*. The President of the Council, in the Absence of the Governor, and his Deputy, supplies his Place; and every Counsellor sits in the Court of *Chancery* with the Governor, and is stiled Honourable, by Virtue of his Place.

The present Members of the Council are,

Geo. Lillington, Esq;
Wil. Sharp, Esq;
Patrick Meine, Esq;
Richard Scot, Esq;
Samuel Cox, Esq;
John Mills, Esq;
Alex. Walker, Esq;
Middleton Chamberlain, Esq;
Tho. Alleyne, Esq;
The Rev. Mr. *Samuel Beresford*.

These following are lately put in by Mr. *Crow*.

William Wheeler, Esq; *John Colliton*, Esq;
Timothy Salter, Esq;

Clerk to the Council, Mr. *Coffin*.

The Manner of electing Assemblies, of their sitting, voting, and passing of Laws, is, as near as possible, like that of the House of Commons in *England*.

As to their Power and Privileges, they are at large set down in the Laws of the Plantations; to which we refer the Reader, and also for an Account of such as are now in Force and

The History of Barbados.

and Use in this Island; where the Laws of *England* are always valid, as far as consists with the Custom of the Colony.

For the easier Distribution of Justice, the Island is divided into Five Precincts: Over which there are as many Judges, who preside one in each, and hold their Courts of Common-Pleas, for Trial of all Causes, according to the Laws of *England*, and Customs of *Barbados*.

The first of these Courts is kept at *Oistin's*, the last *Monday* and *Tuesday* in *January*.

The present Judge of it is ―― *Brewster*, Esq;

The second at the *Bridge*, on the *Wednesday*, *Thursday*, and *Friday* following.

The present Judge, *John Sandford*, Esq;

The third at the *Hole*, on the *Monday* and *Tuesday* next ensuing.

The present Judge, *Tho. Warren*, Esq;

The fourth at *Speight's*, on the *Wednesday* and *Thursday* following.

The present Judge, *Alexander Anderton*, Esq;

The fifth in the Parish of St. *Andrews*, on the *Friday* and *Saturday* next ensuing.

The present Judge, *Reinold Allen*, Esq;

They continue their respective Sittings from four Weeks to four Weeks, till the 26th of *September*, yearly, and then adjourn to the last *Monday* in *January*.

From these Courts there lies an Appeal, in all Causes above 10 *l*. Value, to the Governor and Council: And from them, in all above 500 *l*. Value, to the King, or Queen, and Council in *England*. Besides these Courts, they have

A Court of Estreats,

A Court of Exchequer, the present Chief Baron, *John Mills*, Esq;

Court of Admiralty, the present Judge, *Dudley Woodbridge*, Esq;

Two Masters in Chancery, *Robert Stillingfleet*, Esq; and *Gyles Thyer*, Esq;

Clerk of the Crown, *Norman Maccascall*, Esq;

Attorney General, ―― *Hodges*, Esq;

Sollicitor General, *Wil. Rawlins*.

This Gentleman, in the Year 1698. collected the Body of the Laws of *Barbados*, into one Book; which was printed by Order of the Assembly: And that Book of Laws,
by

The History of Barbados.

by an Act passed by them, *is to be deemed and held a good lawful Statute-Book of this Island of* Barbados. These Laws are all abridged, in the Treatise we have had frequent Occasion to speak of.

Clerk of the Assembly, *James Cowes*, Esq;
Register in Chancery, *Wil. Walker*, Esq;
Provost Marshal, *Geo. Gordon*, Esq;

Which are the Chief Officers in the Law, and in the State; the first next to the Governor, and those we have before-mentioned, is,

The Treasurer of the Island, *John Holder*, Esq.
The Secretary, *Alexander Skeyne*, Esq;
The Governor's Secretary, —— *Merchant*, Esq;

Besides these the People of the Island have Agents in *England*, to take Care of their Affairs, to whom they allow 250 *l.* a Year; a very handsom Salary: And one would expect from such an Allowance, that the Planters should have no reason to be at so much trouble, to solicite the Business of the Island themselves. There are three of these Agents, who are at this time,

William Bridges, Esq;
Rowland Tryon, Merchant; and
Sir *John Stanley*; Brother-in-law to Sir *Bevill Granville*, the late Governor.

As to the Military Affairs of the Colony, they are, under the Governor, managed by Colonels, in the several Parts of the Island, where are five Regiments of Foot, and two of Horse, besides the Regiment and Troop of Guards, each consisting, when it is full, of above 1200 Men.

In the Time of War the Governor makes General Officers, for the better Conduct of the Forces; as, a Lieutenant General, and Major General. The last Gentlemen who had these Commissions were

Abel Alleyne, Esq; Lieut. General.
John Holder, Esq; Major General.

FOOT.

The *Bridge* Regiment is the biggest, and is called the Royal Regiment, or the Regiment of Foot-Guards. It
consists

consists, when it is full, of 1400 Men, and is commanded by Col. *Hallet.*

Leeward Regiment 1200, commanded by Col. *Thomas Maycock.*
St. *Joseph* Regiment, 1200, commanded by Col. *Robert Yeamans.*
St. *Thomas* and St. *James* Regiment, 1200, commanded by the Honourable *Thomas Alleyne,* Esq;
Oistin Regiment, 1200, commanded by Col. ———.
Windward Regiment, 1200, commanded by Col. *Henry Pierce.*

HORSE.

Leeward Regiment of Horse, 1000, commanded by Col. *Thomas Sandiford.*
Windward Regiment, 1000, commanded by Col. *John Frere.*
The *Gard de Corps,* or Troop of Guards, consists of 130 Gentlemen; and on all publick Occasions attend the Governor's Person.

Their present Captain is Col. *Salmon.*
Keeper of the Stores in the Magazine, Mr. *William Moor.* His Salary 110 *l.* a Year.
Surveyor and Engineer General, Col. *Lilly.*
Commissioners of the Customs, *William Sharp,* Esq; and *Samuel Cox,* Esq;
Naval Officer, Mr. *Cox.*
Receiver of the Casual Revenues, Mr. *Yeamans.*
Collector of the *Hole-Town, Hugh Howel,* Esq;
Collector at *Speight's, William Denny,* Esq;
Clerk of the Markets, *Norman Maccafcall,* Esq;
Receiver of the 4½ *per Cent. Thomas Edwards,* Esq;
Commissioner of the Prizes, *William Cleland,* Esq;
Agent for the Ordnance, *John Merring,* Esq;

The Way of listing, raising, and paying the Militia, comes under that Article in the *Laws of Barbados;* and therefore we shall say nothing of it in this Place, but proceed to the Revenues; which are such as are raised for the King or Queen's Use, and such as are raised for the Use of the Island. As first, the 4½ *per Cent.* upon all Goods shiped off; which is settled on the Crown, and amounts to, *Communibus Annis,* 10000 *l. per Annum.*

The History of Barbados.

The next Duty is 4 Pound of Gun-powder for each Tun, of every Ship that unlades there, and is always paid in Specie, amounting to about 600 *l.*

There is also a Duty on *Madeira* Wines, 4 *l.* 10 *s.* a Pipe, which amounts yearly to about 7000 *l.*

And on all other Liquors, which does not bring in above 2000 *l.*

These are settled Duties; the other are such as are raised by the Assembly for the Service of the Colony; and that is generally done by a Pound-Tax, or Pole-Tax, and some Years have amounted to 20000 *l.* But there is nothing settled on the King or Queen, and their Heirs, except the $4\frac{1}{2}$ per Cent. The other two Duties are appropriated to the Use of the Stores and Forts: And the *Barbadians* say the same of the $4\frac{1}{2}$ per Cent. Duty: With what Reason, will be seen hereafter.

The Parish-Taxes are raised by the Vestry, for the Maintenance of the Minister, and the Poor, and keeping the Churches in due Repair. And this brings us naturally to the Church-Affairs of the Island, which are under the Government of a Surrogate, appointed by the Bishop of *London*, who is the Ordinary of all the *English* Colonies in *America*: Where, in Imitation of his Lordship's Zeal for the Church of *England*, its Faith and Worship are, for the most Part, strictly professed. The Laws of *Barbados* charge and command, that all *Persons inhabiting that Island, conform themselves to the Government and Discipline of the Church of England.*

There are so few Dissenters in this Island, that there has been no publick Meeting established, with a Pastor, since the Year 1690. The last Presbyterian Minister there, was Mr. *Vaughan:* And none of his Opinion, since his Death, have though it worth their while to go so far to propagate it.

The Ministers have good Allowances, the least Benefice being worth 150 or 200 *l.* a Year; and that of the *Bridge-Town* 6 or 700 *l.* The present Minister of that Place, or,

St. *Michael'*, is Mr. *Berisford.*
Of St. *George's*, Vacant.
Of St. *James,* or the *Hole,* Mr. *Gordon.*
Of St. *Thomas,* Mr. *Hargrove.*
Of St. *Peter's,* or *Speight's-Town,* Mr. *Ball.*
Of *All-Saints-Chapel,* Mr. *Ball.*
Of St. *Lucy's,* Mr. *Tuckerman.*
Of St. *Andrew's,* Mr. *Justice.*
Of St. *Joseph's,* Mr. *Fullwood.*

Of St. *John's*, Mr. *Wharton*.
Of St. *Philip's*, Mr. *Irvine*.
Of *Christ-Church*, or *Oistin's*, Mr. *Ramsey*.

The present Surrogate is the Rev. Mr. *Berisford*, who succeeded the pious and learned Mr. *Cryer*; as he did the Rev. Mr. *William Walker*, Minister of St. *Peter's*, and a Member of the Council; the first on whom the Bishop of *London* was pleased to confer this Reverend and Honourable Office.

The Assembly have lately had it under Consideration, to erect a College, and endow it; towards which great Legacies have been left, for the Education of their Youth: For it is not every Planter who can be at the Charge of sending his Sons to *England* to be educated; which the most wealthy of them have found inconvenient, by the Distance from their Parents and Guardians, and the Indulgence of their Correspondents here. Who, to flatter these young Gentlemen, in Hopes of their Consignations, when they come to their Estates, or to engage them to write kindly of them to their Friends, give them what Money they ask for; and by this they often get a Habit of Extravagance, which ends in their Ruin. This would be prevented, if there were fitting Schools in *Barbados*; which they might easily have.

Mr. *Thomas Tryon*, who understood the Interest of that Island as well as any Man, affirms, that this sending their Children to *England* has been a very great Hinderance to the Redress of their Grievances; for who can think they are under such heavy Loads as they complain of, when they can afford 2, 3, 4, and 500 *l.* a Year to their Sons in *England*, most of them proving Beaus of the first Rate, and distinguishing themselves by the Gaity of their Dress and Equipage: *From whence,* says he, *it is inferred, they are grown wonderful rich, insomuch that it can't be thought amiss, or any Oppression, to lay Impositions upon their Produce or Commodities; but the wiser Sort are Men of other Sentiments as well as myself.* And again, *The loose and extravagant Education of your Youth* (writing to a Planter) *is a sure Indication of Calamity and Misery to your Country, for in a few Years they come to govern the publick Affairs.*

All these Expences and Inconveniences would, in a great Measure, be prevented by the erecting a College and Library at the *Bridge*, with learned and pious Professors in the Sciences, to breed up young Gentlemen, without exposing them to the Hazards of the Sea, and the more fatal Dangers of Temptation and ill Company in *England*; where, having
Money

The History of Barbados.   145

Money at Will, when they are not of Years to know how to make Use of it, they frequently continue in their Profusion and Prodigality, till they have none left to spend.

As the Gentlemen of *Barbados* may suppose the Author is very well acquainted with this Truth, so they cannot but know, that he can give a great many Exceptions to this bad Custom, but not enough to argue against its being abolished.

CHAP. VII.

Of the Sugar Canes, and the Way of making and refining Sugar, as it is now practised in *Barbados*; together with an Account of the Nature and Use of that Commodity, Rum, and Molasses.

WE have, in the first Chapter, shewed at what Time Sugar Canes began to be first planted in *Barbados*; we shall now shew as well how those Plants were then cultivated, as how they are managed at present.

'Tis for the Sake of this Plant, that many Thousands of *Englishmen* have transported themselves, their Families, and Estates, to the *West-Indies*; by this they have been raised from mean Conditions to a State of Affluence and Grandeur. By this many Thousands of Families have subsisted, and been enriched in *England*; the publick Revenues, Trade, and Navigation, have been advanced, and the national Stock has encreased above three Millions. In a Word, the Grain produced by this Plant has been said, by very good Judges, to contain a Substance, was it altogether, as big as the whole Island.

Sugar grows in a long Stalk, which we call a Cane, full of Joints, two, three, four, or five Inches asunder, and about six Foot high; the Sprouts and Leaves at the Top rising up so high, as may make it near 8 Foot in all. The Body of the Cane is about an Inch Diameter, seldom more. The Colour of the Cane Tops is a pure Grass-green; of the Cane itself, yellowish, when ripe: 'Tis covered with a thin Skin or Bark, somewhat hard on the Inside, being of a white spungy Substance, full of Juice, which the Servants and others suck, and eat great Quantities of, without injuring their Health; nothing is pleasanter than this Sap, when the Cane is ripe; it is also very nourishing and wholesom, if taken with Moderation. Their Way of eating it is thus:

They

They cut the Skin or Rind off, and put the Pith or spungy Parts into their Mouths, when the Juice will come out more freely than Honey out of the Comb; and this Sweetness as far exceeds that of Honey, *as a Pippin does a Crab.* 'Tis not surfeiting, but the cleanest and best Sweet in the Universe. The Nature of this Juice is much like to that of Apples, but something thicker, it is yellow when the Cane is ripe, clean, and without any ill Taste or Hogo, and goes off the Palate as sweetly as it came on. Of this Juice Sugar, Rum, and Molasses are made.

The Season for planting of Sugar Canes is from *August* to the Beginning of *December* sometimes; which Canes don't arrive to Maturity, till they have been a Year and a Quarter, or a Year and an half in the Ground.

Their Manner of growing is in Sprouts, three, four, or five, from one Root. They are not all of a Size, either in Bigness or Length, according to the Goodness of the Soil, and the Seasons. Some Canes will not rise above 3 Foot high, and others 6, and the Flags or Cane Tops of them exceed 9 Foot high, Stalk and all, and sometimes are under 6. These Cane Tops make very good Food for Horses and black Cattle; but the solid Canes are carried to the Mill, for the Uses we shall mention hereafter.

The Manner of planting them, is by digging long Trenches in the Earth, about 6 Inches deep, and as many broad, and laying a double Row of Canes along in the Trench one by another, from one End of the Trench to the other; then the Earth is thrown in, and another Trench dug, and so another, at about two Foot Distance, till all the Land is planted, by laying the Canes along. Thus they produce the greater Number of Sprouts; for this Way a Branch shoots out of every Joint of the Cane, whereas the first Planters used to thrust a Piece of Cane perpendicularly into a Hole at certain Distances, which yielded no Shoot but from the Top; and having three or four Sprouts, whose whole Weight depended on one Root, when they grew tall and heavy, the Storms loosened the Roots, and so they rotted, and became good for nothing. By this new Way of Planting, the Root is secured, and the Produce encreased. They come up in a little while after they are planted; in about 12 Weeks they will be 2 Foot high.

The next Care of the Planter is to keep his Canes well weeded, Weeds being very apt to grow among them, and formerly the *Withies* in particular, a Creeper that runs along the Ground, and fastens to the Canes, by which they hinder their Growth.

The History of Barbados.

The Roots muſt alſo be examined to ſee if any have failed, that they may be ſupplied in Time with others, leſt the Ground ſhould yield ſomething hurtful to the Plant.

If the Withy had over-run a Plantation, or the Planter had neglected to fill up the Vacancies of the Roots that failed in Time, by which Means the Crop was ſome ripe and ſome green, and could never be ſeparated but by much more Labour than they were worth, the Planter burnt the Canes on the Ground. By this tho' he loſt ſo much Time as his Canes had grown, yet he did not loſe his Planting, for the Fire did not touch the Root, which ſhoots out again preſently; and it bettered the Soil, and deſtroyed the Rats. They did this by kindling the Fire on the Outſides of the Field, in a Circle quite round the Piece of Ground; the Rats retired from the Borders to the Centre, and the Flames reaching at laſt to that, conſumed a Swarm of them together.

Theſe Vermine were brought thither by the *Engliſh* Ships, and will ſo gnaw and ſuck the Canes, that they rot after it. In the Time of the Turnado, in *November* and *December*, the Rats flew to the Houſes, where they would have done as much Miſchief, but that they were more eaſily deſtroyed.

The Practice now is to dung the Canes, which is done either when they are planted, or when they come up, and are two Foot high, and this is the greateſt Trouble and Expence the Planter is at; for if it was not for this dunging, a third Part of the Negroes would do.

When the Canes are ripe, which is known by their Colour, they are cut up by Hand with a Bill, or other Tool, by one at a Time (for they are too big to be mowed with a Scithe, or cut with a Hook) as they cut them, they trim them, chop off the Top, and cut or ſtrip off the Leaves or Flags on the Sides, which are ſaved for the Uſes we have already ſpoken of.

The Canes thus cut were bundled up in Faggots, and tied up with the Withies that grew among them, but are now only tied with the Tops of the Canes. Then they are carried to the Mill by Aſſnegoes, in Carts, or drawn by Horſes.

The Mills that were at firſt in Uſe there, were Cattle-Mills; but lately every ſubſtantial Planter has one or two Wind-Mills, and ſome three, as at Sir *Richard Hacket*'s, Sir *Samuel Husband*'s, and Col. *Drax*'s Plantations.

Their Cattle-Mills and Wind-Mills are made after the ſame Manner as ours in *England*, and they grind the Canes thus in the Cattle-Mills: The Horſes and Cattle being put to their Tackle, go about, and turn by *Sweeps* the Middle Roller; which being cogged to turn others at the upper End,

turn

turn them about. They all three turn upon the same Centres, which are of Brass and Steel, going so easily of themselves, that a Man, taking hold of one of the Sweeps with his Hand, may turn all the Rollers about; but when the Canes are put in between the Rollers, it is a good Draught for five Oxen or Horses. A Negro Woman puts in the Canes on one Side, and the Rollers draw them through on the other Side, where another Negro Woman stands, receives them, and returns them back on the other Side of the Middle Roller, which draws the other Way.

This Operation presses out the Juice, and the *English* do no more to the Canes: But the *Spaniards* have a Press to squeeze out the Remainder of the Liquor, after both the former Grindings. Their Works are small, and they are willing to make the most of them.

Mr. *Ligon*, from whom some Part of this Account of the Cattle-Mill is taken, speaks more largely of it; but these Cattle-Mills are almost quite out of Use, there being 40 Wind-Mills to one Cattle-Mill. The Rollers are of Wood, cased with Iron, and they press out the Juice so thoroughly, that there is no Occasion of a Press to squeeze them; for in an Hour's Time the Sun dries the Canes so much, they are fit to burn.

Under the Rollers there is a hollow Place, into which all the Juice that runs from the Canes is received, and by Pipes of Lead, or leaden Gutters covered over close, conveyed into a Cistern, near the Stairs, as you go down from the Mill-House into the Boiling-House.

The bruised Canes, which are called *Trash* in *Barbados*, are dried in the Sun; and since Wood is grown scarce, be-
See his Let- come the principal Fuel there. *It makes*, says Mr. *Tryon*, *a*
ters. *weak and uncertain Fire, much inferior either to Wood or Coals, in the boiling of Sugars.*

When Sugar was first planted in this Island, one Acre of Canes yielded more than now, for four, five, six, or seven Years together, without any farther planting or dunging; the same Root would shoot forth new Branches, and those be fuller of Sap than the Canes are at this Time; when the Sugar being of so great a Substance, and containing such a Quantity of rich Juices, and the Planters being limited to a small Proportion of Land, pressing it so often with the same Plant, and never letting it lie still, the Soil is so impoverished, that they are now forced to dung and plant every Year; insomuch that 100 Acres of Cane require almost double the Number of Hands they did formerly, while the Land retained its natural Vigour, which also then did not only bring
forth

forth certain Crops, but fewer Weeds too, the Weeds having been encreased by frequent Dunging.

Most of the Sugar Islands, *Barbados* especially, have a kind of white chalky Gravel, called *Marl*, two or three Foot deep, which of it self is of so hot a Temper, and that is encreased so much by dunging, that their Crops in all dry Seasons are sure to fail; and on the other Hand, in a wet Year the Canes grow rank, and never come to Maturity.

Some Objections will certainly be made to this at *Barbados*; for what is said of the Uncertainty of the Fire of the dried Canes, can only relate to the Negligence of Servants, in feeding it, for if there's Fuel, it will always be a constant and vigorous Flame.

As to the Marl, said to be frequent here, it is so rare, that I have been told by an Inhabitant of the Island, he rarely or never saw any, nor met with a Soil too hot, or a Season too rank for his Canes.

We have before treated of the Growth of the Canes, and the squeezing out the Juice in a Cattle-Mill; the Practice is much the same in a Water-Mill; but this relates to *Jamaica*, and those Islands, where Rivers are more common than here. The chief Difference between the one and the other consists only in the Way of turning the Rollers, either by Draught or Wind.

When the Liquor is in the Cistern, it must not remain there above one Day, lest it grow sour: From thence it is conveyed through a Gutter, fixed to the Walls of the Boiling-house, to the clarifying Copper, or Boiler, and there boiled, till all the Filth or gross Matter rising on the Top, is skimmed off. This is the largest Copper in the Boiling-house; and as the Liquor is refined, 'tis taken out of the Copper, and carried into the second, and so into a third, fourth, fifth, sixth, and seventh. The least is called the *Tach*, where it boils longest. It is continually kept stirring and boiling, till it comes to a Consistency; and yet all this Boiling would reduce it only to a thick clammy Substance, without kerning or turning to a Grain, were it not for the *Temper* that is thrown into it. This *Lye* or *Temper* was many Years ago made of the Ashes of the *Withy*, which in the Field was so destructive to the Cane, steeped and boiled in Water to a certain Strength; and of this a small Quantity was thrown into the Boiler, when the Sugar was boiling, upon which it would presently kern, and grow hard.

The Quality of the *Temper* is sharp, and this Acid causes the clammy Substance to part, curdle and kern; and so it candies, and becomes Sugar. A Drop of this thrown into
the

the Copper when the Liquor was firſt boiling, would have quite ſpoiled it, and it would never have made Sugar.

The *Temper* now uſed is made of Lime infuſed in common Water. The Boiler makes his Liquor ſtronger or weaker according to the Goodneſs of the Canes; and there is never any brown nor white Sugar made without this Lime Water, or its Equivalent, Pot-Aſhes, which yet is very rarely uſed, being neither ſo good, nor ſo cheap, as Lime-Water is found to be.

Muſcovado Sugar, a Term borrowed from the *Portugueſe* of *Brazil*, which is the browneſt Sort, requires ſometimes ſtronger Lime-Water than our Sugar-bakers or Refiners uſe, in refining White Sugar: And without this Operation, as has been ſaid, the Juice of the Canes could never be made into a firm ſubſtantial Body, nor acquire a ſparkling Grain, but would remain a dull flat *Syrup*, of a heavy groſs Nature, neither wholeſom nor pleaſant. For as the Juice of the Cane is a compleat Sweet, wherein the ſaltiſh, aſtringent, bitter, and ſharp Qualities, are weak and impotent, ſo without their Aſſiſtance it cannot obtain a Body: Wherefore Lime-Water, which includes them all, is thrown into it, when the Sugar begins to riſe up with a turbulent ungovernable Fury, occaſioned by the Fermentation of the Liquor of the Lime-Water, and the vehement Heat of the Fire.

To prevent its running over the Copper, they throw in a Piece of Butter no bigger than a ſmall Nut. This, though there are two or three hundred Gallons of Liquor in it, will preſently make it fall down within its Circle in the Boiler, which proceeds from a kind of Antipathy between the ſalt nitral Property of the Juice of the Cane, and the animal Sulphur of the Butter. From the *Boiler*, when it is reduced to a proper Subſtance, the Liquor is carried to the Cooling-Ciſtern, called the *Cooler*; where it remains till it is fit to be put in Pots, which are now made of Earth, and the Form of them known to every body, they being daily to be ſeen in the Sugar-Houſes in *London*, and elſewhere. They are wide at Top, and taper downwards; where a Hole is left for the Molaſſes to run out: A Commodity which always is in Demand in *England* among the Diſtillers.

Of the Skimmings of all the Coppers the Planters diſtil the famous Spirit known by the Name of *Rum*; which by ſome Perſons is preferred to Brandy. It is a hot Spirit, and has an offenſive Smell and Taſte with it; it is ſaid to be very wholeſom, and therefore it has lately ſupplied the Place of Brandy in Punch. Indeed it is much better than Malt-

ſpirits,

The History of Barbados.

fpirits, and the fad Liquors fold by our Diftillers. But a fine Spirit extracted from Molaffes, or Raifins, will certainly have the Preference of Rum by all nice Palates.

We muſt remember, that the Liquor of the Cane, when put into the Pots, would run out; but they are ſtopped with a Cane-top, till they are ſet upon the *Dripps,* hereafter mentioned.

The Sugar remains in theſe Pots two Days, and two Nights; at the End of which it will be thoroughly cold; and then, if it is good, knock upon the Pot with your Finger, and it will give a Sound. But if the Sugar be bad, it will neither be hard, nor give any Sound.

The Pots afterwards are removed to the Curing-houſe, and ſet upon Earthen-pans, called *Dripps,* about a Foot from the Ground, and the Molaffes run into them, which is afterwards either carried to the Diſtil-houſe, or put into a Ciſtern, where it remains till it riſes to a good Quantity; which is ſometimes boiled again, and a Sort of Sugar made of it, called *Paneels,* worſe than Muſcovado, and ſhipped off in Casks for *England.*

In a Month's time the Planters reckon the Sugar is ſufficiently cured. If the Molaffes did not run from any of the Pots, as it ought to do, they formerly bored a Hole in their wooden Jarrs with an Augre, to open the Paſſages.

From the Curing-Room the Pots are removed to the *Knocking-Room*; ſo called, becauſe the Pots are there turned upſide down, and the Sugar knocked out of them: Which will appear of three different Colours and Qualities, the Top brown, and a frothy light Subſtance for the Depth of an Inch or two; the Bottom black, heavy, moiſt, and full of Molaffes for about a Foot; and the Middle white, dry, and good; and this is generally three Quarters of the whole. The Top is packed up with the Bottom; about half of the whole are boiled, and further refined with the *Paneels.* The Middle is carried to the Store-houſe, as fit for the Market; yet the fineſt of this Sort will have a *Foot*; that is, a Sediment at Bottom, after it is in the Hogſhead, which will be blacker than the reſt, moiſter and fouler, occaſioned by the Molaffes that remain in it.

This is the Sugar that is commonly imported, and is fit for both the Grocer and Sugar-baker. Nine Pound of the Juice of the Cane, which is a Gallon, makes but one Pound of Muſcovado, and one of Molaffes; the reſt is Skimmings and Dregs.

If the Canes be not good, then nine Pounds make but three Quarters of a Pound of Muscovado Sugar, and the like Quantity of Molasses.

The Badness of the Canes was, in times past, caused either by their being planted too thick, which intercepted the Heat from penetrating through them to the Roots, or a wet Season, by which some will be ripe, and some not; and what are of them, will not be so much in Quantity, nor so good in Quality.

There was as much Difference between the Sugar made of such Sort of Canes, and of such as were ripe, as there is between Cyder made of Apples growing on the Out-side of the Trees, and of those that grow under the shady Boughs, where the Sun cannot influence them with its warming Beams. This was when the Soil was too rich; but now there's no such Fault, and the Canes all ripen well, if planted in time.

There are also other Causes of Goodness of the Colour and Grain of some Muscovado Sugar, and the Badness of others: As the Goodness and Badness of the Lands the Canes grow on; the good or bad Times of the Year the Sugar is made in; and the Art and Experience of the chief Boiler. The best Sort is that which is of a lively, whitish and bright Yellow, with a sparkling Grain. I have seen some of this Sort made at Mr. *Walter*'s Plantation at *Apeshill*, so fine and white, that when there was a heavy Duty on first and second Whites, and another on Sugars fit for Use, besides that on Muscovado, which continues to this Day, was past by the Surveyors at the Custom-house for first Whites, and his Correspondent Sir *John Bawdon* was forced to use a great deal of Solicitation to get them off as *Fitts*, a Term the Merchants called the Sort next above Muscovado by, and was the lowest degree of clay'd or purged Sugars. Other Sorts I have seen as bad as *Antego* Sugar, and fit only for a *Dutch* Market.

The next Operation with Sugar, is refining the Muscovado by the same *Lime-Water*, as the Juice of the Cane is refined with; and these Sugars are called *Whites*, or purged Sugar. Clay'd Sugars are made white by claying the Pots of Muscovado: Which is done thus: They take a kind of whitish Clay, somewhat like Tobacco Pipe-clay, and temper it with Water for that Purpose, to about the Thickness of Pancake-batter; they pour it with a Ladle on the Sugar in the Pots, near an Inch thick; which Clay has a wonderful Power over the Sugar, to purge the grosser, flatulent, or treacly Part downward, and to cause the Pot of Sugar, which generally

nerally contains about half an hundred of Brown-sugar, to become less in Quantity, and of several Colours and Goodness. For the first three or four Inches on the Top of the Pot, the Sugar, after it has stood four Months, is very white, near the Whiteness of our Sugar-bakers Sugar; and the next four or five Inches is not so white; and so the whole Pot is in degrees, till you come to the Bottom; every Degree downwards growing worse and worse. For this Reason the Sugar-bakers and Clayers divide the several Sorts into *Firsts, Seconds, Thirds,* and *Fourths*; each of which Sorts is packed in separate Casks from the other, and sold at different Prices, very far short of what they bore in the Infancy of the Colony, White-Sugar selling then for 10 *l.* a Hundred, and now not for 3 *l.*

This Account is given us by Mr. *Tryon*, who was not so well acquainted with the Claying of Sugars, as he was with Muscovado: For the true Way of Claying of Sugars is this; When the Liquor is brought from the *Clarifiers*, it is strained, and then carried into the *Taches*, and made as other Sugars are: But when it comes to be put into Pots, it is kept stirred till it begins to cool. When it has been kept ten Days, it is dug up for five or six Inches deep, and then levelled again, and covered with the Clay, which lies on it, for ten Days; then it is dug up and levelled as before, and a new Clay put on, which lies on it till it is thoroughly purged: After which it is knocked out, and divided into Firsts and Seconds, and the Bottom sometimes makes a Third Sort. There is at least 30 or 35 *per Cent.* waste; but this is made up by the Molasses, which makes a very good *Paneel*-Sugar; and the Molasses of those *Paneels* is distilled into Rum, which of late has been rarely made, because of the excessive Duty. The vast Quantities of purged Sugar that are made here and there, occasion its Cheapness; though the Planters have lately been forced to lay down the claying of Sugars, on account of the high Duties, and low Rates in *England.*

Clay'd Sugar not being refined, that is, boiled over again, is not free from various, gross, Treacly Qualities; which Refining only will purge away, or separate. None of our Sugar-Islands can make this Sort to any Advantage, except *Barbados.* And it is not all Plantations there, that yield Canes whose Juice kern to a Muscovado Sugar, fit for claying, for want of Strength.

If a 100 Weight of Firsts and Seconds should be refined, it would not make above half that Quantity, the rest being, as we have said, Coarse Sugar, Molasses and Skimmings, of a dirty black Substance; which gross excrementitious Matter,

ter, while the Sugar remained entire, was unknown and imperceptible to the moſt curious Eye; and it is the like in Muſcovado, to a larger degree, as to the groſs Matter.

The fineſt purged Sugar that ever came from *Barbados*, was, till within theſe 18 or 20 Years, made of the Growth of Sir *Timothy Thornhill's* Plantation, Sir *John Bawdon's*, and Mr. *Walter's*. The former had a Negro who was allowed to communicate his Art to one of Sir *John Bawdon's*, a Boiler; and he became ſo excellent, that I have heard that Gentleman ſay, he would not ſell him for 500 *l*. This Black inſtructed Mr. *Walter's* Servant, and others have ſince made excellent Whites, but none ſo good as came from thoſe Plantations.

Mr. *Walter's* and Sir *John Bawdon's* Plantations lye both in *Scotland*; and one may thence imagine, that that part of the Iſland produces a Sugar fitteſt for the Clay; though it is to be ſuppoſed, that the Skill of their Servants contributed moſt to the Goodneſs of their Sugars.

There are other Ways of diſtinguiſhing good Sugar from bad, particularly Muſcovado Sugar, that has only gone thro' the Operation of boiling, which is by its keeping; Muſcovado being fouler and groſſer than either clayed or refined, will not keep ſo long. It may be kept ſeveral Years, and be fit for Uſe, though not ſo good the ſecond Year as it was the firſt; and if it is a Year and an half old, it grows of a ſoft yielding Temper, and a ſmall weak Grain or Body. The Refiner will find out its bad Qualities as ſoon as it is in his Pan, and it will neither yield ſo much, nor what it makes be ſo good, as if it had been worked ſooner.

Clay'd Sugar, if well ordered, will keep longer, though not much; for which reaſon *Braſil* Sugar is generally moiſt; and *Barbados* clay'd Sugar will alſo ſink into the ſame Clamminefs, and not keep ſo long as what is refined.

We have ſo often mentioned refined Sugars, the Reader will expect an Account of them, and in what they differ from clay'd.

The clay'd, as is before-mentioned, has no Lime-Water put into it, neither is it boiled again, but only Pots of Muſcovado Sugar clay'd down; which Clay, by its Coldneſs, condenſes, and forces the Moiſture downwards; yet enough is left behind, to make it fouler and groſſer than refined Sugar; which is Muſcovado boiled over again, and clarified with Lime-water, potted and ſtrained; and this Sugar will be drier, and of a more ſparkling White than the brighteſt of the clay'd.

Double

The History of Barbados.

Double and treble refined is only the same Sugar clarified twice or thrice over. By which means I have seen some Sugar whiter than the falling Snow, and of a Grain as fine as Flower; yet of a Sweetness that nothing could equal, which was not of the Juice of the Cane; and this sold after the rate of ten Pound a Hundred; when first Whites fetched but three Pound, or three Pound ten Shillings.

There are no great Quantities of this Sort exported from *Barbados*, the Duty on refined Sugar being no less than 30 *s*. a Hundred in *England*.

The Sugar refined in *Barbados* is infinitely finer and whiter than the Sugar-Bakers Sugar here in *England*; who are a Sort of Men that have adulterated this Commodity, and brew it as much when it is in Liquor, as Hedge-Vintners sophisticate their Wines.

The Grain of the *Barbados* Refined Sugar is very fine, and the Colour a true white, comparable to the best of that Kind in Nature: Whereas the Sugar-Bakers refined Sugar is a blewish sickly white, which looks glaring to the Eye, but will not bear Examination like the *Barbados*. One Reason of this, among many others, may be the whitening the Sugar in *Barbados* in the Sun. Some Planters use *Barbicues* for this Purpose; a Machine made about three or four Foot high, with Drawers to hold the Sugar; and these are drawn out when the Sugar is exposed, and shut in on the Likelihood of wet or misty Weather, which would melt that Commodity.

Sugar dried and whitened by the Sun-beams, in a serene Climate, must of Consequence be a purer White, than what is dried in smoky Rooms by Coal-Fires, or in Stoves, where the Dampness will prejudice the true Brightness of the Sugar, though the Bakers have a way to make it sparkle even more than that of *Barbados*. Since both they and the Planters work up all their Sugar with the Salt Nitre of Stones, infused in Water; which is better understood by Lime-Water, as we have hitherto called it; and that this Ingredient is reckoned unwholesom by several Men and Women, Doctors, Apothecaries, and others, that the dusty, stony Quality of the Lime remains in the Sugar, especially the refined; and will rather use brown, dirty, or clay'd Sugar, it will not be improper to answer this Objection, that many thousands of Persons, who have not given themselves the Trouble of studying this Matter, may be convinced of their Error: In which I shall make use of the Argument of the late Mr. *Thomas Tryon*, an eminent and an ingenious *Barbados* Merchant at *London*, who reconciled Business and Letters, and

shewed,

shewed, that a Man might at once improve his Understanding and his Fortune. His Words are these;

Tryon's Letters.

' The brown or clay'd Sugars are good in their kind;
' they are not to be compared with our white refined Su-
' gars, this being a general and sure Rule, that the whiter
' any Sugar is, the cleaner, finer, and wholesomer it is, and
' is the more purged from all Grossness and Impurity. On
' the other Side, the blacker, duller, and moister any Sugar
' is, the fouler and grosser it must be, and consequently the
' more unwholesom and unhealthy; for the most, if not all
' the Operations of boiling, skimming, clarifying, and
' straining, performed in making the gross crude Juices of
' the Sugar-Cane into Muscovado Sugar, is done by the Re-
' finers, even to a higher Degree, and with great Charge,
' Skill, and Cleanliness, in working Brown-Sugar into White;
' and certainly the more Sugar is freed from its Grossness and
' Molasses, the more compact and harder is its Body, and
' the more Spirits and Life is in it. It will perform all the
' Uses in Housewifery to a greater Perfection, is of a finer
' Taste, of a more excellent Complexion, and causes all
' Things, wherein it is mixed, to be more wholesom and
' pleasant; so that these scrupulous Persons may assure them-
' selves, that the sparkling Grain, and Hardness of White-
' Sugar, are not at all occasioned by any Mixture of Lime,
' but by its own Fineness, as being freed from the grosser
' Part, or Molasses, or treacly Quality, which is soft, gross,
' and of a black or dull Complexion: Besides, the *Sal*
' *Nitral* Powers and Virtues that imbibe and give them-
' selves forth, and incorporate with the Water, are invi-
' sible and spirituous Qualities, as much unseen, and un-
' known to Mankind, as the Powers and Virtues that dwell
' in the Centre of all vegetative and animal Creatures. And
' though we know each Creature encreases, grows, and
' multiplies, yet the inward Power from whence this pro-
' ceeds, remains a Mystery, and wholly invisible to us. Now
' for the Satisfaction and better Information of such as per-
' sist in a Belief that there is some Trick of the Workman
' in preparing a Compost or Mixture of Lime, or some such
' thing in white refined Sugar, let them take common
' Water, as that of the *Thames*, or *New-River*, which for
' the most Part is not very fine nor clear, into which let
' them infuse such a Quantity of slacked Lime as Refiners
' do, in a short Time the dusty Body of the said Lime will
' sink to the Bottom, and the Water will become, as it were,
' purged or rarified from all its Impurities, and thereby be
' rendered much finer and clearer than other Water that
' comes

The History of Barbados.

'comes from the same Spring: Besides, the Lime Water
'will keep sweet, and free from all Kind of stinking Foulness,
'a considerable Time longer than any other common Water
'that is entire, or without this Ingredient of Lime. 'Tis
'with this clear and fine Water, that both brown and
'white Sugars are boiled up, and that which endues both
'Sorts with its sparkling lively Grain, and brisk spirituous
'Body, and without which no Art could raise it to such a
'complete and useful Body, and become so lively and vigo-
'rous in Operation; unto which most or all the best exhila-
'rating Cordials, made by Physicians, Apothecaries, and
'Housewives, owe their Original: So that let them believe
'or not, it is manifest there is no such Mixture of Lime,
'Alum, or any Thing like it in the Refiners white Sugar.'

There is another white Sugar of several Colours, exceeding our Muscovado, called *Lisbon* Sugar, because it came first from *Brasil* to *Lisbon*, but particular Planters have made as good Sugar of that Sort at *Barbados*, as ever was made at *Brasil*; an Instance of which I have given in this Chapter; and the moist *Barbados* Sugar is often sold by our Grocers for *Lisbon*, which the good Women call a *Fat Sugar*, supposing it will sweeten better, but our Refiners white Sugar is much whiter, drier, and cleaner than the *Brasil* white Sugar.

The best Muscovado is whitish; with a sparkling Grain. The next is that which tends towards an Ash Colour, having a large sandy Grain or Body; this is 3 or 4 *s.* a Hundred cheaper than the first Sort, and is generally bought up by the Refiners, as the first is by the Grocers. The third is of a darkish sad Colour, somewhat inferior to the other two, and proper for refining. The worst Sort of all is of a deep redish Colour, has a soft weak Grain and Body, and makes the poorest Work in refining, both in Quality, Colour, and Quantity. The Value of all Muscovado Sugar is always in Proportion to its Colour and Strength; of white Sugar, to its Whiteness and Driness; and the same of refined Sugar; the former of which has always a *Foot*, or Sediment, and the latter very little or none at all.

We have been the larger in our Account of this profitable Plant, because it is the main Article of the *British* Commerce in *America*; we have seen how it rises from a Root to a Plant, and have followed it in all its Operations, till it is fit for the Table, or the Lady's *Conservatory*; by which we may see how painfully and chargeably the Planters work up this Commodity, which we in *England* don't set so great a Value upon as we ought: We have seen how the Cane is carried to the Mill, Cattle-Mill or Wind-Mill, how the Juice is conveyed

veyed to the Ciftern, thence to fix or feven Boilers, thence to the Cooler; how it is then put into Pots, then fet in the Curing-Room, thence removed to the Knocking-Room: All thefe Rooms are built conveniently, one after another, to eafe as much as poffible the Labour of the Servants; who from *Monday* Morning, when they begin to work, to *Saturday* Night, when they always leave off, are kept conftantly at it; but being too hard Work for the fame Men to hold it fo long, they are relieved twice a Day, and take their Turns in the Field. And the like do the Horfes in the Mill, which requires 5 or 6 Horfes at a Time to draw it.

Since Wind-Mills came up, the Planters have not ufed, nor wanted fo much Cattle as before. Affnegoes ufed to carry the Canes, as Carts do now, to the Mill, and the Sugar from the Store-houfe to the Water-fide; where it is fhip'd or fold.

What remains now to be treated of, are the Dregs of the Juice, the Skimmings of the Copper, and the Droppings of the Pots, which are all capable of Improvement. They are carried to Cifterns and Backs, where they ferment; and are then drawn by Pipes into the Stills, in a Houfe adjoining to the former, which is called the *Diftilling-Houfe*. Here they are firft diftilled, and then rectified into the Spirit we have fpoken of, called *Rum*.

The Ways of managing it is much improved, fince the firft Settlement of the Ifland. 'Tis brought to fuch Perfection, that were it not for a certain Twang or Hogo that it receives from the Juice of the Cane, it would take Place next to *French* Brandy; for it is certainly more wholefom, at leaft in the Sugar-Iflands; where it has been obferved, that fuch as drink of the latter freely, do not live long; whereas the Rum-Drinkers hold it to a good old Age.

Rum does not fo foon deftroy the radical Moifture and Digeftion of the Stomach, as *French* Brandy does; whofe thin hungry Leannefs is proved, by putting a raw Piece of Flefh into it, where it will be eaten, and perifh much fooner than a like Piece put at the fame Time into *Barbados* Brandy or *Rum*.

The *Molaffes*, which is the Runnings from the Sugar, is either diftilled at Home, or fhip'd for *England*, and fold to our Diftillers, who make a noble, clean Brandy with it, much better than the Spirit of Malt, or any other Spirit, except what is extracted from the Productions of the Vine.

The Runnings from the Sugar-Pots in the Refiners Curing-Houfes in *England*, are called Treacle; and this is much cleaner than the Molaffes of *Barbados*, but not than the
Barbados

The History of Barbados.

Barbados Treacle; which is also the Runnings of the Sugar-Pots, after the Sugar is refined there.

Treacle makes admirable Brandy, and brown Sugar a finer Spirit still than that. This exceeds all other Brandy, as much as Light does Darkness, being the highest and noblest Cordial that can be made of any Fruit or Vegetable.

Molasses and Treacle are of excellent Use in Medicines, and other Things, particularly in fermented Liquors or Drinks; in which they are to be preferred, by many Degrees, to the Sweets of Malt; and there is no Use which they are put to, but that Sugar, and its Syrrup, will serve much better in its stead.

We must confess, that this excellent Production of the Cane in *Barbados* is one of the most pleasant and useful Things in the World, in many Cases: For besides the Advantages of it in Trade, which will be discoursed of in another Chapter, Physicians and Apothecaries cannot be without it, there being near three Hundred Medicines made up with Sugar; almost all Confectionary Wares receive their Sweetness and Preservation from it. Most Fruits would be pernicious without it; the finest Pastries could not be made, nor the rich Cordials that are in the Ladies Closets, nor their Conserves; neither could the Dairy furnish us with such Variety of Dishes, as it does, but by the Assistance of this noble Juice.

CHAP. VIII.

Of the Trade of Barbados *to and from* England, *to* Africa, *and the other Parts of* America; *and of their running Cash, or Coin.*

THE Trade of *Barbados* is more general than a great many People imagine; who seeing nothing come from thence but Sugar, and a few other Commodities, think all the Merchants there are wholly employed in buying of Sugar, and shipping it Home.

This, it is true, is the main Article, and it is this draws so many Trades after it, as to *England*, for Necessaries for the Subsistence and Clothing of the Planters, and their Families; to *New-England* and *Carolina* for Provisions; to *New-York* and *Virginia* for Bread, Pork, Flower, *Indian* Corn, and Tobacco; to *Guinea* for Negroes; to *Madeira* for Wine;

to *Terceras* and *Fyall* for Wine and Brandy; to the Isles of *May* and *Curassau* for Salt; and to *Ireland* for Beef and Pork; but that Trade is somewhat lessened lately.

'Tis amazing to think what a prodigious Number of Hands this little Spot of Ground employs, which we shall treat of elsewhere, and what great Commerce it occasions in those Parts of the World.

As to its Trade with *England*, it formerly loaded 400 Sail of Ships, most of them of considerable Burthen, with Sugar, Cotton, Ginger, &c. Since the War, that Number is decreased to 250; and even that is much more than all the other Sugar-Islands put together ever loaded Home.

The Inhabitants at first planted Tobacco, and sent it to *England*, but it was found to be so bad, that Necessity, as well as Profit, obliged them to look out for some other Trade, tho' as good Tobacco as any in the World has grown there.

Indigo was shipped thence some Years since, but there is now little or none made in the Island. Of Ginger scraped and scalded they make great Quantities, and have Abundance of Cotton-Shrubs; a Commodity that turns very well to Account.

They also ship *Lignum Vitæ*, Succats, Citron-Water, Molasses, Rum, and Lime-juice, for *England*. The two last Commodities, about 20 Years ago, used to come in Kegs for Presents, so did the Succats; and the Citron-Water in Bottles: But now *French* Wine and Brandy are dear, and Lemons scarce, Rum-Punch has been much used, and Lime-juice supplied the Place of Lemons. These Goods they consign to their Factors or Correspondents in *England*; who have 2 and half *per Cent*. Commission for Sales, and as much for Returns; and one half *per Cent*. Commission, for paying and receiving Money by Bills of Exchange.

The Merchants in *Barbados* have 5 *per Cent*. Commission for Sales, and 5 *per Cent*. for Returns; which, together with other Advantages, make their Business very advantageous; but they are apt to impose upon the Planters in the Prices of what they buy and sell, obliging them to take their Necessaries, which they know they must have, at what Rates they please; and giving them the same for their Sugar, which they know they must sell.

Most of the Merchants there are a Sort of Shop-keepers, and retail their Goods in their Ware-houses. Of late there are several Shop-keepers, who buy whole Cargoes of them at so much *per Cent*. Advance upon the prime Cost in the Invoice,

The History of Barbados. 161

voice, and retail out the Goods afterwards. Thefe Goods, which are all brought from *England* or *Ireland*, are,

Ozinbrigs, which is a chief Commodity, vaft Quantities being confumed by the Servants and Slaves, whofe Clothing is made of this Sort of Linnen.
Linnen of all Sorts, for the Planters and their Families.
Broad Cloth and Kerfies, for the Planters own Ufe, or their Overfeers.
Silks and Stuffs, for their Ladies and Houfhold Servants.
Red Caps, for Slaves, Male and Female.
Stockings and Shoes of all Sorts, for Mafters and Servants.
Gloves and Hats, of all Sorts and Sizes.
Millenary-Ware and Periwigs.
Laces for Linnen, Woollen and Silks.
Beef from *Ireland*.
Pork from *England* or *Ireland*.
Peafe, Beans, Oats, and Bisket. The three former from the *Weft* Country; the latter from *London*, the Bread being better there than in any other Part of *England*, and will keep better; which is a great Convenience now, that good Bisket is bought for 8 *s.* a Hundred. By that Time it gets to *Barbados*, perhaps it will be half Worm-eaten, or at leaft by that Time it is half fpent, the reft will be good for nothing. This Damage is in fome Meafure prevented, by the Goodnefs of the Bread, which the *London* Bakers underftand beft; and tho' it may come cheaper in the Country, yet by that Time it is fold at the *Bridge*, or in the Store-houfe at the Planter's Habitation, there will be fo much Wafte, that the Price is generally double; and it is often fo with *London* Bisket alfo.

Wine of all Sorts, ftrong Beer, and Pale-Ale, Pickles, Candles, Butter and Cheefe, Iron Ware for Mills and Sugar-Works; as Whip-faws, Hand-faws, Files, Axes, Hatchets, Chifels, Adzes, Hoes, Pick-axes, Mattocks, Plains, Gouges, Augres, Hand-bills, Drawing-knives, Nails, and all Sorts of *Birmingham* Ware, Leaden-Ware, Powder and Shot, and Brafiery Ware. As to Brafiery and *Birmingham* Ware, tho' they are good Commodities, yet they are fuch as agree the leaft with the Climate of any. They ruft, canker, and are eaten up in a few Years.

The Air there is fo moift, that if any Inftrument of Steel is never fo clean, let it lie one Night expofed to the Air, it will be rufty by next Morning; which, tho' Things do not

ruft

rust so soon now, occasions the Necessity of frequent Supplies of such Sort of Goods. Copper Ware for the Sugars is a very good Commodity.

Clocks and Watches seldom go right there; but I believe the Watch-makers are as often in the Fault, or the Owners at least in not looking well after them, as the Air, the Dampness of which is said to affect the Springs and Movements, so as to render the Motion uncertain. I know a Gentleman who carried over a Watch to *Barbados*, of *Waters*'s making, ten Years ago, after he had had it four in *England*, and that Watch went well for seven Years there, without wanting to be cleaned or righted: Whereas a Watch made at the same Time by the same Man, of the same Price, and with equal keeping, was spoiled in a much less Time in *England*, without any Accident coming to it; and yet for several Years it went as well, or better, than the other, which has been since another Voyage to *Barbados*, and goes still well without mending. And this is a plain Proof, that the Climate is not such an Enemy to the noble Machine, a Watch, as some ignorant *Voyagers* pretend; who either carried over Trash, or did not know how to use them.

All Sorts of *India* Goods and Toys, Coals, Pan-tiles, Hearth-stones, Hoops; and, in a Word, every Thing that is proper for an *English* Market, or Fair, will sell there, the Difference of the Climates always considered.

Servants will go off well, especially such as are not transported for Crimes, but go voluntarily. Of these many Companies have been sent from *Scotland*; and since the Union has succeeded, it is to be hoped many more will be transported thither. But upon the Disputes between the two Nations, about the *West-India* Trade, at *Darien* and elsewhere, the *Scots* denied the *English* the Advantage which their Colonies drew from their Plenty of Servants, occasioned by the Number of the Poor in that Kingdom.

Mechanicks, as Carpenters, Joiners, Masons, Smiths, Paviers, Coopers, Taylors, go off best; and if very good ones, are worth 25 or 30 *l.* a Piece for their 5 Years Service.

This and the other Islands in King *Charles*'s Reign lay under the Scandal of kidnapping young Men and Boys, that is, forcing or enticing them aboard a Ship without their own or Friends Consents; some great Merchants were charged with it, and Sir *W. Hayman*, a *Bristol* Merchant, actually tried for it by Judge *Jefferies*, but the Fact was never fairly proved upon them, and since the Laws against it have been so well put in Execution in the Colonies, as well as in *England*, that wicked Traffick is quite destroyed. There are
some

The History of Barbados.

some Cautions necessary to be observed by such as would send a Cargo of wasting or perishable Goods to *Barbados*, which are, that they ship their Butter, Oil, Candles, Liquors, and Provisions, as near as they can about the latter End of *September*, and then the Ship on which they are loaden, may arrive about the Middle of *November*, the Length of the Voyage being commonly six Weeks, if the Vessel sails directly thither. I have known a Ship, as particularly the *Richard* and *Michael*, Captain *John Williams* Commander, belonging to Mr. *Richard Walter* and Col. *Michael Terrill*, to make the Voyage homewards in 22 Days, the shortest Passage that was ever heard of from that Island to *England*, which is generally a six or seven Weeks Voyage homeward bound, and a five or six Weeks Voyage outward bound. The Packets generally make it in twenty six or twenty eight Days.

Care also should be taken in the Choice of the Goods that are bought to be sent thither; for if the Factor or Merchant trusts to the Tradesmen in *London*, or other Places, he will often find his Merchandize come out very ill in the Country, where he should have a good Correspondent to give him constant Advice of the Demand of all Sorts of Commodities, some of those we have mentioned always going off better than others, according to their Scarcity, and the Necessity of the Planter. He must be sure to be mindful of their being well packed, especially millenary Ware, Glasses, and all Goods that are easily broken, or he will unload Rubbish instead of Merchandize, when he comes to *Barbados*.

The Freight of Goods homeward before the late War was 5 or 6 *l.* a Tun, and since it has been 12 *s.* a Hundred, which is as good as thirty Pounds a Tun; for many Hogsheads of Sugar weigh 12 and 13 hundred Weight, of which four make 56 Hundred, almost three Tun, of 20 Hundred to the Tun; and I have seen Barrels of 8 hundred Weight a Piece, at which Weight there was 64 hundred Weight to the 8 Tun; which at 12 *s. per Cent.* Freight, from *Barbados* to *London*, amounts to near 40 *l.* a Tun Freight. Outward bound used to be 20 *s.* and is now 4 or 5 *l.* a Tun. These are grievous Burdens to the Planters, which they have no Way to prevent; but of this we must treat more largely elsewhere.

Sugars in King *James*'s Reign sold for 20 and 21 *s.* a Hundred; the coarsest of all for 17 and 18 *s.* and the same Sorts sell now at 30 and 32 *s.* They sold in King *William*'s Reign for near 3 *l.* and Whites proportionably; which Rates being occasioned by bad Crops, Storms, or Captures, the

Planters

Planters muſt not expect to ſee again in their Accounts of Sales, unleſs the ſame Accidents happen.

We ſhall not enter into the Detail of the Prices of all the Commodities that come from *Barbados*, and ſhould not have ſaid ſo much of this, but that it is the capital one, and there is ſomething in the Account that is hiſtorical.

The next Trade to the *Engliſh* in *Barbados* is the *African*, which is managed chiefly by the *Royal African Company's* Agents there, who are at preſent Col. *Butler*, Mr. *Bates*, and Mr. *Steward*, Merchants at the *Bridge*; but that Company do not engroſs the Trade as they did formerly, to the great Loſs of the *London* Merchants, who paid them 40 *per Cent*. Advance Money on their Cargoes to *Guinea*, for Liberty to trade; and beſides that, were obliged to let the Company buy their Merchandize, and charge them at their own Rates; which, with other Advantages, were as good to that Society as 60 *per Cent.* on all the Merchants Invoices, that dealt to *Africa* for Slaves. That Trade is now open, and 10 *per Cent*. only paid by all Merchants, trading to *Guinea* for Negroes, to the *Royal Company*, towards maintaining their Forts and Caſtles.

The Commodities ſent from *England* thither, are Guns, Powder and Arms, Perpetuanoes, Tallow, &c. as elſewhere mentioned; ſome Hats, and other wearing Apparel.

The Price of a Negro in *Guinea* 30 Years ago was 50 *s*. or 3 *l*. and now the *Barbarians* underſtand their Advantage, and our Neceſſities ſo well, that they hold up their Slaves at 9, 10, and 12 *l*. a Head, which occaſions their Dearneſs at the Plantations, where 20 Years ago they were ſometimes ſold at the ſame Rates.

The Planters having been a long Time impoſed upon by the Company's Agents, and private Factors, in the Price of their Negroes, have lately fallen very much into this Trade themſelves. They ſend to *England* for what Cargoes they want for the Voyage, and diſpatch away ſmall Veſſels, either alone, or in Partnerſhip to *Guinea*, to bring them Slaves to ſupply their Plantations; which muſt every Year be recruited with 20 or 30 Negroes, for every 4 or 500 Acres, or their Stock will ſoon come to nothing: For Hands are the Life of all Buſineſs in *Barbados*, and it is the Want of them that keeps the Planters poor, when they fall into thoſe unhappy Circumſtances.

The other conſiderable Trade that remains to be treated of, is that to *Madeira* for Wines, which is the chief Drink of the Iſland that the Gentlemen make Uſe of, either by itſelf, or mixed with Water: Of theſe there are about 3000 Pipes,

The History of Barbados.

Pipes, *Malmsey* and *Vidonia*, imported in a Year, either by the *London* Merchants, or the *Barbadians* themselves. The first Cost at *Madeira* is from 20 to 25 Milrees a Pipe, each Milree worth 6 s. 8 d. of our Money, that is from 7 to 9 l. a Pipe, besides Charges; and the Value at *Barbados*, from 18 to 20 l. a Pipe, according to the Plenty or Scarcity of the Commodity. This is a noble Wine, and has one peculiar Quality, that it keeps the better for being kept hot. That Wine which comes directly from *Madeira* to *England* drinks pall'd, in Comparison of that which comes round by *Barbados*, and so home; which, in Time of War, is the most usual Way of importing it here.

Tho' *Barbados* could never boast of equal Advantages with *Jamaica*, as to the Trade to the *Spanish West-Indies*, and had never such Resort of Pirates, who are the Men that make Silver plenty, yet 4 or 5 Years ago there was a great running Cash in the Island, thought to amount to no less than 200000 l. Sterling in Value, many Merchants at the *Bridge* having paid 10000 l. ready Money upon Occasion; but that Plenty is now so abated, that it is well if there's a fourth Part of that Sum at this Time at *Barbados*. This was occasioned chiefly by the good Weight of their Pieces of Eight; and the Proclamation put forth in *England* in 1702, to reduce Coin to a certain Value by Weight, which tempted many of the Traders to buy up the Silver, and export it to the other Islands, or to *England*, to save the Premium of Bills of *Exchange*; which, on the calling in of the Pieces of Eight, and establishing Paper Credit, rose to 60, and is now 35 *per Cent.* and in Time of Peace, when Trade flourished, was but 10 or 12 *per Cent.* By the Laws of the Country, all Pieces of Eight, *Sevill, Mexico,* and *Pillars,* were to pass for 5 s. and all half and quarter Pieces in the like Proportion. The Eight-Pieces, or seven Pence Halfpennys, are called *Bits,* and is generally the Money that passes in the Markets or Ordinaries. Light Pieces, and those of baser Allay, were forbidden to be imported from *England*, where it was a common Thing to buy up such Pieces, and send them to *Barbados*. Tho' the Currency of this Money was thus settled, yet there was not enough of it to answer all the Necessities of Trade, and the Merchants bartered the Commodities they imported for Sugar, Cotton, Ginger, and the Product of the Island; Muscovado Sugar being the general Medium of Commerce there, as well as in the other Islands.

The only Thing that remains to be treated of under this Head, is the Insurance, which Merchants and Planters make for the Security of their Trade, and this is so extravagant in

Time

Time of War, that the Infurers will have 30 *per Cent.* out and home, when before the War they would have been glad with feven or eight. The Uncertainty of fuch Infurances, moft of the Infurers having been ruined by it, infomuch that of 2000 *l.* in one Policy, I have known 1500 bad before the Lofs happened, makes the Planters run their own Rifk, and fome of them have loft ten thoufand Pound in a Year too by the Venture, which leads us to the next Article.

CHAP. IX.

Of the Riches of the Ifland, in the Time of its Profperity; the Advantage it has been to *England*; the Difadvantages it lies under; and how it may be relieved and improved.

WHEN we examine the Riches that have been raifed by the Produce of this little Spot of Ground, we fhall find that it has been as good as a Mine of Silver or Gold to the Crown of *England,* by the vaft Number of Mouths it feeds in this Ifland and that, the Fleet of Ships it ufed to employ, the Numbers of Mariners it bred, and the Addition it has made to the National Stock, as well as the great Eftates that particular Men have got by it; for (to fay nothing of Men worth 100000 or 150000 *l.* in the Ifland) how many Merchants have in a little Time acquired Lands, Honours, and Offices, by the Credit and Profit of this once thriving Trade, which in the Reign of King *Charles* II. ufed to employ 400 Sail of Ships, of 150 Tuns each, one with another, in all 60000 Tuns, which could not be managed by lefs than 2000 Seamen, nor the Families that fubfifted at Home, by building and fitting out fo many Ships, contain lefs than 8 or 10000 Souls? The Import from the Ifland ufed to come to 30000 Hogfheads of Sugar, of which half was for a Home, and half for a Foreign Confumption; and by the 15000 Hogfheads fpent at Home, no lefs than 10000 Souls more were maintained, and fome of them enriched. The neat Proceed of thefe Sugars might amount to about 250000 *l.* and that of the other Commodities, as Ginger, Cotton, Molaffes, &c. to 100000 *l.* more, in all to 350000 *l.* half of which was returned in Manufactures and Goods from hence; for they eat, drink, and

wear

The History of Barbados.

wear all of the Product of *England*, and by this Means 20000 Mouths more were provided for; besides as many that subsisted by working or retailing these Commodities. In all, by a modest Computation, one may venture to affirm, that the *Barbados* Trade did not subsist less than 60000 Persons in *England*; and there being then 50000 in *Barbados*, this Island maintained 100000 Souls, all *English* or *Europeans*, a 60th Part of the Inhabitants of the *British* Empire; though calculating by the Number of Acres, it is not a thousandth Part as big, reckoning the three Kingdoms only. By the 15000 Hogsheads exported to *Holland*, *Hamburgh*, and the *Streights*, where considerable Quantities of clayed Sugar were sent to *Alicant*, *Genoa*, *Leghorn*, and *Naples*, the National Stock was encreased 150000 *l*. besides what was raised by it in the Exportation of Ginger, Indigo, &c. which all together was a yearly Advantage to the Nation of 200000 *l*. and this for 20 Years together makes four Millions; and allowing but half that Sum for the last 20 Years, two Millions, it will amount to six Millions, which the Publick has encreased its Stock by this Trade in 40 Years time: Besides that, it brings in 30 or 40000 *l*. yearly to the Exchequer, by Customs and Imposts, and has drawn little or nothing out of it for its Defence. On the contrary, 6 or 7000 *l*. yearly has been remitted thence to the Treasury here, for the 4 and a half *per Cent*. Duty; and what Charge the Inhabitants have been at for their Security, has all come out of their own Pockets, excepting some few Guns, and some Ammunition, that have been sent them very sparingly from *England*.

This has occasioned great Complaints in that Plantation, and frequent Petitions for Redress from their Agents here. In the late War they were obliged to go through all without the least Assistance, excepting in one or two Expeditions against the *French*, which put them to more Charge than the Government received Benefit by it.

In this War they have far'd better, which they owe to the present prudent Administration: For Care has been taken to have Supplies of Warlike Stores sent them. But they are still under an unspeakable Want of Hands, which not only occasions their neglecting to manure many thousands of Acres, but also the high Price of Servants and Slaves. This would be in some measure prevented, by sending them 5 or 600 Men, to man their Forts, that they might not fear a Surprize, and be able to employ their own Hands on their Plantations.

Several

The History of Barbados.

Several Regiments have been sent to the Leeward Islands and *Jamaica*, but it has not been the good Fortune of the *Barbadians* yet to have any sufficient Number of Men left among them. On the contrary, they have drained their own Island, to defend the others.

They sent down 1500 Men with Sir *Timothy Thornhill*, &c. against *Martinico*, in King *William*'s Reign, and 1000 with Col. *Codrington* against *Guardaloupe*, in her present Majesty's, of whom many hundreds never returned; yet there never were any Recruits sent in their Places.

The War at home takes up all those spare Men, that would otherwise transport themselves, or be transported thither; and the *Scots*, since their hard Usage at *Darien*, will not furnish our Colonies with Servants, as they used to do at reasonable Rates; which all together has reduced the Island to such a small Strength, that perhaps her greatest Security is, that her Enemies do not know her Weakness.

The Act for the 4 and an half *per Cent.* says in the Preamble of it, that it was given towards the raising and maintaining the Forts, building a State-house, &c.

This Revenue brings in some thousands yearly; and from the Time it was first given, may have amounted to above 300000 *l.* yet there was not a thousand Pound laid out by the Government for the Use of the Island, in all King *Charles*, King *James*, or King *William*'s Reigns. Pensions were granted out of it; and what the *Barbadians* wanted, they were forced to raise themselves by other Taxes. Neither in all this Time have the Agents, though they have good Salaries for minding their Affairs, done them any considerable Service, in getting this Revenue, or part of it, appropriated to the Uses it was given for. Convoys, it is true, have been sent thither, and Ships have lain there some time for the Security of the Commerce; but they have not been able to hinder the *French* Privateers from surrounding the Island, and taking all Ships that come that Way, Homeward or Outward-bound. Twelve Privateers have roved off the Island at a Time, and a Man of War lain all the while in the Harbour; the Captain of which pretending want of Hands, has refused to stir out, though he has been desired to do it in very pressing Terms. For when those Officers get there, and out of the hearing of the Admiralty-Board, they act sovereignly, and think their Power should be directed by their Pleasure.

The Loss of their *Barbados* Ships in the Wars with *France* has been a dreadful Blow to the Planters, Merchants, and all that have any Concerns in that Island. They have suffered

fered more than any other Trade whatsoever. Their Loss by Captures, within the Compass of one Year, of the last War, being computed at 380000 *l.* And in the Year 1704. out of a Fleet of 33 Ships, 27 were taken. Out of another of six Ships, four were taken: And out of a Fleet of 40 Ships, the greatest Number were lost to the *French.*

How to remedy this Evil is apparent enough, but it does not become us to direct our Superiors, whose Wisdoms may have those Reasons for acting otherwise, which we may not be able to answer.

Some light Frigats to cruize off the Island there, and some others in the Chops of the Channels, would perhaps prevent the Loss of so many of our *West-India* Ships; and the Trade is so profitable, it would very well answer the Charge.

Insurances are so high, the Planters cannot afford to pay the Premio's. If they do, the Insurance Money sometimes will not pay the first Cost. But supposing the Insurers stand, the Deductions of 18 and 20 *l. per Cent.* for no manner of reason, the Expence of Meetings, Commission and other Charges, rise so high, that if the Planter has one Hogshead in two come safe, without Insurance, he had better run the Risk.

This is only prevented by the Security of our Trade. And that is a general Article, which would be too tedious to treat of here.

The *Barbados* Trade has nothing particular in this from the others, but that it has been more unfortunate. Another main Disadvantage which they lie under, is the Discouragement that is given to their claying and refining their Sugars, by the heavy Duty that is laid on all First and Seconds, no less than 12 *s.* a Hundred. By which Means they are forced to send home their Sugars unpurged, to their very great Damage; for they could refine their Sugars more easily, and at a cheaper Rate than the Sugar Bakers in *England.*

The low Prices of that Commodity in this War Time, have been another Calamity to the *Barbadians.* During the last War they had terrible Losses, but then their Sugars sold well, from 50 *s.* to 3 *l.* a Hundred; but now they fell for 30 or 32 *s.* a Hundred: And this is occasioned chiefly by the very Thing that one would think should keep up the Price, by the Number of the Ships taken by the *French.* For, as we have said, half of the Sugars imported from *Barbados* is for a foreign Market; and when they were in demand Abroad, they were always so at Home: Whereas now the *French* sell them cheaper than the *English,* and glut the foreign Markets, by the Quantities they export of the Product of our Plantations.

The

The Price of Sugars has lately been very much affected, by the *Dutch* bringing some thousands of Chests from the *East-Indies*. They can afford to do this in Time of War, when the Commodity bears an answerable Price: But in peaceable Times it will not turn to Account. In the mean while, the *Barbadians* feel the Damage of it to their Trade; and the only Way to prevent it, is, by lessening the Duty upon white Sugars, that they may be able to under-sell them Abroad; for all Nations have a Right to plant what they please in their own Soils, and sell the Product of it where they can find a Market, and the cheapest will always have the Preference.

The excessive Freights, 20 and 25 *l.* a Tun, is another vast Disadvantage to the *Barbadians*; and the only Way to remedy it, is to take such Care here of sending them Convoys and Fleets, and furnishing their Ships with Seamen, that Owners may be encouraged to let their Ships out for that Voyage; and if they had Ships enough, Freight would return to its old Rate.

The Exchange of Money which has been 50, 60, and 70 *l. per Cent.* is a great Balk to the Trade; and the protesting the Planters Bills in *England*, of the same ill Consequence to both the Planter and the Merchant. The Planter draws upon his Bill of Lading, and if his Sugar is lost, his Bill comes back, where he is immediately run up 20 *per Cent.* for Interest and Charges; and often brings a Debt on himself, and his Plantation, which he can never clear.

The want of Provisions is also a great Inconvenience to the Inhabitants of this Island. Fifty or sixty Sail of Ships formerly went every Year from *England* and *Ireland*, loaden with Bear, Ale, Bread, Flower, Butter, Cheese, Beef and Fish, and now half that Number is not sent thither yearly, with those Cargoes; neither can they get sufficient Supplies from the Colonies on the Continent, for want of Hands to man Ships for that Trade.

The Act of Navigation prohibiting Foreigners to trade with them, was another severe Discouragement; and tho' some of these were temporary, yet others will be lasting, unless it shall please the great Council of the Nation to look into the Hardships they suffer, and take care to procure them Redress; in which her Majesty, though she is always ready to relieve her Subjects, cannot give them Ease in some Cases, without an Act of Parliament.

And when we consider the vast Charge they are at, that a Man must be in Disburse there 2 or 3000 *l.* before he can make 100 Pound Weight of Sugar, which is not worth
above

above 12 or 14 *s.* in Time of Peace; and muſt have a living Stock of 5000 *l.* to make 100 Hogſheads of Sugar; one cannot but believe it is reaſonable they ſhould be encouraged as much as the State of Affairs at home will permit.

St. LUCIA.

THIS Iſland may, as it is ſaid, be ſeen from *Barbados,* from whence it is diſtant 24 Leagues, only 7 Leagues from *Martinico,* and the like from *St. Vincent*'s. It lies in 13° 40 Minutes of North Latitude, is 22 Miles long and 11 broad, hilly in many Places, but the greateſt Part of it good Land, well watered with Rivers, which give it an Advantage of the Iſland of *Barbados.* The Air is reckoned healthy, and the Reaſon given for it is, its being ſo narrow and the Hills not ſo high, as to intercept the Trade Winds that always fan it from the Eaſtward, whereby the Heat of the Climate, ſays Capt. *Vring, Is mitigated and made rather agreeable than troubleſom.* 'Tis full of tall Trees, among which are great Quantities of good Timber fit for building Houſes and Wind-mills, as the Planters of *Barbados* and *Martinico* find by daily Experience. *Cocoa* is here in Plenty, and Fuſtick in Abundance. It has ſeveral good Bays and Harbours, where there is good Anchorage for Shipping: One of which called the *Little Careenage,* is the Place at which the *Engliſh* lately deſigned to fortify themſelves, it being the fineſt and moſt convenient Harbour in all the *Charibbee Iſlands,* taking its Name from the Convenience of careening Ships there.

Great Numbers of Ships may be ſafe there in all Weathers. So much may be ſaid of the Benefit that might accrue to the *Britiſh* Trade by the Poſſeſſion of this Iſland peaceable and unconteſted, that it does raiſe much Speculation in the Minds of *Engliſh* Readers, acquainted with that Trade in and among the *Charibbee* Iſlands, how it comes to paſs, that this, which has been ſo often aſſerted to be the undoubted Right of the *Britiſh* Crown, ſhould remain unpoſſeſſed by *Britons,* when it is included in every Commiſſion of the Governor for the Iſland of *Barbados.* And the ſaid Governor was wont to aſſert the ſame, ſometimes by going thither in Perſon with great Pomp and Ceremony, hoiſting the King's Colours, firing Guns, *&c.* and otherwiſe. And how that Right is

founded

The History of St. Lucia.

The Right of the English to it. founded will appear by the following State of it, in a *Memorial* drawn up in *England* for the Use of the *British* Ambassador in *France*, after his late Majesty's Grant of it to the Duke of *Montagu*, in the following Words.

'It is agreed by *French* as well as *English* Historians of the best Credit, that the *English* settled on the Island of St. *Lucia* in 1639, and lived there near two Years without any Interruption or Disturbance; but that in 1640, they were driven off from the said Island, and the Governor and most of the Inhabitants killed by the *Charibbeans*, and as the *English* suspected, by the Instigation and Encouragement of the *French*, which the *French* Generals *Parquet* and *de Poincy*, however, both disowned; nor did the *French* at that Time or any other Time make any Sort of Pretension *to the Island. A tacit Acknowledgment of the Right of the* English.

'The civil Wars in *England* breaking out, the *English* neglected this Settlement, and Monf. *du Parquet* sent 30 or 40 *Frenchmen* to take Possession of the Island. The Sieur *de Rousselan* governed here till 1654, and was succeeded by *de la Riviere*, whom the *Charibbeans* killed with several of his Men, and carried off his Wife and two of his Children. He was succeeded by *M. le Briton*, he by *M. Aygremont*, who was also destroyed by the *Charibbeans*.

The French dispossessed. 'After this the *English* made a Treaty with the *Charibbeans* for the purchasing the Island from them, and in 1663, sent 1400 or 1500 Men on Board five Men of War, who being joined by 600 of the *Charibbeans* in 17 Canoes, came before the Island in *June* 1664, which was delivered to them without Resistance, on Condition, that the *French* Governor and Garrison in the Fort, which amounted only to 14 Men, should be transported to *Martinique* with their Cannon, Arms and Baggage.

Mr. Robert Cook Governor. 'In 1666, the *English* Governor Mr. *Robert Cook*, by Reason of the Mortality of his People, Want of Necessaries, &c. abandoned the Island and set Fire to the Fort; yet two Days afterwards a Bark arrived from the Lord *Willoughby* (Governor and Captain General of *Barbados* and the other *English Charibbee* Islands to Windward of *Guardaloupe*) with Provisions, Ammunition and all Necessaries for the Colony.'

The foregoing are Matters of Fact received by Historians, particularly by Father *Tertre*, who is very exact and circumstantial; and as he was a Missionary to the *French Charibbee* Islands and a *Frenchman*, not to be suspected of being favourable in his Narrations to the *English* Rights and Pretensions.

The History of St. Lucia.

tenfions. This Pere Tertre *is the Author, whose Accounts I have made Use of in all that I have said in this Work of the Caribbeans*.

The Memorial proceeds to tell us, that the *French* King by his Treaties with King *Charles* and King *James* II. and by those of *Ryswick* and *Utrecht, stipulated to restore to the King of* Great-Britain *all the Islands, Countries, Fortresses and Colonies, which may have been conquered by the most Christian King, and such as were in the Possession of the King of* Great-Britain, *before the War began*; which shews us that it was taken for granted, that the *English* had the first Possession, and consequently the prior Right to this Island, St. *Lucia* being included in the Words, *all the* British *Dominions*. And this the Governor of *Barbados* asserted, as appears by what he wrote Monf. *Du Quesne*, General of the *French* Islands in Answer to his Letter, which ran thus,

SIR,

I can't dispense with begging Mr. de Valminier, *an Officer of Distinction here, to bring you my Complaints of the Insults which your Men of War have offered at St.* Lucia, *to the King's Subjects, in taking away the Wood which they cut for his Service; this Procedure is contrary to the good Faith and Union which should be between the two Crowns, and very improper to cultivate a good Understanding. It is also surprising, that Mr.* St. Lo, *Commander of the* Valour, *has been capable of such a Procedure. I hope, Sir, that you will not refuse upon this Occasion the Justice which is due. Mr.* de Valminier *has been pleased to undertake to represent to you the just Grounds which we have to complain to you, of the Violences of your Captains against the King's Subjects, who always in Time of Peace, with the General's Passport have gone to St.* Lucia *to cut Wood, without disturbing the Subjects of the King of* England, *who have also gone there. I hope then Sir you will do Justice, by causing to be returned the Wood that has been taken away, and in prohibiting the like for the future,* &c.
Governor of Martinico's Letter to the Governor of Barbados.

Fort-Royal, *in* Martinique,
  Feb. 24, 1715. N. S.   Du Quesne.

P. S. *I am actually informed, that several* English *Vessels go to* Tobago *to cut Wood there: You know that should not be, and that it is not lawful for them.*

To which Mr. President *Sharpe* answered.

Governor of Barbados's Answer about St. Lucia.

SIR,

'I received your Excellency's Letter of the 24th, by Mr. *Valminier*, complaining, &c. The Regard I had for your Excellency's Letter, obliged me to inquire into this Affair, and I cannot find that any of the King's Ships have done what is alledged therein; nor that they have any Ways acted contrary to their Duty.

'The King my Master's *sole Right* of Sovereignty to that Island, St. *Lucia*, cannot be unknown to you, nor is it now to be controverted, and therefore, Sir, it cannot be permitted that any Persons, other than his Majesty's own Subjects, should settle or cut Wood there without his Majesty's Licence: I must therefore earnestly press you to give Order, that such of the King your Master's Subjects as I hear are about to settle there, may forthwith remove, and that none of them re-settle there for the future, least by such a Procedure, the good Understanding between the two Crowns be indeed interrupted.

Forbids the French to settle here.

'The same Right the King my Master has to the Island of *Tobago*, and therefore I can't but be surprized at the Postscript of your Letter, wherein you say it is not lawful for his Majesty's Subjects to cut Wood there.

'It is my Inclination, Sir, to cultivate a good Understanding between the Subjects of the two Crowns in these Parts, as far as is consistent with my entire Devotion to the King my Master. But I think (and I hope when you have re-considered it, you will be of the same Sentiments) to draw Conclusions of Right from some Liberties which may have been occasionally winked at, in (not allowed to) his most Christian Majesty's Subjects, in those the King my Master's Islands, is by no Means a proper Method to establish it, &c.'

Pilgrim in *Barbados*, Feb. 21st, 1714. O. S.

William Sharpe.

This Matter is of so great Importance in the Article of Commerce, that it is well worth the particular Regard of the *British* State in all future Treaties with *France*, to have the Right of the *English* to St. *Lucia* specified and confirmed. The *French* seem to found their Right chiefly on being the next Neighbour. *English* and *French* have landed and planted in several Parts of it: The *English* had once the greatest Number of Inhabitants there, no less than 1500, near 100

The History of St. Lucia.

Years ago, whose Habitations were upon Sandy Bay to the Eastward of *Careening* Harbour. *English* and *French* had formerly at the same Time Habitations on the *North East* and *South East* Coasts of the Island, but that mixed Possession was not of long Duration, for in less than 20 Years, I found all the Island along *Sandy Bay* marked in Capt. *Vring's* Draught for *French* Habitations; and about the Year 1719. the Mareschal *de Estree*, by a Grant of the *French* King, sent a Colony to possess, settle and plant the Country. The Governor of *Barbados* immediately notified to the commanding Officer of the Mareschal's Colony, he should be obliged to dispossess them by Force; but the *British* Ambassador in *France* represented the Matter with so much Spirit and Reason, as a Violation of the Rights of his *Britannick* Majesty, that Orders were sent to the Mareschal *de Estree's* Colony to evacuate the Island, which they did accordingly; and three Years after, his Majesty King *George* I. granted the Islands of St. *Lucia* and St. *Vincent*, to *John* Duke of *Montagu*, by Letters Patent bearing Date the 20th of *June* 1722. His Grace appointed Capt. *Nathaniel Vring*, late Commander of the *West-India* Packet Boat, to be Deputy-Governor of St. *Lucia* and St. *Vincent*; Capt. *John Braithwaite* to be Lieutenant Governor, Mr. *William Falkener* to be Secretary, and others, to supply the Offices requisite for the Management of the Affairs of his well intended Colony.

The Island granted to the Duke of Montagu.

The Preparations made for transporting them to St. *Lucia*, and their Settlement when they arrived, will appear by the following Account,

Ships.	Tons.	Guns.	Officers.	Servants.
Elizabeth	130	4	3	9
Charles and Freemason	200	10	13	108
Griffin Sloop	90	12	3	48
Little George	100	4	8	30
Adventure	200	12	13	141
Hopewell	250	6	11	89
Total	520	48	51	425

Aboard which were shipped great Quantities of all Sorts of Provisions and Stores.

56 Pieces of Cannon.
1163 Muskets and Bayonets.
500 Cutlashes.

1000 Grenado

1000 Grenado Shells fixed with Fuzees.
   4 Brafs Cohorn Mortars.
 100 Barrels of Musket Ball.
  20 Barrels of Bird and Drop Shot.
 100 Barrels of Gunpowder.
 200 Barrels of all Sorts of Nails.

A great Quantity of Tools for *Carpenters, Bricklayers, Smiths* and *Mafons*.
  20 Tons of Bar Iron.
  10 Tons of Cordage.

All Sorts of working Tools, Houfhold Furniture, wearing Apparel, and in Fine, of every Thing fitting for the fecure and commodious Being of a new Settlement.

Aboard the *Leopard*, Capt. *Samuel Foye*, loaden at *Boston* in *New-England*, for St. *Lucia*.

30 *Houfe Frames*, one large *Houfe Frame* for the *Governor*, 50000 Feet of Board, 95000 Shingles, 40 live Sheep, and 2 breeding Sows. The *Winchelfea* Man of War, Captain *Humphry Orme* Commander, was ordered to convoy and attend this Colony, which ftopped in *Ireland* to take in more Stores of Provifions, at *Madeira* for Wine, and at *Barbados* for additional Supplies of Stores. The *Adventure* and the *Hopewell* not being ready to fail with the Convoy and the other Ships from *Ireland*, followed them to St. *Lucia*, but came too late to be of Service to the Colony, the beft provided with Neceffaries that ever any was that went from *Europe* to *America*, to poffefs and fettle a Country.

The *Winchelfea* Man of War, the *Elizabeth*, *Griffin* Sloop, and the *Little George*, Tranfports, arrived at St. *Lucia* the 17th of *December*, 1722, after a long Paffage from *Ireland*. They anchored in *Pilgrim* Ifland Bay, and Captain *Orme* feeing there were Men on the Ifland, fent his Boat to know who they were, and underftood they were *French*, who came from *Martinico* in a fmall Canoe, to catch *Guanoes*; their coming in a fmall Canoe a Pleafuring, fhews that St. *Lucia* is fo near *Martinico*, that the *French* will never admit of any Settlement there while they have Power to prevent or deftroy it, unlefs the Right to it is fpecified and recognized. Some Perfon at *Barbados* advifed Mr. *Vring* to fettle at *Pilgrim* Ifland, but Captain *Orme* himfelf and the Engineer having furveyed it, found the Land a barren fandy Soil, and the River not fafe for Ships; the Wind at *Weft*, therefore they failed to *Petite Careenage*, about three Leagues farther to the Southward. This is a good Harbour, and in it are feveral Places fit for Careening, Ships fheltered from all Winds, and from this Convenience of *Careerning* it

took

The History of St. Lucia. 177

takes its Name. Mr. *Vring* landed 50 Men on a Point which commanded the Entrance into the Harbour, and set them at work to cut down the Trees and Bushes to make Way for raising a Battery at that Place which was called *Montagu-Point*; but there was a Hill so near it as within Musquet Shot, which they also intended to fortifie. Mr. *Vring* dispatched Mr. *Falkner*, Secretary to the Colony, to *Martinico*, with the Duke of *Montagu's* and that of the Admiralty's and his own Letters to Captain *Brown*, Commander of his Majesty's Ship the *Feversham*, and Captain *Brand* of the *Hector*, both of them in that Harbour, the Contents of which were to give the Colony of St. *Lucia* all necessary Assistance. Captain *Brown's* Letter to Mr. *Vring*, shews the desperate Situation of their infant Colony's Affairs.

Feversham, Port-Royal, *Martinico*, Dec. 18. 1722.
Sir,
‘ I congratulate you on your safe Arrival here Abroad,
‘ and am sorry the Settlement of St. *Lucia* is like to meet
‘ with many Difficulties; for you may depend on it, that
‘ last *Sunday* an Order was published in all the Churches of
‘ *Martinico* from the Court of *France*, that after Notice
‘ given, if you do not remove in 15 Days, that then they
‘ are to compel you so to do. Captain *Brand* is much your
‘ humble Servant. We shall wait on you on *Thursday* next,
‘ and am,
Sir,

Your humble Servant,

To *Nat. Vring*, Esq; Governor   Charles Brown.
of St. *Lucia* and St. *Vincent*.

Mr. *Vring* wrote to Captain *Brown* of the *Feversham*, Captain *Brand* of the *Hector*, Captain *Orme* of the *Winchelsea*, to give them formal Notice of the Danger he and his Colony were in, and desired Assistance pursuant to their Instructions from the Admiralty; but he received Answer only from Captain *Brown*, in which he explains the Contents of Mr. *Vring's* to him and the other Captains.

Feversham, at St. *Lucia*, Dec. 23. 1722.
Sir,
‘ This owns the Receipt of yours dated the 22d of *December*,
‘ with the inclosed Letters and Declarations from
‘ Monsieur *Fouquiere*. I have only to answer, that I shall al-
                                                     ‘ ways

'ways be strictly careful in the Execution of my Duty in
'every Thing that relates to his Majesty's Service, and
'am, &c.

Mr. *Vring* had sent him the Copy of the *French* King's Order, which had been read in the Churches at *Martinico*, which the Governor Monsieur *Fouquiere* had sent him, with a Notification of his Intention to obey it, unless he removed in 15 Days. Mr. *Vring* in his Answer to the Governor of *Martinico*, proposed to refer the Matter to the Determination of their Masters in *Europe*, but the *French* Governor kept to the Letter of his Mandate, and it is very plain that Captain *Brown* and the other Commanders of the Men of War, did not think the general Order in the Grant of St. *Lucia* to all the Governors and Commanders to be assisting to the Colony that should be sent to St. *Lucia*, or the like Instructions from the Admiralty, were sufficient to justifie their acting offensively against the *French*, which must have ended in a War between *Great Britain* and *France*, the occasion of which they would not take on themselves, neither would the Governor of *Barbados* or any other Governor of the *British* Colonies in *America* take these general Orders and Instructions to be a sufficient Warrant for them to begin Hostilities against the *French*, for obeying *their King's Mandate*. After what had happened to the Mareschal *de Estrees's* Colony, it seems to have been requisite to have known how the *French* would act in the like Case did the *English* attempt a Settlement at St. *Lucia*, and how far the *English* would be supported by a national Power before they attempted a Thing which the Mareschal *de Estree* and his Colony had been obliged to abandon; for it is most certain the *French* did pretend as well to St. *Lucia* as the *English*, and had actually at that very time Habitations on some part of the Island, though no regular Settlement. But if the *English* had the first Habitations, such seizing gives them a prior Right, which is well worth defending, when the Juncture is favourable, which it did not now seem to be. Notwithstanding these Difficulties that seemed insurmountable, and the Captains of the Men of War declining to act in any Manner that might produce ill Consequences in *Europe*, Mr. *Vring* went on in landing the Cannon, Arms, and Stores, and was very active in forwarding a Fortification raised on the Hill, which he proposed to make defensible before the 15 Days, to which his Removal was limited by the *French* Mandate, were expired.

The History of St. Lucia.

He sent Mr. *Egerton*, and Mr. *Medley*, two of his Colony, to St. *Vincent*, to try what they could do towards a Settlement in that other Island of his Government.

While Mr. *Vring's* Men were very busy in raising their Fort on the Hill, they spy'd *December* 29. 13 Days after their coming to St. *Lucia*, several Sloops standing into *Shoque-Bay*, where they landed Men within an Hour's March of the Hill. The Land about this *Shoque-Bay*, seemed at that very Time to be inhabited by the *French*, for the Governor writes, *two young* Negroes *came to us which were supposed to be* French, *of which the Inhabitants of* Shoque-Bay *were acquainted, and they were claimed and returned to the Owners.* For it appears that the Mareschal de *Estree's* Colony were settled in that Place where Mr. *Vring* intended his Settlement, by what he says, *we found an old Oven* as his Men were working in the Hill, *which we suppose was made by the Duke* de Estree's *Colony when there.* I mention this to shew that it must be well known that the *French* had formerly pretended to claim, nay to possess and settle in this Island; and that there were *French* Inhabitants upon it at this very Time, some of them in Ability to maintain and employ Negroes. However they could not weaken the prior Claim and Possession of the *English*; but before that should have been asserted in so solemn and expensive a Manner, it had been well if any Dispute of that kind had been adjusted, and Measures taken to prevent or effectully to oppose any Molestations from the *French*.

The next Day after the *French* began to land at *Shoque-Bay*, the Governor and Council of St. *Lucia* published a *Proclamation*, which was sent by Mr. *John Braithwaite*, Deputy Governor, to be read to them at the *Shoque.* The Title of it will I believe be enough, considering the present Circumstances of the Colony.

A Proclamation, *requiring all Strangers and Foreigners now within the Islands of St.* Lucia *and St.* Vincent, *or either of them, to submit and conform to the Government therein established, or to depart thereout.*

Mr. *Vring* informs us, the *French* told the Deputy-Governor he *did not understand the* English, *and made light of the Proclamation*, which is not surprizing. In the mean Time, the *English* were raising their Fort on the Hill, and a Barricado on the Point, to secure their Store-houses and Fruits which were there; they carried it from Sea to Sea, and indeed there was no Diligence wanting in the Governor and those he employed to take Care of the Works.

The

The *French* continued landing Men daily from *Martinico*, and being encreafed to about 2000, were joined by 500 Men from *Guardaloupe*; and Mr. *Vring*'s fmall Number was fo diminifhed by Defertion and Difeafe, that he had not above 70 Men fit to bear Arms. The Marquis *de Champigny* who commanded the *French* Troops, moftly *Martinico* Militia, fent Monfieur *de Point Sable* with a Letter to Governor *Vring*, requiring the Evacuation of the Ifland by the *Englifh*; and Monfieur *de Fouquiere*, General of the *French* Iflands, infifting upon it, and rejecting all Propofals for leaving Matters in their prefent State, till Orders fhould come from *Europe* concerning them; Governor *Vring* confulted his Council thereupon, who refolved to draw off and leave the Ifland, and Lieutenant Governor *Braithwaite* was difpatched to the *Shoque*, to treat with the Marquis *de Champigny*, who readily agreed to the reafonable Demands of the *Englifh*. That all their Deferters fhould be reftored, and fufficient Time be allowed for re-imbarking the Cannon, Arms, Ammunition, Provifions, Stores of all Sorts, and whatever had by them been dif-imbarked in that Ifland, which the *French* were alfo to evacuate at the fame Time. The fame Day, *January* 10, the *French* Forces advanced towards the *Englifh*, and the great Detachment marched up the Hill. Mr. *Vring* was of Opinion, if the *Adventure* and *Hopewell* had arrived in Time with the Men they had on Board, near 240, it would *effectually have prevented the* French *from difpoffeffing the* Englifh. But doubtlefs the *French* Forces would have been augmented in Proportion, for according to the Oath of *Robert Bullcock*, taken by *Samuel Cox*, Efq; Prefident of *Barbados*, and fent by him to Mr. *Vring*, the *French* at *Martinico* talked of fending over 10000 Men to St. *Lucia*, rather than they would fail in their Refolution to difpoffefs the *Englifh*. Tho' that might be a Gafconade, yet it was well known they could have fpared many more Thoufands than they fent thither for that Service, had it been neceffary, and there was little Likelihood that the *Englifh*, who with the Reinforcement of 200, had fo many come thither fit to bear Arms, could have defended themfelves in their new Works raifed in Hafte againft a powerful Army: fo they purfued the wifeft Counfels, concluded the Treaty for their peaceable Re-imbarkation, fhipp'd again whatever they had landed, demolifhed their Fort and Barricado, ftruck their Flag and carried it Aboard, and *January* 14th, failed out of the Harbour of *Petite Careenage* for the Ifland of *Antego*, having been a Month upon that of St. *Lucia*, of which

Nathaniel

The History of St. Lucia.

Nathaniel Vring, Esq; was Deputy Governor,
* John Braithwaite, Esq; Lieutenant Governor.
Mr. William Falkener, Secretary.
Mr. Robert Egerton, } Counsellors.
Capt. Watson,

N. B. This Mr. *Braithwaite* was afterwards employed in the *African* Company's Service in *Guinea,* where he acquired some Estate, and afterwards removed to *Carolina,* and is the same Person who behaved so gallantly in an Engagement with the *Spaniards* at Sea, and was barbarously murdered by them after Surrender.

We must now return to the Memorial before cited, where Mention is made of the Evacuation of this Place as follows. ' The *French* at this Time opposed the *English* Settlement, ' but by Article VII. of the Treaty concluded on the Part of ' the *English* by Mr. *Braithwaite,* empowered by Mr. *Vring,* ' the Duke of *Montagu*'s Deputy Governor, and on the Part ' of the *French* by Monf. *de Champigny,* for the Evacuation ' of St. *Lucia, Jan.* 8th, O. S. 1722-3, it is agreed, that ' immediately after the Evacuation of the said Colony of ' Monf. the Duke of *Montagu,* the Sieur Marquis *de Cham-* ' *pigny* obliges himself also to make an Evacuation of the ' *French* Forces, and leave the Island of St. *Lucia* in its ' former State and Condition, till there shall be a Decision of ' it by the two Crowns. To the Rights and Pretensions of ' which the said Sieurs *de Champigny* and *Braithwaite* declare, ' they have neither Inclination or Power to bring any Pre- ' judice to the present Treaty.'

The Treaty between Mr. *Vring* the Duke of *Montagu*'s Governor, and Monf. *Champigny,* can be no Way derogatory to the *British* Title, it being expresly stipulated therein to the contrary, and his Excellency *Henry Worseley,* Esq; has since then been constituted and appointed by his present *Britannick* Majesty King *George* II. Governor and Commander in chief of this Island of St. *Lucia,* by Commission and the following Instructions.

GEORGE R.

' TRUSTY and well beloved we greet you well.
' Whereas the *French* for some Years have claimed a
' Right to the Island of St. *Lucia,* and do insist that the
' Right to the Islands of St. *Vincent* and *Dominico* under
' your Government is in the *Charibbeans* now inhabiting the
' same, altho' we have an undoubted Right to all the said
' Islands;

'Iflands; yet we have thought fit to agree with the *French*
'Court, that untill our Right fhall be determined, the faid
'Iflands fhall be entirely evacuated by both Nations. It is
'therefore our Will and Pleafure, and you are accordingly
'to fignify the fame to fuch of our Subjects as fhall be found
'inhabiting any of our faid Iflands, that they do forthwith
'quit the fame, untill the Right fhall be determined as afore-
'faid. And that they do comply with this our Order within
'thirty Days from the Publication thereof, in each of the
'faid Iflands refpectively, under Pain of our higheft Difplea-
'fure, and you are to ufe your beft Endeavours, that no
'Ships of our Subjects, or of any other Nation, do frequent
'the faid Iflands during the Time aforefaid, except only for
'Wood and Water. But it is our Will and Pleafure, that
'you do not execute this our Order untill the *French* Go-
'vernor of *Martinico* fhall have received the like Directions
'from the *French* Court, and fhall jointly with you, put
'the fame in Execution without any Exception. And you are
'hereby farther ordered to tranfmit to us by the firft Op-
'portunity, a full Account of your Proceedings, as like-
'wife of thofe of the *French* in this Behalf; taking care by
'all Opportunities to inform yourfelf, whether our Subjects
'and thofe of the *French* King do punctually comply with
'the true Intent and Meaning of this Agreement, until
'fuch Time as the Right to the faid Iflands fhall be abfolute-
'ly determined as aforefaid. And for fo doing, this fhall
'be your Warrant. And fo we bid you farewell. Given
'at our Court at St. *James's*, the 30th Day of *November*
'1730. in the fourth Year of our Reign.'

By his Majefty's Command,

Hollis Newcaftle.

The *French* King's Letter to the Governor of *Martinico*,
December 26. 1730.

Monfieur le Marquis de Champigni, *les* Anglois *ont depuis
quelques Annes forme des pretenfions fur l'Ifle de St. Alouzie,
qui m'appartient,* &c.

'Monfieur *de Champigny*, The *Englifh* have for fome
'Years paft laid Pretenfions to the Ifland of St. *Lucia*, which
'belongs to me, and to which I have an inconteftable Right.
'The fame Pretenfions they have laid to the Iflands of St.
'*Vincent* and *Dominico*, which belong to the *Caribbeans*,
'Natives

'Natives of the Country according to the Treaty of the 31st
'of *March*, 1660, and in the Possession of which, it is my
'Intention to support them. I have nevertheless agreed with
'the Court of *England*, that until those Pretensions shall be
'determined, the said Islands shall be evacuated by both Na-
'tions, and this is to acquaint you, that it is my Pleasure, that
'you make it known, *&c*.'

St. Vincent's.

THIS Island being in the same Grant with that of St. *Lucia*, to his Grace the Duke of *Montagu*, was also included in the Commission of Mr. *Vring* as Governor of both Islands; and about 10 Days after his Arrival at St. *Lucia*, he appointed Mr. *Robert Egerton* to go to St. *Vincent*'s as Ambassador, as Mr. *Egerton* phrases it, to the *Indians* and *Negroes* at St. *Vincent*'s, in Order to prepare them for submitting to the Government of Great-Britain.

The *Indians* are the *Aborigines*, the first Inhabitants of this Island; the *Negroes* are the Descendants of a Ship loading of Slaves from *Africa*, who were thrown or ran themselves ashore here 60 or 70 Years ago, and by the Addition of other *Negroes*, either Fugitives from *European* Plantations, or coming voluntarily or involuntarily to this Island in the Course of so many Years, are by Births and otherwise, become a numerous People, and were some Thousands of Men, Women and Children, when Mr. *Vring* sent his Agent to persuade them to submit themselves and their Country to the *English* Proprietor. The same Submission he was to negotiate with the *Indians* who live in Coalition with the *Negroes*, under Chiefs of their own choosing: The *Indians* having particular Chiefs, and the *Negroes* the same with other principal *Indians* and *Negroes* to manage their Affairs under them. Their Government is Republican. They have a just Notion of Liberty, have enjoyed the Sweets of it many Years, are very jealous of losing it, and unanimous and resolute in its Defence, are besides very powerful in their Numbers, the *Indians* being computed to be near 8000, and the *Negroes* 5 or 6000 when Mr. *Egerton* set out on his Embassy. The Tenour of which must be, whatever Terms were made Use of to express it, that they should receive the *English* among them, permit them to take their Lands, plant and settle upon
them,

them, to build Forts and to introduce Soldiers and armed Men, to give them new Laws, and enforce their Obedience to them. The *Indians* and *Negroes* were very sensible of all this, and it had been aggravated to them by the *French* perpetually coming thither from *Martinico* and their other Islands, some of which are nearer to St. *Vincent's* than the *English Charibbees*. The *French* who had been among them, told them that the *English* were settling at St. *Lucia*, and intended to do the like in their Island, after which they would sell them or use them as Slaves: Tho' the *Indians* and *Negroes* might not give entire Credit to their malicious Suggestions, yet they were by no Means disposed to receive the *English* as their Masters and Proprietors of their Lands. Their Country was far from being uninhabited, tho' perhaps not a tenth Part of it was planted by either *Indians* or *Negroes*; however they did not understand that their having not as yet cultivated these Parts of their Land, deprived them of their Property in it, and Mr. *Egerton* was to promise Protection and Denization to all that submitted to them. If *Egerton* or any other Agent, before him, had purchased the Propriety of the Land of the *Indians* the first Owners, and the *Negroes* long Possessors of the same, there doubtless had been no Difficulty in admitting them to take Possession of them, and planting and fortifying them as they thought fit; but neither *Indians* nor *Negroes* could understand how their Right could be asserted by a *Grant* of a Sovereignty to which they did not know, or acknowledge themselves to be subject. This being the natural State of the Case, Mr. *Egerton* succeeded in his Embassy accordingly.

The Beginning of his Report marks the Distance of this Island from St. *Lucia, December* 26. ' Last Night we
' stretched over to St. *Vincent's*, steering *South South East*,
' and *South* by *East*. Between one and two in the Morning,
' we were up with the Land St. *Vincent*, and when Day, in
' a Bay to the *Northward*, we saw several Huts ashore in-
' habited by *Indians*, and three of them in a Canoe paddling
' off to us, we hoisted out our Boat. Mr. *Medley*, who
' came with me to assist me in my Embassy went in her, and
' brought the three *Indians* aboard the *Griffin* Sloop.

' One of the *Indians* spoke very good *French, a Sign of*
' *their being much frequented by, and familiarised with that*
' *Nation*. Medley *informed them that the* English were set-
' tled in the Island of St. *Lucia*, and that if they would come
' under and submit to their Government, they should be pro-
' tected and deemed and dealt with as *Englishmen*. They
' seemed to like it, and informed him that the *French* had
' been

The History of St. Vincent's.

'been with them, and as we understood it prepossessed them 'with a Notion that the *English* were their Enemies, and 'would make them Slaves.' The contrary of which *Egerton* and *Medley* endeavoured to instill into him and his Countrymen: The *Indians* told them, that one of their great Men lived in that Bay, and Mr. *Medley* going with him ashore, brought the great Man aboard, entertained him plentifully, and Mr. *Egerton* made him and near 20 *Indians* that attended him agreeable Presents. The Discourse was to the same Purpose as before, but not much relished by the great Man; the *Negroes* inhabited the Shore to the *North East*, their Hutts near the Water-side, but *Egerton* and *Medley* had no Opportunity to speak with them. To the Eastward of this Island they found a pleasant Prospect, a large Quantity of good Land, tho' hilly, and a great deal of it planted, and the rest fit to plant from the *South West* to the *North East*. In some Places along Shore are Heads of Rocks not very high, but there seemed to be good landing in several Parts, with pleasant Descents to the Water-side in fine green Patches. Much upper Land fit for Plantation lay unmanured. Mr. *Egerton* and Mr. *Medley* went ashore to the *Indian* Dwellings, but finding they were all drunk and in an ill Humour, they got from them as soon as they could. Notwithstanding their Shyness and Aversion to any Treaty of Submission to the *English*, Capt. *Vring* being forced to quit St. *Lucia*, proposed to his Council the removing to St. *Vincent*, and endeavour to bring the Inhabitants to accept the Duke of *Montagu* for their Proprietor and Governor, which could they have done, would doubtless have been for the publick Interest of *Great-Britain*, as well as the particular Interest of his Grace; but I do not see there was the least Shadow of Encouragement, from the Disposition and Situation of the *Indians* and *Negroes* for the Colony of St. *Lucia*, to make any Attempt towards a Settlement at St. *Vincent*'s. For besides the same Objections that were made to the Settlement at St. *Lucia*, were good against St. *Vincent*'s; a much stronger one offered to the Consideration of the *English*, and that was the Island's being already possessed, planted and peopled, and having a great Number of bold daring Inhabitants sufficient to defend it, without the Assistance of the *French*, which however they were sure of. The Council rejected Capt. *Vring*'s Proposal, but agreed that Mr. *Braithwaite*, Lieutenant Governor of St. *Lucia*, should go in the *Griffin* Sloop to St. *Vincent*'s, accompanied with such Persons of the Colony as he thought fit, and make another solemn and certain Trial of the Temper of the *Indians*, *Negroes* and *Mulattoes*, to come under

under the Government of the *English*, and Capt. *Vring*, with the reſt of the St. *Lucia* Colony, would wait at *Antego* for Mr. *Braithwaite's* Return. At *Antego* Capt. *Vring* received freſh Orders from *England*, brought by the *Adventure*, to retire with the Colony from thence and go to St. *Vincent*; but as the State of that Iſland was not ſo well known in *Europe* as the Leeward Iſlands, Col. *Hart*, General of theſe Iſlands, and Col. *Matthews*, Governor of *Antego*, gave their Opinion that Mr. *Vring* would do ill in following theſe new Orders, and offered to give it under their Hands; ſo he reſolved to wait for the Return of Mr. *Braithwaite*, whoſe Report of his Negotiation will give the beſt Light in this Matter. The *Indians* at firſt treated him roughly enough, but being ſoftened by ſome Preſents of Rum and other Things of ſmall Value, he went a ſecond Time aſhore, and was introduced to the General of the *Indians*. I will now uſe his own Words. ' Two principal Men of the *Indians*
' came to me from him, and thanked me for my Preſents,
' and asked Pardon for my former Treatment, *ſuppoſed to be*
' *to pleaſe a* Frenchman, who was then with the *Indian* Ge-
' neral : The two *Indians* had Orders to tell me, that if I
' pleaſed to go aſhore, they were to remain Hoſtages for my
' civil Uſage; I ſent them on Board the *Winchelſea*, and with
' Capt. *Watſon* went myſelf aſhore, and was well received :
' I found the Brother of the General of the *Negroes* with
' the *Indian* General. The *Negro* had with him 500 Blacks
' well armed with *Fuzees*, he told my Interpreter, *They were*
' *informed we came to force a Settlement, or they ſhould not have*
' *been ſo uncivil to us at our firſt landing, as to deny us* Wood
' and Water, *which they had never before denied any* Engliſh,
' *and we might now take what we wanted.* With ſome Diffi-
' culty I prevailed with the *Indian* and *Negro* Generals to go
' aboard the *Winchleſea*, Capt. *Orme* Commander, leaving
' Capt. *Watſon* a Hoſtage. Capt. *Orme* entertained them
' very handſomly, and preſented the *Indian* General with a
' fine *Fuzee* of his own, and the General of the *Negroes* with
' ſomething that was as agreeable to him. The Captain aſ-
' ſured them of the Friendſhip of the King of *England*, &c.
' The *Negro* General ſpoke excellent *French*, and gave An-
' ſwers with the *French* Compliments. I afterwards carried
' them on Board the Duke's Sloop, and having opened their
' Hearts with Wine, for they ſcorned to drink *Rum*, I
' thought it a good Time to tell them my Commiſſion, and
' what brought me upon that Coaſt. They told me it was
' well I had not mentioned it aſhore, for their Power could
' not have protected me. That the Thing was impoſſible,
the

The History of St. Vincent's.

'the *Dutch* had before attempted it, but were glad to re-
'tire. They likewise told me two *French* Sloops had the
'Day before we came been amongst them, gave them
'Arms and Ammunition, and assured them of the whole
'Force of *Martinico* for their Protection against us. They
'told them also, they had driven us from St. *Lucia,* and that
'now we were come to endeavour to force a Settlement
'there; and notwithstanding all our specious Pretensions
'when we had Power we should enslave them, but declared,
'they would trust no *Europeans:* That they owned them-
'selves under the Protection of the *French*, but would as
'soon oppose their settling among them, or any Act of
'Force from them as us, as they had lately given an Instance
'by killing several. And they farther told me, it was by very
'large Presents the *French* ever got in their Favour again.
'This being all I could get from them, I dismissed them with
'such Presents as were ordered for that Service, and a Dis-
'charge of Cannon, and received in Return as regular
'Volleys of small Shot as I ever heard.'

Thus ended the unfortunate Expedition for possessing and settling the Islands of St. *Lucia* and St. *Vincent*: The Preparations and Provisions for it at Home were great and well contrived. Mr. *Vring*'s Prosecution of it at St. *Lucia* diligent and wary; the Men of War attending it sufficient to have prevented the landing of *French* Troops in Sloops, and so gradually. The Governors of *Barbados* and the *Leeward* Islands were well enough disposed to give the Colony at St. *Lucia* their utmost Assistance, but the Instructions both of the Governors and the Commanders of the Men of War, seemed to be in Terms too general to admit of an offensive War, or indeed to run the Hazard of it for the Sake of the Island of St. *Lucia*; which President *Cox* of *Barbados* in his Letter to the *Chevalier Fouquiere*, Governor of *Martinico*, terms *insignificant* and *desert*. President *Cox* must by *insignificant* mean only as it was then without Settlement or Defence, but the Situation shews it to be an Island of very great Significance for the Security and Encrease of the *British* Trade and Navigation in those Parts, was it peopled, planted and fortified.

The same would be St. *Vincent*'s, but I will not determine whether that would be sufficient Reason to dispossess the *Indians*, the natural Proprietors of the Country; or if it were, whether it would be practicable to do it, the Inhabitants in Possession being so numerous, so warlike, and so well protected by their Allies the *French*.

Do-

DOMINICO

IS in the Governor of *Barbados's* Commiſſion; it lies in 50 Degrees, 30 Minutes, North Latitude, and is about 40 Miles long, and 40 Miles over, where it is broadeſt.

There are ſeveral high Mountains in the midſt of it, which encompaſs an inacceſſible Bottom; where from the Tops of certain Rocks may be ſeen an infinite Number of Reptiles of dreadful Bulk and Length.

Though the *Engliſh* pretend to be Lords of this Iſland, they never durſt attempt to make any Settlement upon it, the *Charibbeans* are ſo numerous; and we ſhould have treated of that barbarous Nation under this Head, if we had thought the Place belonged to the *Engliſh*: We have therefore ſpoken of them at large in the Hiſtory of St. *Chriſtophers*, the moſt conſiderable of the *Charibbee* Iſlands, at leaſt of thoſe in Poſſeſſion of the *Engliſh*, to which the Reader is referred. There's none of them ſo populous as *Dominico*. The Natives tell all Strangers, who come to viſit it, a ſtrange Tale of a vaſt monſtrous Serpent, that had its Abode in the before-mentioned Bottom. They affirmed, there was in the Head of it a very ſparkling Stone, like a Carbuncle, of ineſtimable Price; that the Monſter commonly veiled that rich Jewel with a thin moving Skin, like that of a Man's Eye-lid, and when it went to drink, or ſported itſelf in the deep Bottom, it fully diſcovered it, and the Rocks all about received a wonderful Luſtre from the Fire iſſuing out of that precious Gem.

This Story is ſo romantick, we wonder the *French* have not found out a St. *George* to kill this fiery Dragon; and no doubt they would have added abundance of fine Stories of the Amours of theſe gallant *Cannibals*.

They had formerly a King here, or rather Captain, who in all the Wars the Natives had with their Enemies on the Continent, led the Vanguard of their Army, and was diſtinguiſhed by a particular Mark that he had about him.

The *French* have frequented this Iſland more than the *Engliſh*, though the latter ſay it belongs to them; but whatever is the Matter, the *Charibbeans* have always loved the former better; perhaps there is more Agreement between
the

the Dispofition of the *French* and these *Barbarians*, than between the *English* and them. Hither retreated the *Charibbeans* when the *Europeans* drove them out of the other Iflands.

The *French* made Peace with all these Iflanders in the Year 1640. but we do not underftand the *English* ever gave themfelves the Trouble of treating with them, in which perhaps they have been neither juft nor prudent; for the *Dominicans* have conceived fuch an Averfion to them, that they hate them the moft of any Nation, except the *Ariovagues*. This was occafioned by the Treachery of our Countrymen, who formerly, under Pretence of Friendfhip, and treating them, got them aboard their Ships, and when their Veffels were full of them, carried away Men, Women, and Children into Captivity. It is dangerous for any *Englishmen* to be feen upon this Ifland; and feveral whom Storms have driven afhore, have paid feverely for the Treafon of their Countrymen.

There is one remarkable Paffage in the Hiftory of the *Charibbee* Iflands, written in *French*, and done into *English* by Mr. *Davyes* of *Kidwelly*; whereby we may perceive, what Right Princes and States have to the Countries they feize in *America*; and if his Affertion is true, the Title of the *English* to *Dominico* will not appear very plain: *It is a general Rule*, (fays the Author) *that a Country deftitute of Inhabitants, belongs to him who firft poffeffes himfelf of it; fo that neither the King of* France*'s Grant, nor yet that of the Company, does any thing more than fecure thefe Gentlemen againft the Pretenfions of fuch of their own Nation, as might oppofe their Defigns.*

Which Obfervation may be made ufe of in all Cafes, wherein the Nations of *Europe* contend for any part of *America*; and fince all Countries muft be deftitute of Inhabitants, to give any People a Right to poffefs them, fuch as are inhabited fhould be bought of the Poffeffor. It is likely the *Charibbeans* will never part with the Poffeffion of this Ifle; and it may as well be left out of the Governor of *Barbados*'s Commiffion, as the Kingdom of *Jerufalem* out of the King of *Spain*'s Titles.

About the Time that this Ifland was difcovered, a *Charibbean*, whom the *French* called Capt. *Baron*, lived in it, and from hence made Incurfions upon the *English* in the other Iflands: But the *Indians* were afraid of difturbing their powerful Neighbours, who might eafily extirpate them if they pleafed; and we find nothing more material relating
to

to this Island but what Captain *Vring* says in a Voyage to the *West-Indies* 10 Years after my first Impression; that his Ship stopped there to *wood* and *water*, where he found several *French* Families, and during *the Ship's Stay a large Periagua* of the native *Charibbean Indians* came on board; the Men were naked, but the Women had a small piece of Cloth to cover them, and that he entertained them with Drams, with which they were well pleased; and that having wooded and watered there, they departed, and I do not find that the *English* have made any other Use of this Island.

THE HISTORY OF THE Leeward-Iflands.

ANTEGO.

ANTEGO lies between *Barbados* and *Defirado*; in 16 Degrees, and 11 Minutes, North Latitude. It is about 20 Miles long, and as many broad, in feveral Places. The Accefs of it is dangerous for Shipping, by reafon of the Rocks that encompafs it.

There are few or no Springs of frefh Water in this Ifland; on which account it was for a long Time thought to be uninhabitable: But the Lord *Francis Willoughby*, about the Year 1663. procured a Grant of this Ifland of King *Charles* the Second; and about the Year 1666. planted a Colony here.

It is true, the *Englifh*, in Sir *Thomas Warner's* Time, difcovered this Ifland, and fome Families fettled upon it, 30 Years before the Propriety was granted to the Lord *Willoughby*. But fo uncertain was their Settlement, that the *French* intended to have poffeffed themfelves of this Ifland, after the *Spaniards* had driven them out of St. *Chriftopher's*, had they not afterwards recovered their Part of that Ifle.

This Governor *Warner*, we are told by the Voyager *Dampier*, had a Son by an *Indian* Woman, which he bred up after the *Englifh* Manner; he learned the *Englifh* Language alfo of his Mother, but being grown up and finding himfelf defpifed by his *Englifh* Kindred, he forfook his

Father's

Father's House, got away to St. *Lucia*, and there lived among the *Charibbee Indians*, his Relations by the Mother's Side, where conforming himself to their Customs, he became one of their Captains, and roved from one Island to another as they did.

Dampier was in these Parts in the Year 1674, and writes, ‘About this Time the *Charibbees* had done some Spoil on our *English* Plantations at *Antego*, and therefore Governor *Warner*'s Son by his Wife, took a Party of Men and went to suppress these *Indians*, and came to the Place where his Brother the *Indian Warner* lived; great seeming Joy there was at their Meeting; but how far it was real the Event shewed; for the *English Warner*, providing Plenty of Liquor, and inviting his Half-brother to be merry with him, in the midst of his Entertainment, ordered his Men upon a Signal given to murder him and all his *Indians*, which was accordingly performed. The Reason of this inhuman Action is diversely reported: Some say, that this *Indian Warner*, committed all the Spoil that was done to the *English*, and for that Reason his Brother killed him and his Men. Others that he was a great Friend to the *English*, and would not suffer his Men to hurt them, but did all that lay in his Power to draw them to an amicable Commerce, and that his Brother killed him, because he was ashamed to be related to an *Indian*. But be it how it will, he was called in Question for the Murder, and forced to come home and take his Trial in *England*. Such perfidious Doings as these, *continues Dampier*, besides the Baseness of them, are great Hindrances of our gaining Interest among the *Indians*.’

This Voyager writes largely of the Hurricane that happened here in 1681, and of the Signs that it gave of its coming, common with the *Caribbean* Hurricanes; but the most remarkable Accident in it, happened to a Ship of 120 Tons and ten Guns, commanded by Captain *Gadbury*, who had careened his Ship in *Musketo Cove*, in St. *John*'s Harbour but a little before; and being warned by the Planters of the approaching Hurricane, he moored his Ship as secure as he could with all his Cables and Anchors, besides some Cables which he made fast ashore to great Trees; and about Seven that Evening went ashore to a poor Planter's House about half a Mile from the Shore. By the Time he and his Men were arrived at the House, the Wind came on very fierce at North East, and veering about to North and North West, settled there, bringing with it very violent Rains. Thus it continued about four Hours, and then fell flat Calm, and the Rain ceased.

The History of Antego.

In this Calm he sent three or four of his Men down to the *Cove*, to see what Condition the Ship was in, and they found her driven ashore dry on the Sand, lying on one Side, with the Head of her Mast sticking into the Sand; after they had walked round her and viewed her a while, they returned again to the Captain to give him an Account of the Disaster, and made as much haste as they could, because the Wind began to blow hard at South West; and it blew so violently before they recovered the House, that the Boughs of the Trees whipt them sufficiently before they got thither, and it rained as hard as before; the little House could scarce shelter them from the wet, for there was little besides the Walls standing. Yet they staid till the next Morning, and then coming to the Ship, found her almost upright, but all the Goods that were in the Hold were washed out. Hurricanes since that have been frequent in this Island, but there was nothing in them so extraordinary as this.

This Island is divided into five Parishes, four of which are Towns; as St. *John's-Town* to the Northward; and *Falmouth*, *Parham*, and *Bridge-Town* to the Southward. The other Parish is St. *Peter's*.

St. *John's* Harbour is the most commodious. Besides which there are several other good Harbours; as *Five Island* Harbour; so called, from five little Islands to the Westward of the Isle. *Carlisle*-Bay, *English* Harbour, at the Bottom of which is *Falmouth* Town, defended by *Charles* Fort. Next to it is *Willoughby-Bay*. On the *East* Shore is *Bridge-Town*; then *Green-Bay*, off of which is *Green-Island*, then *Nonsuch* Harbour, a spacious Bay.

Of this Coast, on the North East Shore, are several little Islands, called *Polecat-Island*, and *Goat-Island*; and more to the Northward, *Guana-Island*, *Bird-Island*, *Long-Island*, *Maiden-Island*, and *Prickle-Pear-Island*.

The Forts are now in pretty good Repair; *Monk's-Hill* Fort is mounted with thirty Pieces of Ordnance, it has a Magazine with about 410 Musquets, and 800 Bayonets in good Order. The other Fort erected at the Entrance of St. *John's* Harbour, is mounted with 14 Pieces of Canon; there are seven other Batteries raised for the Defence of so many landing Places, in all mounted with 26 Guns.

The Capital of the Island is St. *John's-Town*, which consists of about 200 Houses, and the Number of Souls in all this Colony are computed to be about 8000 Whites, besides the Blacks, which were thrice the Number, but are not now 18000; the Number of Men enrolled in the Militia is now 1500.

The History of Antego.

The want of fresh Springs in this Isle is supplied by Cisterns, in which the Inhabitants catch Rain-water, and save it when they have done. There are some Springs, but no River in the whole Island.

Some Creeks are to be met with here, as two at the Bottom of *Five-Island* Harbour, and one called *Indian-Creek*, between *English* Harbour and *Willoughby-Bay*.

We cannot at most say very much of the *Leeward-Islands*, there having few memorable Events happened in them; and they being all of them separate Governments, under one Governour, or Captain General, the Succession of the Deputy-Governors, appointed by the Governors in Chief, is so uncertain, that we cannot pretend to put them in a true Order; and therefore shall only name them, as we have occasion to mention any Facts wherein they were concerned.

But before we proceed in our Account of *Antego*, we think it not improper to finish what we have to say of the Climate, Soil, Animals, Productions, and Trade.

The Situation of this Island shews it must be hot; and the Heats are indeed more excessive here than even in *Barbados*, though farther from the *Equator*; the Soil being more inclining to Sand, and the Ground not so well cleared of Woods, may be the occasion of it.

Turnados, or Hurricanes, used to be very frequent and troublesom here; and they are but too much so still, as the Inhabitants have experienced this last Year, to their great Loss.

The Animals that may be said to be most peculiar to this Island are first, among the Fish, the Dorado, or Sea-bream, of which Mr. *Davyes* of *Kidwelly*, in his Version of the History of the *Charibbee* Islands, says it is called Dorado, because in the Water the Head of it seems to be a green, gilt, clear Sky Colour. It takes a Pleasure in following the Ships, but swims so swift, that he must be very dextrous who shall take it, either with the Iron-hook, or Long staff with the Casting-net at the End of it. No Man can imagine Fish better furnished for Swimming than this; for it has the Fore-part of the Head sharp; the Back bristled with Prickles, reaching to the Tail, which is forked; two Fins on each side of the Head, and as many under the Belly, small Scales, and the whole Body of a Figure rather broad than big: All which give it a strange Command of the Waters. Some of them are about five Foot in Length. The Meat of this Fish is a little dry, yet no less pleasant to the Taste than Trout or Salmon, in the Opinion of many.

The History of Antego.

The Shark-Fish abounds in the *Charibbean* Seas, and is observed to be as common near *Antego*, as any of the other Islands; wherefore we shall speak of it in this Place. It is otherwise called the *Requiem*, and is a kind of Sea-Dog, or Sea-Wolf, the most devouring of all Fish, and the most greedy of Man's Flesh. He is dreaded very much by such as go a swimming; and that with very good Reason, for he lives by Prey, and commonly follows Ships, to feed on the Filth cast out of them into the Sea.

These Monsters seem to be of a yellowish Colour in the Water. Some of them are of an unmeasurable Length and Bigness, and such as are able to cut a Man in two at a Bite. Their Skin is rough, Files were formerly made of it, to polish Wood. Their Heads are flat, and the Opening of their Mouth is not just before the Snout, but under it; whence it comes, that to fasten on their Prey, they are forced to turn their Bellies almost upwards. Their Teeth are very sharp, and very broad, being jagged all about like a Saw. Some of them have three or four Ranks of these Teeth in each Jaw-bone. They lie within the Gums, but they make them sufficiently appear when there's Occasion. [Ib. p. 102.]

The Shark-fish is commonly attended by two or three Fishes, that go before him with a swift and regular Motion, and either halt, or advance more or less, as they perceive the *Requiem* does. Some call them Rambos and Pilgrims; and the *French* Mariners, the *Requiem*'s Pilots, because those small Fishes seem to be their Guides. They are not much above a Foot long, and of a proportionable Bigness. But their Scales are beautified with so many pretty lively Colours, that, says my Author, it might be said, *They are encompassed with Chains of Pearl, Coral, Emerald, and other precious Stones.*

The Meat of the *Requiem* is not good, at least when it is not very young. The Brains of the old ones are thought to be a Remedy for the Stone or Gravel. The *French* and *Portuguese* call this Fish *Requiem*, or Rest, because 'tis wont to appear in fair Weather. Its Liver, when boiled, yields a great Quantity of Oil, good for Lamps.

We might with as much Reason perhaps have treated of these Fishes, when we wrote of any other Part of the *Charibbee Islands*; but we have placed them here, for that we find others have done so before us.

The *Bucane* found on this Coast, is, like the *Indian* Inhabitants, greedy of Man's Flesh. It resembles a Pike in Figure; but it is seven or eight Foot long, and proportionably big It lives by Prey like the Shark, and furiously fastens on the Man it can reach in the Water. Whatever it feizes, it carries off; and if it did not, its Teeth are fo venomous, that the leaft touch of them becomes mortal, if fome fovereign Antidote be not immediately applied.

There's another Kind of *Bucanes*, by fome called Sea-Woodcocks, from the Figure of the Beak, which is fomewhat like a Woodcock's Bill, excepting that the upper Part is much longer than the lower; and that this Fifh moves both Jaws with like Facility. Some of them are fo big and long, that there are above four Foot between the Head and the Tail; and they are 12 Inches broad near the Head, meafuring fideways.

Ib. p. 106.

The Head is fomewhat like that of a Hog's, but illuminated by two large Eyes, which are extremely fhining. It has two Fins on the Sides, and under the Belly a great Plume, rifing higher and higher by degrees, like a Cock's Comb, reaching from the Head almoft to the Tail, which is divided into two Parts. Befides this long and folid Beak, it has two Sorts of Horns, hard, black, and about a Foot and a half in Length, which hang down under its Throat, and are particular to this kind of Fifh. Thefe it can eafily hide in a hollow Place under its Belly, which ferves them for a Sheath. It has no Scales, but is covered with a rough Skin, which on the Back is black, on the Sides greenifh, and under the Belly white. It is fafe, but not pleafant, to eat the Meat of it.

Another Fifh found on thefe Coafts, is called the *Sea-Urchin*, and well deferves that Name. It is as round as a Ball, and full of fharp Prickles. Some *Europeans* who have taken them, have dried them, and fent them as Prefents to the Curious for Rarities to hang in their Clofets.

Ib. p. 98.

The Sea Parrots, common in thefe Seas, are fcaled like *Carps*; but as to Colour, are as green as Parrots, whence they got their Name. They have beautiful and fparkling Eyes; the Balls clear as Cryftal, encompaffed by a Circle lugent, enclofed with another as green as an Emerald; of which Colour are the Scales of their Backs, and thofe under the Belly of a yellowifh green. They have no Teeth, but Jaws above and below of folid Bone, which is very ftrong, and of the fame Colour as their Scales, divided into little Compartments, very beautiful to the Eye. They live on Shell-fifh; and with thofe hard Jaw-bones they crufh, as between two Mill-ftones, Oifters, Mufcles, and other Shell-fifh, to get out the Meat. The Meat of them is excellent; and fome of them are fo big they weigh 20 Pound.

Ib. p. 101.

The *Efpadon*, or *Sword-Fifh*, is obferved to frequent the Seas off thefe Coafts. It has at the End of the Upper-Jaw

a defenfive

The History of Antego. 197

a defensive Weapon, about the Breadth of a great Cutlass, which has hard and sharp Teeth on both Sides. This Weapon in some of them is about five Foot in Length, about six Inches broad at the lower End; and *palisado'd*, to use my Author's Words, with 27 white and solid Teeth, in each Rank; to which the Bulk of their Bodies bears a Proportion.

The Head of these Sea-Monsters is flat, and hideous to behold, being of the Figure of a Heart. They have near their Eyes two Vents, at which they cast out the Water they swallow. They have no Scales, but a greyish Skin on the Back, and a white under the Belly, which is rough like a File. They have five Fins, two of each Side, two on the Back, and that which serves them for a Tail. Some call them *Saw-Fishes*, some *Emperors*, because there is an Hostility between them and the *Whale*, which they many times wound to Death.

These Fish, and several others mentioned in other Parts of this Treatise, are common also in other Parts of the *Charibbean* Seas. But the Inhabitants are apt to give them other more vulgar Names; and perhaps they will not be known to the meaner sort of them by these, no more than some of the Fowl which we find treated of by Mr. *Davyes* in the above-mentioned History: As the *Canides*, about the Bigness of a Pheasant, of a most beautiful Plumage. This Bird is more frequent at *Curassau*, and therefore we shall say no more of it here. *Ib. p.* 90.

The *Flammans* are great and beautiful Birds; but we should not have mentioned it in this Article, because it delights in Fenny-Places and Ponds, that are not common in this Island, which abounds in all Sorts of Fowl, wild and tame.

It has more plenty of Cattle, and other Beasts, especially Venison, than any other of our *Charibbee-Islands*; the Animals of which are much the same, as also their Productions.

Sugar, Indigo, Ginger, and Tobacco, were the chief Growths and Commodities of *Antego*, when it was first planted; but now Indigo and Ginger are very rarely cultivated there. The Sugar and Tobacco were both bad of the Sort; the former so black and coarse, that one would scarce have thought any Art could have refined it; and as if our *English* Sugar-bakers scorned to put such Dirt into their Coppers, it was generally shipped off for *Holland* and *Hamburgh*, being sold for 16 s. a Hundred, when other Muscovado Sugar fetched 18 or 19 s. a Hundred.

The Planters of *Antego* have since improved their Art, and as good Muscovado Sugar is now made there as in any of our

Sugar

Sugar Iſlands. They have alſo clayed ſome Sugar, which was not known to have been done in *Antego* 20 Years ago.

Tho' there is not much Tobacco planted in this Iſland, what there is, is not ſo bad as it was formerly, when it was ſold for no Uſes, but to make Snuff. The wild Cinnamon Tree is ſaid to grow in the *Lowlands*, or *Savanna* Woods in *Antego*.

Lowth *Vol* 2. p. 685.

We know of no other Productions here, which it has not in common with the other Iſlands; and having treated of them elſewhere, we ſhall proceed in our Hiſtory, which is indeed but ſhort: Our Memoirs for the *Leeward-Iſlands* did not, and perhaps the Facts themſelves would not enable us to enlarge upon it much more.

The Hiſtory of the *Charibbee-Iſlands*, tranſlated by Mr. *Davyes*, mentions, that *Antego* was inhabited by the *Engliſh* almoſt as ſoon as St. *Chriſtophers*; but we cannot get any other Proof of it, and it does not appear that it was planted till after it became the Lord *Willoughby*'s Propriety: It has ſince reverted to the Crown, and is made a Part of the general Government of the *Leeward-Iſlands*, and did not make any conſiderable Figure among them, till about the Year 1680. It has owed moſt of its flouriſhing Condition ſince to the Care and Intereſt of Colonel *Chriſtopher Codrington*; who removing from *Barbados*, where he had been Deputy-Governor, to *Antego*, planted here, and in other *Leeward-Iſlands*, and having a great Knowledge and Experience in the Sugar Plantations, and a great Stock to ſupport it, acquired as good an Eſtate as any Planter had got at *Barbados* or *Jamaica*. Others following his Example, *Antego* throve; and he making it the Seat of his Government, when he was Captain General, and General Governor of all the *Leeward-Iſlands*, this Iſle flouriſhed equally at leaſt with the reſt, and became wealthy and populous.

Among others who came with the Lord *Willoughby* from *Barbados*, was Major *Byam*, whoſe Family ſtill remains on the Place. He was one of the Commiſſioners appointed by that Lord, to treat with Sir *George Ayſcues*, about the Surrender of *Barbados* to the Parliament. His Son Colonel *Willoughby Byam*, was one of the moſt conſiderable Planters in the *Leeward-Iſlands*.

We have not been able to procure an exact Liſt of the Governors of theſe Iſlands, from their firſt Settlement, and much leſs of the particular Governors, or rather Deputy Governors of the particular Iſlands, and therefore ſhall not pretend to give any. Sir *Nathaniel Johnſon* was Governor of all them at the *Revolution*, and not conforming to the Government,

The History of Antego.

vernment, was removed: Upon which, Col. *Codrington* succeeded him in his Government, and Colonel *Rowland Williams* was made Deputy Governor of *Antego*.

In *March*, 1689. there happened a terrible Earthquake in the *Leeward-Islands*, *Monserrat*, *Nevis*, and *Antego*. In *Nevis* and *Montserrat*, no considerable Hurt was done, most of the Buildings being of Timber; but where there were Stone Buildings, they were generally thrown down, which fell very hard on *Antego*; most of the Houses, Buildings, Sugar-works, and Wind-mills being of Stone. Several Sloops felt the Violence of the Shake at Sea.

On the breaking out of the War between *England* and *France*, after the *Revolution*, the Inhabitants of *Antego*, as well as those of the other *Leeward-Islands*, desired Assistance of the Governor and Government of *Barbados*; and when Sir *Timothy Thornhill* had raised his Regiment, he sailed with them to *Antego*, where he arrived on the 5th of *August*, and received the unwelcome News, that the Fort at St. *Christopher's* was surrendered to the *French*, on *Monday* the 29th of *July*, 1689. upon Articles. Sir *Timothy* knowing his Strength to be too inconsiderable to attack an Island so well fortified as St. *Christophers*, and the Government of *Antego* solliciting him to continue with them till the Arrival of the *English* Fleet, which was daily expected; he agreed to their Proposals, and landed his Regiment there, which he quartered in the Town of *Falmouth*, about the same Bigness as that of St. *John's* Town.

After a Month's Continuance in this Island, Lieutenant-General *Codrington* sent three Sloops manned with 80 Men of Sir *Timothy's* Regiment, under the Command of Capt. *Edward Thorn*, from *Falmouth*, to fetch the *English*, with their Goods and Stocks, from the Island of *Anguilla*, where they had been miserably abused and destroyed by some *Irish*, whom the *French* had landed there for that Purpose.

Before Sir *Timothy Thornhill's* Arrival, and during his Stay at *Antego*, the *Indians* of the neighbouring Islands, who were in League with the *French*, landed several Times upon that Island, killing those Inhabitants who lived near the Sea, (to the Number of 10) and then making their Escape in their swift *Periagas*. These Pyratical Excursions were all the People of *Antego* suffered by the Enemy. General *Codrington* ordered several Sloops that were good Sailers to pursue them, but the *Periagas* were too nimble for them: To prevent the like Damage for the future, strict Guard was kept on the Coasts.

About

About the Middle of *September*, a *French* Privateer landed his Men at *Five-Iflands*, near *Antego*, and took off some Negroes. As he was going away with his Booty, he met with two *Englifh* Sloops, one of which, after some Refiftance, he took; the other making her Efcape, came in, and gave an Account of the Action: Upon which Sir *Timothy* fent out two Sloops manned, with a Company of Grenadiers, under the Command of Captain *Walter Hamilton*, who next Day brought her in with her Prize. On board the Privateer were 30 *French* and fix *Irifh* Men; the latter were tried by a Court Marfhal, and four of them hanged. In *November* Sir *Timothy Thornhill* removed to *Nevis*, at the Defire of the People of that Ifland.

The Inhabitants of *Antego* raifed 300 Men, who were commanded by Col. *Hewetfon*; and landing on an Ifland belonging to the *French*, called *Mary-Galanta*, they beat the Inhabitants into the Woods, burnt their Town, nailed down their Guns, demolifhed their Fort, and returned back to *Antego* with the Plunder of the Ifland.

Lieutenant General *Codrington* (for as yet he had not received his Commiffion of Captain General) remained at *Antego*, while Sir *Timothy Thornhill* went from *Nevis* againft St. *Bartholomews* and St. *Martins:* While he was upon the latter, Monfieur *Decaffe* came down with 700 Men from St. *Chriftopher*'s, to the Affiftance of the *French*; the Major General (for fuch was Sir *Timothy*'s Commiffion) difpatched away a Sloop, with an Exprefs to the Lieutenant-General at *Antego*, to acquaint him with his Condition, and defire him to fend fome Ships to his Affiftance. Accordingly General *Codrington* ordered Col. *Hewetfon*, with about 200 Men from *Antego*, aboard three Sloops, under Convoy of three Men of War, one of 40 Guns, and two of 20, fitted out for that Purpofe, to fail to St. *Martins*, where he arrived the 30th of *January*. The *French* Ships who were at Anchor near the Ifland, attacked the *Englifh* Frigats; and after four Hours Difpute, with little or no Damage on Col. *Hewetfon*'s Side, they bore away.

In the following Year, General *Codrington* received a Commiffion from King *William* and Queen *Mary*, to be Captain General, and Commander in Chief of all their *Leeward Charibbee-Iflands*; and Admiral *Wright* arriving from *England* with a ftrong Squadron of Men of War, all the *Leeward-Iflands* raifed Forces for the Recovery of St. *Chriftopher*'s; among which that of *Antego* furnifhed a whole Regiment of 400 Men, who were commanded by the Deputy-Governor, Col. *Rowland Williams*, whofe Son, Mr. *Samuel Williams*,

Williams, was some Time after a Gentleman Commoner of *Christ-Church* in *Oxford*, and a great Lover of the Studies of Humanity; in which he made a good Proficiency in a short Time. The Author owes this Justice to the Memory of his Friend, and the Reader will therefore excuse this Digression.

Nor must we omit doing Justice to *Christopher Codrington*, jun. Esq; the Governor's Son; who distinguished himself in the same illustrious Academy, by his Genius and Judgment in Poetry and Eloquence; wherein he performed several Things with equal Merit and Success: He was a Gentleman Commoner of *All-Souls College*; and when King *William* paid his Visit of Kindness, as his Majesty was graciously pleased to call it, to the University of *Oxford*, Mr. *Codrington* expressed the publick Thanks of that learned Body, in a very elegant Oration. He was a Patron of the famous Mr. *Creech*, who dedicated his *Latin* Edition of *Lucretius* to him. When this Gentleman left the Study of the Arts, he took to the Practice of Arms, signalized himself at the Siege of *Namure*, was made a Colonel of his Majesty's Foot Guards: And more might be said of his Actions and Worth, only we remember we are writing the History of Countries, and not of Persons; but the high Post he afterwards enjoyed in this Island, where he is now an Inhabitant, will excuse us for what we might otherwise be thought to digress in.

The Success of the Expedition of St. *Christopher's*, and other Enterprizes in the *Leeward-Islands*, will be related in the proper Places, where those Actions were performed; only we must correct an Error in the *Gazette*, which on the 18th of *September*, 1690, told us, *Eight hundred Men were raised at* Antego, *for the Expedition against the* French *at St.* Christopher's; whereas, by an exact and faithful Account of it, written by Mr. *Thomas Spencer*, Jun. Secretary to the Honourable Sir. *Tim. Thornhill*, Muster-Master to his Regiment, and Deputy Commissary, we find, the *Antego* Regiment consisted of 400 only; and indeed if this Island could raise 800 Men, and spare them for such an Enterprize, we may very well compute the Number of Souls at this Time to be 14 or 15000, which none pretend there ever was in *Antego*. This Island sent their Quota to all the Forces that were raised against the *French* in the last War.

In the Year 1696, the *Hastings* Frigat was here, and sailed for *London*, Convoy to a small Fleet of 11 Ships, which were above eleven Weeks in their Voyage.

The History of Antego.

General *Codrington* dying in the Year 1698, his Son *Chriſtopher Codrington*, Eſq; of whom we have ſpoken already, was appointed Captain General, and Governor in Chief of the *Leeward-Iſlands*; and in Purſuance of this Commiſſion, he removed from *England* to this Iſland, where he moſtly reſided during his Government, being one of the greateſt Proprietors in it.

In *January*, 1699, Admiral *Bembow* arrived at the *Leeward-Iſlands*, having Col. *Collingwood*'s Regiment on Board, Part of which was quartered in *Antego*, and Part in the other Iſlands. The Governor having received ſome more Forces from *England*, to make up the Loſs of theſe, moſt of them having died in the Iſlands, reſolved, on the breaking out of the preſent War, to attack the *French* at *Guardaloup*.

The Merchants of *Antego* had equip'd ſeveral Privateers; which, in Conjunction with ſome Privateers of the other Iſlands, and a Squadron of Men of War, made a Strength at Sea too mighty for the *French*. He raiſed a Regiment of Soldiers in *Antego*, of which Colonel *Byam* was Colonel; and the other *Leeward-Iſlands* furniſhed Men alſo for this Enterprize.

On the 7th of *March*, 1702, the General came off the Iſland of *Guardaloup*, with the Land and Sea Forces. The *French* ſhot at them from the Shore, but did no other Miſchief than killing one Man, and wounding a Boy aboard the Commodore. The Fleet ſtood off and on till the 10th, waiting the coming up of the *Maidſtone* Man of War, and ſome other ſmall Ships, which lay off of *Mary Galanta*. When they arrived, the Governor came to an Anchor, to the North-Weſt of the Iſland, and ordered a Party of Men to land, and deſtroy ſome ſcattering Plantations on the Coaſt, which they did.

On the 12th, Col. *Byam* with his Regiment, and a Detachment of 200 Men of Col. *Whetham*'s Regiment, landed by Break of Day, at a Place called *Les Petits Habitans*; where they met with ſome Oppoſition, but ſoon obliged the Enemy to retire.

About 9 in the Morning, Col. *Wetham*, with about 800 Men more, landed in a Bay to the Northward of a Town called the *Bayliffe*; where he met with a vigorous Reſiſtance from all the Enemy's Forces, poſted in a very good and advantageous Breaſt-Work. Theſe plyed the *Engliſh* continually with great and ſmall Shot, while they were landing, particularly in a more furious Manner at the Flag; yet notwithſtanding all their Fire, the *Engliſh* bravely marched up to their Entrenchments, with their Muſkets ſhouldered, with-

out

The History of Antego.

out firing one Shot, till they could come up to lay the Muzzles of their Pieces upon the Top of the Enemies Breast-Works. The *English* had 3 Captains killed at the Head of their Grenadiers, before they could make themselves Masters of the first Breast-Work. Col. *Willis* signalized himself in this Action, by his great Bravery; and all the Officers and Soldiers behaved themselves on this Occasion, like *Englishmen* fighting with *French*, we mean, like Men born to conquer.

By Noon they had mastered all the Enemies Out-Works. In an Hour after, the Town called the *Bayliffe* was taken; as also the *Jacobines* Church, which the *French* had fortified, and ten Pieces of Cannon.

About 2 in the Afternoon, they took a Platform, where the *French* had planted three Pieces of Cannon, and a Redoubt with one.

At Night, 400 Men, and the Regiment of Marines, attacked the *Jacobine* Plantation, and the Breast-Work along the *Jacobine*'s River; which was the strongest and most advantageous of any the *French* had in the *West-Indies*, yet they quitted it after the *English* had fired but two Volleys of Small-Shot at them.

The next Day the General marched without any other Opposition, than that of the Enemies Cannon playing upon him, and possessed himself of the great Town, called *Basseterre*, where the *English* stayed about a Week, sending out Parties to burn and destroy the Inhabitants Houses, Works, Sugar Canes, and Provisions. They laid Siege to the Fort and Castle of *Basseterre*, and advanced within Pistol-Shot of the Fort, and within Musket-Shot of the Castle, having 16 Pieces of Cannon mounted for Battery: Into these Forts, and another called the *Dadaw Peck*, the Inhabitants retired with their Families and best Effects, leaving all the open Country at the Mercy of the *English*, who had been taught by the *French* to shew little enough on such Occasions.

But all these Successes were rendered fruitless by some unhappy Differences among the Commanders, and something must be imputed to the vigorous Defence of the *French*, and the Sickness of the *English* Soldiers, which obliged the General to reimbark his Men, after they were so near making a Conquest of this Island.

In the Year 1704, Sir *William Matthews* was made Governor of the *Leeward-Islands*; who dying soon after, Col. *Park* of *Virginia*, who brought the Queen the glorious News of the Victory the Duke of *Marlborough* obtained over the *French* at *Hochstet*, and was his *Aid de Camp*, had

the

the Government of thefe Iflands conferred on him. He arrived at *Antego* the 14th of *July*, 1706, and made this the Place of his Refidence: *Nevis* had been deftroyed by the *French* fome Months before. St. *Chriftopher*'s had alfo fuffered extremely by an Invafion, but *Antego* was not attempted by them.

About the Time that Colonel *Park* arrived, an *Irifh* Veffel from *Belfaft*, having on Board nine Men and fix Boys, was attacked in Sight of this Ifle by an open Sloop with 50 *French* Men aboard, and made fo good a Defence, that 40 of the Enemy were wounded, and the Sloop was taken and brought into *Antego*.

In the following Year, 1707, there happened the moft terrible Hurricane or Turnado, that ever was known in thefe Iflands. It damaged them all, but *Nevis* and *Antego* more than the reft. It blew down Houfes, Works, Trees, tore up Plants, Sugar Canes, and made almoft a general Deftruction; which fell the heavier, becaufe the Inhabitants had had fo many Loffes by the Enemy in their Trade otherwife, that they could ill undergo it: But this Blow coming from Providence, ought to be born more patiently by them all.

We will here infert a Lift of the Officers, Civil and Military, as they ftood at that Time.

Governor and Captain General of all the *Leeward-Iflands*,
Daniel Park, Efq;

Lieutenant Governor of *Antego*, John Yeamans, Efq;

Edward Byam, Efq; Prefident of the Council.

Col. *John Hamilton*,	
Col. *Rowland Williams*,	
Col. *William Thomas*,	
Col. *George Gambell*,	Counfellors.
Col. *Lucy Blackmore*,	
Major *Henry Lyons*,	
Major *Thomas Morris*,	

We have feen another Lift of the Counfellors, wherein the following were added.

Chriftopher Codrington, Efq;
Charles Mathew, Efq;
William Codrington, Efq;
Barry Tankard, Efq;
Lawrence Crab, Efq;

Chief

The History of Antego.

Chief Justice, *Samuel Watkins*, Esq;
Secretary, —— *Rhodes*, Esq;
Judge of the Admiralty, *George Gambell*, Esq;
Commissioner of the Customs, *Edward Pirry*, Esq;
Collector of the Customs, *Richard Buckeridge*, Esq;
Colonel of the Regiment of Foot, Col. *Edward Byam*.
Colonel of the Regiment of Horse, Col. *Lucy Blackmore*.
Ministers of the 3 Parishes supplied with Incumbents, Mr. *James Field*, Mr. *John Buxton*, Mr. *John Powel*.
Commissary of the Bishop of *London* for all the *Leeward Islands*, the Rev. Mr. *James Field*.

Sir *William Matthews* late Captain General and Commander in Chief of the *Leeward-Islands*, was a Gentleman of so courteous and equal a Temper, of so much Honour and Prudence, that Col. *Park* his Successor in that Station, came to his Government with great Disadvantage in Character, *Park* being imperious, arrogant, rash and vicious, and soon giving Proofs in every Kind of these ill Qualities, he became odious to the most sober and most interested Persons of this Island, where he made his Residence.

I avoid entering into the Detail of his Life and Actions, before he had this Government; the Subject is not very agreeable, such as it is, it may be found in the *Political State*, for *April* 1710, *p.* 242. 'Tis true, the Writer says afterwards his Account is *erroneous*, and I must needs own great Caution should be used by such as have Occasion to take any Thing out of his Collection; however, in this Case some of the Facts he mentions relating to Col. *Park*, have come to my Knowledge by other Means, and I can perceive by his referring this Matter entirely to the Board of Trade, and the Queen and Council, what Influence he was under when he mortified himself so far, as to own what he found was full of Error. I shall therefore avoid following him, and have Recourse to other Memoirs for Governor *Park's* unhappy Administration and *tragical End*.

The Government of *Antego* before Col. *Park* arrived, was in the Hands of the Lieutenant Governor and Council, who were

John Yeamans, Esq, President.
John Hamilton, Esq;
Edward Byam, Esq;
Henry Lyon, Esq;
George Gambell, Esq;
William Codrington, Esq;

To these were added,

Thomas Morris, Esq;
Richard Oliver, Esq;
Herbert Pember, Esq;

The

The latter came with him to *Antego*, and was made Attorney General, which gave not so much Offence as his making a private Man of the Regiment of Foot stationed in the *Leeward-Islands*, Provost Marshal, a Place of as great Profit and Trust as any in the Government, and that without giving Security as the Law of *Antego* requires. But one can hardly believe what the Inhabitants alledged against him on this Occasion, in the Beginning of his Administration, that this *Provost Marshal executed all his Commands without Reserve*, and that Col. Park *frequently declared, he would suffer no* Provost Marshal *to act, who would not at all Times impannel such Juries as he should direct*. This being an Article of Complaint against him, he answered by insisting on the Quality of a *Foot Soldier* as a *Gentleman*, and that as he never directed any Thing but what was Law, his so saying could not be exceptionable. I shall say no more of the Articles against him, nor his Answer to them, but refer to his History written by Mr. *George French*, who hazarded his Life in Defence of him, when his Adversaries proceeded to Extremities, but shall content myself with observing, that his Behaviour seems to be very rash and dangerous, in setting the greatest Men in the Island against him, almost as soon as he came among them there, as Col. *Christopher Codrington*, who had the greatest landed Interest, and Mr. *Edward Chester*, who had the greatest trading Interest in the Island. Col. *Codrington*, is that *Gentleman Commoner* of *Oxford*, who composed and pronounced an elegant and spirited *Latin* Oration to our Deliverer King *William* at his coming to that University. He is the Gentleman to whom *Creech* dedicated his learned Edition of *Lucretius* in an Epistle, wherein this Gentleman's Merit has all the Justice done it that could be expected from so masterly a Pen. This is the Gentleman who gained so much Glory by his Valour at the Siege of *Namur*, that his Majesty rewarded him on the Spot with a principal Command in his Guards, at the same Time and in the same Post with the Lord *Haversham*, and the late Lord *Windsor*. Col. *Codrington* is the same Gentleman who wrote these gallant and harmonious Verses to Sir *Samuel Garth* before his *Dispensary*, of which I cannot forbear repeating this *Triplet*.

I read thee ever with a Lover's Eye,
Thou hast no Faults or I no Faults can spye,
Thou art all Beauty, or all Blindness I.

This Col. *Codrington* is the Gentleman, whose Father was Captain General and Commander in Chief of the *Leeward Islands*, who was himself Chief Governor and Commander of the said Islands; in which and *Barbados*, he had an Interest valued at 10000 *l. per Ann.* This is the Gentleman who by his Will left above 30000 *l.* for promoting Religion and Learning: In fine, this is the Gentleman whom Col. *Park* took the Liberty to vilify and to treat with so much Insolence, that, as his own Historian confesses, he retired to *Barbados* to avoid the like ill Treatment by the Abuse of *Park's* delegated Power; tho' the said *Park* said himself, that Col. *Codrington* intended to make him either one of his Executors, or give him a good Legacy. As to Mr. *Edward Chester*, he was the *Royal African* Company's Factor, and the most considerable Merchant in *Antego*.

It happened that this Mr. *Chester* resenting some provoking Words of one *Sawyer* of *Virginia*, about shipping some Goods, flung a Tankard of Punch, or Punch Tankard at him, which bruised his Head a little, and the Man dying of a Disease soon after, Governor *Park* endeavoured to have *Chester* found guilty of Murder, but the Coroner's Inquest brought in a Verdict of *natural Death*, for which the Deputy Marshal that impannelled the Inquest fell under his Displeasure: *Sawyer* was a *Virginian*, Col. *Park's* Countryman, which no Doubt was not forgotten, in the Care he took to have his Death so curiously sifted; but if the *Antego* Author who wrote against *French's* History is not mistaken, the Governor afterwards took a more pleasant Kind of Revenge, *Pag.* 6. in this Question, *What* English *Subject besides Col. Park, that had a larger or more distant Command, durst have carried away a Gentleman's Wife, and that before the Face of her Husband, and kept her as his Mistress.* The Answer to this being only a flat *Negative*, is not strong enough to dispel any Suspicions that are raised by strong circumstantial Evidences: However, I shall have done with it, it having more Relation to Col. *Park's* Person than his Office, in which chiefly consisted his Relation to the Island of *Antego*; or this particular Article of *Chester's* Wife, might be not a little confirmed by a general Charge, in the Answer to his History written by *French*, wherein the Answerer, speaking of his Commerce with the *Antego* Mens Wives and Daughters, says, *He took Care to people the Island with them.* Now there never was such Charge brought against a Wise and virtuous Governor, since Government was established; and therefore I must think Col. *Park's* Historian does not tread on sure Ground, where he says in his Answer to the *Antego* Writer

Pag.

Pag. 37. *The* Lords of Trade *gave him the Character of the beſt Governor the Queen had, or perhaps ſhould have during her Reign.* But as I am under no Temptation to compliment or vilify the Character of Col. *Park,* I ſhall repreſent Things in their natural Light only.

At his firſt coming the Aſſembly voted him 1000 *l.* a Year for Houſe Rent, but the good Intelligence between him and them laſted not long, and it is very plain, that his affecting rather a Sovereignty than a Superiority over them, was the chief Occaſion of the Diſguſt his Government ſoon gave them: He had not been in it much above a Year, before the chief Inhabitants began to cabal againſt him, and prepare Articles of Impeachment to be tranſmitted to *England.* Whoever reads his own Hiſtorian's Liſt of Names of thoſe that entered into this Party, and knows any Thing of *Antego,* will be convinced, that Men of their Character and Intereſt, would not hazard the Peace and Proſperity of their Country by a Contention with their Governor, unleſs they had been driven into it by the Violence and Injuſtice of his Adminiſtration, not ſufficient however to juſtify Violence and Injuſtice in themſelves. They drew up above thirty Articles to be delivered to her Majeſty and Council, with a Petition thereto ſigned by fourſcore of the principal Inhabitants of *Antego,* as Governor *Park*'s Hiſtorian confeſſes, and that the *Complainants* were the major Part of the Iſlanders. I refer to his Hiſtorian *French,* as well for their Articles as for his Anſwers, and ſhall abridge what ſeems to me the moſt material. 'That he gave out ſoon after his coming to his Go-' vernment, *Let him do what he would, he ſhould be protected* ' *and ſupported by the Lord* Godolphin, Lord Treaſurer, *and* ' *the Dutcheſs of* Marlborough.' This would be very fooliſh as well as very impudent, were it true; for beſides that the Dutcheſs of *Marlborough* was then not ſo high in the Queen's Favour, as when ſhe lived with her at *Sion* and *Berkeley* Houſe, in a Strangeneſs with her Royal Brother and Siſter King *William* and Queen *Mary,* it was not decent for a Governor and Captain General to declare himſelf to be under the Protection of a Court Lady; but Raſhneſs often produces the moſt unguarded Expreſſions.

That by *Methods unheard of, and abhorred in Law,* the Words of the Petitioners, with whom joined alſo their Correſpondents the Sugar Merchants in *London,* he endeavoured to have taken away the Iſland of *Barbuda* from Col. *Codrington* firſt, and afterwards from his Heir the late Sir *William Codrington,* then one of the beſt intereſted Planters in our Sugar Iſlands; tho' Col. *Chriſtopher Codrington*'s Father and
Uncle

The History of Antego.   209

Uncle had been in Poffeffion of it near 30 Years, by feveral Patents, and been at a vaft Expence in peopling and planting it. In Excufe for this Extravagance he urged, that it was in his Inftructions fo to do: Whoever gave him thofe Inftructions muft do it without fufficiently acquainting themfelves with Col. *Codrington*'s Right to that Propriety, tho' the very Poffeffion and maintaining it at fo great Charge, was a Right that Reafon and Juftice fufficiently guarded againft any Claim by an Infertion, *with other Charibbee Iflands*, in the Governor's Commiffion. To claim any Place as one's own becaufe we have called it ours, feems too whimfical; unlefs one has been at the Expence and Trouble of poffeffing it. However, the *Codringtons* Grants muft needs have been known by thofe that would have brought their Right into Litigation, and then their Care for the Intereft of the Crown got the better of their Care for the Property of the Subject; a *Dilemma* that very often happens, when Perfons imagine they greaten or ftrengthen their private Interefts, by affecting a Zeal for thofe of the Publick; the late Sir *William Codrington* being peremptorily required by Governor *Park* to make out his Title to the Poffeffion of his Family, unqueftioned and apparent as it was to all the People in every one of our Sugar Colonies among the *Charibbees*.

The Governor thought it proper to make the Council liable to as much Cenfure as himfelf, and Col. *Codrington* refufing to give any Account to him of his Title, which was fo well known to all the World, the Governor confulted his Council, who advifed him to proceed no farther in the Matter, as he himfelf owns, by publifhing the Anfwer of that Council to this and other Articles againft him. But his Acrimony againft Sir *William Codrington* was fo exceffive, that he forbore not to treat him at feveral Times with the unhandfom Terms of *Wretch*, *infamous*, *villainous*, and *impudent*. Be *Codrington* what he will as to his Morals, *Park*'s certainly were not purer; and this Language to a Gentleman of that Diftinction and Fortune fhews the Tendency of the Man to Paffion and Infolence, very ill Requifites in the Formation of the *beft Governor* in the *Britifh* World, as his Hiftorian fays he was thought, and faid to be by his Superiors at Home. French p. 354, &c. al.

The Complainants fay he altered the Method of electing Members of the *Affembly*, with a View to keep out *Edward Perry*, Efq; Surveyor of the Cuftoms. This was fworn by *Edward Kerby*, Efq; Secretary of the Ifland.

He entered the Houfe of Mr. *Edward Chefter* beforementioned with an armed Force, and feized feveral Gentlemen

men there met for good Fellowſhip, on a Suſpicion that they might be conferring about their Proceedings againſt him: Theſe he ſent to Jail, tho' ſome of the principal Men of the Iſland. He ſent his *Provoſt Marſhal* to the Houſe of *Barry Tankard,* Eſq; 8 Miles from St. *John*'s: The Marſhal's Officers and Followers entered in the Night Time with Files of Musketeers, to apprehend the ſaid Mr. *Tankard,* and hawl him to Priſon for a *Breach* of good Behaviour, as himſelf adjudged it. The Ruffians broke into Mrs. *Tankard's* Bed-chamber Sword in Hand, which ſo frightened her, that it endangered her Life.

The Complainants ſay farther, he called no Aſſembly in eleven Months, and forbad the Lieutenant Governor to call one at a Time when the *French* threatened an Invaſion. He frequently inſinuated in Diſcourſe, that it was uſual for Governors in other Colonies, to be preſented with vaſt Sums to paſs beneficial Laws. That it was become dangerous for the Inhabitants of the Town of St. *John*'s to go abroad about their Buſineſs, for Fear of being inſulted: That he was wont to ſtroll about the Streets in the Night privately armed, liſtening and *Eves dropping,* being jealous of the People's Diſſatisfaction with his Management.

I have not touched on a Quarter Part of the Articles againſt him, the Articles and Anſwers being at large in his Hiſtory: But as his Anſwers turn chiefly on the Extent of his Prerogative, which he ſanctifies with the Name of the *Queen's,* and the Conſent of the Council, as much under his Influence, as Perſons generally are under that of thoſe on whom they depend, I ſhall not enter into the *Pro* or the *Con* of this Conteſt.

The Complainants have doubtleſs exaggerated the Facts in the Articles againſt him, but it was not likely that a wiſe and equal Adminiſtration would have produced ſuch a general Averſion to his Government, that in a few Months Time they were ſo exaſperated againſt him as to attempt his Life; for as he rode in the Highway near Mr. *Otto Byar*'s Plantation, he was ſhot at by *Sandy* a Negro of that Planter's, out of a Piece of Canes, and grievouſly, though not mortally wounded, and himſelf charged Mr. *Jacob Morgan* one of the Aſſembly and others, as he ſays, of that Body, with hiring a Soldier to ſhoot him. *Barry Tankard,* Eſq; a Friend of Mr. *Codrington,* ſent him a Challenge to fight him for ſome inſufferable Provocation, but his Dignity forbad him to deſcend to ſuch Inequality, and to match his Excellency with the Rank of a Gentleman only. Theſe and many ſuch Inſtances of the Peril his Conduct had brought him into, he defied,

thinking

thinking himself secure from all Violence, by the Commission he brought from *England*. He was *armed*, says his Historian, *with the Queen's Commission, and cloathed with the Royal Authority*; which had he used for the Good of her Subjects ought to have made his Person sacred, and in such Case it would have been so thought; and tho' he behaved otherwise, as is well known to all that knew the Truth of the Fact, yet the killing him is less justifiable than the Measures he took to deserve it, as was too often said by the most considerable Men in the Country, who had no Concern in the Action wherein he was killed. But as no Man can deserve Death who is not so adjudged by Law, the *tragical End* of Col. *Park* remains among those Events that were necessary in the Intention, but criminal in the Execution. The getting him removed by all fair and legal Means was necessary, but the killing him was criminal, tho' attended with such Circumstances, that the Queen thought fit to prevent the spilling of more Blood, by a Pardon for those that spilt this.

'Tis impossible to bring a tenth Part of the Matter contained in three or four Volumes, published on one Side and the other, on the Subject of Col. *Park's* Conduct, within the Compass of my Work. Therefore I must only observe, that his Administration was so intolerable to the richer and greater Part of the Inhabitants of *Antego*, that in little more than a Year, they resolved to send an Agent to *England*, on Purpose to set forth their Grievances in the said *Park's* Government and procure Redress. They also wrote to *Richard Cary*, Esq; Merchant in *London*, their stated Agent, to be assisting to their Sollicitor Mr. *William Nevin*, and to enable *Nevin* to make the Voyage and negotiate this Affair, a large Sum of Money was raised to defray his Expence, by the Party who signed the Articles and Petition against Governor *Park*, who knew well what was doing; and yet, even by the Account of his own Historian, abated nothing of his arbitrary overbearing Behaviour towards the Assembly and the Party that adhered to them, which he knew to be the most substantial Interest in the Island; and as if his Authority was really originally *royal*, always interposed his *Delegation* as the Sovereignty itself. He encroached on the most valuable Branches of the Assembly's Privileges, and awed that Body the Representatives of the People with the Army, such as it was then in *Antego*, which probably was the Occasion that his Historian tells us, Mr. *Perry* Surveyor of the Customs remembered the Governor of *Charles* the Ist's Government, and the Catastrophe that followed it.

The History of Antego.

The Indiscretion of Col. *Park*, as well as the Impetuosity of his natural Temper, are apparent in his exposing the Honour of the Crown, by setting himself up against the whole Island he was sent to govern; not to flatter his Pride and Vanity, by clothing himself on all Occasions with the *Authority Royal:* His Historian is so frank as to name the chief Persons which his haughty and irregular Conduct provoked to be on their Guard against it, by inciting the main Body of the People in Defence of their Liberties and Privileges, as

    Col. *Christopher Codrington*, late General.
      Barry Tankard, Esq;
      William Thomas, Esq;
      Edward Perry, Esq;
Rev. Mr. *James Field*.
    Samuel Watkins, Esq; Chief Justice.
    Nathaniel Crump, Esq; Speaker of the Assembly.
Dr. *Daniel Mackennen*.

The whole Assembly, one only excepted.

William Hamilton Esq;
John Gamble, Esq;
Capt. *John Pigott*.
Capt. *John Painter*.
Thomas Williams, Esq;
Aril. Cochran, Esq;
Mr. *Jacob Morgan*.
Mr. *Edw. Chester*, Merchant.
Mr. *William Glanville*.
Francis Carlisle, Esq;

Mr. *John Tomlinson*.
Mr. *Isaac Horsefoot*.
Mr. *Samuel Philips*.
Mr. *John Frye*.
Mr. *John Kerr*.
Mr. *William Pearn*.
Mr. *John Elliot*.
Mr. *James Baxter*.
Mr. *Samuel Frye*.

Principal Planters and Merchants.

John Otto Byar, Esq;
Thomas Kerby, Esq;
Mr. *Thomas Trant*.
Mr. *John Burton*.
Mr. *William Osborn*.
Mr. *Baptist Looby*.
Mr. *John King*.
Mr. *Joseph Adams*.
Mr. *Richard Smith*.
Mr. *Bartholomew Sanderson*.
Mr. *Richard Sheerwood*.

Mr. *Charles Dunbar*.
Mr. *William Fenton*.
Mr. *Mark Monk*.
Mr. *John Englefield*.
Mr. *Samuel Meares*.
Mr. *Ob. Bradshaw*.
Mr. *John Codner*.
Mr. *Edward Horne*.
Mr. *William Grantham*.
Mr. *Ambrose York*.

These and a Hundred more such Names the Historian prints, to be revenged of them for their opposing Colonel *Park*, in whose Defence he fought stoutly and received some Wounds in the Action, which thro' all his Book he calls a *Rebellion*. If that Writer had had the Judgment, Experience and Talent of *Jeremiah Dummer*, Esq; late Agent for *New-England*, he would have forborn much of his Bitterness both in Thought and Expression. Mr. *Dummer* in a Discourse, addressed to the Lord *Carteret* then Secretary of State, speaking of ill Governors says, *I suppose with Respect to Mr.* Park's *Fury and Fate, other* Governors, *have fallen Victims on the Spot, not to the Fury of a* Faction *or a* Rabble, *but to the Resentment of the whole Body of the People rising as one Man to revenge their Wrongs.* Mr. *Dummer*'s Discourse of ill Governor's will be better relished in our *American* Colonies than at Home, and being of very great Importance to all Persons therein concerned, I shall give it *Verbatim*.

'It is a general received Opinion, that the People in the
'Plantation have an Interest distinct from that of the Crown,
'when it is supposed at the same Time, that the Interest of
'the *Governors, they being the King's Representatives*, is one
'with the Crown, and from these Premisses it is concluded,
'there can't be too much Power given to the Governors, or
'too little to the People: Whereas, with humble Submission,
'I conceive this to be a very wrong Judgment, and that
'the Reverse of it is true. The only Interest of the People
'is to thrive and flourish in their Trade, which is the true
'Interest of the Crown and Nation, because they reap the
'Profit of it. When on the other Hand, the View that
'Governors generally have is private Gain, which being too
'often acquired by discouraging and oppressing *Trade*, it is
'not only an Interest distinct from that of the *Crown*, but
'extremely prejudicial to it. The proper Nursery for that
'Plant is a free Government, where the Laws are sacred,
'Property secure, and Justice not only impartially but expeditiously administered.' *This will serve at* Home *as well as Abroad*.

'That *Governors* are apt to abuse their Power, and grow
'rich by Oppression, Experience shews us. We have seen
'not many Years since, some Governors seized by their in-
'jured People and sent to *England*; others have fallen Victims, *&c. as before*. Indeed it can hardly be expected but
'these Corruptions must happen, when one considers that few
'*Governors* will cross the Seas for a Government, whose Circumstances are not a little streight at Home, and that they
'know

'know by how light and uncertain a Tenure they hold their
'Commissions, from whence they wisely conclude, that no
'Time is to be lost, &c.' And as Lust of Power often puts
them upon Acts of Oppression as well as that of Lucre, the
latter seems to be the Rock on which Governor *Park* split.

Col. *Park* in his Answer to the Articles against him, and
his Historian every where in his Apology for him, screen all
his Actions with the *Royal Prerogative*, of which they suppose him to have been in as full Possession as Queen *Anne* herself. This is the grand Air he gave himself on all Occasions; to oppose him by Complaint was *Sedition*, and by Resistance *Rebellion*; for which his Historian would have had the best Men in the Country hanged; and Mr. *Douglas*, who came to this Government after him, when he found the Inhabitants preferred Mr. *Hamilton* to him in their Affection and Esteem, talked of *Rebellion*, *Rebels* and the Gallows, as Col. *Park* and his Adherents had done, a Way of thinking and speaking equally insolent and impolitick. The *Authority Royal*, and the *Prerogative* of the *Crown*, are guarded in *France* from all Approach, as was the *Sanctum Sanctorum* of the *Jews*; but so great is that despotick Government's Care of their Colonies, on which their Commerce so much depends, that they will not suffer their Governors to insult and oppress their Fellow Subjects, under the Pretence of the *Prerogative of the Crown* or the *Royal Authority*, as will plainly appear by the following History.

About the Time of Mr. *Park*'s being made General of the *Leeward Islands*, Monsieur *Philippeaux*, a Minister himself, or nearly related to a great Minister in *France*, was General of *Martinique* and the *French* Sugar Islands; and being in Disgrace at Home, so highly resented his being sent to the *Charibbees*, tho' as General, that he took it for a Sort of Banishment, and formed a Project to cast off the Dependency of these Islands on the Crown of *France*, and to erect a Republican Government on the Plan of that of *Venice*, the worst he could have pitched upon. He had prepared the chief Inhabitants for it; but his Death, which happened not without some Suspicion of foul Play from a Physician sent from *France*, prevented it: This Project was said to be found among his Papers, and my Author pretends to have seen the Heads of it. He had not been dead long before the Inhabitants of *Martinique* broke out into open Rebellion, seized on their *General* and *Intendant*, and by Force sent them both to *France*. See the rest in the Words of my Author, 'Yet
'the Court thought proper to overlook it with as good a
'Countenance as it could, for tho' it declared them *Rebels*,
'and

The History of Antego.

'and obtained Orders from the *British* Court and others not
'to relieve or assist them,' yet their Punishment was winked
at. The killing Mr. *Park* was a horrid Crime, but 'tis plain
he tempted his Fate, by daring the Power of a Number of
desperate Men, who were determined to do by him as the
French had done by the Governor of *Martinique*, and send
him Home by Force since he would not go without it. But
the Endeavour of Mr. *Douglas* and others to have the Chief
Justice *Watkins* and Dr. *Mackennen*, a Member of the
Council, hanged for *Rebellion* against Mr. *Park*, shews they
were to learn Justice, Politicks, and Moderation, even of
their Neighbours the *French*.

This cannot justly be termed a Digression, since it has so
near Relation to the Tragedy that was acted at *Antego* in the
Death of the Governor.

I find all his Exorbitancies were much extenuated by his
great Pretences to Zeal for his delegated *Prerogative*, and refusing the *Assembly* their old Custom, to have all their Acts
signed by their Speaker after the Governor had signed them,
which Mr. *Park* called a *Negative* Voice; and tho' this
seeming to be affected only, to disguise his own obstinate
imperious Humour, with a Pretence of his Concern for the
Rights of the Crown; yet he and his Creatures from thence
took Occasion to call all that thought otherwise *factious*, and
even *rebellious*.

Having mentioned the Persons that composed the *Council*,
I shall here insert the then Assembly of *Antego*.

Rich. Oliver, Esq; Speaker.   John Brett, Esq;
William Grear, Esq;   Jeremiah Blizard, Esq;
John Paynter, Esq;   William Thomas, Esq;
William Peara, Esq;   Edward Perry, Esq;
William Byam, Esq;   Francis Rogers, Esq;
Baptist Looby, Esq;   Samuel Philips, Esq;

There could not be many Alterations in this List afterwards,
considering that during Col. *Park*'s short Government, he for
near a Year of it had no Assembly; the Truth is, that the Un-
easiness the People were in on Account of their Disgust with
his Government, hindered a due Application to the Dispatch
of all publick Affairs; Jealousie, and Disturbances were every
where prevalent, the Country Party were perpetually complaining of the Governor's browbeating, insulting and menacing; the latter conceived Hopes by the Dilatoriness of Mr.
Nevin's Negotiation, and gave out that the Governor would be
too hard in *England* for all his Opponents; but they were mistaken,

taken, for Mr. *Nevin* returned, and brought the Queen's Letter, directing that the Witnesses should be examined, to prove the Allegations in the Articles against Mr. *Park*, and his Answers to them. The Complainants not doubting of their making good their Complaints by Evidence, rejoiced extremely at *Nevin*'s Success in *England*, and the People grew so mutinous upon it, that the Governor did not think fit to appear at the examining his Witnesses, for Fear of the Effects of their Animosity and Resentment: Yet he in nothing condescended to bring them into a better Temper, the *Royal Prerogative* of which he was so chary, that he would not suffer the Assembly to breath upon it, was in all his Speeches and Writings, and justified in his Sense of it the worst Things laid to his Charge. There was no Exception to the Behaviour of the Complainants as to Loyalty and Affection to her Majesty's Person and Government, except what relates to the rash and imperious Behaviour of this Governor, and her Majesty's re-calling him is a Proof of her disapproving it. The Depositions concerning the Articles and Answers were sworn before *Edward Byam*, Esq; one of the Council, and *Nathaniel Crump*, Esq; Speaker of the Assembly of *Antego*, and were ordered to be sealed with the *Broad Seal* of the Island, and transmitted to *England* at the same Time; but some Difficulty arising on the Governor's Part, he refused to seal the Affidavits to the Complainants Articles, alledging his own were not ready, occasioned by the Delay of the Justices that took the Affidavits. So the Complainants sealed them with great Care and Formality with another Seal, and gave them to their Agent to carry to *England*. But the Governor missing the Opportunity of returning thither by the Ship that then offered for his Conveyance, and they mistrusting he intended not to remove as he was directed, it made them desperate, and they looked upon him as a Governor *per Force*, and not regularly possess'd of her Majesty's Commission, by his keeping it, and staying upon the Island after his being re-called, or to use his own Historian's Phrase, *directed to come by the first Man of War bound from* Antego *to* England. This Management could not but alarm and irritate the Inhabitants, and in that Disposition, they doubtless put the worst Construction on every Thing he did or said. He was sensible of the Danger he was in, but the Pride of his Heart could not submit to healing and pacifick Counsels. A small Portion of Discretion and Moderation would have induced him to have temporized with the People's Impatience, and have treated their Distemper rather with Lenitives than Inflammatories; so he continued in the
delightful

The History of Antego. 217

delightful Exercife of Acts of Power, till the Inhabitants looking upon him as a Kind of *Ufurper*, by ftaying with them after he was ordered Home, they refolved to compel him to obey thefe Orders, or to quit the Government.

He diffolved the Affembly, but they continued fitting, in an Opinion that the Governor being re-called, his Proceedings were invalid, and it was their Duty to take Care of the Safety and Peace of the Ifland, when it was threatened with a *French* Invafion; upon which the Governor thought convenient to authorife their Meeting by a new Summons, or fummoning a new Affembly of the fame Perfons, who came together with the fame Difpofitions and Refentments as when he parted with them; and he knew very well that they would infift on their Speaker's figning all Bills which they fhould pafs, as had been the Cuftom, to fhew their Affent to them, as the Governor's figning fignified the Affent of himfelf and Council, or at leaft his own Affent including alfo the Council. This he called the *negative Voice*, the *Authority Royal*, the Prop and Pillar of all *French* Laws, *the Rights of the* Britifh *Crown*, which the Affembly had no more Inclination than they had Power to infringe. Hoping to make a Merit of his gratifying his Luft of Power by a Zeal for that of the Sovereign, he not only declared his Refolution to perfift in refufing them that Privilege, but alfo that of appointing their own Clerk. He and his Council being met in the *Court-Houfe* at St. *John's*, the Affembly went thither attended by a Number of *Townfmen* and *Planters*, which his Hiftorian terms an *unruly Mob*, and fome high Words paft between them; upon which one *Worthington* a Lieutenant of the regular Troops then in Garrifon there, haftened to the *Guard-Houfe*, and fetched a Party of Grenadiers led by a Serjeant which he brought to the *Court-Houfe*. The *Affembly* terrified by the Appearance of the Soldiers, left the Place and adjourned themfelves. This Innovation could not but ftill more provoke and even enrage the People, who faw their Laws and Liberties were trampled under Foot, and the Army, as they phrafed it, were made Ufe of to awe the *Reprefentatives*. The Members of the *Affembly* in this Alarm gave Notice to their Electors of the Peril they thought themfelves in. Let me now copy Governor *Park's* Hiftorian. ' That Night
' and the next Day was fpent in fummoning the Inhabitants
' in Col. *Edward Byam's* Name, to come armed to Town
' the *Thurfday* following to protect their Reprefentatives;
' but whether Col. *Byam* iffued out fuch a Summons or no,
' he can beft tell; but 'tis certain he was acquainted there-
' with, and never contradicted it; and when they were af-
' fembled

'sembled together at St. *John's*, never once offered to un-
'deceive them, or defired them to difperfe, though it is very
'probable that he whofe Name had Influence enough to
'bring them together, might eafily perfuade them to de-
'part.' *Park's* Hiftorian charges Colonel *Chriftopher Codrington* with being the firft that fpirited the People againft him, and he owns Mr. *Codrington* to be poffeffed of a greater Intereft in the Ifland than 100 others of the moft leading Planters; and here he infinuates at leaft a Charge againft Colonel *Byam*, the moft difcreet and popular Man in the *Leeward-Iflands*, with countenanceing of the Infurrections which proved fo fatal to his Party. Let the Reader judge whether it is likely that this Governor fhould be the *beft* in all the *Britifh* Colonies, whofe Government provoked two Men of the beft Heads and beft Fortunes in the *Britifh America*, to come to fuch Extremity againft him. I am not ignorant that fome Years after Mr. *Codrington's* good Head was difordered, but I have not heard it fo was when Mr. *Park* came firft to *Antego*. The Hiftorian owns the *Affembly* gave out *that the General's Life was not at all aimed at, that they defigned to take him Prifoner, and fend him off the Ifland.*

On *Thurfday* the 7th of *December*, 1710. early in the Morning, three or four hundred Men appeared armed in the Town of St. *John's*, where Colonel *Park* had been making Provifion for Refiftance if they offered to attack him. He got all the Soldiers that were in the Town to his Houfe under Captain *Nevin*, Lieutenant *Worthington*, and Enfign *Lynden*. He had alfo there with them Mr. *Pember*, whom he had made Attorney-General; Mr. *Galewood*, whom he had made a Juftice of Peace, Mr. *Ayon*, whom he had made Provoft Marfhal, both obnoxious to the Inhabitants: Mr. *French*, Author of this Hiftory, who could not think much to hazard his Reputation for him after he hazarded his Life; Mr. *Rofengrave* and three others, whom Mr. *French* calls Gentlemen. He fent Mr. *Ayon* with a Proclamation to be read to the People to difperfe immediately, it was eafy to forefee that fuch a Proclamation was *Wafte-Paper*. *Ayon* was not very civilly ufed by them, they let him know their Strength, then about 500 Men well armed, that they did not value the Governor's Army, and were refolved to feize him, and fend him Prifoner off the Ifland. However to prevent the Effufion of Blood, they fent their Demands to him by *Nathaniel Crump*, Efq; Speaker of the Affembly, and *George Gamble*, Efq; one of the Council, *That he fhould difcharge his Guards and quit the Government.* His Anfwer
was,

was, *That neither Threats nor Death should make him do it*; his alledging that the Queen had *intrusted* him with it was very unseasonable, because that Trust was vacated by his being ordered Home; and though while he stayed on the Island for want of Opportunity to ship himself for *England*, he was still lawful Governor and in very great Trust; yet he did not seem to be in that Situation after he had neglected an Opportunity that offered for him to obey the Orders he had to return. He bid the Assembly sit at *Parham*, seven Miles from St. *John's*, if they were afraid of the Soldiers, and said he would pass what Laws they made for the publick Good, as also that he would dismiss his Soldiers if six of the principal Inhabitants would remain with him as Hostages. Mr. *Gamble*, and Mr. *Crump*, offered to be two of the Hostages, and said they would endeavour to fetch four more, for the Governor's Proposal seemed to them preferable to Hostilities, as it did to many of the People there in Arms, who laid them down; but the much greater Part suspected the Execution of any Agreement that should be made with him, and fearing Delay might tempt more to drop off from them, they resolved to secure the Governor's Person, and marched in two Parties to his House, the one commanded by Captain *John Piggot*, the other by Captain *John Painter*, a rich Planter and a Member of the Assembly, and in these two Divisions were all the Assembly Men as the Governor's Historian acknowledges. The Governor had posted an Out-guard at *Church-hill*, an Eminence that commanded his House, but his Guard deserted that Fort, and the House was surrounded by *Piggot's* and *Painter's* Men; the Serjeant and Soldiers posted at *Church-hill* were of Captain *Rokesby's* Company, in Colonel *Jones's* Regiment; Captain *Rokesby* refused to head them himself as the Governor commanded, and forbid his Men at their Peril to fire or oppose the Country, of which Party Colonel *Jones* had declared himself on several solemn Occasions. Both of the Divisions making a brisk Fire on the House, those within it returned it as briskly, but Numbers soon prevailing, the Assailants broke into the House, and *French* writes that Captain *Piggot* fell by the Hands of the Governor; but it was the general Report and Belief of the Inhabitants, that *Ayon* the Provost Marshal came behind him and shot him in the Back. Governor *Park* received a Shot in his Thigh which disabled him, and he fell into the Hands of the enraged and armed People; many of his Soldiers were killed, as were several of his Followers and Creatures. It is not agreed by the Writers on both Sides, which it was that fired first, neither Side
is

is willing to take it on themselves, because nothing could excuse the firing on either Side but *Self-defence*. *French*'s Account of the barbarous Treatment of the Governor's wounded and bleeding Body, and which is too full of Horror to be related or read without Emotion far from being agreeable, we leave the Relation as we found it. He adds, every Scoundrel *insulted him in the Agonies of Death*, meaning *Andrew Murray*, Esq; *Francis Carlisle*, Esq; Captain *Painter*, and Mr. *Tomlinson*, who are said to have spoken to him, and if insolently when in the Agony, it was Scoundrel enough to do it. He said to them according to Mr. *French*, Gentlemen, *If you have no Sense of Honour left, pray have some of Honesty*. After his Body had lain a little Time stript in the Street, and as some write *dismembred* by Persons who thought their Beds had been injured by him, he was removed into the House of Mr. *John Wright*, where he expired. Two or three Days after his Body was buried in the Church, but the People demolished the Regent's Pew where he was used to sit; notwithstanding *John Yeamans*, Esq; Lieutenant Governor, Colonel *John Hamilton*, and Colonel *Thomas Morris*, Members of the Council, earnestly dissuaded them from it. Of the regular Forces which Colonel *Park* prevailed upon to assist him against *the Country*, as the Complainants called themselves, Ensign *Lyndon*, and 13 or 14 Soldiers were killed. Captain *Newel*, Lieutenant *Worthington* and six and twenty Soldiers wounded. *Ayon* was shot through the Body by Mr. *Cochran*, but recovered, as did Mr. *George French* the Historian, who received several Wounds, one of them in the Mouth; Captain *Boileau* was killed, Mr. *Pember*, Mr. *Rosengrave*, Mr. *Galeward*, Mr. *Bonnin*, were only beaten and bruised. On the Assembly's Side was killed Captain *Piggot*, Mr. *Young*, Mr. *Turton*, and Mr. *Rayne*, about 30 wounded.

It had been very extraordinary if the Clergy of *Antego*, as few as they are, had not taken Part on one Side or other in the Division between the Governor and the Country, in that especially at a Time when so excellent an Example was set them by the Reverend Dr. *Sacheverell* in *England*. Mr. *James Field*, Minister of the Capital of St. *John*'s-*Town*, sided with the Country, and Mr. *Baxter*, Minister of *Parham*, with the Party of Governor *Park*; but I do not find that either of the *Parties* governed themselves by their Lectures.

On the Death of Colonel *Parks*, the Government of the *Leeward-Islands* fell of course to *Walter Hamilton*, Esq; Lieutenant Governor of *Nevis*, who was also at that Time
Lieutenant

The History of Antego.

Lieutenant General of the *Leeward-Iflands*; Mr. *French's* Account of him is too partial to be trufted to, occafioned by Mr. *Hamilton's* good Opinion of the Intention of the Party that oppofed Mr. *Park's* Male-Adminiftration, till the Caftatrophe defiled it with Blood; and as he did not impute the Crime to a premeditated Defign formed againft the Sovereign Authority, or the Life of its Delegate, but only to remove the faid Delegate from a Government which he had abufed, and from which he was recalled, he did not look upon the Gentlemen in the Country Intereft as Enemies to the Queen's Government, or that of her Generals and Government in thofe Iflands behaving prudently and in another manner than did Colonel *Park*; fo Mr. *Hamilton* refolved to carry himfelf towards the Affembly Men and their Friends, as the Characters and Intereft in the Country deferved. *John Yeamans*, Efq; Lieutenant Governor of *Antego*, who had their chief Government there on the late Chief Governor's Death, had pitched upon four Perfons who had been devoted to him to go to *Nevis*, and invite the Lieutenant-General, now Captain General of the *Leeward-Iflands*, to come to *Antego*, and affume the general Command; but believing thofe Men would not be very welcome to Mr. *Hamilton*, he changed his Mind, and fent four Gentlemen in the Affembly or Country Intereft on that Errand. Their Deputation was received very gracioufly by Mr. *Hamilton*, who complimented and careffed them, and accompanying them back to *Antego*, took up his Refidence at the Houfe of Dr. *Mackennen*, who was afterwards fent Prifoner to *England* to be tried for the Death of Colonel *Park*. Mr. *Hamilton*, as Chief Governor of the *Leeward-Iflands*, called a General Council, confifting of Deputies from all the Iflands in his Government, to examine into that Matter; the Deputies for *Antego* were four Gentlemen in the Country Intereft, and thofe for the other Iflands in much the fame Way of thinking, which did not anfwer the Expectations of the oppofite Party. Nay, the Council of that Ifland drew up an Addrefs, which Mr. *French* complains *palliated* and excufed the Proceedings againft *Park*; which not contenting the Adherents of the Deceafed, they figned another, for which they met privately, and told the Queen, *their Lives are in fo much Danger, that they dare not truft the Acquaintance of their Meeting even with their Friends.*

Thefe Addreffers were,

Col. *John Hamilton*, and he refufed to fign the Council's Addrefs.

Walter Hamilton, Efq; Captain General.

Jofeph

Joseph French, Esq;
W. Matthews, Esq;
Richard Buckeridge, Survey-
  or of the Customs.
Mr. John Brett.
Mr. Isaac Royal.
Mr. John Wickham.
Mr. Jeremiah Blizard.
Mr. John Roe.
Mr. Cæsar Rodeway.
Mr. John Hadder.
Mr. Thomas Turner.

The Address of the Council and this secret one shews, how the People here endeavoured to keep up Division and Animosity even after the chief Cause of both were removed; and as this perpetual jangling must needs be perpetually troublesom to them, so it cannot be pleasant to Readers to meet with nothing but Affirmatives and Negatives took from one to the other, to the Hinderance of all other Business for several Years successively. I shall therefore conclude with observing, that Mr. *Walter Hamilton* was succeeded in this Government by *Walter Douglas*, Esq; who suspended *Hamilton* from the Exercise of all Offices. For it was then thought by many he would have proceeded to this Suspension soon after his Arrival; but he found the Party of *Hamilton* supported by that against the late Governor's so powerful, that he was at first afraid of venturing on so bold a Measure; but being at last provoked to it by some Disregard which he imagined Mr. *Hamilton* had shewn to himself, took Heart and turned *Hamilton* out of all Offices, the Effects of which he felt soon after in an Opposition and Prosecution that ended only in the End of his Government also. For Mr. *Hamilton* going to *England* to manage his Affairs, Mr. *Douglas* turned his Activity against the Gentlemen who had complained against Colonel *Park*, and issued out his Warrant to seize the late Chief Justice *Watkins* and Dr. *Mackennen*, notwithstanding the Proclamation of Pardon sent from *England* for former Crimes, under Pretence of another intended Rebellion; but *Watkins* and *Mackennen* got safe to *England*, as did also *Edward Kirby*, Esq; where they were apprehended and committed to Prison on the Informations that were sent against them; but the Proceedings in *England* were not so rash as those in *Antego*. Let their Crime be what it would, the Proclamation before-mentioned having cleared them of it, and they pleading it accordingly, were discharged without a Trial; but *Douglas*'s Warrant to seize them, which drove them off the Island, was one of the Articles the Inhabitants signed and sent home against him.

Walter Douglas, Esq; Chief Governor. 1712.

Mr. Henry Smith tried and cleared. Ensign *Henry Smith* lay in *Newgate* several Months for Rebellion, as it was termed, against Colonel *Park*, which in

Law

The History of Antego.

Law Phrase was making War on the Queen, but whatever it was, the Jury brought him in *Not Guilty*; and this Jury was as creditable a one as could be pitched upon by the Sheriffs of *London* and *Middlesex*.

Sir *Thomas Halton*.
Alexander Pitfield, Esq;
Joseph Ivry, Esq;
Richard Brown, Esq;
Matthew Holworthy, Esq;
Daniel Dolins, Esq;

Alexander Ward, Esq;
William Northey, Esq;
John Elwick, Esq;
Henry Emmet, Esq;
John Furness, Gent.
James Williamson, Gent.

Ensign Smith's Jury.

In the mean Time Governor *Douglas* became almost as ungrateful to the Country Party, as Governor *Park* had been, as appeared by the Behaviour of the Inhabitants on the Rejoicing-Day for the *Utrecht Peace*. Mr. *French* writes, *there was a Riot little short of a Rebellion* at St. *John's* by *Francis Carlisle*, Esq; Mr. *Jacob Morgan*, Mr. *John Gunthorp*, Mr. *Andrew Murray*, a noted Merchant and others, who being at a Tavern, went to the Governor's House in a Body of 50 or 60 Persons, calling out for the *Pope's Head Boys*. These *Pope's Head Boys* were a certain Division of the Island, inhabited by a boisterous Sort of People who delighted in Bustle and Broils. General *Douglas* had now been insulted by them notwithstanding his Guards, had they not been dissuaded from it by Mr. *William Hamilton*, a leading Man of the Assembly, whom the General ordered to be taken up for Colonel *Park's* Business, and was lately bailed.

Complaints were sent Home against General *Douglas*, and the late General *Hamilton*, who seconded the Endeavours of the Complainants for his Removal; at last prevailed so far as to be restored to his Government of the *Leeward-Islands*. *John Yeamans*, Esq; was removed from being Lieutenant Governor of this Island, and Colonel *Edward Byam* put in his Place. The General being returned to *Antego* in 1715. removed Mr. *Yeamans* from the Bench as Chief Justice, and put in his Place *John Gamble*, Esq; who says Mr. *French* could scarce write his Name. He gave *Daniel Mackennen*, Esq; a Seat at the Council-Board, and did the same by *Nathaniel Crump*, Esq; late Speaker of the Assembly. The Court and Assembly past an Act for 1000 *l.* a Year for the General's House Rent. Governors of Colonies being forbidden by their *Instructions* to receive any Presents or Gratuities, stated Perquisites being not so deemed, and House Rent of 1000 *l.* a Year, where there is not a House to be had worth a 20th Part of the Money,

Walter Hamilton restored.

is,

is, it seems no Gratuity nor Present. Before Col. *Douglas* was removed from this Government, he received Orders from the Queen to see the Act of the 6th of her Reign, concerning the Coin, put in Execution thro' all the *Leeward Islands*, where indeed every Thing ran into Confusion as might well happen under such Changes of Governors.

The Currency of Species according to that Act is mentioned in the Article of *Jamaica*, so I shall here only touch on the Deviation from that Law, by the Practice of the *Antego* Money Jobbers. The Currency here had been according to the Act, till about the Time of Mr. *Hamilton*'s being turned out of this Government, for the greater Pieces of Money but *Bits* and half *Bits*, Sevenpenny Halfpenny Pieces, past so as they had always done in marketing and retailing; but in the *Leeward Islands* a very great Disregard to the Law of Queen *Anne* happened in 1715, which will come more properly in the Article of St. *Christopher*'s.

There was no Grievance more complained of by the Traders of *Antego*, than the Difficulty of recovering Debts, by Want of good Laws for it, and a due Execution, as appears by the following Memorial or Petition of the Merchants, Factors, &c.

Deficiency in the Law for Debts.

Your Petitioners *being disabled by the ill Compliance of Debtors to answer their Correspondents Expectations at Home, in making their Returns according to their respective Promises and Compacts, are, without any Fault of their own, not only suspected of Injustice, but wounded in their Reputations, upon Supposition, that they are paid here by the Persons who deal with them, and that your Petitioners detain their Effects, or that at least, they are highly to be blamed for not prosecuting their Debtors at Law, and by that Means enable themselves to make better and more punctual Remittances, and are deprived of making or improving their own private Fortunes, the Proceedings at Law being so very* dilatory, &c. For which Reasons they pray, that an Act may pass for the more speedy Recovery of Debts, and the Petition was signed by

James Nisbet.
Robert Joyce.
Barth. Sanderson.
John Barnes.
Edward Chester.
Math. Bermingham.
Christopher Stoodly.
John Roach.
Samuel Procter.

John Barbotan.
John Bourke.
Andrew Murray.
John Sweetenham.
John Combes.
Charles Dunbar.
Thomas Trant.
John Brett.
William Glanville.

Edward

Edward Chester, Junior.	Hope for Berdall.
Joseph Adams.	Jacob Thibou.
Richard Sherwood.	Thomas Doleman.
John Rose.	Pat. West.

Names which argue a flourishing Trade at that Time in *Antego*, and I thought the inserting of this Petition the more proper, because the Complaint in it may serve for the other Sugar Colonies as well as this. And indeed the general Practice of the Law there, as well as at Home, is so tedious and expensive, that it is one of the greatest Discouragements Trade lies under, and the Redress of this Grievance is too much in the Hands of those that occasion it.

The Attorney General, *Thomas Bretton*, Esq; had in 1711, drawn up an Act for settling Law Courts, which would in a good Measure have remedied this Evil. The Council and Assembly were so pleased with it, that they ordered him 100 *Pistoles*, passing there for 28 s. each, for drawing it, but they altered it so much for the worse in the passing it, that a new Act to regulate the Practice, especially in *Executions* became necessary.

Mr. *Hamilton* continued in this Government till the Year 1721, when *John Hart*, Esq; late Governor of *Maryland*, was preferred to the Government of the *Leeward* Islands. By the Speeches to the Council and Assembly here, we find a good Agreement between them all, which had been a rare Thing in this Island. The Assembly made a Provision for his Support, which seemed to be more than competent, by his Sense of it, and the Thanks he gave them. [margin: 1721. John Hart, Esq; Governor.]

This Gentleman received Captain *Vring* and his disappointed Colony of St. *Lucia* with great Humanity, and took particular Care of them and the Duke of *Montagu's* Effects which they brought from thence, for which good Work he had the ready Assistance of Col. *Matthews* Lieutenant Governor.

There being now no Contest between the Governors and the governed here, there is nothing remarkable in the Events, and the People were at Leisure to follow Trade and planting, in which they were now only disturbed by Hurricanes, very frequent and terrible in these Islands. To this Governor succeeded the Lord *Londonderry*, Son to Mr. *Pitt*, distinguished by the Diamond he brought from the *East-Indies*, which this Lord sold to the *French* King. He died in his Government of the *Leeward* Islands, and was succeeded by *William Matthews*, Esq; who arrived at *Antego*, October 1733, and soon after presented his additional Instruction to the [margin: Lord Londonderry, Governor. William Matthews, Esq; Governor.]

the Council and Assembly of that Island, and is as follows. *Whereas it has been represented to us, that the Salary of* 1200 l. *Sterling per Ann. which we have hitherto thought fit to allow out of the Duty of four and a half per Cent. arising in our Leeward Islands, for our Governor in Chief of those Islands, is not at present sufficient for his Support and the Dignity of that our Government, we have taken the same into our Consideration, and are graciously pleased to permit and allow, that the respective Assemblies of our said Islands may, by any Act or Acts, settle upon you such Sum or Sums, in Addition to your Salary of* 1200 l. *per Ann. as they shall think proper; and you are hereby allowed to give your Assent to any Act or Acts of Assembly to that Purpose. Provided such Sum or Sums be settled on you and your Successors in that Government, at least on you during the whole Time of your Government there, and that the same be done by the first respective Assemblies of our said Islands after your Arrival there.*

In Compliance with which the Council and Assembly settled on him during the Time of his Government, 1000 l. a Year *Antego* Currency.

In the Chapter of St. *Christopher's* we have mentioned some Proceedings of the Governor there relating to the Coin, which had been regulated by a Proclamation and an Act of Parliament in Queen *Anne's* Time, to ascertain the Currency in the Colonies. We have seen in the Article of St. *Kit's*, how the Proclamation and the Act of Parliament were there broke in upon, and here we shall see how they met with more Indignity and Contempt; for the Assembly took upon them to declare, that Statute *useless* and *impracticable*, and passed an Act of their own in these Words, *It is hereby enacted and ordered, that all Gold Coins of* Great-Britain *shall be taken or paid at* an Advance of 75 *per Cent. on their respective* Sterling *Values and not otherwise, and all* foreign Gold *shall be received or paid* at the Rate of 3 Pence Halfpenny per Grain.

Be it also enacted, that all Silver Coins whatsoever *shall be received or paid at the Rate of nine Shillings and three Pence per* Ounce and not otherwise. But this Act of Assembly not being likely to be confirmed in *England,* Governor *Matthews* and the Council and Assembly then sitting at *Parham,* had another Contrivance to evade the Law for the Coin. Two Gentlemen of the Assembly, brought to the Governor an *Instrument* of Writing, ' purporting an Agreement and ' Association to pay and receive Gold at three Pence Half-
' penny *per* Grain as in the intended Act, which was read
' publickly in Council, but not entered in the Minutes, and
' there

'there figned by the faid Governor and all prefent, except
'the Deputy Secretary who refufed to fign the fame. The
'whole Bench of Lawyers who are moſt of them, if not all,
'of the Affembly, foon after agreed, not to take a Fee from
'any Man that refufed to receive the Gold at that Rate, but
'to be concerned againſt them, and have promiſed to appear
'and defend the other Side gratis.'

Since which a Piftole full Weight, that is 104, paffes at 1 l. 10 s. 4 d. that ufed to pafs for no more than 28 s. full Weight or over. Portuggl Moidores that ufed to pafs for 42 s. pafs for 48 s. an Engliſh Guinea that ufed to pafs for 33 s. now paffes for 37 s. and other Pieces in Proportion. This illegal and exorbitant Rife brought the Exchange for 100 Sterling from 160 to 175 per Cent.

MONTSERRAT.

THE *Spaniards* gave this Ifland its Name, and called it fo for the Refemblance it has to a Mountain in *Catalonia*, not far from *Barcelona*, famous for a Chapel dedicated to the Bleffed Virgin; in greateft Reputation with the *Roman* Catholicks of any, except that of *Loretto*.

The *Engliſh* have not thought fit to give it another Name, fince they were Maſters of it. It lies in 17 Degrees, North Latitude; is about 3 Leagues in Length, and almoſt as much in Breadth, fo that it feems to be of a round Figure.

It was difcovered by the *Europeans* at the fame Time with St. *Chriſtopher's*, but no Settlement was made upon it till the Year 1632. At which Time Sir *Thomas Warner*, firſt Governor of St. *Chriſtopher's*, procured a fmall Colony to fettle there, of the Subjects of *England*; for we cannot affure our felves they were *Engliſhmen*, this Ifland being generally look'd on as an *Iriſh* Colony.

It had the fame Governors as St. *Chriſtopher's*; but we fuppofe they put in Deputy Governors, as has been the Practice fince. We could not get a good Account of either the general or particular Governors, and a bad one we would not impofe upon the Reader.

This Ifland flouriſhed at firſt more than *Antego*; but fince the Lord *Willoughby's* Time, the latter has got and kept the start of it. There were 700 Men in *Montferrat* 90 Years ago, which was 16 Years after it was first inhabited.

The Rolls of the Militia at this Time amounts to 360. We find but one Battery for the Defence of the Coast, and other old dismounted Cannon at several landing Places.

As to the Climate, Soil, Animals, Trade and Productions of this Isle, they are much the same with those of the other *Charibbee* Islands, only this is fuller of Mountains, which are covered with Cedars and other Trees, that make it a lovely Prospect from the Sea. The Valleys are fruitful, and better stored with fresh Water than those of *Antego*.

The Reader will not think it tedious to see a farther Account of the strange Animals in all the Elements peculiar to the *Charibbees*, and other Places in *America*. We range these in the Article of *Montferrat*, for that they are said to be most common here.

Davyes of Kid. Pag. 105. On this Coast, as we find in the *History of the Charibbees* beforementioned, are taken a very hideous Sort of Monsters, from thence called *Sea-Devils*, by my Author and others. This Monster is about 4 Foot long, and proportionably big. On its Back it has a great Bunch of Prickles, like those of a Hedgehog. The Skin of it is black, hard and rugged, like that of the *Sea-Dog*. Its Head is flat, and on the upper Part has many little Risings; among which is to be seen two very little black Eyes. The Mouth, which is extremely wide, is armed with several very sharp Teeth, of which two are crooked, and bent in like those of a Wild-Boar. It has four Fins, and a broad Tail, forked at the End. But all this would not have got it the Name of *Sea-Devil*, was it not for its having above the Eyes two little black sharp Horns, which turn towards its Back, like those of a Ram. Besides that this Monster is as ugly as any Thing can be imagined, the Meat of it, which is soft, and full of Strings, is absolute Poison.

There's another Kind of Sea-Devil, no less hideous than the other, tho' of another Figure. The largest of this Kind are not above a Foot long from Head to Tail, and the Breadth is almost equal to the Length; but when they please they swell themselves up so, that they seem to be as round as a Bowl. Their wide Mouths are armed with many little, but very sharp Teeth; and instead of a Tongue, they have only a little Bone, which is extremely hard. Their Eyes are very sparkling, and so small, and deep set in the Head, that the Ball can hardly be discerned. Between the Eyes they have a little Horn, which turns up, and before it a large String, that has a little Button at the End of it. Besides, their Tail, which

The History of Montferrat.

which is like the broad End of an Oar, they have two Plumes, one on the Back, which stands almost upright, and the other under the Belly. They have also two Fins, one on each Side, over against the Midst of the Belly, having at the Extremities something like little Paws, each of which is divided into eight Claws, armed with sharp Nails. Their Skin is rough and prickly, like that of a Shark's, except under the Belly, which is of a dark red Colour, and marked with red Spots.

The Meat of it is not to be eaten; they may be easily flead, and the Skin being filled with Cotton, or dried Leaves, is preserved by some of the Curious as a Rarity.

The *Lamantine* is often caught in these Seas. This is the best Fish to eat of all the Sea-Monsters, and is kept for Provision, as Salmon and Cod in *Europe*. The *Spaniards* call it *Namantin*, and *Manaty*, from its two little Paws like Hands. Ibid. 103. 'Tis a Monster, that, at its full Growth, is 18 Foot long, and 7 in Bigness. Its Head has some Resemblance to that of a Cow; from whence it is sometimes called the *Sea-Cow*. It has small Eyes and a thick Skin, of a dark red Colour, wrinkled in some Places, and stuck with small Hairs. Being dried, it grows so hard, it might serve for a Buckler against the Arrows of the *Charibbeans*; and some of the Savages use it to ward off the Blows of their Enemies, when they go to Battle. It has no Fins, but instead of them the two little Paws or Hands above-mentioned, under its Belly; each of which has four Fingers, very weak to support the Weight of so heavy a Body. It has no other defensive Weapon. It lives on the Grass and Herbage that grow about the Rocks, and on the shallow Places, that have not much above a Fathom Water.

The Females are disburthened of their young Ones much after the same Manner as Cows are, and have two Teats with which they suckle them. They bring forth two at a Time, which never leave the old one till they have no longer Need of Milk, and can feed on the Grass as she does.

Two or three of these *Lamantines* load a Canoo. The Meat or Flesh is of a Vermilion Colour; it eats short, and does not cloy or surfeit. The most wholesom Way of eating it, is after it has lain in Salt two or three Days.

These Fish are more commonly taken at the Entrance into fresh Water Rivers than in the Sea. Some highly value certain small Stones found in the Heads of these Monsters, as having the Virtue when reduced to Powder to cure the Gravel, and dissolve Stones bred in the Kidnies. But the Remedy is violent, and not much to be depended on, says my my Author, who perhaps has led me into an Error, in treating of the *Lamantine* in this Place. However his Account of this Fish pleased my Curiosity, and I hope will have the same Effect on the Readers.

This Isle produces every Thing that grows on the other *Leeward Islands:* As Sugar, Indigo, Ginger, Cotton, *&c.* especially *Indigo*; of which great Quantities used to be exported from hence to *England*. The Sugar was not so coarse and black as the *Antego*, nor so fine as the *Barbados* and *Jamaica*.

The Trade of this Place is the same with that of the other *Charibbee* Islands. 'Twas so much resorted 60 Years ago, that the Inhabitants had built a very fair Church, by the Contribution of the Governor, Merchants and Planters. The Pulpit, the Seats, and all the Joiners and Carpenters Work within it were of the most precious and sweet-scented Wood that grew in the Country.

There were then also 3 or 4000 Souls, *English, Scots*, and *Irish*; and since that the Number has rather encreased than decreased: For another good Church has been built, and the Island is now divided into two Parishes, one of which only is supplied by a Minister at this Time.

In King *Charles* II. especially in King *James* the IId's Reign, the *Irish* Papists drove a considerable Commerce to this Place; where Mr. *Terence Dermot*, afterwards Sir *Terence Dermot*, and Lord Mayor of *London* when King *James* was at *Dublin*, lived and got an Estate; as did also Mr. *Thomas Nugent*, and other *Roman* Catholicks that were originally of *Ireland*. When Col. *Codrington* was made Governor of the *Leeward Islands*, Col. *Blackstone* was Governor of *Montserrat*.

In the Year 1692, there was a dreadful Earthquake at this, and indeed almost all the *Leeward Islands*. The Inhabitants raised a Regiment of 300 Men, to assist General *Codrington* in his Expedition against St. *Christopher*'s : Which Regiment was commanded by Col. *Blackstone*. What they and the other Soldiers did on this Occasion will be found in the Histories of *Antego*, St. *Christopher*'s and *Nevis*.

To Col. *Blackstone* succeeded Col. *Hill* in the Government of this Island, who being sickly removed to *England* in the *Mary* Yatch, in the Year 1697, and landing at *Milford-Haven*, died at *Pembroke*, the 24th of *August*; who was his Successor we have not learned.

Part of Col. *Collingwood's* Regiment of Foot, that was sent from *England* in the following Year, was quartered in this Island, of which we can give no farther Account.

It

The History of Montserrat.

It was not so sickly as the other *Charibbee* Islands, and has encreased its People and Trade equally with any of them. The *French* did not attack it when they fell upon *Nevis*. As to the Number of the Inhabitants we can only make a Guess; for if they raised 300 Men in 1690, we may suppose they did not spare above one third Part of their whole Number; and granting they were then able to muster 1000 fighting Men, there would not, by the usual Methods of Computation in Political Arithmetick, be less than between 4 and 5000 Men, Women, and Children; and to those may be added 8000 Negroes: For it is a poor Sugar-Island where the Blacks are not twice as many in Number as the Whites.

The Island of *Montserrat*, as one of the *Leeward Islands*, is Part of Col. *Park's* Government; but he has a Deputy here, as well as in the other Isles. The Names of the other Officers that have come to our Knowledge shall be inserted in the usual Place.

Lieutenant Governor, *Anthony Hodges*, Esq;

Thomas Lee, Esq;
William Try, Esq;
John Dawley, Esq;
Joseph Little, Esq;
Will. Beddingfield, Esq;
George Milward, Esq;   ⎬ Counsellors.
George Lyddel, Esq;
Charles Matthew, Esq;
William Broderick, Esq;
George Wicks, Esq;
William Geerish, Esq;

Speaker of the Assembly, *George Milward*, Esq;
Colonel of the Militia Regiment, Col *Anthony Hodges*.
Chief Justice, *George Wicks*, Esq;
Judge of the Admiralty, *Anthony Hodges*, Esq;
Secretary, *Jonathan Warner*, Esq;
Commissioner of the Customs, *William Geerish*, Esq;
Provost Marshal, Mr. *William Martyn*, Deputy.
Minister of the Church of *England*, the Rev. Mr. *Wright*.

Not long after Col. *Park's* Arrival at *Antego*, which he chose for his Residence, News came thither that the *French* at *Martinico* were preparing to make a Descent on *Montserrat*; upon which a Sloop belonging to *Anthony Patch* and *Francis Monteyre*, was dispatched away to that Island, with
Orders

Orders to the Lieutenant Governor Col. *Anthony Hodges* to be upon his Guard, and on the first Appearance of any Number of Vessels making for that Island, to send away immediately an Advice Boat with an Account of it, that the Men of War and the Regiment at *Antego* might be dispatched to the Assistance of *Montserrat*. This Sloop was taken by a *French* Privateer as she went out of the Harbour of St. *John's*, but it had this good Effect, that when the *French* came from *Martinico* and understood by Col. *Park's* Letter to Col. *Hodges*, that he was coming to his Relief with a Man of War and a Regiment of regular Forces, they precipitately left that Island; but about two Years after returned to it with a much greater Force, consisting of several Men of War under Monsieur *Cossart*, having on Board 3500 Men, and anchoring in *Car's* Bay, put them on Shore there. They soon made themselves Masters of the whole Island, except *Dodon* Fort, which stands on an inaccessible Hill, to which the Inhabitants fled with their best Effects that were portable. The *French* took and burnt all the Vessels in the Road, except the *Speedwel* Capt. *George Moulton*, who cut his Cables and made to *Nevis*. The *French* were 10 Days in Possession of this Island, which they plundered and wasted at Pleasure, and then removed to *Guardeloupe* to refresh, when Mr. St. *John* Secretary of State heard of this Depredation, at a Time when the Duke of *Ormond* had refused to act against the *French* in *Flanders*, and himself and the Ministers in *England* were doing every Thing *France* could desire, the Secretary himself appeared somewhat surprised, but contented himself with saying, *Had we thought* Cossart *was sent against our Sugar Islands, we would have sent such a Squadron to guard them, as should have cleared those Seas of him*, or Words to that Effect. I have not heard what Satisfaction, if any, was made the *English* Sufferers for their Losses by the Rapine of the *French* in this Island; and as I never met with any Instance of the *French* having effectually made good the like Damage on the like Occasion, I suppose these Sufferers fared no better than others, notwithstanding the Plenipotentaries at *Utrecht* consented to what the *British* proposed for the Relief of their Fellow-Subjects in this Island. *Article* XI. *Commissaries shall inquire into the Damages last Year in the Island of* Montserrat; comfortable News for those that sustained it, which however was like to be made good by the *English* themselves, for the same Commissaries were to bring in an Account of the Infringments made by the *English* in the Capitulation of *Nevis*, by which the *French* pretended to be very much injured.

The History of Montserrat.

One may suspect, that the Inhabitants of *Montserrat* were not so fond of Col. *Park's* Government towards the Close of it, as when he had not been long in it; for not only the Masters of Ships in the Harbour of *Antego*, but the Council and Assembly of this Island, drew up and signed Addresses in Praise of him. The Masters of Ships hearing of certain Complaints against him in respect of Trade, say in their Address, *That in the strictest Enquiries and Observations they could make, Governor* Park *had exerted his Power to the utmost, in protecting their Rights and Liberties,* of which they must needs be excellent Judges, by their extraordinary Capacities, and their living so little in the Island. The Council and Assembly of *Montserrat* address the Queen's Majesty, and assure her, *They knew not any one Action of Governor* Park's *since his coming to the Government, which deserves Complaint.* The Gentlemen lumping the Matter and not finding one Mismanagement, is a plain Proof that this Address was dictated more to flatter the Party concerned in it, than to let her Majesty into the whole Truth of the Matter. The Members of the Council and Assembly who set their Names to it were

Thomas Lee, Esq; President.
William Frye, Esq;
John Daly, Esq;
George Lyddall, Esq;
William Geerish, Esq;
Edw. Buncomb, Esq; Speaker.

John Brambly, Esq;
John Hart, Esq;
Anthony Ravill, Esq;
William Finch, Esq;
Dennis Daly, Esq;

This and other such Addresses procured in like Manner, hindered not the Representations of the Inhabitants of *Antego*, who having perfected their Articles against General *Park*, sent them to *England* by a Ship from this Island, as well as by another from *Antego*.

I find not the Name of Col. *Anthony Hodges* Lieutenant Governor of this Island, among the Addressers; which probably induced Col. *Park's* Advocate to represent him as a *Smuggler*, a *clandestine Trader*, and no Friend to *Park*, who would not indulge him in that illicite Trade, as is insinuated by that Writer.

The Generals of this as well as the other *Leeward-Islands* that came after Col. *Park*, are spoken of in the Chapter of *Antego*, and we have no perfect Account of the Succession of Lieutenant Governors of *Montserrat* to this Time, nor of any Thing relating to it that is remarkably particular, till we come to the Hurricane, which happened in the Time of

The History of Montserrat.

the Government of General *William Matthews*. The very furprizing Account of this Hurricane is in the following Letter from *Montserrat*.

1733.
A violent Hurricane.

'On the 30th of *June* we had as violent an Hurricane
'here as the oldeft Perfon in this Ifland can remember. For
'3 Months together we had one continued Series of fcorch-
'ing dry Weather till the 29th of *June*, when about 10 in
'the Evening it began to rain very plentifully, and lafted the
'greateft Part of the Night, which gave us the pleafing
'Hopes of a fine Seafon; but about 5 o'Clock the next
'Morning the Wind arofe, and blew prodigious hard at
'N. E. and N. E. by E. and held till 7, when there fol-
'lowed Gufts and Flaws, the Noife of which founded more
'like Thunder than Wind; the Force of it too was fuch,
'that it blew down about ¼ of the Houfes in this Ifland, and
'not one in twenty of thofe which were not entirely de-
'ftroyed, efcaped without the Lofs of fome Part, or at leaft
'fo left upon the Careen, that the next fmall Gale will level
'them with the Ground.

'A Store-Houfe built oppofite to the Cuftom-Houfe, and
'about 45 Foot diftant being left uncovered, the Wind
'blew the Rafters thereof different Ways; part was carried
'with fuch Force, that it broke thro' the Side of the Cuftom-
'Houfe, making a Hole fo large, that had not Mr. *Webb*
'the Collector acted with the greateft Conduct, moft Part,
'if not the whole would have been demolifhed.

'A Cattle Mill Houfe belonging to Mr. *James Huffey*,
'weighing at leaft 20,000 *lb.* was taken fairly up into the
'Air, carried fome Diftance from its proper Place, lodged
'in a Piece of Canes, and broke in ten Thoufand Pieces by
'the Force of the Fall.

'An empty Sugar Hogfhead was taken off the Ground by
'the Wind, and carried 30 or 40 Yards over a Dwelling
'Houfe.

'A large Copper, capable of containing 240 Gallons,
'was by the Wind carried over a high Wall, and by the
'Force of the Fall jammed clofe together.

'A large Mill-Cafe (weighing 400 *lb.*) lying on the Ground,
'was lifted up on End, and large Trees of 4, 5 and 6 Feet
'Diameter were blown up by the Roots. We had on the
'29th 34 Windmills flying in this Ifland, many of which
'were totally deftroyed, and not above 5 or 6 have received
'lefs than 3 or 400 *l.* Damage, *&c.*

'Such Havock is made among our Sugar Canes, as would
'fhock the hardeft Heart and enforce Pity to the Owners;
'fome who had a Profpect of making 200 or 300 Hog-
'fheads

‘ sheads of Sugar next Year, would now gladly compound
‘ for 60 or 80. Col. *Lyddel*, a worthy Gentleman, was so
‘ bruised by the Fall of his House that he died 7 Days after.
‘ My Dwelling Houses are entirely demolished, my Pro-
‘ vision is blown up by the Roots and carried into the Sea, as
‘ was also about 14 Acres of Sugar Canes just fit for Sugar.
  ‘ The Damage sustained in this Island exclusive of the
‘ Shipping, is on a moderate Computation 50,000 *l.* this Cur-
‘ rency, and many Gentlemen are 2 or 3000 *l.* poorer than
‘ they were the 29th of *June.*'

About 3 Years after this General *Matthews* being here in 1736.
Person, the Governor, Council and Assembly passed an Act,
For the more effectual preventing all Trade in these Parts, be- Act against
tween his Majesty's Subjects and the French. Something of French
this illicit Trade has been mentioned in the Chapter of *Trade.*
Barbados. It is directly contrary to the fifth and sixth
Articles of the Treaty between *England* and *France*, concluded on the 6th of *November*, 1686, and to the Act of
Parliament of the 6th of the Reign of his present Majesty
intituled, *An Act for the better securing and encouraging the*
Trade of his Majesty's Sugar Colonies in America, and to all
royal Instructions to Governors of Sugar Colonies, and
particularly to an Article, in General *Matthews's* Instructions, by which he is commanded to take Care that *none of*
the French *Subjects be allowed to trade from their said Settle-*
ments, to any of the Islands under his Government, or Fish upon
the Coasts thereof.

The *French*, who are always watchful for preserving the
Security and Trade of their Sugar Colonies, took early Care
to prevent this unlawful Traffick, by an Edict of *October*
1727, but they seemed to carry their Care a little too far, by
limiting the *British* Navigation to within a League of their
Coast, within which Limits all *British* Ships were seizable,
unless forced by Weather or Pyrates, and in such Case if
they broke Bulk to be Prize. *Barbados* and the other Sugar
Islands had too much connived at the Infraction of these
Orders, and *Montserrat* was the first that exerted the Vigour
of its Constitution, in confirming them by a Law of their
own. Pursuant to this Act, a *French* Ship of 5 or 6000 *l.*
Value was seized here and condemned, in the Court of
Admiralty, and several other less Seizures were made in this
Island. A good Example in this for all the *Charibbees.*

NEVIS

NEVIS.

THE next Island to *Monferrat*, following the Distance from the *Equator*, which is the Method we have taken, is *Nevis*, anciently, and now vulgarly called *Mevis*.

It must have been discovered at the same Time with St. *Christopher's*, because 'tis not above half a League from it. It lies in 17 Degrees, 19 Minutes, North Latitude, and is not above six Leagues in Circumference.

There's but one Mountain, and that is in the Midst of it, very high, and covered with great Trees up to the Top. The Plantations are all round the Mountain, beginning from the Sea-side, and ending only at the Summet of the Mountain, the Ascent being commodious enough.

There are several Springs of fresh Water in it, of which some are strong enough to make their Way to the Sea, and may deserve the Name of Rivers. One Spring here is a Mineral, and the Waters hot. Baths were made not far from the Source, and frequented with good Success, for the Cure of those Distempers that the Baths at the Bath in *England*, and *Bourbon* in *France*, are famous for curing.

Before we enter farther into the Geographical and Natural Account of *Nevis*, we must let the Reader a little into the Historical.

Sir *Thomas Warner*, who made the first Settlement on St. *Christopher's*, made also the first at *Nevis*, in the Year 1628. But in the following Year *Don Frederick de Toledo*, who drove the *English* and *French* out of the former Island, seized all the Ships, to the Number of 15, that were at *Nevis*. It was aboard these Ships the *Spaniards* put the *English*, whom they forced to leave St. *Christopher's*.

The *English* Settlement at *Nevis* went on so prosperously, that in 20 Years time there were between 3 and 4000 Men there, who subsisted, and lived handsomly by the Trade they drove in Sugar.

After Sir *Thomas Warner's* Death, we find mention made of one Mr. *Lake*, who was Governor of this Island, and is remembered as a Man of great Piety and Prudence; insomuch that *Nevis* was said to be the best governed of any of the *Charibbee-Islands*. All manner of Profaneness, Impiety and Debauchery, were severely punished. There were even then three Churches in the Island; not very fine indeed, but convenient and decent for performing Divine Service.

The History of Nevis.

Charles-Town was built, and the Houses were large, the Shops well stored, and Forts were erected to defend the Place against all Invaders. There is but one Fort mounting 19 Guns, which were they in a better Condition, would scarce be a sufficient Defence. The Rolls of the Militia amount to 300 here, and this Island is by no Means in so flourishing a State as when we first treated of it. The Governor and Council at first set a Price upon all Goods, and assigned Times of Payment for them; but that was too great an Imposition on the Liberty of the Market, to be of any long Continuance.

Sir *George Ayscue* reduced *Nevis* with the other *Charibbee-Islands*; and having no certain List of the Deputy-Governors, nor indeed of the Governors-General, we shall not pretend to give any to the Publick, but take some farther Notice of the Climate, Soil, Animals, Trade and Productions.

The Climate is hot, and I have been informed by People who have frequented both Islands, that it is rather hotter than *Barbados*, though the latter is much nearer the Line.

The Soil is fertile, especially in the Valleys. The rising Ground is stony, and the Plantations grew worse and worse in Fertility, the higher the Planters settled on the Mountain. Land was much cheaper there than in the Vale, being coarser, and not so easily cultivated. It is the same with us in *England*, and for the same Reasons: So this Observation might have been spared.

The Rains here are violent, and the Tornado's so in a very high Degree, as we shall observe hereafter.

As to the Product of the Country, and its Trade, what has been said of *Barbados*, *Antego*, and the other *Charibbee-Islands*, will also serve for this. Sugar is the staple Commodity here, as well as there, and serves for all the Uses of Money: For all the Trade of the Island is managed by Sugar. Pounds of Sugar, and not Pounds of Sterling is the Balance of all their Accounts; and, exchanging that Commodity for others, did the Inhabitants Business as well as if they had had Silver.

This Sugar was, generally speaking, Muscovado, of a little finer Grain than that of *Antego*: But they have lately endeavoured to clay. Sir *John Bawdon* ordered his Overseers to attempt it, two or three and twenty Years since, in that Plantation, in this Island, which is now Mr. *Richard Merriweather's*. He sent Mr. *Hacket*, Brother to Sir *Richard Hacket* of *Barbados*, and an excellent Refiner, from that Isle to this. But, through Negligence in those that were employed, the

Project

Project failed, and no white Sugar was made in *Nevis*, but what was for a home Consumption, Presents, or Experiments, till within a very few Years.

Tobacco was at first much cultivated; there's now little or none planted, nor has there been any considerable Quantity this 30 or 40 Years.

Cotton and Ginger have been also planted here; but of late Years those two Commodities have been neglected, and Sugar only taken Care of; of which great Quantities have been made, and 50 or 60 Ships loaden in a Year from this Island to *Europe*.

As to the Animals here, it is a hard Matter to say there are any peculiar to it; however, since we find some taken Notice of as such, we shall give the Reader an Account of them.

Lizzards are said to be more frequent here than in any of our other Sugar-Islands. There are several Kinds of them; the greatest of them are those which the *Charibbeans* call *Ouaymaca*. They are five Foot long at their full Growth, measuring from the Head to the Extremity of the Tail, which is as long as all the rest of their Body.

Dav. *p.* 74. As for their Bigness, they are a Foot about, their Skins are of several Colours, according to the different Soils they are bred in. The *Portuguese* call them *Cameleons*, thinking they were a Species of that Creature. In some Places the Females are of a light green, checkered with black and white Spots; and the Males are green. In others the Males are black, and the Females of a light grey, intermixt with black and green. And others, both Males and Females, have all the little Scales of their Skin so glittering, and as it were studded, that at a Distance one would think them clothed in rich Cloth of Gold and Silver. On their Backs they have Prickles like Combs, which they force up, and set down as they please, and appear less from the Head to the End of the Tail. They go on four Feet, each of which has five Claws, with very sharp Nails. They run swiftly, and are excellent in climbing of Trees. But whether it be that they love to look on Men, or are of a stupid, unapprehensive Nature, when they perceive the Hunter they patiently expect him, without stirring till they are shot. When they are angry, their Craw under their Throat swells, and makes them seem the more formidable. Their Jaws are very wide, their Tongues thick, and they have some very sharp Teeth, which when once they have fastened on any Thing, they will hardly let it go. Their Teeth are not at all venomous. The Females lay Eggs, about the Bigness of
Wood-

The History of Nevis.

Woodquifts, but the Shell is foft. They lay them deep on the Sea-fide, under the Sand, and leave them to be hatched by the Sun. From whence fome Authors have ranked them among the amphibious Creatures.

The Savages taught the *Europeans* the way to take thefe *Lizzards*, and by their Example encouraged thofe that came firft among them to eat them. They are very hard to kill, infomuch that fome having received thtee Shots of a Gun, and by it loft fome Part of their Entrails, would not fall. Yet if a fmall Stick be thruft into their Nofes, or a Pin between their Eyes, where there's a little Hole, into which the Pin eafily enters, they prefently die. Their Flefh is lufcious, but not fafe to eat often: Their Eggs have no White, but are all Yolk.

The *Annolis* is another Sort of *Lizzard*, and at the firft Ib. 75. fettling this Ifland they were very common in all the Plantations. This Reptile is about the Bignefs of an *European* Lizzard, but its Head is longer, its Skin yellowifh, and on its Back it has certain blew, green, and grey Streaks, drawn from the Top of the Head to the End of the Tail. Its Abode is in Holes under Ground, whence in the Night it makes a loud Noife. In the Day-time, it is in perpetual Exercife, and wanders about Cottages, to get fomewhat to fubfift on.

The *Land-Pike* is another ftrange Reptile, which has been met with in this Ifland; it is fo called from its Likenefs to that Fifh: But inftead of Fins it has four Feet, fo weak, that it only crawls on the Ground, and winds its Body as a Pike newly takan out of the Water. The longeft of thefe Creatures are about 16 Inches, and proportionably big. Their Skins are covered with little Scales, which fhine extremely, and are of a Silver grey Colour. Some of the Curious ufed to have young ones in their Clofets, and took them for Salamanders. In the Night-time they make a hideous Noife from under the Rocks; it is more fharp and grating to the Ear than that of Frogs and Toads; and they change their Notes according to the Variety of the Places where they lurk. They are feldom feen but a little before Night; and when any of them are met in the Day-time, thofe that meet them are apt to be frightned with their Motion.

There have been many curious Infects feen in this Ifland, P. 78. and none more fo than that called the *Soldier*, a kind of Snail. The Name given it is taken from the *French*; and the Reafon of it is fo whimfical, we are glad it did not come from an *Englifhman*. Thefe Infects have no Shells proper

proper to themselves; but to secure the Weakness of their little Bodies from the Injuries of the Air, and the Attempts of other Animals, they take Possession of a Shell, commonly that of Perriwinkles; within which they accommodate themselves, as Soldiers, who having no settled Habitation, take up their Quarters in other Mens Houses; wherefore they are termed *Soldats* or *Soldiers*. As they grow bigger, they shift their Shells, and get into larger, as they find them on the Sea Shore, and some have taken up their Quarters in the Claws of great dead Crabs. They are of several Forms and Figures, according to the Diversity of the Shells they possess themselves of. Their Bodies are very tender, except their Heads and Claws. For a defensive Weapon, and instead of a Foot, they have a Claw, like that of a great Crab, wherewith they close the Entrance of their Shells, and secure their whole Body. It is all jagged within, and holds so fast whatever it fastens on, that it takes away that Piece with it. This Insect marches faster than the common Snail, and does not with its Foam or Slime foul the Place over which it passes. When the *Soldier* is taken, it grows angry, and makes a Noise. When it is put near the Fire, it forsakes its Quarters; if its Shell is presented to it, to enter it again, it goes in backwards. My Author adds, (I will give it in his own Words, because there's something extraordinary in them.)

P. 79. *When there are many of them met together, with an Intention at the same Time to quit their former Lodgings, and to take up new ones, which they are all much inclined to do, they enter into a great Contestation, there happens a furious Engagement, which is managed with their Claws, till at length the weaker is forced to submit to the victorious, who presently possess themselves of the Shells of the vanquished, which afterwards they peaceably enjoy as a precious Conquest.*

P. 84. The Reader must be informed, that the History of the *Charibbee-Islands*, an Edition of which Mr. *Davies* put out in *English*, is looked upon to be very authentick; and, as far as we have compared it with Things within our own Knowledge, the Account is very just, allowing for the Distance of Time; and if the modern Inhabitants should happen not to meet with these Creatures in the *Charibbee-Islands*, they are not therefore to conclude there never were any of them, but rather that they are cleared by the Industry of their Predecessors. There are two other Sorts of small Snails, which are very beautiful; one is flat and of a dark Colour, the other is sharp, and has small, red, yellow, or blew Streaks or Lines.

The History of Nevis. 241

There's another Insect, called the *Flying-Tyger*, because its Body is chequered with Spots of several Colours, as the Tyger's is. It is about the Bigness of the Horned Beetle. Its Head is sharp, and it has two great Eyes, as green and sparkling as an Emerald. Its Mouth is armed with two hard Hooks, extremely sharp, with which it holds fast its Prey, while it gets out the Substance of it. Its whole Body is covered with a hard and swarthy Crust, which serves it for Armour. Under its Wings, which are also of a solid Matter, there are four lesser Wings, which are as thin as any Silk. It has six Legs, each of which has three Joints, and they are bristled with certain little Prickles. In the Daytime it is continually catching other Insects, and in the Night it sits singing on the Trees.

The *Horn-Fly* is a Reptile that has two Snouts, like an Elephant, one turning upward, and the other downward; its Head is blew, like a Grasshopper's; its two Eyes green; the upper Side of its Wings of a bright Violet, damasked with Carnation, with a small Thread of Silver; the Colour so lively and shining, that Art can never imitate it.

The same Author, with what Reason I cannot tell, says, *Ibid.* p. 83. there's a certain monstrous Spider in these Islands, so big, that when its Legs are spread abroad, it takes up a larger Place than the Palm of a Man's Hand. Its whole Body consists of two Parts, one of which is flat, and the other round; smaller at one End, like a Pigeon's Egg. It has a Hole on its Back, not unlike a Navel. Its Mouth cannot easily be discerned, because it is in a manner covered over with Hair, which commonly is of a light grey, but is sometimes intermixed with red. It has two Weapons like Tusks, of a solid Matter, and black, so smooth and shining, that some curious Persons have set them in Gold for Toothpicks; and Experience, or the Fable, says, they have a Virtue P. 84. to preserve from Pain, and all Corruption, those Parts that have been rubbed with them. When these Spiders are grown old, they are covered all over with a swarthy Down, which is as soft and close as Velvet. Their Body is supported by ten Feet, that are a little hairy on the Sides, and have below certain small Points or Bristles, that help them to fasten more easily on those Places on which they climb: All these Feet issue out of the Fore part of the Insect, having each of them four Joints, and at the Ends they are armed with a black and hard Horn, which is divided into two Parts like a Fork. They every Year shift their old Skins, as the Serpents do; as also the two Tusks which serve them for Teeth, and are their defensive Weapons. Their Eyes are very little,

and

and lie so deep in their Heads, that they seem to be only two small Points. They feed on Flies, and it has been observed that in some Places their Webs are so strong, that the little Birds caught in them have had much ado to get away.

P. 83. The Worm called by the *French Millepied*, (thousand-footed) and *Palmer Worm* by the *English*, has been met with here: The Number of its Feet is almost infinite, from whence it takes its *French* Name. They are like Bristles under its Body, and help it to run along the Ground with incredible Swiftness, especially when it finds itself pursued. It is about six Inches long. The upper Part of its Body is covered all over with swarthy Scales, which are hard, and jointed one within another, like the Tiles of a House. It has a kind of Claws both in its Head and Tail, that sting cruelly, and with so much Venom, that the Pain remains 24 Hours, or more, after the Patient has received the Hurt.

We must take some Notice of the rare Birds in these Islands; and many Years since there was brought from thence a Bird like a Swallow, only the two great Feathers of the Tail was a little shorter, the Beak turned down like a Parrot, the Feet were like a Duck's; it was black only under the Belly, with a little white like our Swallows.

The *Fly Catcher* is a very pretty Creature, of a small Size, and with four Legs. Some seem covered with fine Gold or Silver Brocade; others with a Mixture of green Gold, and other charming Colours. These Birds are familiar, coming boldly into Rooms, which they clear from Flies, and such Vermin, and do it with such Art and Speed, that the Huntsman's Dexterity is not comparable to it; for they lie down on a Plank, where they hope the Flies will come, and have their Eyes fixed upon them, putting their Heads into as many different Postures as the Flies shift Places. They stand also on their Fore-feet, and gape after their Prey with their Mouths half open. Though a Noise be made, and one should come near them, nothing disturbs them. When they have at last found their Advantage, they start directly on their Prey, and rarely miss it. They are so tame, that they will come upon the Table while Persons are eating at it, and attempt to catch Flies there, or upon their Hands or Clothes. They are very neat clean Things. They lay small Eggs as big as Pease; which, having covered with the Earth, they leave to be hatched by the Sun. When they are killed, all their Beauty vanishes, and they become paler. This Animal has something of the Nature of the Camelion; for it assumes the Colour of those Things on which it resides; for being about Palm-Trees,

The History of Nevis.

it is green; about Orange-Trees, yellow; and the like by other Trees.

If these Animals are particular to this, or common to all the *Charibbee-Iſlands*, they are ſo rare, that the Curious cannot but be pleaſed with our Deſcription of them; and will not look upon this as a Digreſſion from our Hiſtory, which we ſhall now continue.

After the *Reſtauration*, when Trade flouriſhed with Peace, this Iſle enjoyed its Share of the Benefit of it with others, and encreaſed in Inhabitants and Riches. The only Enemy they had to ſtruggle with was the Hurricane, which generally viſited them once a Year. On the 19th of *Auguſt*, 1667. there was a terrible one in this Iſland; at which Time Sir *John Berry*, Captain of the *Coronation* Man of War, was in the Harbour, with that and ſeveral other Ships; of which one was commanded by Captain *Langford*, who having learnt ſome of the *Prognoſticks* of a Turnado from a *Charibbean*, perceiving them, he told Sir *John*, and the other Commanders, of it; who, depending on his Intelligence, made their Ships ready for the Sea, and in the Morning about Four of the Clock, the Wind coming very hard Northerly, they put to Sea, and came all back within four or five Days time ſafe to the Road again. Captain *Langford* was aſhore, and being confident of the Hurricane's coming, took ſuch Care before-hand to ſecure his Sugars, and Goods in the Store-houſe, that when the Hurricane had carried away the Roof of the Houſe, all, except one Hogſhead of Sugar, remained ſafe.

Lowth. *Vol.* II. p. 106.

When Sir *William Stapleton* was Governor of theſe Iſlands, he uſually made this the Place of his Reſidence. Here the Courts were kept; and the Governor living upon it, moſt of the Affairs of this Government were tranſacted here.

Every one of theſe Iſlands have a particular Lieutenant-Governor, Council, and Aſſembly; and the general Government centers only in the Authority of the Captain-General.

We find a wonderful Loyal Addreſs handed to Court in King *Charles* the IId's Reign, to congratulate that Prince on his eſcaping the bloody Effects of the famous *Rye-Houſe Plot*. It was delivered by Colonel *Netheway* and Col. *Jefferſon*; the latter deſcended from that *Jefferſon* mentioned in the Hiſtory of St. *Chriſtopher's*.

On the 28th of *March*, 1685. Sir *William Stapleton* proclaimed King *James* the IId. at *Nevis*, with great Solemnity. The Provoſt Marſhal officiated as Sheriff, Drums

beating

beating, and Trumpets founding, attended by Vollies of all the Ordnance in the five Forts, of the Horfe and Foot, and the Ships in the Road.

Sir *William Stapleton* made Sir *James Ruffel* Lieutenant-Governor of this Ifland, and he enjoyed the Place till his Commiffion was fuperfeded by that of Captain General, granted to Sir *Nathaniel Johnfon*, who alfo refided at *Nevis*; and at this Time none of the *Leeward-Iflands* flourifhed fo much as this. It fupplied the others with almoft all their Wines and Negroes; and it is computed to have contained at that Time near 2000 fighting Men; which will make the Number of Souls, by common Computation, to be above 10000, befides Negroes, of which Number there were not lefs than 20000; a prodigious Improvement of an Ifland fcarce fix Miles long, to maintain between 30 and 40000 Men, Women, and Children. This may feem incredible at the firft View, but we fhall give farther Proof of it in the Courfe of this Relation.

A dreadful Mortality raged in *Nevis*, in the Year 1689. efpecially among the Men, which reduced that Sex to the Moity of its ufual Number, and forced the Inhabitants to make their Addreffes to Sir *Timothy Thornhill*; who then lay at *Antego* with his *Barbados* Regiment, to come down to *Nevis* for their Defence; for the *French* being then Mafters of St. *Chriftopher*'s, they expected every Day to be attacked. Sir *Timothy* was loth to venture his Men, during the Violence of the Diftemper; but hearing it was abated, he removed thither with his Regiment in *November*, landed, and encamped them on a commodious Plain, clofe adjoining to a little River.

In the Beginning of *December*, a Council of War was called, at which affifted,

Chriftopher Codrington, Efq; Lieutenant General.
Sir *Timothy Thornhill*, Major General.
Col. *Charles Pym*, } Colonels of the two *Nevis* Regiments.
Col. *Earl*,
Col. *John Thomas*, Lieutenant Col. to Sir *Timothy Thornhill*.
Major *John Stanley*, and other Field-Officers

By whom it was refolved, that the Major General, with 300 *Barbadians*, and 200 *Nevifians*, to ufe the Term of my Author, fhould go down and attack St. *Martin*'s, and St. *Bartholomew*'s, two of the *Charibbee-Iflands* belonging to the Enemy, where they raifed a Stock, for the Support of their Sugar Iflands.

The History of Nevis.

On the 15th of *December* Sir *Timothy* embarked his Forces on board a *Brigantine*, and nine Sloops, and went aboard himself the next Day, when he also set sail for those Islands. On the 18th they past by St. *Bartholomew*'s, and about Four in the Afternoon, being within four or five Leagues of St. *Martin*'s, they spy'd a small Sloop standing up towards them; but upon sight of the *English* she tacked, and put into one of the Bays. When they came up with the Bay where she lay, Sir *Timothy Thornhill* sent Lieutenant *Dowden* with three Files of Musketeers, in a Boat, to go up to her to board her, and if she were floating, to bring her out. When the Boat was got near the Sloop's Side, the Enemy, who lay hid in the Bushes on each Side, (the Bay being *landlockt*) fired very thick upon the *English*, and forced them to retreat, two of them being wounded. The Major General being very desirous to have the Sloop, after it was dark, sent 30 Men in four Boats and Canoos, under the Command of Captain *Walter Hamilton*, again to attempt the bringing her out, but the *French* discovered them, and fired hotly upon them. The Canoo which Captain *Hamilton* was in, rowed up close to the Sloop, and found her run aground, the Men being all gone out of her; so he was obliged to leave her, and return to the Vessels. Captain *Hamilton* received two Shots in one of his Legs, four Persons more were wounded, but none killed. That Night the *English* stood off and on, as though they designed to land the next Morning.

Sir *Timothy* on the 19th called a Council of War, on Board the *Brigantine*, by whom it was determined, first to attack St. *Bartholomew*'s, to which Island the Sloops stood up in the Night. The next Mornng, before Day, Major *Stanley* landed with 80 Men, notwithstanding the Opposition of the Enemy, beat them out of their Breast-Works, and by Break of Day he had planted his Colours on a Battery of two Guns, which he had taken from them. Not long after, the Major General went ashore with all the Forces, which he divided into three Bodies, himself leading his own Guard of Gentlemen Volunteers, and two Companies of Foot, through the Middle of the Island.

After a Mile's March, the *English* discovered a large Fortification, which appeared to be well man'd: But Sir *Timothy* with his Men charging the Enemy resolutely, they quitted it after 2 or 3 Volleys, and fled into the Woods. The Fortification was Quadrangular, consisting of about two Acres of Land, encompassed with double Rows of Stakes 6 Foot high and 4 Foot distant; the Intervals being filled with Earth,

Earth, and a wide deep Trench without it. On each Corner there was a Flanker, in one of which were planted four great Guns. The Entrance into it was a Lock admitting but one at a Time. In the Middle of it was the Governor's House, and a Guard-house for the Soldiers, also a large Cistern with Store of fresh Water, seven or eight Barrels of dried Fish, Bread proportionable, and two Barrels of Powder. It was situate in a Bottom by the Side of a Lake, through which the *English* were to pass to come at it, and on the other Side was a very high Hill. After Sir *Timothy Thornhill* had entered it, he sent his Secretary Mr. *Spencer*, my Author, with 4 Files of Men to gain the Top of the Hill, which he did, finding it fortified with two great Guns loaden and prim'd, with the Match lighted, and several Bags of Partridge-shot lying by them; but the *French* were in so much Haste they did not stay to fire upon him.

About 4 Miles Distance from the Fortification, on the Side of a Hill, there appeared a large white Building, resembling a Fort, to which the Major General sent 300 Men, under the Command of Col. *Charles Pym*, with Orders if he found it strong, to sit down before it and wait his coming. Accordingly a few Hours afterwards he followed Col. *Pym*, with the rest of the Forces, having left a sufficient Guard in the Fortification.

When Sir *Timothy Thornhill* came up to it, he found it to be only a Stone Platform laid shelving, for the Conveyance of Rain-Water into a Cistern. The Reader should know the Occasion of these Cisterns, which is, the Islands being destitute of Rivers, Wells, or other Conveniences of fresh Water, it forces the Inhabitants to make Use of all Opportunities to catch the Rain, each House being furnished with one or more of these Cisterns, some of them capable of holding 14 or 18 Tuns of Water. Here the Major General encamped that Night, and the next Day marched back to the Fortification.

On the 22d Day of *December* two *French* Captains came in with a Flag of Truce, bringing Articles from their Governor, upon which they offered to surrender themselves. Sir *Timothy* returned an Answer in Writing, and sent it by two Gentlemen who spoke *French*, amounting to a Denial of his Proposals: For he replied, if he and the Inhabitants came in with their Arms in two Days, he should find the Major General was a Gentleman: But if he stood out longer he was to expect no Quarter.

The two *Englishmen* who went to the Governor returned the same Day, and brought his Answer, That in 4 Days
Time

Time he would come in, but it could not be sooner, because some of the Inhabitants were hid in the Woods, to whom before that Time he could not communicate his Design.

The two following Days the *English* marched round the Island, burning all the Houses as they past along. The *French* fired upon them from the Woods in some Places, but did no Damage. On the Day appointed the *English* spied a Flag of Truce coming towards them with the Governor, and a great Company of the Inhabitants. Upon which the Major General leaving his own Company of Guards in the Fortification, and the rest of his Forces drawn up round it, sent the two Gentlemen who had before been with the Governor to meet him. At the Entrance into the Fortification he was received by Lieutenant Colonel *John Thomas*, who conducted him to the Major General, who sat in the House; a poor one indeed, but it served the *French* Governor's Turn: It rather resembled a Pigeon-House than the Pavilion (as the *French* term it) of a Governor, it consisting only of one Room, about 12 Foot square below, and another above.

The Governor was accompanied by a Frier and some of his Officers, who were all very civilly received by Sir *Timothy*. The Prisoners were between 6 and 700 Men, Women, and Children. The Men were sent as Prisoners to *Nevis*, with the Live-Stock, Negroes, and Merchandize. The Women and Children were transported to St. *Christopher's*. Sir *Timothy* restored the Governor his Horse, Arms, Apparel, and some of his Negroes, and permitted him to send them also to St. *Christopher's*. There were but 10 Men of all the *English* killed and wounded in this Enterprize.

While Sir *Timothy Thornhill* staid upon St. *Bartholomew's*, 8 or 9 Sloops came to him from some of the neighbouring Islands, with about 50 Men to reinforce him. Upon this he sent the *Brigantine* with 9 Sloops, under the Command of Captain *Walter Hamilton*, to alarm the Island of St. *Martin's*, and make a false Attack on the Windward-side. Captain *Hamilton* sailed on the 19th of *January*; and the same Day the Major General embarked all his Men, and sailed at Night for the same Island, where he and his Forces landed the next Morning on the Leeward Side without any Opposition; the Enemy having drawn all their Forces to the other Side of the Island.

About 20 of the *French* that were posted in a Breast-Work on that Side fired once, and then quitted it. When Sir *Timothy's* Men were all landed, they marched entirely through the Body of the Country, and after two Miles March, were

drawn

drawn up in a convenient Plain, the Enemy being in Sight, and, as they thought, advancing towards them.

After they had continued an Hour in this Posture, the *French* retired and burnt a great Building upon a Hill, about a Mile distant, which seemed to be a Fortification. Upon which the Major General marched up to it with all his Forces, but found it only to be a large House which they burnt, because it should not serve the *English* for Shelter. However, the Stone-Walls that remained standing proved serviceable to them, in covering them from their Shot.

There was a large Cistern of Water here, but the *French* had rendered it unfit for Drinking, by throwing Salt into it. They also poisoned an adjacent Pond with Tobacco.

The *English* had not been long here, before the *French* began to fire upon them from a Breast-Work, where they had two great Guns planted a Quarter of a Mile off, there being a Valley between them; on the left Hand low and bushy Ground, and on the Right a Ridge of Mountains, with a very thick Wood.

Sir *Timothy Thornhill* sent Captain *Burt* with a Company of Men to gain the Top of the Mountain, which had the Command of the Fort he was at. That being done, he left 100 Men there under the Command of Capt. *Geoffry Gibbs*, to maintain that Post, and marched back into the Plain with the rest of his Forces to secure the Avenues, and hinder the Enemy from coming upon the Backs of the *English*.

Being come into the Plain, himself with several Officers, and about 100 Soldiers went to drink at a Well; where when they were drinking, they received a Volley of about 30 Shot from the Enemy, who lay hid in the Woods; yet there was but one Man hurt tho' they all stood close together. After which Major *John Stanley* was sent with a Party to scour the Woods, which he did, beating them from two strong Breast-Works they had upon a *Saddle*, between two Hills (opposite to those the *English* had before gained:) In which Works Major *Stanley* posted himself. The Passages being both Ways secured, Sir *Timothy Thornhill* encamped that Night with the main Body of his Forces in the Middle of a Plain; and the next Morning his two Brass Field Pieces with Carriages, and two Iron ones without, were brought ashore. The Iron ones were planted in the Plain, but the Brass ones were drawn up to the burnt House; whither Sir *Timothy Thornhill* removed his Camp: And about three in the Afternoon on the 21st of *January*, they began to play on the Enemy.

In the Evening Captain *Bartholomew Sharp* was sent with one Company of Men to cut a Path thro' the Wood, that the

The History of Nevis.

the *English* might make an Attack on the Enemy that Way: For in the Valley they had 4 great Guns planted directly in the Road; but being without Carriages, they could not bring them to bear upon the *English* as they lay encamped.

Captain *Sharp* was discovered before he had made any Progress in his Work, and so hotly dealt with that he was forced to retreat. The *French* kept firing all Day upon the *English* from their Breast-Work, both with their great Guns and small Arms; but in the Night they silently quitted it.

The next Morning Sir *Timothy* left Lieutenant *James Smith*, with 30 Men at the burnt House, marched to the Breast-Work and demolished it; as also their Line, which ran down to a Well in the Valley near their 4 great Guns.

A Mile off of this he came to a fine Plain, encompassed with Orange and other Fruit Trees where he encamped. Here was Store of Cattle grazing and some Houses, where the *English* took some Prisoners; from whom they understood the Enemy had had near 20 Men killed and wounded.

The Major General left Mr. *Spencer* in the Plain with a Guard to take Care of the Plunder, and marched with the main Body of his Forces against the Enemy's chief Fort about two Miles distant; which he took without any Loss, having but one Man wounded in the Action. Indeed the Enemy quitted it after one or two Volleys. It consisted of 6 great Guns mounted on a Platform without Carriages, with Banks of Earth thrown up.

After he had nailed down the Guns, he proceeded in his March about four Miles farther, and then encamped in a pleasant Valley, where were a House and Garden belonging to a Frier. There he found the Governor's Horse saddled and bridled, he having left him and fled into the Mountains with the Inhabitants.

The same Day being the 23d of *January*, Major *Stanley* marched over the Hills, on the other Side of the Island, and engaged a Party of the Enemy, beating them out of a Breast-Work and demolishing it. At Night he returned to his Post on the *Saddle*.

The 24th Sir *Timothy Thornhill* continued his March round the Island without Opposition; and at Night returned to the Burnt-House, where he again encamped, and ordered the Plunder to be removed thither.

On the 25th the *English* saw three great Ships, a Brigantine and a Sloop standing in with the Island, and understood, by some Prisoners, that Monsieur *Du Casse* was come down from St. *Christopher's*, with 700 Men, commanded by the Governor of that Island.

The

The History of Nevis.

The Major General immediately commanded away Guards to all those Bays where he thought the Enemy would land; but they seeing the *English* Sloops perceived he was already upon the Island, and so came not to an Anchor, but gave chase to those Sloops, which made the best of their Way to get clear. One of them being in great Danger, ran ashore to prevent being taken, but was hawled off again by the Enemy, who found no Men in her, for they had all got off.

The Master of one of the Sloops being at the Camp when the Prisoners were brought in, who gave this Account, Sir *Timothy* dispatched him with an Express to the Lieutenant General then at *Antego*, to acquaint him with the Condition the *English* were in, and desire him to send Ships to their Assistance.

Du Casse stood off and on all Night, and in the Morning coming close in with the Shore, fired several Guns to give the Inhabitants Notice of his Arrival. About Noon he came to an Anchor before the Windward Part of the Island, hanging out bloody Colours.

The Inhabitants encouraged by the coming of these Ships, came down out of the Mountains, and finding their Fort unmaned they again took Possession of it, replanting and drilling their Guns. In the Night *Du Casse* landed his Soldiers. Of which the Major General having Advice, he brought his Field-Pieces from the Burnt-House into the Plain, and planted them on the right and left Wing of the Body which was there encamped; the Iron Pieces being planted before towards each Road. He placed strong Guards upon the *Saddle* at the Burnt-House, and the Mountain which commanded it.

In this Posture of Defence he continued the 27th, 28th, and 29th of *January*; the Enemy not daring to attack him, tho' they had received a farther Reinforcement of 3 Ships, and more Men from St. *Christopher's*.

On the 30th of *January* in the Morning, Col. *Hewetson* arrived from *Antego* with 3 Ships, which the Lieutenant General had sent to Sir *Timothy Thornhill's* Assistance.

The *French* Ships at Anchor, perceiving *English* Colours, weighed and stood out to meet them. About Noon they engaged, and after four Hours Dispute with little Damage on the Side of the *English*, the *French* bore away; the *English* Ships also standing off all Night, but in the Morning on the 31st of *January* they returned. The *French* Ships also appeared in Sight, but kept off at a Distance. The Major General having sent the Plunder and Field-Pieces on board, ordered all his Out-Guards to quit their Posts, and march down
into

The History of Nevis.

into the Plain in order to embark, which the Enemy perceiving, they marched down also, and both Parties engaged to the great Loss of the *French*, who were beaten into the Woods and fled in Confusion.

Sir *Timothy Thornhill* afterwards made an honourable Retreat, and embarked safe with all his Men, except about 10 who were killed in the whole Action; and 3 who were taken Prisoners by being asleep in one of the Breast-Works, when the *English* quitted them. One of them made his Escape, got down to the Sea-side, and a Boat went and brought him off clear. The other two were afterwards exchanged. There were about 20 Men wounded, who with the rest arrived safely at *Nevis* on the 2d of *February*.

After the Major General's Regiment returned to *Nevis*, the Inhabitants considering the Service they had done, and their Willingness to continue there in their Defence against the expected Invasion of the *French* at St. *Christopher's*, in the Month of *April* 1690, allowed that Regiment Pay 6 Months, except the *English* Fleet should arrive; and if it did arrive, allowed them one Month's Pay after their Arrival.

The Inhabitants of this Island could not have done more prudently, for their Danger was very great from the Neighbourhood of St. *Christopher's*, where 5 Men of War more were arrived from *Europe*; and it was reported, the Enemies were drawing their Forces together to attack *Nevis*; but the Lieutenant General had, with Sir *Timothy Thornhill's* Regiment, 1200 Men very well armed to defend the Island, there being two *Nevis* Regiments then on Foot, Col. *Pym's* and Col. *Earl's*, of 300 Men each. The Forts, Lines, and Breast-Works were also in very good Repair, and the Men in such Heart, that nothing was talked of, but *rooting the French Interest out of these Parts of the World*, as soon as the Fleet arrived that was expected from *England*, which happened in *June* following: Then Preparations were made with all possible Dispatch for an Expedition against St. *Christopher's*, in which all the *Leeward-Islands* belonging to the Crown of *England* were concerned. They all sent their Quota's of Men to *Nevis*, which was appointed to be the Place of general Rendezvous, it lying most convenient for that Purpose.

On *Monday* the 16th of *June*, 1690, Col. *Codrington*, who had now received a Commission from King *William* and Queen *Mary*, to be Captain General and Commander in Chief of all their *Leeward-Islands*, ordered a general Muster in the Island of *Nevis* of all the Forces raised for the Expedition

pedition againſt St. *Chriſtopher's*, and there were found to be 3000 Men, according to the Muſter Rolls then given in, *viz.*

In the Duke of *Bolton*'s Regiment, commanded by Lieutenant General *Holt*,	700 Men.
In Major General *Thornhill's*, commanded by Sir *Timothy Thornhill* himſelf,	500 Men.
In the *Antego* Regiment, commanded by Col. *Williams*, Governor of that Iſland,	400 Men.
In the *Montſerrat* Regiment, commanded by Col. *Blackſtone*, Governor of that Iſland,	300 Men.
In the two *Nevis* Regiments, commanded by Col. *Pym* and Col. *Earl*,	600 Men.
In the *Marine* Regiment, being a Detachment out of the Men of War, under the Command of Col. *Kegwin*, Capt. of the *Aſſiſtance*,	400 Men.
In the Captain General's Life-Guard, under the Command of Col. *Byam*,	100 Men.

3000 Men.

On the 17th and 18th of *June*, the Forces were embark'd, and on the 19th ſailed from *Nevis* under Convoy of Capt. *Wright*, Commodore of the Squadron of Men of War that was arrived from *England*. We ſhall give a farther Account of this Expedition, when we treat of St. *Chriſtopher's*.

Some Time before the Forces and Fleet arrived from *England*, viz. on *Sunday* the 6th of *April*, about 5 a Clock in the Evening, a ſtrange hollow Noiſe was heard for ſome few Minutes, which was thought to proceed from the great Mountain in the Middle of this Iſland. The Inhabitants were ſuprized and amazed at it; and immediately after, to their greater Amazement, began a mighty Earthquake, with ſo much Violence, that almoſt all the Houſes in *Charles-Town*, which were of Brick or Stone, were in an Inſtant levelled with the Ground, and thoſe built of Timber ſhook: Every Body made what Haſte they could to get out of them. In the Streets the Ground in ſeveral Places clove about a Foot aſunder, and hot ſtinking Water ſpouted out of the Earth to a great Heigth. The *Sea* left its uſual Bounds for more than the third Part of a Mile, inſomuch that very large Fiſh lay bare upon the Shore; but the Water preſently returned again, and afterwards the ſame ſtrange Motion happened ſeveral Times, but the Water retired not ſo far as at firſt. The Earth in many Places was thrown up in great Quantities, and Thouſands of large Trees went with it, which were

buried

buried and no more seen. 'Tis usual almost at every House in this Island to have a large Cistern to contain the Rain Water, of about 9 or 10 Foot deep, and 15 or 20 Foot Diameter; several of which, with the Violence of the Earthquake, threw out the Water 8 or 10 Foot high, and the Motion of the Earth all over the Island was such, that nothing could be more terrible.

Several Sloops that passed from this Island to *Antego* felt it at Sea, between St. *Lucia* and *Martinico*, in their Way to *Barbados*, the Agitation of the Water being so violent, that they thought themselves on Rocks and Shelves, the Vessels shaking as if they would break in Pieces.

Others passing the uninhabited Island, or rather Rock, called *Redunda*, found the Earthquake so violent there, that a great Part of that rocky Isle split and tumbled into the Sea where it was sunk, making as loud a Noise as if several Cannon had been fired. A very great Cloud of Dust ascended into the Air at the Fall. Two very great Comets appeared in these Parts of the World, and in an Hour and a Quarter's Time the Sea ebbed and flowed thrice to an unusual Degree. There happened nothing remarkable here from this Time to the Peace of *Reswycke*, which restored Peace also to the *Europeans* in *America*.

The Reader may observe, that the Island of *Nevis* raised 600 Men for the publick Service against St. *Christopher's*, and we cannot suppose they were above one third of all the fighting Men; if so, there must be 1800 Men in the Island, after so many had been swept away by a Mortality among them: And it is very probable, the Number might be 25000, when the Island was in its most flourishing Condition; in such Case, the Number of fighting Men, old Men, Women and Children, must be 11 or 12000, which will make this little Isle very populous.

The War and Sickness having depopulated it, King *William*, for its Security, ordered Col. *Collingwood's* Regiment of Foot to embark aboard the Ships under the Command of Rear-Admiral *Bembow*, who arrived at *Nevis* the 12th of *January* 1698, and Part of that Regiment was quartered here. The Seamen, the Soldiers, and the Inhabitants were then in good Health.

In the same Year, Col. *Christopher Codrington*, Jun. succeeded his Father (who was lately dead) in the Government of these Islands; who, on the Death of King *William*, having received Orders for proclaiming her present Majesty Queen *Anne*, he commanded the Forces that were in *Nevis* to be drawn up on the Shore towards the *French* Part of

St. *Christopher's*, and the Forces in that Island to draw out facing their Fort also. Himself went on Board the Frigate attending this Government, waited on by 12 Sloops and Brigantines, and held in pretty near the *French* Town of *Baffe Terre* to proclaim the Queen aboard, he being Vice-Admiral of these Seas. Upon a Signal given, her Majesty was proclaimed first at *Nevis*: The Fire of the Cannon began at the Windermost Part of the Island, passed on through the several Forts and Platforms along the Shore, 15 stout Merchant Ships in the Road took it from them, and the Frigats succeeded, being between the two Islands, and the Artillery at St. *Christopher's* took it from the Frigats. This was done thrice, and her Majesty's Companies of Foot, with the Militia of both Islands in two Lines, made as many running Fires.

As soon as the War broke out, this Island and *Antego* fitted out several Privateers to cruize on the *French* Coast, and they were very successful in securing their own Trade and endamaging the *French*: But the Inhabitants of this Island paid severely afterwards for this Success. The *French*, in the Year 1705, made great Preparations to attack the *English Charibbee-Islands*, and threatened *Barbados* itself; but that Island being too strong for them, the Storm fell upon the *Leeward-Islands*, and upon *Nevis* in Particular. The Enemy's Squadron consisted of 12 or 14 Men of War, under the Command of Monsieur *Ibberville*. Their Land Forces were at least 3000; and having made a Descent upon St. *Christopher's*, they came before *Nevis* the 21st of *March*, where they landed their Troops by Night. The Inhabitants had Notice of their coming, and prepared as well as they could for their Defence: They armed some of their Negroes, but that did them more Mischief than Good. Being over-powered by the Numbers of the Enemy, they fled to the Mountain. The *French*, fearing they should never master the Island unless they could reduce the Blacks, tempted them by fair Promises to lay down their Arms, assuring them they should live as well as their Masters; and not a little flattering them with Hopes of Liberty, or at least a very pleasant and easy Servitude. Upon which those false Slaves submitted, and the *French* marching to attack the *English* in the Mountain, the latter beat a Parly, and a Capitulation was concluded on the 24th of the same Month, by which they were to be Prisoners of War, but to remain in the Island, procuring a like Number of *French* Prisoners to be released by Way of Exchange, either in *America* or in *Europe*. In the mean Time they were to be civilly used, and their Houses and Sugar-Works preserved; but the Enemy broke several Articles

The History of Nevis.

Articles of the Capitulation, contrary to the Law of Nations and the Usage of Arms, treating the People most barbarously, and burning their Houses and Sugar-Works. By Threats and Barbarity they forced several of them to sign a second Agreement the 6th of *April* 1706, promising the Enemy in six Months Time to send down to *Martinico* a certain Number of Negroes, or Money in Lieu of them. After which they left the Island, carrying away about 3 or 4000 Negroes, whom they made believe they were going to the *French* Islands to live at Ease; whereas when they had them aboard, they shut them fast down in the *Hold*, and gave out they would carry them to the *Spanish West-Indies*, and sell them to the Mines as they intended, and really did. One of these Negroes, making his Escape to Land, informed those that remained there, how basely the *French* had dealt by them. Upon which the Blacks took Arms, fell on the *French* in the Island, cut their Throats, and in Part revenged their Masters for what they had suffered by them.

The Agents for *Nevis* and *St. Christopher's* at *London*, solicited the Lords of Trade, &c. to have a Consideration for their Losses, which they represented to be several hundred thousand Pounds; and in order to it, those Lords sent one of their Clerks to the *Leeward-Islands*, to take an exact Account of the Damage sustained by this Invasion.

The People of this Island met with as terrible an Enemy this Year 1707 in a Hurricane, which almost entirely destroyed their Sugar-Works, threw down their Houses, tore up their Trees and Plants by the Roots, and left them in a most miserable Condition.

When Col. *Park* arrived at the *Leeward-Islands* he stayed here some Time, and called an Assembly 'Tis said there has been some Differences between him and them, and some Mal-Administration, but having not the Certainty and Particulars of those Matters, we shall say no more of them, nor of the Success of the Representation of the Island to be compensated for their Damages. 'Tis not likely so great a Sum should be given them, while the *British* Empire is at such prodigious yearly Expences to maintain the War against the common Enemy. What may be done for them in Time of Peace will come easily; till then we fear they must look on their Losses as a Debt, but as uncertain a one as some Debts owing in the *Leeward-Islands* to the Merchants in *London*.

Under Col. *Park*, Captain General of this and the other *Leeward-Islands*, are the following Ministers and Officers in *Nevis*.

Lieutenant Governor, *Walter Hamilton*, Esq;

William Burt, Esq; President.

John Smergin, Esq;
Azarias Pinney, Esq;
James Bevon, Esq;
William Butler, Esq;
William Ling, Esq;
Daniel Smith, Esq;
Richard Abbot, Esq;
Philip Broome, Esq;
Thomas Butler, Esq;
Thomas Belman, Esq;
Laurence Broadbelt, Esq;
James Melliken, Esq;
} Counsellors.

Speaker of the Assembly, *Samuel Brown*, Esq;
Chief Justice, *Thomas Belman*, Esq;
Colonel of the Militia Regiment, Col. *Richard Abbot*.
Judge of the Admiralty, *Thomas Belman*, Esq;
Secretary, *Michael Nowell*, Esq;
Commissioner and Collector of the Customs, *John Norwood*, Esq;
Provost Marshal, Mr. *Thomas Denbow*, Deputy.

Tho' Col. *Park* could not have been long in his Government of the *Leeward-Islands*, yet it appears by what Information I had of his Government even 30 Years ago, that it gave Discontent to the People he was to govern, almost as soon as he came among them; but the Council and Assembly in their Address to Queen *Anne* upon his being killed in *Antego* say, *they never complained of him*, and do as good as own, his Death was *occasioned by his Mal-Administration*, their own Words with this softning only, *as they say at* Antego. Neither do they say, they abhor the *Rebellion* of those People and the Murder of Mr. *Park*, but they *abhor* and *detest* all violent Proceedings, Murders and Rebellions, and disown any manner of Concern in the *heinous Crime* at *Antego*. Col. *Walter Hamilton*, General of the *Leeward-Islands* after Col. *Park*'s Death, received the News of it in this Island, where he had married the Lady *Stapleton*, Relict of Sir *William Stapleton*, General of these Islands, and famous in them for nothing more than procuring that excellent Address to King *Charles* II. on his miraculous Escape of the *Ryehouse* Plot.

Col

The History of Nevis.

Col. *Hamilton* did not at all encourage Addresses to Queen *Anne*, in Abhorrence of his Predecessors untimely End at *Antego*, probably that was the Reason of the Softnings in that of *Nevis*, signed by

The Council.	The Assembly.
Daniel Smith, Esq; President.	*John Symonds*, Esq; Speaker.
Col. *Richard Abbot*.	Mr. *Samuel Gardiner*.
John Bevan, Esq;	Mr. *John Butler*.
Azarias Pinney, Esq;	Mr. *John Horn*.
Laurence Broadbelt, Esq;	Mr. *Richard Broadbelt*.
John Norwood, Esq;	Mr. *Solomon Israel*.
John Richardson, Esq;	Mr. *John Smith*.
Michael Smith, Esq;	Mr. *Thomas Bridgwater*.
Robert Ellis, Esq;	Mr. *Roger Pemberton*.
Charles Bridgwater, Esq;	Mr. *Michael Williams*.

This Address, according to Mr. *French*, was offered to General *Hamilton* to be signed by him, but instead of signing it, he reproved them for so doing.

As we have mentioned the Succession of Generals of the *Leeward-Islands* in *Antego*, which of late has been mostly their Place of Residence, and in that Chapter and others, treated at large of the Sugar, Product and Trade, all which are much the same here as in the other Islands, we have nothing to enlarge upon in this. The present General *William Matthews*, Esq; made some Stop at this Island at his first coming to the Government. He summoned the Council and Assembly, and, which probably was the chief Business, recommended to them the Salary Affair: Some of the lower House were for settling 400 *l.* a Year upon him, some 300 *l.* others (who were for fixing no Settlement at all) proposed 1000 *l.* and one 1500 *l.* a Year. After long Debate it was carried for 300 *l. per Ann.* to be paid in Money or at the Country Produce at Currency. This not giving Content, the Council proposed to the Assembly at their next Meeting to enlarge the Settlement, but the Assembly would not hear of it.

The 300 *l.* is to be raised on Slaves (the Number of which is said to be near 7000) at 1 *s.* 6 *d. per* Head, which amounting to more than 300 *l.* the Overplus was to defray some Charge, together with the Rent of an House for the Governor's Reception for the 1st Year, at 100 *l.* which by the Act that grants the Settlement, is limited to one Year only.

THE

THE
HISTORY
OF
St. *CHRISTOPHER*'s.

CONTAINING

An Account of its Discovery, Settlement, Events, Climate, Soil, Product, Trade and Inhabitants, *Charibbeans* and *English*.

THIS Island is called *Liamuiga* by the Savages, and was discovered by *Christopher Columbus*, in the first Voyage he made to *America*. He gave it the Name of St. *Christopher*'s, not from his own, but from the Figure of its Mountains; there being in the upper Part of the Island a very high Mountain, which bears as it were on its Shoulders another less Mountain, as St. *Christopher* is painted like a Giant, with our Infant Saviour on his Back.

'Tis in the Latitude of 17 Degrees, and 25 Minutes on this Side the Line, and about 75 Miles in Circuit.

The *Charibbeans*, who are the *Indigenæ* of the Island, and possessed it before the Discovery of the *West-Indies*, inhabited it when Sir *Thomas Warner*, an *English* Adventurer, came thither.

Monsieur *Desnambue*, a *French* Gentleman, of the ancient House of *Vauderop*, who commanded for the *French* in *America*, arrived at St. *Christopher*'s on the same Day with Sir *Thomas Warner*, and both took Possession of the Island in the Name of their respective Masters, that they might have a Place of safe Retreat, and a good Haven for the Reception

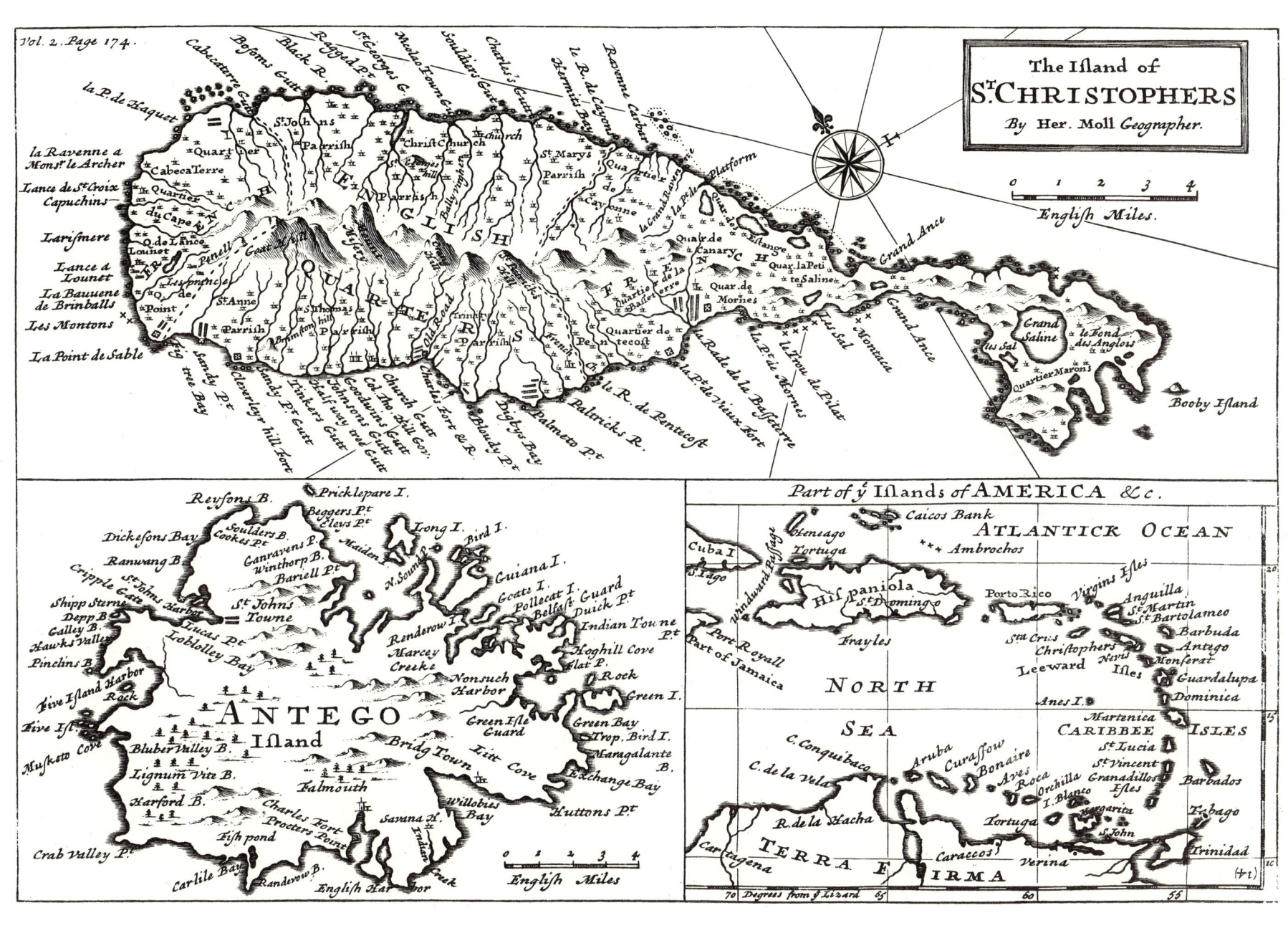

The History of St. Christopher's.

ception of such Ships of both Nations as should be bound for *America*, it being well stored with Harbours. The *Spaniards* used to put in there in their *West India* Voyages, to take in fresh Water; and they were in so good Terms with the *Charibbeans*, that sometimes they left their Sick there, to be looked after by them.

These two Gentlemen considering, that by possessing themselves of this Island, they should very much incommode the *Spaniards*, resolved to leave Colonies of both Nations here; and without entering into Disputes about who came first, and who had the best Title to the whole, they agreed to divide the Island between them. They accordingly became Masters of it, and forced the Inhabitants to submit: But before they left it, having cause to fear there might be some secret Intelligence between the *Indians* and the *Spaniards*, the *Charibbean* Magicians having advised the *Savages* to take their Opportunity, and cut the Throats of all the *Europeans*, the *English* and *French* fell upon the most factious of the Natives by Night, killed them, and drove the rest out of the Island. Then the two Gentlemen left some of their Men upon the Place, and returned, Sir *Thomas Warner* to *England*, and Monsieur *Desnambue* to *France*, for Recruits.

Their Masters approved of their Conduct, and sent them back with Supplies of Men and Provisions, and Commissions to be Governors of the new Settlements. *Sir* Tho. Warner, Governor.

Monsieur *Robbe* in his Account of St. *Christopher's*, says, Monsieur *Desnambue* found several *English* and *French* Fugitives upon the Place when he came thither; to whom he proposed to establish a Colony, and they consenting, chose him for their Governor: Which Design, on his Return to *France*, he communicated to Cardinal *Richlieu*; by whose Means an *American* Company was set up in the Year 1626. And Captain *Warner*, who was there at the same Time, on the like Occasion, gave Rise to a like Company in *England*. Robbe, p. 379. 4 Edit. Par.

This Company continued in *France* till the Year 1651. when they sold St. *Christopher's*, and the other Islands, to the Knights of *Malta*. But in the Year 1664. the *West India* Company, by the King's Orders, bought out the last Proprietors, and are still in Possession of those Islands.

Sir *Thomas Warner* and Monsieur *Desnambue* sailed in the Year 1626, and the latter arrived there about *January*, 1627. having had a long sickly Voyage. The *French* were about 300 in Number: The *English* Colony as many. Sir *Thomas* had proceeded a good way in his Settlement before Monsieur *Desnambue* arrived; and the two Governors, to prevent Differences among their People, about the Limits of their

their Territories, signed Articles of Division, on the 13th of *May*, 1627. They then set those Boundaries to their several Divisions, which remain to this Day, with this particular Proviso, that Fishing and Hunting should be equally free to the Inhabitants of both Nations; That the Salt-Ponds, and most valuable Timber should also be in common, together with the Mines and Havens: Also a League offensive and defensive was concluded between them against all their Enemies. After which they set themselves to work, each in his Station, to advance his Settlement.

The *English* received constant Supplies of Men and Provisions from *London*; by which Means they thrived better than the *French*, and not only became strong enough to keep what they had, but to be able to spare Men for new Plantations at *Nevis*, which Sir *Thomas Warner* took Possession of, and left People upon it for a Settlement, in the Year 1628. And in that which followed, *Don Frederick de Toledo* was sent with a Fleet from *Spain* of 24 great Ships of Burden, and 15 Frigats, to dispossess the *English* and *French* of the Island of St. *Christopher's*.

The *Spaniards* were alarmed at the Progress of the *English* in the *Charibbee-Islands*, and thought it concerned the Safety of their own Plantations to prevent these Nations from settling in their Neighbourhood.

Don Frederick meeting some *English* Ships lying near the Isle of *Nevis*, seized them, and then came and cast Anchor in the Road of *Marigot*, under the Cannon of the *Basse Terre*, where Monsieur *Rossey* commanded.

Neither the *French* nor the *English* Forts were in a Condition to oppose such an Enemy. Their Stores of Ammunition fell short, and their Numbers were no Match for the *Spanish* Army, had they been never so well provided with Powder and Shot. *Rossey*, after a small Opposition, abandoned the *Basse Terre*, and retreated to *Cabes Terre*, another Fort, where Monsieur *Desnambue* was in Person, who could not prevail with his Men either to defend themselves there, or to retire to the Fastnesses in the Forests and Mountains, where a few Men might have resisted a thousand. He remonstrated to them, that *Don Frederick* could not afford to spend much Time in following them, for that he was bound to the *Havana*, to bring home the *Flota*: Yet this, and a great deal more which he said to them, was to no Purpose. Nothing would content them but embarking, and leaving the Place; which he was forced to comply with: And so all the *French* deserted their Settlement, as did their Allies the *English*, who were in a great Consternation; and the
Disorder

Disorder encreased, upon News of *Desnambue's* being gone with his Colony Some endeavoured to escape by Sea, others fled to the Mountains; and all of them who left, finding it was in vain to resist such a powerful Enemy, sent Deputies to treat with the *Spaniards*. The *Don* knowing he had them in his Power, commanded them, *en Maitre*, to leave the Island immediately, or he would put them all to the Sword. He sent them their own Ships, which he had taken at *Nevis*, to embark on, and was persuaded to give Leave to those to stay that had not Room in the Ships for themselves and their Families, till they could be transported. Upon which *Don Frederick* weighed Anchor, carried with him 600 *English*, who were fittest for his Service; and he was no sooner gone, but the *English* rallied, and resolved to go on with their Settlement.

The *French*, who were got no farther than *Antego* and *Montserrat*, sent a Ship for Intelligence to St. *Christopher's*, and understanding the *Spaniards* were gone, and the *English* busy in rebuilding and replanting, rejoiced at this happy and unexpected Turn of Fortune, sailed back to St. *Christopher's*, and retook Possession of their former Habitations.

The *English* continued carrying on their Colony, till they were in a Condition to spare more Men for Settlements at *Barbuda*, *Montserrat*, and *Antego*; which Sir *Thomas Warner* peopled and planted: And the same Year the *Dutch* made themselves Masters of St. *Eustace*, and the *French* took Possession of some other Islands. 1623.

The *English* built themselves good Houses at St. *Christopher's*, and had Wives and Families: Whereas the *French* contented themselves with Huts, after the *Charibbean* Manner. Few of them were married, and consequently took little Pains to furnish themselves with all Things necessary and convenient in Life.

Monsieur *Desnambue* died about the Year 1637. and Sir *Thomas Warner* did not long survive him. Before the *English* Governor's Death, the Colony was so encreased, that there were between 12 and 13000 Souls of his own Nation in the Island. He was succeeded in his Government by Col. *Rich*; who by following his Predecessor's Steps, in well governing the Colony, invited more People to come and settle there. *Col. Rich Governor.*

The chief Employment of the first Planters was cultivating Tobacco; by which they got a competent Livelihood, but afterwards the Quantity that was made, bringing down the Price, they set themselves in several Places to plant Sugar, Ginger, Indigo, and Cotton; and in a little Time became

a rich

a rich and flourishing People, both *French* and *English* living very lovingly together, till the late Wars in *Europe* blew up a Flame there, which is likely to end in the dispossessing of the one or the other of them.

Let us now take a farther View of the Country; for which, in the Sequel of our History, we shall find a great deal of Blood shed by the two contending Nations.

The Island is extremely delightful, and the Mountains lying one above another, afford a lovely Prospect over all the Plantations, to the Sea Coasts, all round the Island. Between the Mountains are dreadful Rocks, horrid Precipices, thick Woods, and hot sulphurous Springs at the Foot of them, in the South-West Part of the Island. There's an Isthmus at the South-East End, which runs into the Sea, within a Mile and an half of *Nevis*; on the same Shore is a Salt-Work.

The Air is good and wholesom, but much disturbed with Hurricanes. The Soil is light, sandy and fruitful, as the vast Quantities of Sugar, and other Commodities which it has produced, sufficiently prove.

This Soil produces Sugar of a finer Grain than that of *Barbados* or any other of the *Charibbee-Islands*, insomuch that I have been informed that the Muscovado here turns out as fine without claying, as in those Islands it does with it, which is a vast Advantage to the Planter, saving a great deal of Waste and Labour.

The Middle of the Island is hardly passable, because of the high and craggy Rocks and Precipices in the Mountains, and the Thickets and Forests, where it is easy for Companies of Men to lose themselves, though it is to be hoped, that that Inconvenience will be remedied in Time, the *English* being as dextrous as any People in the World at clearing of Ways, and felling of Woods.

The Mountains are divided, as it were, into Stories, one above another. And from the highest of them the Eye is wonderfully charmed, to see the Trees always green, which are planted round every Ground as Boundaries. The Plantations look like so many Gardens, and Nature is always gay and smiling.

The fine Houses in this Island add to the Beauty of the Prospect, there being no finer Buildings in *America*: Many of them are covered with glazed Slate. The first that are mentioned of this kind to be built here, were Sir *Thomas Warner*'s, Colonel *Rich*'s, his Successor in the Government, Mr. *Everard*'s, and Colonel *Jefferson*'s.

The History of St. Christopher's.

The *English*, for the Convenience of planting, live scattered up and down the Country. Their Houses are of Cedar, and the Walks and Groves about them of Orange and Lemons. They are divided into five Parishes, three on the South-Side, and two on the North-Side.

In each of which is a very handsom Church wainscotted within, and the Pulpits and Pews made of variety of precious Wood, as Cedar, Ebony, Red-Wood, Brasil, and others, curious for Colour, and delightful for Scent.

The *French* built a fine Town, under the Cannon of the Citadel of *Basse-Terre*, of good Brick, Free-stone, and Carpenter's Work. There's a large Church, a Town-house, and an Hospital. The Church there was formerly in the Hands of the *Capuchins*; but in the Year 1646. upon some Distaste, they were dismissed by the Inhabitants, and *Pere du Vivier*, with his Jesuits, had the Superintendency of Ecclesiastical Affairs. The *Basse-Terre* is now an *English* Town and Parish, as that Part which the *French* possessed is now entirely *English*.

The Castle in this Town where the *French* Governor resided, is the most noble Edifice in the Island; but for the Planters and Merchants Houses, those of the *English* were more stately than the *French*.

The Rivers are a great Refreshment to the People and Country; this Island is indifferently well fortified, having three good Forts and several Batteries.

On the Mountain, about three Miles North of *Fort-Charles*, is a Place called the *Silver-Mine*; and the People of the Country say there is such a one, but they have not Hands, nor indeed Hearts to work it; for their Sugar Plantations turn to so good an Account, that they do not care to quit a certain for an uncertain Profit, finding they can grow rich at a cheaper Rate: And it must be confess'd, that with due Encouragement our Plantations would bring us in as much Treasure as the Mines of *Peru* and *Mexico* have brought into the King of *Spain*'s Treasury; for besides his own Subjects, the *English*, *French*, and *Dutch*, have always had more than their Share with him. The *Sulphur-Mine* is between *Fort-Charles* and *Point-Sable*, near the Shoar.

The Verge or Out-sides of the Island may be travelled round, the Country being all a Level; but, as has been said, some Parts of the Middle are inaccessible. It is out of the Rocks there that several Springs of hot Water issue, and one Part of the Hills goes by the Name of the *Sulphur Mountain*.

The Fort on *Brimſton-Hill* mounts 49 Pieces of Cannon, it contains a Magazine ſupplied with 18,000 Pounds of Powder, 800 Firelocks, 600 Bayonets and other Military Stores. *Charles-Fort* is furniſhed with 40 Pieces of Ordnance and a ſufficient Quantity of Military Stores. *Londonderry-Fort,* ſituated on the Eaſt of the Town *Baſſe-Terre,* ſecures that Part of the Iſland, as do alſo ſix Batteries raiſed at ſo many Landing-places, in all mounted with 43 Pieces of Ordnance.

The Beaſts in this Iſland are the ſame with thoſe in *Barbados,* and the other *Charibbee-Iſlands* ; a few there are which are more frequently met with here, as the *Rocquet,* an Animal, whoſe Skin is like a withered Leaf, marked with little yellow or blewiſh Points. It has four Feet, the Foremoſt higheſt, has ſparkling Eyes, holds up its Head conſtantly, and is in continual Motion. Its Tail is turned up towards its Back, making a Circle and half. It loves to ſtare upon Men ; and when purſued, puts out its Tongue like a Grey-hound.

As for Birds, the moſt particular are, the *Orinoco,* a large Bird, ſhaped like an Eagle ; his Feathers light grey, ſpotted black, the End of his Wings and Tail yellow. He never ſets upon Birds, but in the open Air, and thoſe who have Beaks and Tallons like himſelf.

The *Crawfoul* is another Bird, about the Bigneſs of a great Duck, aſh-colour, has a long flat Back, a great Head, ſmall Eyes, and ſhort Neck, with a Craw, which will contain two Gallons of Water. They ſit upon Trees by the Sea to catch Fiſh, which they diſcover at a great Diſtance ; and are ſo intent on their Prey, that they are eaſily ſhot, but not eatable.

The *Colebry* or *Humming-Bird,* is admirable for its Beauty, Bulk, ſweet Scent, and Manner of Life. It is no bigger than the greateſt Sort of Flies, yet ſo beautiful, that the Feathers on the Neck, Back, and Wings, repreſent a Rainbow. Under its Neck is ſuch a bright red, that it reſembles a Carbuncle. Its Belly is yellow as Gold ; its Thighs green, like an Emerald ; the Feet and Beak black, like poliſhed Ebony ; its Eyes like Diamonds ſet in an Oval ; its Head of a ſhining green ; the Male has a Tuft on his Head, of all the Colours we have mentioned. He makes a Noiſe with his Wings like a little Whirlwind. He ſucks Dew from the Flowers, ſpreading abroad his little Creſt, which looks like ſo many precious Stones. The Female lays but two Eggs, of an oval Form, as big as a Pea or ſmall Pearl : Some Ladies wear them for Pendants, when dead, though then they loſe much of their Beauty. Their Smell is like that of the

fineſt

finest Musk. This is also found in *Virginia*, *Barbados*, and other Places in *America*.

Before we return to our History, from which we have made this long Digression, if we may be said to digress in what we have written of the Product and Country of St. *Christopher's*, it will not be improper to say something of the *Charibbeans*, who were the Natives of the Island.

They are the same Sort of People with the Inhabitants of the other Islands, tractable and credulous. They were willing enough to live peaceably with the *Europeans* who first landed there, and were upon the Place, when Monsieur *Desnambue* came thither; but upon his Landing, their Boyez or Conjurers, telling them, in a general Assembly met on Purpose, that the Foreigners were come to take away their Country from them, and destroy them Root and Branch, it was resolved to massacre them, as we have hinted already, and the *English* and *French* drove them out of St. *Christopher's*. After which they had long Wars with both Nations, and made Descents on the Islands they had lost, from those to which they retired.

An Account of the Charibbeans.

These *Charibbeans*, say some Authors, were descended from *Arouagues*, a People of *Guyana*; their Ancestors rebelling against their King were forced to fly from the Continent to the Islands, which were till then uninhabited.

Our Country-man, Mr. *Brigstock*, who travelled much in *Florida*, and spoke the Language of the Country, derives them from the *Apalachites* in *Florida*, where there is a Nation who to this Day are called *Charibbeans*, the Island of St. *Cruz* being the first they landed upon after they were forced, by the Narrowness of their own Limits, or the Power of their Enemies, to quit the Continent. These *Apalachites* or *Apalicheans* are at the back of *Georgia*, *Carolina*, &c.

Dav.

They are a handsom well shaped People, not an One-eyed, lame, crook-backed, bald, or deformed Man to be seen amongst them. They are black-haired, and keep it combed nicely. They pluck up their Beards by the Roots as fast as they grow. They go stark naked, both Men and Women; and the *French*, who are a very complaisant People, to shew these *Barbarians* how well bred they are, when they go among them, strip themselves, to be of the Mode. They dye their Bodies with a Tincture, which makes them red all over. They wear a little Hat of Birds Feathers of different Colours, and sometimes a Crown of Feathers. They make Holes through their Lips, and put a kind of little Bodkin through them, made of the Bone of some Beast

P. 254.

Beast or Fish. They do the same by their Nostrils, in which they hang a Ring or Grain of Crystal, or some such Toy. The Men wear Bracelets on the brawny Parts of their Arms, the Women about their Wrists. They adorn their Legs with Chains of Rossada, instead of Garters. Those of them who have no Acquaintance with the *Europeans*, commonly wear Whistles about their Necks, made of the Bones of their Enemies. The most considerable of all their Ornaments are certain large Medals of fine Copper, extremely well polished, without any graving on them; which are made in the Form of a Crescent, and enchased in some kind of solid and precious Wood. These in their own Language they call *Caracolis*. It is the Livery or Badge by which the Captains and their Children are distinguished from the ordinary Sort of People. The Women paint the whole Body, and wear a kind of Buskins, which fall no lower than the Ankle.

 The *Charibbeans* have an ancient and natural Language, and a kind of bastard Speech; in which they have intermixed several *European* Words, especially *Spanish* : The last they speak among the *Christians*, and the first among themselves. Though the *Charibbeans* of all the Islands do generally understand one another ; yet there is in several of them some Dialect different from that of the others. Their Language is extremely smooth, and has few or no *Gutturals*. The *Charibbeans* of the Islands have a sweeter Pronunciation than those of the Continent.

 Some *Frenchmen* have observed that they have a Kind of Aversion for the *English* Tongue, and carry their Aversion so far, that they cannot endure to hear it spoken.

 They are shy of teaching their Language to the *Europeans*, even after they have embraced the Christian Religion. The Men have many Expressions proper only to themselves, which the Women understand well enough, but never pronounce: As for Example; *Amac* a Bed is the Man's Word, and *Nekera* a Bed the Woman's; a Bow, *Oullaba*, the Man's, *Chimala* the Woman's; the Moon, *Nonum*, the Man's, *Kati* the Woman's ; the Sun, *Huyeyou* the Man's, *Kachi* the Woman's; and many others. The Women have also their Words and Phrases, which if the Men should use they would be laughed at.

 The Savages say this Distinction of the Mens and the Womens Language was occasioned thus: When 'the *Charibbeans* came to inhabit these Islands, they were possessed by a Nation of *Arouagues*, whom they absolutely destroyed except the Women, whom they married to repeople the Country ; the
Women

Women retaining their own Language, taught it their Daughters, and this is practised to the present Times by Mothers towards their Daughters: The Male Children thus imitate their Father's, and the Female their Mother's Speech.

The *Charibbeans* of the Continent, Men and Women, speak the same Language. The old Men in the Islands have affected Terms and Phrases not used by the young ones.

They have a certain particular Language made Use of only in their Councils of War, which is very sounding and full of Fustian: The Women and Maids know nothing of it, but else they understand the Mens, and the Men their Language very well, though they do not speak it.

They have few Words of Injury, and had none for several Vices, till the *Europeans* supplied them with them. Before they were taught by them, they had no Words for the Virtues, Sciences and Arts. They can name but four Colours, White, Black, Yellow, and Red, to which they make all the rest agree.

Of other Nations they say, the *English* and *Spaniards* are not good at all; that the *Dutch* have as much Goodness as a Man's Hand as far as the Elbow; but like true Barbarians, that *the* French *are as both Arms*, which they stretch out to shew the Greatness of their Worth. A *Frenchman* tells us so, and as all of that Nation are very ready to wrong ours, so are they as well disposed to do themselves too much Justice.

The *Charibbeans* are naturally pensive and melancholy, but affect to appear chearful and pleasant, especially when they have drunk a little too freely. They take it as a great Affront to be thought *Savages*, saying, that Term belongs only to Wild Beasts: Nor do they like the Name of *Cannibals*, tho' they eat the Flesh of their Enemies, which they say they do out of Revenge. Perhaps they have learnt so much Delicacy from the *French*, who have conversed with them more than any other *European* Nation. They are pleased with the Name of *Charibbeans*, looking on it as an Acknowledgment of their Generosity and Courage; for in the *Apalachites* Tongue, that Word signifies as much as warlike and valiant Men.

They are of a tractable Disposition, and so compassionate among themselves, that some have died of pure Grief, when they heard any of their Countrymen who were Slaves to *Europeans*, have been ill used by them.

They reproach the Christians with their Avarice, for all their Care is for moderate Food. They wonder the *Euro-*

peans prefer Gold to Glafs and Cryftal. They alfo lay Injuftice to their Charge, in taking their Iflands from them.

They have not only an Averfion to travelling into any other Country, but they would not willingly fuffer any of their Countrymen to be carried out of their own, yet they are very curious to fee every Thing a Stranger brings among them.

In their Traffick they are apt to fall off from their Words; however, if they are reflected upon as light and inconftant, they are afhamed of it.

Theft is a great Crime among them: They leave their Houfes and Plantations, without any Body to look to them, and are not afraid of a Thief. If a Knife is taken from them they mourn for a Week. and are eager to be revenged. They are very loving one to another till they are injured, and then never forgive.

Their young Men have no Converfation either with Maids or married Women. The Men are lefs amorous than the Women, both are naturally chafte; and if they had not been debauched by the Example of the *Europeans*, Luft would have been one of the Words which the *Charibbeans* had no Term for. The Chriftians have taught them Diffimulation, Lying, Treachery, Luxury, and feveral other Vices, which were unknown in thefe Iflands, before they had any Commerce with them.

The *Savages* are civil and courteous to Strangers, fays my Author; and if they have fo many other good Qualities, why are they called *Savages* ? They are very fimple, and fhew it in nothing more, than in the extraordinary Fear they conceive at the Sight of Fire-Arms, not being able to imagine how they go off, but believe the evil Spirit *Maboya* does it, who they think eats up the Moon when fhe is eclipfed. They cry *Maboya*, or the Devil's here, if they fmell any ill Scent. Not long ago they believed Gun-Powder was the Seed of fome Herb, and fome were fo foolifh as to fow it. They reckon Salt prejudicial to Health, and therefore are afraid to make any. They will not eat Swines Flefh nor Tortoife; the former for Fear of having fmall Eyes, and the latter leaft they might participate of that Creature's Lazinefs and Stupidity; yet they are fo ftupid, they cannot count a Number exceeding that of their Fingers and Toes. The Captains, the *Boyez*, and the moft ancient among them who have more Underftanding than the common Sort, count the Months by Moons, and the Years by the feven Stars, yet there's no Monument of Antiquity among them. They can't tell how long it is fince their Anceftors left the Continent, nor can they

they ever tell what Age they are of, nor give any Account of the Time when the *Spaniards* came into their Country.

As to their Religion, they say the Earth is the indulgent Mother, who furnishes them with all Things necessary to Life. They hearken to what is said to them of a God, the Creator of all Things, and of the Mysteries of Faith; all the Answer they make is, *Friend, thou art a cunning Fellow, I wish I could talk as well as thee.*

The *Charibbeans* of the Continent have no more Religion than those of the Islands: Some of them have a certain Respect for the Sun and Moon, yet they do not worship them. All that looks like Religion among them is, they have a natural Sentiment of some Divinity, who is content quietly to enjoy the Delights of its own Felicity, without being offended at the ill Actions of Men; that it is endued with so great Goodness it does not take any Revenge even of its Enemies, whence it comes that they neither honour nor adore it.

They think there are two Kind of Spirits, some Good and some Evil. The good Spirits are their Gods, and every one imagines there's one of them particularly designed for his Conduct. They say their Abode is in Heaven, but they know not what they do there.

When an *Englishman* or *Frenchman*, or any other *European* talks to them of the God that made Heaven and Earth they reply, *True, thy God made the Heaven and Earth of* England *or* France, *or any other Country which they name, and causes thy Wheat to grow there, but our God made our Country, and causes our Manioc to grow.*

Thus their natural Sentiment of a superior Power is intermixed with so many Extravagancies, and involved in such Darkness, that it cannot properly be said, these poor Wretches have any Knowledge of God.

They have no Temples nor Altars particularly dedicated to their Gods or good Spirits, but they bring their Offerings of *Cassava*; and when they think they have been cured by them of any Disease, they make a kind of Feast in Honour of them. They invocate them when they desire their Presence to demand Revenge, to be cured of some Disease to be advised in their Wars, or to drive away *Maboya*, or the evil Spirit; and this their *Boyez* or Priests do for them. Every *Boyez* has his particular God, which he invokes by the Singing of certain Words, accompanied with the Smoke of Tobacco, as a Perfume very grateful to him. The *Boyez* alway invocate their Gods or rather Devils, by Night; but all that is said of the Spirits entering into the Bones of dead

Men, or poffeffing Women to pronounce Oracles, let thofe report who believe it.

When any of thefe Savages are taken ill, they believe the Gods of their Enemies fend the Diftemper. They apply to their *Boyez*, and they tell them whofe Gods did it, which occafions Enmity between the Perfons; for there are other Priefts befides the Popifh, that make it their Bufinefs to fet People together by the Ears. Their *Boyez* are alfo Magicians.

As to their *Maboyas* vifibly appearing among them, beating them, and playing other Pranks, we think the Reader would believe us as filly as thefe *Americans*, if we give Credit to it or reported it, tho' we find it done by other Hiftorians, who are fond of Miracles.

'Tis faid the Spirits of Darknefs take Occafion in the Night Time by hideous Apparitions and dreadful Reprefentations to frighten the miferable *Charibbeans*, that they keep them in a fervile Fear of their Power, charm their Senfes by Illufions, and oblige them to facrifice to them on all emergent Occafions.

The *Charibbeans* believe they have every one of them as many Souls as they feel Beatings of Arteries in their Bodies; the principal Soul they think is in the Heart, and after Death it goes to Heaven with its particular God, who carries it thither to live in the Company of other Gods; and they fuppofe it lives the fame Kind of Life as Man lives here on Earth. As to the other Souls which are not in the Heart, they believe fome after Death go and live on the Sea-fide, and that they caufe Veffels to turn. The others live in the Woods and Forefts, and are their *Moboyas* or evil Spirits.

They are extremely afraid of Thunder and Lightning, and thofe of them that feem not to be concerned at it when they are among the Chriftians, have been found to be as much terrified as the reft, when they have been at Home.

As for their Habitations, they require only a Tree and a Hedgebill to build them. Their Houfes are near to one another, in the Form of a Village, and for the moft Part they plant themfelves upon fome little Afcent, as well for the Goodnefs of the Air, as to fecure themfelves againft thofe peftilent Flies, called Muskettos and Maringoins. They love to dwell near Springs, Brooks, and Rivers, becaufe of wafhing themfelves every Morning, before they put the red Paint on their Bodies.

Their Houfes or Huts are made in an oval Form, of Pieces of Wood planted in the Ground, over which they put a Roof of Plantane Leaves or Sugar-Canes, or fome Herbs; which they can fo difpofe and intermix one among another,

The History of St. Christopher's.

another, that under that Covering which reaches to the Ground, they are secured against Rain and all the Injuries of Weather. This Roof will last three or four Years, unless there happens to be a Hurricane.

They make Use of small Reeds fastened a-cross for Palisadoes. They have as many Partitions under every Covering as they would have Rooms. A Piece of Matting serves instead of Doors, Bolts and Locks. There's nothing above their Heads but the Roof itself, and the bare Earth only is under their Feet; but they are so cleanly, they sweep as often as they see the least Filth upon it.

Besides the little Room where they take their Rest and entertain their Friends, every considerable Family has two other little Rooms, the one is their Kitchen, the other their Storehouse. They have a Sort of Hanging-Beds like Coverlets, made of Cotton neatly woven, which is fastened to certain Pillars, and there they swing as in a Hammock if they please, or fix them in a settled Place as they think fit.

They breed great Numbers of Poultry, and have about their Habitations good Store of Orange-Trees, Citron-Trees, Guavas, Fig-Trees, Bananas, and other Fruit-Trees.

Their Gardens are full of Manioc Potatoes, several Sorts of Pulse, as Pease, Beans, Maize, Millet, and others. They have also Melons, Citrons, Cabbage of very delicious Taste, and Ananas.

They often change their Habitations as the Humour takes them, either on Account of their Health or Cleanliness, or the Death of one of the Family. The Men for the most Part spend their Time abroad, but their Wives keep at Home, and do all that is requisite about the House.

The Men hunt and fish, but the Women fetch Home the Venison from the Place where it was killed, and the Fish from the Water-side. They also get in Manioc, prepare the Cassava and the Ouicou, or ordinary Drink, dress the Meat, set the Gardens, keep the House and Houshold-stuff clean, paint their Husbands with Roucou, spin Cotton, and are continually employed.

In the Islands of St. *Vincent* and *Dominico*, there are some *Charibbeans* who have many Negroes to their Slaves. Some of them they got from the *English*, and some from *Spanish* Ships cast away on the Coasts; and the Blacks serve them as obediently as if they were the most civilized People in the World.

The *Charibbeans* are temperate and cleanly in their Meals, at least the greatest Part of them. They often eat publickly together, the Women never eat till their Husbands have
done.

done. They patiently endure Hunger, they dress all their Meat with a gentle Fire, and are not the worst Cooks in the World. They commonly eat sitting on low Stools, and every one has his little Table to himself. Instead of Table-Cloths they use fair and large Banana Leaves newly gathered. They wash their Hands before Meals, and before they dress their Meat. Their ordinary Bread is a thin Cake, which they call *Cassava*, made of the Manive Root. They have another Kind of Bread made of Maze, and some of them instead of Bread eat Potatoes.

Their common Food are Lizards, Fish, Pulse and Crabs. Their Desert are Figs, Bananas or Ananas. Sometimes the *Charibbeans* on the Continent have a detestable Kind of Seasoning to their Meat, which is with the Fat of the *Arouagues*, their irreconcileable Enemies.

Their Drink is generally Mobby, made of Potatoes boiled with Water; as the *Ouicou* is of *Cassavia*. In several Places delicious Wine is to be met with, as Palm Wine, Couscou and Cane Wine, made of Sugar-Canes; and there was more of this Wine made by the *Charibbeans* of St. *Christopher's*, than by any other Savages, because this Island abounded most with Sugar-Canes.

The *Europeans* have taught them to forsake several of their barbarous Customs, particularly of their Severity to their Wives; for of late they are seldom seen to fetch Home the Fish and Venison taken by their Husbands, and when they have been a fishing, the Husband and Wife eat together: Besides, the Women go oftner to the *Carbet*, or House of publick Feasts and Rejoicings than formerly; neither are the Barbarians such Enemies to the Flesh of Tortoise, Lamantine, and Swine, as they were before. An Instance of which is reported in a *French* History of the *Charibbee-Islands*. A Gentleman of that Nation who lived in one of them, being visited by a Cacique or Captain of the Savages, entertained him and his Company in Jest, with Lamantine's Flesh. The Cacique mistrusting the *Frenchman* would put a Trick upon him, prayed the Gentleman not to deceive him; and the other upon his Honour assured him he would not. Then the Cacique fell to it, and eat heartily. After Dinner the *Frenchman* confessed the Deceit, to see how the Cacique and his Followers would behave themselves: But the *Charibbean*, the least Savage of the two, replied, *Well Friend, we shall not die of it*: And he and his Followers put a good Face on the Matter, but went Home resolving to be revenged. Accordingly some Time after, the Cacique invited the Gentleman to an Entertainment at his Village;

The History of St. Christopher's.

Village, and the latter went thither attended by some of his Countrymen. The *Charibbean* gave them a plentiful Feast, but had ordered his People to put into all the Sauces some Fat of their dead Enemies, of which the chief *Charibbeans* are always well provided. When Dinner was over, the Cacique asked the Gentleman and his Companions, how they liked their Treatment? They all highly commended it, and thanked him for his Kindness. He then acquainted them with the Trick he had put upon them. Most of the *Frenchmen* were so shocked at hearing it, that they could not retain what they had eaten, and growing sick of the Fancy, the *Charibbean* laughed and said, *I am now revenged of you.*

The Savages take Pains even in their Pleasures. The chiefest of their Exercises are Hunting and Fishing, especially the latter. They are wonderful expert in using their Bows and Arrows. They do not take their Wives with them when they hunt or fish, as some Basilians do.

Their ordinary hunting is for Lizards. They are the best Fishermen in *America*, either with the Hook or Dart, or other Inventions. They weave Beds, make Baskets of Bull-Rushes, Wooden-Chairs all of one Piece, little Tables wove of the Leaves of the Latanier-Tree, Streining-Cloths, Carocolis, several Kinds of Vessels for eating and drinking, Girdles, Hats and Crowns of Feathers. The Women make Buskins, or Half-Stockings of Cotton for themselves.

The Men are very neat in ordering and polishing their Arms, and take a great deal of Pains about the Periagas or Boats, some of which are so large, that they will carry 50 Men. They make earthen Pots of all Sorts, as also Plates. They delight much in handling Joiners and Carpenters Tools, and would make good Mechanicks. They are great Lovers of Diversion and Recreation, and take a particular Pleasure in keeping and teaching a vast Number of Parrots and Parakets.

The *Charibbeans* have musical Instruments, but indeed very far from deserving that harmonious Name. Their Drums are made of hollow Trees, over which they put a Skin only at one End. They have a rude Kind of Organ made of Gourds. As soon as they are up in the Morning, they tune a Pipe well polished, and handsomly made; some of them of the Bones of their Enemies. While they are tuning their Pipes, their Wives are busy in getting them their Breakfasts. They sing certain barbarous Airs over their Fish while it is broiling. Most of their Songs are bitter Satyrs in their Way, on their Enemies. They have also Songs on Birds, on Fishes and Women. In the latter they would give Offence

fence to Mr. *Collier*, for like the Barbarians of *Parnassus*, they are full of *Smut*.

The *Charibbeans* Dancing is chiefly at their Corbet, or Place of publick Entertainment. At such Times they spend the Day and Night in Eating, Drinking, Dancing, Talking, and Laughing. Both Men and Women then make a shift to get drunk, but they are seldom so beastly except on those solemn Occasions. As when a Council of War is held, when they return from any Expedition, no Matter whether fortunate or unfortunate; on the Birth of their First-born, when their Childrens Hair is cut, when they are at Age to go to the Wars, when they begin a Building, launch a Boat, or are recovered of any Disease. They have on the contrary their solemn Fasts, but it would be too tedious to give all their ridiculous Reasons for them.

They receive Strangers who come to their Islands to visit them, with great Tokens of Kindness and Affection. They are very much afraid of being surprized by the *Europeans*, and driven out of the Islands they possess; and to prevent it have Men posted on the Sea-Coasts and on the high Mountains, to discover who comes and give Notice. Immediately they send away a Canoo, to see if they are Friends or Foes, for they will not trust any People's Colours, having been deceived by the *Europeans*. If they are Enemies and land, they lay Ambuscades, fall upon them from thence, and then on a sudden, joining all together, let fly a Shower of Arrows, and afterwards come to Handy-blows with their Clubs. If the Enemy is too hard for them they fly to Rocks, or even the Sea, and some diving down will rise 200 Paces off. They often rally again after they are routed, meeting all at a certain unknown Place of Rendezvous.

Their having no Arithmetick is the Occasion that they cannot tell what Number of them there is in any of their Islands: But it is supposed where they are most numerous, they cannot make above 1500 fighting Men.

The Strangers that come like Friends are entertained as such, with equal Chearfulness and Plenty. Their Government is as barbarous as their Customs, or rather as strange; for why should they be called barbarous for any Thing we have said of them, except it is their eating the Flesh of their Enemies?

There are several Sorts of Captains in every Island belonging to them, the Captain of the Carbet or Village, which is generally the Father of a numerous Family; the Captain of the *Periaga*, or Boat, and an Admiral, who commands the whole Fleet; the grand Captain, or Captain General, who

The History of St. Christopher's.

is also called Cacique. His Office is during Life, he is preferred by Election, leads their Armies, and is always highly esteemed among them.

There are seldom above two Caciques in an Island. None of these Caciques have any Command over the whole Nation, nor any Superiority over the other Captains after the War is over, and none of them command twice in chief, unless he has distinguished himself eminently.

Let us see what are the Qualities that a new Man must be Master of, to give any a Pretence to stand for the Office of Captain General among the *Charibbeans*. He must have been several Times in the Wars, and have behaved himself bravely in them. He must surpass all his Competitors in running, in Swimming and Diving. He must be able to carry a greater Burthen than the rest of the Pretenders, and to endure Pain; which Experiment is made by cutting and hashing his Flesh, and his best Friends make the deepest Incisions. But this Ceremony is not used every where, and those *Charibbeans* who have much Commerce with the *Europeans*, have quite left it off, with several other Customs, at which they laugh.

The Cacique being chosen makes War, prepares for it, and leads the Army. He appoints Assemblies of Counsellors, and of the Carbet.

As for Laws they have none, and no Magistrates. He who thinks himself injured, is his own Judge, and gets what Satisfaction he will or can of his Adversary. If he does not revenge himself, he is despised as a Coward. They are such Strangers to Law and Lawyers, that they have no Words in their Tongue for *Justice* and *Judgment*. And if they knew what they meant in ours, or how they are abused, they would with Reason turn the Barbarians upon us.

They carry some Women to their Wars, to dress their Meat, and look to their Periagas. Their Canoos are less Boats, fit for Rivers or Bays only. Their Custom is to go from Island to Island to refresh themselves, and to that End, they have Gardens in those which are desert.

The *Arouagues* a Nation of *Guyana*, are their irreconcileable Enemies, who cruelly persecuted the *Charibbeans* of the *Continent*, the Relations of those of the Islands. The latter sail once or twice a Year in their Periagas to find them out, and be revenged on them.

The *Arouagues* never make any Attempt on the Islanders, but always stand on their Defence only. The Island-Savages coast along all the other Islands from St. *Cruz*, the furthermost of the *Charibbees*, which is 300 Leagues distant from the

the *Arouagues*: When they land if they are difcovered they take it for an ill Omen, and retire. If not, they feek their Enemies and engage them. The Prifoners they take are not immediately flain, but chained and carried Home.

Next to the *Arouagues* they hate the *Spaniards* and *Englifh*. A *French* Author gives this for a Reafon of their Hatred to the *Englifh*, that the latter, under the Flags of other Nations, got feveral *Charibbeans* aboard their Ships; when they had firft made them drunk, carried them to their Plantations, and kept them as Slaves; which, it is very probable, is a fcandalous Reflection on our Countrymen by our Enemies the *French*.

They have made feveral Incurfions upon the Iflands of *Montferrat* and *Antego*, burnt Houfes, deftroyed Plantations, and carried away Men, Women, and Children; but we do not underftand they eat any of them, the *Arouagues* being their only Difh of that Kind.

About 50 Years ago they had fome *Englifh* Boys and Girls in the Ifle of St. *Vincent*'s, who being carried thither very young, were bred up by the Savages with equal Gentlenefs as their own, and had fo accuftomed themfelves to their Way of living, that they were only diftinguifhed from the *Charibbeans* by their fair Hair.

They have the fame Averfion for the *Spaniards*, and for the fame Reafon; but the *French*, according to my Author, a *Frenchman*, are in the good Graces of the *Charibbeans*.

The Reader will not be difpleafed to have a particular Account of their Treatment of their Captives, or Prifoners of War, it being from thence they are called Cannibals, and are perhaps the only People upon Earth that eat Man's Flefh out of Choice. For though the *French*, who converfe moft with them of any Nation in *Europe*, gives us fuch a Defcription of them, that one would think they were become as polite as themfelves; yet it is certain, they often feaft themfelves with that abominable Repaft, which but to think of, makes Nature ftart, and the Blood curdle in ones Veins with Horror.

When they bring Home a Prifoner of War from among the *Arouagues*, he belongs of Right to him who feized him, and that Savage keeps him at his Houfe, fecures him there in Bonds, and after he has been kept fafting four or five Days, produces him at the Carbet to ferve for a publick Victim, to the immortal Hatred of his Countrymen towards that Nation.

If there be any of their Enemies dead upon the Place, they eat them before they leave it. The young Maids and Women taken in War are only defigned for Slavery. They do not eat the Children of their Female Captives, but formerly

had

had good Stomachs for all the Male-Captives, as well of other Nations, as of the *Arouagues*.

We are not entirely convinced of the Truth of this, but in the History of the *Charibbee-Iflands*, tranflated out of *French* by Mr. *Davyes*, the Author pretends this is not only true, but fays there was a great deal of Difference between a Ragout made of a *Frenchman*, and one made of a *Spaniard*. His Words are, as they are rendered in our Tongue; *They have heretofore tafted of all the Nations that frequented them, and affirm, that the* French *are the moft delicate, and the* Spaniards *of hardeft Digeftion*; *but now they do not feed on any Chriftians at all.* Wherein the Vanity of the *French* Nation is the moft confpicuous that ever we met with; for they are not only content to fay in other Places, they fight the beft, write the beft, talk the beft, paint the beft, fing the beft, dance the beft, &c. but this *French* Author avers, they *eat the beft* of any People whatever; which is a Compliment on his Nation, the Cannibals perhaps learnt to put on them, fince they were civilized by them; for there's no doubt, but among other of their Talents, they taught them that of Flattery.

They ufed to torture their Captives before they killed them, but now they give them the *Coup de Grace*, knock them on the Head, broil, and then eat them. As foon as the unfortunate Prifoner is laid dead upon the Place, the young Men take up the Body, wafh it, and cut it in Pieces, then they boil Part, and broil Part of the Flefh; the Women licking the very Stick on which the Fat of the *Arouague* dropped. Each there prefent has his Portion. All the Greefe that is produced by this diabolical Cookery is carefully faved, and diftributed among the chiefeft of them, who keep it in *Gourds* to relifh their Sauces with it.

They rub the Bodies of their Children with the Blood of thefe miferable Victims, to animate them to future Cruelties, and thus they make their Revenge hereditary. But the *French* Author does all he can to excufe thefe Cannibals, by Examples of others more cruel than they. And indeed there feems to be a great Difpofition in him to forgive the *Charibbean* Man-Eaters, who had fo highly extolled the favoury Difh of a *Frenchman*.

When thefe Savages defire to marry, they have a Privilege to take all their Coufin-Germans, and make no more ado about it, than to fetch them and enjoy them. After which they are their lawful Wives. They may have as many as they pleafe, and the Captains value themfelves much on the Number of theirs.

They build a particular Hut for each Wife, continue with her they like most, and the rest conceive no Jealousy at it. She whom they honour most with their Company is very assiduous in waiting upon them. They love their Wives very passionately while it lasts, but leave them when they please, with or without Reason; yet it is seldom known that they forsake their first Wives, especially if they have had Children by them. They often make their young She-Prisoners of War their Wives. Their Children by them are accounted free, but their Mothers are still reckoned Slaves. If any one of them has no Cousin-Germans, he may marry such as are not a-kin to him, demanding them of their Fathers and Mothers. They are then, provided Consent is obtained, *ipso Facto*, their Wives, and Home they carry them. Those young Men that have signalized themselves in the Wars, are much importuned by the Fathers and Mothers of the young Maids, to take them to be their Wives, and as often as they return victorious from War, new Wives are offered them. The young Men never converse with either Maids or Women till they are married. If a Woman was formerly inconstant to her Husband, he knew not how to punish this Crime, but since the *Europeans* have made it better known among them, if a *Charibbean* finds his Wife prostituting herself to another, he does himself present Justice, by beating out her Brains with his Club, or cutting her open with a Razor.

Their Customs at the Birth of their Children are too obscene to be reported. One merry enough is, that the Man lies in instead of the Wife, and is dieted for 10 Days; and at the Birth of the First, the Father is scarified, and fasts a long Time.

As soon as the Children come into the World, the Mothers make their Fore-heads flat. They do not swath them. They name them 10 Days after their Birth, and give them Names from some Accident that happened to the Father while the Wife was with Child: As for Instance, a *Charibbean* of *Dominico* having been at St. *Christopher*'s, in the Time of his Wife's being with Child, and seen the *French* General, named the Child he had at his Return *General*, in Remembrance of the kind Entertainment he had met with from him. These first Names are changed by the Male Children, when they grow up to be Soldiers.

The *Charibbean* Women suckle their Children, and are very good Nurses. Their Children are bred up in a great Reverence of their Parents, they are carefully educated in the

Exercise

Exercife of the Bow, and other Arms, to fifh, fwim, make Baskets, Clubs, Bows, Arrows, Beds, and Periaguas, which is all they think is neceffary they fhould underftand.

Thefe *Charibbeans*, by their natural Temperament, Sobriety and Exercife, enjoy Health and long Life. 'Tis faid, they are fo vigorous in their old Age, that it is common for them to get Children at fourfcore and ten Years old. Many among them have not a grey Hair at above 100 Years old. They live, fays the above-mentioned Author, commonly Ibid. p. 150 Years, and fometimes longer; for about 50 or 60 Years 342. ago, there were fome Perfons living among them, who remembered the firft Arrival of the *Spaniards* in *America*. Thofe very old Perfons are Bed-riden, immoveable, and reduced to meer Skeletons.

When they are at any Time fick, they have Recourfe to Herbs, Fruits, Roots, Oils, and Gums, by the Affiftance of which they foon recover their Health, if the Difeafe be not incurable. They have an infallible Secret to cure the ftinging of Snakes, a great Skill in their Kind of Phyfick, and if it fails, apply themfelves to their *Boyez* or Conjurers, who by their devilifh Myfteries pretend to cure them. 'Twas formerly a great Act of Friendfhip among them, to kill fuch as were old and ufelefs, but it is not thought fo now.

They bury their Dead with many ridiculous Ceremonies, reckoned holy among them, and fometimes kill Slaves to wait on the Ghofts of the deceafed.

Thus we have in a little Compafs, given the Reader a diftinct Idea of the Origin, Hiftory, Cuftoms, Manners, Religion, and Way of Living of the *Charibbeans*, the firft Inhabitants of thefe Iflands; and this Account is to ferve for all the other Iflands as well as St. *Chriftopher's*, of which we are treating; and that being one of the biggeft, we thought we could not infert it in a more proper Place.

Before we continue the hiftorical Events of this Ifland, we fhall take fome farther Notice of the Climate and Country, by other Informations. 'Twas formerly much troubled with Earthquakes, which, upon the Irruption of the *Sulphur* Mountain there many Years ago, have in a great Meafure ceafed, and have feldom been felt there fince. Hurricanes are ftill frequent here, and it was fome Time fince the Cuftom of both the *Englifh* and *French* Inhabitants in this and the other *Charibbee-Iflands*, to fend about the Month of *June*, to the Native *Charibbees* of *Dominico* and St. *Vincent*, to know whether there would be any Hurricanes that Year; and about 10 or 12 Days before the Hurricane came, they conftantly fent them Word, and it very rarely failed.

An

Lowth. Vol. II. p. 105.   An *Indian* who lived with Capt. *Langford* several Years, gave him these Prognosticks, to know when a Hurricane was coming. It comes either on the Day of the full Change, or Quarters of the Moon. If it will come on the full Moon, you being in the Change, then observe these Signs: That Day you will see the Skies very turbulent, the Sun more red than at other Times, a great Calm, and the Hills clear of Clouds or Fogs over them, which in the High-Lands are seldom so. In the Hollows of the Earth or Wells, there will be a great Noise, as if you were in a great Storm; the Stars at Night will look very big with Burs about them, the North-West Sky very black and foul, the Sea smelling stronger than at other Times, as usually it does in violent Storms; and sometimes that Day for an Hour or two, the Wind blows very hard Westerly, out of its usual Course. On the full of the Moon you have the same Signs, but a great Bur about the Moon, and many Times about the Sun. The like Signs must be taken Notice of on the Quarter-Days of the Moon. In the Months of *July*, *August*, and *September*, for the Hurricanes come in those Months; the soonest that had been ever heard of was the 25th of *July*, and the latest the 8th of *September*, not many Years since, for the Month they usually come in is *August*.

We have nothing farther to say of St. *Christopher's*, as to the Natural or Geographical Account of it, so we shall return to the Historical; in which, if we are not more exact, the Reader will excuse us, considering the Difficulties we were obliged to struggle with: For having much less Acquaintance with the *Leeward Islands*, than with the other Plantations, we could not procure so many Memoirs, as we have done for other Parts of our History of the *British* Empire in *America*.

Mr. Everard, Governor.   To Mr. *Rich*, the second *English* Governor of St. *Christopher's*, succeeded Mr. *Everard*, who continued in the Government several Years; and by what we can understand, was in that Office when the Rump usurped the supreme Power in *England*. The *Leeward-Islands* refusing to acknowledge their Sovereignty, King *Charles* the IId. appointed Major General *Poyntz* to be Governor, and he was in Possession of St. *Christopher's*, when Sir *George Ayscue* arrived at *Barbados* and reduced that Island: After which he sailed to *Nevis* and St. *Christopher's*; but Major General *Poyntz* not being strong enough to defend himself against the Power Sir *George* brought with him, withdrew before his Arrival, and ship'd himself for *Virginia*, the only Retreat for Cavaliers.

Who

The History of St. Christopher's.

Who the Parliament put into this Government, we cannot tell, but after the *Restoration*, the Lord *Willoughby* was made Governor of the *Leeward-Islands*, as well as of *Barbados*, and he resided there some Time.

Who was his immediate Successor is not come to our Knowledge, unless it was Sir *William Stapleton*, whom we find not long after the Lord *Willoughby's* Death, in Possession of this Government, in which he continued to his Death; and in his Stead King *James* made Sir *Nathaniel Johnson* Governor of the *Leeward-Islands*, who enjoyed it till King *William's* Accession to the Throne; when, through Discontent or Fear, he withdrew to *Carolina*, and made Way for Colonel *Codrington* in the Government of these Islands, who being a great Proprietor here, was the more acceptable to the Inhabitants.

There had not been any declared War between *France* and *England*, since the Settlement of the Island of St. *Christopher's*; yet the *English* and *French* had not been without Skirmishes there upon their particular Quarrels, but they never made any Attempt to dispossess each other till the last War, which followed the *Revolution* in *England*; for King *Charles* and King *James*, in their Treaties with *Lewis* the XIVth, agreed, that in Case of a Rupture in *Europe*, the Subjects of both Kings, in the *West-Indies*, should be Neutral, that they might not be involved in Wars, to which they did not in the least contribute in the Cause of them, and that their Trade might not be interrupted, which would be very fatal to their growing Settlements: But the *French*, who were never famous for observing their Treaties, broke this; and before any Declaration of War was made in *England* or *France*, they entered the *English* Pale, and destroyed it with Fire and Sword, forcing the Inhabitants to fly to the Forts for Safety. It is true, the Animosities between the two Nations were grown to a great Heigth; and it is said, the *Irish* Papists, and others of the Popish Faction in St. *Christopher's*, instigated the *French* to break the Peace there, before it was broken in *Europe*.

In King *William's* Declaration of War against the *French* King, the Invasion of the *Charibbee-Islands* by the *French*, is mentioned as one of the Reasons of it.

When they had reduced the *English* to great Streights, the latter applied to the Government of *Barbados* for Succours; but before those Succours arrived, the *English* surrendered the Forts, and their Part of the Island of St. *Christopher's* to the Enemy, on the 29th of *July*, 1689. and could obtain no better Conditions, than to be sent to the adjacent Island of *Nevis*. We

The History of St. Christopher's.

We must now leave the *French* in Possession of the whole Isle, and the *English* Inhabitants of it dwelling in other Places. This proved a terrible Loss to the Merchants of *London*, and other Parts of *England*, trading to the *Leeward-Islands*; for the Factors at *Nevis* took great Part of their Merchandize, their Negroes especially, to the Planters of St. *Christopher's*; and this made their Debtors incapable of paying them. Some dishonest Factors took hold of this Opportunity to balance their Accounts with their Principals; and a Merchant of *Nevis*, who owed his Correspondent 10000 *l.* paid off the greatest Part of it with Debts at St. *Christopher's*; for many Persons being ruined in this deplorable Calamity, it was a Temptation to an unfair Correspondent to sink his good Debts with the bad; and the Author is but too well convinced, that there's a great deal of Truth in this Conjecture.

Eight Months after the *French* were sole Masters of St. *Christopher's*, there happened an Earthquake here, which was felt in the other Islands. The Earth opened nine Foot in many Places, and buried solid Timber, Sugar-Mills, &c. It threw down the Jesuits College, and all other Stone-Buildings.

The *French* had two Men of War here; and having equipped 15 small Vessels, they put 4 or 500 Men aboard, and went down to *Stacia*, out of which Island they drove the *Dutch*.

We have mentioned Sir *Timothy Thornhill's* being at *Antego*, and his going thence to *Nevis*, to wait for the Arrival of Commodore *Wright*, with the regular Troops expected from *England*. It is said in our Account of *Nevis*, that the Forces rendezvoused there; and all that remains for us to say here, is, what they did when they arrived at St. *Christopher's*.

The Captain General, *Christopher Codrington*, Esq; commanded in this Expedition in Person, and sailed from *Nevis*, with the Land Forces, on *Thursday* the 19th of *June*, 1690; and the same Evening the Fleet came to an Anchor before the Island of St. *Christopher's*, in *Frigat-Bay*. In the Night, eight Frigats weighed, and fell down three Leagues to leeward, to amuse and harass the Enemy; and the next Morning they returned. That Day the *English* ply'd their great Guns from some of the Frigats, which lay nearest in with the Shore, upon the *French* in their Trenches, and received some Shot in Exchange from a Battery of five Guns they had there, but without any Damage on the Side of the *English*. At Night a Council of War was held

aboard

aboard the Commodore, at which affifted the General and Field Officers, and the chief Commanders of the Men of War.

According to the Refolutions by them taken, Major General *Thornhill*, with 400 of his own Regiment, and a Detachment of 150, out of the Regiments of *Nevis*, *Antego*, and *Montferrat*, landed the next Morning between two and three of the Clock, with the Forelorn, at the little *Salt-Pits*, about a League to the Windward of *Frigat-Bay*. The Field-Mark were Matches about their Left Arms. The Enemy made no Oppofition, having left that Place unguarded by Reafon of its Situation, it lying at the Foot of a Hill, which is almoft inacceffible, and over which they thought it impoffible for Men to march. The *Englifh* mounted this fteep Afcent, by a Path frequented by none but wild Goats, and in fome Places fo near a Perpendicular, that they were forced to ufe their Hands as well as their Feet, in climbing up. About break of Day they gained the Top, where they received a Volley of about feven or eight Shot, from fome Scouts placed there, who immediately upon their firing retired. Two Officers were wounded by thofe Shot, and one of them died of his Wounds foon after. Sir *Timothy Thornhill* left one Company to fecure the Pafs upon the Hill, and led his Men down a third Part of it, before they were difcovered by the *French*, who then fired briskly upon the *Englifh* from their Trenches, wounded feveral Men, and among others Major General *Thornhill* himfelf, who was fhot through the Small of his Left-Leg, which obliged him to ftay the Binding of it up: But his Men, *Creoleans* moft of them, ran refolutely down upon the Enemy, and flanked them in their Trenches; at the fame Time that the Duke of *Bolton*'s Regiment, and the *Marines*, landed at *Frigat-Bay*. In which Action Colonel *Kegwin* received a mortal Wound, of which he foon after died.

Colonel *Holt*, who commanded the Duke of *Bolton*'s Regiment, and acted here as Lieutenant General, charged the Enemy fo bravely, that he forced them to quit their Poft in Diforder, and leave the *Englifh* Mafters of the Field. Fourteen *French* and *Englifh* were killed in this Difpute.

Sir *Timothy Thornhill* and the wounded Men being fent on Board the Ships, and the Forces all landed, were drawn up into four Battalions. Colonel *Holt*, who led the Van, was ordered with his Regiment to take the Road adjoining to the Sea. Lieutenant Colonel *John Thomas*, at the Head of the *Barbados* Regiment, marched thro' the Country; and Col. *Williams* with the *Antego* Regiment, marched at a Diftance, as a Referve to that Body. The other four Regiments kept their Pofts, and waited for farther Orders. After

After an Hour's March, Colonel *Holt* came up with a small Party of the Enemy, and routed them. The Companies of *French* which ran from *Frigat-Bay*, joining with the rest of their Forces, they all advanced against the *English*, and having the Advantage of the Ground, and three to one in Number, they charged the *Barbados* Regiment. After a sharp Dispute of half an Hour, the *French* had almost surrounded the *English*; but Colonel *Williams* coming up with the Reserve, and attacking them vigorously, and unexpectedly, the *Barbadians* were so encouraged, that they pressed resolutely on, and beat the Enemy out of the Field in Confusion, one part flying to the Mountains, and the rest betaking themselves to the Fort, which formerly belonged to the *English*. The four Regiments at *Frigat-Bay* were upon this ordered to march up, and Colonel *Holt's* Regiment also joined Colonel *Thomas*. After which the whole Army was drawn up into one Body, and the Soldiers were permitted to drink by Companies at the adjacent Wells and Cisterns.

While the Army was thus refreshing, the Cockswain of the Commodore came with Advice to the Captain General, that the Men of War having fallen down before the Town and Fort of *Basse-Terre*, the *French*, after firing two or three Rounds, struck their Flag, set the Town on Fire, and quitted it, but by the Diligence of the Seamen, who came ashore from the Frigats, it was extinguished.

Upon which General *Codrington* marched immediately to *Basse-Terre*, designing to quarter the Army there that Night; but the Enemy having left Store of Wine, and other Liquors behind them, and he fearing the Disorders it might breed among the Soldiers, altered his Resolutions, and only halted there, placing his own Company of Guards, commanded by Colonel *Byam*, in the Mass-house. He then ordered the Army to march to the Jesuits Convent, lying about a Mile above the Town; where they were drawn up again, and Orders were given to lie by their Arms all Night.

Guards were set, and Parties sent out to drive in Cattle. The *English* found Store of Flower, Bread, &c. in the Convent. The Night proved wet, and it rained without Intermission till Morning; but the Officers generously shared the Weather with the Soldiers, scarce any, except the general Officers, going into the Convent for Shelter.

The next Morning the Army marched down to the Town, the Commissary General having secured the Liquors in a convenient Store-house: The Soldiers had free Liberty to plunder the Town, and the Commiffary of each Regiment diftributed alfo Wine and Brandy among them. The Fort here was mounted with 16 Guns, which the Enemy had nailed and fpiked; but the *Englifh* cleared them again.

In the Afternoon Major *Gunthorp* was fent with 150 Men out of the *Antego* Regiment, to gain and fecure a Pafs, which was thought to be poffeffed by the Enemy. It lay in the Way to the *Englifh* Fort, and the *French* quitted it before Major *Gunthorp* came up.

The next Day the *Englifh* continued in the Town; and in the Evening, the Country all round it was in Flames, being fired by the *Englifh* Negroes, who came from the Mountains; where they had lain fince their Mafters the *Englifh* were beaten off the Ifland.

The Day following General *Codrington*, with the whole Army, marched towards the Fort, and that Night encamped about three Miles from it, having the like ill Fortune of rainy Weather. The fame Day the Men of War weighed from *Baffe-Terre*, and fell down to *Old-Road*; and the Wheel-barrows, Shovels, Pick-Axes, &c. were brought afhore.

On *Thurfday* Morning, the 20th of *June*, the *Englifh* marched within a Mile of the Fort, and encamped under Covert of a high Hill; a Detachment out of Colonel *Earl*'s Regiment being fent, under the Command of Captain *William Butler*, to fecure the Top of it.

The next Day the Commodore's two Chafe-Guns, and fix Pounders, were brought afhore, in order to be drawn up to the Top of the Hill; and the Marine Regiment, under the Command of Colonel *Kirby*, Captain of the *Succefs* Man of War, was employed to cut and clear a Path for the drawing them up; which was done in two Days time, a Platform laid, and the Guns mounted on it. Baskets of Earth were thrown up, for a Covering from the Enemy's Shot, it lying open to the Fort. On which they began to play on the 30th of *June*, the very firft Shot doing Execution. The Frigats alfo weighed from *Old-Road*, ftood down to the Fort, and battered it; the whole Army at the fame Time marching into a deep and wide Ditch, between the Hill and the Fort, within Musket Shot of it.

In the Afternoon the Frigats ftood up again to *Old-Road*; but the Guns from the Hill kept playing inceffantly till Night: At which Time the *Englifh* began their Entrenchments, running (from the Ditch where they lay encamped) a Trench, with a Half-Moon at the End, capable of holding 400 Men.

One

On the 1st of *July*, one of the *Nevis* Regiments, and part of the *Antego* Regiment, was sent under the Command of Colonel *Charles Pym*, to take a small Fort of the Enemy's about three Miles distant from the Camp; which they surprized, and made 50 Men Prisoners.

In the Evening, Lieutenant General *Holt* having given Orders to the Out-guards that were placed towards the Fort, to fire, without challenging any one who should come that Way: Himself afterwards riding by them in the Dusk, to view the Works, was shot into the Body by one *Gibbons*, an *Irishman*, who was one of the Soldiers upon Duty. He returned to the Camp, and languished long of the Wound, with little Hopes of Recovery. *Gibbons* was tried by a Court-Marshal, but after a full Hearing, acquitted.

The Guns on the Hill proving so serviceable, on the 2d of *July* four more, of a larger Size, were drawn up; but one of them splitting at the first Firing, and the rest being incommodiously planted, they were no more made use of. The same Day four Companies of the Enemy marched out of the Fort, and drew up before the Gate; but in a Quarter of an Hour they marched in again.

The *English* having finished their Half-Moon, ran another Trench about a Quarter of a Mile below it, able to contain a like Number of Men. And at a like Distance below that, they began another, wide enough to draw the Carriages of the great Guns through.

The four following Days they continued quiet in their Trenches, and at Night ran on their Works. The *French* fired Day and Night upon them with great Guns and small Arms, but did them little Damage: Whereas the Guns on the Hill extremely galled the Enemy, leaving no Corner of the Fort unsearched. Some Hundreds of *French* being out in the Mountains, headed by one Monsieur *Pinelle*, Parties were daily sent abroad, commanded by the Officers in their Turns, to scour them out. And the Major General, Sir *Timothy Thornhill*, being returned, went himself, on the 7th of *July*, at the Head of 200 Men, on the same Design; but could not meet with any Enemy to engage him, the *French* lurking sometimes in one Place, and sometimes in another. However he took some Prisoners, many Negroes, and store of Cattle.

After Sir *Timothy Thornhill*'s Return to the Camp, a Proclamation was made by beat of Drum, in several Places of the Island, by the Command of the General, that all who would come in, in three Days Time, should receive his Protection, to secure their Persons from the Outrages of the Soldiers,

The History of St. Christopher's

Soldiers. Several Families surrendered themselves; of whom many were permitted to return to their Houses, and keep some small Stock, till farther Orders. Monsieur *Pinelle* also sent in a Flag of Truce from the Mountains, to acquaint General *Codrington*, that he could not come in without Leave from the Governor. However he assured him, he would remain quiet, and give free Passage to any of the *English* he should meet with.

The Army continued in their Trenches the 10th and 11th of the same Month, having run them within Pistol Shot of the Fort. They had a Half-Moon over against the Gate, on which they planted several Colours, two 18 Pounders, and four 12 Pounders; but before they were mounted, on *Saturday* the 12th of *July*, the Drums beat a Parley in the Fort, and four Persons marched out with a Flag of Truce. They were met in the Pasture, between the *English* Trenches and the Fort, by Major *Legard*, and by him conducted to General *Codrington*.

After some Treaty Hostages were given on both Sides: A *French* Major continued with the *English*, and Lieutenant Colonel *Not* was sent to the *French*. Captain *Hamilton* went also with him, as an Interpreter. Notwithstanding the Treaty, General *Codrington* continued in his Works, joining his Trench to the Enemy's Trench, through which they used to come from the Fort to the Well. Out-Guards were placed under the Walls, and at the Gates of the Fort: And in the Evening the *English* mounted their Guns on the Battery. About 12 a Clock in the Night, there was a Canoo let over the Fort-Walls, (it being situate by the Sea-side) which ran aboard a Sloop that came close in with the Shore, under Covert of the dark Night. The *English* let fly a whole Volley upon them, which made them hasten away.

Captain *Hamilton* came to the Centry, at the Fort-Gate, and ordered him to acquaint Sir *Timothy Thornhill*, that there was a Ship seen off. Upon which Mr. *Spencer*, his Secretary was dispatched away to *Old-Road*, to give Commodore *Wright* Notice of it; but in the Interim, a Brigantine was sent in Pursuit of the Sloop.

The Commodore immediately ordered two Frigats to weigh, and put out in Search of the said Ship, a Sloop; which they did: And the next Day they returned, without seeing any Vessel.

All the while the *English* were attacking the *French* at Land, there were two Men of War that cruized about to take any *French* Ships that might arrive there, either by Design or Chance; but they met with none.

The History of St. Christopher*'s.*

On the 14th of *July,* the Fort was surrendered to General *Codrington,* upon the same Articles that the *English* had, when they delivered up the Fort to the *French.*

After the Enemy marched out, the *English* Flag was put up, the King's and Queen's Health were drank, the great Guns thrice fired, and three Volleys made by the whole Army.

The Fort was quadrangular, consisting of four Flankers, with three Curtains between each. On each Flanker were mounted five Guns. The Walls were of Stone, about 20 Foot high, surrounded with a deep Ditch, 12 Foot wide, over which was a narrow wooden Bridge. In the Middle of the Fort were two Mounts, thrown up for Batteries. There was also a Well, but upon firing the Guns, the Water presently dried away. There was store of Provisions, Liquors, and Powder; but they wanted Shot.

The *English* had about 100 Men killed and wounded, in re-taking this Island; which in general is very strong, there being several small Fortifications and Breast-Works all round, except where it is naturally fortified with Hills and Shoals.

The Inhabitants were about 1800 Men, besides Women, Children, and Negroes, who were all, (except the Negroes, who were to be divided as Plunder*)* transported to the Island of *Hispaniola* ; only some particular Persons had the Favour granted them, to be carried up to *Martinico.*

After a few Days Refreshment, Sir *Timothy Thornhill* embarked with his own Regiment in the Sloops, and the *Marines* on board the Frigats, and set sail for the Island of St. *Eustace.*

The same Day, the 20th of *July,* he came before the Island, and sent Captain *Hamilton* ashore, with a Flag of Truce, to summon the Governor and Inhabitants to surrender : But the Governor returned Answer, That he would defend the Place to the utmost.

The next Morning the Frigats began to batter the Fort; and the Major General landed with his Men, at the same Time under a high Cliff, which they ascended. They had not marched far, after they got up, before they perceived some *Dutch* Colours in the Woods. Upon which a Party was sent to discover them ; who returned with an Account, that it was Colonel *Scorer,* (the Governor of the Island for the *Dutch,* when the *French* took it) with a 100 Men under his Command ; who came from *Saba,* and landed there three Days before ; but not having Strength enough to take the Fort, (into which the Inhabitants were fled) he designed to get what Plunder he could, and so go off again. He refused to join with Sir *Timothy Thornhill,* because he was

first

The History of St. Christopher's.

first landed, and so accordingly he went off the next Day. The Major General proceeded in his March towards the Fort, and encamped within Musket-shot of it, under the Rising of a small Hill.

The next Day the *Marine* Regiment landed, and the Shovels, Pick-axes, &c. being brought ashore, the *English* began their Entrenchments, running their Trench along by the Fort, within Musket-shot of it. After five Days Siege, the Governor sent out a Flag of Truce, with Articles; but he was so high in his Demands, that Sir *Timothy* refused them, and returned for Answer, That if he did not descend to more reasonable Terms within three Days, he would give him and his Men no Quarter. Within the prescribed Time, another Flag of Truce came out of the Fort, and the Governor surrendered it upon Quarter for Life, and to march out with their Baggage. The Fort was mounted with 16 great Guns, was surrounded with double Rows of Stakes, the Intervals filled with Earth, and without that strong Pallisadoes. On the one Side of which was a deep Ditch, and over it a very narrow Bridge, leading to the Gate, admitting but one at a Time. The besieged were about 60 Men, (the Women and Children being sent off some Time before.) They had a Well for Water, about 20 Barrels of Flower, some Salt-fish and Pork, and a small Quantity of Ammunition. They behaved themselves very bravely during the Siege, especially the Governor, who was very active in firing the great Guns. Sir *Timothy Thornhill* had but eight Men killed and wounded in taking this Island, where he left one Company, under the Command of Lieutenant *John Mackarthur*, and then returned to St. *Christopher's*, with the whole Fleet, carrying the Inhabitants with him Prisoners, and from thence they were transported to *Hispaniola*. Lieutenant *Pilkington* was afterwards sent down with a Company of the Duke of *Bolton's* Regiment, to relieve Mr. *Mackarthur*.

The Inhabitants of the Island of St. *Bartholomew's*, who were brought up Prisoners from thence to *Nevis*, being sent down to St. *Christopher's*, before that Island was retaken, there met with their Wives and Families; and after that Island was recovered by the *English*, were desirous to live under an *English* Government. Upon which General *Codrington* gave them Liberty to return to their Island, transported them thither, and granted a Commission to one Captain *Le Grand*, a former Inhabitant among them, to be their Governor, and to keep and defend the Island in the

Name

Name of their Majefties King *William* and Queen *Mary*, under which Government it continued feveral Years.

The *Englifh* thus far went on fuccefsfully, and great Talk there was that they would drive the *French* quite out of the *Charibbee-Iflands*.

The next Expedition was to be againft *Guardaloup*. General *Codrington* ordered the Forces to be muftered in *October*, and be in a Readinefs to embark. Commodore *Wright* was reinforced with fix ftout Merchant Men, fitted out for Men of War at *Barbados*, and more Men were fent from that Ifland, under Colonel *Boteler* and Colonel *Salter*. The Troops rendezvoufed at St. *Chriftopher's*, where Lieutenant Colonel *Not* was left with a Garrifon, to fecure the Inhabitants as well againft the *French* and their Negroes, who had fled to the Mountains, as againft any Enemy that might invade the Ifland. This Precaution was very neceffary; for the *French* and their Slaves in the Mountains often defcended into the Valleys, and in one Defcent killed 15 Soldiers out of one Company of Foot, that was left there.

Captain *Wright* was accufed of being very remifs in his Duty; and that through Jealoufy of General *Codrington*, or Fear of the *French*, he was the Ruin of the Expedition to *Guardaloup*. He took no Care to fcour the *Charibbean* Seas of *French* Privateers, which almoft furrounded *Barbados*; and what he did at *Guardaloup*, is not worth mentioning, though he had a good Fleet, well man'd and equip'd. *He and General* Codrington (as a Man of Honour wrote to his Friend) *deferted* Guardaloup, *without any Reafon, only their Jealoufies, and Fear of the* French *Fleet, when we had three times the Number of Men that the* French *had. They left their Mortar Piece behind them. The* French *at the fame Time deferted it alfo, concluding we were going to attack* Martinico; *fo that any body might for a Time have poffeffed the Ifland*.

We have fpoken of this Enterprize in the Hiftory of *Barbados*, fo we fhall fay no more of it here. The *Englifh* continued Mafters of all St. *Chriftopher's*, and the *French* defpaired of recovering their Part, but by a *Peace*.

On the 23d of *March*, 1694. Commodore *Wilmot* arrived here, with the Fleet and Land-Forces defigned for *Jamaica*, and from thence he proceeded on his intended Voyage.

On the 23d of *January*, 1696. the Addreffes and Affociations of the Chief Governor, Deputy Governors, Councils, Affemblies, Officers Civil and Military, and all the principal Inhabitants of his Majefty's Leeward *Charibbee-Iflands*, which had been fent over by Colonel *Chriftopher Codrington,*

The History of St. Christopher's.

Codrington, Chief Governor of these Islands, were presented to King *William,* by the Commissioners for the Affairs of the said Islands.

In 1697. Colonel *Collingwood* arrived at the *Leeward-Islands* with his Regiment; and himself, and Part of his Soldiers were quartered in St. *Christopher's,* where the Colonel's Lady and Family also settled. The Climate did not agree with them, nor much with the Soldiers. Mrs. *Collingwood* and her Children died in the following Year ; at which Time Colonel *Codrington,* Son of General *Codrington,* was in Possession of the Government of the *Leeward-Islands,* his Father being dead.

On the 13th of *January,* that Part of St. *Christopher's,* which had been taken from the *French* in the War, was restored to them, in Pursuance of the Treaty of *Reswick,* but they did not enjoy it long; for in *June,* 1702. Colonel *Codrington* having received Advice of the Declaration of the present War with *France,* attacked the *French* Part of St. *Christopher's,* and after firing but one Volley of Shot, their Fort was surrendered to him.

In the History of *Antego* we have given an Account of Colonel *Codrington*'s Expedition against *Guardaloup,* and the the *French* Islands, of which he took St. *Bartholomew*'s and St. *Martin*'s.

Some Time before the Surrender of the Fort by the *French,* an odd Accident happened in their Part of St. *Christopher's*. Monsieur *de Gennes,* the *French* Governor, had married the Widow of a Protestant Merchant of *Rochelle,* who had a Daughter of that Religion, whom he endeavoured all he could to pervert, and employed a Jesuit to deal with her to that End. The Priest, being convinced by the young Gentlewoman's Arguments or Beauty, went off with her to the *English* Settlement; and Monsieur *de Gennes* demanding them, some *English* Gentlemen took the Lady and the Jesuit in the Night, and conveyed them to *Nevis,* where the Priest professed the Protestant Religion, and married the young Gentlewoman.

In the Year 1704. Sir *William Matthews,* brigadier General in her Majesty's Armies, was appointed to succeed Col. *Codrington* in the Government of the *Leeward-Islands,* and he sailed from *England* about the Beginning of *June,* with six Men of War, and 12 Transport Ships, having on board some Land Forces. Captain *Walker* being Commodore. The Ships Crews proved healthy, all but the *Burford* Man of War, where 200 Men died. Sir *William Matthews* himself died aboard the Commodore; and we hear no

The History of St. Christopher's.

more of these Islands, till Colonel *Daniel Park* was made Governor of them, in the Year 1705. The *French* landed here, before they made their fatal Descent on *Nevis*. Their Forces were embarked aboard five Men of War, and 20 Sloops. They attacked the Fort, and being repulsed, fell among the Plantations, some of which they burnt, and plundered the Inhabitants. The Governor of *Barbados* having Notice of it, sent down a Sloop to the Lieutenant Governor of St. *Christopher's*, to acquaint him, that there was a strong Squadron of *English* Men of War coming to his Assistance; in Hopes that upon this News the *French* would retire, which had the desired Effect: For as soon as the *French* heard of it, they immediately left the Island, taking with them 6 or 700 Negroes, which Monsieur *Ibberville* sold at *Vera Cruz.*

The Inhabitants of St. *Christopher's* solicited to have their Losses made up to them, as well as those of *Nevis*; and they suffered also in the late terrible Hurricane, but not so much as the latter did.

For Want of sufficient Information, I am obliged to be silent as to the Government of Col. *Johnson*, Lieutenant General and Commander in Chief of the *Leeward-Islands*, and having spoken so largely in the Article of *Antego* of the Dissentions in the *Leeward-Islands*, under the Government of Col. *Park*, I shall only touch upon what particularly related to this Island, *Nevis* and *Montserrat*.

That Governor held a General Assembly at St. *Christopher's* in the Year 1710, the Representatives of the Councils and Assemblies of all the other *Leeward-Islands* which were then.

The General Council.

Henry Burrel, Esq;
Stephen Payne, Esq;
James Bevan, Esq;
John Norwood, Esq;

George Lyddell, Esq;
George Milward, Esq;
John Hamilton, Esq;
William Byam, Esq;

The General Assembly.

Robert Cunningham, Esq; Speaker.
Clement Crooke, Esq;
Jasper Verchell, Esq;
Anthony Ravell, Esq;
William White, Esq;
Edward Parsons, Esq;
William Barzey, Esq;

Anthony Fox, Esq;
Samuel Watkins, Esq;
John Painter, Esq;
John Duor, Esq;
Richard Cockran, Esq;
Daniel Mackennen, Esq;
Richard Whillet, Esq;

But

But the Difference that then immediately rose between General *Park* and the *General Assembly* about choosing a Clerk, hindered the Dispatch of any Business. Mr. *Park* had given a Commission to one *Caleb Rawleigh*, to be Clerk of the Assembly met at *Old Road*, in *March* 1710, and they resolved *Nem. Con.* That it is their Right and Privilege to appoint their own *Clerk*, and any Officer or Servant thereto belonging, which is so much in Reason, that all other Usages do not seem to justify the Governor's Obstinacy, in refusing to come to any Temperament with the Representatives met in a critical Juncture; for Fear of giving Way to them in a Punctilio of Prerogative, and he widened this Difference by another, his sending Messages to the Assembly by his *Provost* Marshal's Deputy; tho' it had been the constant Custom for a Member of the Council to bring Messages from the Governor and Council to the Assembly, which they now desired might be continued: But Col. *Park* refused this too, alledging that because the House of Lords in *England*, did not send a Peer with Messages to the Commons, but a Judge or Master in Chancery; therefore he made Use of the Deputy Marshal, an Officer of not much better Rank than that of a *Bumb-Baily* in *England*. The Council, who well knew that the Members of the Assembly were every whit as honourable as themselves, excepting only their Seat at their own Table, were not so stiff as General *Park*, and declared they were ready to carry Messages from the *General* to the *Assembly.*

The Assembly having chosen Mr. *Giles Cokes* to be their Clerk, the Governor threatened to send him to Jail if he durst act as such; and when they then pitched upon Mr. *Clement Crooke*, one of their Members, to take their Minutes, he gave them to understand, no *Assembly* Men could be admitted to do it according to the Practice in *England*, which he insisted upon strenuously to be his Rule of Government, himself as Sovereign, the Council as the House of Lords, the Assembly as the House of Commons. 'Tis plain, that the *Prerogative* was the delightful Part of the Constitution to which he adhered so inflexibly, because he is clothed with it by Commission; but he ought to have remembered they required him to proceed according *to the Custom and Usage of the said* Islands, and that the Assembly asserted the Usage and Customs to be what they claimed in the Choice of their Clerk. What he said in Answer to their Claim of Privilege, shews that he was not so much in Love with Assemblies as with the sovereign Power.

You will find, fays he, *even in* Antego *no Affemblies for feveral Years, and St.* Chriftopher's *was governed all the late War by a Governor and Council of Militia Officers, and the Fort of* Brimftone-Hill *was then built,* Anguilla, Spanifh *Town, and* Tortola *have no Affemblies, and defire none.* Thefe three Iflands are in the Government of the *Leeward-Iflands.*

I leave it to the Reader to judge, whether fuch Infinuations were proper to come from the Mouth of an Officer, commiffioned by a *Revolution* Government to govern a free People. Three or four Days after the above-mentioned Speech or Meffage, he prorogued the Affembly.

The Lieutenant Governor and Council of St. *Chriftopher's,* tranfmitted a Petition to *England* to clear themfelves of the Death of Col. *Park,* and pray that their Privileges may not be retrenched. This was figned by

Michael Lambert, Efq; Lieutenant Governor.

Henry Burrel, Efq;	*J. Peteres,* Efq;
J. Panton, Efq;	*J. Bourycan,* Efq;
Francis Phipps, Efq;	*Jofeph Elbridge,* Efq;

Thefe Gentlemen offered their Petition to General *Hamilton,* who fucceeded General *Park* in this Government, to join with them in it; but *Hamilton* difliking fome harfh Expreffions in the Affembly Men of *Antego,* who oppofed General *Park,* refufed to fet his Hand to it, telling them it was a *Bufinefs that did not belong to him.*

This Ifland was in a terrible Confternation on the Appearance of the *French* Fleet on their Coaft, after the Misfortune of *Montferrat* in 1712, but the Expulfion of the *French* out of this Ifland by the Treaty of *Utrecht,* by which the *French Quarters* of St. *Chriftopher's* were yielded to the *Englifh,* abated very much their Fears of a *French* Neighbourhood.

'Tis very grating to a good *Englifhman,* to have Occafion to fpeak of the Treaty of *Utrecht.* The 12th Article fays, *The Ifland of St.* Chriftopher's *is to be poffeffed alone by the* Britifh *Subjects,* who had before driven the *French* off of it, and we fhall fee prefently what induced the *French* King to be fo generous to *Britifh* Subjects in this Particular.

Upon the Ceffion of thefe Lands and the Evacuation of the Ifland by the *French,* many Projects were offered to the Publick for the Difpofal of thofe Lands for publick and private Ufe. And before the Parliament of *England* took this Affair into Confideration, and voted that the faid Lands

fhould

should be disposed of solely for the Use of the Publick, the Generals of the *Leeward-Islands* for the Time being, made Grants of the *French* Lands, for what Considerations they thought fit, and took them away again; sometimes after such as had Possession of them had been at great Expence to cultivate and plant. This is particularly laid to the Charge of General *Hamilton,* who dispossessed *John Thornton,* Esq; late Chief Justice of *Nevis,* of a Plantation of these *French* Lands by a forcible Entry; and did the same by Mr. *Christopher Stoddart,* of a Plantation adjoining to Mr. *Hare*'s in *Basse-Terre.* Mr. *Stoddart* says in his Petition to one of the principal Secretary's of State, *General* Hamilton *sticks at nothing to gratify his tyrannical Humour and provide for his Creatures, tho' at the Expence of my Labour and Industry; and took such Methods to gain his corrupt Ends, as must fill all his Majesty's Subjects in his Government, with dismal Apprehensions of the Precariousness of their Properties, when they see a Chief Justice,* Clement Crook, *Esq; removed for not being treacherously complying with his Purpose in so unjustifiable a Proceeding, as the ejecting of me out of my just Possession, without any other Ground for it than the Pleasure of the said General, and another Judge* Matthew Mills, *Esq; put in his Place, on whom he could depend for the Execution of all his Commands.*

Mr. *French* the *Charibbee* Historian has no Restraint upon his Pen, when he compliments Col. *Park*'s Friends, or censures their Opponents; what he says here of Mr. *Mills* is very injurious to the Reputation of one whose religious Education and honest Life I had perfect Knowledge of, and can hardly think the Air of the *Charibbees* can so change the Constitution of a Man's Mind as well as Body, as to corrupt the soundest in the Manner this Writer paints it. And that the Air is not so unhealthy to the Body as some say it is, the same Mr. *Mills* may prove, it being three and fifty Years ago that I myself went with him, when he was to embark at *Gravesend* for *Nevis.*

Ten thousand Acres of these *French* Lands are reckoned some of the best Ground in the Island, and 5000 other Acres of them of less Value. I know not what Sums have been raised by the Sale of them, but 80,000 *l.* of that Money was in Bank, and appropriated by Parliament for the Payment of a Dower to her Royal Highness the Princess of *Orange.* But let the Sale of them amount to what it will, if the *national Merchant* is right in his Argument, the Cession of the *French* Part of this Island to us, was among the false Steps taken by the Managers of the *Utrecht* Treaty, tho' they
boasted

boasted much of the great Advantage they had procured by it for *Great-Britain*. See his own Words.

<small>*Letters, p. 29. & seq.*</small>

'Some will say, was not the *French* Part of the Island of St. *Christopher*'s yielded up to *Great-Britain* by *France*, and is not the whole Island become our Property by the Treaty of *Utrecht?* Yes, yes, there lay the Game, the *French* knew it,——we did not. To explain what I mean, it is necessary to advance what I fear at first will look like a Paradox, *That even this very* Cession *of the* French *Part of St.* Christopher's *to us, was a Point that turned more in Favour of* France *than of* Great-Britain, *which I prove thus.*

'*France* has for very many Years had two Things in View; One, the fully peopling *Martinique, Guardaloup*, and the adjacent Islands in the *Charibbees*, and the possessing herself of *Hispaniola*, and peopling that Island also with great Numbers of Inhabitants: Secondly, to remove all her Subjects off from the smaller Islands, as St. *Martin*'s, St. *Bartholomew*'s, and *Santa Cruz*, and to settle them in the great Islands. But St. *Christopher*'s being the first of her Settlements, she found it no easy Matter to remove her Inhabitants from thence. They would not leave their *old* Habitations and Neighbours for *new* ones, being too well fixed; notwithstanding all the Temptations and Encouragements that were offered them. The Cession therefore of the *French* Part of St. *Cristopher*'s exactly answered the Wishes and Designs of *France*, by furnishing the great Islands with such a Number of seasoned and experienced Planters, who have been of excellent Service to strengthen them, and instruct the raw *European* Supplies of Inhabitants in the making of Sugar, *&c*. Is it not as plain to be seen as the Sun, that at the Treaty of *Utrecht* we took the very Bait the *French* had proposed for us, and thereby also took off all the Odium from the *French* Court: For the *French* Subjects at St. *Christopher*'s looked on the *English* as the sole Authors of all their Troubles, and the Cause of their Removal from their ancient Habitations. In short by this Treaty of *Utrecht*, we did more for the *French* than they could do for themselves. We contented ourselves with four or five small Islands for the Sake of a present Advantage, which the *French* did not think worth keeping.'

In the Year 1715, the Government of St. *Christopher*'s made a bold Attempt in raising the current Coin of the Island, contrary to the Proclamation and the Act of Parliament in Queen *Anne*'s Reign, from 6 *s*. to 7 *s*. the *French* Crown, as by this Minute.

<small>*Coin raised by the Lieutenant General.*</small>

At

The History of St. Christopher's.

At a Meeting of the Council the 23d of August, 1715, *Present the Honourable the Lieutenant General, and eight Counsellors.*

'The Council were of Opinion, that it would be of Be-
'nefit to this Island, to raise the Value of *French* Crowns to
'7 s. and so in Proportion for *Half Crowns* and *Quarter*
'*Crowns*, upon which the following Order was directed to
'be affixed in the several Towns of this Island.'

By the Honourable the Lieutenant General *in* Council.

'It is this Day ordered in Council that *French* Crowns
'pass *current*, and be taken in Payment after the Rate of 7 s.
'a-piece, and all *French Half Crowns* and *Quarter Crowns*
'in Proportion to the aforesaid Rate, and of this all Persons
'are required to take due Notice.'

It appears by another Minute of Council the 15th of *January* 1715-6, that the Lieutenant General began to reflect on his late Transaction, and to be suspicious of the Penalty of it, which made him call his Council to his Assistance, to whom he proposed this Question, *whether the Order he had made* against the Proclamation, the Act of Instrument, and his Queen's Instructions, *was regular?* We shall see by their Answer how implicitly Colony Councils do for the most Part follow the Opinion or Directions of Governors. They ingeniously answered, *That* French Crowns *having been current several Years in the other Islands for* 7 s. *it could not be said he altered the Coin, but only followed the Practice of the other Islands*; equally weak and equivocal, for *Barbados* did not go contrary to the Statute directing the Currency of Coin in the Sugar-Islands; and if it had, no Practice could have warranted the plain Breach of the Law and the Governor's Instructions. However, the private Advantage made by him, his Counsellors and others, who had heaped up Money at 6 s. the Crown, reconciled the raising it to 7 s. both to his Conscience and Understanding.

This extraordinary Proceeding, so unlawful in itself, and so prejudicial to the Traders, was taken Notice of to the Governor in a Letter even from the Secretary, wherein he pressed him in very strong Terms to pursue the Act of the 6th of Queen *Anne* as to the Coin, but without the least Effect, or without being able to obtain one single Word in Answer. The Secretary, after entreating the Governor as to other Matters, writes.

That your Excellency will be pleased to issue your Proclamation requiring Obedience to be paid to her late Majesty's Proclamation relating to the Coin, enforced by an Act of Parliament.

That

That *myself*, as well as others of his *Majesty's Subjects*, may not be any longer defrauded of the 6th Part of their Due, nor the royal Proclamation, nor the *Act* of Parliament, suffer any longer that Indignity they have hitherto been treated with in *these Parts*. The Secretary's Request being thus rejected by the Governor, and the Affair being of the last Importance to the Trade of the Island, he made a Voyage to *England* on Purpose, to set the Matter forth to his Majesty.

Governor *Matthews* coming to this Island called the Council and Assembly, and made the customary Speech, having in it nothing more remarkable than recommending the Instruction relating to the Salary, which they settled at 800 *l*. a Year Currency in Money, to be raised on Slaves at that Time about 17000, at 1 *s*. 9 *d*. per Head for the first Year, and 1 *s*. 2 *d*. for the Remainder of his Government.

When Mr. *Hart* and the Lord *Londonderry* were Governors here, there was a Duty of 3 *s*. per Hogshead laid on Sugar exported, to discharge the Addition made to their Salaries. But as that affected the Sugar-Factors in *England*, as well as the Planters here, the Factors opposed the passing of it at Home; 'Whereas did the Sugar Factors in *England*
' consult the Good of their Employer and of the Publick,
' *to use the Words of a Planter of St*. Kit*'s*, as well as their
' own, they would oppose the raising of any such Salary Set-
' tlement at all, whether on the Sugar or the Slaves, or any
' Thing else here, but rather apply to the Government, to
' find out some Means for supporting the Governor, *&c.*
' But so far are these Gentlemen from shewing that Kindness
' to the Sugar Colonies or the Nation, that some of them
' have earnestly enough recommended it to their Friends here,
' to promote the making of such Settlements. (The *French*,
' our Rivals in the Sugar Trade are so sensible of this, that
' their Governors have almost all along had very liberal Ap-
' pointments out of their King's Coffers, and none of them
' are suffered on any Pretence whatever, to draw any Profits
' from the People in these Parts.)

' Nay we seem, continues the Planter, to be so sensible of
' it ourselves, that one of the Instructions of our present
' Governor, expresly condemns the Grievance complained
' of, which Instruction was not made publick here till after
' the Bills of Settlement had passed through both Houses in
' the several Islands.' We are willing to insert this Instruction here, because we have before inserted another in *Antego* to the same Governor, which is not of the same Nature.

Whereas several Inconveniences have arisen to our Governors in the Plantations by Gifts and Presents made our Governors

nors by the Assemblies, 'It is our Will and Pleasure, that
'neither you nor any other Governor or Commander in
'Chief of our *Leeward-Islands* for the Time being respec-
'tively, do give your or their Consent to the passing any
'Law or Act, for any Gift or present to be made to you
'or any of them by the Assembly or Assemblies of all or
'any of our said Islands, and that neither you nor they do
'receive any Gift or Present from any of the said Assemblies,
'on any Account or in any Manner whatsoever, on Pain of
'being recalled from that our Government.'
House Rent not exceeding 400 *l. per Ann.* is excepted.

We should here finish the History of the *English Leeward-Islands*, because these are all that are within this Government: But there are two other small *Charibbee-Islands* belonging to the *English*, which remain next to be spoken of; and as to their Situation, they may be as well called *Leeward-Islands* as the others, we mean *Barbuda* and *Anguilla*.

Of BARBUDA.

THIS Island, which is by some called *Barbouthos*, lies in 17 Degrees 30 Minutes North Latitude. It is about 15 Miles long, lying North East from *Montserrat*.

The Land is low and fruitful, and the *English* began to plant it as early as *Nevis*, *Montserrat*, or any other of the *Leeward-Islands*, St. *Christopher*'s excepted; for Sir *Thoma. Warner* who first settled there, placed a small Colony in this Island, but the *Charibbeans* disturbed them so much, that they were often forced to desert it and their Plantations. There hardly passed a Year, but they made one or two Incursions, and that generally in the Night, for they durst not attack them by Day: But the Damage the *English* sustained by them made them weary of dwelling in a Place where they were so much exposed to the Fury of the *Barbarians*, who diminishing daily in Number, and the *Europeans* increasing, the *English* again possessed themselves of *Barbuda*, and were 500 Inhabitants 60 Years ago. There are now 1000 or 1200 Souls upon it.

The Proprietary is the Honourable *Christopher Codrington*, Esq; and he puts in a Governor here, having the same Prerogative as the other Lords Proprietaries in their several Jurisdictions in *America*.

This

The History of Anguilla.

This Island has bred great Store of Cattle, and the Inhabitants employ themselves mostly in that Sort of Husbandry, Corn and Provisions coming almost always to a good Market in the Sugar Islands.

There's Plenty of all Sorts of tame Cattle as in *Europe*, and the *English* live here much after the same Manner as they do in the Counties of *England*; only their Labour in the Field is not so hard as here, the Country being so much hotter. Col. *Park*'s Attempt to dispossess the *Codrington*'s of this *Island*, is spoken of in *Antego*. Next to it is,

ANGUILLA.

*A*Nguis Insula, or *Snake Island*, so called from its Figure, being a long Tract of Earth, but narrow, winding almost about rear St. *Martin*'s: From whence it may easily be seen. *I.* lies in 18 Degrees, 21 Minutes.

The Country is level and woody, the Soil fruitful, and the Tobacco that grew there formerly was reckoned very good in its kind. There's not a Mountain in it. Where it is broadest, there's a Pond, about which the *English* settled in the Year 1650. Their Business, like the Inhabitants of *Anuilla*, was to plant Corn, and breed tame Cattle; for which Purpose they brought Stock with them. They were poor, and continue so to this Day, being perhaps the laziest Creatures in the World. Some People have gone from *Barbados*, and the other *English Charibbee-Islands*, thither, and there they live like the first Race of Men, without Government or Religion, having no Minister nor Governor, no Magistrates, no Law, and no Property worth keeping, if a *French* Author is to be believed *L'Isle n'est pas estimee valoir la peine qu'on la garde, ny qu'on la cultive*. The Island is not thought worth the trouble of defending or cultivating it: In which perhaps the *Frenchman* is out; for the Soil being good, if an industrious People were in Possession of it, they would soon make it worth defending.

The way of the present Inhabitants is to take no Care for any Thing but Food and Rayment, which are both ordinary enough, though of the two their Food is best. They generally marry here, and are given in Marriage, after the good old Fashion. They have no Lawyers to put them to the

Expence

The History of Anguilla.

Expence of Jointures; nor Priests, to pick Money out of their Pockets for Licences; they trust to Honour, and it being difficult for any Man or Woman here to make their Condition better or worse by Change, there are seldom any Divorces: And if there is any Reason for them, the People have good Nature enough to put it up, every Man being his own Master, at least every Master of a Family. This is a sort of Primitive Sovereignty, where no Man's Power exceeded the Bounds of his Houshold.

One would think such a poor People as this should live quietly, and that no Enemy would pretend to invade them; indeed it was worth no Nation's while, but the *Wild Irish*, we call them so, to distinguish them from the *English* of *Ireland*; and these Wretches thinking it was impossible for any Men to be poorer than themselves, landed in the last War, and took away from the Inhabitants of *Anguilla* the little they had. In the Year 1689. the *French* put them ashore, and they not only robbed, but abused, and barbarously treated the *English*.

Sir *Timothy Thornhill*, who was then at *Antego*, hearing of it, sent Captain *Edward Thorn*, with 80 Men, to bring off the *English* that were on this Island, to prevent their being so insulted again.

Whether they removed or not, we have not learnt, but it is certain, there are now 150 Families upon it, and 8 or 900 Souls, who live poorly, and we might say miserably, if they were not contented; and considering they desire no more, and that they want nothing necessary for Life, why are they not as happy as the Inhabitants of *Peru* and *Mexico*?

THE HISTORY OF JAMAICA.

CHAP. I.

Containing an Account of its Discovery, Settlement, the Conquest of it by the *English*; and all other Events to the present Times.

1494.

Columbus here.

1502.

THIS Island had the Honour to be discovered by *Christopher Columbus* himself, Discoverer of the *New World*, in his second Voyage from *Spain* to the *West-Indies*: He landed here in the Beginning of *May*, 1494, and found it the most beautiful and best peopled Place he had yet seen in the *new discovered World*. The Natives endeavoured to hinder his landing, but six or seven of them being wounded by the *Spanish* Cross-bows; they became peaceable, bartered their best Goods with him for Trifles, and a young *Indian* was so fond of going with him to *Spain*, that he could not be hindered by the Entreaties of his Relations; upon which *Columbus* took him aboard, and ordered that he should be civilly treated.

In the Voyage *Columbus* made to the *New World* in 1502, he met with such bad Weather, and his Ships were so Worm eaten and Leaky, that he ran them ashore at this Island. He stranded them as close together as he could, that they might not budge, but lie steady in the Water, which they did almost

moſt up to the Deck. He then built Sheds on the Poops and Forcaſtles for his Men to be in, keeping ſtrict Watch to prevent their being attacked by the Natives. He ſuffered none of them to come on board, nor any of the *Spaniards* to go aſhore, except ſuch as were particularly appointed to encourage the Traffick with the *Indians*, who bartered Gold, *He is wrecked.* Plate, Proviſions, &c. for Bells, Beads, and other ſuch Toys, having neither Money nor Materials to build a Ship out of the Wrecks he bought two large Canoos, in which he ſent his Secretary and others to *Hiſpaniola*, about 20 Leagues diſtant, where the *Spaniards* had then a Settlement for another Ship and Proviſions, but the *Spaniſh* Governor there, envying *Columbus's* ſuperior Authority as General and Admiral in theſe Parts, hindered his Secretary's procuring a Ship to fetch him from *Jamaica* (the *Engliſh* Name of this Iſland, for *Columbus* called it St. *Jago*, and *James* not being *Spaniſh*, *Jamaica*, its augmentative, muſt be entirely *Engliſh*, agreeing with no other Language.) Here *Whence the* he remained ſeveral Months, and was reduced to great *Name of* Streights, tell at laſt his Men mutinied, and moſt of them *Jamaica.* deſerted him; ſeized 10 Canoos which *Columbus* had bought of the Natives, and ſet out from the moſt Eaſterly Point of this Iſland, now Point *Negril*, for *Hiſpaniola*, but were forced back again, and roving up and down the Country, plundered the *Indians* for Subſiſtence. To put a Stop to their Ravages, *Columbus* ordered one of his Brothers with a Party of choſen Men to reduce the Mutineers to Obedience. Several of them were killed, and the reſt ſubmitted, after which one of the Perſons whom *Columbus* had ſent to *Hiſpaniola* returned to *Jamaica* with a Ship in which he and the *Spaniards* that remained here with him, removed to that Iſland, from whence he returned to *Spain*, and there died of Grief, chiefly for the ungrateful Treatment he met with from the Court of *Spain*, for which he had found out a *New World*, as he ſaid himſelf in an Epitaph he directed to be put on his Tomb.

A Caſtilia y a Leon
Nuevo Mondo die Colon.

He had in a former Voyge been ſeized by the *Spaniſh* Governor of *Hiſpaniola*, and ſent to *Spain* in Chains, on a falſe Accuſation; a fine Reward for that Service. He carried the Remembrance and Reſentment of that vile Uſage with him to his Grave, notwithſtanding he came off with Credit in *Spain*, and was employed as before, for he ordered his Chains to be buried with him in his Grave.

It

It was three Years after his Death, before any *Spanish* Colony was settled here. They flocked hither from *Europe*, and built three Cities about the Year 1509. As *Seville* on the North Coast; *Mellila* on the same Coast, and *Oristan* on the South Coast, towards the Western Part of the Island, 14 Leagues from *Seville*, *Delaet* writes *Mellila* was built by *Columbus* himself, but that is plainly erroneous; for *Columbus* needed not to have raised Sheds on the Poops and Forecastles of his wrecked Ships, if he had had a City to have housed his Men in, when he was the last Time in *Jamaica*. It is most likely his Son and his Brethren carried on the Settlement of the *Spaniards*, and built those Cities for them after his Death. His Son *Diego*, who wrote his Life, built the City of *La Vega*, which he called St. *Jago de la Vega*, and the Situation of it being more pleasant and healthful than that of the other Cities, so many of the Inhabitants of the later removed thither, that *Seville*, *Mellila* and *Oristan*, were left almost desolate, and St. *Jago* encreased in Buildings and People, till there were counted in it 1700 Houses, two Churches, two Chapels and an Abbey: *Diego Columbus* was the first *European* Governor of this Island. He also had all, or the greatest Part of it in Property, and his Successors if not himself, Descendants from *Columbus*, were stiled Dukes *de la Vega*, but they exacted such high Rents from the Planters, that it was a great Discouragement to them, and hindered the Growth of this *Colony*, when the *Spaniards* were in Possession of the Island, which lies in 18 Degrees North Latitude, and is at an equal Distance, 20 Leagues from *Cuba* and *Hispaniola*, 50 Leagues in Length from *East* to *West*, and 20 or more in Breadth.

The *Spaniards* lived mostly at *La Vega*, and kept Slaves to plant there: After *Portugal* became subject to *Spain*, the *Portuguese*, a more industrious Nation than the *Spaniards*, would have improved the Culture and Commerce of *Jamaica*, but the *Spaniards* were not very forward in giving them Encouragement.

The *Spaniards* here minded no Sort of Manufacture or Trade, but lived lazily in Town upon what their Slaves brought them from their *Stanchas* or little Plantations in the Country. They sold small Quantities of Sugar, Tobacco and Chocolate, Hides, Pepper, Tallow and Cocoa Nuts, to such Masters of Ships as came hither; yet for the Possession of a Place which they would not be at the Pains to cultivate, they cut the Throats of 60,000 *Indians* Natives of this Island. They were not themselves 1500 Inhabitants and as many Slaves, when the *English* conquered it.

Don

The History of Jamaica.

Don *Pedro de Squibello*, whom *Diego Columbus* had appointed his Lieutenant, was deeply concerned in the maffacring the Natives, fome of whom, as the Bifhop of *Chiapa* writes, were roafted alive by his Countrymen the *Spaniards*, and others torn in Pieces by Dogs. The Barbarities thofe Maffacrers exercifed on the innocent Inhabitants, as related even by a *Spaniard*, cannot be read without Horror.

In 1596, Sir *Anthony Shirly* who had been cruizing on the *Continent* of the *Spanish West-Indies*, landed at *Jamaica*, took St. *Jago*, plundered the Ifland, and then left it. And about the Year 1635, Col. *Jackfon* with a Fleet of Ships from the *Leeward-Iflands*, came hither, landed 500 Men at *Paffage-Fort*, drove 2000 *Spaniards* from their Works, took St. *Jago* with the Lofs of 40 Men, facked the City, and divided the Spoil with his Soldiers. Then putting the Town to Ranfom, he received a confiderable Sum to fave it from Burning, and retreated to his Ships, the Enemy not daring to difturb his Rear.

After which the *Spaniards* poffeffed the Ifland undifturbed, till *Cromwell*, by the Perfuafions of Cardinal *Mazarine*, who politickly contrived it, to make Ufe of his Arms againft the *Spaniards* then at War with the *French*, fitted out a Fleet for the Conqueft of *Hifpaniola*. 2000 Old Cavaliers, and as many of *Oliver*'s ftanding Army, befides Volunteers and neceffitated Perfons embarked for this Expedition.

The Command of the Army was given to Col. *Venables*, and Admiral *Pen*, who were ordered to call at *Barbados* and the *Leeward-Iflands*, to take in more Forces there; it not being doubted, but thofe Colonies would be willing to affift in an Enterprize, by which, in all Probability, they would receive moft Profit.

Col. *Doyly*, Col. *Haynes*, Col. *Butler*, Col. *Raymund*, and other Officers of Note, accompanied the Generals *Venables* and *Pen*, who arrived at *Barbados* in the Year 1655. From whence two Men of War were fent to St. *Chriftopher*'s and *Nevis* to raife Volunteers. They were fupplied with feveral Neceffaries at *Barbados*, where Hundreds of Volunteers joined them, and no lefs than 1300 at the *Leeward-Iflands*.

On the 13th of *April* the Fleet made Land at *Hifpaniola*, and difcovered the Town of St. *Domingo*. The next Day, as it had been concluded at a Council of War, General *Venables* (who had uxoriously carried his Wife with him) landed 7000 Foot, a Troop of Horfe, and 3 Days Provifions; but this Enterprize not having hitherto any Relation to the Hiftory of *Jamaica*, we fhall content ourfelves with a general Account of it; that our Forces were defeated, and their
Com-

Commander *Venables* forced ingloriously to retreat to his Ships, having lost the brave Col. *Haynes*, and a great many Men.

When the Troops were reimbarked, a Council of War was held, and it was resolved to make a Descent on *Jamaica*, where they arrived the 3d of *May*. The Generals landing their Men, marched directly to St. *Jago* the Capital of the Island, intending to storm the Place immediately; and to prevent the same Fate they met with at *Hispaniola* by the Cowardice of their Men, Proclamation was made, That he who saw his Fellow run, should shoot him.

The *Spaniards* had had no Information of the Defeat of the *English* at *Hispaniola*, and were in no Condition to oppose an Army of 10000 Men, and so many they were still: So they made Use of Policy more than Arms to save themselves and their Effects. And when General *Venables* advanced near the City, they desired to capitulate, which being granted, they spun out the Treaty as long as they could, that they might in the mean Time send away their Treasure into the Woods. To amuse the *English*, they furnished the Army with fresh Provisions, and presented Mrs. *Venables* with some of the choicest Fruits and Delicacies of the Island; which had a good Effect on her Husband, and put him in a good Humour till the *Spaniards* had done their Business: Otherwise his Patience might have been worn out before their best Moveables were safe in the Mountains and Coverts up in the Country; to which they fled themselves afterwards, and left the *English* a naked Town to possess, where they found fine Houses without Inhabitants or Goods; which was a terrible Disappointment to an Army who expected Plunder, and had been baulked already.

[marginal note: Hickeringil of Jamaica.]

They removed all they had, their Wives and Children to the Woods and Fortresses. From whence they sallied in Parties and surprized the *English*, of whom they cut off several Bands, before they could tell how to come at them. They came down upon *Venables*'s Men in the Night, and attacked them when they were in no Manner of Expectation of an Enemy, and for Want of Knowledge of the Country, could not pursue them.

At last the *Spaniards* grew weary of their hard Quarters in the Mountains, which did not at all agree with their riotous Way of living at St. *Jago*; and despairing to be able to dislodge the *English*, who began also to find them out in their lurking Places, they retired to *Cuba*, leaving the *Molattoes* and *Negroes* in the Woods to harass the Enemy, and keep Possession of the Island till they returned.

The History of Jamaica. 307

The Vice-Roy of *Mexico* commanded them to return to *Jamaica*, and ordered the Governor of *Cuba* not to let them stay there, sending them Word, that he would supply them with Men and Ammunition to recover what they had lost. Accordingly they came back, and scattered themselves up and down in single Families, that they might be able to subsist the better, and prevent being discovered by the *English*. But this miserable Course of Life killed several of them, and there came no more than 500 Soldiers to their Assistance, who also refused to join with them, when they saw the weak Condition they were in, and retreated to the *North* of the Island, fortifying themselves in a Place called St. *Chereras*, waiting for a Reinforcement.

In the mean Time the *English* possessed themselves of all the South and South-East Parts of the Island: A Regiment was seated about *Port Morant*, to plant and settle there, and others in other Places; over whom Col. *Doyly* was left Governor with between 2 and 3000 Land-Forces, and about 20 Men of War, commanded by Vice-Admiral *Goodson*. _{Heath. Chron.} _{Col. Doyly Governor.}

Venables and *Pen* returned Home, and arrived in *England* in *September*, where they were both imprisoned for their scandalous Conduct in this Expedition; which would have been an irreparable Dishonour to the *English* Nation, had not the Island of *Jamaica*, which Chance more than Council bestowed upon them, made amends for their Loss at *Hispaniola*.

Cromwell bore this Misfortune with an heroick Temper, which he was always Master of; and to put the best Face upon the Matter, highly extolled the Advantage of this new Acquisition in the *West-Indies*, resolving to maintain the Footing he had got there; and not liking Col. *Doyly* so well as *Venables* had done, he commanded a Squadron of Men of War to be fitted out for *Jamaica*, whither he sent Major *Sedgewick*, to take upon him the Government in the Room of Col. *Doyly*.

With *Sedgewick* went Col. *Humfreys*, the Son of him who carried the Sword before President *Bradshaw* at the King's Trial, and 1000 fresh Men.

Col. *Doyly*, before the Arrival of these Troops, had discovered where the *Spaniards* had fortified themselves, and marched to attack them. Thirty Companies more of *Spaniards* were by this Time sent to reinforce the former, who had raised several strong Works for their Defence at *Rio Novo*, in St. *Mary's* Precinct, having received Cannon and Stores of Ammunition from *Cuba* and the *Continent*. However, Col.

Col. *Doyly* in a few Days beat them out of their Entrenchments, and demolished their Fortification.

This great Loss, with others that happened much about the same Time at *Point Pedro*, where a Party of them had again seated themselves and were driven thence, made the *Spaniards* despair of ever recovering the Island; so they put their Wives, Children, and Treasure aboard a Ship, and abandoned it to the *English*.

In this Action at *Rio Novo*, the *English* regained the Reputation they had lost at *Hispaniola*. The *Spaniards* were twice their Number and strongly entrenched, yet Col. *Doyly* drove them to their Ships, and they never made any considerable Attempt against the new Comers afterwards.

Their *Negroes* finding their Masters were either knocked on the Head by the *English* or dead of Distempers, cut the Throat of the Governor who had been set over them, and chose one of their Comrades to command them.

Hick.

These lived a while in the Mountains by Game and Robbery, but finding they were not able to keep their Ground long, they sent to Col. *Doyly*, and offered to submit on Terms of Pardon; which being granted, their Captain came in with his Company, and laid down their Arms. Some *Molattoes* and *Spaniards* still stood out, most of whom Col. *Doyly* destroyed, by employing the Slaves to hunt them out of the Woods. The *Spaniards* instead of thinking of chastizing the revolted *Negroes*, desired some Assistance from them. To such a wretched Extremity of Fortune were they reduced.

The Slaves were so far from helping them, that to shew their Loyalty to their new Masters, they either murdered them themselves, or discovered the Places of their Retreat to the *English*, who in a Year's Time cleared the Island of them wholly, except 30 or 40 *Negroes* and *Molattoes*; who either out of Hopes of procuring their Liberty by it, or Love to their old Masters, or Hatred to their new, kept in the Mountains, and stayed there living by Robbery and Game.

They committed several Murders, and fearing they should be severely punished if taken, the greatest Part of them made their Escape to *Cuba* in *Cauka's*; since which there have been no Attempts against *Jamaica* by the *Spaniards* worth Remembrance.

The *Spanish Negroes* who remained in the Mountains were afterwards joined by the *English* rebellious *Negroes*, and from thence made frequent Descents into the Valleys; which forced the Government of *Jamaica* to build Forts, and keep

The History of Jamaica.

keep Guards, to defend the *English* against being surprized. Some of them, about 20 Years ago, came down upon the *English*, and murdered Mrs. *Coates* and her Family. She was the Wife of Judge *Coates*, who afterwards lived at *Barbados*; and it is said these Slaves or their Descendants, lurk in the Hills to this Day. To prevent their doing Mischief, several Laws have been made against the *Negroes* travelling without Passes.

We hope the Reader will not think this a Digression, since we did it only to follow the *Spaniards* and their Slaves, as far as we could.

The *English* seeing they were Masters of the Island, fell to Planting with equal Industry and Success, and they received constant Supplies of Men, Provisions and Necessaries from *England*.

When the *English* had no more foreign Enemies to deal with, they quarrelled amongst themselves, and the Soldiers fell into a dangerous Mutiny; for what my Author, Parson *Hickeringill* of *Essex*, who was a Captain in the Army in the *Hispaniola* Expedition and wrote of *Jamaica*, does not let us know. The chief of the Mutineers was Col. *Raymund*, who had debauched almost all the Soldiers, being a Man in high Esteem among them. He drew Lieutenant Colonel *Tyson* into the Conspiracy, which it is likely was to seize the Government themselves.

Col. *Doyly* discovering the Plot, had them both tried by a Court Marshal, who passed Sentence on them to be shot to Death. Col. *Raymund* died with a great deal of Resolution, but *Tyson* with Regret and Sorrow.

Major *Sedgewick* died a few Days after his Arrival, of a Distemper that then raged in the Island. Col. *Fortescue* followed him, and Col. *Humphreys* was forced to return to *England*.

Cromwell, who resolved to have a Governor that should be his Creature at *Jamaica*, sent Orders to Col. *Brayne* in *Scotland*, to ship off 1000 Men from *Port Patrick*, and sail for *Jamaica*, where he was to take upon him the Government; for *Oliver* did not at all like Col. *Doyly*, who was a Sort of an old Cavalier: Yet that Gentleman kept in his Place till after the King's Restoration, for Col. *Brayne* did not long survive his Arrival at *Jamaica*; and the Rump continued Col. *Doyly* in his Government after *Cromwell's* Death, and *Richard's* Abdication.

Col. Brayne Governor.

Col. Doyly Governor.

This Gentleman brought the Colony into Order, encouraged the People's Industry, and put the Soldiers upon Planting. Most of the first *English* Inhabitants of this Island were

were military Men, and it was necessary it should be so, because lying so near the *Spaniards*, it was expected they would have been forced to have fought for what they had; but they were very quiet from any Invasion for above thirty Years. Some of them who did not care to turn their Hands to the Culture of the Earth, nor leave their Military Life, turned Privateers, and cruizing on the *Spaniards*, got many rich Prizes, which grew to such a Trade afterwards, that when *Spain* had given up *Jamaica*, and Peace was concluded between the two Nations, yet the *English* could not forbear Privateering; and thence rose the *Buccaneers*, so famous in the Reign of King *Charles* II. at *Jamaica*.

Lord Windsor Governor. Colonel *Doyly* was recalled upon the King's Restoration, and the Lord *Windsor* sent Governor thither. Several Gentlemen removed from the other Colonies thither, as Sir *Thomas Modiford* from *Barbados*, where he had got a vast Estate; but desirous to get more, with greater Ease and Pleasure than he could do at home; he removed to the new Settlement, where he was very serviceable to the young Planters, by his *Sir Tho. Modiford Governor.* Instruction and Government, when the King advanced him to that honourable Office, which he did about the Year 1663. And in his Time the Settlement was encreased so much, that there were between 17 and 18000 Inhabitants. As,

		Families.	Inhabitants
1	Port-Royal Parish,	500	3500
2	St. *Katharine*,	658	6270
3	St. *John*,	83	996
4	St. *Andrew*,	194	1552
5	St. *David*,	80	960
6	St. *Thomas*,	59	590
7	*Clarendon*,	143	1430
8	St. *George*,		
9	St. *Mary*,		
10	St. *Anne*,		2000
11	St. *James*,		
12	St. *Elizabeth*,		

17298

After which there were several other Parishes added, and the Number of Inhabitants of those above-named were very much encreased.

This Governor set up a Salt-work in the Parish of St. *Katharine's*, planted Coco-Groves; and by his Example put the People upon Industry, and Improvements in Planting and Trade.

The

The Island began to abound in Money, which was brought thither by the *Buccaneers*, as the Pyrates in the *Spanish West-Indies* are called. And the Government of *Jamaica*, tho' they were far from encouraging any such wicked Courses, yet winked at them, in Consideration of the Treasures they brought thither, and squandered away there.

The first of these who was famous in *Jamaica*, was one *Bartholomew*, sirnamed the *Portuguese*, who was accompanied by several *Englishmen*. This Man, in his last Expedition, was cast away, as he was making to *Port-Royal* with a Prize, on the Sands called *Jardines*. He was succeeded in the Command of the *Buccaneers* by a *Dutchman*, born at *Groninguen*, in the *United Provinces*; and, for having lived most part of his Time at *Brasil*, called *Brasilano*.

When the *Portuguese* drove the *Dutch* out of *Brasil*, this Fellow came to *Jamaica*, where not being able to maintain himself according to the Extravagance of his Nature, he turned Pyrate. While he was a private Man he had got such a Reputation among his Companions, that a Company of Mutineers of them chose him for their Captain. In his first Voyage he took a great Ship, bound home with Plate, and other Treasure from *New Spain*, which he carried to *Jamaica*; and as soon as these *Buccaneers* landed, they fled to the Stews and Gaming-houses, to ease themselves of the Load which they had scraped together with so much Hazard. They have given 500 Pieces of Eight for a Favour from a Strumpet, who would have bestowed it on another for a Bottle of Ale. They would buy Wine by the Pipe, force all that came by to drink, and throw away as much as was drunk. By such Practices one of them spent 3000 Pieces of Eight in less than a Month.

Brasiliano, by such Ways, having reduced his Pocket to almost a solitary Pistole, put to Sea again, took a Ship bound from *New Spain* to *Maracaibo*; but in a second Voyage was taken, as he landed on the Coast of *Campeche*, carried before the Governor, and condemned to be hanged, together with all his Companions: However he got off so far by a Wile, that their Lives were spared, and they were sent to *Spain* to the Galleys; from whence, by another Wile, they made their Escape, and got again to *Jamaica*, where they returned to their old Trade.

Lewis Scot, a *Welshman*, plundered the Town of *Campeche*, *Mansfeld* took the Island of St. *Katharine's*, *John Davies* sacked *Nicaragua*, and returned with 50000 Pieces of Eight to *Jamaica*; and in his next Voyage took and plundered the Town of St. *Austin's*, in *Florida*, though there was a Garrison

rison of 200 Men in the Castle: But the most renowned of all the *Buccaneers*, was *Henry Morgan*, the Son of a *Welsh* Yeoman, of a good Estate; who not liking his Father's Employment, enter'd himself aboard a Vessel, bound for *Barbados*, where he was sold, and served his Time in that Isle. When his Time of Servitude expired, he came to *Jamaica*, and engaged himself with some Pyrates there; amongst whom he had such Success, that in three or four Voyages, he got a good Stock of Money before-hand, joined with others, bought a Ship, and went for *Campeche*, where he took several good Prizes. After this he was chosen by *Mansfeld*, an old Pyrate, to be his Lieutenant, and they sailed from *Port-Royal* with 15 Ships, manned with 500 stout Men, who attacked the Isle of St. *Katharine's*, made themselves Masters of it, and *Mansfeld* left one Monsieur *Simon* Governor of it, with 100 Men. *Mansfeld's* Design was upon *Panama*, but hearing the *Spaniards* were prepared to give him a warm Reception, he contented himself with the Conquest of St. *Katharine's*; which Island was so fruitful, so pleasant, and so conveniently situated for invading or roving on the *Spanish* Coasts in *America*, that he would fain have made a Settlement there; but Sir *Thomas Linch*, then Governor of *Jamaica*, Sir *Thomas Modiford's* Successor, durst not consent to it, it being too notorious a Breach of the Peace between the two Crowns of *England* and *Spain*. *Mansfeld* in Discontent retired to *Tortuga*, an Island in the Gulph of *Mexico*, about 15 Leagues from the Continent, where the Pyrates nested themselves, and used to refresh after their Expeditions.

Sir Tho. Linch, Governor.

In the mean Time, Monsieur *Simon*, for want of Supplies, was forced to surrender the Isle of St. *Katharine's* to the Governor of *Costa Ricca*; which he had scarce done, before a Ship arrived from *Jamaica* with Provisions, 14 Men and two Women, to begin a Plantation by their own Authority. *Mansfeld* died at *Tortuga*, and Captain *Morgan* became Chief of the *Buccaneers*.

1669.

In his first Voyage he took *Puerto Del Principe*; but one of his Men having killed a *Frenchman*, so disgusted all his Followers of that Nation, that they left him. Captain *Morgan* divided 50000 Pieces of Eight among his Companions, who hastened to *Jamaica* with the Purchase, to spend it on Women, and other Debaucheries.

In the next Expedition, he took *Puerto Velo*, one of the finest Cities in the Government of *Panama*. The Treasure they divided here amounted to 250000 Pieces of Eight, besides Cloth, Linnen, Silk, and other Merchandize; with

The History of Jamaica.

which the *Buccaneers* failed chearfully to *Port-Royal*, and scattered it about after their usual Rate: By this Means Money grew plenty, and Returns easy to *England*, where many hundred thousand of those Pieces of Eight have been imported.

When he undertook his next Enterprize, he had no less than 15 Ships, and 900 Men with him. He landed at the Port of *Occa*, near Cape *de Lobos*, but met no Booty. He also made an unsuccessful Attempt on *Hispaniola*; and being at a Loss whither to go, one of his Followers, who had served *Lolonnois*, a famous *Buccaneer*, whom not spending his Money at *Jamaica*, we have omitted speaking of, though he was a mighty Man among the Pyrates, advised him to fall upon *Maracaibo* in *Terra Firma*, which *Lolonnois* had before plundered. *Morgan* attacked and took the Town, sacked both that and *Gibraltar*, and destroyed three *Spanish* Men of War who lay off the Harbour, to intercept his Retreat. This Booty also amounted to 250000 Pieces of Eight, besides rich Merchandize and Slaves, which were disposed of at *Jamaica*, and the Money spent in a convenient Time.

These Successes so encreased his Fame, that when he rendezvoused the next Year at *Tortuga*, he had 2000 desperate Fellows, and 37 Ships at his Service. His first Attempt was upon St. *Katharine's* Island, of which he again made himself Master. He detached Captain *Brodely* to take the Castle of *Chagre*, which facilitated his Design on *Panama*, and secured his Retreat. *Brodely* having taken that Castle, a Garrison of 500 Men was left in it; and Captain *Morgan* with the rest, about 1400 effective Soldiers, advanced towards *Panama*, defeated 500 Horse, and 1000 Foot, sent to oppose him, assaulted the City, and took it, after a Dispute of three Hours. When he was Master of the Town, he set it on Fire, without consulting his Soldiers, or letting them know who did it, for what Reason no body can tell. The Houses most of them were built with Cedar, very magnificently and richly furnished. There were 7000 Houses in the City, besides 200 Ware-houses.

Captain *Morgan* stayed here four or five Months, sending out Parties to scour the Country, and bring in Prisoners and Plunder.

On the 24th of *February*, 1671. he left the Town, or rather its Ruins, loading 175 Beasts of Carriage, with Silver, Gold, and other precious Spoils, and carrying away with him 600 Prisoners. He took and plundered the Town of *Cruz*, on the River *Chagre*, where Captain *Morgan* obliged the Prisoners to ransom themselves, threatning

threatning to sell them for Slaves, if they did not; and when he had raised as much Money as he could, he divided it among his Followers; but the Dividend not coming to above 200 Pieces of Eight a Man, they believed he had been too hard for them; and *Morgan* fearing a Mutiny, taking with him three or four Ships, wherein were Men he could trust, left them at the Castle of *Chagre*, which he demolished, nor durst the Pyrates venture to fall upon him, as some proposed, to be revenged on him for his Treachery. It is believed that he had not played them fair; and it is no wonder to find a Pyrate guilty of unfair Play. The Treasure he brought to *Jamaica* now was valued at near 400000 Peices of Eight.

After this Enterprize, Captain *Morgan* gave over the *Buccaneer* Trade: He had a Project to fortify the Island of St. *Katharine's*, to settle it with *Buccaneers*, make it a Harbour for Pyrates, and himself to be their Prince; but before he could bring his Project to bear, a Man of War arrived from *England* with a new Governor, *John* Lord *Vaughan*, and Orders from the King and Council for the late Governor, Sir *Thomas Linch*, to appear at Court, and answer to such Articles as were presented against him by the *Spanish* Ambassador, for maintaining Pyrates in those Parts, to the great Loss of the King of *Spain's* Subjects.

John Lord Vaughan Governor.

The new Governor sent to all the Coasts of *Jamaica*, to acquaint all Sea-faring Men, that his Majesty intended to observe the Peace between himself and the Catholick King religiously, and commanded his Subjects not to commit any Acts of Hostility on the *Spaniards*; however some of them ventured to land on the Isle of *Cuba*, committing all manner of Cruelty and Rapine, for which, as fast as they could be taken, they were hanged at *Jamaica*; where Sir *Henry Morgan*, for so we must now call him, the King having conferred the Honour of Knighthood on him for his Bravery, was made one of the Commissioners of the Admiralty, *Robert Byndlofs* and *William Beeston*, Esq; being joined in Commission with him. The Character of this Man shines brightly as to his Valour, and certainly his taking of *Panama* is an Action that is hardly to be parallel'd; but whether his Honesty was equal to his Courage, and the Scandal of Pyracy which he brought on the *English*, be what we ought to value ourselves upon, is not so easily decided, as I find it done by Sir *Dalby Thomas*, who, speaking of Sir *Henry Morgan*, and his Misfortunes, afterwards says, *He was as great an Honour to our Nation, and Terror to the* Spaniards, *as ever was born in it.*

Hist. Account of the West-Indies.

' Not-

' Notwithstanding he had done nothing but by Commis-
' sion from the Governor and Council of *Jamaica*, and had
' received their formal and publick Thanks for the Action,
' he was, upon a Letter from the Secretary of State, sent
' into *England* a Prisoner, and without being charged with
' any Crime, or ever brought to a Hearing, was kept here
' three Years, at his own great Expence, not only to the
' wasting of some Thousands he was then worth, but to the
' Hindrance of his Planting, and Improvement of his For-
' tune by his Industry, towards which none in *Jamaica* was
' in a fairer Way: So he wasted the remaining part of his
' Life, oppressed by a Court Faction, and a lingring Con-
' sumption, brought upon him by his Troubles here, and
' the Coldness of the Climate. This happened several Years
' afterwards, during the Government of the Lord *Vaughan*.'
One of the great Difficulties that happened, was the arbitrary
Proceedings of a new Company, calling themselves the
Royal African Company of England. The King granted
them a Charter, bearing Date the 26th of *September*, 1672,
to trade to *Guinea, Binny, Angola,* and *South Barbary,* exclusive of all others. The Duke of *York*, Prince *Rupert*,
the Earl of *Shaftsbury*, and other Persons of the first Quality, being of the Company; who, by Virtue of this Charter,
pretended to monopolize the Trade, and make Prize of all
Ships that came from any of those Parts of *Africa*, with
Negroes, or other Merchandize, without their Licence.

The Duke of *York* entered so far into the Interest of this
Corporation, as to threaten Sir *Jonathan Atkins*, Governor
of *Barbados*, to turn him out of his Place, for but seeming
to give Countenance to *Interlopers*; a Name they gave those
Merchants, who, contrary to that unjust Monopoly, traded
to *Africa*.

Several Ships were taken by them from the Owners forcibly, the Men of War having Orders to seize all private
Traders; and they took from one Merchant, Sir *John Bawdon*, at Times, to the Value of above 10000 *l*. They were
so severe, that they seized Ships, whether they had a Right
to do so by their Charter or not; and Merchants were afraid
to try their Causes, for fear of being thought to oppose
the King's Prerogative, a Bug-bear Word in that Reign.

Their Agents, in the Lord *Vaughan*'s Government, detained the St. *George*, a Ship belonging to the above-mentioned *Bawdon*, and consigned to *Samuel Bernard*, Esq; one
of the present Council of *Jamaica*; but that worthy Merchant asserting his Right before Sir *Thomas Modiford*, then
Chief Justice, was too hard for the Company's Agents, and
put

put them to near 1000 *l*. Expence to defend themselves for their Rapine.

It would be endless to give an Account of all the wicked Practices of these Agents in *Jamaica*, if we had had a perfect History of them transmitted to us. Their Tyranny was one of the greatest Grievances to Trade that ever it was oppressed with, and threatned to ruin all the Sugar Plantations, had not the Parliament in *England* regulated the Company, and laid the Trade of *Africa*, in a great Measure open.

About this Time, Mr. *Cranfield*, Mr. *Dukenfield*, and and Mr. *Brent*, Commissioners for removing the *English* Colony from *Surinam*, according to a Treaty concluded between King *Charles* and the States-General, arrived at *Jamaica* from that Plantation, with the *English*, Men, Women, Children, and Negroes, to the Number of 1200 Persons, whom the Governor, the Lord *Vaughan*, received very graciously, according to Instructions he had from Court, and provided Land in St. *Elizabeth*'s Precinct, as much to one as to another, for them to plant. The Addition of so many Hands was a great Service to *Jamaica*, and the Goodness of the Soil, beyond that of *Surinam*, made the Planters amends for leaving their old Habitations.

Charles, Earl of Carlisle, Governor.

To the Lord *Vaughan* succeeded the Right Honourable *Charles*, Earl of *Carlisle*, who arrived at *Jamaica* in the Year 1678. The Lord *Vaughan* removing to *England*, the People of this Island were very free with his Lordship's Character, and it is to be hoped more free than just; for they did not stick to charge him with selling his own Servants; a Story equally false and absurd, which should not have been mentioned, but to clear that noble Lord from the Aspersion which the Malice of his Enemies laid upon him. It may perhaps be true, that he made haste to grow as rich as his Government would let him; and when Governors are of that Opinion, the Inhabitants are generally Sufferers by it.

During the Lord *Carlisle*'s Government, the People of this Island were alarmed with groundless Fears of an Invasion from the *French*, the Count *D'Estree* being in those Parts, with a Squadron of *French* Men of War; but the Apprehensions of the *English* here were founded on Reports of Plots and Massacres in *England*, the Popish Plot being then lately discovered.

Sir Hen. Morgan, Deputy Governor.

The Country not agreeing very well with the Earl of *Carlisle*, he returned to *England*, in a Merchant Ship, and arrived at *Plymouth* in *September*, 1680. having left Sir
Henry

Henry Morgan Deputy Governor, for he was not yet fallen under the Displeasure of the Court.

Sir *Henry* being informed that *Jacob Everson*, a *Dutchman*, (a most notorious Pyrate) rid then in *Cow-Bay* with a Sloop, and a *Barqua Longa*, having about 100 Men with him, he presently ordered a Sloop, that was an excellent Sailer, and very fit for the Service, to be manned with 50 Men, besides Officers, and set Centinels to hinder any Boats or Men from going off, to give the Pyrates Advice. The Sloop was ready, and sailed in an Hour's Time. On the 1st of *February* she came before *Cow-Bay*, where the Pyrate rid, and as she stood in without Colours, and with most of her Men in the Hold, several of the Pyrate's Men that were ashore, returned aboard their Sloop and Bark, which were to Windward of the Governor's Sloop. As soon as she was within Shot of the Pyrates, the Commander in Chief ordered the King's Colours to be hoisted, and laid them aboard. The Pyrates at first fired a few Small Arms, but did the Soldiers little Damage; and when they saw them enter with Resolution and Authority, many of the Pyrates leaped into their Canoes, which overset, and they were drowned. Their Fellows made some Resistance after they were boarded, but in the End the Governor's Men mastered them and the Sloop. In the mean time, the Bark riding to leeward, cut, and got under Sail, though not without visible Damage, 3 or 4 of her Men, who were mending a Top-Sail, disordered by a Shot from the Governor's Sloop, being seen to fall over-board. The Sloop chaced her, but to no Purpose, she being a better Sailer.

The Captain was killed in the Engagement, but his Men who were almost all *English*, Sir *Henry Morgan* sent to the Governor of *Carthagena*, by Captain *Haywood*, that they might receive due Punishment for the Pyracies they had committed on the *Spaniards*.

About the Year 1682, Sir *Thomas Linch* returned to *Jamaica*, with a new Commission to be Governor again, a Person who was eminently loyal. *Sir Tho. Linch, Governor.*

In those Times, when the *Presbyterian Plot* was most talked of in *England*, News of the Discovery of it was with all possible Speed conveyed to the *West-Indies*; and Sir *Thomas* having Notice of it, he communicated it to the Assembly then sitting, who immediately came in a full Body to the Governor and Council, to desire a Day might be set apart to give Thanks to *Almighty God* for so great and signal a *Deliverance.* Sir *Thomas* invited the Council and Assembly that Night to Supper, and treated them again on the

Thanksf-

The History of Jamaica.

Thanksgiving-Day. But what shewed the Loyalty of this Assembly much more, was their continuing his Majesty's Revenue 21 Years longer in this Island.

The *Ruby* Man of War about this Time, cruised several Months to the Windward to defend those Parts from Pyrates, whose chief Captain *Van Horn* lost one of his Ships, which was taken by the *Spanish* Fleet, but most of the Men escaped.

The Assembly before-mentioned passed several good Laws which are printed at large and well abridged, in a Treatise often spoken of in this History of the Plantations.

Besides the *Ruby*, the *Guernsey* Man of War cruised also to Windward, for those Seas were full of Pyrates, who pretended to have *French* Commissions; and when they met with any *Jamaica* Men were very civil, suffering them to pass and repass untouched.

The Governor to wipe off the Scandal thrown upon him formerly of encouraging Pyrates, was now very zealous against them, and built a Galley with 54 Oars, which was launched with great Solemnity the 12th of *June*, and was of great Use in securing the Coast.

The *Buccaneers* however continued their Pyracies on the *Spaniards*: They were Crews of all Nations, *English, Dutch,* and *French.* In Sir *Thomas Linch*'s Time, one *Laurens* and one *Michael Tankers* headed them, and the *Spaniards* at *Carthagena* having Notice that they cruized off their Coasts, the Governor there sent out 3 Men of War, one of 40, one of 36, and another of 20 Guns to take them; and they were all three taken by the Pyrates, who killed 400 *Spaniards*, with the Loss of 14 Men in *December*, 1683.

There happened nothing farther remarkable in Sir *Thomas Lynch*'s Government, which he held about 3 Years, and was succeeded by Col. *Hender Molesworth*, a Man of great Worth and Honour, whom King *William* afterwards created a Baronet. Col. *Molesworth* was Governor when News came hither of the Death of King *Charles*, and King *James* the IId's Accession to the Throne. He resided at *St. Jago de la Vega*, or *Spanish Town*, and performed the Proclamation of the King with all possible Solemnity, himself appearing at the Head of the Militia before the King's House; about which several great Guns were planted, and fired on this Occasion. From thence he went to *Port Royal*, and before the King's House there drew up his own Regiment, and at the Head of them made the like Proclamation; which he afterwards did for K. *William*, with as loud and much more unaffected Joy.

The Governor and Council transmitted a very loyal congratulatory Address to King *James*: And this must be said

Col. Hender Molesworth Governor.

for

The History of Jamaica. 319

for the Gentlemen of the Plantations, they have been as forward on such Occasions, as various as the Humours of them have been, as the People of *England*.

In the same Year 1689, the Pyrates in the *South Seas* were in very great Distress; for having landed there at the Instigation of the *Indians*, the latter deserted them, and their Return Home by Land was by that Means cut off, and that Company perished by Want or the Enemy. Another, commanded by Monsieur *Grammont* took *Campeche*, where they found nothing but *Indian* Corn. *Grammont* took a Sloop belonging to *Jamaica*, and forced the Men to serve him; but the *English* taking the Advantage of some Disorder among the Pyrates, got away in the Night.

The *French* King hearing of this Pyrate's Robberies, sent strict Orders to all his Governors in *America*, to recall the Commissions they had granted them, and forbid them to commit any more Pyracies on the *Spaniards*, or any other Nation; in which they had been till then encouraged.

In the Year 1687, a Post-Office was erected in *Jamaica*, and Mr. *James Wale* made Post-Master; and the same Year the King appointed his Grace *Christopher* Duke of *Albemarle* Governor of this Island, and he sailed from *Spithead* in the *Assistance* Man of War, the 12th of *September*, his Lady the Dutchess being on Board. *Christopher Duke of Albemarle Governor.*

They arrived at *Barbados* in *November*, and at *Jamaica* in *January* following, and were received with great Pomp. It was said this Lord was sent hither as to a Sort of Banishment, for his Zeal against Popery: But that seems to be a very favourable Report, for the Duke of *Albemarle* was no such Zealot in Religion, to make the Court uneasy on that Account, nor a Man of such Interest in *England*, that the Government should entertain any Jealousies of him.

The Truth is, he had lately got a great Sum of Money by Sir *William Phips*'s fishing for Silver, and he had formed several Projects for fishing for more, which he intended to put in Execution, and thought if he was at *Jamaica*, he might forward it by his Presence. He had also contracted so many Debts, that the Silver Sir *William Phips* brought him Home, was not sufficient to clear them, and his Government he thought would help to discharge them.

These and other Considerations prevailed upon him to accept it; but being a Man of Pleasure and intemperate in his Drinking, it was expected the Country would not agree with that Excess, and so it proved.

On *Sunday* the 19th of *February* 1687, there was an *Earthquake* in *Jamaica*. It came by Shocks; there was
three

three of them, with a little Paufe between. It lafted about a Minute's Time in all, and was accompanied with a fmall Noife. It was generally felt all over the Ifland. Some Houfes were cracked, and very near ruined; others being uncovered of their Tiles; very few efcaped fome Injury, and the People were every where in a great Confternation. The Ships in the Harbour of *Port Royal* felt it, and one that was *Eaftward* of the Ifland coming hither from *Europe*, met with, as he faid, a *Hurricane* at the fame Time. One riding on Horfeback was not fenfible of it. A Gentleman being at that Time abroad in his Plantation, faw the Ground rife like the Sea, in a Wave, as the Earthquake paft along, and then it went *Northward*.

The *Spaniards* who inhabited this Ifland and thofe neighbouring, built their Houfes very low, and they confifted only of Ground-Rooms, their Walls being made of Pofts, which were as much buried under Ground as they ftood above, on Purpofe to avoid the Danger that attended other Ways of Building, from Earthquakes: And Dr. *Sloan* writes, *I have feen in the Mountains afar off bare Spots, which the Inhabitants told me were the Effects of Earthquakes throwing down Part of the Hills, which continued bare and fteep.*

Lowth. Phil. Tranf. Vol. II. p. 410.

The terrible Earthquake that happened 4 or 5 Years afterwards, makes this to be the lefs remarkable.

While the Duke of *Albemarle* was in *Jamaica*, King *James* granted a Commiffion to Sir *Robert Holmes* to fupprefs Pyrates in *America*; and Sir *Robert* procured a Proclamation to be publifhed *for the more effectual reducing and fuppreffing Pyrates and Privateers in* America. He alfo appointed *Stephen Lynch*, Efq; Conful in *Flanders*, to be his Agent a *Jamaica*, whither he carried the before-mentioned Proclamation and fent it to the *Spanifh* Parts, as well on the *North Sea*, as to *Panama* on the *South Sea*, being furnifhed with all Neceffaries and Paffports from the Crown of *Spain*.

The Duke did not live long in his Government, and his Death is fuppofed to be haftened as much by the Alteration of his Wine, as by that of the Climate; for coming to drink *Madeira* Wine, which is many Degrees hotter than *French* Wine, and not abating of the Quantity, it foon threw him into a Diftemper that carried him to his Grave.

An eminent Merchant of *London* now living, being offered a Policy of Infurance on the Duke's Life to fubfcribe at a good *Premio* he refufed it, and gave that for a Reafon before the Duke embarked, his drinking *Madeira* Wine with the fame Excefs as he had done Claret, which we have given, for the fhortning his Arrival in *Jamaica*.

Col.

The History of Jamaica. 321

Col. *Hender Molesworth* was chosen Governor again on the Duke of *Albemarle*'s Death. The Duke's Body was embalmed and brought to *England*, in the same Ship in which the Dutchess, the present Dutchess of *Montague*, returned.

Col. Hender Molesworth Governor.

There was an Agreement made between the *English* and *Spaniards*, for a Trade in *Negroes* between *Jamaica* and the *Spanish West-Indies*. This Treaty was managed by *Don Santiago del Castillo* in *London*, and he was appointed by the King of *Spain* to be Commissary General at *Jamaica*, for supplying the *Spanish* Dominions in the *West-Indies* with Slaves.

King *William* III. who then reigned in *England*, conferred the Honour of Knighthood on the *Don*, better known by the Name of Sir *James de Castillo*, and he resided several Years in that Island. His Majesty gave the Government of it to the Earl of *Inchiqueen*, who embarked in *May* 1690, and arrived there in due Time.

The Earl of Inchiqueen Governor.

On the 29th of *July*, the *Negroes* belonging to Mr. *Sutton*'s Plantation in the Mountains, being about 400, broke out into Rebellion, and having forced the House, and killed the Man who looked to it, seized upon 50 Fuzees, Blunderbusses, and other Arms, and a great Quantity of Powder and Shot, four small Field-Pieces, and other Provisions, and marching to the next Plantation killed the Overseer, and would have engaged the *Negroes* there to have joined with them, but they hid themselves in the Woods. Then they returned back, and prepared to defend themselves in Mr. *Sutton*'s great House.

The Alarm was immediately given to the adjacent Quarters, and 50 Horse and Foot marched against them. In their March they were joined by other Parties, who making all together a good Body of Men, attacked the *Negroes* the next Day; the latter took to the Canes, firing them as they went, but a Party of *White Men* falling on their Rear routed them, and pursued them several Miles. Many of the *Blacks* were killed, and 200 of them threw down their Arms, and submitted: The rest were afterwards either killed or taken, and the Ringleaders of this Rebellion hanged as they deserved.

In 1691, the Lord *Inchiqueen* sent the *Swan* and *Guernsey* Men of War, with the *Quaker* Ketch and a hired Merchant-Man, to endeavour to destroy what *French* Ships they could find on the Coasts of *Hispaniola*, from the Isle of *Ash* to *Porto Point*, as likewise their Settlement on Shore.

Mr. *Obrian* commanded in chief in this Expedition, in which were employed 900 Soldiers; and tho' their Success did

did not answer the Peoples Expectation, yet they took and destroyed several *French* Ships; and landing on the Coasts did the Enemy some Damage hardly enough to quit Cost.

The most terrible Calamity that ever befell this Island or perhaps any other, was the dreadful Earthquake which happened the 7th of *June* 1692, a most amazing and tremendous Judgment of the Almighty: For without presuming to enter into a natural Description of such wonderful *Phenomena* of Nature, our Religion requires us in all these Cases, to look up to the Omnipotent, the great Judge of the Hearts of Men, as well as the strict Observer of their Ways, and to read a severe Lesson of Repentance to ourselves, from his Proceeding with others in so extraordinary a Manner.

It began between 11 and 12 a Clock at Noon, shook down and drowned 9 Tenths of *Port Royal* in two Minutes Time, and all by the Wharfs-side in less than one, very few escaped there.

There is something very remarkable written by a Gentleman from thence soon after, in *Lowthorp*'s Abridgment. *I lost all my People and Goods, my Wife, and two Men, Mrs. B. and her Daughter. One white Maid escaped who gave me an Account, that her Mistress was in her Closet 2 Pair of Stairs high, and she was sent into the Garret where was Mrs. B. and her Daughter when she felt the Earthquake, and bid her take up her Child and run down; but turning about, met the Water at the Top of the Garret-stairs, for the House sunk downright, and is now near 30 Foot under Water. My Son and I went that Morning to* Liguania, *the Earthquake took us in the Midway between that and* Port-Royal, *where we were near being overwhelmed by a swift rolling Sea, six Foot above the Surface, without any Wind. Being forced back to* Liguania, *we found all the Houses even with the Ground, not a Place to put our Heads in but in Negroes Huts. The Earth continues to shake* (June 20th) *5 or 6 Times in 24 Hours, and often trembling, great Part of the Mountains fell down, and falls down daily.*

All the Wharfs at *Port Royal* sunk down at once, and several Merchants were drowned with their Families and Effects, among whom was an intimate Friend of the Historian's, Mr. *Joseph Heminge.* There were soon several Fathoms of Water where this Street stood, and all that in which was the Church was so overflowed, that the Water stood up as high as the upper Rooms of the Houses that remained. The Earth when it opened swallowed up People, and they rose in other Streets; some in the Middle of the Harbour, and yet were saved, tho' at the same Time about 2000 *Whites* and *Blacks* perished in this Town. At the *North* above 1000 Acres

The History of Jamaica.

Acres of Land funk, and 13 People with it. All the Houses were thrown down over the Island, and the surviving Inhabitants were forced to dwell in Huts. The two great Mountains at the Entrance into 16 *Mile Walk* fell and met, and so stopped up the River, that it was dry from that Place to the *Ferry* for a whole Day; by which Means vast Quantities of Fish were taken up, to the great Relief of the Distressed.

At *Yellows* a great Mountain split and fell into the level Land, covered several Settlements, and destroyed 19 *white* People. One of the Persons whose Name was *Hopkins*, had his Plantation removed half a Mile from the Place where it formerly stood. The Water of all Wells from one Fathom to six Fathom, flew out at the Top with the violent Motion of the Earth.

Another Account of this deplorable Judgment gives us a lively and lamentable Idea of it. The Writer's own Words will be most satisfactory, as we find them in a Letter in the above-named Treatise. *Between* 11 *and* 12, *we felt the Tavern where I then was shake, and saw the Bricks begin to rise in the Floor: At the same Time we heard a Voice in the Streets cry, An Earthquake, and immediately we ran out of the House, where we saw all People with lifted up Hands begging God's Assistance. We continued running up the Street, while on either Side of us we saw the Houses some swallowed up, others thrown on Heaps; the Sand in the Street rising like the Waves of the Sea, lifting up all Persons that stood upon it, and immediately dropping down into Pits. At the same Time a Flood of Water broke in, and rolled these poor Souls over and over, some catching hold of Beams and Rafters of Houses: Others were found in the Sand that appeared when the Water was drained away, with their Legs and Arms out. Sixteen or eighteen of us who beheld this dismal Sight, stood on a small Piece of Ground, which Thanks be to God did not sink. As soon as the violent Shake was over, every Man was desirous to know if any Part of his Family was left alive. I endeavoured to go towards my House upon the Ruins of the Houses that were floating upon the Water, but could not. At length I got a Canoo, and rowed up the great Sea-side towards my House, where I saw several Men and Women floating upon the Wreck out at Sea, and as many of them as I could I took into the Boat, and still rowed on till I came where I thought my House had stood, but could hear of neither my Wife nor Family. Next Morning I went from one Ship to another, till at last it pleased God I met with my Wife and two of my Negroes. She told me when she felt the House shake, she ran out and called all the House to do the same. She was no sooner out but the Sand lifted up, and her Negro Woman*

Ibid. 412.

Woman grasping about her, they both dropt into the Earth together, when at the very Inftant the Water came in, rolled
them over and over, till at length they caught hold of a Beam,
where they hung till a Boat came from a Spanifh *Veffel* and took
them up.

The Houfes from the *Jews-ftreet* to the *Breaft-Work* were
fhaken down, except 8 or 10 which remained, from the
Balcony upwards above the Water.

As foon as the violent Earthquake was over, the Watermen and Sailors did not ftick to plunder thofe Houfes; and
in the Time of the Plunder, one or two of them fell upon
their Heads by a fecond Earthquake, where they were loft.

When as the firft and great Shake was over, the Minifter
defired all People to join with him in Prayer, and among
them were feveral *Jews*, who kneeled and anfwered as they
did, and it was obferved they were in this Extremity heard to
call upon Jefus Chrift.

Several Ships and Sloops were over-fet and loft in the
Harbour. Among the reft a Man of War, the *Swan* Frigat
that lay by the Wharf to careen. The violent Motion of
the Sea and finking of the Wharf, forced her over the Tops
of many Houfes, and paffing by that where a Perfon called
my Lord *Pike* lived, Part of it fell upon her and beat in her
Round-houfe; fhe did not over-fet, but helped fome Hundreds in faving their Lives.

A great and hideous Noife was heard in the Mountains,
infomuch that it frightened many *Negroes* who had run away
from their Mafters, and been feveral Months abfent, and
made them come Home. The Water that iffued from the
Salt-Pan Hills forced its Paffage from 20 or 30 Places,
fome more forcibly than others; for in 8 or 10 Places it
came out with fo much Violence, that had fo many Sluices
been drawn up at once, they could not have run with greater
Force, and moft of them 6 or 7 Yards high from the Foot of
the Hill; 3 or 4 of the leaft were near 10 or 12 Yards high.
The *Salt-Pans* were quite overflowed. The Mountains between *Spanifh-Town* and *Sixteen Mile Walk*, as the Way lies
along the River, are almoft perpendicular about the Mid-
Way. Thefe two Mountains joined together, which ftopped
the Paffage of the Water, and forced it to feek another,
that was a great Way in and out among the Woods and
Savana's.

'Twas 8 or 9 Days before the People had any Relief from
it: The People concluding it was funk like *Port-Royal*,
thought of removing to fome other Part of the Country.

The

The History of Jamaica.

The Mountains along the River were so thrown on Heaps, that all People were forced to go by *Guanaboa* to *Sixteen Mile Walk*. The Weather was much hotter after the Earthquake than before, and such an innumerable Quantity of *Muskettoes*, that the like was never seen since the Island was inhabited. A great Part of the Mountains at *Yellows* falling down, drove all the Trees before it, and wholly overthrew and buried a Plantation at the Foot of them. The Sand in *Port-Royal* cracking and opening in several Places where People stood, they sunk into it, and the Water boiled out of the Sand, with which many People were covered.

The Houses that stood were so shattered, that few of them were thought fit or safe to live in, and most of them remained empty a Year afterwards.

Those Streets that were next the Water-side were the best in the Town, full of large Warehouses, stately Buildings, and commodious Wharfs; close to which Ships of 700 Tuns might lie and deliver their Lading. Here the principal Merchants lived, and now alas! is 6, 7, and 8 Fathom Water.

The Part that was left standing, was Part of the End of that Neck of Land which runs into the Sea and makes this Harbour; at the Extremity of which stands the Fort not shook down, but much shattered by the Earthquake. 'Twas afterwards a perfect Island.

The whole Neck of Land from the Fort to the Pallisadoes or other End of *Port-Royal*, towards the Land, which is above a Quarter of a Mile, being quite discontinued and lost in the Earthquake, and is now also, with all the Houses which stood very thick upon it, quite under Water. This Neck was at first nothing but Sands, which by the People's driving down Timber, Wharfing, &c. were by little and little gained in Time out of the Sea, which now has at once recovered all again. On this sandy Neck of Land did the Inhabitants great heavy Brick Houses stand; whose Weight on such a light Foundation contributed much to their Downfall, for the Ground gave Way as far as the Houses stood only, and no farther.

The Shake was so violent, that it threw People down on their Knees, and sometimes on their Faces as they ran along the Streets to provide for their Safety; and it was a very difficult Matter for them to keep on their Legs.

One whole Street, a great many Houses of which stood after the Earthquake, was twice as broad then as before; and in several Places the Ground would crack, and open and shut quick and fast.

Major

Major *Kelly* of this Island, reported he saw 2 or 300 of these Openings at one Time; in some of which many People were absorpt, some the Earth caught by the Middle and squeezed to Death, the Heads of others only appeared above Ground; some were swallowed quite down and cast up again with great Quantities of Water, while others went down and were never more seen. These were the smaller Openings, the larger swallowed up great Houses, and out of some of them issued whole Rivers, spouting to a vast Heigth in the Air, accompanied with ill Stenches and offensive Smells. The Sky, which before was clear and blew, became in a Minute's Time dull and reddish, compared to a red hot Oven. Prodigious Noises were made by the Fall of the Mountains, and terrible Rumblings were heard under Ground.

While Nature was labouring with these Convulsions, the People ran up and down pale and trembling with Horror like so many Ghosts, thinking the Dissolution of the whole Frame of the World was at Hand.

The Shake was stronger in the Country than in the Town, where it left more Houses standing than in all the rest of the Island. People could not stand on their Legs in other Places, but fell down on their Faces, and spread out their Arms and Legs to prevent a greater Mischief by falling by the Earthquake. It left not a House standing at *Passage-Fort*, but one at *Liguania*, and none at St. *Jago*, except a few low Houses built by the wary *Spaniards*. In several Places of the Country, the Earth gaped prodigiously. On the North Side, the Planters Houses with the greatest Part of their Plantations were swallowed, Houses, People, Trees, and all in one Gap, instead of which appeared a Lake of 1000 Acres over: Afterwards it dried up, and there remains not the least Appearance of House, Tree, or any Thing else that was there before.

In *Clarendon* Precinct, there were great Gapings and Spoutings of Water 12 Miles from the Sea. Many Marks of these Gapings remain to this Day. In the Mountains were the most violent *Shakes* of all, and it is a general received Opinion, that the nearer the Mountains the greater the *Shake*. The *Blue Mountains* were the greatest Sufferers, and for two Months together so long the Shake lasted, they bellowed out hideous loud Noises and Echoings. Part of a Mountain not far from *Yellows*, after having made several Leaps, overwhelmed a whole Family and great Part of a Plantation lying a Mile off; and a large high Mountain not far from Port *Morant*, is quite swallowed up: In the Place where

The History of Jamaica. 327

where it stood, there is now a vast Lake 4 or 5 Leagues over.

Some were of Opinion that the Mountains sunk a little; certain it is, the Beauty of them is quite changed: For whereas they used to look always Green, above half of the Prospect now lies bare; and how can that be otherwise, when they were so rent and torn, and such prodigious Quantities of Trees rooted up and driven into the Sea by the Earthquake, on which several hundred thousand Tun have been computed to float sometimes?

Some think this whole Island is sunk a little; others, that *Port-Royal* sunk a Foot, and several Wells in *Legany* do not require so long a Rope to draw Water out of them now, as before the Earthquake by 2 or 3 Foot.

The Water in the Harbour of *Port-Royal* was suddenly raised with such a strange Emotion, that it swelled as in a Storm; huge Waves appeared on a sudden, rolling with such a Force that they drove most Ships from their Anchors, breaking their Cables in an Instant.

Capt. *Phips* and another Gentleman happening to be at *Legany* by the Sea-side at the Time of the Earthquake, the Sea retired so from the Land, that the Bottom appeared dry for 2 or 300 Yards; in which they saw several Fish lie, and the Gentleman who was with him ran and took up some, yet in a Minute or two's Time the Sea returned again, and overflowed Part of the Shore. At *Yall-House* the Sea retired above a Mile. It is thought near 3000 People perished in all Parts of the Island.

After the *great Shake*, those that escaped got on board the Ships in the Harbour, at least as many as could; where some of them continued above two Months, the Shakes being all that Time so violent and thick, that they were afraid to venture ashore. Others removed to *Kingston*, where from the first clearing of the Ground, and from bad Accommodations, the Huts built with Boughs, and not sufficient to keep out Rain, which in a great and unusual manner followed the Earthquake, lying wet, and wanting Medicines, and all Conveniences, they died miserably. Indeed there was a general Sickness, supposed to proceed from the noxious Vapours, belched from the many Openings of the Earth all over the Island, insomuch that few escaped being Sick, and it is thought it swept away 3000 Souls, the greatest Part from *Kingston* only, which is not even now a very healthy Place. Besides, the great Number of dead Bodies floating from one Side of the Harbour to the other, as the Sea and Land Breezes drove them, sometimes a 100 or 200 in a Heap, may be thought to add something to the Unhealthfulness of this Island. Half the People who escaped at *Port-Royal*, died at *Kingston*; where were 500 Graves dug in a Month's Time, and two or three buried in a Grave.

The Assembly appointed every 7th Day of *June* to be observed as a Day of Fasting or Humiliation, unless it falls on a *Sunday*, and then the Day after, in Remembrance of this dreadful Earthquake.

The Loss the Merchants suffered, both in *Jamaica* and *England*, was much more than is pretended to be lost by the Inhabitants of the *Leeward-Islands*, yet they never solicited for any Help; it is true they did not suffer by an Enemy: However the Assembly considered several of them, particularly Mr. *Benjamin Way*, Mr. *Joseph Sergeant*, Mr. *William Hutchinson*, Mr. *Francis Hall*, and Mr. *Edmund Edlyne*, who owing Customs for great Quantities of Wine, which were destroyed in the Earthquake, were by an Act indemnified from Payment of what Sums were due on that Account.

Nor did this Calamity come alone, for the *French* about the same Time landed 300 Men on the North-Side of the Island: Upon which the *Guernsey* Man of War, and several Sloops, were sent against them, and repelled the Enemy, burnt their Ships, and took or destroyed all their Men, both by Sea and Land, except 18, who escaped in a Sloop.

There was a strong Report in *London*, some Time after News came of the first *great Shake* in *Jamaica*, that there had happened a second, by which the greatest Part of the Island, and most of the Inhabitants were said to be destroyed, and all who had Interests there were in a terrible Consternation; but the next Letters thence proved that Report to be false and groundless.

Sir William Beeston *Governor.*

The Lord *Inchiqueen* dying in this Island, his Majesty, on News of it, was pleased to appoint Colonel *William Beeston* Lieutenant-Governor, and Commander in Chief of it, in *October*, 1692. He also conferred on the new Governor the Honour of Knighthood.

Sir *William* embarked aboard the *Falcon* Frigat, and arrived in *Jamaica* the 9th of *March*, 1692, where he set about reforming several Abuses crept into the Government there during the Lord *Inchiqueen*'s Administration.

In *November*, 1693. the *Mordaunt* Man of War, Convoy to a Fleet of Merchant Men, homeward bound from *Jamaica*, was cast away on the Rocks, near the Island of *Cuba*, and was lost, but all the Men were saved.

The History of Jamaica.

This Year the Assembly appointed Agents to sollicit their Affairs in *England*, who were, Mr. *Gilbert Heathcot*, Mr. *Bartholomew Gracedieu*, and Mr. *John Tutt*, of *London*, Merchants; and 450 *l.* was ordered to be raised, and remitted to them, for their solliciting the publick Affairs of *Jamaica*. Commissioners were also appointed in the Island for the Management of that Agency, who were,

Samuel Bernard,
Nicholas Law,
James Bradshaw,
William Hutchinson,   } Esquires.
Thomas Clark,
James Banister,
Modiford Freeman,

In the following Year, the Governor, Sir *William Beeston*, had Advice that four *French* Men of War had taken the *Falcon* Frigat before-mentioned, and carried her to *Petit Guaves*, where the Enemy were making Preparations, in order to some Attempt upon this Island: For being encouraged by several disaffected Persons to invade it, they had resolved to put their Design in Execution, having received an additional Strength, by the Arrival of three Men of War from *France*, carrying about 50 Guns each; of which Design Sir *William Beeston* had the first certain Advice from Captain *Elliot*, who being a Prisoner at *Petit Guaves*, made his Escape from thence, and arrived at *Port-Royal* the last Day of *May*, 1694. with two Persons besides, in a Canoe which could carry no more.

On this Notice, the Governor, Sir *William Beeston*, assembled the Council, and such Resolutions were taken, as were judged most proper for putting themselves in a Posture to receive them. It was ordered, That the principal Forces of the Island should be posted about *Port-Royal*.

On the 17th of *June*, the *French* Fleet came in Sight, consisting of the three Men of War before-mentioned, several Privateers, Sloops, and other small Vessels; in all about 20 Sail, commanded by Monsieur *Du Casse*, the *French* Governor in *Hispaniola*. Eight of them stay'd about Port *Morant*, and 12 Sail anchored in *Cow-Bay*, seven Leagues to Windward of *Port-Royal*, where they landed their Men, and plundered and burnt all before them for several Miles Eastward, killed the Cattle, drove several Flocks of Sheep into Houses, and then fired them, committing the most inhuman Barbarities. They tortured some of the Prisoners

soners they took, murdered others in cold Blood, after two Days Quarter, caused the *Negroes* to abuse several Women and dug up the Bodies of the Dead; for such are the *French* when they are Masters. They designed to have done the like in other Parts of the Island, and during their Stay at Port *Morant*, sent five or six Vessels to the North Side, where they landed at St. *Mary's* and St. *George's*; but upon the Appearance of some Forces that were sent thither, they withdrew, and returned to their Fleet.

On the 21st, the Wind blowing very hard, Monsieur *Rollon*, in the Admiral Ship, riding in deep Water, his *Anchors came home*, and he was driven off, with another in his Company, and could not get up again with the Fleet, but bore away to *Blackfield-Bay*, towards the West End of this Island, where he landed 60 Men. Upon which Major *Andress*, who was left there to take Care of those Parts, fell upon them, killed several of them, and the rest ran away to their Ship in haste, that they left their Provisions behind them. As soon as they could get up their Anchors, they sailed away.

The Enemy having done what Mischief they could at Port *Morant*, their whole Fleet sailed from thence the 16th of *July*. The 17th in the Morning, some of them came in Sight of *Port-Royal*, and in the Afternoon they went all to an Anchor again in *Cow-Bay*; and to amuse the *English*, landed their Men very fast, and made Fires along the Bay; but in the Night they all returned to their Ships, reimbarked, and on the 18th they were seen from *Port-Royal*, standing to the Westward; from whence it was concluded they designed for *Carlisle-Bay* in *Vere*; and to prevent their doing the same Damage they had done at Port *Morant*, two Troops of Horse were immediately ordered that Way, together with the Regiment of St. *Catharine's*, Part of the Regiment of *Clarendon* that were in Town; and Part of the Regiment of St. *Elizabeth*, which lay in the Way. The *French* anchored in *Carlisle-Bay* that Afternoon, and the next Morning landed 14 or 1500 Men, who attacked a Breast-work that was defended by 200 *English*. A great Fire was made for a considerable Time on both Sides; but the latter finding the Work could not be maintained, at last retired, and repassed the River, after having killed many of the Enemy. In this Action, Colonel *Clayburne*, Lieutenant Colonel *Smart*, Captain *Vassal*, and Lieutenant *Dawkins* were killed; and Captain *Dawkins*, Captain *Fisher*, and some other Officers wounded. In the mean Time, four or five Companies of Foot, and some Horse, advanced against the

the *French*. The *English*, though they had marched 30 Miles the Night before, and were very much fatigued, charged the Enemy with such Gallantry, that they not only put a Stop to their Pursuit of the *English*, who had quitted the Breast-work, but made them retreat. Here many of the *French* were killed, as also some *English*; and Captain *Bakestead*, and other Officers were wounded.

The 20th and 21st, there passed some Skirmishes between small Parties. The 22d the Enemy came to a Brick House belonging to Mr. *Hubbard*, and attacked it. There were 25 Men in it, who killed and wounded several of the *French*; among whom were some Officers of Note. Major *Lloyd* hearing of the Dispute, marched with some Horse and Foot to the Relief of Mr. *Hubbard*'s Men, and came in Time enough to help them to beat off the Enemy, who resolved to try their Fortune again the next Day against the same same Place, with a stronger Party and Cannon. Upon Notice of which, Major *Lloyd* put 50 Men into Mr. *Hubbard*'s House, and laid the rest of the *English* in Ambuscade, expecting the *French* would, as they gave out, renew the Assault: But the Enemy changed their Resolution; and finding they had lost many of their Men, and several of their best Officers, and that they could make no further Advance into the Country, they went all on board again the Night following; and the 24th their whole Fleet set Sail. Monsieur *Du Casse*, with two or three Ships more, made the best of his Way home, and 17 Sail went into Port *Morant* to Wood and Water, which they did with all the Speed they could. On the 28th they put ashore most of the Prisoners they had taken, and sailed homewards.

The *French*, according to the Report of the Prisoners who returned from them, lost above 350 Men, in their several Engagements with the *English*, besides many who died of Sickness; so that their whole Loss was computed to be 700 Men while they were in this Island. On the Side of the *English* 100 of all Sorts, *Christians*, *Jews*, and *Negroes* were killed and wounded.

Captain *Elliot*, who gave the Governor Notice of the intended Expedition of the *French*, had a Medal and Chain of 100 Pounds Value given him, by Command of King *William*, and 500 Pounds in Money, and 50 Pounds to each of the Men who escaped with him, as Rewards of their good Service. His Majesty was further pleased to order, that Captain *Elliot* should be recommended to the Lords Commissioners of the Admiralty for an Employment in the Navy.

The Council and Affembly fent over an Addrefs, which was prefented to the King; *moft gratefully acknowledging his Majefty's Royal Care of them, in ordering a fpeedy Relief and Affiftance to be fent thither, for the Defence and Security of their Perfons and Eftates againft a cruel and barbarous Enemy; who in their late Attempt upon that Ifland, had no other Advantage over them, but what was owing to the Inequality of their Numbers, and not to the Valour of their Men, which chiefly fhewed itfelf, in burning deferted Plantations, murdering Prifoners in cold Blood, and offering Indignity to Women.*

The King ordered a Body of Forces, under the Command of Colonel *Lillington*, for *Jamaica*; who arrived in the Year 1694. with about 1200 Men. The Governor having received fo ftrong a Reinforcement, refolved to be revenged of the *French* for their Barbarity in the late Invafion; the *Swan* Frigat was difpatched away to *Hifpaniola*, with an Agent, to concert Meafures with the *Spaniards* for attacking the *French* in that Ifland; and Captain *Wilmot*, Commodore of a Squadron of Men of War then at *Jamaica*, failed for St. *Domingo*, with Colonel *Lillington* and the Land-Forces aboard. When they came there, it was agreed, that the Governor of St. *Domingo* fhould march with the *Spaniards* to *Manchaneel-Bay*, on the North-fide of *Hifpaniola*, where the Ships were to meet him. Captain *Wilmot* failed accordingly to *Cape Francis*; and Colonel *Lillington* landed his Men within three Leagues of the Cape, and Captain *Wilmot* with his Men of War went within Gun-fhot of the Fort. The 18th the *Englifh* going near the Shore, the Enemy fired both great and fmall Shot upon them, which was anfwered by the Ships; and it was refolved, that as foon as the Land-Forces could march to one Side of the Town, the Seamen fhould affault it on the other, while the Ships battered the Fort.

Captain *Wilmot* went that Evening with feveral Boats, to find a convenient Landing-place; and going clofe into a Bay, a Party of Men lay under Cover, and fired very thick on the *Englifh*, but without killing a Man.

The next Evening he went with a greater Strength; which the Enemy perceiving, and believing he was going to land, they blew up the Fort, burnt the Town, and went off in the Night, leaving behind them at the Fort-Batteries and Breaft-Work above 40 Pieces of Cannon.

The *Englifh* entered the Town next Day, and found a good Booty there. After this they refolved to attack *Port Paix*, where Captain *Wilmot* ftaid feveral Days, to expect

the

The History of Jamaica.

the coming up of the Land-Forces, the *English* and *Spanish* Forces marching thither by Land. Before they came up, Captain *Wilmot*, with a Party of Seamen, landed about five Miles to the Eastward of *Port Paix*; where he received some little Opposition by an Ambuscade; but quickly forced the Enemy to retire, and burnt and destroyed the Plantations as far as the Fort, whither the *French* fled, and then the Seamen returned a Ship-board.

On the 15th, Captain *Wilmot* understanding the Land-Forces were come near *Port Paix*, he landed again with 400 Seamen. The four following Days were spent chiefly in putting the Cannon and Mortars ashore,

The 21st the Men of War sailed to the Westward of the Castle, and landed some more Guns. The 22d the *English* raised a Battery on a rising Ground, and play'd it the same Evening. The next Day they began another Battery, which they finished by the 27th. Both of them very much annoy'd the Enemy, and made a great Breach in the Castle.

The 3d of *July*, at Night, Colonel *Lillington* and Captain *Wilmot* were informed, that the *French* designed to leave the Castle, as they did accordingly, marching out to the Number of 310, besides 200 armed *Negroes*, and 150 without Arms. But the *English* and *Spaniards* being ready to receive them, killed many; among whom were most of their commanding Officers, took several Prisoners, and then made themselves Masters of the Castle, which it was thought fit to demolish; but they brought off the Artillery, Provisions, and Stores. After this the *English* reimbarked, and Captain *Wilmot* who directed his Course to *Jamaica*, where he arrived the 21st of *July*.

The Confederates thus ruined two of the *French* Settlements in *Hispaniola*, killed 350 Men, brought away 150 Prisoners, with 80 Pieces of Cannon, and a great deal of Booty, with inconsiderable Loss on their Side.

The Castle was situated at the Bottom of a Bay, upon a flat rocky Hill, very high, steep towards the Land, and sloping towards the Sea. It was built in the Form of a Square, with four Bastions. The Wall was Cannon-proof; on the Top of it were 12 small Pieces of Artillery, and this Fortress was of great Importance to the *French* at *Hispaniola*. Indeed *Jamaica* lies so convenient for annoying the Enemies of the Crown of *England*, in *Hispaniola* and the Continent, that we wonder the *English* have made no more Advantage of its Situation. It is certainly their own Fault, if the *French* at least are suffered to possess any Thing in *America*, where the *English* are near ten Times as numerous as their Enemies.

About

About this Time the Assembly past an Act, appointing Commissioners to give Freedom to such *Negro-Slaves*, as could prove they had done any remarkable Service against the *French*; which Commissioners were,

Rich. Lloyd, Esq;
Fran. Rose, Esq;
James Banister, Esq;

Tho. Bindlos, Esq;
John Walters, Esq;

Their Power was general; but those that follow, were only Commissioners for the Parishes of *Kingston*, St. *Andrew's*, St. *David's*, and St. *Thomas's*, to the Windward, *viz.*

Nicholas Laws, Esq;
Edward Stanton, Esq;
Modiford Freeman, Esq;

Josias Heathcot, Esq;
James Bradshaw, Esq;

This Year the Island of *Jamaica* hired, victualled, and manned two Sloops of War; and raised 200 Men, to reduce the rebellious *Negroes*; for which Services 4303 *l.* was levy'd on the *English*, and 750 *l.* on the *Jews*; which was assessed, collected, and paid by some of their own Nation, as,

Mr. *Solomon Arary*.
Mr. *Jacob de Leon*,
Mr. *Moses Toiro*,
Mr. *Jac. Mendez Guteras*.

Mr. *Jacob Henriquez*,
Mr. *Jacob Rodriguez de Leon*,
Mr. *Moses Jesurun Cardoso*, &c.

The Receivers of this Money were also appointed by the same Act to be,

Col. *Charles Knights*,
Col. *Tho. Clark*,
Capt. *Lancelot Talbot*,
Capt. *Robert Wardlow*,

Wil. Hutchinson, Esq;
Capt. *Josiah Heathcot*,
And,
Capt. *Tho. Clark*.

The Treasurers, or Pay-Masters, were Colonel *Charles Knights*, and *Josiah Heathcot*, Esq;

And the Commissioners who were to receive the Monies, and manage this Affair, were to employ Captain *William Dodington*, to provide Victuals, Arms, and Ammunition, for the Sloops.

Garrisons were put into *Fort William* and *Port Morant*, who were under the Command of Col. *Edward Stanton*.

In

The History of Jamaica.

In the Year 1696. Monsieur *Pointi*, with a *French* Squadron, made a Feint on *Jamaica*, in his Way to *Carthagena*, but understanding the Strength of the Place, bore off to Sea. The Inhabitants, as soon as they saw his Ships, took Arms, and kept strict Guards; being in so good a Posture of Defence, that they rather wished he would attack them, than pass them by. The *French* had indeed got 2000 *Buccaneers* together at *Petit Guaves*, with a Design either to attack the *Spaniards* in *Hispaniola*, or the *English* in *Jamaica*; but the Storm fell on the *Spaniards*.

Admiral *Nevill* was then in those Parts, in search of Monsieur *Pointi*; and the *Monmouth*, one of *Nevill*'s Squadron, took a *French* Privateer, that had just put the Governor of *Petit Guaves* ashore.

Admiral *Nevill* arrived at *Jamaica* the 16th of *May*, 1697. and sailed again the 25th, having staid there for a Wind. Two or three Days after he discovered *Pointi*'s Squadron returning from *Carthagena*, and chased them a Day and a Night; but the *French* out sailing him, got away, except a rich Ship, formerly taken from the *Spaniards*, being Vice-Admiral of the *Burlovento Fleet*, which the Princess *Anne* and the *Hollandia* brought to *Jamaica*, having on board, besides Plate, 800 Barrels of Powder, and 100 *Negroes*. The Ship and Cargo were computed to be worth 200000 Pounds *Sterling*.

Admiral *Nevill* sailed to the Coasts of *Hispaniola*, to look after the *Galleons*. He landed some Men on the Island, made himself Master of *Petit Guaves*, plundered and burnt it to the Ground. He also took seven *French* Privateers.

The Admiral died in *August*. Commodore *Mees*, Capt. *Lytcot*, Capt. *Holmes*, Capt. *Bellwood*, Capt. *Dyer*, Capt. *Stadley*, and Capt. *Foster* died also in this Voyage. They were all Commanders of Men of War, and the Seamen were swept away by the Sickness which raged in the Fleet.

The Squadron was, after the Death of Admiral *Nevill* and Commodore *Mees*, commanded by Capt. *Dilks*, who stoped in his Way home at *Virginia*, where the Seamen recovered their Health.

The *French* soon repaired their Losses this Year by the *English*; for in the next we find they talked of invading *Jamaica*. They had 14 Men of War at *Petit Guaves*, some of which were 70 Gun Ships.

Sir *William Beeston* sent Capt. *Moses* thither in a Sloop, to fetch off a Man, or more, to get Information of their Designs; which he performed very well, landing with four five

Men,

Men, who took one *Grumbles* out of a House, as he was at Dinner, and brought him away.

Grumbles was a Native of *Jamaica*, where he lived till a few Years before, when he ran away to the *French* at *Hispaniola*, where he was the chief Man that instigated the Enemy to invade, plunder, and destroy the Island of *Jamaica* his Native Country.

The *French* were enraged at the Loss of so useful a Man, and if he was hanged, threatened to do the same by Capt. *Price* Commander of a *London* Ship, which they had taken, and kept the Captain Prisoner at *Petit Guaves*. *Grumbles* said the *French* designed for the *Havana*; but the timely Notice the *Spaniards* had of their Preparations broke all their Measures.

In 1698, the Assembly past an Act for fortifying *Port-Royal*: Upon which the Governor removed thither from *Spanish-Town* to see that Work begun.

The *Scots* now settled at *Darien*, and fortified *Golden-Island* at the Bottom of the Gulph, where the Isthmus between that and the *South-Seas* is so narrow, that a few Men might defend it against Multitudes, and deny all Passage that Way to the *Indies:* But King *William* being in a strict Alliance with the King of *Spain* at that Time, this Settlement of the *Scots* was an open Breach of it, and he could not suffer his *English* Subjects to be assisting to the new Colony, without whose Assistance it was impossible for the *Scots* to effect their Design. Orders were sent to the Governor of *Jamaica* and other Governors in the *West-Indies*, not to let them be supplied from thence; so for Want of Provision the *Scots* were forced to abandon their Settlement: For which Loss Satisfaction has been since made them, upon the Conclusion of the late happy Union between the two Nations.

In the Year 1699, Admiral *Bembow* arrived at *Jamaica* with a Squadron of Men of War, the Seamen were infected with a mortal Distemper, which carried off great Numbers of them, as also of the Officers.

The *South Sea Castle* Capt. *Stepney*, and the *Biddeford* Capt. *Searl*, two Men of War were cast away, *Anno* 1700, near *Hispaniola*, and 30 Barrels of Powder blew up in *Fort-Charles* in *Port-Royal*, at saluting a *Scots* Ship.

Major Gen. Selwyn Governor.

Sir *William Beeston* dying in the Year 1700, Major General *Selwyn* was made Governor of *Jamaica* in *April* 1701, at which Time the Island was in a very flourishing Condition, Admiral *Bembow*'s Squadron healthy.

This Commander was very vigilant and brave in the Discharge of his Trust, and had Cruizers always about the Island for

The History of Jamaica.   337

for the Security of Trade; it being expected, that the War between *England* and *France*, which had ceased about 4 Years, would break out again, on the *French* King's seizing the *Spanish* Dominions in *Europe* and *America*.

Major General *Selwyn* arrived at *Port-Royal* in 1701, but died soon after his Arrival, and *Peter Beckford*, Esq; was chosen Lieutenant Governor by the Council; who receiving Advice of the Death of King *William* the IIId of glorious Memory, ordered all the great Guns to be fired at a Minute's Distance, at St. *Jago* or *Spanish-Town*, *Port-Royal* and *Kingston*, the 23d of *June* 1702, from Sun-set to 12 at Night; the same was done by Vice-Admiral *Bembow*, and the Men of War under his Command.   *Peter Beckford, Esq; Lieutenant-Governor.*

The next Day our present Gracious Sovereign Queen *Anne* was, with all possible Solemnity, proclaimed in *Spanish-Town* the Capital of the Island; the Lieutenant Governor, the Council, and most of the Gentlemen of the Place being present and the several Companies of Soldiers and Militia under Arms: All the great Guns in the Town were thrice discharged, and were answered by as many Volleys of small Shot: All the Forts in the Island fired all their Guns thrice, and the Vice-Admiral, the Men of War, and all the Ships in the Port did the like. The Lieutenant Governor gave the Council and principal Gentry a noble Entertainment at Dinner, and the Joy for her Majesty's Accession to the Throne, was as great as their Sorrow for the Death of their late Sovereign.

As soon as Admiral *Bembow* had Notice of the War breaking out again between *England* and *France*, that he might with the greater Advantage infest the Enemy, he detached some of the Ships under his Command, and sailed himself with the rest of his Squadron to insult the *French*, and their new Confederates the *Spaniards*, and intercept the Ships sent to the *West-Indies* under Monsieur *Du Casse*. Some of these Frigats took between the two Capes of *Hispaniola* and *Cuba*, a very rich Ship designed for *France*, mounted with 20 Guns and 190 Men, which they sent to *Jamaica*.

The Admiral and his Officers by their long stay in this Island, were so well accustomed to the Climate, that they were all in a good State of Health. The *Bristol* Man of War took the *Gloriana* a *Spanish* Man of War, and sent her into *Port-Royal*. She was bound for St. *Domingo*, to carry a new Governor from thence to *Carthagena*.

The Admiral with 7 Men of War cruizing off *Leogane* and *Petit Guaves*, put the *French* and *Spaniards* in a terrible Consternation. He drove a *French* Man of War of 40
Guns

Guns aſhore, and the Enemy blew her up, to prevent her falling into his Hands. He with his Boats ſet fire to two great Merchant Ships, and took two more, with a Brigantine and a Sloop; which the *Colcheſter* brought into *Port-Royal* the 14th of *Auguſt*, 1702. After which he ſailed in ſearch of *Du Caſſe*.

The Council and Aſſembly of *Jamaica* having tranſmitted a very loyal Addreſs to her Majeſty in *England*, it was preſented by Sir *Gilbert Heathcot*, and Sir *Bartholomew Gracedieu*, two eminent *Jamaica* Merchants.

In *October* this Year the Queen was pleaſed to appoint the Right Honourable the Earl of *Peterborough*, who has ſince made himſelf ſo famous by his Conqueſts in *Spain*, to be Governor of *Jamaica*, and gave him larger Powers than the Duke of *Albemarle* had. His Lordſhip being declared Captain General and Admiral of all her Majeſty's Settlements in the *Weſt-Indies*, Mr. *Graydon* was ordered with a Squadron to convoy the Lord *Peterborough*, and the Forces he was to take with him thither: And all People concerned in the Plantations were extremely pleaſed to ſee this Commiſſion in ſo good Hands. Why this Lord did not go is a Queſtion we cannot anſwer: And it is therefore enough for us to obſerve only, that Mr. *Graydon* went with the Men of War, and ſome Tranſports; and that the Voyage proved unfortunate both to him and the Kingdom. In the mean Time, Admiral *Bembow* hearing Commodore *Wheſtone*, with ſeveral Ships, was abroad, ſailed to join him; but underſtanding Monſieur *Du Caſſe* was expected at *Leogane*, he went thither in ſearch of him. In his Paſſage he took a *French* Sloop, and forced a *French* Man of War of 50 Guns to run her ſelf aſhore at *Leogane*, where ſhe blew up; he ſunk another of the Enemy's Ships of 16 Guns, took one of 30, another of 16, and a third of ſix.

He afterwards went to *Petit Guaves*, and Cape *Donna Maria*; where he received Advice that Monſieur *Du Caſſe* was ſailed for *Carthagena*, and ſet Sail after him the 10th of *Auguſt*, towards the Coaſt of St. *Martha*, with the *Breda*, Captain *Fog*, of 70 Guns, on board which he was himſelf; the *Defiance*, Col. *Richard Kirby* Commander, of 64 Guns; the *Windſor*, Captain *John Conſtable*, of ſixty Guns; the *Greenwich*, Captain *Cooper Wade*, of 54 Guns; the *Ruby*, Capt. *George Walton*, of 48 Guns; the *Pendennis*, Capt. *Thomas Hudſon*, of 48 Guns; and the *Falmouth*, Capt. *Samuel Vincent*, of 48 Guns.

On the 15th, he came in Sight of Monſieur *Du Caſſe*, who had with him four ſtout Ships, from 66 to 70 Guns, one

great

The History of Jamaica.

great *Dutch* built Ship, of 30 or 40 Guns, and one small Ship, full of Soldiers, with a Sloop, and three other small Vessels. The Admiral immediately made a Signal for an Engagement, and attacked the Enemy very bravely, maintaining the Fight five Days. If the other Ships of his Squadron had seconded him, he would certainly have taken or destroyed all the *French*, but four of his Ships did not assist him. The *Ruby* was disabled on the 21st, and sent to *Port-Royal*, and the whole Burthen lay upon the Admiral and the *Falmouth*; who however took a Prize, being an *English* Vessel, which the *French* had formerly taken. The *Breda* so disabled *Du Casse's* second Ship, that she was towed away, and very much shattered the rest of his Squadron. The Admiral, on the 24th, had his Leg broken by a Chain-shot, which yet did not discourage him from continuing the Fight; but not being able to prevail with his Captains to concur with him in his Design, he was obliged to give it over, and so *Du Casse* got into *Porto Bello*. He ordered the Offenders to be taken into Hold; and when he arrived at *Jamaica*, granted a Commission to Rear-Admiral *Whetstone*, who was then there, and other Officers, to try them. A Court Martial was held, and *Arnold Brown*, Esq; Judge Advocate, officiated in his Place on this Occasion. Col. *Kirby* and Capt. *Wade*, were, for Cowardice and Breach of Orders, condemned to be shot to Death, but the Execution was respited till her Majesty's Pleasure should be known. Capt. *Constable* being cleared of Cowardice, was for Breach of Orders cashiered from her Majesty's Service, and condemned to Imprisonment, during her Royal Pleasure. Capt. *Hudson* died before his Trial.

This Sentence was certainly very just; for during the whole Course of the Wars between *England* and *France*, never did two *Englishmen* bring such Dishonour upon their Country, as *Kirby* and *Wade*, through their Cowardice and Treachery. Besides the great Profit that they hindered the Nation of receiving, by the Destruction of *Du Casse*, and his Squadron, which perhaps would have prevented the *French* in all their Designs on the *West-Indies*, and forwarded the Reduction of the *Spanish* Dominions there: But this fair Opportunity was lost; and without the Gift of Prophecy we can foresee, we shall not soon have such another.

The Admiral lived till the 4th of *November*, and then died of the Wound he received in the Engagement with *Du Casse*. Captain *Whetstone* took on him the Command of the Squadron of Men of War, which was then at *Port-Royal*.

The Merchants there fitted out a great Number of Privateers, and nine or ten of them attacked a Place called *Toulou,* on the Continent, about 10 Leagues from *Carthagena,* which they took, plundered and burnt. From thence they failed to *Caledonia,* went up the River *Darien,* and perfuaded the *Indians* to be their Guides; who in twelve Days carried them to the Gold Mines at *Santa Cruz de Cana,* near *Santa Maria.*

The 9th Day of their March, they fell in with an Out-Guard of ten Men, which the *Spaniards* had pofted at fome Diftance from the Place; of whom they took nine, but the other efcaping, gave Notice at the Mines of their Approach. Upon which the richeft of the Inhabitants retired from thence, with their Money and Jewels. However the *English,* to the Number of 400 Men, being come up, took the Fort, and poffeffed themfelves of the Mine; where there remained about 70 *Negroes,* whom they fet to work, and continued there 21 Days, in which Time they got about 80 Pound Weight of Gold Duft. They alfo found feveral Parcels of Plate, which the *Spaniards* had buried when they left that Place. The *English,* at their Departure, burnt all the Town, except the Church, and returned to their Sloops, carrying away the *Negroes* with them.

Some went farther up the River, having a Defign upon another Gold Mine, called *Chocoa*; and two of the Privateers, commanded by Captain *Plowman* and Captain *Gandy,* failed towards *Cuba,* landed near *Trinidado*; and with 100 Men took the Town, burnt part of it, and brought off a very confiderable Booty.

Col. Tho. Handafyde, Governor. This Year Colonel *Thomas Handafyde* was appointed Lieutenant Governor of *Jamaica*; and Captain *Whetftone* having refitted his Ships, failed with 12 Men of War to look out the Enemy. But before we can give an Accout of this Expedition, we muft take Notice of the dreadful Judgment which fell upon the rich and beautiful City of *Port-Royal,* for it then deferved that Name, and which fo far buried it, that it is now no where to be feen, but in a Heap of Ruins.

On the 9th of *January,* 170 . between 11 and 12 in the Morning, a Fire happened through Carelefnefs in this Town, which before Night confumed it, without leaving a Houfe ftanding. The Place being fituated on a fmall Neck of Land, furrounded by the Sea, and taken up wholly with Houfes, and the Streets and Lanes narrow, admitted not of that Help which might have been otherwife given; and the People could not fave fo much of their Goods as they might have done in a more open Place: However the two Royal
Forts

The History of Jamaica. 341

Forts and Magizines did not receive any Damage, nor any of the Ships at Anchor, except one Brigantine and a Sloop, which were burnt. Most of the Merchants saved their Money and Books of Accompt, and some of them considerable Quantities of Merchandize, through the Assistance of Boats from the Men of War. The Governor, on this sad Occasion, summoned the Assembly to meet at *Kingston*, recommended to them the Case of the poor Inhabitants, and acquainted them, that by the Advice of the Council he had made some Disbursements for that End; several Barrels of Beef, Flower, and fresh Provisions having been sent to them. Upon this Information, the Assembly unanimously resolved, That they would reimburse the Treasury, what had been or should be expended for the Relief and Support of the distressed People, and prayed the Governor and Council to continue their Care of them. They also, with the Concurrence of the Lieutenant Governor, took such farther Resolutions, as were necessary for the Safety and Welfare of the Island in this Exigency. They voted, That *Port-Royal* should not be rebuilt; but that the People should remove to *Kingston*, where Streets were laid out, and soon built and inhabited.

News of Vice-Admiral *Bembow*'s Death coming to *England*, Vice-Admiral *Graydon* was ordered to *Jamaica*, to take on him the Command of the Squadron there. Before he arrived, Capt. *Whetstone* returned to that Island, having been out from the 14th of *February*, to the 9th of *April* following, A. D. 1703. He cruised about five Weeks on both Sides of *Hispaniola*, in hopes of meeting with a considerable Fleet of Merchant Ships; which, as he had been informed, was expected in those Parts, under a Convoy from *France*: But not being able to get any Account of them, he sailed to *Petit Guaves* and *Leogane*, in the Gulph of *Hispaniola*; and for the better preventing any Ships escaping out of that Bay, he divided his Squadron, and sent Captain *Vincent*, who had so bravely seconded Admiral *Bembow* in his Battle with *Du Casse*, with one half to the Southward, and himself steered with the rest to the Northward. As he had conjectured, three *French* Privateers, upon the Appearance of Capt. *Vincent*, and the Ships with him, stood away immediately to the Northward, and so came in the Commodore's View, who chaced one of 12 and another of 14 Guns ashore, where they were burnt, and the third of ten Guns was taken. In the mean Time, Captain *Vincent* with his Boats rowed in the Night undiscovered into the *Cul*, where there lay four Ships, of which the biggest was former-

ly

ly taken from the *English*, and was called the *Selwin*. She had her full Cargo, and was richly laden, but all her Sails were ashore. Captain *Vincent* burnt one, sunk another, and towed out a third, which was a *Consort* of the Privateers; the fourth was boarded by one of the Boat's Crews, but by Accident blew up. This alarmed the Enemy at Land, and put them into a terrible Consternation to see their Ships burning on both Sides of their Bay. The Squadron looked into *Porto Paix*, on the North-side, but found no Ships there. These four Privateers were all the *French* had at *Hispaniola*, and were designed to sail with 500 Men to the North-side of *Jamaica*, to make a Descent, and plunder and destroy the Country. The *English* brought away 120 Prisoners, and the *French* suffered a considerable Loss in their Ships and Goods.

On the 5th of *June*, 1703. Vice-Admiral *Graydon* arrived at *Jamaica*, having on board 2000 Land Soldiers, whose chief Commander was *Ventris Colenbine*, Esq; Brigadier General of Foot, who died on Ship-board, when the Ships were in Sight of the Island. Indeed there had been a great Mortality in the Fleet, and the Disagreement between the two Climates of *England* and the *West-Indies* is such, that it is very discouraging to send Soldiers thither; where they have no Enemy to fear so much as the very Air they breathe. This cannot be said of *seasoned* Men; but no Pretences to the contrary will prevail against a Truth confirmed by so many sad Experiences.

Kirby and *Wade*, the two cowardly Captains above-mentioned, being this Year sent home Prisoners, under Sentence of Death, found a Warrant lodged for their Execution, as soon as they came to *Plymouth*, and they were accordingly shot a Ship-board: A just Example to all those Traitors, who take Commissions only to fill their Pockets, and feed their Debaucheries, and have no Consideration for the Service of their Queen and Country.

On *Shrove-Tuesday*, as the People were at Church at *Kingston*, they felt a *Shake* of an Earthquake, which was small, and did no Damage.

The Men of War here, in 14 Days Time, *A. D.* 1704. took three *French* Privateers, 120 Prisoners, and retook a Sloop of *Jamaica*; so that these Seas were almost entirely cleared of the Enemies Rovers. This Island was then very healthy; and the Merchants traded enough with the *Spaniards*, to fill it with Money. It is to be wished they may have Encouragement in that Trade, and the best Encouragement is to secure it.

The History of Jamaica.

On the 7th of *May*, Captain *Whetstone* (now Rear-Admiral) arrived at *Jamaica*, with six Men of War and 12 Merchant Ships from *England*. He took a Brigantine and a Sloop in his Passage. His Men were healthy, and so continued.

On the 6th of *June* he sailed to cruize, and took off *Carthagena* a *French* Ship of 46 Guns, after a very resolute Defence made by the Captain. One of the *Jamaica* Privateers took another *French* Ship of 24 Guns.

Rear-Admiral *Whetstone* stay'd in these Parts till *September*, 1706. when he left Captain *Kerr* Commander in Chief of the Squadron which remained there.

Before he sailed for *England*, the Cruizers of *Jamaica* brought in there eight Prizes. One of them a *French* Merchant Ship, very richly laden, commanded by one *Cordier*, and taken by the *Experiment* Man of War, a Privateer of *Jamaica* being in Company. A *Dutch* Caper afterwards took a *Spanish* Advice-Boat of 14 Guns, bound for St. *Domingo*, and another of 22 Guns, bound for the *Havana*. Which shews us how advantageously this Island is situated to annoy the *Spaniards* in the *West-Indies*, if proper Methods of doing it were pursued, and due Encouragement given to such as would undertake it.

The Behaviour of several Captains of Men of War in these Parts has been very infamous, and the Nation has suffered much by it.

In *Jan.* 170$\frac{5}{6}$. before the Arrival of Captain *Kerr*, her Majesty's Ships the *Bristol* and *Folkston* met with ten Sail of Merchant Men bound from *Petit Guaves* to *France*, under Convoy of two *French* Men of War, one of 24, and another of 30 Guns; out of which Captain *Anderson*, Commodore of the *English*, took six *French* Merchant Men, laden with Sugar, Cocao, Cocheneal, and Indigo, and brought them to *Jamaica*; where, when he arrived Admiral *Whetstone* held a Court of Admiralty, and Captain *Anderson* and the other Officers were condemned to lose their Commissions, for not engaging the two *French* Men of War.

The Merchants of *Jamaica* having been extremely abused by Capt. *Kerr*, and through his Negligence or Avarice, lost several Sloops bound thither from the *Spanish West-Indies* with Plate, they resolved to apply to the Parliament for Redress; accordingly they employed Mr. *Thomas Wood* to be their Agent in *England* on this Occasion, and he has with great Industry and Prudence prosecuted the Matter, so that Justice has been done the Merchants on the Offenders, and the chief of them had his Commission taken from him, without

Hopes

Hopes of ever being employed in her Majesty's Service more.

I do not think it will be expected, that in the History of the *British Empire* in *America*, I should enter into the various Causes of Differences between the Governors and Assemblies, Councils and Assemblies, publick and private Persons, farther than the general Good or Evil is concerned in them. We find the Governor Col. *Handasyde* and the Assembly in ill Terms or ill Temper in the Year 1611, insomuch that the Governor dissolved the Assembly, as a *Jamaica* Man writes, under a sham Pretence, at the Instigation of *Richard Rigby*, Esq; Provost Marshal General and others of a Cabal with him: And how happy the Inhabitants here were in the Disposition of their Employments in the Case of this Man, will appear by his being at this Time, or soon after, a Member of the Council, Provost Marshal General, and thus he is, by his Deputy Marshal, Executioner both in civil and criminal Cases, Secretary of the Island, by Deputation from Mr. *Baber* the Pattentee, Clerk of Inrollments of all Deeds, Conveyances, Letters, Patents, &c. The executive Power of so many important Offices being in one Hand, it is easy to conceive if it was not an honourable Person, the Inhabitants would be exposed to much Tyranny and Oppression, and if he was a Man of Honour and Integrity, he would not accept of so many and so inconsistent Trusts; to prevent which a Bill past the Assembly, but was not ratified in *England*. However when it was again past with some Modifications, it was confirmed *at Home*, a Term used in the Sugar Colonies for *England*, which the Planters always think of as their Home; which shews their natural Affection to our Country. I wish our Affection for them bore any Proportion to it.

1711. Lord Archibald Hamilton Governor.

In *July* 1711, the new Governor Lord *Archibald Hamilton* arrived at *Jamaica,* and put off the Meeting of the Assembly for some Time. It was suspected that he was influenced therein by the Suggestion of the above-mentioned *Rigby, William Broderick,* Esq; Attorney General, and Dr. *John Stewart*; I know not whether he was a graduate Physician or a Surgeon, or Apothecary only, it being very common in the Sugar Islands for such Kind of Professors to erect themselves into Doctors, and as Docters some have acquired very considerable Estates. But at this Time *Jamaica* was happy in the Advice of a Physician of the most Note in his Profession, Dr. *Thomas Hoy*, Professor of Physick in the University of *Oxford*, who lived here many Years and kept his Professorship at *Oxford* by Favour of that University, who admitted of his holding it by a Deputy, or rather by Proxy. The Attorney General *Broderick* came hither from *Montserrat,*

Montferrat, and we have been told that his leaving that Island was not voluntary. Be that as it will, he was in the special Grace here at this Time, and this Attorney, *Rigby* and *Stewart* were called the *Triumvirate*, to denote the Superiority of their Power, which some pretend was the same with that of the Governor, whose Removal afterwards seems to warrant such an Opinion, as well as the Characters of this *Triumvirate*.

Notwithstanding the Endearments between the new Ministers in *England* and those of *France*, and the Attachment this Governor's Brother Duke *Hamilton* had to the Pretender's Interest, the Inhabitants of *Jamaica* were in dreadful Apprehensions of being attacked by the *French*. Just about the Time that the Duke of *Ormond* declared a Suspension of Arms between the *English* and *French* in *Flanders*, *Cossart* with a Squadron of *French* Men of War plundered *Montferrat*, and it was feared at *Jamaica* he was coming to do the same there. An Embargo was laid on all Shipping, and the *London* Fleet detained in the Harbour; into which the Ships were hawled as close as could be to the Shore, and all Dispositions made for Defence, but no *Cossart* came, to the no little Joy of the Inhabitants, which lasted not long; for they were thrown into a more terrible Consternation, by a furious *Hurricane* of Lightning, Wind and Rain without Thunder. The Wind then at North shifted to the South. It began on the 28th of *August* 1712, about eight at Night, and continued till two in the Morning, during which fourteen Ships belonging to this Island were lost, together with several belonging to *London* and *Bristol*. The Ships of War and all other Ships and Sloops received much Damage, as well at *Kingston* as *Port-Royal*; many Houses and Warehouses were blown down, and very few escaped being shattered in Pieces, and the violent Rains ruined or damaged Abundance of Goods. The Trees were mostly blown up by the Roots, the Sugar Works destroyed or much damaged, the Canes and Negroes Provisions generally blown away. Four hundred of the Ships Crews at *Port-Royal* and *Kingston* were drowned, and several Persons were killed by the Fall of Houses, &c.

On *Monday* the 1st of *September* following, the martial Law was proclaimed, and all the Inhabitants were in Arms to be ready for Defence, if the Enemy should take Advantage of the Distress they were in to invade the Island. On the 18th of *September* there was another violent Tempest, which lasted from 8 a Clock at Night till next Day at Noon. The *Defiance*, *Salisbury* and *Centurion* Men of War escaped the Storm, being cruizing off St. *Martha* and *Carthagena*.

1712.

The

The Governors of *Jamaica* sent the *Spy* Sloop to get Intelligence of the *French*, and at her Return News was brought that they had suffered in the Storm, and had quitted this Coast. As great as was this Storm, that which happened here 10 Years after was much greater.

Labour and Industry are so painful, Idleness and Ease so pleasant to most Men, that it is no Wonder so many throw themselves out of all Means of subsisting themselves by honest careful Business, and follow Courtiers and Ministers for Offices. This Infatuation has carried Thousands out of *England* to *Ireland* and the *West-Indies*, flattering themselves and very often being flattered with vain Hopes of Preferment from the new appointed Governors, as if they were sent to their Governments only to fill up Vacancies; but the Disappointment they generally meet with, is a a good Lesson to others to beware of running into the like Misfortune.

There came with this Governor to *Jamaica*, *David St. Clare*, Esq; Son of the Lord *St. Clare* of *Scotland*, *Robert Paterson*, Esq; Brother of Sir *Hugh Paterson*, *Richard Denham*, Esq; Brother of Sir *Thomas Denham*, Mr. *Robert Douglas*, recommended by his Grace the Duke of *Roxburgh*, Mr. *Elliot* a young Gentleman, Heir to an Estate, recommended by Sir *Gilbert Elliot* of *Stobbs*, Dr. *St. Clair*, Son of Sir *Robert St. Clair*, Physician to the Governor at his landing, Lieutenant *John Mehews*, who was recommended by the Duke and Dutchess of *Ormond*, and I marvel it was not more successful; Mr. *Patrick Hamilton* late Sheriff of *Cork*. The Fate of these Gentlemen and Mr. *Mackenzie* Secretary to the Governor, is too biographical for our compendious History, but may be seen at large in a *Letter from a Gentleman in* Jamaica *to his Friend at* London, printed in the Year 1714, which is written with so much Freedom, that one would think it was never intended for the Press; and if the Facts are true, I should have much wondered the Government of this Island was not put into other Hands, had not the Government of *England* been then in the Hands of Persons, who fell afterwards under Attainders and Impeachments.

The most extraordinary Instance of Oppression and Injustice that ever I met with under *West-India* Governors, who have not spared giving such Sort of Instances, is that of *Escheats*; a Law Term for seizing the Lands and Tenements of the Owners, under Pretence that they had no Right to them, and consequently they were fallen to the Crown. Accordingly several Plantations cultivated and stocked by particular Persons at their great Charge, upon

Titles

Titles of former Purchasers and Grantees, which Titles being set aside, as the rapacious Tools of Government knew how to do, they took the said Lands and Tenements so escheated to their own Use tho' in other Names, and kept them or sold them as they saw fit, but generally sold them to prevent Clamour, and divide the Guilt and Blame of it with others. The Letter above-mentioned charges *Rigby* as the chief Engine in this Work, and what a terrible Thing it is to conceive, that an honest industrious Family, who have laid out their whole Substance upon a Plantation greater or smaller, and brought it into a Condition of subsisting and sometimes enriching them, shall all at once be dispossessed of it, and reduced to Want and Beggary, to gratify the Avarice of Men in Power. Their Way was to get a Jury to appraise the Estate in Question at a small Price, and returning that small Price as the *Escheat* Fee, they sell it or assign it, or take out the Grant in other Names, and have it disposed of for their own Use.

Ruinous Escheats.

In the Parish of *Clarendon* was a Plantation, that belonged to one *Kupuy* a naturalized *Dutchman*, that produced 120 Hogsheads of Sugar yearly, and was farmed at 300 *l.* a Year by Trustees in Behalf of his Grand-daughter and Heir, a *Minor*, who dying soon after her Succession, the Estate was immediately escheated, and tho' it was rented at 300 *l.* a Year, and had 120 Negroes in it worth 25 *l.* a Head, amounting to 3000 *l.* and the 120 Hogsheads of Sugar, valued in the Country at 2 *l.* a Hogshead gross Amount, and had besides very valuable Appurtenances; yet the Jury the Provost Marshal summoned and swore, gave in the Valuation upon Oath at but 1436 *l.*

The Renter of this Plantation Mr. *Swymmer*, a Name well known in the City of *Bristol*, at 300 *l.* a Year, got a very good Estate out of it in a few Years, and this Estate, which at a moderate Computation may be reckoned to have been worth 6 or 7000 *l.* was by that sworn Jury rated at less than a Quarter Part of its real Value to the Crown, by these Officers of the Crown, then in the highest Trust at *Jamaica*, but this is a Trifle to what they accomplished at the Expence of their Oaths and Consciences in other Cases.

A Plantation belonging to *Nathaniel Herring*, Esq; of *Westmoreland* Parish of 540 Acres, was sworn by the Provost Marshal's Jury to be worth but 1 *l* 2 *s.* 6 *d.* to the Crown. However, Mr. *Herring* who had before bought it and paid for it, was forced to pay for an Escheat Patent 300 *l.* besides Composition Money to the *Triumvirate* aforesaid, and Fees to the Provost Marshal *Rigby* and the Attorney General, of

whom

whom I was told such Things by his own Son, that I can easily give Credit to whatever is said of him in the *Jamaica* Letter, where are these Expressions with which I shall drop this invidious Subject. *The Mal-Practices of Mr. R—by, his Confederates, Abettors and Tools, have been so grosly fraudulent and oppressive, to the manifest Prejudice both of the Queen and the Subject, that in the escheating of Estates, whether justly escheatable or not, the private Composition given to the G————rs, besides what these escheat Parties have got themselves, has oftener than once amouted to near* 300 *Times as much as the pretended trifling Value, tho' upon Oath of such Estates brought to the Queen's Account.*

The *Jamaica* Letter would furnish one with Multiplicity of like amazing Instances of Oppression in these *Escheaters,* chief Ministers at that Time in this Island ; but as I believe the Author was injured and consequently angry, the Stile is not always decent enough for an impartial Reader. What he says, which carries a Face of Truth, renders the Change of Government in this Colony 2 or 3 Years after less surprizing, and the more agreeable to those that wish it well.

The Assembly was so sensible of the Grievances of this Administration, that they past three Acts, which would have gone very far towards redressing them. *An Act to prevent any one Person holding two or more Offices and Posts in this Island.* This referred particularly to Mr. *Rigby's* being at once Secretary of State, Provost Marshal General, *&c. An Act for regulating* exorbitant Fees. *An Act for quieting Men's Possessions, and preventing vexatious Suits at Law.* The Reason and Necessity of these good Laws are so obvious, that it would be impertinent to offer Arguments to support them. The *Provost Marshal,* who was concerned chiefly in the Act against exorbitant Fees, as well as that of holding Offices, took one effectual Method to put a Stop to the passing them in *England*; for as Secretary, it was his Business to take Care of transmitting an authentick Copy of all Acts of Assembly, that were sent Home for Ratification, and what made such Copy authentick, was the affixing the Broad Seal of the Island to it, which that sagacious Minister depending on his own Weight and Influence in the Government of *Jamaica,* artfully omitted, and the Copy of these Acts being transmitted without a Broad Seal, could not consequently receive the necessary Ratifications in *England.* The Act for quieting Possessions, related to the *Escheats* before-mentioned.

Mr Rigby's bold Attempt.

The *Jamaica* Men complaining very much of the Disadvantage the Colony has often in prosecuting Suits in Chancery, where the Governor as Chancellor dicides Causes, tho'

tho' he knows no more of Law than of Gospel, instancing particularly in the former Governor Col. *Handaside,* whose Education he says, *was generally confined to Pike and Musket, and it need not be much wondered at, if he understood, without Inspiration, little more of the Office of a Lord Chancellor, and the deciding of abstruse and knotty Law Cases, than he did of what he commonly by Mistake called the Creed of St. Ignatius, meaning that of St.* Athanasius, *to which he said,* he could not be easily reconciled; which Opinions do not seem to disqualify him to judge of Right and Wrong, whatever the Letter would insinuate by it.

It would be an Injury to the Colonies, if we sunk what is told us of the little Care that has been taken, to supply the Courts of Justice with able and experienced Judges. The Letter Writer vouches for the Truth of his Assertions; let it go in his own Words.

' Our present Chief Justice and Chief Judge of the
' *Grand Court,* that is the Courts of *Queen's-Bench, Com-*
' *mon-Pleas,* and *Exchequer* in one, was likewise bred at
' Sea from a Boy upwards, and happening to get the Com-
' mand of a Frigat, had the good or bad Luck, I can't tell
' which, to lose her on a Rock in Sight of *Port-Royal,* with-
' out any Stress of Weather, so that thinking it not con-
' venient to return Home, he settled here and became first
' a *Planter* and then a *Judge.*

' The next Judge was a Soldier in one of the Regiments
' of Foot Guards, and his Captain trusting him to pay his
' Company's *Subsistence* Money, he borrowed a Week's Pay
' of the said Company, drew his own Pass, and made the
' best of his Way to *Jamaica;* some say he sold himself to
' the Master of the Ship that brought him. However, be
' that as it will, he married a Planter's Widow, and is now
' the first of the six Assistant Judges of the *Grand-Court.*
' All the rest of the Assistant Judges are likewise Planters,
' of indifferent Estates and have no Salaries;' insinuating that they make their Market of the Judgments they give. The Author confirms this with other more shocking Instances and Particulars, but I shall not transplant them into my History, since he has not thought fit to warrant them, by setting his Name to his Information, and I should not have given so much of his Letter a Place in it, had I not known the like Grievances to have been complained of in our other Colonies, and particularly the Characters of the Persons he speaks of by other very authentick Information. I write this History for Use and not for Amusement, and my chief Aim in all Events I relate, and all Reflections I make

on

The History of Jamaica.

on them, is to mark, as *Bouys* do in the Water, the Rocks and Shelves where the *Steersmen* of these Colonies have often wrecked the Ships of their Government. And having justly from so many notorious Facts, received an ill Impression of the Management of the Plantation Affairs, I endeavour to shew the ruinous Effects of such Management, that it may be amended and improved for the future.

Col. *Peter Haywood*, a Gentleman of a large Interest in this Island, a Member of the Council and Chief Justice, was removed from his Places by the Governor, as were also Mr. *Chaplin* and Mr. *Blair*, two other Members of the Council. After the Removal of Mr. *Haywood*, I find *Thomas Bernard*, Esq; Chief Justice, I suppose the Son of *James Bernard*, Esq; before-mentioned, a very worthy Merchant. Mr. *Chaplin* whom I just mentioned, was Chairman of the Committee of Assembly, to whom was referred the Consideration of the Money advanced for the Subsistence of Col. *Handaside*'s Regiment, and the two independent Companies of Foot then there. That Committee reported, *that it had been raised without Law, or the publick Faith given for it*, and consequently was not precedented, *and the House voted the said Money to be no publick Debt*. If the House proceeded regularly therein, and only asserted their Right to raise Money, I see no Reason for turning Mr. *Chaplin* out of the Council for asserting the Liberty of his Country. For tho' I have seen more than one solemn Opinion given, that Members of the Council should be displaced to make Governors only; yet I have looked upon it always as the Effect of the Dependance, such as gave that Opinion, had on those to whom it was given. It was very freely owned, that Mr. *Chaplin* and Mr. *Blair*'s Crime, for which they were turned out of Council, was for asserting that *the Parliament*, the Assembly, had the sole Right of framing *Money Bills, and had a Power to adjourn themselves*. I question whether any of the Gentlemen concerned in the *outing* of Mr. *Chaplin* and Mr. *Blair*, will venture to say in *England*, that the Parliament has no such Powers.

The proclaiming of the *Utrecht* Peace here, or rather the declaring a Suspension of Arms between *Great-Britain* and *Spain*, hindered not Robberies and violent Depredations, which probably were committed by Particulars for their private Gains, without any Warrant from the Governments of either Nation. The *English* were charged with landing at *Hispaniola* and carrying off *Negroes*, Indigo and other Goods to a great *Value*; but upon Complaint of the *Spanish* Governor of St. *Domingo*, the Governor and Council of *Jamaica*,

The History of Jamaica. 351

maica, finding good Cause so to do, ordered full Satisfaction to be made to the *Spanish* Sufferers, which the *English* could not procure for their Losses by the *Spaniards,* from the *Spanish* Governors of *Cuba* and *Hispaniola.* The Damages the *English* sustained by the Robberies of the *Spaniards,* amounted to above 200,000 Pieces of Eight in little more than a Year after the *Utrecht* Peace, by which *Spain* through the Favour of *England* only obtained so many Advantages, that she became in a Condition to reward her Benefactors with Pillage and Spoil, and to defend her Usurpations and Piracies by Arms.

About this Time the *Flotilla* from *New Spain* was shipwrecked on the Coast of *Florida* and the *Bahama-Islands* and several Sloops, went to fish on the Wrecks from *Jamaica* and other Places. There were Hostilities committed on the *Spaniards* after the Satisfaction given them. Lord *Archibald Hamilton* saying in his Vindication, ' *Jonathan* ' *Barnes* who commanded the *Snow Tyger,* who made ' an Affidavit against his Lordship, was the first who com- ' mitted Hostilities upon the *Cuba* Shore.'

But inconsiderable were those Excursions of the *English,* compared with the daily Piracies and Acts of Hostilities committed by the *Spaniards* on the *English* after the above Calculations of 200,000 Pieces of Eight Damage. I cannot forbear taking Notice of the great Regard one ought to have not to give Credit to one Party in the Colonies complaining against another, without carrying an even Hand between both. The Opposers of Lord *Archibald Hamilton* made loud and successful Complaints against him, for granting Commissions which had been abused ; but when he was recalled, and these Complainers had less Power in their own Hands, See what his Lordship says in his Vindication, as it was written to his Lordship from *Jamaica. The Agents are going, and do not stick to say that the same Lord* Hamilton *is removed for nothing but to cover the Piracies. So many of their Friends being concerned in* Jennings's, *and robbing the Ships in* Port-Royal *Harbour:* May not this shew us a little into what sort of Hands Opposition and Clamour generally falls. The Letter from *Jamaica* is crammed with bitter Complaints of the like Acts of Oppression with these beforementioned ; but I do not find one of them formed into an Article against his Lordship. The main of the Charge consisting of what relates to his granting Commissions to some Commanders of Ships, equipped as was alledged for the procuring these Commissions to secure the Trade of the Island, upon the Return of all the Men of War to *England,*

land, or to other Stations, which was not only done at the Petition of the Merchants and Owners of Ships, but was in itself a most well advised and necessary Proceeding. If any of these Commanders abused such Commissions, they only were blameable and accountable; and if they or any other Commanders of Ships fished on the Wreck beforementioned, did not Sir *William Phips*, by an ample Commission from King *James* II. fish for and bring away near 400000 Pieces of Eight from the Wreck, in or near the same Place? and I cannot think that the fishing for Silver wrecked in the Sea five Years or 100 Years after it was so lost, alters the Case; the Property of the Money fished up now on the Coast of *Florida* having no more a particular Owner than that brought home by *Phips* had, against which not a Word was said, and what the Council of *Jamaica* says on this Head is very satisfactory.

1715.

9th of *February*, Present.

His Excellency Lord *Archibald Hamilton*, Capt. General.

Peter Haywood, Esq;	*Thomas Bernard*, Esq;
Thomas Rose, Esq;	*John Archibald*, Esq;
John Stewart, Esq;	*John Sadler*, Esq;
John Peck, Esq;	Dr. *Samuel Page*, Clerk of the Council.
Valentine Mander, Esq;	
Richard Rigby, Esq;	

' As to such Part of the *Flota* Ships wrecked on the Coast of
' *Florida*, as remained in the Possession of the Subjects of his
' most Catholick Majesty, of which it is pretended they were
' *dispossessed*,' this is in Answer to a Memorial of Captain *Juan de la Vallee*, Deputy of the *Spanish* Council of Commerce, sent by the Governor of the *Havana* to demand Satisfaction, for that fished Money, &c. ' It is the Opinion of his Excel-
' lency and the Council, that the Dispossessors are Robbers
' and ought to be punished; but concerning such Part of
' the said *Flota's* if any, lying *derelict* the Subjects of his
' Catholick Majesty were not drove and forced out of Posse-
' on, but it belonged to the first Occupant.'

This is so plain, that the Claim both in Matter and Expression, shews only the Weakness of the *Don's* Judgment, and the Impertinence of this Deputy's Errand.

On the Acceptance of the *Assiento* Contract by the *South-Sea* Company lately established in *England*, they obliged themselves to sell to the *Spaniards* yearly, 4000 Negroes

at

The History of Jamaica.

at ―― a Head. The Factors they employed here, were Meſſieurs *Morris* and *Pratter* Merchants at *Kingſton*. In the Interval between *February* 1715-6, and *June* 1716, happened the Removals in the Council before-mentioned. 1 find an Order of the 9th of *June* 1716. Preſent,

1716.

William Broderick, Eſq; *Francis Roſe,* Eſq;
Richard Rigby, Eſq;   *John Peeke,* Eſq;
John Stewart, Eſq;   *Thomas Bernard,* Eſq;

A plain Indication from what has been ſaid before, that the Majority of this Council was not difficult to be procured, if the Government here wanted Opinions to ſupport it in any Caſe whatſoever.

On King *George* the Ift's happy Acceſſion to the Throne, as ſoon as Notice of it arrived at *Jamaica,* his Majeſty was proclaimed with the uſual Solemnity and Acclamation. And it muſt be ſaid to the Honour of all Governors, Councils and Aſſemblies in our Sugar Colonies, that they have upon all ſuch Occaſions behaved with exemplary Zeal, as well on the Acceſſion of *James* II. as of *William* III. The Governors who influence all ſuch Things, knowing very well how much it behoves them to be well with thoſe that can put them in and put them out. The *Utrecht* Peace was introduced here with equal Joy, tho' the People of *Jamaica* were as ſenſible as any, how the *Engliſh* Intereſt in the *Weſt-Indies* was mortally wounded by it, leaving the *Spaniards* and their Confederates the *French,* in a Condition to aſſert what Claims they pleaſed in theſe Countries and Seas, and to defend them by Arms.

The chief Gentlemen of *Jamaica* were Malecontents with the Adminiſtration here in the Queen's Time, but they had little Proſpect of Succeſs in their Attempts to relieve themſelves, while the Miniſtry in *England* were ſo enamoured with the Name of the Governor *Hamilton,* on Account of the late Duke's great Merits in Abhorrence of Revolution Principles, and in a conſtant Attachment to the Intereſt of King *James* the IId. and on the Proteſtant Succeſſion's taking Effect at Home, the *Jamaica* Gentlemen reſolved to make the true Uſe of that Bleſſing, and apply at Home for the Redreſs of their Grievances, and in Order to it, they raiſed among themſelves above 1000 *l.* to defray the Charge of ſuch an Application, the Management of which was entruſted to Mr. *Bendiſh,* who went to *England* and to their Correſpondents at *London.* Mr. *Chaplin* and Mr. *Blair,* Mr. *Rigby,* Mr. *Thomas Beckford,* Col. *James,* who took the Subſcriptions

for

for Money, and *Peter Haywood*, Efq; were at the Head of this Affair, and it feems to be a rafh Proceeding at fuch a Juncture, to turn Mr. *Haywood* out of his Office of *Chief Juftice*.

I obferve in the Governor's Anfwer to the Articles againft him, that what he did himfelf is faid to be done by the King, as in this Inftance of Mr. *Haywood* and the Counfellors the Governors turned out; the Words are, *Perfons whom his Majefty thought fit before to difplace*. As far as royal Stile is ufed in this and other Governments in Declamations and Law Proceffes, it is doubtlefs neceffary; and fo perhaps in the State Papers of Colony Governments, but to fay the King thought fit to turn out Perfons whom he never heard of, and whom he put in again as foon as he had due Information of them, feems to me to have more of Form than Subftance. I obferve, that the Governor, in his Vindication, fupports himfelf chiefly by the Majority of *the Council:* Counfellors of his own making or recommending were without Doubt ready to fall in with whatever he required of them, and this is no Plea againft his being accountable for what he did by the Advice and Warrant of fuch Counfellors.

Peter Haywood, Efq; Governor.

On the Removal of the Lord *Hamilton* from the Government of *Jamaica*, *Peter Haywood*, Efq; was made Governor and Commander in Chief of the Ifland, and a new Council was alfo named, of which were two of the difplaced Members as is before related, Mr. *Chaplin* and Mr. *Blair*, and three leading Members of the Affembly, Mr. *Rigby*, Mr. *Bennett*, and Mr. *Thomas Beckford*, a Name of great Account and Efteem in this Ifland, and when we find the *Beckfords* and fuch Men as thefe ftanding up in Behalf of their Country, againft fuch a Man as the Attorney General, who was enriching himfelf by fuch Oppreffion, it muft give us a very ill Opinion of thofe that countenanced the Oppreffor. The Author of the new Hiftory of *Jamaica*, tells us Col. *Peter Beckford* had 20 Plantations, above 1200 Slaves, and a Million and half in Bank Stock, &c. which doubtlefs is looking on his Fortune thro' a magnifying Glafs; but if the Quarter Part of it were true, all the Governors that are fent from *England* to *Jamaica*, the Peers excepted, could not together have made a Capital equal to Mr. *Beckford's*. Dominion is founded in Property as Philofophers pretend, and it is with a very ill Grace that Colony Governors give themfelves an Air of Empire over fuch Men. The Lord *Archibald Hamilton* was taken into Cuftody at *Jamaica*. I do not wonder it was carried in Council by one Vote only, as his Lordfhip obferves, confidering the Characters

The History of Jamaica.

racters of some of the Members that still remained in it, tho' considering also that Sir *Nicholas Lawes* was at that Time actually the commissioned Governor and Captain General of this Island, I do not see any Thing extraordinary in the Commitment of the late Governor, under the heavy Charge exhibited against him: Heavy in the Sound of it, *encouraging Piracy*, but the very contrary as to the Substance, the granting Commissions to Commanders of Ships on Purpose to secure the Trade against Pirates.

Dr. *Samuel Page*, Clerk of the Council, was very busy in the Prosecution of Lord *Hamilton*, and his Lordship was so sensible of it, that he refused to sign his Ticket for shiping himself for *England* on that Occasion; there is something remarkable at this Time with Respect to *Doctorship*. The Governor's Party had Dr. *Stewart* at their Head. The Country Party's chief Manager was Dr. *Samuel Page*; Dr. *Stewart* was a Member of the Council, Dr. *Page* Clerk of the Council, but Lord *Hamilton* says, so little qualified for it, that the Members of the Council were forced to take the Minutes of it themselves, and neither of them was more a graduate Doctor of Physick, than the Chief Justice, a Master of a Ship, and the Assistant Judge, a Foot Soldier before mentioned, were Barristers at Law. This I hope will put the *Jamaicans* on their Guard against admitting such Sort of Persons into so useful and important Employments for the future.

Lord *Archibald Hamilton* was sent Prisoner to *England*, bailed when he came there, and was so fully cleared of the Charge relating to his Difference with the Assembly about their Right as to Money Bills, that the Board of Trade took it on themselves, by saying in their Report of that Matter and others, that they had recommended to him to take Care, *that the Council should not be denied any Right of amending Money Bills*. If by adding 40 or 50000 *l*. to be raised on the Subject, or the easing some Persons in the levying it more than others, contrary to the Sense of the Assembly, that is there the Sense of the Nation, is *to amend a Bill*, let every *English* Man versed in Parliamentary Rights judge. I do not take the Minutes inserted by his Lordship on this Occasion to be the strongest Part of his Vindication, but I do think if the *Jamaica* People had nothing but the Sea *Commissions* to complain of against him, his Lordship had very hard Measure from them, and there is nothing on which they insist so much in their Complaint, as these Commissions.

In *July* 1717, his Majesty was pleased to appoint *Nicholas Lawes*, Esq; Governor of *Jamaica*, and to confer on him the Honour of Knighthood. The People here could not but

1717. Sir Nicholas Lawes Governor.

but with great Satisfaction hear their Government was given to a *Planter* of this Island, whose Interest was the same with theirs. True it is

The Interest of the King and Country is in Effect the same, and consequently the true Interest of every Colony Governor and the Colony he governs is in Effect the same, when the Governors are of the Country, as every King is, or is supposed to be. But most of the Governors sent to the Plantations from *England*, to govern Places where they have not a Foot of Land, and go thither with Intention to use their utmost Skill and Industry, to raise Fortunes out of the Inhabitants of the Island or Provnice they govern; such are apt to think their Interest is quite different from that of the Inhabitants, and that their Interest is to get as large Appointments as they can, and it is certainly the People's to keep their Money in their Pockets as much as they can. From which different Interests and Views are perpetually rising Differences between Governors and Assemblies, Jarrings and Jealousies, that are a perpetual Hinderance to the Prosperity and Peace of the Country; as for those Governors, that like the Duke of *Portland* at *Jamaica*, the Lord *How* at *Barbados*, spend out of their *European* Stock to become popular in *America*, they ought no more to be sent to *West-India* Governments than the greedy and the griping, for their Profusion and Gaiety soon infect the Planters, naturally subject to such Contagion; and many of them, in Imitation of their Governors, run into Pleasures and Expence, very inconsistent with the necessary Oeconomy and Industry of a Planter's Life.

About the Time of Sir *Nicholas Lawes*'s Arrival, there were three Men of War on this Station, the *Diamond*, the *Adventure* and the *Ludlow Castle*, 40 Gun Ships, and it is to be hoped there will never be fewer, except in Cases of Cruize on the neighbouring Coasts and Continent.

Among the many Pirates that now infested the *American* Seas, none made himself more terrible than *Edward Toutch* of *Jamaica*, commonly called *Blackbeard*. He was born in this Island, where his Mother was living at *Spanish-Town* within these two Years, and his Brother was then Captain in the Train of Artillery: *Blackbeard*, a Monster of Cruelty, was attacked by an *English* Lieutenant of a Man of War on the Coast of *Virginia*; he took a Glass of Wine, and drank *Damnation* to them that gave or asked Quarter. He was killed and his Head cut off, and stuck upon a Pole on that Coast.

In 1718, *John Knight*, Esq; was made Secretary of this Island. This often is granted by Patent, and the Deputy here when the Principal is in *England* makes it worth 1000 *l.* per Ann. the Principal in *England* farming it sometimes for 6, 7 or 800 *l.* a Year. As such Principal Secretary has no Manner of Relation to the Interest in *Jamaica* but what his Farm gives him, it seems very reasonable that *Jamaica* should have no Manner of Relation to him. There are so many Hazards and so much Expence in Plantation Business, that it is Pity a Penny that is raised by it should be diverted from the Planters Use, for the Commodity of such as are in another World.

A new History of *Jamaica* having been published at the Time I was writing this, whose Author arrogates to himself a Privilege of chastising all Writers that touched upon this History before, as imperfect and incorrect, I hoped to have had great Helps from his Works, where my Memory fell short, and should very thankfully have received his Rebuke, had he not been himself so very defective and incorrect; when I had Recourse to his Labour for some Assistance in Sir *Nicholas Lawes's* Government, I found only 6 or 7 Lines relating to the Hurricane, which we shall give an Account of in its Place, and of which the most remarkable Thing he says is, the Assembly appointed the 28th of *August* a Day of solemn Fasting and Humiliation to be observed for ever. Three Years before this Hurricane happened, War had been declared between *Great-Britain* and *Spain*. On Notification of it to the Governor here, he summoned an Assembly, to whom he recommended to take Order for the Execution of *martial Law*, and to take into Consideration the military State of the Island. He informed them he had taken Care to repair the Fortifications of *Port-Royal*, and added, *I think the Rock Line and the decayed Port of* Carlisle-Bay, *worth your immediate Consideration. I have addressed to the Minister at Home, for an Engineer to be sent upon the Establishment, to oversee the Works and direct where to raise new ones.*

This Governor, Sir *Nicholas Lawes*, had besides the Publick so large a private Interest in this Island, that it was not likely he would omit any Occasion of shewing his Zeal for its Security and Welfare; and the *Spaniards* from *Cuba* and the Continent having committed many Depredations on the *English*, he sent Captain *Chamberlain*, Commander of the Snow *Happy*, to *Trinadado* in *Cuba*, to demand Satisfaction of the *Alcades* or commanding Officers of that Town, which they call a City. Commodore *Vernon*, Commander in chief of all his Majesty's Ships in the *West-Indies*, in a Letter to the said

said *Alcades*, sent by Mr. *Joseph Lawes*, Lieutenant of the *Snow Happy*, made the like Demand of Satisfaction. The Governor and Lieutenant's Letters will set this Matter in the best Light.

Governor Lawes's Letter to the Alcades of Trinadado.

Gentlemen,

'The frequent Depredations, Robberies, and other Acts
' of Violence, which are daily committed on the King my
' Royal Master's Subjects, by *Bandittis*, who pretend to
' have a Commission from you, and in Reality are sheltered
' by you, is the Occasion of my sending the Bearer, Capt.
' *Chamberlain*, Commander of his Majesty's *Snow Happy*,
' to demand Satisfaction for the Robberies your People
' have committed on the King's Subjects of this Island, by
' those Traitors *Nicholas Brown*, and *Christopher Winter*,
' to whom you have given Protection. These Proceedings
' are not only a Breach of the Law of Nations, but must appear
' to the World of a very extraordinary Nature, when consi-
' dered that the Subjects of a Prince in Amity with another,
' should encourage such vile Practices. I have had long
' Patience, and declined using any violent Measures to
' obtain Satisfaction, hoping the Cessation of Arms so hap-
' pily concluded between our Sovereigns, would have put a
' Stop to these Disorders; but I find the Port of *Trinadado*
' a Receptacle for Villains of all Nations.

' I therefore assure you in the King my Master's Name,
' if I meet with any of your Rogues upon the Coasts of this
' Island, they shall be hanged without Mercy. I demand
' of you to make ample Satisfaction to Captain *Chamberlain*
' for all the *Negroes* which the said *Brown* and *Winter* have
' taken from these Islands, since the Suspension of Arms,
' and that you will deliver up to the Bearer such *Englishmen*
' as are detained at *Trinadado*, and that you forbear granting
' Commissions to, or suffer any such notorious Villains to
' be equipped from your Port, otherwise those I can meet
' with shall be treated as Pirates.'

Mr. *Joseph Lawes*'s Letter was as follows

Lieutenant Lawes's Letter.

Gentlemen,

' I am sent by Commodore *Vernon*, Commander in Chief
' of all his Majesty's Ships in the *West-Indies*, to demand, in
' the King our Master's Name, all the Vessels with their ef-
' fects, &c. and also the *Negroes* taken from *Jamaica* since
' the Suspension of Arms; likewise all *Englishmen* now de-
' tained or otherwise remaining in your Port of *Trinadado*,
' particular-

The History of Jamaica.

'particularly *Nicholas Browne* and *Christopher Winter*,
both of them being Traitors, Pirates and common Enemies to all Nations. And the said Commodore hath ordered me to acquaint you, that he is surprized that the Subjects of a Prince in Amity with another should give Countenance to such notorious Villains.'

Off of the River of Trinadado, *Feb.* 8. 1720.

Answer of the *Alcades* of *Trinadado*.

'Capt. *Lawes*,
'In answer to yours, this serves to acquaint you, that *The* Alcade
neither in this City nor Port are there any *Negroes* or *of* Trina-
Vessels which have been taken at your Island of *Jamaica*, *swer*.
nor on that Coast, since the Cessation of Arms; and what
Vessels have been taken since that Time have been for trading in an *unlawful Commerce* on this Coast; and as for these
English Fugitives you mention, they are here as the other
Subjects of our Lord the King, being brought voluntarily to
our holy Catholick Church, and have received the Water of
Baptism; but if they should prove Rogues, and should not
comply with their Duty in which they are bound at present,
then they shall be chastised according to the Ordinance of
our King. And we beg you will weigh Anchor as soon as
possible, and leave this Port and its Coast, because on no
Account you shall be suffered to trade, or any Thing else,
for we are resolved not to admit thereof.'

Lieutenant *Lawes* answered this insolent Letter, in the Stile
and Sentiments of a good *Englishman*.

'*Gentlemen*,
'Your refusing to deliver up the Subjects of the King my
Master is somewhat surprizing, it being in a Time of
Peace, and the detaining of them consequently against the
Law of Nations, notwithstanding your trifling Pretence,
for which you have no Foundation, but to forge an Excuse
to prevent my making any Inquiry into the Truth of the
Facts I have alledged in my former. I must tell you my
Resolutions are to stay on the Coast till I have made
Reprisals, and should I meet any Vessels belonging to
your Port, shall not treat them as the Subjects of the
Crown of *Spain*, but as Pirates, finding it a Part of
your Religion in this Place to protect such Villains.

To this one of the *Alcades* answered.

Captain *Lawes*,

'You may assure yourself I will never be wanting in the
'Duty of my Post; the Prisoners that are here are not in
'the Prison, but only kept here to be sent to the Governor
'of the *Havana*. If you, as you say, command at Sea,
'I command ashore. If you treat the *Spaniards* you meet
'as Pirates, I will do the same by every one of your People
'I can take up. I will not be wanting in good Manners
'if you will do the same. I can likewise act the Soldier
'if any Occasion should offer that Way, for I have very
'good People here for that Purpose. If you pretend any
'Thing else, you may execute it on this Coast;' by this will
be seen the Obstinacy and Rodomantado Spirit of the
American Spaniards, and their Opinion of and Disposition
towards the *English* 20 Years ago; as also the Conduct of
the *English* towards the *Spaniards*, who were then complaining of illicite Trade on the Part of the *English*; but
it is to be noted that the *Spaniards* in *America* were always
so desirous of that Trade, that they ran as great a Risk to
have it, as the *English* did to bring it to them, and taught
the *English* how to manage it.

The *Spaniards* having refused to deliver up *Brown* and
Winter, the Governor of *Jamaica* issued a Proclamation
against them. The Beginning of it I insert to shew the
Stile of such Pieces there which run in the King's Name.

*Whereas several Treasons, Piracies and Robberies have been
lately committed on the High Seas, adjoining to our said Island of*
Jamaica, *by the Subjects of* Great-Britain, *and particularly
by* Nicholas Brown, *and* Christopher Winter, *late of our
said Island Mariners; and though we have used such Methods
as we thought most effectual for the taking and suppressing of
the said Traitors, Pirates and Robbers, yet we having such
Acts of Villainy in the utmost Abhorrence, and for the greater
Encouragement of such Persons of our Subjects as shall be
active in the apprehending the said* Nicholas Brown, *and*
Christopher Winter, *so as that they or either of them may be
brought to Justice, we have thought fit, by and with the
Advice of our Council of our said Island, to promise that if
any Person shall discover, or seize, or cause or procure to be
discovered, he shall have the Reward following; for the said*
Nicholas Brown 500 *l. of current Money of* Jamaica, *and
for the said* Christopher Winter 500 *l. of like Money, to
be paid by the Receiver-General.*

Four

The History of Jamaica. 361

Four Days after the Date of this Proclamation, Sir *Nicholas Laws* the Governor made the following Speech to the Assembly, which shews the Temper of both the Governor and the governed in some Measure, and will let the Reader into a better Light than a barren Journal of Facts, and give him an Idea of the want of a thorough Union of Sentiments and Intentions of both at this Time.

Mr. Speaker, and Gentlemen of the Assembly,

'I had sent for you sooner after the late Prorogation of your own begetting, but that I find by Experience you are all *too wise* for me to think of talking you into any Thing I would have you do, though never so apparently your Interest. And I wish you were all so prudent and discreet, as not to be talked out of what you ought to do in Justice to your Country and Duty to his Majesty; and that by false Reasoning and mistaken Politicks. I am at Length convinced that there are some who would be glad to continue the old Breaches, or to see or make Divisions amongst us, and it is not to be wondered that those who obstinately refuse to serve the King and Country, will be active in doing Mischief; but I would have these Gentlemen remember, by whose Tenure they hold their Lands, and know under whose Influence and Protection they enjoy at least their well Being. But you Patriots, such as I hope you will appear to be, know how to govern yourselves on such Occasions, and Wisdom will ever be justified by her Children.'

Gentlemen and Brother *Planters,*

'Let it suffice that I can say for myself, that I have been known to your Fathers, and am not unacquainted with most of you, and that my Interest and my Posterity stands upon the same Foundation with yours, and therefore I can have no Designs or Views, otherwise than what I must be equally concerned with you in the Event. I have done all Things in my Power to settle the present and future Peace and Prosperity of this Island; and I wish you had all joined with me in the same Measures. I may be allowed to say what your own Journals will say to my Honour, *that I have pointed out to you* many more Particulars for the Publick Welfare, Security, and Advantages of the Country, than ever any of my Predecessors did.

'And now I challenge your whole Body to propose to, or lay before me any Thing that you in your Wisdom can desire or devise for your own Good, or the real Interest of this Island, consistent with my Duty and his Majesty's just Prerogative,

'Prerogative, to grant, which I will not heartily concur with
'you in. I hope for all our Sakes you will readily fall
'into your Duty in the ordinary and ufual Way agreeable to
'our happy Conftitution, otherwife it may be eafily fore-
'feen, without the Spirit of Prophecy, that his Majefty's
'wife and able Minifters will rightly counfel and inform
'him, how and by what Ways and Means he may make his
'Government eafy here, and his People truly happy under it,
'and I know we are all in Love with *Englijh* Laws.'

'But were I capable, or might be thought worthy of ad-
'vifing you, it fhould be not to contend with the King and
'Miniftry, *or kick againft the Pricks*, but to *prefer Obedience
'before Sacrifice*, which I am confident would be moft
'acceptable to his moft Sacred Majefty, and in Confe-
'quence make us the happieft Subjects in all his Do-
'minions.'

After this the Affembly was adjourned. The Behaviour of this Reprefentative to the Governor at this Time was not well relifhed by him as appears by his Speech, and this Governor being, as he ftiles himfelf, a *Brother Planter*, it may be well conjectured that the Occafion of whatever Difference there was then between them, was more their Fault than his. The Intereft Sir *Nicholas Lawes* had in the Ifland was probably ten Times more valuable than his Government could be rated at; and as he was a wife experienced Man, it is not to be fuppofed he would act contrary to the *Jamaica* Intereft to ingratiate himfelf with the Miniftry in *England*.

Dreadful Hurricane 1722.

The dreadful Earthquake which laid in Ruins fo great a Part of the Buildings in this Ifland 30 Years before, has been amply related, and a Hurricane almoft as dreadful and ruinous as that happened here *Tuefday* the 28th of *Auguft*, 1722. It began at *Kingfton* at Eight in the Morning, and continued till Ten at Night. The Heigth of it was from Eleven at Noon till One, during which Time it rained very hard, and the Wind often fhifted. Near one half of the Houfes were thrown down or fhattered to fuch a Degree, that they were irreparable, and few or none efcaped without fome Damage. *Port-Royal* was once more a Heap of Rubbifh, but the People had fo much Time and Convenience to efcape, that not above four or five Perfons loft their Lives. The Wharfs were all deftroyed, and moft of the Sugar and other Commodities that were there were wafhed away. The moft melancholy Account came from the Shipping. Of 26 Topfail Veffels and 10 Sloops then in the Harbour, no more than 10 were to be feen after the Hurricane, and of thefe ten but five or fix were repairable. At *Liguania* moft of the

Sugar

Sugar Works and Houses were blown down, and a Plantation entirely destroyed by an Inundation of the Sea and Sand. Great was the Damage done at St. *David's, Wagwater,* St. *Mary's,* and St. *Thomas's* in the East. The Hurricane began in these Parts the Night before about Seven o'Clock, and lasted till Eight the next Morning, at what Time it began at *Port-Royal* and St. *Jago de la Vega* where the King's House and the Secretary's Office were much damaged, but very few Persons were hurt in this Calamity. It was remarkable that those Houses which had been built by the *Spaniards* 80 or 90 Years before received very little Damage, which gave Reason to believe that the *Spaniards*, having been accustomed to such Tempests, had provided against them better than the *English* had done, by the Manner and Materials of their Building. The Houses and People at *Old Harbour* were almost all destroyed, and those at *Sixteen Mile Walk* suffered very much, as did also those at St. *Thomas* in the *Vale.* The Inhabitants had some Prognostick of it before they felt its Fury. The Weather being very unsettled, the Wind often shifting, and more than both these a prodigious uncommon Swell of the Sea, which threw them into a terrible Consternation, it throwing up the Day before several hundred Tons of Stones and large Pieces of Rocks over the Wall of the East End of *Port-Royal*, though at the same Time there was very little if any Wind. The Town was overflowed with Water the Night before, occasioned by the driving of the forementioned Swell. The Wind was at North East when the Hurricane began, and there was a very hard Rain. The Water was 5 Feet deep all over the Town by eleven a Clock; about three in the Afternoon the Wind abated by Degrees, and the Water fell away. The Town appeared afterwards almost in as frightful a Condition as after the *Earthquake*, the Streets being covered with Ruins of Houses, Wrecks of Boats and Vessels, and great Numbers of dead Bodies, for *Port-Royal* did not fare so well as *Kingston*. The Inhabitants, fond of the advantageous Situation of that Spot of Ground for shipping and unshipping their Merchandize, did not take sufficient Notice of the Warnings given them by the Sea, which, as if it looked on the Building of a Town there as an Incroachment on its Element, had often in this terrible Manner reclaimed its own, that Town having no better Foundation for the most Part than what Art had contrived on the sandy Shore. The Inhabitants who were preserved, were reduced to great Extremity for Want of fresh Water and Provisions, their Stores being destroyed in the Hurricane, and many must have perished

rished by that Want, had they not been supplied by the Men of War that rode out the Storm. *Fort-Charles* suffered very much, several of the Guns were dismounted and some washed into the Sea. The *Church* and the Row of Houses to the East of the Town were so washed away, that there remained very little Appearance of a Building. Above half of *Port-Royal* was destroyed, and near 400 Persons lost their Lives. The Magistrates were very diligent in burying the dead Bodies, and for the Comfort of the living, prevented the Sale of Provisions at higher Rates than before the Hurricane. Three Men of War, the *Falkland* Captain *Harris*, the *Swallow* Captain *Ogle*, the *Weymouth* Captain *Lawes*, and the Sloop *Happy* before-mentioned, lost all their Masts; the Duke of *York* of *London* Captain *Sanders* was cast away near *Green* Bay, the Master and all the Men except three were drowned.

The *Chriftobella* of *Briftol* Captain *Griffin* drove ashore, broke her Back, the Men and Part of the Cargo saved. The *King William* of *Briftol* Captain *Raddish* stranded, the Men saved. The *Kingfton* Captain *Mafters*, in the Service of the *South Sea* Company with 200 Slaves aboard foundered, the Master and most of the Men and Negroes drowned. The *Frederick* of *Briftol* Captain *Good* stranded, the Men saved. The *Onflow*, and another of the Prizes taken by Capt. *Ogle* from the Pirates on the Coast of *Guinea* were lost; the other Prize called the *Ranger* rid out the Storm after cutting away her Masts; 14 Sloops most of them belonging to *Jamaica*, were lost.

The Hurricane was as violent in St. *Anne*'s Parish and that Part of the Island, as about *Kingfton* and *Port-Royal*, that Part of the Town situate on the Shore excepted. The *Froft* Frigate of *London* Captain *Kingfton* drove ashore and was lost, the Men saved.

The Parishes of St. *Mary*'s and St. *Thomas*'s in the *Eaft* received the least Damage, *Port-Royal* the most. Some were of Opinion, that the Hurricane 10 Years before was as violent as this, but it does not appear so by the Relations of both transmitted to *England*. The Men of War lost all their Boats, but recovered their Anchors, and were brought to proper Births and again moored. The three King's Ships *Lancafter*, *Adventure*, and *Mermaid*, Part of the Squadron under Commodore *Harris*, were then at Sea; the naval Storehouse being blown down, Capt. *Harris* sent some of the Men of War's Crew to clear away the Rubbish and assist the Inhabitants.

The History of Jamaica. 365

In this Time of Extremity of general Affright and Confusion, Pilferers were busy at *Port-Royal* and elsewhere to embezzle the Goods of the Sufferers, and make their Markets of the publick Calamity. The Governor issued a Proclamation, commanding the *Provost Marshal* to seize all such embezzled Wares and Goods, in Order to their being restored to the right Owners. It was on this Occasion that he summoned the Assembly, which ordered a Day of Fast and Humiliation, as had been done for the Earthquake the 7th of *July* yearly. He also joined with the Council in an Address to the King, which I insert as the most authentick Account of this deplorable Accident. — They say, 'We beg
'Leave humbly to represent to your Majesty, the deplorable
'Circumstances we are reduced to by a dreadful Storm, which
'happened on the 28th of *August* last. The Violence of it
'is inexpressible. It has thrown down and shattered all our
'Houses to such a Degree, that for some Time we were
'exposed to the Extremity of the Weather; it has blown
'down Part of your Majesty's Fortifications, dismounted
'the Guns, destroyed the Carriages, and damaged most of
'the Powder in the Magazines and the *Fire Arms*, and the
'Calamity has been so general, and the Loss sustained so
'great throughout the Island, that the poor Inhabitants are
'utterly unable to put themselves into a Posture of Defence
'without some Aid, &c. We humbly beseech your Majes-
'ty to send us such Aids of Guns, Fire Arms, Carriages and
'Ammunition, and such a Number of Ships of War, as
'your Majesty in your Wisdom shall think necessary, &c.'

Sept. 13, 1722. Nicholas Lawes.

Joseph Maxwell, Clerk of the Council.

Upon this humble Application, his Majesty ordered 12 Men of War to be put in Commission for the *West-Indies*, and all Necessaries to be shipped for the Supply of this and the other Colonies.

The Beginning of *May*, Captain *Chandler* Commander of the *Launceston* Man of War, cruizing on the *Spanish* Pirates, for so the *Jamaicans* called the *Guarda Costas*, took one of them with 58 *Spaniards* aboard, who had a little before taken a *Snow* belonging to this Island six Leagues off of *Hispaniola*.

Sir *Nicholas Lawes* the Governor, assisted by the Council and the Commanders of the King's Navy Ships in *Jamaica*, held a Council of War to try these Pirates. The Attorney
General

General Mr. *Kelly*, and Mr. *Norris*, Regifter of the Court of Admiralty, proceeded againft them, and no fewer than 43 of thefe Pirates or *Guarda Cofta* Men were convicted of Piracy and Robbery, condemned and hanged. The *Launcefton*, the *Adventure*, and the *Mermaid*, all King's Ships, were at Sea when the Hurricane happened, and it was well for them or they would have run the Extremity of Danger had they not perifhed in the Storm.

Guard de Cofta Men hanged.

Notwithftanding Sir *Nicholas Lawes* was their Countryman as well as their Governor, the moft bufy Men in and out of the Affembly, by their unreafonable Oppofition, made him very uneafy in his Government, as appears by his laft Speech to the Affembly.

The rebellious Negroes had nefted fo long in the Mountains, that they were become powerful and formidable, they had raifed a Fortification in the *Blue Mountains* called *Nauny*, of fo difficult Accefs, that a few could defend it againft Thoufands. They often broke down into the low Country and came once fo near *Spanifh-Town*, that the Inhabitants were in a mortal Fright; feveral Parties had been fent againft them in their Faftneffes without Succefs. It was therefore thought advifeable to hire fome *Mufchetoes*, an *Indian* Nation on the Continent between *Traxillo* and the *Honduras*. They fubmitted themfelves to *England* when the Duke of *Albemarle* was Governor of *Jamaica*. They were never conquered by the *Spaniards*, but ftill retain their natural and original Liberty. If their Country was worth the having, no Doubt the *Spaniards* would long ago have been their Mafters. What Right they have to *Honduras* and the Logwood there feems by this Submiffion of the *Mufchetoes* to be transferred to the *Englifh*. But this Submiffion is in Truth without Subjection, and they are ftill governed by Kings and Captains of their own, who prefer the Protection of the *Englifh* to any other *European* Power.

Mufcheto Indians depend on Jamaica.

Capt. *Vring*, who was fome Time among them, gives this Account of them. Thefe *Mufcheto Indians* inhabit a marfhy Country on a fandy Bay, beyond Cape *Gracia de Dios*, not far from the Bay of *Campeachy*. They live under a Kind of monarchical Government, but tho' the whole Natives do not confift of above 1000 fighting Men, yet they have feveral petty Kings under their chief King. They were driven to their Marfhes by the *Spaniards*, and the *Indians* who fubmitted to them; they have frequently Wars with thofe *Indians*, which are moftly hafty Irruptions, wherein they furprize and carry off Men, Women and Children, and fell them at *Jamaica*, or keep them for their own Ufes. Some of thefe

Of the Mufcheto Indians.

The History of Jamaica.

these Women Slaves have been so kindly treated by their *English* Masters, that they have brought them Children in Return for their Kindness to them. There lived among them 20 Years ago, ten or twenty *English* Men who had *Muscheto* Wives; among whom was *Luke Haughton*, a Drougar Man of *Jamaica*, his Business to carry Sugars in a Kind of *Hoy* from the River, and Sea Coast to the shipping Place. These *Englishmen* live exactly after the Manner of the *Indians* by fishing and hunting, and some casual Traffick with the *Logwood* Cutters for Liquors and *Ozinbrigs*. The *Logwood* Cutters at both the Bays of *Honduras* and *Campeachy*, living the same Manner of Life, I shall content myself with an Account of those in the Bay of *Honduras* in the Sequel.

The *Muscheto Indians* had a considerable Victory over the *Spanish Indians* about 30 Years ago, and cut off a great Number of them, but gave a *Negro* who was with them his Life, purely on Account of his speaking *English*, which shews the good Will they bear our Nation. The *Jamaicans* had a Project of inviting them to live in their Island, and assigning them certain Lands for their Subsistence, with the Liberties of *Englishmen*; but the *Muschetoes* would not quit their *Morasses*, nor their Manners every whit as filthy, though they swarm with *Sockeys* or Priests who are Conjurers, and live more lazily and get more plentifully than other People, which a cunning *Morooner*, so the *English* are called that live among them, observing, he turned *Sockey* or Priest, and soon became in great Vogue among them. About the Year 1720, pursuant to the Act of Assembly, 200 of them were invited to *Jamaica* to their Assistance against the rebellious Negroes. Sloops were sent to transport them, and being arrived in that Island, they were formed into Companies under their own Officers, and were paid 40 s. a Month with Shoes. They staid in the Island several Months, and did very good Service, for which they were well rewarded, and returned to their Marshes well pleased. When they were out in Search of the runaway Negroes with white Men for their Guides, one of the *Jamaicans* shot a wild Hog, which much displeased the *Muschetoes*, who said, ' That was not the Way
' to surprize the *Negroes*, for if there were any within hear-
' ing of the Gun, they would immediately fly, and they
' should not be able to take any of them, and if they wanted
' any Provisions they would kill some with their Lances or
' Bows and Arrows which made no Noise.' They are exquisite Hunters and Fishers, and no People are so expert at striking Fish as they are, insomuch that they look upon it as the greatest ill Luck if they miss a Fish when they have a fair
Stroke

Stroke at it; and in such Case they are wont to rally him who mist by saying, *Brother your Hand is crooked, somebody has lain with your Wife.* Few of the *Jamaica* Sloops go to Sea without one of these *Muscheto* Men, to whom they give good Wages and treat them in the friendliest Manner, the Commanders make them their Companions, and call them *Brother.* The Governor of the Island has a particular Article in his Instructions to shew Kindness to them, and assure them of his Protection. As often as a new Governor comes, their King or some of their Chiefs go up to compliment him on his Accession to the Government, and he kindly entertains them and sends them away with Presents.

We see by a Speech made by Sir *Nicholas Lawes,* that this Governor's being a *Jamaica* Man and a Planter, did not suppress the Spirit of Opposition, nor reconcile the Assembly to his Administration, so far as to prevent those Differences and Discontents which Subordination is apt to create in the Minds of the proud and envious. But I do not understand that the Discontents occasioned the Removal of Sir *Nicholas Lawes* from the Government, which was given to the Duke of *Portland,* a Nobleman of fine Accomplishments, both of Person and Mind.

The Assembly here were in as ill Temper with their Neighbour of St. *Dorothy's* Parish, which they excluded from the Right of electing Members, but my Information reaches not so far as the Cause of the Offence that was taken.

Duke of Portland Governor, Col. Dubourgay Lieutenant Governor.

When his Majesty appointed the Duke of *Portland* Governor of *Jamaica,* Col. *Dubourgay* was made Lieutenant Governor, to be Assistant to his Grace in the Discharge of so weighty a Trust. The Duke and Dutchess of *Portland* made some short Stay at the Island of *Barbados,* where they were magnificently received and entertained, and arrived here with their Family and Retinue the 22d of *December,* 1722. Their Graces were received here also with all imaginable Pomp and Splendor; the Character of this Lord having endeared him to the Inhabitants, by the Report of him before his Arrival, it being the Reverse of that of *Christopher Monk* Duke of *Albemarle,* who excepting his Title had nothing noble in his Composition to gain him either Affection or Esteem. The Assembly voted his Grace a double Salary to what any of their Governors had before, no less than 5000 *l.* a Year, which tho' the Duke of *Portland* might merit by his good Qualities, yet they could not afford to give without burthening themselves too much. What follows are the Words of one on the Spot.

Never

The History of Jamaica.

Never did a Governor recommend himself more, or kept such a handsom Court; he was remarkably civil, of easy Access and affable to all. The Island grudged no Expence to oblige him, and if any Fault could be at all found with his Government it is only this, that the Planters, who could not well afford such extraordinary Expences, spent too profusely, by endeavouring to imitate the Duke.

With the Duke of *Portland* came Col. *Dubourgay* just mentioned, and in the first Speech his Grace made to the Assembly, he was pleased to recommend him to them in these Words. *I am farther to signify to you*, Gentlemen, *that his Majesty has been pleased to appoint Col.* Charles Dubourgay, *a Person of great Merit and Honour, to be your Lieutenant Governor. His long and earnest Services in War, and his sincere Attachment to his Majesty, have prepared his Way to this particular Mark of the royal Favour, and I am commanded to let you know, that it is expected from you that you receive him with the Honour due to his Commission, and provide him the Support which his Credentials will acquaint you with.* The Arrival of this Gentleman seemed to be unacceptable to the Colony. His Grace their Governor made a very long Speech, but the Assembly returned a short Answer, however they doubled the Governor's Salary as is before observed, and gave Col. *Charles Dubourgay* 1000 *l.* to defray his Charges, and the Colonel returned to *England* in the same Ship that brought the Duke and him to *Jamaica*, the *Kingston* Man of War. It was said in a Letter from *Jamaica* that came by the *Kingston*, ' The ' Assembly thought such an extraordinary Magistrate un-
' necessary, especially during their Governor's Residence ' with them, and were apprehensive of the Consequences of ' admitting new *erected Officers*, in which they guarded well ' against future Inconveniences of the like Nature.' It is somewhat extraordinary that the Agents of *Jamaica*, who had handsom Salaries to have an Eye on what concerned her Interest, and those other Gentlemen to whose Care the Affairs of the Colonies are particularly committed, did not find Means to have this Novelty prevented, by representing it to his Majesty in its just Light, which no Doubt would have prevented the Duke of *Portland's* putting that ungracious Paragraph in his Speech, and Col. *Dubourgay's* carrying thither so unnecessary and disagreeable a Commission.

On the Duke's Arrival here, *Edmund Kelly*, Esq; and *James Haywood*, Esq; Members for the Parish of St. *Dorothy*, presented a very dutiful Address from the Freeholders there, congratulating and complimenting his Grace on his entering upon the Government. His Grace's Answer to it was very

St. Dorothy's Address.

engaging,

Duke of Portland's Answer.

engaging. 'Gentlemen, I thank you for the hearty Expressions
'of Affection to me and my Family contained in this Ad-
'dress. I am sorry to perceive by some Part of it, that there
'is not that Harmony between you, the Assembly and your
'Parish, which I could wish. I will endeavour to make my-
'self acquainted with the real Cause of it. You may pro-
'mise yourselves that my Interposition in Order to reconcile
'you, and my Readiness to do what I can to contribute to
'your Ease and Satisfaction, shall not be wanting.'

The King of the *Muschetoes* coming to pay his Duty to his Grace the Governor of *Jamaica* soon after his Arrival, I must add a few Words more of their History. They are implacable Enemies to the *Spaniards*, and by sudden Excursions and Surprize do them as much Mischief as they can; they term the *murdering* them *hiding* them, and kill them when they fall in their Way. They are not much afraid of the *Little Breeches*, so they call the *Spaniards*, their Country being surrounded by inaccessible Mountains and Morasses. By their Commerce with the *English* they have learnt a little of their Language; they are an inoffensive People in their Carriage to all but *Little Breeches*; never forfeit their Word, a very great Reproach to the *English*, who have no where that Character. They have but one Wife, and have the highest Veneration for the Ceremony of Marriage. They adore the Sun, and truly the *Sun* has a much better Claim to Adoration, than the Stocks and Stones in *Popish* Idolatry. When any of them die they put them into a Mat, and place them strait with their Faces to the *East*. The King, says the *Jamaican* Historian, has his Commission from the Governor of *Jamaica*, and therefore at every new Governor's Arrival, they come over to know his Pleasure. During their Stay they are maintained at the publick Charge and clothed in a very rich Dress. When they depart they have a few trifling Presents made them, with which they are extremely well satisfied.

Advantage to be made of the Muschetoes.

The same Historian tells us, 'great Advantage might be
'made of the friendly Disposition of this People in Case of
'a War with *Spain*, and it is not to be doubted but in Case
'of a Rupture, the Government will improve so fair an
'Opportunity of advancing the Interest of the *British* Na-
'tion' —— as these *Muschetoes* border on *Honduras*, and have probably a Right to the Growth of Logwood, and besides, are possessed of a Country little known to or frequented by *Europeans*. If this Account of them written in *Jamaica* is true, the Advantage that might be made of their friendly Disposition to the *English* is so obvious, that it is amazing one hears of no Steps taken to procure it. The

The History of Jamaica. 371

The King of the *Muschetoes* was received by his Grace the Duke of *Portland*, with that Courtesy which was natural to him, and with more Ceremony than seemed to be due to a Monarch, who held his Sovereignty by his Commission, as the *Jamaica* Historian says. He invited his *Muscheto* Majesty to dine with him, and that Writer informs us, *The poor King knew not which Way to go up Stairs, but jumped up Step by Step*, which doubtless is rather Raillery than History. *The King used such indecent Expressions, that the Dutchess was obliged to remove from Table.* However, he was dismissed very civilly, and went Home to his Subjects proud of his Entertainment.

The Assembly past a Bill in their Session after the Duke of *Portland's* Arrival, for making their *Laws perpetual*; I have not learnt what were his Grace's Reasons for objecting to it, but I observe he was confirmed in them by that Opinion of the Ministry in *England*. For in his Speech of the 1st of *October*, 1723. his Grace tells them *the* same *Objections have been made at home, and they are thought to be of that Weight that it would be deceiving you, should I give you the least Room to expect that that Bill can receive his Majesty's Approbation.* If Liberty, Property, and the very Lives of the People who past that Law, were interested in the Perpetuity of their *Laws*, it is reasonable to think they were the best Judges of the good or ill Consequences of such a Law; and if the Royal Approbation was denied it by any Representations of Persons entire Strangers to this Country and Constitution; it may well happen that the Assembly and People of *Jamaica* made a better Judgment of their own Affairs, than those who were not at all concerned in them.

1723.

Having Occasion to speak here of the Alteration in the *Of Coins* Currency of the Coin contrary to Queen *Anne's* Proclamation to regulate it in all the Sugar Islands, it is proper to particularize the Value of the Silver Species as they were to pass by that Proclamation, confirmed by the Act of the 6th of that Queen.

	l.	s.	d.
Seville Pieces of Eight Old Plate, to pass for	00	06	00
Ditto, New Plate	00	04	09½
Mexico Pieces of Eight	00	06	00
Pillar Pieces of Eight	00	06	00
Peru Pieces of Eight	00	05	10½
Cross Dollars	00	05	10½
Ducatoons of Flanders	00	07	00
Louis of France, Silver Louis	00	06	00

	l.	s.	d.
Crufados of *Portugal*	00	03	09½
Rix Dollars of the *Empire*	00	06	00
Three Guilder Pieces of *Holland*	00	06	10¾

Notwithstanding a positive Law to ascertain the Value of Money as here mentioned, the People of *Jamaica* raised their Money by agreeing to tender and receive it at 6 s. and 3 d. the Piece of Eight. Several Merchants sent home a Representation against it, and the Government was so far from giving the least Countenance to the least Disregard of this Law, that the Lord *Carteret*, then Secretary of State, wrote to the Duke of *Portland* by his Majesty's Command, in a Letter dated 22 *October*, 1722. wherein his Lordship tells his Grace, ' That the Articles of Complaint, in *the Repre-*
' *fentation*, deserve his Grace's most serious Consideration,
' and the King directs his Grace to use his utmost Care to
' see proper Remedies applied. That the Trade and Credit
' of the Island will be lost if the Valuation of the Coin be
' not rectified. *It is*, adds his Lordship, a bold Attempt,
' *that those who advised have undertaken it*, being ex-
' pressly contrary to the Act of the 6th of Queen *Anne and*
' *your 47th Instruction, which I am commanded to repeat to*
' *you, should be strictly obeyed.*'

The Duke of *Portland* restored the Currency to the Tenure of the Act, which was never infringed in the Island of *Barbados*, either by Act of Assembly or common Practice of Merchants.

That the Inhabitants of *Jamaica* made good Use of their Water-Carriage as well by River as by Sea, to convey the Growth of the Island to the Shipping, may be imagined by the little Care they took of their Land Carriage; for if *Roads.* their Roads were impracticable for Horsemen and Footmen, they must much more be so for Carts and Carriages of Burthen. His Grace takes Notice of this in his Speech.

' There is another Neglect not unequal to this, *the uncul-*
' *tivated Lands*, I mean that of the Roads in *general*, and
' particularly those by which a Communication should be al-
' ways kept open between the great Towns. One would think
' the Inconveniencies which their impassable State bring upon
' the Inhabitants daily, should be a sufficient Motive to re-
' pair them; but the Danger which the Publick are from
' thence exposed to in the Case of any unexpected Alarm,
' which does render it very difficult, if not always impracti-
' cable, for the Forces of the Island to join for its Defence,
' will accuse and condemn you should any unhappy Conse-
' quences

'quences refult from it. Will it be of any Avail to plead,
' that the Parifhes to which thefe Roads belong were o-
' bliged to keep them in a good Condition? The late dread-
' ful *Hurricane* has made the Expence too great for the
' Parifhes, &c.'

In the Law for Highways and Roads, I meet with fome few Paffages that will give a little Infight into the Parifh Geography of this Ifland. ' The *Path* or *Road* now ufed
' from the *Orange* River Plantations in the Parifh of St.
' *Mary's*, into the Plantation late of *Andrew Holloway* at
' *Wagwater*, and fo into the Parifh of St. *Andrew's*, fhall
' be a publick Road or King's Highway, between the two
' Parifhes of St. *Mary's* and St. *Andrew's*. The Path or
' Road from *Annotta River Bay*, to the Parifh of St. *George's*
' leading towards St. *Andrew's*, fhall by its neareft Courfe fall
' into the Path coming from the faid *Orange Plantation*,
' this to be the Highway between the Parifhes of St. *George's*
' and St. *Andrew's*. The Surveyors of St. *Mary's* Parifh
' to mend the Road from the *Orange* River, to the Field at
' the Foot of the Hill at *Little Tom's River*; and St. *George's*
' Parifh to clear the Road from *Annotta Bay* to the faid
' Place: The Parifh of St. *Andrew's* to clear the Ford and
' Road from thence to *Holloway's* Plantation.'

Having taken this Paffage out of the Laws of *Jamaica*, as it helps to defcribe the Country, I fhall refer to the Laws themfelves for other Matters, and only mention the Endow- *Minifter's* ments to Minifters by it. *Income.*

Port Royal to pay to the Minifter,	250 *l. per Annum.*
St. *Catharine's* ——— ———	300
St. *Thomas's* ——— ———	200
St. *Andrew's* ——— ———	200
St. *John's.* ——— ———	200

All the other Parifhes 150 *l. per Ann.* very moderate Allowances confidering the Dearnefs of all Neceffaries, but then Perquifites are very confiderable, and it is amazing that in a Place where there was fuch a flaming Zeal in feveral Affemblies for maintaining all Rites of the Church of *England* in Matter of Worfhip, there has been fuch an unaccountable Careleffnefs in the Miffion of their Miniftry, who for the moft Part have been very unworthy of the Character they went with; of which I have had fo much Knowledge with Refpect to this and other Colonies, that I very often regret the fruitlefs Pains and Expence fuch well defigning Perfons have been at, to propagate the Gof-
pel

pel in thefe Parts. This pious Work has been carried on many Years, (and how the Cafe ftands in *Jamaica*, and fuch has been the Cafe ever fince it was reckoned Part of an *Englifh* Diocefe) fee by the Account the Author of the *New Hiftory of Jamaica* gives of it, *p.* 303. ' The *Clergy* here ' are of a Character fo vile, that I do not care to mention ' it; for, except a few, they are generally the moft finifhed ' of all Debauchees. Meffieurs *Gulpin, Johnfton,* and *May*, ' are indeed Men, whofe unblemifhed Lives dignify the Cha-' racter they bear. They generally preach either in their ' own Churches, or to a few in fome private Houfes every ' *Sunday*, but for others their Church Doors are feldom ' opened.'

His Grace the Duke of *Portland* continued in this Government to his Death, about four Years reckoning from the Date of his Commiffion, and about three Years and a half, reckoning from the Day of his Arrival to that of his Death. His Adminiftration was the moft eafy to the Governor and Governed, that had been yet known in this Ifland, where Admiral *Hofier* arrived with a Squadron of Men of War, to fecure the *Britifh* Commerce in thefe Seas, and demand Satisfaction of the *Spaniards* for the frequent Infults and Loffes the *Englifh* had fuffered by them in their Navigation and Trade, particularly their detaining the *South Sea* Company's large Ship the *Royal George* at *Porto-Bello*. As foon as the Admiral came before the Place, the Governor fent to know what he wanted; he anfwered the *Royal George*, which was immediately difcharged; but the Admiral ftill lying off the Place, the Governor fent again, defiring him to be gone, who anfwered, *he fhould ftay till farther Orders*, and ordered a Man of War to lie within Reach of the Guns at *Porto-Bello*. There was at that Time 24 Millions of Pieces of Eight, ready in that Place to be fhipped aboard the Galleons for *Spain*, which was removed up into the Country on the Appearance of the *Englifh* Men of War. It is well known, that that Treafure was intended to have enabled the *Spaniards* to anfwer their Stipulations for large Subfidies to feveral Powers of *Europe*, for raifing a new War, particularly againft *England*, and the interrupting the Conveyance of fo much Treafure, as alfo 16 Millions of Pieces of Eight, in the whole near 40 Millions; then fhipped and to be fhipped aboard the Galleons and *Flota*, none of which came to *Spain* in Time to anfwer that Occafion, was the only Caufe of preventing that War, which probably would foon have extended into a general one by Sea and by Land. That Service was furely owing to the ftationing the *Britifh* Squadron at the *Baftimentos*

off

off of *Porto-Bello*; a sickly Station it is true, and so is the Situation of *Porto-Bello*; insomuch that the *Spaniards* who trade there, reside in it only in the *Fair* Time, about six Weeks once in two or three Years, according as the Galleons arrive with Goods from *Old Spain*. This Fair happens always in the most unhealthy Seasons, but Traders do not then avoid the Place because it is sickly; and if the *Spaniards* think fit to bring their Treasure there, the *English* will never forbear seeking it in Time of War, because the Air is not so wholesom as were to be wished. Extremity of Air and Change of Air will always affect Constitutions, but I never met with an Instance that a Nation at War with another, suffered an Enemy to gather Strength in a Country, because the Air of it was incommodious. If it is so for the one, it is for the other, and War on both Sides must alike stand all Chances. The *Spaniards* do not think their being seasoned in *America* is a Protection to them, for those Merchants who come hither to trade and do carry on the chief Trade, stay no longer than the Fair lasts, and when it is over hasten back to *Lima, Panama,* and other Places.

His Grace the Duke of *Portland* was taken ill of a Fever the 29th of *June*, which carried him off the 4th of *July* 1726. A Paragraph of a Letter from *Jamaica* on that Occasion will best shew the Sense of the Inhabitants under so great a Loss. ' A melancholy and universal Misfortune has
' befallen us here, which has thrown us into the utmost Grief
' and Confusion. My Lord Duke of *Portland* is dead!
' This may be remote and unaffecting to you at a Distance of
' almost half the Globe, but it is impossible for us who
' lived under his mild Government, and participated of the
' Gentleness of his Nature, the Complacency of his Tem-
' per, the Refinement of his Manners, the Generosity of his
' Living, the Tranquillity, Lenity and Equity of his delight-
' ful Administration, not to be forcibly touched and grie-
' vously afflicted, &c.' All the Gentlemen of *Jamaica* went into deep Mourning, and three Members of the Council, by Order of the Board, waited upon her Grace the Dutchess of *Portland* with the following Message,

Death of the Duke of Portland. 1726.

May it please your Grace,

We are directed by the honourable the President and Council to wait upon your Grace, to condole with you upon the late unhappy Occasion, and to assure your Grace, that as we have a very sensible Share in the Loss, so likewise in the Affliction.

The Council, may it please your Grace, will do every Thing in their Power that may contribute to your Ease. They are in-

The Council address the Dutchess.

formed

formed of your Grace's Intentions of quitting speedily this Island, and as there is no Ship of War in Harbour to convoy your Grace through these Seas, they have resolved to fit out a Vessel for that Service; and where they can be farther useful to your Grace, they will readily embrace the Opportunity, and upon every Occasion endeavour to shew their Gratitude, and the Value and Regard they have for your Grace's Person and Character.

Her Grace expressed her Thanks in Terms suitable to the Civility, Respect, and Affection, to the Council's Address.

<small>John Ayscough, Esq; Governor.</small>

The Government of *Jamaica* devolved of Course on the President of the Council *John Ayscough*, Esq; a windward Planter of fair Character and Fortune. About 7 Weeks after the Duke of *Portland's* Death, the Dutchess Dowager with her three Daughters and the Corpse of her late Consort, sailed from *Jamaica*, *August* 21, on Board the *Essex*, Capt. *Henry Geering*, and met with very bad Weather, insomuch that the Ship lost her main and mizen Masts: However, she arrived off *Dover* the 14th of *October*, landed there, and the next Day came safe with her Grace's three Daughters to *London*, and two Days after received Compliments of Condolence from his Majesty, and their Royal Highnesses the Prince and Princess of *Wales*.

<small>General Hunter Governor.</small>

The President Mr. *Ayscough* held the Government till the Arrival of Major General *Hunter*, who had been Governor of *New-York* and *Virginia*, and was much better acquainted with the Affairs of the Continent Colonies, than those of the Sugar Islands. He laid an Embargo on all Shipping; which, says the *Jamaica* Historian, *proved of infinite Disadvantage to the Island*. No Doubt that Embargo was in the Governor's Instructions, and then the Blame lies on those by whose Advice it had a Place there, for this Gentleman was of himself well intentioned. Several necessary Laws were made for suppressing the rebellious Negroes, and as it was then feared that the Island abounded with *Papists* in Disguise, the Assembly past an *Act*, obliging all, from *sixteen* to *sixty*, to abjure the Church of *Rome*. General *Hunter* was a very hearty Protestant, of Revolution Principles, a great Enemy to Popery and Priestcraft; he promoted this Bill by his Party in the Assembly, where too many warmly opposed it, by which Heats were fomented, but the Governor's Party prevailed. He died in the Year 1734, and the Government again devolved on *John Ayscough*, Esq; in which Year a Reinforcement of six independent Companies were sent to *Jamaica* to act against the Negro Rebels. The Rebellion

The History of Jamaica.

of Negroes was now become fo formidable, that it required the whole Strength of the Island to reduce them.

The Exercise of *civil Law* was suspended, and the *martial Law* took Place, several Parties of Militia and regular Forces were sent against those Rebels. Capt. *Stoddart* with one of them attacked their Town *Nauny* in the *Blue Mountains*. He had carried with him three small Field Pieces, and made his Approaches with great Caution and without the least Noise, he reached the Foot of the Mountain a little before Night, and when it was dark scaled the narrow Passage, and with very great Difficulty got up his Field Pieces, and mounted them on an Eminence, from whence he played on the *Negro* Town with Musket-Ball, which killed and wounded a great Number of the Rebels who offered to make Defence. In fine, he obtained a complete Victory here, the Negroes took to Flight. He slew many more of their Number in the Rout, demolished their Town, destroyed their Provisions, and did them more Hurt than had been done them in 20 Years before, with little or no Loss of his Party.

The Rebels were also hard pressed in other Parts of the Island. They presumed at *Bagnels* to attack a large Party commanded by Col. *Edward Charlton*, and Capt. *Ivy*, whose Men had not kept enough to close Order, of which the Rebels having quick Intelligence, they laid an Ambuscade to intercept them as they straggled, and when the Officers were at Dinner, and few of the Party near, they rushed out and attacked the Hut where they were. Several Pieces were discharged which killed a few, but the firing had this good Effect, that it alarmed those of the Party that were nearest, who immediately took to their Arms, and came up in Time to save the Lives of their Officers. The Negroes fled, but the Pursuit by the *English* was very faint, and the latter lost Sight of the Runaways. The *English* not knowing whither they ran, the Plantations nearest the Mountain were terribly alarmed, and tho' *Spanish Town* was above 30 Miles from thence, yet News came about one a Clock in the Morning, that the Negroes had escaped Col. *Charlton*'s and Capt. *Ivy*'s Party and were coming that Way. Mr. *Ayscough* the President immediately ordered the Trumpets to sound and the Drums to beat, and before six a fresh Party of Foot, with a Troop of Horse, were ready to support the former under the Command of more experienced Officers. In two Days they came up to a Place, where by the Fires which remained unextinguished, they knew the Negroes had lodged the Night before, and having followed the Track got Sight of them soon after. Capt. *Edmunds* disposed of his Men for

A Skirmish with the Negro Rebels.

an

an Engagement, but the Rebels had not Courage to venture a Battle, they difperfed and fled feveral Ways, however, a good many were killed and more taken, which fo difheartened them and broke their Strength, that they never appeared in any confiderable Body afterwards.

About this Time Port *Antonio* on the North Side of *Jamaica* was ordered to be fortified, and Store-houfes erected there for the Ufe of the Ships of War. A little Ifland lies fo near it, that a Man of War's Yards touch the Branches of the Trees, on the two Sides of the Harbour's Mouth, which when entered is very fafe, and capacious enough to receive a confiderable Fleet. Admiral *Stewart*, who commanded a Squadron then there, faw this Work in good Forwardnefs, and it will be of infinite Advantage to the *British* Commerce in thofe Parts, if it can be perfected and maintained; but the Air is unhealthy, tho' to clear it the Admiral had ordered the Trees in *Navy* Ifland to be burnt. The Defign was good and well profecuted, but there was no guarding againft the Malignity of the Air; however, there is a Company of Soldiers at this Time in Garrifon, Part of which was under Capt. *Newton* in the *Porto-Bello* Expedition, and they would fain have been in that of *Chagre*, but the *Jamaicans* abofolutely refufed to let them go, alledging that as they paid them Subfiftence Money, they fhould remain there for the Defence of the Ifland. Not far from this Place, a fmall Town was lately begun to be built called *Tichfield*, from a Manor in *Hampfhire* belonging to the Dutchefs of *Portland*.

It is well known that the Heat of the Sugar Colony Climates, has an Influence on the Spirits of the People, which are foon enflamed, and therefore great Caution fhould be ufed in Company to keep every Thing calm and cool; but the Heat is general, and confequently when it begins to kindle, there are more ready to catch than to extinguifh. This happened in the Cafe of Mr. *Stevens* a Merchant at *Kingfton*, and Mr. *Vale* a Barrifter at Law. Mr. *Stevens* having fpoken offenfively to or of Mr. *Vale*, fome Gentlemen were fo weak and indeed fo wicked, as to incenfe them, and blow the heated Fewel into a Flame. Mr. *Vale* meeting Mr. *Stevens* one Morning at the Coffee-houfe, beat him with a fmall Stick; the Standers by let them grapple in Wrath, and Mr. *Stevens* falling with his Head upon a Stone fractured his Skull and he died foon after. 'Tis certain *Vale* knew nothing of a Stone nor intended a Fracture, but intending Harm to *Stevens*, the Law interpreted it Murder: *Vale* was tried, and tho' he pleaded his own Caufe with great Reafon and Vivacity, and tho' the Jury was fhut up two Days before they

agreed

agreed on a Verdict, yet in the End they brought in *Vale* guilty, and he was condemned to be hanged; and tho' the Case does not appear to have more aggravating Circumstances than are here mentioned, *Vale*, despairing of Mercy, cut his Throat the Night before the Day appointed for his Execution.

Soon after the President died, *John Gregory*, Esq; who had been Chief Justice succeeded him in the Government, in which he contiuued till the Arrival of *Henry Cunningham*, Esq; whom his Majesty had appointed Governor of *Jamaica*, a Gentleman of great Parts and Worth, of a sound Judgment and happy Temper. He had great Knowledge of the *British* Constitution, and was zealous in the Support of it in and out of Parliament, of which he had almost always been a Member ever since the *Union*. See what the *Jamaica* Historian writes of him, ' Tho' Governor, he
' never lost the Affability of a private Gentleman. Never
' was one more beloved or caressed with more Justness, he
' knew the Blessings of Liberty, and had he lived, would
' have redressed many Grievances under which the Poor la-
' boured. It was his Fault to begin too soon to cure the In-
' solence of the Planters, and a Difference with one of the
' most considerable of them hastened his Death.' The Author does not explain whether it was to accommodate or prosecute this Difference; but other Accounts say, The Governor was at an Entertainment with some of the principal Persons of the Place, and that there was such an Abundance of good Wine as well as good Humour, that Mr. *Cunningham* soon felt the Effects of it in a violent Fever in a few Days, if not Hours, about six Weeks after his Arrival.

Upon his Death, *John Gregory*, Esq; President of the Council, resumed the Government, and about that Time died *James Hay*, Esq; Chief Justice, of a Character so different from that of the Chief Justice spoken of in Lord *Hamilton*'s Time, that whatever Impurities the Judgment Seat might then be defiled with, this Gentleman's Conduct cleared it of all Blemish. The Author says, ' tho' he re-
' sided upwards of 20 Years in so wicked a Place, he was
' never known to give into any of its Debaucheries, an Oath
' he was never heard to swear, nor ever neglected his Fa-
' mily Devotion.'

The same Author introduces the Government of *Edward Trelawney*, Esq; with some Reflections on the Misbehaviour of the *Spaniards* toward the *English* in *America*, of which reiterated Accounts had come from thence by almost all Shipping, and which could not but end in a Rupture. The

Jamaica

Jamaica Author writes, ' The War between *Great-Britain* and *Spain* was an Event long wished for by all good *Britons*, ' and particularly by the People of this Island, who wanted ' nothing more than to be left at Liberty to revenge the ' Cruelties and Depredations they have so long suffered from ' the insulting *Spaniards*, thro' the great Lenity and Forbear-' ance of the Gentlemen at the Helm of Affairs in *Great-* ' *Britain*, who at length appear roused out of the Lethargy ' their Enemies attributed to them, to avenge the Insults of-' fered, not only to the Subjects of the Crown of *Great-* ' *Britain*, by an Enemy not considerable enough to appear ' in Sight of the *Flag* they have long defied.'

1738.   Upon Mr. *Trelawney's* Arrival, he was honourably received by the Council and Gentlemen of the Island. The Assembly allowed him the same Salary which any of their former Governors had, except the Duke of *Portland*, which doubtless will never be brought into Precedent. The first Act of his Administration was to put the Island into a better Posture of Defence, than it had been for some Years before. He ordered the several Forts to be viewed, and took effectual Care that such Repairs as were necessary should be instantly set about: He appointed Officers of Experience and Resolution to command the *Militia*, by whom they were better trained in Arms than ever they had been before; and it is to be noted, that the Colony Militia, whether *Creolians* or *Europeans*, are better exercised and regulated than our *English* Train Bands ever were since *Cromwell's* Time. Governor *Trelawney's* next Care was to reduce the rebellious Negroes, who for 50 Years past had put the Colony to a great Expence, as well of Blood as Treasure, and tho' the Rebels were frequently very much distressed, yet they found Means to maintain themselves in their almost inaccessible Fastnesses.

The Island was in Arms nine Months together in 1735, and 1736 to guard against them, but yet they little prevailed towards clearing the Country, and none would cultivate Land nor settle near the Place where they nested, and those Lands that had been cultivated and settled were deserted; which Lands were some of the most fertile in the Island, but being now overgrown with Woods and Shrubs were a Shelter for the Runaways. The Governor taking into Consideration the Damage, Distress and Terror occasioned by them, and the ill Success of all Attempts hitherto to reduce them by Force, he resolved to put milder Methods in Practice, and by Offers of Pardon and Security he brought them to such reasonable Temper, that they laid down their Arms, and all to a Man chearfully submitted. By the Articles of Surrender

Rebellious Negroes submit.

The History of Jamaica.

Surrender they are allowed a Chief to govern them, but he is to do nothing without the Consent of the Governor of the Island, and several *white Men* live among them to observe their Actions.

As soon as the Governor of *Jamaica* was authorised from Home to grant Letters of *Marque* and *Reprisal*, for Satisfaction of the Injuries done the *English* by the *Spaniards*, he issued out such Letters, and immediately the Merchants and Planters fitted out many Privateers, which brought several good Prizes to this Island; one of the Privateers landed a few Men on *Cuba*, took a Town and plundered it, before the Arrival of Admiral *Vernon*, September 1739, with six Men of War; who with these six Men of War only has done more Execution on the Enemy, than has hitherto been done by all other *British* Squadrons. These indeed are the Seas and Coasts most proper to turn the Superiority of the *British* maritime Power to the most Advantage to our Trade and Navigation, and why so little has been effected with it in all our late Ruptures with *Spain* and *France*, none can so well answer as those that were entrusted with the Care of the Plantations, which I hope will never be committed to such as have not been long and well acquainted with them and their Affairs.

1739.

The taking and destroying *Porto-Bello*, one of the Bulwarks of the *Spanish West-Indies*, was an Action of so great Glory and Advantage to the *British* Nation, that the Name of *Vernon* is now as terrible to the *Spaniards* in *New Spain*, as ever that of *Blake* was in *Old*. What the Consequences of that glorious Action might have been, had his Strength enabled him to improve it, let Connoisseurs determine.

The Town of *Porto-Bello* is not so large as might be expected, from the great Resort of People to trade to it in and out of *Fair* Time, tho' the latter is inconsiderable in Comparison of the former, and only to take off the Gleanings of the Fair. The Unhealthiness of the Air has been and always will be, a Hinderance to the Increase of this Town, in Building and Inhabitants. It consists of about 500 Houses, it has two Churches, a Treasury, a Custom-house and Exchange. The Fair is here every two or three Years, and lasts about six Weeks, according as the *Galleons* happen to arrive from *Carthagena*, where they always first dispose of Part of their Cargo of *European* Goods, which are for the Trade of *Mexico* and other Cities in that Part of *America*. From *Carthagena* they come hither, and dispose of the rest of their Cargoes. Here they are met by the Merchants from the great Cities of *Lima* and *Panama*, Capitals of *Peru*,

Of Porto-Bello.

which

The History of Jamaica.

which have the Trade of the *South Sea*, which is plainly to be seen on a Mountain not far from *Panama* between *Chagre* and that City. In *Fair* Time Warehouse Room can scarce be got for the Chests of Money brought from these Cities, for the King's Account and the Merchants; some of the Inhabitants have made 10,000 Dollars in the Time of the *Fair* for the Use of their Houses. It lies on the *North* Side of the Isthmus of *Darien*, a Name I always read and mention with Grief, when I reflect on the infinite Damage the *British* Nation sustained, in neglecting the fair Opportunity that was once offered them, to possess and maintain that *Isthmus* against all maritime or *American* Power that could oppose them; and I refer to the *Connoisseurs* again to determine, what an Encrease of Trade, Riches and Power, such a Situation would have become to the *British* Empire. Whatever political Reasons might have been started in *Europe* against it, are very easily refuted were this a Place for it. *Panama* is but 54 Miles from *Porto-Bello*, which has a commodious Harbour with good Anchorage for Ships, it is narrow at the Mouth and spreads wider within, at the Bottom of it is the Town, bending about the Shore like a Halfmoon. It is long and narrow, having two principal Streets besides Lanes, which go across with a small *Parade* about the Middle of it; the Houses are handsom, the Town lies open to the Country, and at the East End of it in the *Panama* Road, there is a long Stable for the King's Mules which bring his Treasure from the Capitals. The direct Road to *Panama* would be to the *South*, but the Hills there hinder it: The East Side is low and swampy, which much contributes to the Unhealthiness of the Air, and the *Bastimentos* where our *English* Squadrons are wont to be when they block up this Harbour, being so near as almost within Gun shot, must needs participate plentifully of these noxious Vapours, which the fervent Sun-beams continually exhale from the swampy and slimy Shore, for the Sea at low Water leaves it bare a great Way from the Houses. The Slime is filthy and stinking, and in all Parts of the World as well as in *America*, where are such Slimes, Stinks and Heats, there can be no Health. Only I say in Case of a War, the *English* have as good a Chance to stand it there as have the *Spaniards* who come from *Europe*, and those that do not, are in no Condition to defend their Coasts or their Country against *Europeans*, who are Masters at Sea.

'Tis pretty well known now in *England*, that this Town was defended by three Forts. The *Iron Fort* on the *North* Side of the Mouth of the Harbour with 100 Guns, *Gloria Castle*

The History of Jamaica.

Castle on the *South* Side of the Harbour with 120 Guns, a Mile from the *Iron Fort*, and Fort *Hieronymo* with 20 Guns. Mr. *Trelawney* Governor of *Jamaica* was very forward and diligent in giving Admiral *Vernon* all the Assistance for his Enterprize that the Island could afford, in which the Inhabitants bore a proportionable Part. The Admiral shipped 200 Men only at that Island, which shews he could lay no Scheme for keeping if he should conquer it, nor for extending his Conquests at that Time. He sailed from *Port-Royal* Harbour the 5th of *November* 1739, with the following Ships.

The *Burford*, Admiral *Vernon*.
The *Hampton-Court*, Captain *Brown*.
The *Norwich*, Captain *Herbert*.
The *Worcester*, Captain *Main*.
The Princess *Louisa*, Captain *Waterhouse*.
The *Stafford*, Captain *Trevor*.
Two seventy Guns, three sixty Guns, one fifty Guns.

On the 10th of *November*, the *English* took a Sloop from *Carthagena* bound for *Porto-Bello*, a happy Accident, for none of Admiral *Vernon*'s Pilots were acquainted with the Coast Westward of *Chagre*. Near *Porto-Bello* they came in Sight of 4 Sail of *Spanish* Ships bound thither, but they got into Port, and alarmed the People before the *English* could come up with them. The *Spaniards* put on their best Airs, and none have better if *Rhodomontade* is good for any Thing, and hoisted a Flag of *Defiance*.

Captain *Brown* in the *Hampton-Court* was the first who began the Attack, which he continued with great Courage and Conduct. The Wind falling away, he was obliged to drop Anchor near the Fort, from whence the *Spaniards* fired very briskly, and he received their Fire with Firmness and but little Loss, at but about a Cable's Length Distance, and how briskly he returned it may be imagined, by his firing above 400 Shot against the Fort in a few Minutes Time. The *Norwich* came up next, and met with the like warm Reception, and returned the Fire of the *Spaniards* so well, that it gave a Check to their first Fury, insomuch that they made not one Fire to Captain *Herbert*'s three. The *Worcester* Captain *Main* got up in less than half an Hour, and anchoring near the other two, did a great deal of Damage to the Fort, beating down the higher Part of it, and driving the *Spaniards* from their Guns. The Admiral's Ship came up soon after with the Blue Flag at her Foretopmast-Head, and the bloody Flag at the Mainmast-Head; the Admiral ordered the An-

chor

chor to be dropt within half a Cable's Length of the Caftle, notwithftanding they had difcharged but very few Guns for fome Minutes before; yet as if their mighty Spirits highly difdained to fee the *Englifh* Flag waving as it were over their Walls, they welcomed it with a terrible Volley which did little Execution. One Shot ftruck away the Stern of the Barge, another broke a large Gun on the upper Deck, a third went thro' the Foretopmaft, and the fourth thro' the Arning, within two Inches of the Mainmaft, and beat down the Barricado of the Quarter Deck very near the Admiral's Perfon, killing three Men and wounding five; but this brisk Fire was fo briskly returned, that it abated of their Heat, and they did little or no Damage with it afterwards, contenting themfelves with a few random Shot. The Fire of the fmall Arms foon commanded the Enemy's lower Battery and drove away the *Spaniards*, which gave the *Englifh* the Opporportunity of landing. As the Boats came near the Admiral's Ship, he called to them to go afhore directly under the Walls of the Fort, though there was no Breaches made, which threw the Enemy into fuch Confternation, that the Officers and Soldiers who had ftood at the lower Battery fled to the upper, and put out a Flag of Capitulation, which the Admiral anfwered with a like, but it was with the greateft Difficulty he could reftrain his own and the *Stafford's* Men from firing. In the mean Time the Soldiers and Seamen that were landed, climbed the Walls of the lower Battery in this Manner. One Man fet himfelf clofe under an *Emboffier*, while another climbed upon his Shoulders and entered under the Mouth of a great Gun; all the Boats Crews were in the Platform in three Minutes after their landing, they immediately ftruck the *Spanifh* Flag of Defiance, and hoifted the Flag of *England*; fome *Spanifh* Officers and Soldiers fhut themfelves up in a ftrong Lodgment, but Lieutenant *Broderick* of *Jamaica*, firing a Gun or two through the Door, they opened it and yielded themfelves Prifoners, five Officers and thirty five Soldiers all that were left of 300, the reft being killed or wounded. Thus was the *Iron-Fort* taken by five *Englifh* Men of War only, and the *Spaniards*, who were once a warlike Nation, muft be funk into the moft daftardly Spirit, to abandon fo eafily the Defence of a Fort, which their Affailants would have defended a long Time againft all the naval Power of *Spain*. Let the *Englifh* Reader be furprifed at this glorious Action of his Countrymen, but call to Mind the Bravery and Fortune of the bold and adventurous *Morgan* 60 or 70 Years before that, who marched but with 1200 Men from *Chagre* to *Panama*, attacked and took that great City,

Porto-Bello taken.

The History of Jamaica.

City, then as big as *Briftol* and kept it feveral Months, and with a Recruit of as many fuch Men more, would doubtlefs have driven the *Spaniards* into the *South Sea*, or maftered all their Mines. There are *Britons* ftill who have as good Hearts and as good Hands, and as good Heads too, if they had as good Encouragement.

Gloria-Caftle and Fort *Hieronymo*, continued firing after the *Iron Fort* had given it over, but moft of their Shot fell fhort or flew over the Rigging. The Admiral tried fome of his lower Tire againft thefe Forts, and that Tire being new Guns anfwered beyond Expectation, carrying over *Gloria-Caftle* into the Town, none of the Shot falling fhort, and one of them went thro' the Governor's Houfe, and others thro' feveral Houfes in the Town. The next Morning the Admiral went aboard the *Hampton-Court*, to confult with Captain *Brown* and the other Captains, about warping the Ships up the next Night in Order to attack *Gloria-Caftle*, but was prevented by the Enemy's putting up a white *Flag*, and fending a Boat with a Flag of Truce to the Admiral, with the Governor's Adjutant and the Lieutenant of a Man of War, who brought Conditions figned on which they would furrender. Admiral *Vernon* digefted thefe Conditions as he thought fit, and fent Captain *Newton*, who commanded the *Jamaica* Soldiers, with them to the Governor, who accepted of them, and the Forts and Towns were delivered to the *Englifh* with all the Shipping in the Harbour. Dr. *Walfh* the *South Sea* Company's Factor at *Panama*, and other Servants of that Company detained by the *Spaniards*, were fet at Liberty.

In *Gloria-Caftle* were 120 Guns, 200 fmall Arms and Blunderbuffes, 200 Swords, 200 Barrels of Powder, 4 large Mortars, Thoufands of Iron and Copper Balls.

In *Iron Fort* 100 Guns, of which 87 were Brafs.

In the Harbour were 2 Men of War, 24 Guns each, one Snow of 14 Guns, 4 good Sloops, a Periagua and half Galley.

The Admiral broke the Trunions of all the Iron Guns, blafted all the Foundations, and burnt the Superftructures of all the Forts and Caftles. The Damage to the *Spaniards* amounting to Millions, and it is next to impracticable to rebuild the like Fortification on the fame Spot of Ground. This Advantage and Glory were gained to the *Englifh* with the Lofs of fix Men only, three were killed on board the Admiral's Ship, and three on board Capt. *Main's*.

The War between *Great-Britain* and *Spain* was carried on in the *Weft-Indies* with good Succefs by the *Englifh*, the

Privateers of the Sugar Islands and the Continent took so many Prizes, that they almost ruined the Trade of the *Spaniards* in the *American* Seas. None of their Plate Fleets durst venture out with them, and now and then a Runner or a single Ship brought a few Pieces of Eight to *Spain*, bearing a small Proportion with the many Millions that used to be the Lading of their *Flota's* and *Flotilla's*.

Vice Admiral *Vernon* did not stay long after his Return to *Jamaica*, before he put to Sea again with his Squadron to execute another great Design he had formed against the *Spaniards*. He sailed from *Port-Royal* Harbour the 25th of *February* 1739-40, and got Sight of the high Land of *Santa Martha* on the *Spanish* Main the 1st of *March*. He ordered Captain *Windham* in the *Greenwich* to ply up in the Night and lie to Windward of the Port, to intercept any Thing that might be coming in there the next Day, and then bore away with an easy Sail for *Carthagena*. On the 3d at Noon he was joined by the *Falmouth* Captain *Douglas* off Point *Canoa*, and that Evening anchored with the Squadron before *Carthagena* in nine Fathom Water, in the open Bay called *Playa Grande*, and on the 6th he ordered in all the Bomb Ketches and the small Ships and Tenders for covering and assisting them, and continued bombarding till nine in the Morning. The Squadron received no Damage from the Town, but the Shells fell into the Town pretty successfully, particularly into the principal Church, the Jesuit's College, the Custom-house, and beat down several Houses between them, and a Shell that fell into the South Bastion, silenced a Battery of 10 Guns there for a long Time.

Carthagena bombarded.

On the 9th he drew off his Bomb Ketches and small Craft, and weighed with his Squadron on the 10th in the Morning, and making the Signal for the Line of Battle, he coasted the Shore towards *Boca Chica*, they fir'd at him from the three small Castles without *Boca Chica*, but none of their Shot reached him, and having left the *Windsor* Captain *Berkley*, and the *Greenwich* Captain *Windham*, to cruize off the Port of *Carthagena* for 20 Days, he made sail for *Porto-Bello* to repair there the Damages the small Craft had received, and on the 14th anchored with his Squadron in *Porto-Bello* Harbour, detaching his Cruizers from Time to Time to lie off *Chagre* to block up the Enemy; and having got his Ships watered put to Sea on the 22d with his Squadron, except the *Louisa* and *Falmouth*, which had not compleated their Watering, but had his Orders to hasten it and follow him. But an Accident in the Foretopsail Yard of his Ship the *Strafford* retarding her Progress, he ordered Captain *Herbert*, in the *Norwich*,

to

The History of Jamaica. 387

to make all the Sail he could in before him, with the Bomb-Ketches and all the Fire Ships and Tenders under his Orders, and Capt. *Knowles*, as Engineer on Board the Bomb-Ketches, for placing them to play on the Caftle and to cover them with his own Ship and the reft; Captain *Knowles* got to an Anchor by Three in the Afternoon, and began bombarding and cannonading that Evening, and by ten a Clock at Night he got alfo to an Anchor with his own Ship the *Strafford*, and the *Falmouth*, and Princefs *Louifa* that followed him the fame Night, and continued bombarding and cannonading with three Ships, firing leifurely only from their lower Tire till *Monday* the 24th, when the *Spaniards* hung out a Flag of Truce from the Fort, and he anfwered it from his own Ship, and ftopped all firing as foon as poffible, and fent Captain *Knowles* on Shore, who foon returned with the Governor, to whom having granted Capitulation, he fent him afhore again with Captain *Knowles*, whom he appointed Governor of the Caftle for his Majefty, and fent a Garrifon along with him of five Lieutenants and 120 Men, and all the Boats of the Fleet to land them, and by 3 a Clock that Afternoon, Captain *Knowles* entered the Fort with his Garrifon. The fame Evening Captain *Knowles* fent and placed a Guard upon the Cuftom-houfe, on the oppofite Side of the River *Chagre*, and Vice Admiral *Vernon* went on Shore himfelf by Day-break the next Morning to give all neceffary Orders, and found the Cuftom-houfe full of Goods for the lading of the Galleons, fuch as Guayaquil, Cocoa, Jefuits-Bark and *Spanifh* Wooll, and gave immediate Orders for their being fhipped off; the Number of Serons and Bags of the before-mentioned Goods amounted to 4300, the two *Guarda Cofta* Sloops in the River (all the *Guarda Cofta's* left in thofe Parts) were funk and deftroyed. The Cuftom-houfe by the 28th was filled with combuftible Matter of the neighbouring Huts, and fet on Fire and burnt to the Ground. On the 29th in the Morning, the Brafs Cannon, which were 11 Guns and 11 Patereroes, being embarked and a good Part of the Garrifon, the Mines were fprung under the lower Baftion which entirely demolifhed it. Then two Mines were fprung to blow up fome of the upper Parts of the Works, and afterwards all the inner Buildings of the Caftle were fet on Fire; and on the 30th Vice Admiral *Vernon* put to Sea to return to his Cruize off *Porto-Bello*.

Chagre bombarded.

Chagre demolifhed.

'Tis well known that this Place was of great Importance to the *Spaniards*, and a Check to the Trade and Navigation of the *Englifh* in thofe Parts. The River *Chagre* carries fmall Veffels within 15 Miles of *Panama*, fo that the Goods

which

which they carry back are only carried by Land thofe 15 Miles to the Shore of the South Sea; from whence they go by Sea either to *Lima* or any other Port upon the Coaſt of *Peru* or *Chili*; and the Fortification Admiral *Vernon* deſtroyed, cut off the *Engliſh* from any Communication between the two Seas, by that River and the Paſſage from it to the South Sea.

CHAP. II.

Containing an Account of the Precincts, Towns, Forts, Climate, Soil, Product, Commodities, Animals, Diſeaſes, &c. at *Jamaica*.

WE have already ſpoken of the Situation of this Iſland, to which we think fit to add here, that it is 140 Leagues from *Carthagena* to the South Weſt, 160 Leagues from *Rio de la Hache* in the ſame Country; of an oval Figure, and according to the lateſt Surveys is 170 Miles long where it is longeſt, and 70 broad where it is broadeſt, which is about the Middle of the Iſland. Towards the two Ends it grows narrower by Degrees, till it terminates in two Points. It is ſaid to contain about five Millions of Acres, of which one half are planted.

There's a Ridge of Hills which divides it into two Parts, running from Sea to Sea, and out of them flow Abundance of Rivers, that render the Soil very fruitful, and are a great Help to the Inhabitants.

It abounds in excellent Bays on the Southern Coaſts; as *Port Royal, Port Morant, Old Harbour, Point Negril, Port St. Francis, Michael's Hole, Miccary Bay, Allegator Pond, Point Pedro, Parattee Bay, Luana Bay, Blewfield's Bay, Cabarita's Bay*, and many more, all very commodious for Shipping.

The Iſle is now divided into 16 Pariſhes which lie thus, proceeding from Point *Morant* round the Iſland. The firſt is the

Pariſh of St. *David's*. In which is a little Town called *Free-Town*, and a Salt Work in *Yallah* Bay. Port *Morant* is in this Precinct, a ſafe and commodious Bay, where Ships ride ſecure from the Weather, and the Country about it is well planted. This Precinct ſends two Members to the Aſſembly,

The History of Jamaica.

bly, and is fortified by a small Fort, where in War Time 12 Men are kept in Pay. Wood and fresh Water are plenty in this Parish. And next to it is the

Parish of *Port-Royal*; in which stands the Remains of one of the most beautiful and wealthy Towns in *America*, which gave its Name to the Parish. The Town of *Port-Royal* was formerly called *Coguay*; and when it was in Being, stood on that long Neck of Land which ran above 10 Miles into the Sea, but is so very narrow, that it is not a Bow-shot over in some Places.

On the very Point of this Neck the *English* chose to build their capital City, for it deserved the Name 15 Years ago. There were so many Houses upon the Neck then, that it looked like one City. The Reason of their building here, was for the Convenience of the Harbour; for the Shore is so bold and the Sea so deep, that Ships of the greatest Burthen laid their Broad-sides to the Merchants Wharfs, and loaded and unloaded with very little Trouble or Charge. This Point of Land makes the Harbour, which is as safe as any in *America* for Shipping, having the *Main Land* on the *North* and *East*, the Town on the *South*; so it is open only to the *South-West*.

A thousand Sail of Ships may ride here, and be secure from all Winds that blow. The Entrance into it is fortified by *Fort Charles*, the strongest Fort in the *English American* Dominions, with a Line of Battery of 60 Pieces of Cannon, a Garrison of Soldiers maintained by the Crown in constant Pay. The Harbour is about three Leagues broad, and so deep, that it is able to receive the largest Fleet of the greatest Ships in the World.

The great River on which St. *Jago* or *Spanish-Town* stands, runs into the Sea in this Bay. Here the Ships generally take in their Wood and fresh Water. The Convenience of Anchorage and Depth of Water, by which Means a Ship of 1000 Tuns may put Plank ashore here, made this the chief Port and Town of the Island for drawing Merchants hither. They were soon followed by Shop-keepers, Vintners and other Trades, insomuch that when the dreadful Calamity of the Earthquake happened, there were 2000 handsom Houses in the City; the Rents of which were as dear as those in *London*. It raised a whole Regiment of Militia, and yet, excepting the Convenience of the Harbour, the Situation of it is neither good nor commodious, there being no Wood nor fresh Water, Stone, nor Grass on the *Neck*. The Soil is a hot dry Sand, and the Resort of Merchants, Mariners and others for Traffick thither, rendered it always like a Fair, which made every Thing extremely dear there. There

was

390   *The History of* Jamaica.

was a very large Church with a Minister, who had an Allowance of 250 *l.* a Year by Act of the Assembly, to which this Parish sends three Members.

This Town, as has been said, was destroyed by an Earthquake in the Year 1692, and ten Years after, when it was rebuilt by a Fire. Upon which the Assembly voted that it should not be built again, but that the Inhabitants should remove to *Kingston* in St. *Andrew*'s Parish, which was made a Town and Parish of itself. They also prohibited any Market for the future at *Port Royal*, but the Convenience that invited the People to build there first, will it is probable in Time tempt them to rebuild, and make them forget the terrible Judgments which seem to forbid any future dwelling on a Place that Heaven dooms to Destruction. Next to it is

St. *Andrew*'s Parish; in which stood the Town of *Kingston* on the Harbour of *Port Royal*, but now that Place is made a Parish of itself. This Precinct sends two Representatives to the Assembly, and allows the Minister 100 *l.* a Year.

Parish of *Kingston*, to which, by an Act of the Assembly in the Year 1695, the Quarter Sessions for the Peace and Court of Common Pleas were removed. The Secretary, Receiver General and Naval Officer, were obliged to keep their Offices there; and it had the Privilege of sending three Representatives to the Assembly. It is much encreased since *Port Royal* was burnt, and is now a large Town of 7 or 800 Houses. It lies on the Harbour of *Port Royal*, the Parish is bounded by it to the South West, and North by the Lands of the late Sir *William Beeston*, and continued from a Calabash on the North East Corner by a strait Line to the Foot of the long Mountain, and from thence till it meets with the Bounds of the Parish of *Port Royal*.

St. *Katherine*'s Parish, in which is the little Town of *Passage Fort*, situated at the Mouth of the River that runs up to St. *Jago* six Miles from that Town, and as many from *Port Royal*. There are about 200 Houses in the Town, which was built chiefly for the Entertainment of Passengers from *Port Royal* to St. *Jago*. There's a Fort mounted with 10 or 12 Guns for the Security of that River. 'Twas called *Passage*, from Passage-Boats coming always thither to land such as went from one Town to the other. This Precinct sends three Representatives to the Assembly, and allows the Minister 100 *l.* a Year. There's a River in this Parish called *Black River*, over which is a Bridge. Six Miles up in the Country is the Parish of

St.

St. *John's*, one of the most pleasant, fruitful, and best inhabited Spots of Ground in *Jamaica*, as one may imagine by the Names of three Plantations contiguous to one another, *Spring Vale, Golden Vale,* and *Spring Garden.* It sends two Representatives to the Assembly, and allows the Minister 100 *l.* a Year; but is most famous for being in the Neighbourhood of

Spanish Town, or St. *Jago;* the Capital of the Island when the *Spaniards* were Masters, as it is also at present. Before the *English* burnt it when they conquered it, it contained above 2000 Houses, had 16 Churches and Chapels; but after they had exercised their Fury upon it, there were left only the Remains of two Churches and about 5 or 600 Houses, some of which were very pleasant and habitable.

'Twas founded by *Christopher Columbus,* who called it *St. Jago de la Vega,* as we have hinted before; and he reciprocally received the Title of *Duke de la Vega* from this City.

There is a *Savana* or Plain which faces the Town, where Thousands of Sheep, Goats, Calves and Horses grazed, when the *Spaniards* owned it. The Back-side of the Town is washed by a fair but unnavigable River, which falls into the Sea at *Passage Fort.* 'Tis a fine large Stream and runs by the Sides of the Town, serving all the People for drinking and other Uses. The *Spaniards* called it *Rio Cobre,* or the *Copper River,* from its running over that Mineral. This Town or rather City, is 12 Miles from *Port Royal,* and the *English* like it so well, that they have made it the Capital of the Island. The Governor and his Successors at first chose it for the Place of their Residence, the principal Courts of Judicature are kept here. The chief Officers are obliged to attend here, where the Seat of the Government is; and by this Means and the Fate of *Port Royal,* this City is so much enlarged, that there are now 2000 Houses in it, as there were before the *English* conquered it.

'Tis a very pleasant City, and the Inhabitants live in a great deal of Pomp and Luxury. The *Savana* before the Town is the Place of Rendezvous every Evening for the People of Fashion, as the *Park* is at *London,* and the *Cours* at *Paris.*

The Night Guard here consists of Horse as well as Foot, three Troopers and a Corporal, and six Foot Soldiers and a Corporal. It sends three Representatives to the Assembly. The supreme Court of Judicature is kept here. Capt. *Vring* writes, that this Town and the greater Towns are very dirty in wet, and dusty in dry Weather, not being paved. Next to it is

St. *Dorothy*'s *Parish*; in which is *Old Harbour*, about four or five Leagues to the leeward of St. *Jago*. 'Tis a good Road and a little Gulph, which may as conveniently serve *Spanish Town* as *Port Royal*. Four or 500 tall Ships may ride there, without Danger of falling foul upon one another. This Precinct sends two Representatives to the Assembly, and allows the Minister 80 *l. per Ann.* as do all the following Parishes bordering on St. *Dorothy's*. On the same Shore is

Vere Parish; in which is a small Place called *Carlisle* of 10 or 20 Houses, and *Maccary Bay*, very safe for Shipping. It also sends two Representatives to the Assembly. Next to it is

St. *Elizabeth's Parish*, which sends two Representatives to the Assembly, and is the last Parish on the Southern Coasts of the Island. In the Bay into which *Blewfeld*'s River runs not far from the Shore, was the Town of *Oristan*, which the *Spaniards* built when they first settled upon this Island.

There are Abundance of Rocks off this Coast, and some Isles among the Shoals; as *Seruavilla*, *Quitesvena*, and *Serrana*. 'Tis said *Augustino Pedro Serrana* was cast away here, and himself only saved; that he lived three Years in this Island by himself, that then there was another Seaman thrown ashore, who was the only Man of all his Company that was saved, and that these two lived four Years more before they were taken off. There are several Plantations to the Westward as far as *Point Negril*, which is the Lands End of *Jamaica*, it is a good Harbour, and Ships are sheltered there from the Weather. It lies convenient in Case of a Rupture with *Spain*, for our Men of War to wait there for the *Spaniards* passing to or from the *Havana*; and it was there that Admiral *Bembow* waited for *Du Casse*, when *Kirby* and his other Captains deserted him.

A little farther to the North West stood the City of *Seville*, situated on the Northern Coast near the Sea. 'Twas the second Town built by the *Spaniards*. There was formerly a Collegiate Church there, the Head of which was honoured with the Title of an Abbot. *Peter Martyr*, who wrote the *Decades of the West-Indies*, was Abbot of this Monastery.

Eleven Leagues farther Eastward was the City of *Mellila*, the first the *Spaniards* built. Here *Columbus* suffered Shipwreck, in his Return from *Veragua* in *Mexico*. The City stood in

St. *James*'s Parish; which sends two Members to the Assembly. This Precinct is but thinly inhabited, as is also the next to it,

St *Anne*'s: It sends two Representatives to the Assembly. The same does

The History of Jamaica.

Clarendon; an Inland Precinct, better peopled and planted. St. *Mary's* is next to St. *Anne's*, and sends also two Members to the Assembly. To *Rio Novo* in this Parish, the *Spaniards* retreated when the *English* had driven them from the South Coast of the Island. Bordering on this Precinct is St. *Thomas in the Vale*, which is pretty well planted, and sends two Representatives to the Assembly. Next to this is St. *George's Parish*; which sends two Members to the Assembly: As does St. *Thomas*, in the North East Part of the Island. On the Northern Coast is *Port Francis*, by some called *Port Antonio*, one of the best Ports in *Jamaica*. 'Tis close and well covered, and has but one Fault, which is the Entrance into it is not very easy; the Channel being straitened by a little Island that lies at the Mouth of the Port. 'Tis called *Lynch Island*, but belonged to the Earl of *Carlisle* of the Family of the *Howards*, who was once Governor of *Jamaica*.

There are several good Harbours on the Northern as well as on the Southern Shore; as *Cold Harbour*, *Rio Novo*, *Montega Bay*, *Orange Bay*: But the South Parts being best peopled are most frequented; and there is nothing more in any of these Northern Precincts worth the Reader's Curiosity, unless we entered into the Natural History of the Country, which the learned Dr. *Sloan* has published, after he had been several Years about it.

The Difference in the Riches of these Counties or Parishes, will be seen by their Valuation, in a Tax of 450 *l*. laid upon the whole Country for their Agents in *England*.

	l.	*s.*	*d.*
Port Royal,	49	10	10
St. Andrew's,	52	17	5
St. Katherine's,	56	16	3
St. Dorothy,	25	3	1
Vere,	47	1	8
Clarendon,	42	1	8
St. Elizabeth,	51	6	8
St. Thomas in the N. E.	27	10	0
St. David's,	16	11	0
St. Thomas in the *Vale*,	29	9	0
St. John,	15	8	3
St. George,	3	15	6
St. Mary's,	11	13	7
St. Anne's	7	2	6
St. James's,	2	16	8
Kingston,	19	5	0

The History of Jamaica.

The Soil of *Jamaica* is good and fruitful every where, especially in the Northern Parts, where the Mould is blackish, and in many Places mixed with Potters-Earth; in others, as towards the South East, the Soil is reddish and sandy. Take it all together it is extremely fertile, and very well answers the Industry of the Planter. The Plants and Trees are always blooming, and always green of one Sort or another; and every Month there resembles our *April* and *May*.

There is Abundance of *Savanas* or Lands of *Indian* Corn. These *Savanas* are found up and down even among the Mountains, particularly Northward and Southward; where there are great Numbers of wild Beasts, tho' not so many as when the *English* came first there.

The *Indians* used to sow Maze in those *Savanas*, and the *Spaniards* bred their Cattle which they brought from *Spain*; as Horses, Cows, Hogs and Asses, which multiplied to such a Degree, that not many Years ago Herds of wild Cattle were found in the Woods, as also wild Horses.

The *English* killed vast Quantities of Oxen and Cows when they were Masters of the Island, yet there were an incredible Number still left in the Woods, whither the *Spaniards* drove them from the Conquerors.

The *Savanas* are now the most barren Parts of the Island, which proceeds from their not being at all cultivated: However there grows such Plenty of Grass, that the Inhabitants have been forced to burn it.

As *Jamaica* is the most Northerly of all the *Charibbee-Islands*, the Climate is more temperate, and there is no Country between the *Tropicks* where the Heat is more moderate and less troublesom. The Air is always cooled by the Eastern Breezes, frequent Rains, and nightly Dews, which before the terrible Revolution in the Course of Nature by the Earthquake made the Place very healthy, and all Things look smiling and pleasant there in all Seasons.

The Eastern and Western Parts of the Island are more subject to rainy and windy Weather, than the Northern and Southern; and the thick Forests there render them not so agreeable as the Southward and Northward, which is a more open Country, and less subject to Wind and Rain. The Air in the mountainous Parts is cooler, and frosty Mornings have been often known upon the Hills.

Before the dreadful Hurricane, which overwhelmed so many Hundreds of its Inhabitants in 1692, this Island was not troubled with Tempests like the other *Sugar Islands*, neither were their Ships driven ashore in their Harbours, nor their Houses blown down over their Heads; as at *Barbados*
and

and the *Leeward Iflands*, but they can now no more boaft of that Advantage over their Neighbours.

The Weather ufed to be more various and uncertain than in the *Charibbee Iflands*. The Months of *May* and *November* are wet Months, and *Winter* is known from *Summer* only by Rain and Thunder, which are then more violent than at other Times of the Year. The Eafterly Breezes begin to blow about nine a Clock in the Morning, and grow ftronger as the Sun rifes, by which Means People may travel or work in the Field all Hours of the Day.

The Nights and Days are almoft of an equal Length all the Year long, and there's hardly any Difference to be perceived. The Tides feldom rife above a Foot high. Storms are very rare, and few or no Ships were ever caft away on thefe Coafts. But there being a curious Account of the Weather, Soil, Water, Diet, and other Things relating to *Jamaica*, communicated to the *Royal Society* by Dr. *Stubbs*, who made thefe Obfervations, I fhall for the Satisfaction of the Reader give him an Abftract of it.

The Wind at Night blows off the Ifland of *Jamaica* every Way at once, fo that no Ship can any where come in by Night, nor go out but early in the Morning, before the Sea Breeze comes on. As the Sun declines the Clouds gather and *fhape* according to the Mountains; fo that old Seamen will tell you each Ifland towards the Evening, by the *Shape* of the Cloud over it. *Lowth. Abridg. Phil. Tranf. Vol. III. p. 548. & feq.*

As there are certain Trees that attract the Rains, fo as the Woods are deftroyed, the Rains are alfo deftroyed or at leaft abated. At *Port Morant* the Eaftermoft Part of the Ifland, there's little of Land Breeze, becaufe the Mountain is remote from thence, and the Breeze coming thence, fpends its Force along the Land thither.

In the Harbour of *Jamaica* there grow many Rocks, fhaped like Bucks and Stags Horns. There grow alfo feveral Sea Plants, whofe Roots are ftony. At the *Point* in *Jamaica* where *Port Royal* ftood, fcarce fall 40 Showers a Year. From the *Point* towards *Port Morant*, and fo along to *Liguanee* fix Miles from *Port Royal*, there's fcarce an Afternoon for eight or nine Months together, beginning from *April*, in which it rains not. At *Spanifh-Town* it rains but three Months in a Year, and then not much. At the *Point*, wherever one digs five or fix Foot, Water will appear, which ebbs and flows as the Tide; not falt but brackifh, unwholefom for Men but wholefom for Hogs.

Paffengers when they firft come to *Jamaica*, fweat continually in great Drops for three Quarters of a Year, and then

then it ceafes; yet they are not more dry than in *England*, neither does all that fweating make them faintifh. If any one is dry, his Thirft is beft quenched by a little Brandy. Moft Animals drink little or nothing there. The hotteft Time of the Day is about Eight in the Morning, when there is no *Breeze*.

In *Magotti Savana* in the midft of the Ifland, between St. *Mary*'s and St. *John*'s Precinds, whenever it rains, the Rain as it fettles on the Seams of any Garment, turns in half an Hour to Maggots, yet that Plain is healthy to dwell in: Tho' Water is found every where five or fix Foot deep at the *Point*, yet there rifes no Steam into the Air from the Sands; for Men often lie all Night and fleep on them, without receiving any Hurt.

The Sea *Breeze* comes not into *Jamaica* till eight or nine in the Morning, and commonly ceafes about four or five in the Evening. But fometimes the Sea *Breeze* blows in the Winter Months 14 Days and Nights together; and then no Clouds gather but Dews fall. But if a North Wind blows, which fometimes in the Winter Months lafts as long, then no Dews fall nor Clouds gather. The Clouds begin to gather at two or three of the Clock in the Afternoon at the Mountains; the reft of the Sky being clear till Sun-fet.

As for the Produd of the Ifland, it is much the fame with *Barbados*. We fhall take Notice in what it differs, as we proceed in our Difcourfe on this Subjed.

The Sugar of *Jamaica* is brighter and of a finer Grain than the common *Barbados* Mufcovado, and fells in *England* for five or fix Shillings in the Hundred more, being fit for Grocers, whereas the *Barbados* unpurged Sugars muft generally pafs thro' the Refiners Hands firft. So long ago as the Year 1670, there were 70 Mills in *Jamaica*, which made about 2000000 Pound of Sugar; but that Quantity is encreafed to ten Times as much fince.

p. 554. At *Jamaica*, the Sugar cures fafter in 10 Days than in fix Months at *Barbados*; and this happens on thofe Places, where it rains for many Months together. Rains are fudden here, and make no previous Alterations in the Air before they fall, nor do they leave it *moift* afterwards.

There is more Cocoa comes from thence than from all our Colonies. But it is now no longer a Commodity to be regarded in our Plantations, tho' at firft it was the principal Invitation to the peopling *Jamaica*. For thofe Walks the *Spaniards* left behind them there when we conquered it, produced fuch prodigious Profit with little Trouble, that Sir *Thomas Modiford* and feveral others, fet up their Refts to

grow

The History of Jamaica. 397

grow wealthy by it, and fell to planting much of it, which *Sir* Dalby the *Spanish* Slaves who remained in the Island, always foretold Thomas's would never thrive, and so it happened; for tho' it promised *Hist. Acc.* fair, and throve finely five or six Years, yet still at that Age, *and Growth* when so long Hopes and Care had been wasted about it, it *of the West-* withered and died away by some unaccountable Cause, tho' *nies.* they impute it to a black Worm or Grub, which they find clinging to its Root.

The Manner of planting it is in Order like our Cherry Gardens. They place a Plantain by every Tree, and when it is grown up, it resembles a Cherry Tree. It delights in Shade, and for that Reason has the Plantain set by it. The Cocoa Walks are kept clear from Grass by Hoing and Weeding. The Trees begin to bear at three, four, or five Years old; and did they not almost always die before, would come to Perfection at 15 Years Growth, and last till 30; which renders them the most profitable Trees in the World, one Acre of them having cleared above 200 *l.* in a Year: But the old Trees planted by the *Spaniards* being gone by Age, and few new thriving as the *Spanish* Negroes foretold, little or none now is produced, worthy the Care and Pains in planting and expecting it. Those Slaves ascribe its not coming to Perfection to a superstitious Cause, many religious Rites being performed at its planting by the *Spaniards*, which their Slaves were not permitted to see: But it is probable that wary Nation, as they removed the Art of making *Cocheneal* and curing *Venelloes* into their Inland Provinces, which were the Commodities of the Islands in the *Indians* Time, and forbad the opening any Mines in them, for Fear some maritime Nation might be tempted to conquer them; so in transplanting the Cocoa from the *Caraccas* and *Quatamela* on the Continent, they might conceal wilfully some Secret in its Planting from their Slaves.

Cocoa grows on the Trees in Bags or Cods of greenish, red or yellow Colours, every Cod having in it three, four or five Kernels, about the Bigness and Shape of small Chesnuts; which are separated from each other by a very pleasant refreshing white Substance, about the Consistence of the Pulp of a roasted Apple, moderately sharp and sweet, from which its Nuts are taken when ripe, and by drying cured.

The Body of a Cocoa Tree is commonly about four Inches Lowth. *Vol.* Diameter, five Foot in Heigth, and above 12 from the II. *p.* 662. Ground to the Top of the Tree. These Trees are very different one from another, for some shoot up in two or three Bodies, others in one. Their Leaves are many of them dead, and most discoloured, unless on very young Trees. A bearing

ing Tree generally yields from two to eight Pound of Nuts a Year, and each Cod contains from 20 to 30 Nuts.

The Manner of Curing them is to cut them down when ripe, and to lay them to fweat three or four Days in the Cods; which is done by laying them on Heaps. After this the Cods are cut, the Nuts taken out and put into a Trough, covered with Plantain Leaves; where they fweat again about 16 or 20 Days. The Nuts that are in each Cod are knit together by certain Fibres, and have a white Kind of Pulp about them, very agreeable to the Palate, as has been hinted before. By the Turning and Sweating their little Strings are broken, and the Pulp is imbibed and mingled with the Subftance of the Nut. After this they are put to dry three or four Weeks in the Sun, and then they become of a reddifh dark Colour. The Cods grow only out of the Body or great Limbs and Boughs, at the fame Place there are Bloffoms and young and ripe Fruit.

The greateft Crop at moft of the Cocoa Walks in *Jamaica*, is in *December* or *January*; but at one of Col. *Modiford's* Walks they bear moft in *May*, yet it is not above five Miles from thofe Walks that bear in *December* always; but thofe that bear then have fome Fruit in *May*, as the others have in *December*. 'Tis planted firft in the Night, always under Shade. Some fet them under *Caffave*, others under Plantane Trees, and fome in their Woods. The *Spaniards* ufed a certain large fhady Plant, called by them *Madre di Cocoa*, the Mother of Cocoa. The *Englifh* ufe the others only. It muft always be fheltered from the North Eaft Winds.

The People at *Jamaica* feldom tranfplant it, only where it falls, as it does often in open, poor and dry Lands; for this Tree requires to have a flat, moift, low Soil, which makes them to be planted commonly by Rivers and between Mountains. 'Tis an Obfervation, that it is ill living where there are good Cocoa Walks. In a Year's Time the Plant becomes four Foot high, and has a Leaf fix Times as big as an old Tree, which as the Plant grows bigger falls off, and a leffer comes in its Place. The Trees are almoft always planted at two Foot Diftance, and fometimes at three Years old where the Ground is good and the Plant profperous, it begins to bear a little, and then they cut down all or fome of the Shade. The Fruit encreafes till the 10th or 12th Year, when the Tree is fuppofed to be in its Prime. The Root generally fhoots out *Suckers*, that fupply the Place of the old Stock when dead or cut down, unlefs any ill Quality of the Ground or Air kill both.

The History of Jamaica. 399

Cocoa was originally of these *Indies* and wild. Towards *Maracajo* are several Spots of it in the Mountains, and it is said the *Portuguese* have lately discovered whole Woods of it up the River *Maranon*. The Cocoa passes for Money in *New Spain* and the Silver Countries.

The following Account is a Calculation of the Charge and Profit of a Cocoa Walk, as it was drawn up by Sir *Thomas Modiford*, Bart. who had the best in *Jamaica:*

	l.
For the Patent of 500 Acres of Land, when the Country was first conquered,	10
For three Men and three Women Negroes, at 20 *l.* a Head,	120
Four White Servants, their Passage and Maintenance, at 20 *l.* a Head,	80
20 Hatchets, 20 Pick-Axes, and 20 Spades,	5
The Maintenance of six Negroes six Months, till Provisions can be raised for them,	18
For an Overseer, 40 *s.* a Month.	24
	257

These Men must begin to work the first Day of *March*, and build themselves Huts, plant Potatoes, Corn and Plantains, and when the Plantation is ready to receive them, there must be bought five Negro Men and five Negro Women more at 20 *l.* a Head, 200 *l.* And at the latter End of *March* the Planter must plant his Cocoa, either in the Nut or Seed, between Rows of Plantains of six Foot high. Twenty one Acres will be proper to be planted every Year, and by the first of *June* in the following Year, the Walk will be full of Cocoas; which in four Years Time will bear Fruit, and in the fifth be fit to gather. Every Acre will produce 1000 Weight yearly, which was then worth 4 *l.* a Hundred in the Island. Thus every 21 Acres will every Year produce to the Value of 840 *l.* Sterling.

The Charges of Gathering and Housing the Fruit is inconsiderable, a few Bags, and some other odd Things, which in all amount to 43 *l.* 10 *s.* So that the whole Expence is but 500 *l.* and the Charge lessens every Year, but the Profit encreases according to the Number of Acres planted. 'Tis to be observed that this Calculation was made when the Place was first settled, but it will serve to give the Reader some Idea of the Advantage of such a Walk at this Time, for in most Things it holds the same. Land and Negroes are dearer,

but

but the latter is a temporary Scarcity, and the former not hard to be come at, for enough may be had in the Northe Precincts on eafy Terms.

As to Indigo, there is more produced in *Jamaica* than i any other Colony, by Reafon of the great Quantity of *Savan* Land; for it thrives beft in light fandy Ground, as fuch thoi *Savanas* or great Plains are. The Seed from whence it i raifed is yellow and round, fomething lefs than a Fitch o Tare. The Ground is made light by Hoing, then Trenche are dug like thofe our Gardners prepare for Peafe, in whic) the Seed is put about *March*. It grows ripe in 8 Week' Time, and in frefh broken Ground will fpire up to abou: three Foot high, but in others to no more than 18 Inches. The Stalk is full of Leaves of a deep green Colour, and will from its firft fowing yield nine Crops in one Year. When it is ripe it is cut, and fteept in proportioable Fats 24 Hours, then it muft be cleared from the firft Water, and put into proper Cifterns; where when it has been carefully beaten, it is permitted to fettle about 18 Hours. In thefe Cifterns are feveral Taps, which let the clear Water run out, and the thick is put into Linnen Bags of about three Foot long and half a Foot wide, made commonly of Ozenbrigs, which being hung up all the liquid Part drips away. When it will drip no longer, it is put into Wooden Boxes three Foot long, 14 Inches wide, and one and a half deep. Thefe Boxes muft be placed in the Sun till it grows too hot, and then taken in till the extreme Heat is over. This muft be done continually till it is fufficiently dried.

Ibid.

In Land that proves proper for Indigo, the Labour of one Hand in a Year's Time, will produce between 80 and 100 Weight, which may amount from 12 to 15 *l.* to the Planter, if no Accident happen, for Indigo as well as other Commodities in thofe Parts is fubject to many. The moft common are Blafting and Worms, by which it is frequently deftroyed.

Piemento is another natural Production of *Jamaica*, from whence it is called *Jamaica Pepper*, alluding to its Figure and the chief Place of its Growth. The Trees that bear it are generally very tall and fpreading.

Lowth. *Vol.* II. p. 663.

' Its Trunk is as thick as one's Thigh, as Dr. *Sloan* who
' lived in *Jamaica* informs us. It rifes ftrait above thirty
' Foot high, is covered with an extraordinary fmooth Skin of
' a grey Colour; it is branched out on every Hand, having
' the End of its Twigs fet with Leaves of feveral Sizes, the
' largeft being four or five Inches long, and two or three
' broad in the Middle where it is broadeft, and whence it
' decreafes to both Extremes, ending in a Point fmooth, thin,
' fhining,

The History of Jamaica. 401

'shining, without any Incisures, of a deep green Colour,
' and standing on *Inch long Foot-stalks*; when bruised very
' odoriferous, and in all Things like the Leaves of a Bay
' Tree. The Ends of the Twigs are branched into Bunches
' of Flowers, each Foot-stalk sustaining a Flower bending
' back; within which Bend are many *Stamina* of a pale
' green Colour. To these follows a Bunch of crowned
' Berries, the Crown being made up of four small Leaves,
' which are bigger when ripe than Juniper Berries; at first
' when small, greenish, but when they are ripe black, smooth,
' and shining, containing in a moist green Aromatick Pulp,
' two large Seeds separated by a Membrane, each of which
' is a Hemisphere, and both joined make a spherical Seed.
' It grows on all the hilly Part of the Island of *Jamaica*,
' but chiefly on the North Side; and wherever these Trees
' grow they are generally left standing, when other Trees
' are felled: And they are sometimes planted where they ne-
' ver grew, because of the great Profit from the cured Fruit
' exported yearly in great Quantities into *Europe*.'

How this Planting can be reconciled to what Sir *Dalby* Hist. Acc.
Thomas writes of the cutting down these Trees, let the *of the Rise and Growth*
Knight and the Doctor adjust between them. *of the West-*

The Knight says, the Trouble of Gathering would make *India Colo-*
it incredibly dear, had not the People of *Jamaica* found out *nies.*
an easier Method of coming at it. The Trees that are left
grow generally in Mountains and Woods, which are not
taken up for Planting, but remain in the Queen's Hands; and
the Inhabitants go with their Slaves into the Woods where
it is plenty, and cutting down the Trees pick it off from the
Branches.

Thus no *Piemento* comes into *Europe* twice from one
Tree, and it happening to miss for two or three Years together, what it produces at present must be counted an acci-
dental Benefit to the Planters, rather than any Thing to be
relied on as a national Advantage or constant Encouragement.
The same may be said of *Lignum Vitæ*, *Guaiacum*, of *Red-
Wood*, and several other Sort of Trees which come from
thence, for the more comes the less remains: And the Time
required for the growing of these Woods, in the Room of
such as are cut down, is in human Reason so many Hundreds of Years, that the proposing to plant them would be
rather Madness than Foresight.

The *Jamaica* Pepper-Tree according to Dr. *Sloan*, flow- Lowth *Vol.*
ers in *June*, *July* and *August*; but sooner or later accord- II. p. 663.
ing to their Situation and different Season for Rains, and after

ter it flowers, the Fruit soon ripens: But it is to be observed, that in cleared open Grounds it is sooner ripe than in thick Woods. There's no great Difficulty in the curing or preserving this Fruit for Use. 'Tis for the most Part done by the Negroes. They climb the Trees and pull off the Twigs with the unripe green Fruit, and afterwards carefully separate the Fruit from the Twigs and Leaves; which done, they expose them to the Sun from the rising to the setting for many Days, spreading them thin on Cloths, turning them now and then, and carefully avoiding the Dews which are there very great. By this Means they become a little wrinkled, and from a green change to a brown Colour, when they are fit for the Market, being of different Sizes, but commonly of the Bigness of Black-Pepper, something like in Smell and Taste to Cloves, Juniper-Berries, Cinnamon and Pepper; or rather having a peculiar mixt Smell, somewhat akin to all of them; from whence it is called *All-Spice*.

The more fragrant and smaller they are, they are accounted the better. 'Tis deservedly reckoned (adds the Doctor) *the best and most temperate, mild and innocent of common Spices, and fit to come into greater Use, and to gain more Ground than it has, of the* East-India *Commodities of this Kind; almost all of which it far surpasses, by promoting the Digestion of Meat, attenuating tough Humours, moderately heating and strengthning the Stomach, expelling Wind, and doing those friendly Offices to the Bowels, which we expect from Spices.*

The *Wild Cinnamon Tree*, commonly, tho' falsely called *Cortex Winteranus*, grows in this Island. Its Trunk is about the Bigness of that of the *Piemento Tree*, and rises 20 or 30 Foot high, having many Branches and Twigs hanging downwards making a very comely Top. The Bark consists of two Parts, one outward and another inward. The outward Bark is as thin as a milled Shilling, of a whitish, ash or grey Colour, with some white Spots here and there upon it, and several shallow Furrows of a darker Colour, running variously through it, making it rough, of an Aromatick Taste. The inward Bark is much thicker than Cinamon, being as thick as a milled Crown Piece, smooth, of a whiter Colour than the outward, of a much more biting and Aromatick Taste, something like that of Cloves, and not glutinous like Cinnamon, but dry and crumbling between the Teeth. The Leaves come out near the Ends of the Twigs without any Order, standing on *Inch long Foot-stalks*, each of them two Inches in Length, and one in Breadth near the End, where broadest, and roundish, being narrow at the Beginning; from
whence

whence it augments in Breadth to near its End, of a yellowish green Colour, shining and smooth, without any Incisures about its Edges, and somewhat resembling the Leaves of *Bay*. The Ends of the Twigs are branched into Bunches of Flowers, standing something like *Umbels*, each of which has a *Foot-stalk*; on the Top of which is a Calix made up of some little Leaves, in which stand five scarlet or purple *Potala*, within which is a large *Stylis*; to these follow so many *Calycalated* Berries of the Bigness of a large Pea, roundish, green, and containing within a mucilaginous, pale, green, thin Pulp, four black shining Seeds of an irregular Figure.

All the Parts of this Tree, when fresh, are very hot, aromatick and biting to the Taste, something like Cloves; which is so troublesom, as sometimes to need the Remedy of fair Water. It grows in the *Savana* Woods very frequently on each Side of the Road, between *Passage-Fort* and the Town of St. *Jago de la Vega*, The Bark of the Tree is what is chiefly in Use, both in the *English* Plantations between the *Tropicks* in the *West-Indies* and in *Europe*, and is without any Difficulty cured, by only cutting off the Bark, and letting it dry in the Shade. The more ordinary Sort of People use it in the *West-Indies* instead of all other Spices, being thought very good to consume the *immoderate Humidity of the Stomach, to help Digestion, and expel Wind*, &c. Rum loses its loathsom Smell if mixed with this Bark.

The true *Cortex Winteranus*, for which the Druggists sell this wild Cinnamon, was brought by Capt. *Winter*, who accompanied Sir *Francis Drake* in his Voyage round the World from the Streights of *Magellan*.

The so famed Tree called a *Cabbage-Tree*, is (says Dr. *Stubbs*) nothing else than a Palm-Tree, and all that is eaten in the Cabbage, is what sprouted out that Year, and so is tender. If eaten raw, it is as good as any new Almonds, and if boiled, excels the best Cabbage, when that Top is cut off the Tree dies. The Timber will never rot, and when it is dried, grows so hard that one cannot drive a Nail into it. [Ibid. *Vol.* III. *p.* 554.]

There's a Tree in *Jamaica* called the *Bastard Cedar*, whose Wood is so porous (tho' none would guess so upon View) that being turned into Cups, Wine and Brandy will soak through at the Bottom in a short Time.

There's a Tree called *Whitewood*, of which if Ships are built, they will never breed any Worm. The *Soap Tree* grows at the *Spanish Town*, with Berries as big as Musket-Bullets; which of themselves, without any mixt Ingredient whatsoever, washes better than Castle-Soap, but they rot the Linen in Time.

The Juice of *Caſſavi* is rank Poiſon, all Hogs and Poultry that drink it ſwell and die preſently. If the Root be roaſted it is no Poiſon, but only occaſions Torſions in the Belly.

The *Palma* yields a prodigious Quantity of Oil, and it might eaſily be made a ſtaple Commodity. 'Tis the only Remedy of *Indians* and *Negroes* for the Head-ach.

The *Manchinel Tree* is a Wood of an excellent Grain, equalling the *Jamaica* Wood, but large to four Foot Diameter. The *Spaniards* turn it into Beds, and the *Engliſh* uſually floor their Rooms with it in *Jamaica*.

The *Manchinel Apple* is one of the beautifuleſt Fruits in the World to the Eye, one of the agreeableſt to the Smell, and of the pleaſanteſt to the Taſte (being thence by many called the *Eye Apple*) but if eaten certain Death. The Wood of it yet green, if rub'd againſt the Hand, will fetch off the Skin or raiſe Bliſters, and if any Drops of Rain falling from this Tree light upon one's Hand, or other naked Part of the Body, it will alſo have the ſame Effect.

There's Plenty of Cotton and Ginger in *Jamaica*, and it is finer than that of the *Charibbee-Iſlands*. The Tobacco that was planted there was better than at *Barbados*, but there's ſo little it deſerves not the Name of a Commodity.

Very good tan'd Leather is made there. The Tanners have three Barks to tan with, *Mangrave*, *Olive* Bark, and another. They tan better than in *England*, and in ſix Weeks the Leather is ready to work into Shoes. There's Abundance of Dyers Woods, as Fuſtick, Redwood, Logwood, and others, with ſeveral Sorts of Sweet-Woods.

'Tis not doubted but that there are Copper Mines in the Iſland, and the *Spaniards* ſay, the Bells of the great Church of St. *Jago* were made of *Jamaica* Metal. 'Tis ſuppoſed there may be Silver Mines in it as well as at *Cuba*, and on the *Continent*: And there is a Place in the Mountains of *Port Royal* or *Caguag*, where it is reported, the *Spaniards* dug Silver, but the *Engliſh* have not been ſo happy as to find it. The *Spaniards* alſo found *Ambergreaſe* on the Coaſt, but the *Engliſh* have not often had that good Fortune: Yet ſome Years ago an ignorant Fellow found 180 Pound of Ambergreaſe daſhed on the Shore, at a Place called *Ambergreaſe Point*, where the *Spaniards* came uſually once a Year to look for it. This vaſt Quantity was divided into two Parts, ſuppoſed by rolling and tumbling in the Sea. Some ſay it is produced from a Creature, as Honey and Silk; and Mr. *Tredway* who viewed this Piece writes, he ſaw in ſundry Places of this Body, the Beak, Wings, and Part of the Body of the Creature, which he preſerved for ſome Time. He was alſo

Ibid. *Vol.* II. *p.* 492.

told

told by a Man that he had feen the Creature alive, and believed they fwarmed as Bees on the Sea-fhore or in the Sea. Others fay it is the Excrement of the Whale, and others that it iffues out of the Root of a Tree. *Ibid.*

Abundance of Salt might be made in *Jamaica*, for they have three great Ponds; however they make only enough for their own Ufe. 100000 Bufhels were made thirty Years ago in a Year, and Capt. *Noye*, who was the Undertaker, faid he could make 500000 Quarters if he could fell it. Salt-Petre is found here, and their Long-Pepper is in great Efteem in the *Weft-Indies*.

The Ifland abounds in Drugs and medicinal Herbs, as *Guaiacum*, *China*, *Salfeparella*, *Caffia*, *Tamarins*, *Venilloes*, many Sorts of *Miffeltoe*; as alfo in falutary Gums and Roots. But for thefe Things we muft refer the Curious to Dr. *Sloan's* Natural Hiftory.

The Plant of which *Cocheneal* is made grows in *Jamaica*, and yet the Inhabitants for want of Knowledge how to cure it make no Advantage of it; befides the Eaft Wind blafts it, fo that it never comes to Maturity.

'Twill not be improper to give an Account of this excellent Dye, *Cocheneal*. 'Tis generally believed that it comes out of a Fruit called the *Prickled Pear*, bearing a Leaf of a flimy Nature, and a Fruit Blood-red and full of Seeds, which give a Dye almoft like to *Brafiletto Wood*, that will perifh in a few Days by the Fire. But the Infect engendered of this Fruit or Leaves gives a permanent Tincture, as every one knows.

An old *Spaniard* in *Jamaica*, who lived many Years in that Part of the *Weft-Indies*, where great Quantities of *Cocheneal* is made, affirmed, that this Infect is the very fame which we call the *Lady Bird* or *Cow Lady*. It appears he fays at firft like a fmall Blifter or little Knob, on the Leaves of the Shrub on which they breed; which afterwards by the Heat of the Sun becomes a *live Infect* or *fmall Grub*. Thefe *Grubs* in Procefs of Time grow to Flies, and being come to full Maturity, which muft be found out by Experience in collecting them at feveral Seafons, are killed by making a great Smother of fome combuftible Matter, to Windward of the Shrubs on which the Infects are feeding (having before fpread fome Cloths under the Plants) by which all the Infects being fmothered and killed, by fhaking the Plants will tumble down upon the Cloths, and thus are gathered in great Quantities with little Trouble; then they are wiped off the fame Cloths in fome bare fandy Place or Stone-Pavement, and expofed to the Heat of the Sun till they are dry, and their Bodies *Ibid. Vol. II. p. 784.*

dies shriveled up; which being rubbed gently between one's Hands will crumble into Grains, and the Wings separate from them which must be garbled out. Others, it is said, expose them to the Sun in broad and shallow Copper-Basons, in which the Reflection of the Sun dries them sooner.

The *Prickled Pear*, or *Indian Fig*, is easily propagated, by putting a single Leaf above half it's Depth into the Ground, which seldom fails to take Root. Others say they may be raised from the Seed, which is something like a Fig, arising out of certain Flowers that grow out of the Tops of the uppermost Leaves; which Fruit is full of a red Pulp, that when ripe stains the Hands of those that wash it like Mulberries, with a purple Colour: On which, or the Blossoms, the Insects feed, and perhaps that causes the rich Tincture they bear within their Bowels.

There are few Colonies in *America* who have such Store of Cattle as there is at *Jamaica*. Horses are so cheap, that a good one is sold for 8 or 10 *l*. The Oxen and Cows are large, and till the *English* came, who minded Planting more than Grasing, there were great Quantities of them; but now they cannot boast of their Stock, and are supplied with Flesh from the other Colonies as well as the *Leeward Islands*.

Asses and Mules are cheaper at *Jamaica* than any where else in the *English* Dominions in *America*. Their Sheep are generally large and fat, the Flesh is good, but the Wooll worth nothing. 'Tis long and full of Hairs. There's Abundance of Goats and Hogs, and the Flesh of the latter is as pleasant as that of *Barbados* Pork.

Their Bays, Roads and Rivers, are full of excellent Fish of all Kinds, *European* and *American*. The *Tortoise* is the chief, because it is the most advantageous on Account of its Shell. They abound on the Coasts about 20 or 30 Leagues to the left of *Port Negril*, near the Isles of *Camaros*. There come several Vessels in a Year from the *Charibbee-Islands* to take them, for the Flesh of them is esteemed the best and wholesomest Food in the *Indies*.

Lowth. *Vol.* III. p. 553, 557, 559.

The *Tortoises* float asleep in a calm Day a long Time, insomuch that the Seamen row gently to them, and either strike them with Irons, or ensnare their Legs with a Rope and Running-Net, and so take them. If their Blood be heated they die, for to maintain Life, it must not be hotter than the Element they live in. They bite much more of the submarine Grass than they swallow, by which Means the Sea is sometimes covered with the Grass, where they feed at the Bottom. Once in about half an Hour they come up, fetch one Breath like a Sigh, and then sink down again. When they

The History of Jamaica.

they are out of the Water, they breath somewhat oftner. If they are hurt on Shore as they lie on their Backs, the Tears will trickle from their Eyes.

They may be kept out of the Water twenty Days and more, yet they will be so fat as to be fitting Meat, provided about half a Pint of salt Water is given them every Day. The Fat that's about their Guts is yellow, tho' that of their Bodies be green. The Head being cut off dies instantly, and if the Heart is taken out, the Motion continues not long, but any Quantity of the Flesh will move if pricked, and also of itself many Hours after it is cut into Quarters; and the very Joints of the Bones of the Shoulders and Legs have their Motions, even tho' you prick only the Fat of them. But if you place these Parts of the *Tortoise* in the Sun, they presently die, as the Legs do in a Manner as soon as they are cut off.

The Blood of the Tortoises (says Dr. *Stubbs* in the same Collection) *is colder than any Water I ever felt in* Jamaica; *yet is the Beating of their Heart as vigorous as that of any Animal, and their Arteries are as firm as any Creatures I know: Their Lungs lie in their Belly. Their Spleen is triangular, of a firm Flesh, and floridly red. Their Liver is of a dark green: They have a Sort of Teeth, with which they chew the Grass they eat in the submarine Meadows.* All the *Tortoises from the* Charibbees *to the Bay of* Mexico *repair in Summer to the* Cayman *Islands on this Coast, to lay their Eggs and to hatch there. They coot for fourteen Days together, then lay in one Night about three hundred Eggs with White and Yolk, but no Shells. Then they coot again and lay in the Sand, and so thrice; when the Male is reduced to a kind of Gelly within and blind, and is so carried Home by the Female. Their Fat is green, but not offensive to the Stomach, tho' it is in Broth or stewed. Urine looks of a yellowish green, and is oily after eating it.* Ibid. p. 549, 550.

There is no Sort of Fowl wanting here, wild or tame, and more Parrots than in any of the other Islands.

The Fruits, Flowers and Herbs are much the same with those of *Barbados*, various and excellent in their Kinds. The Fruit of the Trees in this Island of the same Kind, ripen not at one Time. There's a Hedge of Plumb-Trees of two Miles in the Road to *Spanish-Town*, of which some Trees have been observed to be in *Flower*, others with green, others with ripe Fruit, and others to have done bearing at the same Time.

Jasmins have been seen to blow before their Leaves, and also after their Leaves are fallen again. The *Sour-Sop*, a very pleasant Fruit, has a Flower with three Leaves. When these open

open they give so great a Crack, that Persons often run from under the Tree, and think it to be tumbling down.

The Diseases of this Country before the Earthquake, were not so mortal to the *Europeans* as they have been since. Intemperance always was more fatal to the *English* than the Climate, and those Voyagers who were always drinking in the City of *Port-Royal*, might well cry out against the Heat of the Climate, the Fires from without being encreased by their Flames within. Temperance and Exercise would have gone a great Way towards keeping Men well there, before Diseases were brought thither out of *Europe*, and the Air became infected with the pestilential Vapours of the Earthquake. The Distempers to which Strangers are most subject, are the Dropsy, occasioned commonly by hard Drinking and Laziness, Agues and Fevers.

There's a Bird called a *Pelican*, but is a Kind of *Cormorant*. It has a fishy Taste, yet if the Flesh lies buried in the Ground two Hours it loses that Taste.

The Birds called by some *Fregats* are here termed *Men of War*, their Fat is good against Aches.

The *Fire-Flies* in *Jamaica* contract and expand their Light as they fly, and their Light continues some Days after they are dead. These Flies are a Kind of *Cantharides*, looking green in the Day-time, but glowing and shining in the Night, even when they are dead, as we have already observed. Our Author affirms, he applied them dead to a printed and written Paper in the dark and read it.

There are several troublesom Creatures and Insects here, as well as in the other Islands.

The *Wood Lice* eat Covers and Books, and some Sorts of Timber, but not all.

The *Ciron* or *Chego* is a terrible Plague to the *Blacks*, especially if they come among the nervous and membranous Parts, they are very painful and not to be pulled, lest the Surgeons Needles touch the Nerves. No *English* ever get them, but by going in Places frequented by the Negroes; they are incident mostly to such as are nasty about the Feet, and very seldom any else have them; they will spread by little and little over the whole Feet, eat off Toes, and over-run the whole Body of some idle *Blacks*; they are not felt to have got into the Body till a Week after: They breed in great Numbers, and shut themselves up in a Bag, which when the Negroes feel, there are certain skilful Men, who with little Pains take them out, having great Care to take out the Bag entirely, that none of the Brood which are like Nits may be left behind, for Fear of giving Rise to a new Generation.

The History of Jamaica.

We muſt take Notice that the *Swallows* in *Jamaica*, as hot as it is, depart in the Winter Months, and the wild Ducks and Teal come thither then.

The *Manchinella*, in Shape like a *Crawfiſh*, which is ſo common in the *Charibbee-Iſlands*, is alſo frequently met with in *Jamaica*, as are *Adders* and *Guyanas*, but neither of them venomous.

The moſt terrible Creature is the *Alligator*, which commonly lies about their Rivers and Ponds. They live upon Fleſh, after which they hunt greedily, but ſeldom get any Man's Fleſh, becauſe it is eaſy to avoid them; for they cannot ſtir but in a ſtrait Line, which they do ſwiftly and forcibly, whereas they turn with Difficulty and very ſlowly. Some of them are 10 or 15, and ſome 20 Foot long, their Backs are all over ſcaly and impenetrable, and it is hard to wound them any where, except in the Eye or the Belly, they have four Feet or Fins, with which they either walk or ſwim. 'Tis obſerved, that like Fiſh they never make any Noiſe. Their Way of Hunting is thus: They lie on a River's Bank, and wait for Beaſts that come to drink there, which they ſeize as ſoon as they are within their Reach and devour; they deceive them the more eaſily, becauſe they reſemble a long Piece of old dry Wood or ſomething that's dead. The Miſchief theſe Animals do, is recompenced by the Advantage of their Fat, of which an excellent Ointment is made good for any Pains or Aches in the Bones or Joints. They have Bags of Musk ſtronger and more odorous than that of the *Eaſt-Indies*, the Smell is ſo great and ſo ſearching, that it is eaſy by it to diſcover where they lie, and avoid them before a Man ſees them; even the Cattle by a natural Inſtinct ſmell them, and run away from them. They breed like Toads, by Eggs which they lay in the Sand on the Rivers Banks; their Eggs are no larger than a Turkey's, they cover them and the Sun's-Beams hatch them: The Shell is as firm and like in Shape to a Turkey's, but not ſpotted. As ſoon as their Young come out of the Shell, they take immediately to the Water.

Theſe *Alligators* are ſhaped like Lizzards being four-footed, they walk with their Belly at a Diſtance from the Ground like them. Thoſe of full Growth have Teeth like a Maſtiff, as has been before hinted. They may be maſtered and killed by any one dextrous and skilled in the Way of doing it, which is thus: A Man muſt be armed with a good long Truncheon and attack them Side-ways, for if he does it Front-ways they will be too nimble for him, and by leaping upon him (which they can do the Length of their whole Body) ſpoil him; but if he lays his Club on them againſt their Shoulder and behind

hind their Fore-feet, they are eafily lamed there and fubdued.

Some Places in this Ifland are troubled with Gnats and ftinging Flies: There's no avoiding fuch Inconveniencies in the *Weft-Indies*.

There are feveral other Particularities relating to *Jamaica* which are worth obferving, and could not fo well be couched under any particular Article.

Several Sorts of Beans grow in this Ifland, as the *Cacoons*, the *Horfe-Eye* Bean, fo called from its Refemblance to the Eye of that Beaft, by Means of a Welt almoft furrounding it; the *Afh-coloured Nickar*, fo termed from its being perfectly round and very like a Nickar, fuch as Boys ufed to play withal.

Iron and other Metals ruft leaft in *Jamaica* in rainy Weather, as Dr. *Stubbs* in the Tract fo often cited by us obferves.

'Tis a Miftake that any Tobacco grows wild in *Jamaica* at leaft. The nitrous Tobacco, which grows upon Salt-Petre Ground there, will not come to fo good a Colour, nor keep fo long as other Tobacco; infomuch that the Merchants often lofe all their Tobacco in the Voyage for *England* or *Ireland*, by its rotting all away. In fome Ground that is full of Salt-Petre, the Tobacco that it bears flafhes as its fmokes. The Potatoes in the fame Salt-Petre Ground are ripe two Months fooner than in any other Ground, but if they be not fpent immediately they rot, the Salt-Petre fretting the outward Skin of the Root, which is thinner in that Sort of Ground, than in other Places.

<small>Lowth *Vol.* II. p. 550, 554.</small>

The fame Doctor fays elfewhere, *I could never hear of any Hurricane about* Jamaica; but the dreadful Earthquakes that brought the Inhabitants fo near an univerfal Ruin, are worfe than the Tempefts, which are fo frequent in the *Charibbee-Iflands*.

We muft not omit remembring that there are hot Springs, and other mineral Waters in this Ifland, as we find by Information given the Royal Society by Sir *William Beefton*. The *Hot Spring* moft talked of was difcovered many Years ago, but the Diftance and Trouble of getting to it, kept People from trying it till *March* 1695, when two Perfons, the one very much *macerated* with the Belly-Ach, and another with the *French* Difeafe went to it, carried Cloths, built a Hut to keep them from the Rain and Sun, and both prefently by Drinking and Bathing found fuch Eafe, that in about ten Days they returned perfectly cured. It comes out of a Rock in a frefh Current, near to a fine Rivulet of good cool Water; but is fo hot, that all affirm it foon boils Eggs, fome fay Crawfifh, Chickens, and thofe that do not value their Credit much,

<small>Ibid. p. 344.</small>

The History of Jamaica.

much, add even a Turkey: However it is certain, that near where it comes forth, there is no enduring any Part of the Body but it takes off the Skin. It cures Ulcers, and contracted Nerves and Sinews in a few Days to a Miracle. Col. *Beckford*, who was given over by the Physicians for very acute Pains in his Bowels went to it, made use of it and recovered. Another for the Belly-Ach, and a third for the Venereal Disease made the same happy Experiment; which got the Waters such a Reputation, that many afterwards resorted to them. It was tried with Galls before Sir *William Beeston*, and they made the Water in 24 Hours look only like *Canary* or *Old Hock*. He says, *Out of Curiosity we tried the Water of our River at* Spanish-Town *with Galls, and in one Night it turned to a deep Green more inclining to Black.*

Pag. 345.

Mr. *Robert Tredway* wrote from *Jamaica*: *We have lately discovered two hot Springs, one to Windward which seems sulphurous; the other to Leeward is very salt, but as I am told does not partake of Brimstone; and both are very much magnified for the Diseases of these Parts, the dry Belly-Ach, Pains of the Nerves and Yaws.*

Among other Rarities of this Country is one very remarkable, and that is the Plant called *Spirit Weed*; which when its Seed is ripe the Vessel containing it, touched by any Thing whatever if it is wet, instantly opens itself, and with a smart Noise throws its Seed several Ways to a considerable Distance.

Thus we have given the Reader an Account of the most curious Part of the Natural History of this Island, to enter into the Reasons is a Dissertation without our Bounds; and Dr. *Sloan* has in his Tract said enough to give entire Satisfaction to all, whose Curiosity shall carry them into such nice Discussions.

CHAP. III.

Of the Inhabitants and Trade of *Jamaica*, and the Advantages *England* does and may receive from it.

*J*Amaica like *Barbados* has three Sorts of Inhabitants, Masters, Servants and Slaves; to whom may be added a fourth, which tho' they are uncertain, yet by their Resort thither are a good Strength to the Island, Privateers and Water-

Watermen always coasting about it, carrying Goods from one Place to another or cruizing for Prizes. The Privateers were at one Time the best Flower in the Garden of the *Jamaica* Trade, they brought some Millions of Pieces of Eight there, and made the Place so rich, that it out-stript all the Colonies in Wealth in a very few Years; even *Barbados* could only vie with it for Eldership, and having been longer planted.

The Masters of Families in *Jamaica*, Planters and Merchants, live with as much Pomp and Pleasure as any Gentlemen in the World; they keep their Coaches and six Horses, have their Train of Servants in Liveries running before and behind them, and for Magnificence and Luxury they have always got the start of the other Colonies: Whether it had not been better for them to have encouraged Industry and Frugality we shall not take upon us to determine; their natural Advantages above all the other Islands does not make it so necessary for them to be industrious, and the Riches that were brought them by their Trade with the *Spanish West-Indies*, put them in a Capacity of answering their Expences: And both together invited so many People to settle there, that 20 Years ago there were 60000 *English* Souls, and 100000 *Blacks* upon the Island. The War, Earthquake and Diseases since have hindered the Colony's encreasing; but still they are almost that Number, of which 15000 *Englishmen* are able to bear Arms, and the Militia consists of several Troops of Horse and seven Regiments of Foot, making 7000 Men.

The Way of living of both Masters, Slaves and Servants here, is like that of the *Barbados* People, and the Form of Government the same with theirs; but the Trade differs in some Things, as in most of their Dyer's Woods, which the Merchants of *Barbados* have not the Convenience of exporting. The Bay of *Campeche* has been very beneficial to those of *Jamaica*, for they are only at the Charge of cutting and carrying off the Wood, which comes generally to a good Market in *England*; but the *Spaniards* have done what they could to hinder that Trade, insomuch that the Wood-Cutters have been forced to have Guards, and fight for their Prize.

The Trade from *Jamaica* with the *Spaniards* consisted chiefly in Negroes, Stuffs and other *English* Manufactures. The *Spaniards* for several Years were not permitted to deal with the *English*, but after the Revolution a Treaty of Commerce was concluded between King *William* and King *Charles*, for their Dominions in *America*; and Sir *James de Castillo*, whom King *William* had knighted, resided at *Jamaica*

maica as Agent for the *Spaniards*, to buy Negroes for them and ſhip them for the Continent. The Advantages by this Traffick would have enriched our Nation had it laſted, and been carried on wiſely and induſtriouſly; but the War with *France* and *Spain* has interrupted all the Commerce between *Jamaica* and the *Spaniſh Weſt-Indies*, which the *Engliſh* cannot too much encourage.

The other Branches of the *Jamaica* Trade is the ſame with that of *Barbados*, and we muſt refer the Reader to our Hiſtory of that Iſland on this Article.

Indigo and Piemento are the Commodities of this Country, and Cocao Nuts are but a new Experiment at *Barbados*, or elſe the Commodities of that Place and *Jamaica* are all one, and we muſt enter upon needleſs Repetitions, if we pretended to give any particular Account of them. In the general, this Trade has the Advantage of that of *Barbados*, for it brings us in Bullion which is ſo much wanted at Home. *Jamaica* is placed in the Center of the *Spaniſh* Acquiſitions in *America*, no Veſſel can go to or come from the Continent or the Iſlands belonging to them, but they muſt neceſſarily come in Sight of *Jamaica*, or fall into the Hands of our Cruizers if we had enough Ships there, with brave and faithful Commanders to wait for them; and 12 or 15 light Frigats would be ſufficient, which the Benefit it would bring to us by Prizes, or the Inconveniencies it would put our Enemies to, would more than anſwer.

Every Plate Fleet that comes from *Carthagena* puts into *Hiſpaniola*, from whence they cannot ſail to the *Havana* in *Cuba*, without paſſing by one End or the other of *Jamaica*. The *Havana* is the Place of general Rendezvous for the *Flota*; and the Importance of their Junction there for their Security is eaſily to be imagined, which we could ſoon hinder, by being Maſters of the Seas about *Jamaica*.

The Product of this Iſland is generally the beſt in its Kind of any in the *Engliſh* Plantations. Their Sugar, Ginger, Cotton and Indigo, are better than that of the *Charibbee-Iſlands*; and there is Ground enough to ſpare for the Inhabitants to furniſh themſelves with Proviſions of their own raiſing, if they did not think it worth their while to cultivate the Commodities for an *European* Market. All the Proviſions and Neceſſaries that are ſent from *England* to the other Plantations are alſo ſent to *Jamaica*; and there is conſtantly employed in this Trade between 2 and 300 Sail of ſtout Ships, and before the War there were many more.

The Laws of *Jamaica* are very well collected in the Abridgment of the *Plantation Laws*, and the Natural Hiſtory
of

The History of Jamaica.

of the Country is published by Dr. *Sloan*, Secretary to the *Royal Society*, who has an Interest in that Island, which with the History we have here faithfully related, will give the Curious a sufficient Idea of it. But we must here add something relating to the Country, Inhabitants, Trade, &c. as it differs now from our last Account of it.

Jamaica, according to the latest Observations and Surveys, lies in 17 Degrees 40 Minutes North Latitude, 18 Leagues from *Cuba*, 24 from *Hispaniola*, so that it is nearer those Islands than *England* to *Ireland*, except at the Extremities. No Vessel can go to or come from the Continent, but must necessarily sail within Sight of *Jamaica* or fall into the Hands of the *English*, which shews what Advantage it is, and may be to us in all Wars with *Spain*. 'Tis 160 Miles long, 55 broad, contains four Million of Acres, of which if one Million is patenteed, not 200000 Acres are planted. The Island is divided by a Ridge of Hills that run from Sea to Sea, and go by several Names in several Districts. In those Mountains rise several Rivers not navigable but for Canoos, in which Sugars are carried to the Sea-side and shipped in Scooners and Sloops for *Port-Royal* and *Kingston*, to be loaded there for *England*; two of these Rivers run under Ground as the *Mole* in *Surry*. *Rio Cobre* in St. *Thomas* in the *Vale*, and *Rio Pedro* in the same Parish; *Rio Cobre* runs under Ground nine Miles before it appears again; *Rio Pedro* runs two Miles thro' a Mountain; *Rio Pedro* is 12 Miles from *Spanish-Town*, *Rio Cobre* 22 Miles. It rises in the Mountains called *Monte Diabolo* near Mr. *Lord*'s dwelling House. The whole Island is very well watered, but in some Places the Water is brackish, and there the Rain Water is preserved.

Rivers.

The *Jamaica* Historian tells us, not one Part in three of the Island is inhabited, which I fear is a very modest Account of its Settlement, for it contains four Millions of Acres, and if ⅓ or 1300000 Acres were inhabited, laid out and planted, and, as he says, one Acre has produced several Hogsheads of Sugar, the Number of the Inhabitants and the Quantity of the Product, would be more than ten Times as much as they really are now. Nor can we suppose that 100,000 Hogsheads of Sugars are made here yearly as he informs us; but as not a quarter Part of the Island is planted, and as Mr. *Ashley* in his Account of *Barbados* assures us, That and the *Leeward-Islands* can make twice the Quantity of Sugars they do now produce; it is strange that a late Writer upon Trade should make such grievous Complaints of our Want of Sugar Ground in our *American* Islands; that in *Jamaica* Millions of Acres cannot be said to be worn out, having

The History of Jamaica.

having never been broke up; if that in *Barbados* is pretty well worn, a Planter there assures us, the Soil can produce twice as much as it does had it Hands to work it, by which it appears that we need not purchase or conquer other Lands for the Sugar Growth, but supply by Industry and Oeconomy what is wanting for cultivating and manufacturing the Sugar Cane.

There are in *Jamaica* some large *Savanas*, where the *Indians* planted their *Maize* and the *Spaniards* breed their Cattle; it is to be hoped the *Jamaicans* know as well as they how to improve them, and they might have Plenty of Cattle here, if breeding Cattle was as much minded as it deserves to be, considering the many Months they have to feed, and how much fresh Provisions is for their own Health and their Servants.

As the planted Part of this Island is the nearest to the Sea, the Conveniency of its Navigation appears by the great Numbers of Bays all round it.

Bays.

Port Royal.	*Luana Bay.*
Port Morant.	*Blewfield's Bay.*
Old Harbour.	*Cabaretta Bay.*
Point Negril.	*Cold Harbour.*
Port Antonio.	*Rio Novo.*
Michael's Hole.	*Montigo Bay.*
Alligator Pond.	*Orange Bay.*
Point Pedro.	And many others.
Parattee Bay.	

The Towns in this Island have little to be added to the former Account of them. *Towns.*

Port-Royal, which was the fairest and richest Sea Port Town in *America*, is by the Accidents mentioned in this History reduced to a small Place, yet it still consists of three handsom Streets and several cross Lanes. It has a fine Church, an Hospital for disabled Seamen, and a Yard for the King's naval Stores and Ship Carpenters Work. It is guarded by one of the strongest Forts in the *West-Indies*, mounted with 100 Guns, and garrisoned by regular Troops; the Harbour is one of the best in the World, 1000 Sail of Ships may ride there and be secure from every *Wind that can blow*, always excepting a *Hurricane*. The *Receiver General*, the *naval Officer*, the *Secretary* or *Deputy Secretary* are still obliged to keep their Offices here as well as at *Spanish-Town*. No Building is to be here within 30 Feet of high Water Mark, nor farther Northward on the Harbour than Major *Back's* and Capt. *Suimmer's* Houses. *Port-Royal* is distant from *Spanish-Town* five Miles by Water and six more by Land. It is about

Port-Royal.

bout fix Miles diftant from *Kingfton*, which was built after the great Earthquake had deftroyed *Port-Royal*, by a Plan of Col. *Chriftian Lilly*'s, who is now or was very lately chief Engineer of this Ifland, whither he came with Col. *Lillington* near 50 Years before, no Proof this that the Air is unwholefom. By Col. *Lilly*'s Plan, this Town was to be a Mile long and half a Mile broad, laid out into little Squares by crofs Streets, and wants not much of the Extent *Lilly* intended it; here the inferior Courts fit. The Receiver General, *naval* Officer, Secretary and Surveyor, are obliged to have and attend Offices here. Here refide the Merchants for the moft Part fince the Fall of *Port-Royal*, and here are moft of the Sugars fhipped off for *England*. It encreafes daily, and now mufter 10 Companies of Foot and two Troops of Horfe, about 1100 Men; and fuppofing the Militia to be half of the Male Inhabitants of Age fit for Arms, this muft now be a great Town of 1100 or 1200 Houfes. It has one Church with a poor burying Place, which is in this Ifland a very important Appurtenance for Parifh. The *Jews* have two Synagogues, and the *Quakers* a Meeting-houfe. It is bounded by *Port-Royal* Harbour to the *South Weft*, and to the *North* by Lands patenteed by Sir *William Beefton*, and continued to a *Calabafh* Tree on the *North Eaft* Corner, directly to the Foot of the *Long Mountain*, and from thence to the Bounds of the Parifh of *Port-Royal*. 'Tis 18 Miles from thence to *Spanifh-Town*, 12 Miles by Sea and fix by Land; it choofes three Members for the *Affembly*.

St. Jago de la Vega. *St. Jago de la Vega* or *Spanifh-Town* is the Capital of *Jamaica*, and gave the Title of Duke to the Family of *Columbus* the Difcoverer of the *New World*, and this Ifland in particular. It was a large City in the *Spaniards* Time confifting of 2000 Houfes; it has not now above 7 or 800, but they are very good. The Governor refides here; here the Affembly hold their Seffion, as do alfo the grand Courts of Juftice. It retains its *Spanifh* Name *St. Jago de la Vega* in all publick Deeds, is fituated in a fine pleafant Valley on the Banks of the *Rio Cobre*, being an inland Town; the Trade is not confiderable, but feveral wealthy Merchants and Gentlemen have Houfes here and live very gayly, as much like Men of Pleafure as Bufinefs; Coaches and Chariots are perpetually plying, and a great Number of Gentlemen's are feen every where. Here are frequent Balls and Affemblies, a Play houfe and a Company of Players: The *Jamaica* Writer affures us, they are *excellent Actors*, which is more than can juftly be faid of the beft Company now in *England*. The Governor's Houfe faces the *Parade*, one Part of it confifts of two Stories, it was

The History of Jamaica. 417

was rebuilt by the Duke of *Portland*. It has a curious Garden towards the *West*, which is generally kept in excellent Repair, though here is a great Neglect of Garden Ground for the Culture, of which the *Jamaicans* seem to have no Taste; and indeed where there is an eternal Spring, a perpetual *Bloom* and perpetual *Green*, there seems to be little Need of Gardening. The Church is a handsom Edifice and has in it a very good *Organ*. Here is also a Chapel where divine Service is performed. The *Custom-house* is a small Square Building about 40 Feet each Way; here the Chief Justice, who is now or was lately the worthy ——— *Ellis*, Esq; who has five assistant Judges, their Seats are raised almost 10 Feet from the Floor. The *Provost Marshal*, the most beneficial Office in the Island next the Governor's, has a Chair placed for him on the right Hand of the Judges, and opposite to them at a good Distance are seated the Lawyers. The Attorney General has a large Chair placed for him in the Middle. The Houses are generally low, of one Story, with 5, 6 and sometimes more Rooms, being usually lined and floored with *Mahagony*. Each has a Piazza ascended by Steps, which serves for a Screen against the Heat, and is commodious for taking the cool refreshing Air. A few Houses have two Stories, but that Way of Building is disapproved, as too much exposed to the Violence of *Earthquakes* and *Hurricanes*. The other Towns in this Island are inconsiderable; every rich well stocked Plantation is a Kind of little Town, and the Planters Business is very inconsistent with a Town Life, which occasions the Spread of People in all the Colonies except *New-England*, where their Trade is best carried on in Port and Market Towns.

Here are seen the Ruins of *Sevilla* and *Oristan*, two pretty large Towns in the *Spaniards* Time; but the Ground where they and other *Spanish* Towns stood, does in several Places now produce the Sugar Cane. *Towns.*

At *Bagnal's* in the Parish of St. *Ann's* is begun a Town, but how it goes on we know not, and are doubtful of its Success.

Free-Town in the Parish of St. *David's*, is another small Place.

Passage-Fort in St. *Catharine's* Parish, consists of about 50 Houses, and is likely to encrease in Trade and consequently in Buildings, it being the only Place for taking Boat to *Port-Royal* or *Kingston*. Col. *Jackson* landed here with his Men from the *Leeward-Islands*, when he took St. *Jago* in 1635.

Carlisle

The History of Jamaica.

Carlisle in *Vere* Parish, is another inconsiderable Village; a Fort was erected here after the *French* Invasion in 1695, but it is already in Ruins.

Tichfield a small Town, so called from the Dutchess of *Portland's* Manor of *Tichfield* in *Hampshire*, is near Port *Antonio*, which has been spoken of before. The Fort there is very regular, and has always a *Captain's* Guard for its Defence.

The present Division of *Jamaica* is into 19 Parishes.

Parishes.

1. *Kingston.*
2. *Port-Royal.*
3. *St. Catharine's.*
4. *St. Dorothy's.*
5. *Clarendon.*
6. *Vere.*
7. *St. Elizabeth.*
8. *Hanover.*
9. *Westmoreland.*
10. *St. George's.*
11. *St. James's.*
12. *St. Anne's.*
13. *St. Mary's.*
14. *Portland.*
15. *St. Thomas in the East.*
16. *St. David's.*
17. *St. Andrew's.*
18. *St. John's.*
19. *St. Thomas in the Vale.*

Spanish Town Church and Chapel are not in the *Jamaica* Historian's List, probably because as it is the Capital of the Island, it should not be confounded with common Parishes; but as the chief Precinct, it should have been in the Catalogue. We read in the late History of *Jamaica*, that there is a *Custos* over the Parishes, as Col. *Blair* Custos of *Spanish-Town*, Col. *Campbel* of St. *Elizabeth's*, &c. the Nature of the Office may be conjectured, but it is not defined. The Churches in the Town are generally in Form of a Cross with a small *Cupola*, the Walls pretty high. In that of St. *Andrew's* is an *Organ*, the Churches in general are no better than small Houses, scarce distinguishable from others. The Author adds, *The Clergy trouble themselves little, and the Church Doors are seldom opened.* What Pity it is, especially considering how many thousand Pounds yearly the *Jamaicans* pay for their *Churches* and their *Churchmen*. This Complaint is general all over the Colonies, and I never met with one reasonable Word said in Excuse of it.

Pag. 29.

Little is to be added to our History of *Jamaica* concerning the Inhabitants and Trade. The *Jamaica* Historian computes the Number of white Men able to bear Arms at about 17000, and the Negroes at about 100000 Men, Women and Children, and the white Men able to bear Arms, being as he says 17000, the Number of the whole may be computed at between 50 and 60000, a small Computation considering how long this Island has been in *British* Hands,

and

The History of Jamaica.

and how many Thousands have transported themselves and been transported thither since the Year 1656. The Publick Revenues of the Island are reckoned 70000 *l.* a Year. The Riches of particular Persons would be inconceivable, if one could give Credit to what the *Jamaica* Writer says of Mr. *Beckford* only, *Pag.* 267. *He is the richest Subject in Europe, he has twenty two Plantations in this Island, and upwards of* 1200 *Slaves, his Money in the Banks and at Mortgages is reckoned at a Million and a half.* As the Author makes Use of Words at Length and not of Figures, there can be no Mistake in the *summing,* if there is not a prodigious one in the Fact.

He assures us that 500 Sail of Ships are now imployed here in the Sugar Trade, each Ship carrying 200 Hogsheads which swells the Produce to 100000 Hogsheads of Sugar yearly, which doubtless is another Excess in Computation, and must be reduced to less than half. The *Assiento* or Agreement for the *South Sea* Company's Negro Trade to the *Spanish West-Indies* being now suspended, and not likely to be long continued without such Suspension, is not enlarged on here: The Sale of 4000 Slaves yearly would be very profitable to the *British* Subjects, was there any Security for the Returns.

Among the other Products of this Island, must now be reckoned *Coffee,* of which good Quantities are already shipped yearly for *England,* and probably it may produce enough in Time to answer more than the *British* Consumption. It were to be wished that the Affairs at Home did not make it necessary to load every Product of our *American* Colonies with such high Duties, so ruinous to Industry and Commerce.

It may not in this Place be improper to say something of the Trade carried on by the *English* at *Jamaica,* with the *Spaniards* on the Continent, which is thus managed. The Merchant or Master of the Ship bound for this Voyage, being furnished with a proper Cargo of dry Goods and *Negroes,* commonly makes first for the Coast near the Harbour of *Porto-Bello,* and in War Time at the *Grout* within *Monky-Key,* a very good Harbour within four Miles of the Town. From thence it was usual for the Merchant or Master of the Ship to send one who could speak *Spanish* as many of these Traders do, to the Town to give Notice of her Arrival to the Dealers, who appoint the Time and Place for the Ships Canoo to attend them. They come accordingly, and having purchased as many Negroes and as much dry Goods as they think fit, they return to the Town, fetch the Money, bring it aboard and take the Goods. Here such a Ship lies sometimes

Trade from Jamaica *with the Spaniards.*

times five or six Weeks trading with the *Spaniards*, for after the first Market is pretty well over, the Dealers who have soon Information of her being on the Coast, come from *Panama* over the Isthmus to trade, travelling like Peasants, with Mules bearing their Silver in Jars, and if any of the King's Officers meet them nothing appears but *Meal*, which they pretend to be carrying to *Porto-Bello*. But for the most Part they travel thro' Woods in Bye-Ways, for Fear of being discovered by those Officers. When they have bought what *Negroes* and Goods their Money will purchase, which they sell again up in the Country and get very well by it, the Goods are made up in little Packs fit for one Man to carry, and the *English* supply them with as much Provisions as will serve them Home cross the Isthmus to the *South Sea*, for they come far. An *English* Ship lying between *Chagre* and *Porto Novo*, a Signal was given her from the Castle of *Chagre*, and she anchored two Miles from it. The *Spaniards* came to her, and one Merchant bought 70 Negroes and a good Quantity of dry Goods, amounting to 3 or 4000 *l*. which was brought on Mules to the Water-side, Part Gold and Part Silver, from the *Grout*; the *English* Ship sailed to the *Brew* near *Carthagena*, where she lay to trade with the Merchants of that City, from which it is about eight Miles distant. The People of the Island *Brew* gave these Merchants Notice of her Arrival, and they came and traded as the others did at the *Grout*. This trading Ship in about two Months disposed of 150 Negroes and a good Cargo of dry Goods, by which probably the Proprietors cleared 2000 *l*. more than would have been got in any other Market; a plain Proof of the very great Advantage of this Trade between *Jamaica* and *New Spain*, of which we see the *Spaniards* are so fond, that they run as great Hazards in buying the Merchandize, as the *English* do in selling it to them.

Something has already been said of the Trade to the Bay of *Campeachy*, we must now add a Word or two of that to the Bay of *Honduras*.

Logwood cutting.

This Bay has a very difficult Entrance, the Bar being two or three Miles broad, with only 11 Feet Water. As soon as a Ship is entered, Guns are fired to give the Logwood Cutters Notice of her Arrival, and they soon repair to her to truck Wood for strong Liquors, as Madeira Wine, Rum, Spirits, Ozinbrigs, Hats and Shoes, of which 40 Shillings the prime Cost, will buy a Ton of *Logwood*. The Sailors go 30 Miles up the River to fetch it out of the Lagunes or Creeks in Canoos: The Logwood Cutters having picked out a Spot of Ground well furnished with Trees, build Huts

or

or rather Tents there of *Ozinbrigs*, which they find to keep out the Flies beft, they being fadly peftered with many Sorts all over that *Coaft* and *Country*. They cut down the Trees, bark them, log them, and make them fit for fhipping. The *Guarda la Cofta* Ships often difturb the Logwood Traders both in this Bay and that of *Campeachy*, but there are often fo many of them, that the *Spaniards* content themfelves with fpying them and leave them as they found them. Such Ships run great Danger both in and out of the Harbour, when the *Guarda la Cofta* is cruifing. This Logwood Trade and that of *Campeachy* is fo advantageous, and the *Spaniards* as we have feen have fo little Right to thofe Bays by Conqueft or Poffeffion (as we have fhewn in the Hiftory of the *Mufchetoes*, who plainly are the natural Lords of the Soil, and are very defirous the *Englifh* fhould have the Wood) that it is to be hoped the *Spaniards* by any future Treaty, fhall not have any Pretence left to difturb them in it.

THE

HISTORY

OF THE

Isle of *Providence*.

CONTAINING

An Account of its Discovery, Settlement, Climate, Soil, and all Events relating to it, to the present Times.

THIS Island is chief of those called the *Bahama-Islands*, and notwithstanding that Character is so inconsiderable in itself, that it had been well if it had never been discovered; for all the Advantage the Inhabitants can pretend it is to *England* or the other Colonies is, that it lies convenient for *Wrecks*; by which they mean to save such as are driven ashore there, and for Ships forced thither by Stress of Weather: And it being some Hundreds of Miles out of any Ship's regular Course, to or from any of our Colonies and *England*, it is certain we had never lost any Thing by it had it never been heard of.

The Island called *Providence* was discovered by Capt. *William Sayle*, who was afterwards Governor of *Carolina*. He was driven thither by a Storm, as he was on a Voyage to the *Continent*: From him it had the Name of *Sayle*'s Island.

This Adventurer returning to *England* about the Year 1667, gave his Employers, the Proprietaries of *Carolina*, an

Account

The History of Providence.

Account of his Discovery, and they procured a Grant for this and all the *Bahama-Islands* to themselves, their Heirs, &c. The Extent of their Grant reaches from 22 to 27 Degrees N. L. All the Proprietaries of *Carolina* were not concerned in the Grant of *Providence*, but all the Proprietaries of *Providence* were interested in that of *Carolina*. They were six in Number, and continue so to this Day. Their Names and Titles were,

George, Duke of *Albemarle*.   *Anthony*, Lord *Ashley*.
William, Lord *Craven*.   And
Sir *George Carteret*.   Sir *Peter Colliton*.
John, Lord *Berkley*.

Whose Heirs and Assignees enjoy it at this Time.

Providence Island lies in the Center of 4 or 500 Islands, some of them 160 Miles in Length; others no bigger than *Knolls* or little Rocks, rising above Water; so that one may imagine, it must be very dangerous for Ships to be forced among them in Tempests.

The most considerable Profit made by the Inhabitants of *Providence*, was by the Misfortune of poor Adventurers; either such as were shipwrecked, or such as in a Winter-Voyage for the *Continent* of *America*, were driven to the *Bahama-Islands*, and put into *Providence* for Provisions; which, after they had lain a long while beating off the Islands, they used to be in great Distress for Want of. 'Tis true, this Island had little or none but what came from *Carolina*, however, the Traders here kept Store-Houses to supply those that wanted, and they were a great Relief to the unfortunate Mariners of whom we are speaking.

As for Wrecks, the People of *Providence*, *Harbour-Island* and *Eleuthera*, dealt in them as it is said the good Men of *Sussex* do: All that came ashore was Prize, and if a Sailor had, by better Luck than the rest, got ashore as well as his Wreck, he was not sure of getting off again as well. This perhaps is Scandal, but it is most notorious, that the Inhabitants looked upon every Thing they could get out of a Castaway Ship as their own, and were not at any Trouble to enquire after the Owners.

The Isle of *Providence* lies in 25 Degrees N. L. is 28 Miles long, and 11 Miles broad where it is broadest. It had the Name of *Providence* given it by Capt. *Sayle*, after he had been a second Time driven upon it, when he was bound for the *Continent*.

The

The first Governor that was sent thither by the Proprietaries, was ―――― *Chillingworth*, Esq; The Time of his going there we cannot be certain in; it is probable it was about the Year 1672. Several People went from *England* and the other Colonies to settle there, and living a lewd licentious Sort of Life, they were impatient under Government. Mr. *Chillingworth* could not bring them to Reason: They assembled tumultuously, seized him, shipped him off for *Jamaica*, and lived every Man as he thought best for his Pleasure and Interest.

<small>―― Chillingworth, Esq; Governor.</small>

The Proprietaries found they had an unruly Colony to deal with, and it was a very small Encouragement for any one to put himself into their Hands, after the Treatment Mr. *Chillingworth* met with from them: However, six or seven Years after he was sent away, the Lords Proprietaries made ―――― *Clark*, Esq; Governor, whose Fate was worse still than his Predecessor's; for the *Spaniards* 30 Years ago, being jealous of every new Colony of the *English* towards the South, came upon them in the Isle of *Providence*, destroyed all their Stock, which they could not or would not carry off, and took the Governor away with them in Chains, having burnt the few Cottages that were upon the Place. The Inhabitants deserted it after this, and removed to other Colonies.

<small>―― Clark, Esq; Governor.</small>

Mr. *Trot*, one of Governor *Clark*'s Successors, informed the Writer of this Relation, that the *Spaniards* roasted Mr. *Clark* on a Spit after they had killed him; but perhaps that is said to encrease the Terror of the Story, and might do better in a *Poem* than a *History*. 'Tis certain they killed him, and that after this Invasion the Island was uninhabited till about the Time of the Revolution, when several Persons removed thither from *Europe* and the *Continent*; among whom was Mr. *Thomas Bulkley*, who has printed a large Account of his Sufferings there, during the arbitrary Government of one *Cadwallader Jones*, whom the Lord Proprietaries made Governor upon this second Settlement of *Providence* in the Year 1690. He arrived there the 19th of *June*, and was received by all the Inhabitants with the Respect due to his Quality: But says *Bulkely*, he soon discovered the *Weakness of his Judgment, the Wickedness of his Inclination, and his Disaffection to his Majesty's Person and Government*: For the Proprietaries of *Carolina* have not been unhappy in the Choice of their Governors in that Province only. My Author writes of this *Jones, That all his vile Practices were patiently born by the People, till they became so numerous and heinous as to be intolerable.*

<small>Cadwallader Jones Governor.</small>

<small>Appeal to Cæsar, p. 1.</small>

<small>Pag. 10 & seq.</small>

The Inhabitants groaning under the Oppression of this Governor, lived in an abominable Slavery; and that the Reader may form an Idea of the Tyranny of Governors in Proprietary Governments, we shall report some of the most material Crimes this Person was guilty of; and it is Pity his History is not an Example of Terror, to all such as under his Character commit the same Outrages against Reason, Justice, and Virtue.

He endeavoured to erect and maintain in himself an absolute unlimited Power, to govern according to his Will and Pleasure. He assumed royal Prerogatives, and arrogantly used the royal Stile. He confer'd Honours, and invested the Persons so dignified by him, with the Privileges of the Peers of *England*. He pardoned capital Offenders, seized the publick Treasure, wasted and converted it to his own Use. He neglected the Defence of the Island, imbezzled the Stores of Powder, converted the Lords Proprietaries Royalties to his own Use, invited the Pirates to come to the Port. He refused to take the Oaths to King *William* and and Queen *Mary* at his Entrance into his Office, when one of the Lords Proprietaries Deputies tendered them to him. In a Speech he made to the People he declared, *He would have a free Trade, and nothing to do with the King's damned Officers.* He intercepted Letters without Cause, put the most ignorant, indigent and vicious Persons into the greatest Offices of Honour, Power, and Trust. He highly caressed those Pirates that came to *Providence*. He arbitrarily imposed Fines on several Persons; he constituted himself Deputy to the Chief of the Lords Proprietaries, Treasurer, Provost-Marshal, and chief Secretary of the Province, and put his own Creatures into those Places under him. He commonly imprisoned Persons without Cause or Warrant. He denied to grant Writs of Process at Law, when desired against his Favourites, who were usually the *vilest of the People*. He refused to prosecute one of them, who had stoln 14 great Guns belonging to *New Providence*. He pardoned and discharged Pirates without Trial. He gave Commissions to Pirates without, and contrary to the Advice of the Council. *By Colour of one of these Commissions* (according to Mr. *Bulkley*'s Narrative) *a Ship belonging to* Bermudas, *being in* Pensylvania *River was piratically taken, and had been carried out to Sea, if some of the People of that Place had not gone out armed after the Pirates, and forcibly recovered the Vessel from them, they justifying their Villainy by their Commission and Instructions from the said* Jones.

He

He wilfully neglected to call a General Affembly, till fix Months after the Time appointed by the Lords Proprietaries Inftructions, and governed by Orders of a Juncto, which he imperioufly commanded the Affembly to pafs into Laws. While that Affembly was fitting, he directed his Son who was Captain of a Ship in the Port, to lay her fo as to bring all her Guns to bear upon the Houfe where the General Affembly was fitting. He abruptly diffolved them, while Matters of the greateft Importance to the Province were depending. He confpired with his Creatures and Pirates, to banifh fome of the moft virtuous and ufeful Inhabitants, without lawful Caufe or Trial. He faid, it was high Treafon to fign a Petition for the fitting of a General Affembly: In which one may fee, how petty *Plebeian* Tyrants agree with the fovereign imperial ones, in their Dread of Parliaments.

Thefe and many more flagitious Practices, are recorded by *Bulkley* againft *Jones*; and the People being no longer able to bear with him, Mr. *Bulkley* who was then Deputy Secretary, exhibited a Charge of High Treafon againft him, upon which he was feized and imprifoned.

Mr. Gilbert Afhley Prefident. The Government devolved upon the Council, and they declared Mr. *Gilbert Afhley* Prefident, putting out a Proclamation, requiring all the Inhabitants of the *Bahama-Iflands* to yield their ready Obedience to the faid Prefident. This Proclamation was dated the 24th of *January* 1692, and figned by two Deputies of the Lords Proprietaries, and five Affembly Men, who were alfo Counfellors; *viz.* by

Col. *Bowen Clawfon*,
Thomas *Comber*, Efq; } Deputies.

Mr. *Nicholas Spencer*,
Mr. *Thomas Higginbotham*,
Mr. *Ifrael Jones*,
Mr. *John Ogle*,
Mr. *George Dumarifque*, } Affembly-Men.

Jones being thus confined, himfelf and his Friends were alarmed, knowing the Inveteracy of the Accufer, and but too well the Guilt of the Accufed. The Governor defired the Council to permit him to go to Mr. *Bulkley*'s Houfe, and try if he could prevail with him to withdraw his Accufation. He was permitted; and coming to him, promifed to reftore him to all the Offices he had taken from him, to make Reparation of the Damage he had done him, to govern according to his Directions, nor do any Thing of a publick Nature without his Advice. After

The History of Providence. 427

After much Discourse, *Bulkley* replied, *He should have known in due Time, the Things that belonged to his own and the publick Peace and Prosperity, but now it was too late: That his Business was to make the best Preparation he could, to clear himself of the heavy Charge that lay against him;* which if he could do, it would be for his Honour as well as Safety, and the Law would give him Advantage enough against his Accuser, who neither expected nor desired any Favour from him in such a Case. *Bulkley* added, *he should incur Misprision of Treason, by complying with his Desires.* *Jones* answered, *Will you have my Heart's Blood?*

The Accusation against the late Governor was published, and Mr. *Bulkley* bound in 500 *l.* Bond to prosecute him. But *Jones* resolved to save them that Trouble; and to use the Words of his Accuser, *some desperate Rogues, Pirates and others,* gathered together an ignorant seditious Rabble, who on the 27th *of* February 1692, *with Force of Arms rescued the Governor, proclaimed him again, and restored him to the Exercise of his despotick Power.*

Now it was *Bulkley*'s turn to suffer. Whether guilty or not guilty, was not the Question? He was devoted to Persecution; and the same armed Rabble going to his House seized him, shut him up in a close dark Confinement, threatened him with the Torture, and forced him to deliver all the Books having any Relation to his Office of Deputy-Secretary.

The Leaders of this Rabble were,

Daniel *Jackson*.	Charles *Wainwright*.
Thomas *Wake*.	Samuel *Coverley*.
Thomas *Witter*.	Samuel *Dunscomb*.
Martin *Cock*.	Richard *Carpenter*.
Robert *Bolton*.	*Josias Ap Owen*.
Lancellot *Lawson*.	*Blackden Docden*.
William *Smith*.	And

Nathaniel Shepherdson, who was a Rebel to King *William*, having served his Enemies against his Subjects, and shared in the Booty the *French* took from the *English*; of which he was accused by two Witnesses, yet *Jones* permitted him to reside in *Providence*, to take a Man's Wife there, and live in open Adultery with her, if Mr. *Bulkley* may be credited. He was one of this Governor's Confidents, and a main Instrument of his Tyranny, as was also *Bartholomew Mercier*, a *Frenchman*; by whom *Bulkley* and his Wife were inhumanly used, insomuch

insomuch that the latter dying shortly after, declared solemnly on her Death-Bed before several Witnesses, and signed a Declaration to the same Purpose, that *Cadwallader Jones*, *Martin Cock*, *Bartholomew Mercier*, *Thomas Cumber*, *Robert Bolton* and others, were the Occasion of her Death.

John Graves arriving from *England* some Months after Mr. *Bulkley* had procured his Enlargement, upon delivering up his Books accused him of High Treason, for his Proceedings in the Accusation; and *Bulkley* was put in Irons aboard the Governor's Son's Ship, which was lately come from *Barbados*, tho' a pestilential Distemper was aboard.

This was not the worst of their Designs against Mr. *Bulkley*, they conspired to get him by Force aboard a Pirate's Ship, and the Pirate promised to make him away, by leaving him on some desolate Island or otherwise; which he having Notice of, hid in the Woods till the Pirate sailed.

Martin Cock also laid a Design to have him assassinated, which being discovered in Time was prevented. *Jones* then sent to *Harbour-Island* and *Eleuthera*, to see if he could pack a Jury to do *Bulkley*'s Business; which he could not do, the latter being looked upon to be a Sort of Confessor in his Country's Cause.

Bulkley was kept Prisoner till the Arrival of *Nicholas Trott*, Esq; with a Commission from the Lords Proprietaries, to be Governor in the Place of *Cadwallader Jones*. Mr. *Trott* allowed Mr. *Bulkley* a fair Trial, and he was acquitted. After which he charged *Jones* again with High Treason.

What Reason the new Governor had to give his Predecessor Leave to go off the Island, without coming to a legal Trial, we know not: The Fact is true, and to us there seems so much just Cause of Complaint against him, that he ought to have been brought to condign Punishment, for abusing the Power put into his Hands.

Bulkley pretended to have lost 4000 *l.* by the Persecution of this Governor *Jones*: But that seems a little improbable, for an Estate of 4000 *l.* is a Thing that has hardly been heard of in the *Bahama-Islands*.

When he came to *England*, he applied to the King by the Earl of *Portland*, and was ordered to leave all his Papers with Sir *William Trumball*, Secretary of State. What Redress he found we know not, and what he deserved let the Reader judge.

By this Time the Town at *Providence* was grown so considerable, that it was honoured with the Name of *Nassau*; and before Mr. *Trott*'s Government expired, there were 160 Houses: So that it was as big as the Cities of St. *James* and St. *Mary*'s, in *Maryland* and *Virginia*. The

The History of Providence.

The Harbour of *Nassau* is formed by *Hog-Island*, which belongs to Mr. *Trott*. It runs along parallel to it five Miles in Length, lying East and West. At the Entrance of the Harbour is a Bar, over which no Ship of 500 Ton can pass; but within the Bar, the Navy Royal of *England* might safely ride.

In the Town of *Nassau* there was a Church in Mr. *Trott's* Time, and he began a Fort in the Middle of it, which with his House made a Square. This Fort was mounted with 28 Guns and some Demi-Culvers.

In the Year 1695, the *Winchester* Man of War coming from *Jamaica* in Company with other Ships, drove off and on between the *Bahama Shoals* and *Cape Florida*, and had the Misfortune to run ashore on the Rocks called the *Martiers*, lying to the Southward of that *Cape*.

There never was a Man of War at *Providence*, unless *Avery's* the Pirate's Ship may be reckoned one, for it carried 46 Guns, and coming at a Time when the Inhabitants were in an ill State of Defence, it was to no Purpose for them to stand out against him. But by the Character we have had of the People of *Providence*, we cannot think that Pirate who was very rich, was unwelcome to them.

Mr. *Trott* assured the Author, there were but 70 Men at that Time upon the Island both able and disable, and *Avery* had 100 as stout Men aboard as ever he saw. If so, no Resistance the Governor could make, could be supposed to be strong enough to prevent the Pirate's beating down the Town, and taking that by Force, which when he was received as a Friend he paid for, and gave very good Rates to.

Thus we see in what the Trade of this Place chiefly consisted, and who frequented it most. 'Twas very unfortunate that there should be only 70 Men upon the Island at that Time, when a little before and a little after there were 200 Men, which was the greatest Number that could ever be mustered in the *Bahama-Islands*: For besides *Providence*, there are Settlements on *Harbour-Island* and *Eleuthera*. *Harbour-Island* is so called from the Goodness of the Harbour. 'Tis 20 Leagues from *Providence*, and has about 20 Houses upon it. *Eleuthera* is nearer, but has not so many Houses. Sometimes there are two or three Families on some of the other Islands.

The Inhabitants of these Islands, on Elections of Assembly-Men and other publick Occasions, go to *Nassau* in *Providence* to give their Votes. The Assembly consisted of 20 Members, chosen by the Inhabitants of all the Islands met together for that Purpose; for the Province not being divided

into

into Precincts, they had no other Way of choosing their Representatives.

The Fort which Mr. *Trott* built, was such a Security in his Time to the *Island*, that tho' the *French* landed several Times, they could make nothing of their Descent; but the Governor was so hard put to it for Want of Men, that half the People was always upon the Guard at a Time, and Duty was so long and came about so fast, the Inhabitants were terribly fatigued. The *French* made several Attempts in this Governor's Time, but were unsuccessful in all of them.

Mr. *Trott* continued in his Government till the Year 1697, at which Time the Lords Proprietaries nominated *Nicholas Webb*, Esq; Governor of the *Bahama-Islands*, and King *William* was pleased in Council to approve of their Nomination: By which we perceive his Majesty's Approbation was then thought necessary.

<small>Nicholas Webb, Esq; Governor.</small>

The Oaths appointed by the Acts of Trade and Navigation, &c. to be taken by the respective Governors of his Majesty's Plantations, were tendered to Mr. *Web* at the Council Board, and having taken them, he had the Honour to kiss his Majesty's Hand.

There happened nothing memorable in this Governor's Time: The Peace in *Europe* prevented Wars in *America*; Wrecks and Pirates were the only Hope of *Providence*, there being no Product to trade with except *Brasiletto* Wood and Salt. At *Xuma* in this Island, great Quantities of Salt were made, which the People exported to the *Continent* and other Islands.

Carolina being the nearest Colony to this, the People of *Providence* traded most thither. 'Tis about a Week's Sail to *Carolina*, and 10 Days Sail back, because of the strong Current in the Gulph of *Florida*. One would wonder why this Place should not produce Provisions sufficient for 1000 Souls, and more there never were there, since we have been told by a Gentleman who was Governor of *Providence*, that Pease came up in six Weeks Time, and *Indian* Corn in 12.

When this Island was in its most flourishing Condition, there were 3 or 400 Blacks upon it; and Mr. *Lightwood* attempted to set up a Sugar-Work, which he brought to some Perfection, the Soil being fertile but shallow. He built a Sugar-Mill, and others were preparing to follow his Example, when the *French* and *Spaniards* put an End to all their Projects.

<small>Lowth. Vol. II. p. 845.</small>

There have been Whales found dead on the Shore here, with a Sperm all over their Bodies; but my Author who had been upon the Place writes, he could never hear of any of that Sort that were killed by any, such is their Fierceness and

The History of Providence.

and Swiftness. One such Whale is worth many Hundred Pounds. They are very strong, and in-laid with Sinews all over their Body, which may be drawn out 30 Fathom long.

The Fish at *Providence* are many of them poisonous, bringing a great Pain on the Joints of those that eat them, which continues so for some short Time, and at last with two or three Days itching the Pain is rub'd off. Those of the same Species, Size, Shape, Colour, and Taste are one of them Poison, the other not in the least hurtful; and those that are, are only so to some of the Company. The Distemper never grows mortal to Men, Dogs and Cats are sometimes killed by it. In Men that have once had that Disease, upon the first eating of Fish tho' it be those that are wholesom, the poisonous Ferment in their Body is revived by it, and their Pain encreased.

Ibid.

Mr. *Richard Stafford*, whom we have mentioned in our Account of the *Bermudas-Islands* says, in some Observations of his communicated to the Royal Society. *Many rare Things might be discovered in* New Providence, *if the People were but encouraged. 'Tis stored with Variety of Fish and Fowl, and with divers Sorts of Trees and other Plants, whose Qualities are not yet known.*

Ambergreafe has been found here, but in no great Quantities; and the Inhabitants were never in a very thriving Condition.

The Governors talked as big as if they had been Vice-Roys of *Peru*; they told every one they had Power of Life and Limb, and could not bear to be thought dependent on the Government of *Carolina*, tho' it looked something like it: For the Proprietaries used, when any Difference happened between the People of *Providence* and their Governor, to send Orders to the Governor of *Carolina* to inspect Matters, and order them as they should think most convenient.

Here were Courts of Justice of all Denominations, as in *Westminster-hall*, and the Inhabitants were so litigious, that not a Burough in *Cornwall* could compare with them; which is the more amazing, because they had not much to quarrel for or to spare for Law.

To Mr. *Web* succeeded *Elias Hasket*, Esq; in the Government of the *Bahama-Islands*, about the Year 1700. He found an unruly People, and they were the more so, for few Wrecks had happened lately, and the Pirates began to spend their Money elsewhere. Whatever was the Occasion, the Inhabitants were in a little Time so out of Humour with Mr. *Hasket*, that they seized him, put him in Irons and sent

Elias Hasket, Esq; Governor.

sent him away, taking upon them to choose a Governor for themselves; and that Choice fell on *Ellis Lightwood*, Esq; in whose Time the Settlements were destroyed: For in *July* 1703, the *Spaniards* and *French* from *Petit Guaves* landed, surprized the Fort, took the Governor Prisoner, plundered and stripped the *English*, burnt the Town of *Nassau* all but Mr. *Lightwood*'s House, together with the Church, spoilt the Fort and nailed up the Guns. They carried off the Governor and about half the Blacks. The rest saved themselves in the Woods: But in *October* they came again, and picked up most of the Remainder of the Negroes.

Ellis Lightwood, Esq; Governor.

Mr. *Lightwood* having procured his Liberty by Exchange or Ransom, came to *Carolina*, and going off thence in a Vessel on some Adventure was never since heard of.

The *English* Inhabitants of the *Bahama*'s after this second Invasion, thought it in vain to stay longer; so they removed some to *Carolina*, some to *Virginia*, and some to *New-England*.

The Proprietaries however appointed ―――― *Birch*, Esq; to go over Governor of *Providence*; who not hearing that the Inhabitants had deserted the Island went thither, but finding it a Desert, he did not give himself the Trouble to open his Commission. He tarried there two or three Months, and was all that while forced to sleep in the Woods. After which he came back, and left the Place uninhabited, as it remains at present: But it is expected, that as soon as the Government of the Island is settled, and Measures taken to defend it, the Wrecks and other Advantages will tempt People to venture upon a third Settlement.

―*Birch, Esq; Governor.*

There was a Project on Foot, warmly sollicited by *John Graves*, one of *Bulkley*'s Persecutors, to get the Nomination of the Governor out of the Hands of the Proprietaries. We shall see how it was effected.

The Proprietaries then were,

William, Lord *Craven*, Palatine of the Island of *Providence*, &c.

Henry, Duke of *Beaufort*.
William, Lord *Berkley*.
John, Lord *Carteret*.
The Honourable *Maurice Ashley*, Esq;
Sir *John Colliton*, Baronet.

The History of Providence. 433

This and the other *Bahama-Islands* were looked upon to be so necessary for the Security of our Trade in the *West-Indies*, that the Parliament of *England* have not thought it unworthy of their Care, as well to have it cleared of Pirates, as to defend it against both *Spaniards* and *French*, who find its Situation very convenient to annoy or befriend their Commerce. In Queen *Anne's* War, both *Spaniards* and *French* overrun and plundered the *Bahama-Islands* twice, upon which in *March* 1714, at a Time when the Administration in *England* was in the Hands of those who had not its Interest, especially as to Commerce, very much at Heart. Yet the House of Lords addressed her Majesty, that the Island of *Providence* might be put into a Posture of Defence. Their Lordships observing, *It would be of fatal Consequence, if the* Bahama-Islands *should fall into the Hands of an Enemy*. They therefore humbly pray her Majesty to take the said Islands into her own Hands, and give such Order for their Security as in her royal Wisdom she should think fit. But nothing was done, and for the future Guidance of such as have it in their Power to do good Offices for our *American* Colonies, it is not improper to remember, that their Lordships four Years after took Notice of that Neglect, in an Address to his late Majesty King *George*. *There were not any the least Means used in Compliance with that Advice for securing the* Bahama-Islands, *and that then the Pirates had a Lodgment with a Battery on* Harbour-Island, *and that the usual Retreat and general Receptacle for the Pirates are at* Providence. Hereupon his Majesty was pleased to give Directions for dislodging these Pirates, and make Settlements and a Fortification for its Security and Defence.

Pursuant to this Address, Capt. *Woodes Rogers* was appointed Governor, the same Person which went with the Duke and Dutchess of *Bristol* to the *South Sea* and made a prosperous Voyage eight Years before. He sailed for *Providence* in *April* 1718, taking with him a naval Force for subduing the Pirates. In the mean Time Col. *Bennet* Governor of *Bermudas* sent a Sloop to that Island, requiring them to surrender themselves pursuant to the late Proclamation. The Pirates who were then on the Island very gladly accepted of the Mercy offered them thereby, and promised to surrender themselves as soon as they could get Passage to the *English* Colonies, adding they did not doubt but their Fellows, who were at Sea, would gladly do the same after their Example; accordingly Captain *Henry Jennings* and 15 others, immediately followed the Sloop to *Bermudas* and surrendered themselves, and Captain *Leslie* and Captain *Nichols* with a good Number of their Pirates,

Captain Woodes Rogers Governor.

rates, sent Word that they would also surrender. The above-mentioned Proclamation was brought hither by Capt. *Peers* in the *Phenix* Frigate, lately stationed at *New-York*. Besides the above, surrendered Capt. *Hornigold*, Capt. *Burges*, and in the whole as many of their Men as amounted to 114, which were followed by many more; however Piracy was not suppressed, nor did *Woodes Rogers* answer the Expectations of those that employed him, tho' at his Arrival here he seemed very zealous in the Service he was sent for. He arrived at *Nassau* in *Providence* in *July* 1718. *Vane* one of the Captains of the Pirates knowing what Errand he came upon, to reduce those Robbers by the Proclamation or by Force, caused a *French* Ship of 22 Guns which he had taken to be set on Fire, intending to make Use of her as a Fireship, to burn the *Rose* Frigate which came with *Woodes Rogers*; and indeed the *Rose* would have been in great Danger, had she not got off in Time by cutting her Cables. But *Vane*'s bold and rash Attempt could not have secured him, for besides the *Rose* there were at Hand the *Milford* Man of War, and the ——— aboard which was the Governor; these were soon after seen standing in for the Harbour of *Nassau*, upon which *Vane* and about 50 of his Men made off in a Sloop. The Governor sent a Sloop with sufficient Force after them, but the Pirates got off, and the *Milford* and the ——— ran aground coming into the Harbour, which shews its Entrance to be very dangerous, or the Pilot very ignorant or careless; one of the King's Ships being under his Pilotage, and aboard the ——— a Navigator, who ten Years before had rounded the World, as did Sir *Francis Drake*.

The 27th of *July*, Mr. *Woodes Rogers* came ashore, took Possession of the Fort, and caused his Majesty's Commission to be read in Presence of the Officers, Soldiers and about 300 People, whom he found there at his Arrival, which had been almost daily exercised in Arms for their Defence, in Case of Attack by *Spaniards* or *French*. As for the Pirates, they were not in so great Fear of them, most of them having been themselves of the Fraternity who had surrendered and made their Peace with the Government. *Woodes Rogers* brought with him above 100 Soldiers, and this joint Force, which was and might easily have been still farther recruited, was sufficient to secure the *Bahama-Islands* against any Enterprizes of the *French* and *Spaniards*.

Mr. *Rogers* set himself to regulate the Government, and restore Order in it which had been neglected several Years past. Of the Adventurers who came with him, six were nominated to be of the Council, as were also six of the In-

habitants

The History of Providence.

habitants who had never been Pirates themfelves, but one cannot conceive that in a Place where thofe Robbers were almoft always Mafters and always welcome, that any one of the Inhabitants had not rendered himfelf criminal in the Eye of the Law. Thefe Counfellors are diftinguifhed from the new Comers by the *Italick* Character.

The Governor and Council of the *Bahama-Iflands* in the Year 1719.

Captain *Woodes Rogers*, Governor.

Counfellors.

Mr. Robert Beauchamp. Mr. *Nathaniel Taylor.*
Mr. William Fairfax.   Mr. *Richard Thompfon.*
Mr. Wingate Gale.   Mr. *Edward Holmes.*
Mr. George Hooper.   Mr. *Thomas Barnard.*
Mr. Chriftopher Gale. Mr. *Thomas Spencer.*
Mr. Thomas Walker.   Mr. *Samuel Watkins.*

Judge of the Admiralty Mr. *William Fairfax.*
Captain of the Independent Company, Capt. *Woodes Rogers.*
Collector of the Cuftoms, Mr. *John Graves.*
Secretary Mr. *Richard Beauchamp.*
Chief Juftice and Regifter, Mr. *Chriftopher Gale.*
Provoft Marfhal, Mr. *William Watkins.*
Naval Officer, Mr. *George Hooper.*

Thefe Officers had their Powers from *England* directly.

As foon as the Governor and Council had fettled their Board, about 200 of thofe that had been Pirates furrendered themfelves to them, had Certificates of their Surrender, and took the Oaths of Allegiance, as did voluntarily the greateft Part of the Inhabitants of *Providence*; where in a few Years after, were computed to be near 1500 Souls. Out of thefe are formed three Companies of Militia, under Officers of their own Ifland. Thefe Companies take their Turn every Night in the Town Guard at *Naffau*, and the independent Company are always upon Duty in the Fort here, and another of eight Guns erected at the Eaftermoft Entrance into the Harbour. There is or was lately a Guard Ship in the Road well provided for Defence. If there is Deficiency in any of thefe Articles, every one of which is of the laft Importance, the concerned will doubtlefs take

Care

Care to have it amended. The Inhabitants did not only set their Negroes at Work upon the Repairs of Fort *Naſſau* and the erecting the other at the Harbour Mouth, but worked alſo themſelves upon the Forts and clearing the Ground within Gun-ſhot from Bruſhwood and Shrubs, as alſo paliſading the ſaid Forts which are or were in good Condition and very defenſible. The Number of Houſes are increaſed according to that of the Inhabitants, and are computed at near 300 in the Town of *Naſſau*. There are here great Convenience for Building, as Stone, Lime and Timber in Plenty; neither would there be any Want of Bread, the Soil being very productive of Corn was it well cultivated, nor of freſh Proviſions if the Inhabitants will by their Induſtry anſwer the Bounty of Nature.

At *Eleuthera-Iſland* are now about 60 Families. Here is a Company of Militia formed out of the Inhabitants, under Command of Mr. *Holmes* as Deputy Governor.

At *Harbour-Iſland* are about 70 Families and a like Company of Militia, under the Government of Mr. *Thompſon*, both theſe Governors being at their Eſtabliſhment Members of the Council of *Providence*. In each of theſe Iſlands is a ſmall Fort of ſix or eight Guns.

As a Proof of the ſtrong Propenſity of the People of this Iſland, to make their Market by Piracy, we muſt add, that *Vane* the Pirate before-mentioned, after his Eſcape from *Providence*, took two good Prizes belonging to *Carolina*. A *Merchant* of *Naſſau*, as he is called, having obtained Leave of the Governor to go a Turtling, went in a Sloop under that Pretence to trade with *Vane*, and accordingly traded with that Pirate; in queſt of whom was ſent from this Harbour Capt. *Hornigold* before-mentioned, who had been a Pirate himſelf: He found *Vane* too ſtrong for him, but he met with and took the *Turtling* Sloop, and the Merchant's illicite Trade being plainly proved, he was ſent in Chains to *England*.

We have mentioned that the Propriety of this and the *Bahama-Iſlands* was in the Proprietaries of *Carolina*, but by what legal Title they pretended to it, or what Reaſon they had to aſſert a Right, which their ſo little Care of the Iſlands was alone ſufficient to have vacated, we know not. The Government of *England* had been at a very great Expence for the Security and Improvement of theſe Iſlands, and as the original Right ſeems to be there lodged, we ſuppoſe a Grant of them was iſſued to the Lord *Londonderry*, Brother in Law to Earl *Stanhope*, which was litigated by the Lord *Craven*, in Behalf of the Proprietaries of the *Carolina* Charter.

The History of Providence.

Charter. I must confess it is in me against the Grain, to treat of transforming the Right of the Liberty and Property of *Englishmen* from one to another without their Consent, and very often against it by Grants and Charters for the Profit of particular Persons, very far from deserving them by their publick Services.

In the Year 1715, one Capt. *Juan de la Valle* Deputy of the *Spanish* Commerce, being sent by the Governor of the *Havana* to *Jamaica* to demand the Money fished up out of the wreckt *Flota's* on the Coast of *Florida* and the *Bahama-Islands*, pretended in a Memorial he delivered to the Governor and Council of *Jamaica*, that these *Bahama-Islands* belonged to the King of *Spain* and were Part of his Dominions. The Governor and Council say in Answer, *We can no Ways admit that the* Bahama-Islands *are Part of the Dominions of the King of* Spain, *but look upon the same to be his* Britannick *Majesty's*. A very just Answer, but not spirited enough to correspond with the Insolence of the *Spaniards* Claims. The *Dutch* and *French* have the same Right to the *Bahama-Islands* as the *Spaniards*, having been often thrown ashore and wrecked upon these Islands. If the seizing and possessing Part of them for a certain Time give a Title, the *English* have a good one to the best Parts and Places in the *Spanish West-Indies*. The pretended Claim of the *Spaniards* to the Empire of *America*, is exactly in the Spirit and Stile of their Countryman Don *Quixot*: The brave *Vernon* is now teaching them more Moderation and Sobriety in this Article.

The Inhabitants of *Providence* did for several Years make good Advantages of the *Salt Pans* in the *Bahama-Islands*, but the Disturbances and Changes here put a Stop to that Work, which we hear is now revived to the great Benefit of our Colonies.

Mr. *Rogers* before-mentioned, returned to *England* some Time after to solicite Recruits of all Kinds for this Colony, which as he told me himself he had great Hopes of obtaining. But whether it was he or his Successor Capt. *Fitzwilliams* that procured an independent Company to be sent thither we cannot tell. But certain it is such a Force was very necessary there, and indeed will always be so, considering the *Spaniards* and *French* look on the Possession of those Islands by the *English* with an envious Eye, not for the Beauty of the Country or the Fertility of the Soil, but for the Commodiousness of their Situation to annoy and distress them in their Navigation.

The History of Providence.

This independent Company of Soldiers continued there some Years, but having no Augmentation of Pay as in *Jamaica*, &c. they first murmured and then mutinied.

1736. Mutiny of the Soldiers. On the 27th of *March* 1736, a little after eight at Night, several Soldiers of this Garrison (who it seems for some Time before, had been combining to rise and take the Fort, in Order to facilitate their Dissertion) knocked down the Corporal and several Soldiers, who they imagined would not be of their Party, seized the Fort Gate, surprized the Centinels at their Posts and took Possession of the whole Garrison.

The Governor who was then in his own House drinking a Glass of Wine with two or three Gentlemen, being informed of this Mutiny by one of the Centinels who made his Escape over the Fort Wall, immediately snatched up a Sword, and ordered the Centinels that guarded his House in the Night to follow him, and ran down to the Fort, imagining that if he could by any Means get in with three or four People, his Presence would with the Loss of one or two, form a Party strong enough to overpower the Mutineers: But he no sooner approached the Fort Gate, and called out to one of the Serjeants who was just before him to endeavour to secure it, than half a Dozen Muskets were fired at him, whereupon he ordered those Soldiers he brought with him to return the Fire; which one of them had no sooner done, than a Volley was fired from the Bastions between which the Governor and the few People with him were, whereby the Serjeant beforementioned just before him was shot through the Arm, and many Places through his Clothes, and the Centinel almost close at his left Hand received a mortal Wound whereof he soon died, and the Gentlemen who followed the Governor from his House, being but a little Way from him were much endangered, for by this Time the firing from all Parts of the Garrison became general, occasioned it is believed by the Governor's being overheard to order People to run to some Buildings in the Town for Ladders, in order to endeavour to get over the Fort Walls.

The first Battle being over, and the Mutineers having secured all the Arms and Ammunition in the Fort, they began to fire the great Guns at two or three Vessels in the Harbour, with Design to make them come down near the Fort, and also at the Governor's House. In the mean Time he was getting as many of the Inhabitants as he could together in order to invest the Fort, but finding he could not suddenly get a sufficient Number of them to perform that Service, he had Recourse to a Stratagem, which was as follows. The Governor having detached Mr. *Stewart*, his Surgeon, with a few

The History of Providence.

few Men to reinforce and command a small Number of the People of the Country who were gone to the Magazine, went about a Mile to the Eastward of the Town, where Capt. *Charles* of this Island had removed a Scooner of his out of Sight of the Fort, and on Board this Vessel the Governor put some Powder and Ball, brought on Purpose from the Magazine, and ordered about 35 chosen Men of the Island to be under the Command of Capt. *Walker* and Mr. *Sam. Lawford*, with Directions to get under Sail at a Moment's Warning; for by this Time the Governor had Notice that about 18 of the Mutineers had seized a small Sloop in the Harbour, and that a Party of them had broke open the common Jail and taken out a *French* Seaman (committed a Week before for endeavouring to carry off some Soldiers) to be their Pilot, and that they purposed farther to get the Governor into their Possession if possible. But finding themselves disappointed in this last Part of their Scheme, and having been repulsed at the Magazine which they went to blow up, they to the Number of 42 broke open the Provision Storehouse and a Place where there was some new Clothing (and having equipped themselves and the Sloop, and nailed up some of the Guns that pointed to the Harbour's Mouth) went on Board, and set sail about three a Clock the next Morning; at the same Instant Capt. *Walker* weighed, pursued and kept in Sight of them all Night, without being seen by them till Day Light, which was such a Surprize and bred such a Confusion among them, that they were soon taken without any Damage or Loss on either Side.

Upon this they were carried back, and the next Day every Man of them was convicted and sentenced to Death, 12 of the most notorious and the *French* Pilot were forthwith executed, the latter at the Mast Head of his own Vessel.

These poor Wretches declared upon their Death, that they intended to spill no more Blood than might happen in their own Defence, and that their View in attempting to take the Governor, was only to secure him and thereby their own Escape, and Mr. *Stewart*, as being one always active to execute the Governor's Commands on Emergencies of this Kind, their whole Design being only to get from a Place where the Pay is scarce sufficient to support human Nature, there being no additional Allowance for them here as in *Jamaica* and other Places.

THE HISTORY OF THE BERMUDAS OR Summer-Islands.

CONTAINING

An Account of the Discovery, Settlement, Growth, and present State of the Colony: A Description of the Country, Climate, Soil, Productions, &c.

THE first Mention we find any where made of these Islands by *English* Authors, is in Captain *Lancaster*'s Voyage for Discoveries in the *East-Indies* in 1593. The Captain sent one *Henry May* to *England* from *Hispaniola*, having obtained Passage for him aboard a *French* Ship, commanded by Monsieur *de Barbotiere*, who was driven ashore on the Island commonly called *Bermudas*; and this was the first of our Countrymen who had been upon it.

As to the first Inhabitants, it is very probable there were none before the *English*, the Place being so far from any Part of the Continent of *America*, that the *Indians* did not understand Navigation enough to reach it.

Oviedas

The History of Bermudas.

Oviedas writes, he was near *Bermudas*, and had Thoughts to have set some Hogs ashore for Encrease, but he was driven thence by Tempests, it being extremely subject to furious Rains, Lightning and Thunder.

The Name of *Bermudas* is said to be given them from *John Bermudas* a *Spaniard*, who discovered them in his Way to the *Spanish West-Indies*, several Years before Mr. *May* was cast ashore there; but we do not read that he landed upon any of them, tho' it is certain the *Spaniards* had been on Shore, not willingly but forced by Shipwreck: And indeed several Wrecks of Ships were found in the Water among the Rocks, which were easily known to be some *Spanish*, some *Dutch*, some *Portuguese*, and some *French*; and in the Year 1572, King *Philip* gave them to one *Ferd. Camelo*, who never took Possession.

Mr. *May* and his Company having a little refreshed themselves on the biggest of these Islands, which now goes by the Name of St. *George*'s, when the Weather permitted got off their broken Ship, to see what they could save out of her, and with the Remains of that Vessel and the Cedar they felled in the Country, they built a new Ship; and after various Adventures, arrived at the several Ports of *Europe* to which they belonged.

This *May*'s Relation of these Islands occasioned their being talked of, and Sir *George Sommers* and Sir *Thomas Gates* suffering the same Fate there in the Year 1609, revived the Discourse of them, yet no Body thought it worth their while to adventure thither, till after Sir *George*'s second landing and breathing his last there.

We have spoken of Sir *George*'s being shipwrecked on these Islands, where two Women that were delivered, the one of a Boy who was christened *Bermudas*, and the other of a Girl who was named *Bermuda*: We have related how he and his Companions got off in the History of *Virginia*, whither he was bound: We have also hinted how he was sent by the Lord *de la Ware* to fetch Provisions hence for the *Virginians*, *Bermudas* abounding in Hogs and Turtles. Sir *George* mist the Coast, and fell in with that of *Sagadahoc* in *Norembegua*, where he took in fresh Water and Provisions, and proceeded in Search of these pleasant and fruitful Islands: At last he found them, and being extremely harassed with the Fatigues of the Sea above what his great Age, upwards of threescore Years, could bear, he died as soon as he came ashore.

'Twas observable, that the Vessel he went in had not an Ounce of Iron about it, except one Bolt in her Keel, and all her Timber and Planks were of Cedar. From

From him these Islands are called *Sommer's-Isles*, which our Mariners, very dextrous in corrupting Terms and Names of Places, call the *Summer-Islands:* A Name they very well deserve indeed, on Account of their Pleasantness and Fertility.

Sir *George* enjoined his Men to return to *Virginia* with black Hogs, for the Relief of that Colony; but they resolved otherwise after his Death, and storing their Cedar Ship with such Provisions as they had, they set sail for *England,* where they arrived at *White-Church* in *Dorsetshire* having Sir *George Sommers*'s Corpse aboard, only the Heart and Bowels they left at *Bermudas,* where Capt. *Butler* 12 Years afterwards built a handsom Monument over them.

These Persons at their Return gave such an Account of the Country to the *Virginia* Company, that they thought it worth their while to establish a Correspondence between *England* and it; accordingly they sold these Islands to 120 Persons of the same Society, who obtained a Charter of King *James* and became the Proprietors of them.

We must not omit relating the following Part of this History, tho' it seems a little too romantick to be true; but since we find it reported as a Truth, we think fit to let the Reader know and judge of it for himself, without trusting to our Sentiments.

'Tis said, that when Sir *George Sommers* was first here, two of his Men stayed behind him; these having committed some Crime, for which they would have been put to Death if they had gone, fled into the Woods, and would not accompany him to *Virginia.* They were still here when Sir *George* returned, and had ever since his Departure supported themselves on the Productions of the Place, such as it naturally yielded; they had built them a Hut, and taken Possession of St. *George*'s Island.

These two Men, whose Names were *Christopher Carter* and *Edward Waters,* stayed still behind Sir *George*'s second Company, of whom they persuaded one *Edward Chard* to remain there with them; and now *Carter, Waters* and *Chard,* were sole Lords of the Country, but like the Kings of the World they soon fell out among themselves; *Chard* and *Waters* were coming to a pitched Battle, but *Carter,* tho' he hated them both, yet not liking to be left alone prevented it, by threatning to declare against the Man who struck the first Stroke: At last Necessity made them good Friends, and they joined together in making Discoveries; in one of which Expeditions they found the greatest Piece of Ambergrease among the Rocks, that ever was seen in one Lump, weighing 80 Pound,

The History of Bermudas.

Pound, besides other smaller Pieces. This Treasure made them almost mad. The Value of it turned their Heads, they grew giddy with the Thoughts of it, and that they might have an Opportunity to make Use of it, resolved on the most desperate Attempt that Men in Distraction could run upon, which was to build a Boat after the best Manner they could, and sail to *Virginia* or *Newfoundland*, according as Wind or Weather should present. But before they could put their extravagant Project in Execution, a Ship arrived from *England*; for Capt. *Matthew Sommers*, Sir *George*'s Brother, had promised to come to them or send a Vessel to their Relief, or they had not stayed neither the first Time nor the last. The Ship they discovered standing in with the Shore was the *Plough*, which had 60 Persons aboard, sent by the *New Bermudas Company* to make a Settlement, over whom they placed one Mr. *Richard Moor* for Governor; who was an honest industrious Person. He pitched upon a Plain in St. *George*'s Island to settle on, and there first built himself a House or rather Cabin, for the Building was only of *Palmeto* Leaves, yet he made it large enough for him, his Wife and Family; and the rest of the Adventurers following his Example, it became a Sort of a Town, which in Time grew to a considerable Bigness, and is now St. *George*'s Town, one of the strongest and best built in all our *American* Colonies, for the Houses are of Cedar, and all the Forts of hewn Stone.

1612. *Mr. Richard Moor, Governor.*

Mr. *Moor* was a Man of ordinary Condition, being but a Carpenter. He was a good Architect and Engineer, and fitter in the Infancy of the Colony for the Post he was in, than an unexperienced Gentleman would have been. He spent the most Part of his Time in fortifying the Islands, and carried on the Work of the Plantation with all imaginable Zeal and Capacity. He drew out the Model of the Town as it stands at present. He trained the People in martial Exercises, built 9 or 10 Forts, and furnished them all with Ammunition. He also built a Church of Cedar, which being blown down by a Tempest, he raised another of *Palmeto* Leaves, in a Place better sheltered from the Weather.

In the first Year of his Government, another Ship arrived with a Recruit of Provisions and 30 Passengers. He by this Time had found out the Booty of Ambergreafe, which *Carter*, *Waters* and *Chard* had concealed, and seized it as belonging to the Proprietors. He sent one third of it to the Company at *London* by the Ship that brought the Supply, and the rest by the next Opportunities that offered, in the same Proportion; which gave such Encouragement to the Adventurers,

turers, that they continued to supply them with Provisions, Stores, and more Company, till they were in a Condition to defend and support themselves by their own Strength and Plantations.

Mr. *Moor* made very good Returns Home in Ambergreafe, Drugs, Cedar, Tobacco, and the Product of the Islands.

1614. In the third Year of his Government the *Spaniards* shewed themselves on the Coast, with a Design to supplant them; but finding them better provided to receive them than they imagined they were, they bore away after the *English* had fired two Shot at them; tho' had they made an Attack then, they had probably ruined the Settlement, Powder falling so short that there was not a whole Barrel in St. *George's*, the Game having consumed that Part of their Stores.

'Twas also in the Time of this Governor that the famous *Rat Plague* began in *Bermudas*, which lasted five Years. They came thither in the Ships, and multiplied so prodigiously ashore, that such Numbers were hardly ever seen in the World. They had Nests in every Tree, and all the Ground was covered with them. They eat up the Fruits, and even the Trees that bore them. They devoured the Corn within Doors and without, and neither Cats, Dogs, Traps, nor Poison, availed any Thing towards clearing the Country of them. They not only swarmed in St. *George's* Island, but in many of the other whither they swam over, and made the same Havock of every Thing that lay in their Way. At last they disappeared all on a sudden, and went as strangely as they came.

'Tis remarkable, that during this Rat Plague there were seen vast Numbers of Ravens in the Island, which had not been observed to be there before or since.

When the three Years of Mr. *Moor's* Government were expired, Capt. *Daniel Tucker* was sent over to succeed him.

Capt. Daniel Tucker, Governor. This Gentleman much encouraged the improving of the Soil, the planting of Tobacco, and did all Things he could think of to promote the Good of the Colony, which he saw brought into a flourishing Condition before he left it.

The Houses that were built of *Palmeto* Leaves, were for the most Part taken down, and others of Stone raised in their Places, several Fruit Trees were planted, Fields and Woods cleared of Rubbish, and a regular Form of Government established. But the Severity of his Discipline was so grievous to some licentious Persons, that five of them executed as desperate a Design to escape him as *Waters* and his Companions had projected to get away from the Island. They knew the Governor would not give them Leave to go off, and

The History of Bermudas.

and therefore invented this Contrivance to effect it: Hearing Capt. *Tucker* had a great Desire to go a fishing out at Sea, but was afraid to do it, because several Fisher-Boats had been driven off by the Weather and the Men perished, they proposed to him to build a Boat of two or three Tuns for him with a Deck, and so fitted that she should live in all Weathers. The Governor consenting to it, they fell to building it in a private Place, pretending it was convenient for their getting Timber and launching the Boat. They finished it sooner than it was expected, and the Governor sent Hands to fetch it, intending to go in it aboard a Ship which he was then dispatching for *England*. When his Men came to the Place, neither the Boat nor the Builders were to be found. All that they could hear of them was, that the Boat being finished the Night before, those that built it went off to Sea in it to try how it would sail. At last they found by some Letters they left behind them, that they were gone for *England*. And the Story of their Adventure is told us in this Manner: They borrowed a Compass-Dial of a Neighbour on some Pretence or other, and went aboard the Ship bound for *England*, where they trucked with the Seamen such Things as they had on Board for Provisions. One of them at parting told the Mariners, that *tho' they were forbidden to go with them, yet they hoped to be in* England *before them*: At which the Master of the Ship laughed; and away these fearless Adventurers sailed, with fair Wind and Weather for one and twenty Days. They then met with a Storm which reduced them to Extremity for eight and forty Hours; and obliging them to bear up afore it, drove them a little out of their Course to the Westward; but the Wind coming fair again and continuing so ten Days, they went on chearfully. In that Time they met with a *French* Privateer, where they went aboard to beg some Relief; but instead of helping them, he plundered them of the little they had, took away even their Instrument of Navigation and turned them adrift. In this miserable Condition they sailed on, growing daily weaker and weaker. Their Provisions were almost spent, their Fire-Wood quite gone, not a Drop of fresh Water left, nor Food for above a Day, when at last in the very Hour they expected to perish, they made Land to their unspeakble Joy. This Land was *Ireland*, where they went ashore in the County of *Cork*, and were nobly entertained by the Earl of *Thomond*, to whom they related their Voyage which lasted 42 Days.

The Men were Mr. *James Barker*, a Gentleman; *Richard Sanders*, the Contriver of the Design; *William Goodwin* a Ship Carpenter, chief Builder of the Boat; *Thomas Barker* a Join-a Joiner; and *Henry Puet* a Sailor, whose Enterprize was so daring, that it may well recommend their Names to Posterity.

<small>1619.
Capt. Butler
Governor.</small>
Capt. *Tucker* resigned his Government in the Year 1619, to Capt. *Butler*, who arrived there at that Time with four good Ships, in which he brought at least 500 Passengers, and there being as many *English* already on the Island, the Colony began to make a considerable Figure; and the more, because the *English* had not any so numerous in *America*, nor indeed any other except that at *Virginia*, and a small Settlement in *New-England*.

Capt. *Butler*, as has been hinted, raised a noble Monument over the Remains of Sir *George Sommers* that were left in the Island, depositing them in the Church at St. *George*'s Town, with an Inscription in *English* Rhimes as barbarous as the Place he then governed.

He divided the Islands into Districts; and now the Government, by Governor, Council and Assembly was established, which before had been only by Governor and Council. The Laws of the Country were also settled as near as the Circumstances and Conveniencies of the Place would admit, to the Laws of *England*, as is done in all the Colonies in *America*.

<small>Mr. Bernard
Governor.
1622.</small>
When the three Years of Capt. *Butler*'s Government were out, the Proprietors sent over one Mr. *Bernard* to supply his Place.

The Country did not agree with this Gentleman, as it had done with his Predecessors; for in less than six Weeks after his Arrival he died, and the Council made Choice of Mr. *Harrison* to preside till the Arrival of a new Governor or fresh Orders from *England*.

<small>Mr. Harrison President.
M Delaet calls him Woodhouse.</small>
The Settlement was so well peopled, that in this Gentleman's Presidency there were reckoned three thousand *English*; and their Affairs went on prosperously then, having no less than 10 Forts and 50 Pieces of Cannon mounted.

We have had so little Acquaintance with, and Information of these Islands, that we cannot pretend to continue the Succession of the Governors, nor give a large History of the Events that happened under their Government. 'Tis true there have not been many, and had our Information been the best that is to be procured, we know enough of the *Bermudas-Islands* to be very well satisfied, that much could not be said of them.

The most considerable Person that ever visited these Islands, was *Edmund Waller*, Esq; a Proprietor of them, one of the most gallant Men, and one of the finest Wits in the Courts of King *Charles* the Ist and King *Charles* the IId;

and one of those to whom Mr. *Dryden* confessed he owed the Harmony of his Numbers.

This Gentleman being a Man of Fortune as well as Wit, was chosen a Member of the *Long Parliament*; and at first fell in with the Party against the King, tho' he afterwards entered into the Conspiracy against the Parliament, for which Mr. *Chaloner* and Mr. *Tompkins* were executed; but Mr. *Waller* got off for a Fine of 10000 *l.* and Banishment. After which he went to the *Bermudas-Islands*, where he stayed some Time, and from thence to *France*. When *Oliver* prevailed, Mr. *Waller* returned to *England*.

By his being in this Country, *Bermudas* has the Glory to be sung by one of the most harmonious Poets that ever beautified the *English* Tongue; and that is an Honour to which none of the other Islands, or any Part of the *American* Continent can pretend.

The Inhabitants of this Island were never any great Traders. They contented themselves with what they could raise out of the Earth for their Subsistence, and found enough for Nourishment and Pleasure.

The Healtiness of the Air invited several Persons from other Places, and by this Means it was computed that about 20 or 30 Years ago, there were 8 or 10000 Souls of *English* Extraction. Whether that Number has diminished since we cannot tell; but we are inclined to believe it is rather less than more.

The Government in King *William*'s Reign, sent over a very loyal Address; as also the *Association*, signed by the Governor, Council, Assembly, and principal Inhabitants, which Sir *William Trumball*, then Secretary of State, presented to his Majesty *Feb.* 15, 1696.

The King, two Years afterwards, was pleased to appoint *Samuel Day*, Esq; to be Governor of these Islands; who embarked aboard the *Maidstone* Man of War in *May*, and arrived in *July* at St. *George's*. He either was recalled or died in his Government in two Years Time, for in 1700, Capt. *Bennet* was made Governor of his Majesty's *Bermudas* or *Summer-Islands*: Of which we can say little more, except what relates to the Geographical or Natural Account of them; and we therefore proceed to it, hoping it will make some Amends for what we fall short of in the History.

We come now to the Geographical Description of these Islands, and the other Parts of our Account of them.

There are such a vast Number of them, that most of them yet want a Name, and indeed are so small, they are not worth it. Some Writers say there are 300 of them,

The History of Bermudas.

others 400, and others 500; but not to stand to determine what is transmitted to us with so much Uncertainty, we shall only venture to be positive in that they are above 400, because the major Part of the Writers who make any Mention of them agree in that Point.

From Spain 1000 Leagues, from London 1100, from Roanoke 500. Del.

They lie some Hundreds of Leagues from any Land; the nearest Part of the *Continent*, which is *Cape Hattoras* in *Carolina*, being 300 Leagues from them, the Island of *Hispaniola* 400, *Madeira* 1000, and *England* 1600; their Latitude is between 32 and 33 Degrees N. L.

The Eighth Part of them are not inhabited; and all but St. *George's*, St. *David's*, and *Cooper's Isles*, have only a few Houses scattered up and down. They all together make the Figure of a Crescent, and are within the Circuit of six or seven Leagues at most. There are none of them of any considerable Bigness, yet some much bigger than others, as Time and the Sea continually washing upon them, have worn them away in different Proportions.

The Main or great Island of all is called St. *George's*, and is about 16 Miles in Length from E. N. E. to W. S. W. 'Tis not a League over in the broadest Place, but is fortified by Nature all around, the Rocks every Way extending themselves a great Way into the Sea. To which natural Strength, especially towards the Eastward where it is most exposed, the Inhabitants have added that of Forts, Batteries, Parapets and Lines; the Cannon of the Forts and Batteries being so disposed, as to command the several Channels and Inlets into the Sea.

There are no more than two Places where Shipping may safely come in, and it is not easy for a Man to find those Places out. The Rocks lie so thick in such a Manner, and some so undiscovered, that without a good Pilot from the Shore, a Vessel of 10 Tuns would not find the Way into those Harbours; which being once known, the biggest Ships in the World may enter. These two Havens are so fortified, that if an Enemy should light of them, he might easily be kept out.

The Rocks in most Places appear at low Water. It ebbs and flows there not above five Foot; the very Shore itself is for the most Part a Rock, and it is impossible to find out an Island better guarded by Rocks than this; indeed they are all of them so invironed with them, that they seem to threaten all Ships who venture on that Coast with present Destruction; and so many have been shipwrecked upon them, that the *Spaniards* gave them the Name of *Los Diabolos*, the Devil's Islands; this Place having been fatal to them and all Nations.

The

The History of Bermudas.

The Town of St. *George*'s stands at the Bottom of the Haven of the same Name, which has no less than six or seven Forts and Batteries; as *Kings Castle*, *Charles Fort*, *Pembrook Fort*, *Cavendish Fort*, *Davyes Fort*, *Warwick Fort*, and *Sandy*'s *Fort*, mounted with above 70 Pieces of Cannon; and they are so disposed, that they can be all brought to bear upon any Ship before she can make her Entrance.

In this Town there is a fair Church with a fine Library, for which the Inhabitants are indebted to Dr. *Thomas Bray*, the Patron of the *American* Learning. There are near a Thousand Houses in it; it is very handsomly built, and has a State-House for the Meeting of the Governor, Council and Assembly.

Besides the Town and Division of St. *George*'s, there are eight Tribes, *Hamilton Tribe*, *Smith*'s *Tribe*, *Devonshire Tribe*, *Pembrook Tribe*, *Paget*'s *Tribe*, *Warwick Tribe*, *Southampton Tribe*, and *Sandy*'s *Tribe*; of which *Devonshire* in the North, and *Southampton* in the South are Parishes, have each a Church and a particular Library. In the whole Island there are Plantations of Oranges, Mulberries, and other Productions of the Country, which render it a very beautiful Prospect.

There is a Haven in *Southampton* Tribe or District, which is also called *Southampton*, and other Harbours; as the *Great Sound*, *Harrington*'s *Inlet* in *Hamilton Tribe*, *Paget*'s *Port* in *Paget*'s *Tribe*, and others.

There are no Parish-Churches in any of the lesser Islands, and all of the Inhabitants are ranged under one or the other of the eight Tribes.

As to the Climate, it was for fourscore Years reckoned one of the healthiest Countries in the World; and the sickly used to remove thither from the *Sugar Islands* in *America*, as they do from the Northern Parts of *France* to *Montpellier* for the Air. But within this 20 Years there have been dreadful Hurricanes, which have had such an ill Effect on the Air, that the *Bermudas-Islands* have had their Share of Sickness as well as the *Antilles* and the *Charibbees*. However the Face of the Heavens, the Serenity and Beauty are still the same. The Weather is generally fine and pleasant, and the Air temperate and calm.

Here is a Sort of perpetual Spring, and tho' the Trees throw off their old Leaves, there are new ones always coming out at the same Time. The Birds breed all the Year round, or at least in most Months, and the Country is alike *fruitful and charming, yet not so much more charming and fruitful*

Hæ Insulæ n c Cœli, nec Soli bo- ntate cum via (Anglia) ullo modo sint compa- randæ. Del. fruitful than England, as to tempt People who can live here, to transport themselves thither.

'Tis true, the Thunders and Lightnings are here very dreadful, Rocks having been split asunder by the latter. The Storms come with every new Moon, and it is particularly observed, that if a Circle is seen about the Moon, a prodigious Tempest certainly follows. These Circles are larger there than any where else, and the Storms are more terrible. The N. and N. W. Winds are most predominant, and when they blow turn Summer into Winter. The Rains are not frequent but violent, and the Sky is then darkened in a frightful Manner. Seldom any Snow is to be seen there. The Soil of the Isle of St. *George*'s and the other Islands, are of several Colours and Tempers; the Brown is the best; the Whitish which is like Sand, the next to it; and the Red, which resembles Clay the worst. Two or three Foot under the Mould lies a solid white Body, which the Inhabitants call the *Rock*, tho' with very little Reason, for it is as soft as Chaulk and porous like a Pumice-Stone. Those Pores contain Abundance of Water, and as much a Rock as it is, the Trees fasten their Roots in it, and draw their nourishing Sap from it. Clay is often found under it, and the hardest Kind of this Rock is met with under the red Mould; in this there's little or no Water, and it lies in the Ground in Quarries, like thick Slates one upon another.

There's rarely any fresh Water in these Islands, what they have comes through the Pores of the Slate or Rock; in which there are as many salt Particles as in that which comes from the Sea after it has soaked through the Sand. These two Sorts of Water are all they have, except Rain Water caught in Cisterns. Both of the other Sorts are a little brackish.

The *English* have dug several Wells within four or five Paces of the Sea, that held a Correspondence with the Sea, and ebbed and flowed as that did; yet the Water was as fresh as that which was drawn up farther within Land.

The Soil is very fruitful and yields two Crops a Year, for what they sow in *March* they gather in *July*; and what they sow in *August*, in *December*; and the chief Product of the Country is Maize or *Indian* Corn, the common Grain of *America*, which is the main Support of the People.

Their Fields yield Abundance of other Plants; as Tobacco, not a very good Sort, and consequently of no great Advantage to them. They have most Kinds of other Plants, which are peculiar to the *West-Indies*, and such as are brought from *Europe*, and are cultivated there, thrive to Perfection. They
also

alſo have the *Poiſon Weed*, which is like *Engliſh* Ivy, and the Touch of it cauſes a Pain and Tumour for the preſent, but it goes off again as the *Red Reed*, the Juice of whoſe Root is a forcible Vomit. The *Sea Feather* grows upon the Rocks at the Bottom of the Sea, like a Vine Leaf but broader, with Veins of a paliſh Red. Excepting the *Poiſonous Weeds*, there's no venomous Thing in theſe Iſlands, neither among Animals nor Vegetables, and if any venomous Beaſt is brought thither it will not live. Some Lizards were ſeen before the Wild Cats, bred in the Time of the Rat Plague, deſtroyed them. But theſe Lizzards had no Poiſon in them ; neither have their Spiders any, tho' they are of a large Size, of which we ſhall have Occaſion to ſpeak more in this Chapter. * We have run over their Fields and muſt now viſit their Foreſts, where we firſt find the Glory of *Libanus* of old.

The Cedar is a finer Tree than any of the Sort in the other Parts of *America*. 'Tis harder and more durable, will bear the Extremities of wet and dry Weather as well as Oak, is found to be an extraordinary Timber for Shipping, and they build the beſt Sloops, Brigantines, and ſuch like Veſſels at *Bermudas*, of all the *Weſt-Indies* either for Service or Sailing.

Theſe Trees *Palmetos*, *Pepper Trees*, bearing a Fruit like our *Barberries*, *Laurel*, *Olive Trees*, *Mulberry Trees*, and many others, for which the *Engliſh* knew no Names, were the natural Growth of the Iſland.

Their *Palm Tree* is a Sort of wild Palm, reſembling the true *Indian* Palm in all Things but the Fruit, which is black and round like a Damſin. 'Twas obſerved, that Abundance of Silk Worms lodged in their Leaves, and there being alſo great Plenty of *Mulberry Trees*, the Silk Manufacture might have been improved more than it is, had the Inhabitants known their Intereſt or purſued it better.

There are great Variety of odoriferous Woods, ſome black, ſome of a yellow, and ſome of a red Colour. The Berries of theſe Trees have the ſtyptick Quality of a Sloe, and are much uſed by the *Engliſh* to cure the Flux, which they frequently get by eating the luſcious Palm Berries too greedily.

Their other Fruits are *Dates* ; their *Prickled Pear* like an *Engliſh Katharine* in Shape and Size, full of Juice like a *Mulberry*: It grows upon the Rocks. And near the Sea-ſide is found a Kind of *Woodbind*, bearing a Fruit reſembling a Bean, and another Shrub like a Bramble, whoſe Fruit is a hard tough Berry in a hard Shell.

The moſt famous Fruit, and one of the moſt delicious in the *Univerſe* is their Orange, much larger than any that grow elſewhere of ſuch a Fragrancy both in Taſte and Smell,

that

that it may compare with the richest Fruit in the World.

There grows a Berry in *Bermudas* called the *Summer-Island Redwood*, which Berry is as red as the *Prickle Pear*, giving much the like Tincture. Out of which Berry come first Worms, which afterwards turn into Flies, somewhat bigger than the Cochineal Fly, feeding on the same Berry. In which it is said, there has been found a Colour nothing inferior to that of the Cochineal Fly, and a medicinal Virtue much exceeding it.

<small>Lowth. Phil. Tranf. *Vol.* II. *p.* 784.</small>

As for the Animals in these Islands there were none but Hogs, Insects and Birds, when Sir *George Sommers* was shipwrecked there. He found out that there were some Hogs in the Island, by sending out two or three of his own to feed, and when they rambled Home a huge wild Boar followed them, and being killed was found to be excellent Meat.

The Hogs they killed afterwards were all black, and from thence it is concluded that the *Spaniards* had left them there to breed, because they were of the same Kind with those they carried to the *Continent* of *America*.

Some have fancied the Islands derived their Name from thence, *Bermudas* signifying in the old *Castillian* Dialect a *Black Hog*. Waving that as a foolish Imagination, it is certain the Island was stored with them, and that the *Portuguese* and *Spaniards* used to leave some on uninhabited Islands in their Way to the *West-Indies*, that in Case they were driven ashore there, or were forced to put in, they might be sure to meet with fresh Provisions. They now fat them at *Bermudas* with Palm and Cedar Berries, but their Number is very much decreased.

These Islands abound in more and greater Variety of Fowl than any in *America*. There are Hawks of all Sorts, Herons, Bitterns, Offpreys, Cormorants, Baldcoots, Moor-Hens, Swans, Teal, Snipe, Duck and Widgeon.

Bats and Owls are also very common here, with Multitudes of small Birds, as Woodpeckers, Sparrows, &c.

The *English* at their first coming, found a Sort of Fowl here called *Cohows*, which bred in the Holes of the Rocks and in Burrows like a Coney, and were so numerous and gentle, that they were taken by Hand. They are now almost all destroyed, being very easy to be caught. 'Tis of the Bigness of a Sea-mew.

There are also the *Tropick Bird*, and the *Pemlico* seldom seen by Day, and the unwelcom Foreteller of a Storm.

Fish here is as Plenty as Fowl, of which there are so many Sorts, that Authors have not yet found out Names for them.

The History of Bermudas.

They have of the scaly and the shelly Kind, the Whale, the Sword-Fish and the Thresher; but particularly the Tortoise abounds to a Wonder, and is as good and great of the Sort as any in the World. Whale-Fishing has been attempted but without Success.

The Whales about *Bermudas* are to be found only in the Months of *February*, *March* and *April*. One *John Perinche* found one dead there driven upon an Island, and tho' ignorant in the Business, yet got a great Quantity of *Sperma Cæti* out of it. [Ibid. p. 844.]

Their Whales have not as much Oil as some others, what they have is at first like *Sperma Cæti*, but they clarify it by Fire.

The Reader will not be displeased with the following Account of the Whales at *Bermudas*, communicated by Mr. *Richard Stafford* to the Royal Society.

'We have in these Seas about *Bermudas* great Store of [Ibid. p. 847.]
' Whales, which in *March*, *April* and *May* may use our
' Coasts. I have myself killed many of them. Their Fe-
' males have Abundance of Milk, which their young ones
' fuck out of the Teats that grow by their Navel. They
' have no Teeth, but feed on Grass growing on the Rocks at
' the Bottom, during these three Months and at no other Sea-
' son of the Year. When that is consumed and gone, the
' Whales go away also, those we kill are for Oil. But there
' have been *Sperma Cæti* Whales driven upon the Shore,
' which *Sperma* (as they call it) lies all over the Bodies
' of those Whales. These have divers Teeth, which may
' be about as big as a Man's Wrist.'

Ambergrease and *Sperma Cæti* have been found here in great Quantities, and Pearl; all which are almost as rare here now as elsewhere.

The Spider in these Islands is a beautiful Insect, looking as if it was adorned with Pearl and Gold. Its Web is in Colour and Substance a perfect raw Silk, and so strongly woven, that running from Tree to Tree like so many Snares, small Birds are sometimes caught in them, as Capt. *Smith* reports, whose Authority was very good in his Day.

Musketoes, Bugs, Ants and other Insects are here, and some of them very troublesom and mischievous.

We have little more to say of this Place, the Government of which resembles (as has been said) that of the other Colonies, by a Governor, Council and Assembly.

They have fewer By-Laws than any of our other Settlements, which we impute to the Smallness of their Trade: For this Colony produces no considerable Commodity, by
which

which the Inhabitants may be enriched; and their Commerce confists chiefly in Timber and Provisions, which they send to the other Parts of *America* that stand in Need of them, and some *Tobacco* imported to *England*.

Several Families retired thither formerly, on Account of their Religion or Health from *England*, and carried confiderable Effects with them. There is a Sort of pedling Retail Trade between *England* and those Islands, by which neither the Inhabitants of the one Place or the other grow much the richer.

The Building of Ships and Sloops is the moft advantageous Branch of their Traffick, and the People of *Bermudas* seem to content themselves with the Pleasure and Plenty of their Country, with a safe and quiet Retreat from the Troubles and Cares of the other Parts of the World, without any Ambition to enrich themselves; and if they had any such Desire, it is to be questioned whether they have any Opportunity of gratifying it.

Mr. *Norwood* and the before-mentioned Mr. *Stafford*, having given a farther Account of *Bermudas*, we shall communicate it to the Reader in their own Words.

Lowth. *Vol.* III. p. 561.
'I never saw any Sand in the *Bermudas*, such as will grind Glass or whet Knives, &c. as in *England*, but a Subftance like Sand tho' much softer. Neither have we any Pebble-Stones or Flints. The Inhabitants here at *Bermudas* live some to an hundred Years, and something upwards. Many live till they are nigh an Hundred, but few above. And when they die, Age and Weakness are the Cause, and not any Disease that attends them. The general Distemper that is yearly among us is a Cold, and that is moft gotten in the hotteft Weather. The Air is here very sweet and pleasant. Our Diet is but ordinary: The People are generally poor, and I observe that poor People are moft healthful.

'That *Weed* which we call *Poifon Weed* grows like our *Ivy*. I have seen a Man who was so poisoned with it, that the Skin pealed off his Face, and yet the Man never touched it, only looked on as he paffed by. But I have chewed it in my Mouth and it did me no Harm: It is not hurtful to all.

'Here are Spiders, that spin their Webs between Trees ftanding seven or eight Fathom asunder, and they do their Work by spirting their Web into the Air, where the Wind carries it from Tree to Tree. This Web, when finished, will snare a Bird as big as a Thrush.

'We cover our Houses with the Leaves, not the Bark of a Tree, which is the Palmeto; without which Tree we could

'could not live comfortably in this Island. The Leaves of
'some of these Trees are eight or ten Foot long, and nigh
'as broad.'

We shall conclude what we have to say on this Head with Mr. *Waller's* Verses in Praise of these Islands, which are to be found in the first *Canto* of his Poem, called,

The Battle of the SUMMER-ISLANDS.

BERMUDAS *wall'd with Rocks, who does not know*
That happy Island where huge Lemons grow,
And Orange Trees, which golden Fruit do bear,
The Hesperian *Gardens boast of none so fair;*
Where shining Pearl, Coral, *and many a Pound,*
On the rich Shore, of Ambergrease is found?
The lofty Cedar which to Heaven aspires,
The Prince of Trees, is Fewel for their Fires.
The Smoak by which their loaded Spits do turn,
For Incense might on sacred Altars burn:
Their private Roofs an oderous Timber born,
Such as might Palaces for Kings adorn.
Their sweet Palmetos *a new* Bacchus *yield,*
With Leaves as ample as the broadest Shield;
Under the Shadow of whose friendly Boughs,
They sit carousing where their Liquor grows.

Figs there unplanted thro' the Field do grow,
Such as fierce Cato *did the* Romans *shew;*
With the rare Fruit inviting them to spoil
Carthage, *the Mistress of so rich a Soil.*

The naked Rocks are not unfruitful here,
But at some constant Seasons, every Year,
Their barren Tops with luscious Food abound,
And with the Eggs of various Fowl are crown'd.

Tobacco is the worst of Things, which they
To English La*ndlords as their Tribute pay.*
Such is the Mould that the blest Tenant feeds
On precious Fruits, and pays his Rent in Weeds.
With candid Plantines and the juicy Pine,
On choicest Melons and sweet Grapes they dine,
And with Potatoes fat their wanton Swine.
Nature these Cates, with such a lavish Hand,
Pours out among them, that our coarser Land
Tastes of that Bounty, and does Cloth return;
Which not for Warmth, but Ornament is worn:
For the kind Spring, which but salutes us here,
Inhabits there, and courts them all the Year.

Ripe Fruits and Blossoms on the same Trees live,
At once they promise what at once they give.
So sweet the Air, so moderate the Clime,
None sickly lives, or dies before his Time.
Heav'n sure has kept this Spot of Earth uncurs'd,
To shew how all Things were created first.
The tardy Plants in our cold Orchards plac'd,
Reserve their Fruits for the next Ages Taste:
There a small Grain, in some few Months, will be
A firm, a lofty and a spacious Tree.
The Palma Christi, *and the fair* Papah,
Now but a Seed (preventing Nature's Law)
In half the Circle of the hasty Year,
Project a Shade, and lovely Fruits do wear.
   The Rocks so high about this Island rise,
That well they may the num'rous Turks *despise,* &c.

The critical Reader will consider these Verses were written 90 Years ago, and must excuse what there is in them that tastes of Antiquity, for what there is that may teach the Moderns. They are not Mr. *Waller's* best Verses, neither are they his worst; be they what they will, they serve to give those that read them a very lively Idea of the Country we are treating of, and that is all we propose by inserting them.

The Government of these Islands is, as has been said, like the rest, by Governor, Council and Assembly. The Names of the former we have procured, but could not learn those of the latter.

Governor ———— *Bennet*, Esq;

Richard Penniston, Esq;
John Tuker, Esq;
Anthony White, Esq;
Thomas Harford, Esq;
Michael Burroughs, Esq;
St. George Tucker, Esq;   } Counsellors.
Benjamin Hinson, Esq;
Patrick Downing, Esq;
Capt. *Brooks.*
Capt. *Jenner,*
Col. *Trimingham,*

Our Materials for the continuing the History of this Province are very inconsiderable, we having learn'd nothing remarkable since our former Impression. The State of it in every

every Article is much the fame, except that the Inhabitants by the Ufe of Cedar in Ship Building have fo leffened that Product, that there are not near the Number of Ships built here as there were 20 or 30 Years ago.

For fome Time they had a pretty good Vent for their Straw, of which they made very fine Hats, and do ftill make the neateft in the World, but the Fafhion has now taken another Turn in *England*.

This Ifland had fome Years ago an independent Company of Soldiers, which being removed to the *Bahama-Iflands*, the Negroes here grew mutinous, and being much more numerous than the white Men the latter were thrown into a great Confternation, increafed by the Death of Numbers of them who were poifoned by the Slaves, feveral of which were convicted at the Affizes here 1730 and executed.

THE

INDEX

TO

Both VOLUMES.

A.

ACCOMACK County, in *Virginia*, defcribed, Vol. I. Page 413.
Albany, Town of, Vol. I. 372. Congrefs there, 253.
Albany River, in *Hudfon*'s-*Bay*, Vol. I. 560.
Albemarle, *George* Duke of, firft Palatine of *Carolina*, Vol. I. 462.
Albemarle, *Chriftopher* Duke of, made Governor of *Jamaica*, Vol. II. 319.
Albemarle County, in *Carolina*, defcribed, Vol. I. 508.
Alexander, King of the *Wauponaags* in *New-England*, his Revolt, Vol. I. 106. and Death, *ib.*
Aligator, a Defcription of it, Vol. II. 409.
Alliluja, a Word ufed in the *Indian* Songs, Vol. I. 37.
Aloes Tree, of *Barbados*, defcribed, Vol. II. 115.
Ambergreafe, found at *Jamaica*, Vol. II. 404. At *Bermudas*, 453.
Amelia Ifland, in *Georgia*, Vol. I. 537.
Amidas and *Barlow*, firft Adventurers to *Virginia*, Vol. I. 346.
Anguilla, Why fo call'd, Vol. II. 300. Situation, Climate, and Soil, *ib*. Settlement there, *ib*. Diflodg'd by the wild *Irifh*, 301. *Englifh* there, *ib.*
Annapolis, in *Maryland*, defcrib'd, Vol. I. 338.
Ann-Arundel County, in *Maryland*, defcrib'd, Vol. I. 337.
Annolis, Defcription of it, Vol. II. 339.
Antego, defcribed, Vol. II. 191. The Story of Governor *Warner*'s Son by an *Indian* Woman, 192. Remarkable Hurricane here, *ib*. Parifhes, 193. Climate, Soil, Animals, 194, *et feq.* Trade, 197. Sir *Tim. Thornhill*, with Forces from *Barbados*,

affifts

INDEX.   459

affifts it, 199. General *Codrington* Governor, *ib.* Admiral *Bembow* and Col. *Collingwood* arrive there, 202. Sir *William Matthews* Governor, 203. Col. *Park* Governor, 204. Council, 205. Col. *Park* quarrels with the Inhabitants, 206. His troublefom and tragical Story, 207, *et seq.* Is kill'd, 219. *Walter Hamilton*, Efq; Governor, 220. *Walter Douglas*, Efq; Governor, 222. Mr. *Smith* tried for *Park*'s Death, and cleared, *ib.* His Jury, 223. *W. Hamilton* again Governor, *ib.* Deficiency in the Law for Debts here, 224. *J. Hart*, Efq; Governor, 225. Lord *Londonderry* Governor, *ib.* *William Matthews*, Efq; Governor, *ib.* His Salary fettled, 226. The Act about Coin broke in upon, *ib.*

Apple-Prickle defcrib'd, Vol. II. 109.

Argal, Sir *Samuel*, fteals the *Indian* Princefs *Pocahonta*, Vol. I. 365. Made Governor of *Virginia*, 367. His Expedition againft the *French* and *Dutch*, 368.

Ariatomakaw, a King of the *Carolina Indians*, his Bravery, Vol. I. 478.

Afhley River, in *Carolina*, Vol. I. 509.

Affnegoes, in *Barbados*, Vol. II. 118.

Avery, the Pirate at *Providence*, Vol. II. 429.

Augustino, in *Florida*, taken by Col. *Robert Daniel*, Vol. I. 477.

Augusta, Town in *Georgia*, its advantageous Situation for the *Indian* Trade, Vol. I. 537.

Ayfcue, Sir *George*, reduces *Barbados* for the Parliament, Vol. II. 17, 18.

B.

BACON, Col. his Rebellion in *Virginia*, Vol. I. 381. The Caufes of it, 382. His Character, *ib.* Chofen General, 384. Quarrels with the Governor, 385 Brings an Army to *James* Town, and forces the Governor to give him a Commiffion, 386. Proclaim'd a Rebel, *ib.* Gentlemen join with him, *ib.* His Death, 387.

Baffin, Mr. his Voyage and Difcoveries in *Hudfon*'s-*Bay*, Vol. I. 544.

Baltimore, *Cecilius* Lord, his Grant of *Maryland*, Vol. I. 323.

Baltimore, *Charles* Lord, Governor of *Maryland*, 329. Has the Government taken from him by King *James*, 331.

Baltimore County defcribed, 337,

Baltimore, Bird, why fo call'd, 340.

Banana Tree, in *Barbados*, defcrib'd, Vol. II. 114.

Banks of *Newfoundland*, Vol. I. 20.

Barbados, when and by whom difcover'd. Vol. II. 2. Its Name whence derived. 3. Firft Settlement. 4. Capt. *Cannon* Governor, *ib.* Granted to the Earl of *Carlifle*. 5. Which Part firft fettled upon, *ib.* Sir *Henry Hunks*, Governor. 6. Names of the firft Planters, *ib.* Sugar made there. 7. Fortify'd. 11. Government fettled and Increafe, *ib.* *Yarico*, her Story.

13.

13. *Francis* Lord *Willoughby* Governor. 15. Taken by the Parliament Forces, 17, 18. Col. *Allen*, the Parliamentarian Officer kill'd, 17. ——*Searle*, Efq; Governor, *ib.* Col. *Modiford* Governor, 19. Supported by the *Dutch*, *ib.* Col. *Tufton* Governor, 20. H. *Hawley*, Efq; Governor, *ib.* Lord *Willoughby* again Governor, *ib.* Earl of *Clarendon*'s Account of Lord *Carlifle*'s Grant and the 4 ½ *per Cent.* 21. Hump. *Walrond*, Efq; Prefident, 24. Acts paffed, *ib.* Why the Affembly made the 4 ½ *per Cent.* perpetual, 25, *et feq.* Henry *Willoughby*, Efq; H. *Hawley*, Efq; *J.* Berwick, Efq; Governors, 27. Hardfhips to the Sugar Iflands by the Act of Navigation, 19. *William* Lord *Willoughby* Governor, 28. *Chrift. Codrington*, Efq; Deputy-Governor, 31. Sir *J. Atkins* Governor, *ib.* Attack'd by the *Dutch*, 33. Hurricane there, *ib.* Sir *Richard Dutton* Governor, 37. *Henry Walrond*, Efq; Governor, 38. Hardfhips by the heavy Tax on Sugars, 40, *et feq.* Col. *Kendal* Governor, 45. Forces raifed and fent againft the *French* Sugar Iflands, 46. Agents in *England* appointed, *ib.* Charge of them, 47. Sicknefs there, 51. Commiffion for Trade fet up, *ib.* More Forces raifed, 54. Col. *Francis Ruffel* Governor, 56. *Francis Bond*, Efq; Prefident, 58. *Ralph Grey*, Efq; afterwards Lord *Grey*, Governor, 59. Col. *J. Farmer* Prefident, 63. Sir *Bevill Greenvill* Governor, 63. A Female Miniftry then, 64. *Mitford Crow*, Efq; Governor, 65. *Robert Lowther*, Efq; Governor, 66. *William Sharp*, Efq; Prefident, *ib.* Governor *Lowther* profecutes feveral Gentlemen, 67, *et feq.* Is recall'd, 71. *Samuel Cox*, Efq; Prefident, *ib.* Conteft about the Government, *ib.* Henry *Worfeley*, Efq; Governor, 74. Duke of *Portland* here, *ib.* His noble Entertainment by all Parties, 75, *et feq.* Governor of *Barbados* Inftructions about *St. Lucia*, 77. Governor *Worfeley*'s Proceedings againft Prefident *Cox*, 78, *et feq.* Affembly againft the Negro Tax, 83. Grievances complained of, *ib. et feq.* Remarks on Addreffes there, 85. Proceedings againft the Provoft Marfhal, 87. *Samuel Berwick*, Efq; Prefident, *ib.* *French* Trade with our Northern Colonies, 88. Steps towards redreffing Plantation Grievances, *ib.* Lord *Howe* Governor, 89. Mr. *Gel Mc. Mahon* tried for a Murder, 90. A *Romifh* Prieft turns Proteftant, 91. Lord *Howe*'s Death and good Character, *ib.* The Affembly give Lady *Howe* 2500*l.* 93. *James Dotten*, Efq; Prefident, 92. *Robert Byng*, Efq; Governor, 95. Dies, *ib.* Lift of the chief Officers here, *ib.* Geographical Defcription of it, 96, *et feq.* Climate, Soil and Product, 106, *et feq.* Trees, 107, *et feq.* Birds, Beafts, Fifh, Infects and other Animals, 118, *et feq.* Of the Inhabitants, and their Way of Living, 124, *et feq.* Government, Courts, Offices and Revenue, 138, *et feq.* Of making Sugars, 145, *et feq.* Molaffes and Rum, 158. Of the Trade, 159, *et feq.* Money, 165. Its former Riches and Advantages to *England*, 166, *et feq.* Hardfhips, 170.

Barbuda,

INDEX. 461

Barbuda, Island of, describ'd, Vol. II. 229. *Christopher Codrington*, Esq; Proprietor, *ib.* Col. *Park* endeavours to dispossess him, 300.
Barnstable County, in *New-England*, described, Vol. I. 200.
Bartholomew the Buccaneer his Actions, Vol. II. 311.
Baths in *Nevis*, Vol. II. 236. In *Jamaica*, 410.
Bawdon, Sir *John*, his Loss in the Hurricane at *Barbados*, Vol. II. 33. By the Royal *African* Company, 36. Opposes the Monopoly Project, 43.
Beckford Peter, Esq; Lieutenant-Governor of *Jamaica*, Vol. II. 337. His vast Riches, 354.
Bembow, Admiral, his Actions in the *West-Indies*, Vol. II. 336.
Berkley County, in *Carolina*, Vol. I. 509, *et seq.*
Berkham County, described, Vol. I. 283.
Bermudas, disover'd, Vol. II. 440. Whence its Name, 441. Sir *G. Somers* shipwreck'd, *ib.* Mr. *R. Moor* Governor, 443. The famous Rat-Plague, 444. Capt. *Daniel Tucker* Governor, *ib.* A desperate Adventure thence by Sea, 445. Capt. *Butler* Governor, 446. Mr. *Barnard* Governor, *ib.* Mr. *Harrison* President, *ib. Edmund Waller*, Esq; the Poet there, *ib.* His Verses in Praise of it, 455. Geographical Description of it, 447, *et seq.* Climate, 449. Soil, 450. Healthfulness and Pleasantness, *ib.* Trees, 451. Animals, 452. Whales, Ambergrease and *Sperma Cæti*, 453. Number of Inhabitants, 447. Shipbuilding here, 454. Diminish'd, 457. *Bermudas* Hats, ib. Mutiny of the Negroes, *ib.*
Birkenhead's Conspiracy in *Virginia*, Vol. I. 379.
Blake, Mr. Brother to the famous Admiral, settles in *Carolina*, Vol. I. 466.
Blenman, Jon. Esq; persecuted by Governor *Lowther*, Vol. I. 68.
Boston, City of, in *New-England*, built, Vol. I. 61. Large and populous, 194. The Bay, 195. Describ'd, *ib. et seq.*
Brasiliano, the Buccaneer, his Actions, Vol. II. 311.
Bridge-Town, in *Barbados*, great Mortality there, Vol. II. 51. The Town described, 98, *et seq.*
Bridgwater, in *New-England*, attack'd by the *Indians*, Vol. I. 123. Bravery of the Garrison, *ib.*
Bristol Town and County, in *New-England*, describ'd, Vol. I. 201.
Bristol, in *Pensilvania*, described, Vol. I. 298.
Bucane, a Fish so call'd, describ'd, Vol. II. 195.
Buccaneers in *America*, their Actions, Vol. II. 311, *et seq.*
Buckinghamshire, in *Pensylvania*, describ'd, Vol. I. 298.
Burlington, in *West New-Jersey*, describ'd, Vol. I. 288.

C.

CABBAGE-Tree, in *Jamaica*, describ'd, Vol. II. 403.
Cabot, Sebastian, said to discover *Florida*, Vol. I. 456.

Calvert,

INDEX.

Calvert County, in *Maryland*, Vol. I. 336.
Cecil County, in *Maryland*, Vol. I. 338.
Callibash-Tree, in *Barbados*, Vol. II. 111.
Cambridge, in *New-England*, Town of built, Vol. I. 63. 78. 192. Synod there, 102. College there, an Account of, 213, *et seq.*
Canada, the Right of the *English* to it, Vol. I. 39. The *French* there attempt to draw off the *Indians* in Friendship with the *English*, 243. Assist the Savages against the *English*, 121.
Canida, Birds so call'd, Vol. II. 197.
Cape-Britain Isle, given to the *French*, Vol. I. 37.
Cape-Cod, in *New-England*, Vol. I. 200.
Carolina, discover'd, Vol. I. 456. Old *Carolina* describ'd, 459. King *Charles* II his Grant of it to Proprietaries, 460. Mr. *Locke*'s Draught of a Constitution for it, 462. Sir *W. Sayle* Governor, 464. Sir *J. Yeomans* Governor, 465. *Joseph West*, Esq; Governor, *ib.* again, 469. *Joseph Moreton*, Esq; Governor, 466. *J. Colliton*, Esq; Governor, 469. Mr. *Archdale*'s Description of *Carolina*, *ib.* *T. Smith*, Esq; Governor, 470. Col. *Robert Quarry*, Governor, *ib.* Mr. *Southwell*, Col. *Philip Ludwell*, *Thomas Smith*, Esq; Governors, *ib.* *John Archdale*, Esq; Governor, *ib.* *Joseph Blake*, Esq; Governor, 473. Col. *James Moor*, 474. An Expedition against *St. Augustino*, 476, *et seq.* Sir *Nathaniel Johnson* Governor, 480. A Schism Bill set up there, 481. And occasions great Troubles, 482, *et seq.* Opposed by the Parliament of *England*, 487, and by Queen *Anne*, 489. Major *Tynte* Governor, 491. —— *Gibbs*, Esq; President, *ib.* *C. Craven*, Esq; Governor, *ib.* *Robert Daniel*, Esq; Governor, *ib.* *Robert Johnson*, Esq; Governor, *ib.* Again, 501. *James Moor*, Esq; 491. *Francis Nicholson*, Esq; Governor, *ib.* Pyrates on the Coast, *ib.* —— *Middleton*, Esq; President, 492. Negro Plot, *ib.* Verdict of Juries by Ballot, 493. Abolish'd, *ib.* An *Indian* War, 494, *et seq.* The Charter surrendered and Soil purchased by the Crown, 498. Sir *Alexander Coming*'s Conference with the *Indians*, 499. *Indians* submit to King *George*, 500. Governor *Johnson*'s Interview with them, 502. The new Province of *Georgia* taken out of it, 504. Mr. *Oglethorpe* arrives there, *ib.* Forwards the new Settlement, *ib.* A Contest amongst the Lawyers, 505. *Purrysburg*, a *Swiss* Town built, *ib.* *Thomas Broughton*, Esq; Lieutenant-Governor, 506. Geographical Description of this Province, 508, *et seq.* Again, 519. Product, *ib.* The great Increase of the Rice Trade, *ib.* Silk 517. 520. Trade 521. People, *ib.* Churches and Ministers, 522. Money, 523. Method of settling, *ib.* First Charge, *ib.* Price of Labour, 524.
Cassavia Tree, in *Barbados*, describ'd, Vol. II. 107.
Cassia Fistula Tree, its quick Growth, Vol. II. 108.
Cedar Tree, in *Barbados*, Vol. II. 109. Of *Bermudas*, 451. Of *Maryland*, Vol. I. 342.
Chactaw Indians trade with the *English*, Vol. I. 533, *et seq.*
Chagre, taken by Admiral *Vernon*, Vol. II. 387. Its important Situation, *ib.*

INDEX.

Charibbeans, an Account of them, Vol. II. 265, *et seq.*
Charibbee Iflands, *Davye's* Hiftory of them authentick, Vol. II. 240.
Charles County, in *Maryland*, Vol. I. 337.
Charles-City County, in *Virginia*, Vol. I. 406.
Charles-Town, in *Carolina*, defcrib'd, Vol I. 510. *et seq.*
Charles-Town, in *New-England*, built, Vol. I. 69. Defcrib'd, 192.
Charles-Town, in *Nevis*, Vol. I. 252.
Charleton Ifland in *Hudfon's-Bay*, Vol. I. 546.
Chegos, of *Jamaica*, what, Vol. II. 408.
Chefeapeak-Bay, defcrib'd, Vol. I. 341, 405.
Chefter Town and County, in *Penfylvania*, Vol. I. 302.
Chichefter, in *Penfylvania*, Vol. I. 303.
Chub treacheroufly delivers up *Pemaquid* Fort, Vol. I. 161. Is kill'd, 164.
Clarendon County, in *Carolina*, Vol. I. 509.
Clarendon Parifh, in *Jamaica*, Vol. II. 393.
Cinnamon Tree, in *Jamaica*, wild, Vol. II. 402.
Citron Tree, in *Barbados*, Vol. II. 108.
Cochineal, how made, Vol. II. 405.
Cocoa Tree, in *Jamaica*, Vol. II. 397, *et seq.*
Coco Tree, in *Barbados*, 110.
Cock-Roches, in *Barbados*, 122.
Coin in *Barbados*, 165. In the *Leeward* Iflands, 297. In *Jamaica*, 371.
Cohows, Birds in *Bermudas* fo call'd, Vol. II. 452.
Colebry, a Bird fo call'd, Vol. II. 264.
Colliton County, in *Carolina*, Vol. I. 513.
Coloquintida Tree, in *Barbados*, Vol. II. 108.
Columbus Chrift. difcovers *Jamaica*, Vol. II. 302. Is wreck'd, 203. His ill Ufage, his Epitaph, *ib.*
Connecticut Colony, in *New-England*, fettled, Vol. I. 66. Confederated with the other Colonies, 88. Its Conftitution, 204.
Corn, Indian, fee *Maize*.
Cornwal County, in *New-England*, Vol. I. 189.
Cotton Tree, in *Barbados*, defcribed, Vol. II. 112.
Craven County, in *Carolina*, Vol. I. 509.
Crawfoul, a Bird fo call'd, Vol. II. 264.
Creolians, why fo call'd, Vol. II. 126.
Cuftard-Apple-tree, in *Barbados*, Vol. II. 111.
Cyprefs, in *Maryland*, defcrib'd, Vol. I. 342.

D.

DALE's Gift, in *Virginia*, built, Vol. I. 364.
Darien, *Scots* Colony fettled, Vol. II. 336.
Darien, in *Georgia*, fettled, Vol. I. 535.
Devil's Sea, defcrib'd, Vol. II. 228.

Dogwood,

INDEX.

Dogwood, in *Maryland*, Vol. I. 342.
Dominico Island, describ'd, Vol. II. 188, *et seq.* Since the Account of it was printed, Lord *Cathcart*'s Fleet put in here.
Dorado, a Fish so call'd, Vol. II. 194.
Dorchester, in *New-England*, describ'd, Vol. I. 198.
Dorchester County, in *Maryland*, Vol. II. 339.
Dorchester, in *Carolina*, Vol. I. 513.
Dover, in *Pensylvania*, Vol. I. 304.
Drake, Sir *Francis*, the first Man that landed in *New England*, Vol. I. 39.
Dungan, Col. a Papist, Governor of *New-York*, a true Lover of his Country, Vol. I. 240.
Dunstan, Hannah, of *New-England*, her masculine Spirit, Vol. I. 162.

E.

EARTHQUAKE, dreadful one, Vol. II. 322, *et seq.*
East New-Jersey, how bounded, Vol. I. 282. And divided, 283, *et seq.* Trade, 289.
Ebenezer, Old and New, in *Georgia*, Vol. I. 536.
Elizabeth Town, in *East New-Jersey*, describ'd, Vol. I. 284.
Elizabeth City and County, in *Virginia*, describ'd, Vol. I. 409.
Essex County, in *New-England*, Vol. I. 190.
Essex County, in *East New-Jersey*, Vol. I. 284.
Essex County, in *Virginia*, Vol. I. 411.

F.

FAIRFIELD County, in *New-England*, Vol. I. 209.
Falmouth Town, in *Antego*, Vol. II. 193.
Fig, *Indian*, how propagated, Vol. II. 406.
Fire-Arms, use of, first taught the Savages, Vol. I. 55.
Fishery at *Newfoundland*, Advantage of, Vol. I. 19, 20.
Fly-Catcher, describ'd, Vol. II. 405.
Flies, fire, in *Jamaica*, Vol. II. 408.
Freggats, Birds so call'd, Vol. II. 408.
Frederica Town, in *Georgia*, describ'd, Vol. I. 536.
French, their ridiculous Complaisance for the *Charibbeans*, Vol. II. 265. And Vanity, 277.
Frobrisher's Streights, where and when discover'd, Vol. I. 543.

G.

GEORGIA, its Charter and Bounds, Vol. I. 525. Trustees, 526. First Imbarkation, *ib.* *Savannah* Town built, 527. *Indian* Nations submit to the *English*, 529. Articles of Trade with

INDEX.

with them, 531. First Ship here from *England, ib. Indian* Chiefs brought over by Mr. *Oglethorpe,* 532. *Chactaw Indians,* 533. Trade with the *English,* 534 *Darien,* 535. Greater Imbarkation, *ib.* Old and *New Ebenezer* laid out by *Saltzburghers,* 536. *Frederica* built, *ib.* St. *Andrew's* Fort, on *Cumberland* Island, 537. *Amelia* Island, *ib. Augusta* well seated for the *Indian* Trade, *ib. James Oglethorpe,* Esq; General of the Forces of *Carolina* and *Georgia,* 538. Fifty five Children born in the Camp here last Year, *ib.* Situation and Soil, 539. Its Security to our Colonies, *ib.* Product and Trade, 540. Wages and Price of Provisions, 541.

German Town, in *Pensylvania,* Vol. I. 302.
Gillam, Capt. *Zach.* first settles in *Hudson's-Bay,* Vol. I. 544.
Ginger Plant, in *Barbados,* describ'd, Vol. II. 113.
Gloucester County, in *Virginia,* Vol. I. 411.
Gosnold, Capt. his early Voyage to *New-England,* Vol. I. 29. To *Virginia,* 353.
Guaver Tree, describ'd, Vol. II. 110.
Guildford, in *New-England,* Vol. I. 208.

H.

HAMPSHIRE, *New,* Province of, in *New-England,* describ'd, Vol. I. 70.
Hampshire, New, County, Vol. I. 199.
Hartford, in *New-England,* built, Vol. I. 66. Town and County described, 207.
Harvard College, founded, Vol. I. 78. Description of, 212, *et seq.*
Henrico County, in *Virginia,* Vol. I. 405.
Henricopolis Town, Vol. I. 406.
Hiaccomes, an *Indian* Preacher, converted, Vol. I. 95.
Hole Town, in *Barbados,* describ'd, Vol. II. 100.
Horn-Fly, describ'd, Vol. II. 241.
Howe, Lord, Governor of *Barbados,* Vol. II. 89. His Death and good Character, 91.
Hudson, Capt. discovers *New-York,* and sells it to the *Dutch,* Vol. I. 236. Discovers *Hudson's-Bay,* 543.
Hudson's-Bay, a wretched Place, Vol. I. 542. *Hudson,* the Discoverer, is kill'd, 543. How the *English* came to settle it first, 544. First Proprietaries, 545. Situation and Extent, *ib.* Streights describ'd, *ib.* Air, Soil, 547. Standard of the Trade, *ib.* First Governor, 549. And Traders, *ib.* Disturbed by the *French, ib.* How the *English* live, *ib.* The Settlement in great Distress, 556. A Governor at Port *Nelson,* 559. Five Settlements in the Bay, 561. Lose all, *seq.* Restored by the *Utrecht* Peace, 567.
Hurricanes, Prognosticks of them, Vol. II. 280.
Huskanawing, what it is, Vol. I. 424.

Jamaica,

I.

Jamaica, difcovered by *Chriftopher Columbus*, Vol. II. 302. Who is wreck'd here, 303. Whence its Name, *ib.* Firft *Spanifh* Settlement, 304. And Trade, *ib.* Maffacred 60000 *Indians* there, 305. Sir *Anthony Shirly* plunders it, *ib. et feq.* Col. *Jackfon* takes and leaves it, *ib.* Reduced by *Cromwell's* Forces, *ib.* Col. *Doily* Governor, 307. Col. *Brayne* Governor, 309. Col. *Doily* continued Governor, *ib.* Lord *Windfor* Governor, 310. Sir *Thomas Modiford*, *ib.* Great Increafe of the Inhabitants, *ib.* Buccaneers begin their Enterprizes, 311. Sir *Thomas Linch* Governor, 312. Captain, afterwards Sir *Henry Morgan's* Succeffes againft the *Spaniards*, 312, *et feq.* Takes *Panama*, 313. Lord *Vaughan* Governor, 314. Sent Prifoner to *England*, 315. Earl of *Carlifle* Governor, 316. Sir *Henry Morgan* Deputy-Governor, *ib.* Sir *T. Linch* again Governor, 317. Col. *Hender Molefworth* Governor, 318. Duke of *Albemarle* Governor, 319. A terrible Earthquake, 320. Col. *Molefworth* again Governor, 321. Earl of *Inchequin* Governor, *ib.* The prodigious Earthquake, 322, *et feq.* Sir *William Beefton* Governor, 328. The *French* land there and are beaten off, 330, *et feq.* Rebellious Negroes, 334. General *Selwyn* Governor, 336. *Peter Beckford*, Efq; Lieutenant-Governor, 337. Earl of *Peterborough* appointed Governor, 338. Capts. *Kirby* and *Wade*, their Cowardice, 339. Col. *Thomas Handafide* Governor, 340. Admiral *Graydon* and Col. *Colenbine* arrive here with Forces, 342. Lord *Archibald Hamilton* Governor, 344. Complaints of Male Adminiftration here, *ib.* The pernicious Practice of Efcheats, 347. Mr. *Rigby*, Provoft-Marfhal; his Oppreffion, 348. Chief Juftice *Haywood*, &c. turned out, 350. *Spanifh* Depredations, 351. Council, 352. Frivolous Complaints of the *Spaniards*, *ib.* Peter *Haywood*, Efq; Governor, 354. Lord *Hamilton* fent Prifoner to *England*, 355. Sir *Nich. Laws*, a Planter, Governor, *ib.* Pirates infeft here, 356. Commodore, now Admiral *Vernon*, demands Satisfaction of the Governor of *Trinidado* for *Spanifh* Depredations, 358. Governor *Law's* good Speech, 361. A dreadful Hurricane, 362, *et feq.* Guarda-Cofta Men hang'd, 366. Of the *Mufcheto Indians*, *ib. et feq.* Their Friendfhip to the *Englifh*, &c. *ib.* Duke of *Portland* Governor, 368. Col. *Dubourgay*, Lieutenant-Governor, difcharged, 369. Advantage to be made of the *Mufcheto's*, 370. Of the Coin, 371. Of the Roads, 372. Minifter's Income, 373. Duke of *Portland's* Death, 375. The Council addrefs the Dutchefs, *ib.* J. *Afcough*, Efq; Prefident, 376. General *Hunter* Governor, *ib.* Skirmifh with the Negro Rebels, 377. *John Gregory*, Efq; Prefident, 379. *Henry Cuningham*, Efq; Governor, *ib.* His Death, *ib.* *Edward Trelawney*, Efq; Governor, *ib.* Rebellious Negroes fubmit, 380. Admiral *Vernon* arrives here, 381. Takes *Porto-Bello*

and

INDEX.

and *Chagre*, 384. *et seq.* Towns, Forts, Parishes in *Jamaica*, describ'd, 388, *et seq.* Climate and Soil, 394, *et seq.* The *Sugar* here, 396. *Cocoa*, Manner of planting it, 397, *et seq.* *Piemento*, 400. *Cabbage*-Tree, Account of, 403. *Cochineal*, describ'd, 405. Fish, Fruits, Animals, *&c.* 406, *et seq.* *Manchinello*, 409. The Alligator describ'd, *ib.* Of the Inhabitants, 411, *et seq.* Trade, 413. Product, *ib.* Latitude, 414. Rivers, *ib.* Bays, 415. *Port-Royal*, *ib.* *St. Jago de la Vega*, or *Spanish* Town, 416. Other Towns, *ib.* Parishes, 418. Number of Inhabitants, *ib.* What the *Spaniards* call the illicit Trade, describ'd, 419. Of Logwood cutting, 420.
James River, in *Virginia*, Vol. I. 410.
James City, in *James* County, describ'd, Vol. I. 406.
Indians, see the Accounts of them in their respective Colonies.
Indigo, Description of it, Vol. II. 400.
Isle of *Wight* County, in *Virginia*, Vol. I. 405.

K.

KENT County, in *Pensylvania*, Vol. I. 304.
Kent County, in *Maryland*, Vol. I. 339.
Kent-*New* County, in *Virginia*, Vol. I. 411.
Kingston, in *Jamaica*, great Mortality there, Vol. II. 328. Describ'd, 390.
King William County, in *Virginia*, Vol. I. 411.
King and *Queen*'s County, *ib.*

L.

LAMENTINE, a Fish so call'd, Vol. II. 229.
Lancaster County, in *Virginia*, Vol. I. 412.
Landgraves, in *Carolina*, Vol. I. 463.
Lemon-Tree, in *Barbados*, Vol. II. 110.
Liguania, in *Jamaica*, destroyed by an Earthquake, Vol. II. 326.
Lizards, in *Nevis*, describ'd, Vol. II. 238.
Lime-Trees, Vol. II. 109.
Locke, the Philosopher, his Draught of a Constitution for *Carolina*, Vol. I. 462.
Logwood, of the cutting it, Vol. I. 420.
London New County, in *New-England*, Vol. I. 207.
Long-Island, in *New-England*, Vol. I. 79. In *New-York*, 274.

M.

MACOW Tree, describ'd, Vol. II. 111.
Main County, in *New-England*, Vol. I. 70.
Maize, or *Indian* Corn, its Growth, Vol. I. 189, *et seq.*

Mangrave

INDEX.

Mangrave Tree, describ'd, Vol. II. 111.
Manchineal Tree, in *Jamaica*, Vol. II. 404.
Manchineal Apple, *ib.*
Manteo, a faithful *Indian* brought to *England*, Vol. I. 347. Chriſtened and rewarded, 351.
Martha's Vineyard, Iſland of, planted, Vol. I. 86. Deſcrib'd, 201.
Martinico, attack'd by the *Engliſh*, Vol. II. 54.
Maryland, Bounds by the Grant, Vol. I. 323, *et ſeq.* By whom named, 324. Firſt Adventurers thither, *ib.* Government ſettled, 328. Settlement, 325, *et ſeq.* Diviſion into Counties, 329. Liberty of Conſcience there, 330. Churches built there, 332. State of it, *ib.* Geographical Deſcription, 335. Climate, 339. The Tobacco, 340. Soil, *ib.* Trade, *ib. et ſeq.*
Maſſachuſet Colony founded, Vol. I. 57. Firſt Proprietors, *ib. et ſeq.* Geographical Deſcription of it, 224, *et ſeq.*
Melaſſes, how made, Vol. II. 158, *et ſeq.*
Middleſex County, in *New-England*, Vol. I. 192.
Middleſex County, in *Eaſt New-Jerſey*, 284.
Middleſex County, in *Virginia*, 411.
Miſſiſſipi, the *Engliſh* have as much Right to it as the *French*, Vol. I. 412. *French* there not ſo dangerous as repreſented, 496.
Montſerrat, why ſo call'd, Vol. II. 227. Its Situation, *ib.* Climate, Soil, 228. Deputy-Governor and Council, 231. *French* land there, 232. *Engliſh* retire to Fort *Dodon*, till the *French* leave the Iſland, *ib.* A prodigious Hurricane, 234. Act againſt *French* Trade, 235.
Morgan, Sir *Henry*, the Buccaneer, his Actions, Vol. II. 312, *et ſeq.* Takes *Panama*, 313. Ill uſed, 315. Made Deputy-Governor of *Jamaica*, 316.
Moſe, the Way of hunting it, Vol. I. 187.
Mount-Joy, in *Penſylvania*, Vol. I. 303.
Mount-Hope, in *New-England*, Vol. I. 202.
Muſchetoes, Account of, Vol. II. 122.

N.

NANSEMUND County, in *Virginia*, Vol. I. 405.
Nantucket Iſland, inhabited by *Chriſtian Indians*, Vol. I. 201.
Narraganſets, their King taken, Vol. I. 87. Subdued by the *Engliſh*, 120.
Naſſau, in *Providence*, deſcrib'd, Vol. II. 429, 435.
Nelſon Port, in *Hudſon*'s-*Bay*, Vol. I. 545. A Governor there, 559.
Nevis, deſcrib'd, Vol. II. 256. Sir *G. Ayſcue* reduces it, 237. Climate and Soil, *ib.* Product and Trade, *ib. et ſeq.* Animals, 238, *et ſeq.* Sir *Tim. Thornhill* and General *Codrington* here,

INDEX.

here, to act against the *French* Islands, 244, *et seq.* The *French* land and plunder it, 255. Lieutenant-Governor and Council, 256. Governor's Salary settled, 257. Address against the Death of *Park, ib.*

Newcastle Town and County, in *Pensylvania*, Vol. I. 303.

New-England, Vol. I. Capt. *Gosnold*'s first Voyage in Queen *Elizabeth*'s time, 39, *Popham* and *Gilbert*'s, 41. Call'd *New-England, ib.* Capt. *Hunt*'s Villainy to the *Indians*, 42. *Squanto* the faithful *Indian*, 43. First Settlement, 45. Betrayed by *Hollanders, ib.* Instrument of Association, *ib.* Mr. *J. Carver* Governor. 46. *Plimouth* Colony settled, 47. *Indians* and their King *Massasoit* visit the *English*, 47, 48. *William Bradford*, Esq; Governor, 48. *Indian* Princes submit, 49. The ill Fate of *Weston* and his Colony, 51. *Peirce*'s Treachery, 52. Mr. *Winslow* takes out the first Patent, 53. First neat Cattle, *ib.* Capt. *Woolaston*'s Settlement frustrated, 55. *Morton*'s Mutiny, *ib.* Teaches the Savages the Use of Fire-Arms, *ib.* Distribution of Land, 56. The *Massachuset* Patent, 57. *Matthew Cradock*, Esq; Governor, *ib. J. Endicot* Deputy-Governor, *ib.* The grand Imbarkation, 58. *Separatists* there, *ib. J. Winthrop*, Esq; Governor, *T. Dudley*, Esq; Deputy-Governor, 59. *Salem* built, 59. Sir. *R. Saltonstal*, &c: remove to *Massachuset*, 60. *Charles-Town* built, *Boston* built, 60, 61. Sir *R. Gardiner* there, 62. *Cambridge* built, 63. University founded, 77. *Indians* murder the *English*, 63. *Indians* Lands purchased, 64. Persecution there, 65. Sir *H. Vane* there, *ib. Connecticut* Colony settled, 66. *Ed. Hopkins*, Esq; Governor, *ib. Oliver Cromwell* and others, about to remove thither, 68. *New-Haven* Colony, 69. *Theop. Eaton*, Esq; Governor, *ib. New-Hampshire* and *Main* Government, 70. The *Pequot* War, 71, *et seq.* The good Behaviour of an *Indian* Princess, 74. *Pequots* subjected, *ib.* Sedition about the Covenants of *Grace* and *Works*, 75. *New-England* Synod explained, 76. *Antinomians* banish'd, 77. Settle at *Rhode-Island*, 77. Confederacy of the four Governments here, 78. *Long Island* inhabited by the *English*, 79. Puritans remove hither, 81. *Martha*'s Vineyard planted, 86. War between *Indian* Kings, 87. Capt. *Atherton* seizes the King of the *Narragantsets, ib. Indians* converted to *Christianity*, 90. *et seq.* Mr. *Elliot* preaches to them, *ib.* He translates the Bible into their Language, 95. *Hiaccomes*, an *Indian* Preacher, *ib.* Mr. *Mayhew*'s Mission, 97. *New-England* Society for propagating the Gospel, 99. Names of them in *New* and *Old England*, 100. *et seq.* Synod at *Cambridge*, 102. Baptists persecuted, *ib.* Again, 112. Cruel Laws against Quakers, 103, 105, *et seq. T. Prince*, Esq; Governor, 104. *F. Newman*, Esq; Governor, 105. *Venner* the 5th Monarchist there, *ib. Massasoit*'s two Sons take the Name of *Alexander* and *Philip*, 108. Synod at *Boston*, 106. The Beginning of putting People to Death for Witchcraft, 110. *Connecticut* and *New Haven* Colony united, 111. *J. Leveret*, Esq; Governor

INDEX.

Governor, 113. *J. Sanfaman*, King *Philip*'s Secretary, becomes a Preacher, and is murder'd, *ib.* The War with King *Philip* begins, 116, *et feq.* Capt. *Beers*, &c. kill'd, 119. Governor *Winflow* fubdues the *Narragantfets*, 120. Six *Englifh* Captains kill'd, 121. A great Slaughter of the *Indians*, *ib.* The *French* affifts them, *ib.* The Queen of *Pocaffet*'s Bravery, 125. King *Philip* fhot by an *Indian*, *ib.* The War in the Eaft, 126, *et feq. W. Leet*, Efq; *Sim. Bradftreet*, Efq; and *Robert Treat*, Efq; Governors, 128. *New-England* Charter taken away, *ib. H. Cranfield*, Efq; Governor, 129. *Jof. Dudley*, Efq; Governor, *ib.* Sir *Edmund Andros* Governor, *ib.* Seized, 136. Council refume the Government, 137. Capt. afterwards Sir *William Phips*, brings home immenfe Treafure, 130. Made High Sheriff, 134. Third *Indian* War, 132. *Indians* take *Pemmaquid*-Fort, 138. Bravery of two *Englifh* Boys, 139. Sir *William Phips*'s unfortunate Expedition to *Quebec*, 140. The Difference between the old and new Charter, 144. Sir *William Phips* Governor, *ib.* Capt. *Convers*'s Bravery, 145. *Pemmaquid* New Fort built, 146. Peace with the *Indians* concluded there. 147. Witch Plague, 148, *et feq.* Mr. *Boroughs*, a Minifter, tried and hang'd as a Witch, 149, 151. Numbers more hang'd, 151, *et feq.* Dog hang'd as an Accomplice, 156. Dr. *Mather*'s and Sir *William Phips*'s Relations accufed of Witchcraft, *ib.* A Stop thereupon to the Perfecution, *ib.* Difcontents againft Sir *William Phips*, 158. *W. Stoughton*, Efq; Governor, 159. The *Indians* fet on by the *French* againft the *Englifh*, 159. A War, and their King *Bomafeen* taken, 160. Major *Hammond* taken and fold, and redeemed by Count *Frontiniac*, 161. *Indians* firft ride a Horfeback, *ib. Chub* delivers up *Pemmaquid* Fort, *ib.* Kill'd 164. *Hannah Dunftan*'s Stoutnefs rewarded, 162. Earl of *Belmont* Governor, 164. *Indian* Sachems fubmit to *England*, 165. *New-England* affifts *Jamaica*, 167. *G. Dudley*, Efq; Governor, *ib.* General *Hill* and Admiral *Hovenden*, their fatal Expedition to *Canada*, 169. *Samuel Shute*, Efq; Governor, 171. *New Haven* Univerfity fet up, 173. Pirates tried and hang'd, 174. *W. Burnet*, Efq; Governor, *ib. J. Belcher*, Efq; Governor, 175. Contefts about the Governor's Salary, 176, *et feq.* Salary fettled, 179. Woods for Mafts laid out, 180. Climate, Soil and Product, 181, *et feq.* Hunting the Mofe, 187. Geographical Defcription of Counties, Towns, &c. 189, *et feq. Bofton* defcrib'd, 193, *et feq.* Number of Inhabitants, 196. Trade and Way of Living, 197. *Rhode-Ifland* defcrib'd, 203. *Martha*'s Vineyard, 201. *New-England*, its Inhabitants, Fruitfulnefs and Pleafantnefs, 205. Its Laws and Government, 210, *et feq. Harvard* College, 212, *et feq.* Of the *Indians*, 223, 224, 225. Number of Inhabitants in *New-England*, 227. *Englifh* Title to the *Miffiffipi*, 228. Trade of *New-England*, 229. Plenty of Naval Stores, 231. Exports thence to the Sugar-Iflands, 234.

New-

INDEX.

Newfoundland, its Situation, idle Pretences of the *French* to the Difcovery, Vol. I. 2. Sir *H. Gilbert* takes Poffeffion for Queen *Elizabeth*, 3. Caft away, 4. Firft *Newfoundland* Company, 5. Dr. *Vaughan* purchafes and fettles, 7. Sir *G. Calvert*'s Grant, 8. Number of Inhabitants, 14. Climate, Way of Living, and Soil, 16. The *Spaniards* pretend to the Fifhery, 17. Product, Meats, Fifh, 19. The *Banks*, 20. *Indians*, 21, 22. Wars between the *French* and *Englifh*, 22, 23, 24. Sir *J. Norris* here, 24. Ceffion of the Ifland by the *French* to the *Englifh*, 26.

Newhaven Colony, in *New-England*, fettled, Vol. I. 69. Join'd to *Connecticut*, 111. County defcrib'd, 208.

New-Jerfey defcrib'd, Part of *Nova Belgia*, Vol. I. 281. *Swedes* here, 282. Divided into two Proprieties, *ib*. Their Bounds, *ib*. Divifion, Eaft and Weft, 283. Why not encouraged, *ib*. Counties, *ib. et feq*. Iron Works, 286. No Churches, *ib*. Dr. *Cox*, Proprietor of *Weft Jerfey*, *ib*. Number of Inhabitants, 289. Second Proprietaries, 290. *Robert Barclay*, Efq; the famous Quaker, Governor, 291. *Gawen Lawrie*, Efq; Deputy-Governor, *ib*. Terms of Sale of Lands, *ib*. Sir *Neal Campbell* Governor, 292. Col. *Andrew Hamilton* Governor, 293. *Edmund Byllings*, Efq; Governor of *Weft New-Jerfey*, *ib*. Charter furrender'd, 294. Trade here, 295. Increafe of Slaves, *ib*. *Lewis Morris*, Efq; Governor, *ib*.

New-Scotland, its Difcovery and Settlement, Vol. I. 28, *et feq*. That and *Canada* belongs to the *Englifh*, who drive out the *French*, 31, 32. Mr. *de la Tour* his Purchafes there of the *Englifh*, *ib*. Yielded together with *Canada* by *Charles* II. to the *French*, 33. Sir *W. Phips* retakes it, *ib*. Governor *Nicholfon* calls *Port-Royal Anapolis*, 34. *Indians*, 36. Their Mufick, 37. Cape *Briton* Ifland, its great Advantage for the Fifhery, *ib*. Better for the *French* than *Newfoundland*, *ib. et feq*. Given up to them by the *Utrecht* Treaty, *ib*.

New-York, Dutch firft Poffeffors, Vol. I. 236. Bounds, 237. Climate and Soil, 238. The *Englifh* take Poffeffion of it, *ib*. Defcrib'd, 239. *Hudfon*'s River, *ib*. Capt. *Nichols* Governor, 240. Sir *Edmund Andros*, *ib*. Col. *Dungan*, *ib*. Col. *Schuyler*'s Expedition againft *Quebec*, 241. *Scheneclada* burnt by the *French*, 242. Col. *Lefley* Governor, by Ufurpation, *ib*. Condemned and executed, 243. Col. *Fletcher* Governor, *ib*. Count *de Frontinac* enters and quits the Province, *ib*. Col. *Slaughter* Governor, *ib*. *Jof. Dudley*, Efq; Deputy-Governor, 244. Earl of *Bellamont* Governor, *ib*. Mr. *Nanfan* Deputy-Governor, *ib*. Lord *Cornbury* Governor, 245. *Indian* Kings of the five Nations at *London*, 247. *New-York* joins in the Expedition againft *Canada*, 248. *Palatines* fettle there, 249. The Charge of it, 250. Brigadier *Hunter* Governor, renews the Alliance with the Kings of the five Nations, *ib*. *W. Burnet*, Efq; Governor, 251. *Peter Schuyler*, Efq; Prefident, meets the *Indian* Segamores at *Albany*, *ib*. Another Congrefs with them

INDEX.

at *Albany*, 253. Their Speeches, *ib. et seq. John Montgomery*, Esq; Governor, 256. *Rip. Van Dam*, Esq; President, *ib. W. Cosby*, Esq; Governor, 257. His Quarrel with Mr. *Van Dam, ib. et seq.* And with Chief Justice *Morrice*, 259. Orders *Zenger* the Printer to be prosecuted, 263. Tried and acquitted, 268. Mr. *Hamilton, Zenger's* Council, highly honoured by the City of *New-York*, 269. Geographical Account of the Province, 271, *et seq.* The Five Nations, 273. *Long-Island*, 274. Climate and Soil, 276. *Indians, ib.* Number of Souls, *English* and *Indians*, 279. Trade a very profitable one, *ib.*

New York Town, first called *New-Amsterdam*, Vol. I. 39. *et seq.*

Norfolk County, in *Virginia*, Vol. I. 405.

Northumberland, ib. 412.

O.

OIL, Train, how made, Vol. I. 20.

Oppecancanough, Emperor of the *Virginia Indians*, formidable to the *English*, Vol. I. 370. Massacres them, *ib.* Defeated by the *English*, 371. Massacres them again, 373. Is taken, 374. His Magnanimity and Death, *ib.*

Orange Trees, in *Barbados*, describ'd, Vol. II. 109. In *Bermudas*, 451.

Oronoco, a Bird so call'd, Vol. II. 264.

Oystins, in *Barbados*, why so call'd, Vol. II. 103.

P.

PALM Tree, in *Bermudas*, Account of, Vol. II. 451.

Palmer Worm, Vol. II. 242.

Palmeto Tree, Vol. II. 113.

Paneel Sugars, what they are, *ib.* 153.

Papa Tree, in *Barbados, ib.* 110.

Park, Col. Governor of the *Leeward Islands*, Vol. II. 204. His tragical End, 219.

Parrot Fish, in *Barbados*, Vol. II. 123. In *Antego*, 196.

Passage Fort, in *Jamaica*, destroyed by an Earthquake, Vol. II. 326. Described, 417.

Pear prickled, in *Barbados*, described, Vol. II. 109. In *Bermudas*, 451.

Pelican, in *Jamaica*, Vol. II. 408.

Pemlico, a Bird in *Bermudas* so call'd, Vol. II. 452.

Pen, William, Esq; procures a Grant of *Pensylvania*, Vol. I. 297. Goes thither, 310. Buys the Country of the *Indians, ib.* Leaves the Place, 315. Government taken from him, *ib.* His Troubles, 317. Dyes, 318.

Pen, William, Esq; Junior, goes to *Pensylvania*, Vol. I. 321.

Pensberry, in *Pensylvania*, describ'd, Vol. I. 299.

Pensylvania, the Grant promised to Sir *William Pen*, Vice-Admiral, Vol. I. 297. Given his Son, *ib.* Extent and Bounds, *ib.*

INDEX.

ib. Lands not yet laid out, 298. Counties, *ib. et seq.* *Swedes* and *Dutch* here, 299. *Philadelphia*, fine Plan of it, *ib.* A Church of *England* there, 301. *Swedish* Churches, 302. Number of Inhabitants, 304. Climate and Soil, 305. Product, 306. Indians, *ib.* Why the *Indians* have flat Heads, 307. *Swedes* furrender to the *Dutch*, 309. Col. *W. Markham* Governor, *ib.* Rates of Land at firſt and now, 310. *William Pen*, Eſq; Governor, *ib.* Buys the Country of the *Indians*, *ib.* The *Indians* get by the coming of the *Engliſh*, 311. The Conſtitution, *ib.* Alter'd, 311. Mr. *Pen*, a Court Favourite, 312. Col. *Fletcher* Governor, 313. Capt. *Blackwell* Governor, *ib.* Tobacco not to be preferred here, *ib.* *Thomas Lloyd*, Eſq; Governor, *ib.* The Ballot aboliſh'd, 314. *George Keith*, the Convert Quaker, offends, *ib.* Col. *And. Hamilton* Deputy-Governor, 315. Col. *Evans* Governor, approved by the Queen, *ib.* Mines, 316. Trade and Labour, *ib.* *William Keith*, Eſq; Governor, 318. New Comers taxed, *ib.* Fire at *Philadelphia*, 318. Credit, Aſſociation, 319. Major *Gordon* Governor, 320. Acts paſs'd, *ib.* More new Comers, 321. Number of Inhabitants, 321. Mr. *Pen*, Junior, arrives, *ib.* League with the *Indians*, 322.

Pepper, red, the Plant in *Barbados*, Vol. II. 113.

Pepper Tree, in *Jamaica*, deſcrib'd, Vol. II. 401.

Pequot Indians, War with the *Engliſh*, Vol. I. 71, *et seq.*

Perth, Amboy, in Eaſt *New-Jerſey*, Vol. I. 285.

Philadelphia City, deſcribed, Vol. I. 299, *et seq.* Fire there, 318. Number of Inhabitants, 321.

Philadelphia County, *ib.* 299.

Philip, King of the *Wampanoags*, his Wars with the *Engliſh*, Vol. I. 116, *et seq.* Sets the *Maquas* againſt him, 123. Is kill'd, 125.

Phips, Sir *William*, finds a Wreck, Vol. I. 130. Made High Sheriff of *New-England*, 134. Reduces *New-Scotland*, 33. His Expedition againſt the *French* at *Canada*, 140. Puts an End to Witch-burning, 156. Sent to *England*, 159. His Birth, 190.

Phyſick Nut, Vol. II. 107.

Piemento, in *Jamaica*, deſcrib'd, 410.

Pike, Land, Vol. II. 239.

Pine Tree, in *Barbados*, deſcrib'd, Vol. II. 114.

Plantine Tree, *ib.* 113.

Plimouth Colony, in *New-England*, ſettled, Vol. I. 47. United with the other Colonies, 88. The Town deſcribed, *ib.*

Pocahonta, an *Indian* Princeſs, in *Virginia*, her Kindneſs to Capt. *Smith*, Vol. I. 361. Stoln by Sir *Samuel Argal*, 365. Chriſtened, 366. Married to Mr. *Rolfe*, and carried to *England*, *ib.* Her Treatment at Court, 367. Her Death in *England*, *ib.*

Poiſon Tree, in *Barbados*, deſcrib'd, Vol. II. 107.

Poiſon Weed, in *Bermudas*, *ib.* 454.

Pomgranate Tree, Vol. II. 110.

Portland, Duke of, Governor of *Jamaica*, Vol. II. 368. His Death, 375.

INDEX.

Porto-Bello defcrib'd, Vol. II. 381. Taken by Admiral *Vernon, ib.*
Port-Royal, in *Jamaica,* deftroyed by an Earthquake, Vol. II 322, *et feq.* Its prefent Defcription, 415.
Port-Royal, in *New-Scotland,* Vol. I. 34.
Port-Royal, in *Carolina,* Vol. I. 516.
Powaw Indian, in *Hudfon's-Bay,* what it is, Vol. I. 553.
Powhatan King, wars with the *Englifh,* Vol. I. 360. His Daughter turns Chriftian, and marries an *Englifh* Gentleman, 366. He makes Peace with the *Englifh, ib.*
Powhatan Town, *ib.* 359.
Prince George County, in *Virginia,* defcrib'd, Vol. I. 406.
Prince George County, in *Maryland, ib.* 337.
Princefs Ann County, in *Virginia, ib.* 405.
Providence and *Bahama* Iflands, their Difcovery, Vol. II. 422. Proprietaries, 423. Mr. *Chillingworth* Governor, 424. Mr. *Clark* Governor, *ib. Cadwallador Jones* Governor, his Tyranny, *ib.* Mr. *Gilbert Afhley* Prefident, 426. A Sedition there, 427. *Avery* the Pirate there, 429. Mr. *Trot* Governor, *ib.* Houfe of Lords petition Queen *Anne* about it, 433. Mr. *Webb* Governor, 430. Mr. *El. Hafket* Governor, 431. Mr. *Lightfoot* Governor, 432. Mr. *Birch* Governor, *ib.* Capt. *Woodes Rogers* Governor, 433. Council and chief Officers, 435. Number of Inhabitants, 436. Infolent Claim of the *Spaniards* to thefe Iflands, 437. Mutiny of the Soldiers there, 438.

Q.

Quebec, attack'd by Sir *W. Phips,* Vol. I. 140.

R.

RATTLE-SNAKE, in *New-England,* Vol. I. 187.
Rat-Plague, in *Bermudas,* Vol. II. 444.
Rawleigh, Sir *Walter,* difcovers *Virginia* by his Servants, Vol. I. 346. Said to go there himfelf, 350.
Reading, in *New-England,* defcrib'd, Vol. I. 193.
Rhode-Ifland, defcrib'd, Vol. I. 203.
Rice Trade, great Increafe of, Vol. I. 519.
Richmond County, in *Virginia,* Vol. I. 412.
Roenoke Ifle, the firft Land made by the Adventurers to *Virginia,* Vol. I. 346.
Rolfe, Mr. marries the *Indian* Princefs *Pocahonta,* Vol. I. 366. Call'd in Queftion for it, 367.
Rocquet, an Animal, defcrib'd, Vol. II. 264.
Roxbury, in *New-England,* defcrib'd, Vol. I. 199.
Rum, how made, Vol. II. 150, *et feq.*
Rupert's River, in *Hudfon's Bay,* firft fettled upon, Vol. I. 544.

INDEX. 475

S.

ST. *Andrew*'s Parish, in *Barbados*, Vol. II. 102.
St. *Andrew*'s Parish, in *Jamaica*, Vol. II. 390.
St. *Bartholomew*'s Island, taken by Sir *T. Thornhill*, Vol. II. 245, *et seq.*
St. *Criftopher*'s, Discovery, Vol. II. 158. Settled by *English* and *French*, 259. Sir *Thomas Warner* Governor for the *English*, 260. Col. *Rich* Governor, 261. Climate, Soil and Product, 262. Parishes, 263. A full Account of the *Charibbeans*, 265, *et seq.* Mr. *Everard* Governor, 280. Sir *William Stapleton* Governor, 281. Sir *Nath. Johnson*, *ib.* *English* surrender to the *French*, *ib.* Recover'd by General *Codrington* and Sir *Tim. Thornhill*, 288. Sir *William Matthews* Governor, 291. The Cession of it to the *English* by the Treaty of *Utrecht*, 294. Lands left by the *French*, 295. Coin raised by the Lieutenant-Governor against the Act, 296. Governor's Salary settled, 298.
St. *David*'s Parish, in *Jamaica*, Vol. II. 388.
St. *Dorothy*'s, *ib.* 392.
St. *Elizabeth*'s *ib.*
St. *George*'s Parish, in *Barbados*, Vol. II. 100.
St. *George*'s Parish, in *Jamaica*, Vol. II. 393.
St. *George*'s Isle, one of the *Bermudas*, Vol. II. 448, *et seq.*
St. *Jago de la Vega*, in *Jamaica*, built, Vol. II. 304. *Chrift. Columbus* made Duke of it, *ib.* Plunder'd by Sir *Ant. Shirley*, 305. By Col. *Jackson*, *ib.* Destroyed by an Earthquake, 326. Describ'd, 391.
St. *James*'s Parish, in *Barbados*, Vol. II. 100.
St. *James*'s Parish, in *Jamaica*, Vol. II. 392.
St. *John*'s Parish, in *Barbados*, Vol. II. 102.
St. *John*'s Parish, in *Jamaica*, Vol. II. 391.
St. *John*'s Town, in *Newfoundland*, Vol. I. 13. Destroyed by the *French*, 14.
St. *John*'s Town, in *Antego*, Vol. II. 193.
St. *Joseph*'s Parish, in *Barbados*, Vol. II. 102.
St. *Katharine*'s Parish, in *Jamaica*, Vol. II. 390.
St. *Lucia*, describ'd, Vol. II. 171. The Right of the *English* to it, 172. The *French* dispossess'd, *ib.* First Settlement abandoned, *ib.* *French* complain of the *English* taking Wood there, 173. Governor of *Barbados* forbids the *French* to settle there, 174. A Grant of it to the Duke of *Montague*, 175. Preparation for a Settlement, *ib.* The *English* begin it, and are opposed by the *French*, 177, *et seq.* *English* and *French* leave the Right to it contested, 181.
St. *Lucy*'s Parish, in *Barbados*, Vol. II. 101.
St. *Mary*'s Parish, in *Jamaica*, Vol. II. 393.
St. *Mary*'s County, in *Maryland*, Vol. I. 336. City, *ib.*
St. *Michael*'s Parish, in *Barbados*, Vol. II. 98.
St. *Peter*'s Parish, in *Barbados*, 101.
St. *Thomas*'s Parish, 100.

St.

INDEX.

St. Thomas's, in the *Vale*, Vol. II. 393.
St. Vincent's, inhabited by *Indians* and *Negroes*, Vol. II. 183, *et seq.* Granted to the Duke of *Montague*, *ib*. His Agent there unsuccefsful, 184.
Salem, in *New-England*, built, Vol. I. 59. Defcrib'd, 199.
Savannah Town, in *Georgia*, Vol. I. 527.
Saybrook, in *New-England*, built, Vol. I. 67.
Schenectada, in the Province of *New-York*, burnt by the *French*, Vol. I. 242.
Schuyler, Col. *Peter*, of *New-York*, his Expedition againft *Quebec*. Vol. I. 241.
Seafonings, in *Maryland*, Vol. I. 328.
Shark Fifh, defcrib'd, Vol. II. 195.
Soap Tree, in *Jamaica*, defcrib'd, Vol. II. 403.
Soldier, a Reptile fo call'd, defcrib'd, Vol. II. 239.
Somerfet County, in *Maryland*, Vol. I. 339.
Speight's Town, in *Barbados*, defcrib'd, Vol. II. 101.
Spiders of *Bermudas*, defcrib'd, Vol. II. 453.
Spiders, monftrous, in *Nevis*, Vol. II. 241.
Spotfilvania County, in *Virginia*, Vol. I. 414.
Stafford County, in *Virginia*, Vol. I. 412.
Suffolk County, in *New-England*, Vol. I. 193.
Sugar, when firft made in *Barbados*, Vol. II. 7. A grievous Tax upon it, 40. Canes, how planted, 145, *et seq.* How made, 148, *et seq.* How clay'd, 152. How refined, 154. *Jamaica* Sugar, 396.
Surinam Colony, abandoned by the *Englifh*, Vol. II. 316.
Surry County, in *Virginia*, Vol. I. 405.
Suffex County, in *Penfylvania*, Vol. I. 304.
Sword-Fifh, defcrib'd, Vol. II. 197.

T.

TALBOT County, in *Maryland*, Vol. I. 339.
Tamarine-Tree, in *Barbados*, Vol. II. 108.
Tobacco, firft brought into *England*, Vol. I. 347. Severe Tax upon it, 394. How made, 442. Of *Maryland*, 340. Of *Jamaica*, Vol. II. 410.
Tobacco, fweet-fcented, Vol. I. 410, 442.
Tortoife, the Fifh fo called, Account of it, Vol. II. 406.
Treacle, how made, Vol. II. 158.
Tygers, flying, defcrib'd, Vol. II. 241.

U.

Vere Parifh, in *Jamaica*, Vol. II. 392.
Virginia, its Difcovery by Sir *Walter Raleigh's* Direction, Vol. I. 346. *Amidas* and *Barlow's* Voyage, *ib*. Tobacco firft brought into *England*, 347. Mr. *Ralph Lane*, firft Governor, 348. Sir *Francis Drake* here, 349. Firft Settlement ends, 350. Second

INDEX.

cond Settlement, *ib.* Destroyed, 351. Third Settlement, *ib.* Mr. *J. White* Governor, *ib.* The *Indian* Manteo christened, *ib.* An End of the third Settlement, 352. Capt. *Gosnold*'s Voyage, 353. Capt. *Pring*'s Voyage, 354. Capt. *Weymouth*'s Voyage, *ib.* The South *Virginia* Company, 355. Capt. *Newport* here, 356. First Colony that remained, *ib.* Mr. *Wingfield* President, 357. Capt. *Radcliffe* President, *ib.* Capt. *Smith* President, 359. Sir *Thomas Gates,* Sir *George Somers,* Capt. *Newport,* Deputy-Governors, 360. Capt. *Smith*'s Adventures, 361. The Friendship of *Pocahonta, ib.* Miserable State of the Colony, 362. Lord *Delaware* Governor, 363. Sir *T. Dale* Marshal General, *ib.* Sir *T. Gates* Governor, 365. *Pocahonta* seized by Capt. *Argal, ib.* Married to Mr. *Rolfe,* 366. Arrives in *England, ib.* Her Treatment and Behaviour at Court, 357. Dies in *England, ib.* Capt. *Yardly* Deputy-Governor, 366. Sir *Samuel Argal* Governor, 367. His Expedition against the *Dutch* and *French,* 368. Capt. *Powel* Deputy-Governor, 369. Sir *G. Yardly* Governor, *ib.* The first Assembly, *ib.* Sir *F. Wyat* Governor, *ib.* The *English* massacred by the *Indians,* 370. The Company dissolved, 372. Present Constitution, *ib.* Sir *J. Harvey* Governor, 373. Sir *W. Berkley* Governor, *ib.* Another Massacre, *ib.* King *Oppecancanough* kill'd, 374. Sir *W. Berkley* submits to the Parliament, 375. Col. *Diggs* Governor, 377. Mr. *Bennet* and Mr. *Matthews* Governors, *ib.* Col. *Francis Morrison* Deputy-Governor, 378. Sir *W. Berkley* again Governor, *ib.* Clamours here, 379. Adventurers, 381. Discoveries towards the Mountains, *ib.* Col. *Bacon*'s Mutiny, *ib.* The Causes of it, 382. The *Indians* stir, 383. *Bacon* chosen General by the People, 384. Quarrel with the Governor, 385. Enters *James* Town with his Army, *ib.* The Governor flies from him, 386. Gentlemen join with him, *ib.* Dies, 387. *Herbert Jeffreys,* Esq; Deputy-Governor, 389. Sir *W. Berkley* dies in *England, ib.* Peace with the *Indians, ib.* Sir *H. Chickley* Deputy-Governor, 390. Lord *Colepepper* Governor, *ib.* Salary 2000 *l.* a Year, *ib.* Riot about Tobacco, 391. Lord *Colepepper* gets the *Northern Neck,* 392. Lord *Howard,* of *Effingham,* Governor, 393. The Impost on Tobacco, 394. *Nath. Bacon,* Esq; President, 395. A College set on Foot, *ib. Francis Nicholson,* Esq; Lieutenant-Governor, *ib.* Sir *Edmund Andros* Governor, 396. Col. *Nicholson* Governor, 398. Earl of *Orkney* Governor, 400. *Edward Notte,* Esq; Deputy-Governor, *ib.* Col. *Spotswood* Deputy-Governor, 401. His Scheme for a general Housing of Tobacco, *ib.* Pirates hang'd, 402. *Hugh Drisdale,* Esq; Governor, *ib.* Major *Gouge* Governor, 403. Geographical Description of it, 404. *Chesapeak* Bay, 405. Sweet-scented Tobacco, 410. *Williamsburgh* describ'd, *ib.* and 436. Hills in *Virginia,* 414. Of the Inhabitants, *English* and *Indians,* 416, *et seq.* Government, 430, *et seq.* Church Affairs, 434, *et seq.* Climate, Soil, Product, 438, *et seq.* Beasts, Birds and Fish, 443, *et seq.* Coin and Trade, 447, *et seq.* State, 452.

University;

University, in *New-England*, an Account of it, Vol. I. 212, *et seq.*
Voyage, a very dangerous one, by Sea, Vol. II. 445.
Urchin, Sea, a Fish so call'd, describ'd, Vol. II. 196.

W.

WALES, new, in *Hudson's-Bay*, Vol. I. 545.
Waller, Edmund, Esq; at *Bermudas*, Vol. II. 446. His Verses upon it, 455.
Warwick County, in *Virginia*, Vol. I. 409.
Weathersfield, in *New-England*, built, Vol. I. 66.
Weed, Spirit in *Jamaica*, Vol. II. 411.
Westmoreland County, in *Virginia*, Vol. I. 412.
West New-Jersey, the History of, Vol. I. 293, *et seq.*
Whales about *Bermudas*, Vol. II. 453.
Whitewood Tree, in *Jamaica*, Vol. II. 403.
Williamsburg, Town of, in *Virginia*, describ'd, Vol. I. 406.
Wilton, in *Carolina*, Vol. I. 513.
Wind-mills, in *Barbados*, an Account of them, Vol. II. 147, *et seq.*
Witches persecuted in *New-England*, Vol. I. 148, *et seq.*
Wood, Ant, in *Barbados*, describ'd, Vol. II. 122.
Wood, Iron, ib. 113.

Y.

YARRICO, a *Charibbean* Maid, her Story, Vol. II. 13.
York County, in *Virginia*, describ'd, Vol. I. 409.
York River, *ib.* 410.

FINIS.